Translational Systems Sciences

Volume 39

Jeffrey Yi-Lin Forrest

Systemic Principles of Applied Economic Philosophies II

Value, Decision, and Large-Scale Business Forces

Springer

Jeffrey Yi-Lin Forrest
Dept. of Accounting Economics Finance
Slippery Rock University
Slippery Rock, PA, USA

ISSN 2197-8832 ISSN 2197-8840 (electronic)
Translational Systems Sciences
ISBN 978-981-99-7938-7 ISBN 978-981-99-7939-4 (eBook)
https://doi.org/10.1007/978-981-99-7939-4

This Springer imprint is published by the registered company Springer Nature Singapore Pte Ltd.
The registered company address is: 152 Beach Road, #21-01/04 Gateway East, Singapore 189721, Singapore

Paper in this product is recyclable.

Preface

Continuing what is left off from the first volume, this book, as the sequel of the previous one, focuses on how a wide range of applied economic and business studies can be more or less unified within the framework of systems science in terms of the logical reasoning and methodology of the science. This imagined unification is practically carried out in this book in two fronts: (a) all topics of applied business studies visited in this book should be examined in the light of and relevant conclusions restated in the language of the newly developed economics in the first volume; (b) the holistic thinking, as well advocated and developed in systems science, should permeate the effort of both reestablishing previously known and/or developing brand-new conclusions and selecting appropriate methods to deal with the particular problem in hands.

The significance of accomplishing (i) is very obvious to me, because, as a trained mathematician, I have a strong educational background and professional interest in mathematics and natural science. Specifically, in mathematics, when a particular theory does not work as expected when applied to address a real-life problem, scholars generally scrutinize carefully why the application failed. And then, if needed, scholars would simply go to the identified problematic areas of mathematical theory and see how the theory can be improved so that a greater collection of topics from a wider range of inquiries can be investigated successfully. In contrast, scholars in applied economic and business areas do not seem to put in such efforts, due more or less to the reason that many issues of concern involve business events and/or processes that had already occurred or finished. In other words, a large amount of scholarly endeavors in such applied areas represent 20–20 hindsight guess works based on speculations of what had caused the appearance of a particular event or process. One representative example of such scholarly efforts is the studies on what had led to the appearance and success of the Industrial Revolution. By looking at the revolution from different angles and perspectives, various theories had been proposed, while these theories are inconsistent with or even contradictory to each other. For more details about this end, see, for example, *The Stages of Economic Growth: A Non-communist Manifesto*, by W.W. Rostow (1960,

Cambridge University Press) or *The Making of an Economic Superpower: Unlocking China's Secret of Rapid Industrialization*, by Yi Wen (2016, World Scientific).

The importance of accomplishing (ii) above can be clearly seen when we seriously consider the recognition that each of the methods commonly employed in economic and business studies experiences its specific deficiencies, for more details, see Chap. 10 of the first volume of this monograph series. Hence, system-based holistic thinking can help a researcher effectively choose the most relevant methodology(-ies) to deal with issues in hands.

This book represents the first step toward the imagined unification of applied economic and business studies. It leaves a door open for scholars to look backward to revise and to improve the theories that have been already developed when they experience failures and inadequacies in their practical applications.

I hope you will enjoy reading and referencing to this book in your scholarly exploration and academic pursuit while making your new theories of economics and business more real-life relevant and practically useful than the conventional ones. If you have any comments or suggestions, please let me hear from you by sending an email to: jeffrey.forrest@sru.edu.

Slippery Rock, PA, USA
June 23, 2023

Jeffrey Yi-Lin Forrest

Acknowledgements

This book contains many research results previously published in various sources. We are grateful to the copyright owners for permitting us to use the material. They include

Alexandru Ioan Cuza University, România

Decision Sciences Institute

Elsevier

Emerald Publishing

IGI Global (Hershey, Pennsylvania)

International Institute for General Systems Studies, Inc. (Slippery Rock, Pennsylvania)

Kluwer Academic and Plenum Publishers (Dordrecht, Netherlands, and New York)

National Association of Business, Economics and Technology

Pennsylvania Association of Economics

Sciendo (Warsaw, Poland)

Springer Nature

and Taylor and Francis, Ltd.

Contents

About the Editor

Jeffrey Yi-Lin Forrest also known as Yi Lin, holds all his educational degrees in pure mathematics and had one-year post-doctoral experience in statistics at Carnegie Mellon University. He had been a guest professor of economics, finance, mathematics, and systems science at several major universities in China, including Nanjing University of Aeronautics and Astronautics. And currently, he is a professor of mathematics and research coach for the School of Business at Slippery Rock University, Pennsylvania, and the president of the International Institute for General Systems Studies, Inc., Pennsylvania. He serves either currently or in the past on the editorial boards of thirteen professional journals, including "Kybernetes: The International Journal of Systems, Cybernetics and Management Science," "Journal of Systems Science and Complexity," "International Journal of General Systems," "The Journal of Grey Systems," etc. Currently, he serves as a co-editor-in-chief of the international journal "Advances in Systems Science and Application," the editor- or co-editor-in-chief of four book series, "Series on Grey System" (Springer, Singapore), "Systems Evaluation, Prediction, and Decision-Making" (CRC Press, New York), "Communications in Cybernetics, Systems Science and Engineering" (CRC Press, Balkema), and "Communications in Cybernetics, Systems Science and Engineering—Proceedings" (CRC Press, Balkema).

Some of his research was funded by United Nations, State of Pennsylvania, National Science Foundation of

China, and German National Research Center for Information Architecture and Software Technology. As of the end of 2022, he has published well over 500 research works, including over 50 monographs and special topic volumes. Some of these monographs and volumes were published by such prestigious publishers as Springer, Taylor and Francis, World Scientific, Kluwer Academic, Academic Press, etc. Over the years, his scientific achievements have been recognized by various professional organizations and academic publishers. In 2001, he was inducted into the Honorary Fellowship of the World Organization of Systems and Cybernetics. His research interests are wide ranging, covering areas like data analytics, economics, finance, management, marketing, prediction, mathematics, systems research and applications, philosophy of science, etc.

Part I
The Overview

Chapter 1
Potential Unification of Applied Economic and Business Studies

Jeffrey Yi-Lin Forrest

Abstract This chapter outlines our initial attempts to unify several different areas of applied economic and business studies. Other than endeavoring to fill a good number of gaps that exist in relevant literatures, as individual research projects aim at accomplishing generally, this chapter sketches how this book fulfills this grand purpose in two aspects. The first aspect is on how to place at least some of the known conclusions and all new results of related areas of business research on a common theoretical ground and a convenient visual intuition. And, the second aspect is the demonstration on how the holistic thinking of systems science can be directly or indirectly employed to develop generally-true conclusions, some of which might be statistically confirmed previously. After having accomplished the aforementioned objectives, this chapter turns its attention to look at the major contributions the following chapters make to their respective literatures both theoretically and methodologically.

The rest of this chapter is organized as follows. Section 1.1 outlines the issues to be addressed in this book. To make this volume as self-contained as possible, Section 1.2 introduces the basics of systems science. Section 1.3 points to the major contributions this book makes to the literature. Section 1.4 describes how this volume is organized.

Keywords Irrational decision · Reflexive nature · Systems methodology · Systemic yoyo model

1.1 Issues This Book Attempts to Address

This section describes how this book addresses a list of different issues encountered in applied economic and business studies. It consists of three subsections with the first focusing on how to understand the creation and capture of values. The second subsection looks at issues related to decision-making in the modern business world. And, the third subsection examines how large-scale economic forces interact with each other.

J. Y.-L. Forrest, *Systemic Principles of Applied Economic Philosophies II*, Translational Systems Sciences 39, https://doi.org/10.1007/978-981-99-7939-4_1

1.1.1 Understanding the Creation and Capture of Values

Innovatively deciphering market signals generally helps place a firm in an advantageous position in terms of market competition. However, in practice, such theoretical advantage can be materialized only when other players in the firm's supply-chain ecosystem (Adner et al., 2013) can provide sufficient and adequate supports. For example, flying cars surely represent a solution to the problem of traffic jams in many U.S. metropolitans (Lemoussu et al., 2018). However, to make this idea a reality, the making of such cars needs different suppliers to provide necessary parts, and related agencies to develop appropriate road conditions and air traffic controls so that such cars can move and fly around in an orderly manner. So, in terms of value creation and capture, a natural question arises: When a firm creatively interprets a market signal, how will the consequent design of the firm's new product(s) pose challenges to other players within its ecosystem? In other words, how will the firm's consequent success depend on the success of other players in its ecosystem?

This question is important both theoretically and practically. In particular, any attempt to answer this question requires the researcher to holistically look at the firm of concern both internally and externally. When looking at itself internally, the firm needs to know how to make adjustment in order to embrace the newly recognized opportunities, while externally it needs to identify environmental challenges and develop corresponding countermeasures to overcome environmental difficulties. This question is addressed in Chap. 2 with the development of a series of general conclusions.

When a firm looks at itself internally, it is suggested (e.g., McGrath, 2013) that the firm need to develop the necessary organizational culture and capability to effectively ride waves of transient competitive advantages. To accomplish this, the firm can strategically look either (1) inwardly at its nascent, heterogeneous resources and dynamic capabilities or (2) outwardly at product markets and consumer demands. In particular, task (1) helps the firm see what values it can create for consumers (e.g., Barney, 1991; Eisenhardt & Martin, 2000), while task (2) can potentially reveal where consumer synergies are located and what can then be potentially developed (Drucker, 1954). No matter whether to look inwardly or outwardly, the essence is for the firm to find potentials of different competitive advantages (Porter, 1985; Santalo & Becerra, 2008; Ye et al., 2012). One way to achieve this end is for the firm to create economies of scope by diversification at either the producer side (Porter, 1985; Santalo & Becerra, 2008) or the demand side (Ye et al., 2012) or both. If a firm adopts this approach, then the firm has to address several different, while related, questions: (1) How can producer-side synergies be created when using the strategy of economies of scope? (2) How can demand-side synergies be developed by making use of simultaneous consumer utilities and multi-sided markets, after all it is consumers who determine the success of companies (Penrose, 1959)? (3) What are the most fundamental decisions a retailer can make in terms of its offers to consumers? (4) How can collocating products and/or services lead to simultaneous consumer utilities? (5) When can the firm develop a positively correlated multi-sided market? Aiming at addressing these questions, this book develops a cohesive theory on how to potentially develop synergistically innovative ideas at either the producer side or the demand side by developing simultaneous consumer utilities, two-sided markets, and addressing related issues.

With the development of economic globalization, new ways for wealth creation, such as the emergence of virtual markets, have appeared (Forrester Research Report, 2000). This new era of business has greatly changed the conventional way of market competition and provided unprecedented opportunities for entrepreneurs. It has also made once accustomed form and rule of competition transformed so that businesses and individuals have to adapt to the emerging formats of decision-making and inter-organizational interactions. These and other related changes in the business world have attracted the attention of scholars, front-line managers, and entrepreneurs (Hitt & Ireland, 2017), leading to enhanced information acquisition, knowledge development and sharing of know-hows (Amit & Zott, 2001). By comparing what is realistically happening and how the literature of scholarly works expands, one can see that most studies on value creation and capture provide managerial suggestions of limited validity instead of general recommendations due to various constraints inherently existing with the tools of analysis employed. Hence, this book addresses the following naturally arising question: Based on original, empirical studies on issues and matters of value, which consist of a dominating part of the literature, can generally-true conclusions be established so that they do not suffer from the inherent constraints of data- and anecdote-based analyses?

This question is very important epistemologically, because addressing it will definitely help introduce new methodologies into studies of business-related topics and issues that can be employed widely to develop useful conclusions instead of suggestions as currently done. At the same time, this question is also practically significant due to the fact that competitive advantages, at least some of which were once sustainable, have become mostly transient, short-lived. That is, the business world is currently in the era of transient competitive advantages; consumers have become less patient than ever before, while their preferences evolve rapidly (Forrest & Tallapally, 2018; McGrath, 2013).

To respond adequately to the fast-changing political and geographical environment of the world, many leading nations have made their strategic adjustments by zooming in on artificial intelligence (AI) as their next strategic direction. For example, the following two important documents, which plainly put out seven chief stratagems for the advancement of AI in the United States of America, were published in 2016 by the Obama White House: (1) Preparing for the Future of Artificial Intelligence (OWH, 2016a); (2) The National Artificial Intelligence Research and Development Strategic Plan (OWH, 2016b). To keep up with the movement started in the United States, in May of 2018, the European Commission (EC (European Commission), 2018) submitted its corresponding document, entitled "Artificial Intelligence: A European Perspective." It pronounces the EU's place in the international AI competition, while presenting a plan for corresponding actions. That plan involves the goal of increasing investment in AI related R&D and ideals on how to update the European system of education and training in order to maintain development strength of European talents. Parallel to the United States and Europe, the Japanese government also assigns great importance to AI and relevant development. In its "Report on the 5th Science and Technology Basic Plan (2016–2020)" (Government of Japan, 2015), the Japanese government recommends to establish at the national level a relatively complete R&D promotion mechanism to center on internet of things, big data, AI, and other technologies, and the materialization of a superintelligent society through extending AI to all aspects of life. As the fastest growing nation in the world, the importance of AI also catches China's attention. The term of AI appears in the 2017 Report of the 19th National Congress of the Communist Party of China (Xi, 2017), reflecting the Chinese ambition of keeping up with the international development and to stimulate the economic restructuring by profoundly fusing internet, big data and AI with the real economy. To possibly help understand this international push for AI and its applications, this book investigates how AI may impact technological innovation by first establishing a series of general conclusions, and then confirming these conclusions empirically by using the industrial robot data from the International Federation of Robotics and the panel data of China's 14 manufacturing sectors from 2008 to 2017.

In terms of effectively organizing itself initially, surviving the next and succeeding eventually in the present increasingly fast-evolving markets, it has been widely recognized (Day, 1994; Forrest et al., 2017; McGrath, 2013; Webster, 2002) that market sensing and market reaching, particularly customer value propositions (CVPs), are important capabilities for a company to have. It is on specific understandings of market signals and effective CVPs that a firm creates values for customers and captures values from the market (Forrest & Liu, 2022; Payne & Frow, 2005). However, the existent literature on CVPs is mostly on how to define the concept of CVPs (Payne et al., 2017), while the literature on market-sensing points to inconsistent findings. For example, Ardyan (2016) finds that such capability does not have any positive effect on companies' profitability; and Lindblom et al. (2008) reveals some effect but not significant. In terms of its impacts on the quality of market entry and the creation of knowledge, scholars find the capability has either some positive or quite significant impacts (Alshanty & Emeagwali, 2019; Sugiyarti & Ardyan, 2017). Hence, this book attempts to develop a general theory of CVPs by answering the following question: what do these inconsistent empirical results on market sensing mean in theory and in practice?

The discussion in the previous paragraph indicates that this goal is both theoretically and practically important. For example, for either a manager or an entrepreneur, knowing the future direction of consumer demands is essential for a firm to plan and position itself strategically in advance. It is especially so within the current landscape of the business world where once sustainable competitive advantages have become transient (McGrath, 2013). To potentially achieve the aforementioned objective, this book adopts unconventional methodologies. The logic behind this adoption is that the existent literature is frequently empirical, and in many circumstances, inconsistencies and contradictory discoveries are simply results of the tools of analysis employed (Einstein, 1997). Additionally, beyond attempting to accomplish the objective above, this book also enables us to look at profit opportunities in stagnant industries, as case studies, without much market growth and shows how market knowledge and relevant innovative understanding of the knowledge can assist a company to construct effective CVPs.

In terms of corporate governance, there is clearly a need to holistically understand how various decision-making units of a firm work together, interact with each other, and how stakeholders with inconsistent objectives put in their efforts to accomplish their respectively different, or even divergent goals. This book represents a first step toward the eventual materialization of this important effort.

Before developing a specific analytic model, this book first establishes a systems foundation based on the systemic yoyo model to understand some of the relevant empirical discoveries. On such a qualitative foundation, an explanation is provided for, among others, (1) why an elaborate legal system is needed for venture capital to flow smoothly and why certain governments around the world are willing to go extra miles to establish such as legal system; (2) why the agency problem, existing between the large shareholders and the CEO, cannot be resolved completely and the best one can do about this problem is to reduce its severity; (3) why outside financers still leave their money to managers in all market economies from around the world even with the knowledge of the unsolvable agency problem; and (4) why there are boards of directors in the first place.

With these new and deepened understandings about the mutual interactions and restrictions between the board of directors and the CEO, this book then turns its attention to establish a simple analytic model, on which it studies the price behaviors of different investment projects, the dynamics between long-term and short-term projects and assets, and the power struggle between the board and the CEO. The developed analytical reasoning indicates that when assets are undervalued, the mispricing of the long-term asset in equilibrium is worse than that of the short-term asset. When the assets are overpriced, the mispricing of the short-term asset in equilibrium is worse than that of the long-term asset. With this result in place, an explanation is given to illustrate why CEOs would prefer, among different kinds of projects, undervalued short-term investment projects.

1.1.2 Decision-Making in the Modern World

With the blossoming of online retail businesses, traditional, storefront-based retails get hit big time. Currently, a massive number of retail stores are closing and a huge number of employees are laid off from the retail industry ..., as the news goes. That is only a snapshot of avalanche changes in the present business world, where markets change faster, competitive advantages of companies become much shorter lived, and business entities are reconfigured as more cohesive wholes than before. Looking at the dramatic development in the business world, other than mustering comprehensive conjectures about what is underneath the fast-changing practices behind magnificent successes and devastating failures based on anecdotes and data, a natural question for decision-making managers and entrepreneurs arises as follows: can a general theory be developed, from which managers and entrepreneurs can plausibly and deductively explain what is happening with reliability?

This book addresses the question theoretically by examining such issues as (1) how firms compete for customers who switch from the product of one company to that of another by adjusting prices; (2) how firms' expected profits stay stagnant; and (3) why firms' bases of loyal customers deteriorate while customers become less patient than ever before. By employing the intuition of systemic thinking and the rigor of game theory, this book establishes the following results, among others: (1) Within an oligopoly market, in the Nash equilibrium, when the competition of the market grows with an increasing number of firms entering the market, the base of loyal customers for each incumbent firm will gradually diminish; (2) in a developed market place, risk neutrality would lead to stagnation in profits and irrational decision on pricing. And, it uses systemic models to explain why competitive advantages of the past seem to be sustainable, while present competitive advantages transient.

Although change is considered by many as a good thing, it does cause difficulties for people to cope with. Generally, change means uncertainty; and uncertainty brings forward unexpected risks along with the potential of unanticipated benefits. Such uncertainty and unexpected risks challenge the established status quo, while they can easily appear and do occur. Nevertheless, the modern world of business is changing fast, and evolving faster than ever before. And, competition in the marketplace is increasingly intensifying due to the globalization of international economies and unification of international finances. With these accelerating changes and developments, once sustainable competitive advantages have become transient, short-lived (McGrath, 2013). In other words, if a business organization does not or cannot transform itself along with the shifting landscape of the business world, it will be obsolete and become history in no time. In the 1980s, Michael Porter (1985) developed a theory of competitive advantages, which soon since then has been widely used by managers and entrepreneurs when they need to find "a way to conceptualize the firm that would expose the underpinnings of competitive advantage and its sustainability."

Looking at the long list of once-storied business organizations that are either gone or no longer relevant, a natural question arises: Are there necessary steps that a firm need to go through in order for the firm to ready itself potentially for successfully riding waves of transient competitive advantages?

One characteristic of the market economy is the constantly and widely existing competition in the marketplace. To continuously find a new profitable market niche, an entrepreneurial mentality that makes competition increasingly intensive is the key for successfully running business enterprises. So, two natural questions arise as follows for anyone who dreams to acquire success in the business world: (1) what characterizes a market that begets new opportunities or competition? And, (2) how should a firm motivate and compensate its sales force in order to win market competitions against its rivals? To possibly address these questions, this book investigates such a condition under which market competition will intensify, how the existing loyal consumer base of an established firm will start to deteriorate, and how a firm can gain an upper hand in the market competition internally by looking at how a firm's sales associates should be appropriately compensated (or the problem of sales force compensation).

These and other related questions have been active areas of research with a great potential of direct applications in real life. And, from a specific angle this book attempts to jointly address these questions and several other issues, such as (1) when the consumer surplus of the market, which is the totality of all price switchers, is sufficiently large, market competition will intensify with additional profits to be made; (2) when the number of competing firms increases, the number of loyal customers will decline and eventually approach zero; (3) how different pricing strategies could be employed to potentially double expected profits; and (4) how the competitive spirits of a firm's sales associates can be lifted to a different height.

The importance of innovation has been acknowledged since the time of Smith (1776) when he treated innovation as a critical factor in enhancing wealth. Owing to the fierce world-wide competition in manufacturing, innovation is inevitable for manufacturing companies' survival and healthy growth (Stock et al., 2002). Hence, it is compelling for decision-making managers, entrepreneurs, and scholars alike to find answers to the following questions, given that organizational culture, structure, leadership, and what strategy to employ represent the crucial foundation of an organization: (1) what are the main strategic tactics that underlie the innovative activities of a manufacturing firm? (2) How do the organizational culture, corporate structure, and leadership of a manufacturing firm influence the firm's degree of innovativeness?

In the present business world, innovation is increasingly inevitable for every company that wishes to remain competitive, develop comparative advantages, and enter profitable markets (Stock et al., 2002). That explains why the topic these questions represent has remained one of the most popular and hottest ones investigated over many decades by researchers, managers of firms, and policy makers.

International business activities and performance of firms have been a hot topic of research in recent years; and the relevant literature, both empirical and theoretical, has been growing exponentially (Melitz & Redding, 2014; Wagner, 2016). The empirical branch of the literature was initiated by Bernard and Jensen (1995), and the theoretical branch by Melitz (2003). Due to the ongoing globalization of regional and natural economies from around the world, investigations on this research topic have been helping not only relevant academic discussions but also public debates and policy decision-making. Evidently, such studies are vitally important for local, regional, national, and international economic developments. Therefore, it is both theoretically and practically important for us to establish a general theory that integrates the findings reported in the literature while providing guidelines for practical applications and future research. To this end, this book concentrates on the following topics: (1) the dynamics of competition of the domestic market; (2) exports to either less developed markets or more advanced markets or both; and (3) development of a general theory regarding the relationship between international trades and the performance of firms, where such firms' outcomes as productivity, profitability, employees' wages, and survival are specifically considered.

1.1.3 Interactions of Large-Scale Economic Forces

Opposite to Becker (1974) famous rotten kid theorem, when the rotten members of the family are the parents instead of the kids (Bommier & Dubois, 2004; Lin, 2009), the question of child labor and its efficiency arises. To this end, this book introduces three independent variables—child labor, formal schooling, and level of maturity—into the study of this question. It shows that as long as children's disutility or utility of labor or formal schooling is concerned, the laissez faire triple of child labor, formal schooling, and level of maturity, which maximizes the parents' utility function, can never be efficient. In fact, such a laissez faire triple is always inefficiently too high. On the other hand, if the efficiency of parent's chosen (for their children) levels of child labor, formal schooling, and level of maturity is determined by the impact on the children's lifetime earnings potential, it then finds that (1) if all externalities of the parents' decision made for the children could be internalized by their interior transfers in terms of savings (if the capital markets are imperfect) and bequests to their children, then the children would have the potential to obtain their optimal lifetime earnings; (2) if the parents could borrow money in the capital markets, and if the child lives below his means when he is an adult, then the parents' decision made for the child, when he was a kid, about the child's labor, formal schooling, and level of maturity, would be efficient in terms of the child's lifetime earnings potential; and (3) if the capital markets are imperfect and if the parents' bequests are at a corner or their savings are at a corner, then the laissez faire triple of child labor, formal schooling, and level of maturity is inefficiently high.

To help resolve some of the inefficiencies, which cannot be resolved by individual families, this book places the systemic yoyo fields of individual families in a much mightier yoyo, representing the government. In this way, the spin field of the government yoyo forces families and individuals to modify their behaviors accordingly. In particular, if a government regulation is introduced to impose a marginal ban on child labor, then such a ban could be either welfare reducing for both the child and the parents or a Pareto improvement for both the child and the parents, under different sets of specific conditions.

Over 50 years ago, economists started to notice stable wage differentials existing inter-industrially over time and across national borders. Some industries pay their workers more than other industries (Slichter, 1950). And, the differentials apply across all occupations. That is, if one occupation in an industry is highly paid, then all other occupations of the same industry tend to be so, too; and such wage differentials appear stably over time and exist internationally. Hence, over these years, many scholars, including Nobel laureates George Stigler of 1982 (Stigler, 1958), Robert Solow of 1987 (Solow, 1979), George Akerlof of 2001, and Daniel Kahneman of 2002 (Kahneman et al., 1986), have contributed to the understanding of this inter-industrial wage pattern. However, it is found (Thaler, 1989) that none of the established theories actually explains the pattern satisfactorily without assuming something difficult to accept. To help ease the situation, this book provides a new theory that not only is intuitive and plausible but also assumes nothing difficult to swallow.

To successfully accomplish the aforementioned goal, this book models each commercial firm as a specific spinning yoyo, and reveals how these economic yoyos interact with each other through combinations and breakups on the basis of the evolution of a flow of such yoyos. Then, it develops a simple profit maximization model to study large and small firms and their differences in the areas of production, determination of the selling prices, and cost bases of their products. By employing this simple profit maximization model to the study of inter-industry wage differentials, it is found that financially resourceful companies have a large array of advantages over those companies that are limited by their resources. One example of such advantage is that the former companies bring in handsome profits in two dimensions—the product dimension and the personnel dimension, while the latter companies could only produce their profits from a single dimension—the products—with an invisible glass ceiling.

According to discussions in the first volume of this monograph series, not all firms attempt to maximize its profit. Instead, they all maximize the realization of their respective missions. However, considering the fact that the present world of business is still mostly composed of such firms that aim at maximizing profits, the simple profit maximization model developed for the described purpose above is appropriate for our purpose.

To maximize their profit in the human resource dimension, financially resourceful companies need to spend extra money on their employees. This end provides the long-sought-after explanation for the stable wage differentials existing inter-industrially over time and across national borders (Thaler, 1989). Beyond this wonderful outcome, the model derived herein also provides plausible economic reasons for other relevant questions, including, but not limited to, (1) why high-wage industries tend to have low quit rates; (2) why profits and market power are reliable predictors of industry wages; (3) why the association between wages and labor's share of costs in an industry is negative; (4) why industries with high capital–labor ratios tend to pay higher wages, and (5) why unionization rate increases wages for both union and nonunion members in a firm. And, what is worth noticing here is that in the labor market, the law of one price does not hold true for job opportunities that look identical in their job descriptions.

Because the present-day regional economies are closely intertwined with each other due to a high degree of globalization, when a nation or geographic region suffers from economic and financial shocks, in terms of their damaging effects and adverse impacts, the shocks tend to possess international and global characteristics. Since the 1920s, there had appeared many large-scale financial crises with cross regional effects (Hein et al., 2016; Wang & Hu, 2005). This book (specifically, Chap. 15) looks at such financial crises that are purposefully caused or created by certain group(s) of people in order to acquire economic and political gains.

For the purpose of this book, by financial crises, they mean all those with respect to, either individually or jointly, currency, credit, bank, debt, and the markets of stocks, bond, and financial derivatives, etc. They generally mean severe fluctuations that appear in the financial area of an economy. The chaos interferes negatively with the operation of the real economy. Each of such crises is accompanied by sudden deterioration of all or most financial indexes, stock market crash, capital flight, credit destruction, extremely tight money supply, rising interest rate, bank runs, bankruptcy of a large number of financial institutions, major decrease in the official reserves, inability to repay the interest and principal of maturing debt, currency devaluation both internally and externally, etc.

This book makes use of the systemic yoyo model, concepts of control theory and Bernanke-Gertler model of fundamental value of capital to show that when a large amount of foreign investments gathers in one place over either a long period or a short period of time and then leaves suddenly and massively, that local economy will suffer through a positive bubble, caused by the increased money supply as a consequence of foreign investments, and then a following negative, disastrous bust, caused by the sudden dry-out of the money supply. Because a large number of economic activities are either unexpectedly delayed or totally impossible to complete, the local investors are actually unable to continue to collect their originally expected dividends for many time periods to come. In other words, foreign investments can be employed as a weapon of mass destruction, if they leave strategically and suddenly, no matter whether they come quickly in a short period of time or slowly over a relatively longer period of time.

By combining the theoretical analysis on how financial crises could be caused or created by certain group(s) of people with the recent cases of speculative attacks in the arena of international finance, the following predicament can be readily seen. When a nation tries to develop itself economically, due to its loosening economic and monetary policies, large amounts of foreign investments would be welcomed; and at the same time, a lot of such foreign investments would strategically rush into the nation in order to ride along with the forthcoming economic boom. Now, what have been shown earlier is that if a large amount of foreign investments leaves suddenly, then the host nation would most likely suffer from a burst of the economic bubble with a large percentage of economic activities interrupted either temporarily or indefinitely. So, a natural question at this junction is: How could policy makers possibly design a measure to counter such sudden leaves of foreign investments in order to avoid the undesirable disastrous consequences? This book addresses this question by providing a possible strategy of defense.

1.2 A Brief Introduction to Systems Science

Based on the previous discussions, this section illustrates the reason why systems science and methodology are appropriate for us to address the large array of questions, as listed above, that appear in a wide range of areas in business studies.

In particular, the contents of this book are presented in a similar fashion as a scientific theory by using the systemic yoyo model as the intuition and playground, and a set of axioms and rigorously established game-theoretic results as the starting points. Here, such a logical reasoning as the one commonly used in mathematics and natural science will be used to derive generally-true conclusions by relating each newly introduced concept to the starting points or previously established conclusions.

This section is included here for the purpose of making this book as self-contained as necessary so that the reader does not have to go back and forth between this and the previous volume within this monograph series.

1.2.1 Numbers and Their Limitations

The concept of numbers appeared initially and naturally in daily lives, as people pursued activities for survival, such as hunting, where recording and counting were necessary. And then in ancient Greece, Pythagoras treated numbers as the origin of everything, while believing that through numbers and their properties, the mankind can comprehend all things under heaven. Such belief in the west led to the development of the traditional science as the religious foundation (Kenny, 2012). At roughly the same time, in ancient China of the east, Zhan Yin, a scholar of the warring states time, realized that the use of numbers is limited, because there are things numbers just cannot describe (Qu, 1985). Such recognition about the limitations of numbers led to how later generations of Chinese people treated numbers and why they did not appreciate numbers as much as Westerners, for more details, see Wu and Lin (2002).

Beyond their limited power to describe things, such as organizations, events and processes, numbers cannot appear before existence, reflecting their original purpose—measurement and recording. This reality greatly affects how well and useful numbers can be employed to predict the future and study the evolution and interaction of organizations, two key issues heavily dealt with in applied business studies. In particular, since the time of Pythagoras, numbers have been identified as points on the real-number line, which is an imaginary linear axis, leading to the appearance of the infinity ∞. That explains why analysis and reasoning based on numbers or numerical variables must be of bounded validity, because the natural world is curved so that it never reaches this imaginary ∞ (Lin, 2009, p. 21–22). That indicates that such a new science and methodology that can be utilized to describe organizations and their interactions need to be introduced to the study of various business issues. While systems science meets this requirement, therefore, it needs to be adopted as the tool of analysis and language of reasoning for the planned theory that will be presented in this book. In particular, by system, it means an organization or a structure where components are related somehow to each other to form an organic whole.

To know how consumer preference evolves and what is going to be favored next, one has to consider the attributes and systemic structures of the forever changing market condition and how they interact with one another. However, in the language of natural science, interactions of different products, market forces and organizations of parts belong to non-inertial systems. That separates the traditional science of the first push, which heavily uses quantities and inertial systems, from systems science of the second stir, which focuses on structures, organizations, and non-inertial systems (Lin & OuYang, 2010).

For things with or without internal structures, their evolution and interaction demonstrate different characteristics (Lin, 2009). For example, when two objects without internal structure collide, the law of action and reaction applies. However, when the colliding objects possess their individually different internal structures, the consequence of the collision can be very different, where the third law of motion does not apply. This end explains why nations in real life need to have their own security systems to protect and maintain their peace and stability. Hence, the logics of thinking and methodologies of analysis needed to handle these distinct evolutions and interactions will have to be different from those widely employed in applied economic and business studies.

As what physics has shown, methods of analysis, such as calculus, statistics, and consequent theories, developed on the formality and generality of quantities, can be reasonably useful when applied to investigate evolution and interaction of things that have no internal structure. However, in terms of economic and business studies, where all economic entities involved do possess internal structures, quantities, and methodologies developed on quantities have experienced great difficulties, for details, see Chap. 10 of the previous volume of this monograph series. To coordinate these two methodological approaches—one quantity-based and the other system-based, one can associate them by using the concept of rotational stirring energies or the systemic yoyo model. Doing so naturally leads to the overall system of a two-dimensional science with the first dimension focusing on the study of things without internal structure and the second dimension on matters involving internal organization (Lin, 2009).

By carefully examining the world systemically or through the lens of systems, one can readily see that the fundamental form of movement in the universe is rotation, no matter whether what is considered is physical, intellectual, or economic (Lin, 2009). To this end, it is Vilhelm Bjerknes (1898) who first recognized that the fundamental form of atmospheric or oceanic motion is rotation, then it is Shoucheng OuYang (Wu & Lin, 2002) who generalized this result to solids. Based on this fundamental, rotational form of movement of fluids and solids, the concepts of stirring energy and second stir (Lin & OuYang, 2010) and the yoyo model (Lin, 2009) are introduced. For a quick introduction to the yoyo model, see Sect. 1.2.3 below.

In short, the methods of systems science are developed to deal with the development of organizations, evolutions, and interactions of organizations; the systemic yoyo model helps managers and entrepreneurs intuitively see how economic entities evolve and interact with each other. Hence, it can be expected that jointly these tools will assist decision makers to effectively process market information and make appropriate decisions (Forrest, 2018; Forrest et al., 2020).

1.2.2 Reflexivity and Need for Systems Science

To possibly resolve the problem of how to innovatively comprehend market information (or cues or signals), let us first examine the concept of information. It was Shannon (1949) who first officially defined information by using probability. Since then, this concept has been jointly investigated with those of uncertainty and greatly helped the debate between determinacy and indeterminacy within the world of learning. While the school of determinacy imposes strong conditions, such as stability or continuity and differentiability, to smooth out specifics that appear with each particular application, the school of indeterminacy removes small-probability events by focusing on stable time series. That is, scholars arrive at the same destination although they take different approaches: they acquire the desirable generality by eliminating either specifics or complexities of the events and processes under consideration. For instance, to produce conclusions of desired generality, one widely used method is to take averages, known as expected values. However, in a lot of real-life cases, such expected values are guaranteed to be not reachable, contradicting the meaning of expected values. Speaking differently, to innovatively understand market information, involved specifics cannot be ignored by decision-making managers and entrepreneurs, although quantitative methods cannot handle them. On the other hand, various unique understandings of the market cue entice managers and entrepreneurs to take their individually different actions, which further alters the meaning of the original market cue. Such reflexive nature (Soros, 1998) between a piece of market information and innovative understandings of it naturally motivates scholars and practitioners to employ systems science and methodology to deal with events and processes (or systems) and explore such issues as how to innovatively understand market information with relevant specifics and how to practically apply such understanding to make more reliable predictions and decisions.

From the angle of systems, it can be readily seen that an innovative understanding of market information is closely related to the interaction of various economic events and agents (Lin & OuYang, 2010). So, by purposely examining the product market from the angle of interacting economic events and agents, one will be able to discover profit opportunities in consumers' forever changing preferences. In other words, specifics of market information represent the dynamic mechanism of evolving underlying structures; their importance in terms of business opportunities goes beyond the formality of quantities; and innovatively understanding them relies directly on the attributes and properties of the systemic structure of the interacting economic entities and agents. The current effort devoted to big data uses the name of quantities to uncover hidden systemic structures. That signals the fact that human exploration of knowledge has gone beyond the limitations of numbers and numerical variables and into the era of systems thinking of events and processes.

In principle, specifics of market information reveal changes taking place in the product market, while knowledge and technologies of big data provide a new approach and capability for dealing with changes and for expecting what is coming up next. Such approach represents another methodology different of those that are calculus-based and/or statistics-based. It marks a new development in the epistemological system of knowing the world through analyzing the underlying systems and their interactions.

Because of the duality of action and reaction and that of spin directions, when a particular piece of market information appears, changes in the original market structure have already occurred. So, considering the fact that the present world of business is in the era of transient competitive advantages (McGrath, 2013), there appears an urgent need for decision makers to generate innovative comprehensions of the market by employing systems science. In this regard, systemic thinking and systemic intuition—the yoyo model—can expediently help managers and entrepreneurs walk out of the realm of quantities and enter that of interacting organizations and non-inertial systems (or systems science).

All methodologies commonly and conventionally employed in economic and business studies have not produced managers and entrepreneurs who can consistently pinpoint to potentials of profit opportunities with appropriate reliability. Specifically, presently available knowledge, developed on either calculus-based or statistics-based approaches or a combination of both, has not dependably helped managers and entrepreneurs to generate innovative understandings of market cues, from which potentials of profit opportunities appear. No matter how this situation is looked at, it has to be a serious challenge that needs to be met urgently due to its theoretical and practical importance and the fact that the present business world is in the era of transient competitive advantages (McGrath, 2013). To answer this challenge, this book comes into being: it attempts to fill the gaps outlined in Sect. 1.1 and to avoid the methodological deficits of calculus-based or statistics-based approaches or any combination of both by employing systems methodology and by considering the specific attributes of the scenario in hands. This book demonstrates clearly that systems are more adequate than quantities when managers and entrepreneurs need to discover potentials and opportunities of value. Additionally, this book shows indirectly how the advantages of the commonly employed methodologies in the literature can be utilized to address applied economic and business issues and challenges based on the guidance of an underlying systemic analysis.

1.2.3 Systems Science and Its Methodology

After the previous two subsections demonstrated the need for scholars and practitioners in the area of applied economic and business studies to adopt systems thinking and methodology, this subsection provides a quick glance of relevant basics of systems science.

Systems science is developed to enable scholars to look at the world holistically by focusing on the investigation of organizations and structures, each of which is known as a system (Klir, 1985; Lin, 1999). Based on the discussions in the previous subsections and the fact that entities involved in studies of applied economics and business generally possess their respectively rich, yet different, internal structures, this book adopts systems science as its way of reasoning and intuitively sees how various business potentials evolve either individually or collectively.

As is defined earlier, a system represents an organization or a structure whose component parts are associated to each other to form an organic whole, where the whole is greater than the sum of parts (Lin, 1999). Hence, system is everywhere in the world, especially in investigations of applied economic and business issues. For example, each consumer is both a complex biological system and an input and output economic system, depending on in which angle the person is seen. At the same time, other than being a member of many larger systems, such as a family, neighborhoods, communities, etc., he also interacts with various man-made systems, such as a car and an ATM machine, and with different social systems, such as the company of employment and sport clubs.

Historically, scholars in different disciplines over the recorded history have either consciously or unconsciously employed the concept of systems by using their respective languages (von Bertalanffy, 1968). And in our modern time, an increasing number of scholars in the area of business, such as Forrest et al. (2020), Klir (1985), Lin (2009), and Porter (1985), also demonstrate the power of holistic thinking and relevant methodology in terms of producing reliable and usable conclusions regarding business entities and how they interact with each other.

Similar to the situation of how numbers item from the physical world, systems can also be abstracted out of any and every physically, intellectual or socially existing object, event, and process. However, beyond their common origin, numbers and systems represent two different aspects of the world. In particular, when a firm is seen as a collection of isolated component parts, then the firm can be described with numbers—*m* staff members, *n* office rooms, etc. When the firm is investigated as a potential place from where opportunities and values emerge, then it becomes a system with its particular culture, philosophical values and beliefs, and missions to be realized, specifically associated talents, operational routines, among others. It is the invisible whole that makes the firm exist both physically and intellectually. Of course, the firm considered in this discussion can be readily replaced by an individual (seen as an economic agent whose behavior is dictated by his value-belief system), a market, an industry, an economy, etc. That implies that behind each business entity, event, and process, there is an abstract, theoretical system within which the relevant whole, component parts, and their interconnectedness are emphasized. Conversely, it is the whole and interconnected parts that the totality is known as a firm, or a market, or an industry, or an economy. That is, other than specific circumstances where numbers play their roles, the business world is dominantly made up of systems (or structures or organizations).

In comparison, numbers, if used in relationships, describe small scale and non-structural phenomena (Wu & Lin, 2002), while the concept of system large-scale and organizational. That is another reason why the systems methodology is more appropriate than all theories developed on numbers and numerical variables for the investigation of applied economic and business issues when the internal structures of involved economic entities cannot be ignored.

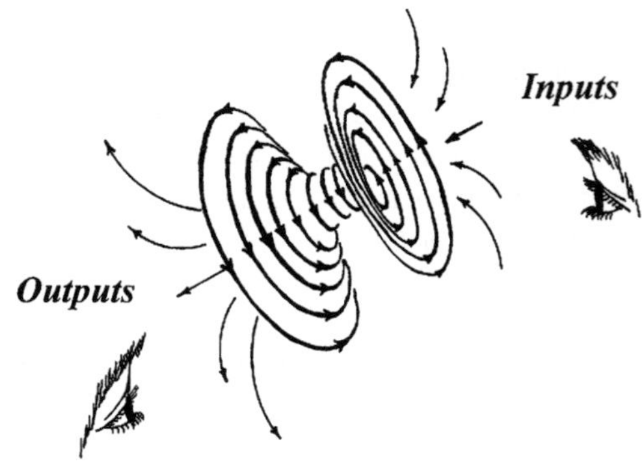

Fig. 1.1 The systemic yoyo model seen in our 3-dimensional space

By systems science, it means the collection of all studies of systems and organizations. It investigates the systemhood of objects, structures (or organizations), and evolutionary processes of organizations. That is what makes systems science different from the traditional science that studies the thinghood of objects. Jointly, systems science and the traditional science constitute a 2-dimensional spectrum of knowledge with the latter being the first dimension and the former the second dimension (Klir, 2001). With systems science—an additional dimension of knowledge—in place, human ability to learn has gained additional strength so that more problems that have been challenging the very survival of the mankind since the beginning of time can be more adequately addressed than ever before. The materialization of such great expectation of systems science relies on the particular speaking language and intuition—the (systemic) yoyo model (Lin, 2007), Fig. 1.1. That is similar to how the Cartesian coordinate system, consisting of intersecting real-number lines, plays its role in mathematics and the traditional science (Kline, 1972). Specifically, any system of concern, be it physical or intellectual, tangible or intangible, a living being or an organization, a culture or a civilization, can be intuitively treated as a spinning field structure. When such structure is seen in the 3-dimensional space we live in, the structure shown in Fig. 1.1 appears. It remains in a continual spin motion, which stands for the internal working of the system; otherwise, it will no longer exist as an identifiable system. For more in-depth discussions, see Chap. 2 in the first volume of this monograph series or Lin (2009).

As expected, this yoyo model has successfully played the role of intuition and playground for scholars who investigate the world and explore new knowledge holistically, just as what the Cartesian coordinate system did for the traditional science (Forrest, 2013, 2014; Forrest & Tao, 2014; Lin, 2009; Lin & Forrest, 2011; Ying & Forrest, 2015). In particular, this yoyo model of general systems has been successfully applied in the investigation of business organizations, civilization, economics, finance, foundations of mathematics, history, management, marketing, Newtonian physics of motion, small-probability disastrous weather forecasting, the concept of energy, the mind, among others.

Along this same line of logical thinking, this book uses this systemic intuition to establish generally-true conclusions regarding a whole list of various topics considered in applied economic and business studies.

To conclude this subsection and to prepare the reader for the rest of this book, let us quickly look at the concept of systems. Symbolically, S is a system, if S is equal to an ordered pair of sets $S = (M, R)$ such that M consists of all component parts of the system, known as the object set of S, each component part in M is known as an element or object of S, and R stands for the set of all relationships of the elements in M, known as the relation set of S. Note that out of the same set M, many different sets of relations can exist. That is, by each choice of sets M and R, a unique system $S = (M, R)$ is defined; for each identified system S, its object set M and relation set R are also specifically fixed.

1.3 Major Contributions of This Book

This section outlines how the following chapters contribute to their relevant literatures. It consists of three subsections with the first one pointing to the contributions to the literature of value creation and capture. The second subsection emphasizes on the major contributions of this work to the literature of business decision-making. And, the third subsection describes the contributions to the literature of interacting economic forces.

1.3.1 Contributions to the Literature of Value Creation and Capture

As a consequence of addressing the question of how a firm's design of new product (s) poses challenges to other players within its supply-chain ecosystem, when the firm creatively interprets a market signal, this book (specifically, Chap. 2) first distinguishes suppliers and complementors so that suppliers provide their outputs for the focal firm to integrate in its effort to offer a complete product to its customers and complementors facilitate necessary conditions for customers to fully utilize the product. Then, it establishes, among others, the following main results: (1) The upper limits of value the focal firm can create and capture are respectively constrained by the challenges facing its upstream components and downstream complementors; (2) the performance advantage of the focal firm over its competitors is positively correlated to the level of challenges the firm's suppliers face and negatively to that of the firm's complementors; (3) when contracting with upstream suppliers, the focal firm has to deal with technological and behavioral uncertainty, where the former affects the firm's creation of value, and the latter impacts the firm's capture of value.

Comparing to previous studies, this work contributes to an array of different literatures, covering business ecosystems, value capture and creation, competitive advantage, and customer adoption of innovation, firm uncertainties (contractual, behavioral, and technological), as well as technology life cycle.

When a firm attempts to find potentials of different competitive advantages by creating economies of scope through diversification at either the producer side or the demand side or both, this book (specifically, Chap. 3) develops a cohesive theory on how to potentially develop synergistically innovative ideas at either the producer side or the demand side by developing simultaneous consumer utilities, two-sided markets, and by addressing related issues. It contributes simultaneously to the literatures of entrepreneurship, innovation, and strategy by emphasizing on the creation of consumer synergies through the collocation of commonly available products and/or services, and by developing generally-true conclusions, such as that, among others, (1) if two offers of a firm facilitate beneficial interactions of two consumer segments, then that firm establishes a positively correlated two-sided or multi-sided market; (2) under the influence of a particular factor, such as location, circumstance, etc., if one of a firm's collocated offers that is necessary for consumers meets a competitive market demand, while other offers provide convenience, then the firm provides simultaneous consumer utilities; (3) mobilizing inconsistent resources generally produce negative synergies.

To address the epistemologically important question—can generally-true conclusions be established based on empirical studies so that they do not suffer from the inherent constraints of data- and/or anecdote-based analyses, this book (specifically, Chap. 4), respectively, considers innovations, resources, the market state of mutual forbearance, inter-organizational networks, platforms that directly connect sellers and buyers. And, it studies how information flows affect the emergence of creative destruction. By doing so, this book establishes the following generally-true conclusions, among others: (1) with free competition, innovation can effectively help create value, if protective property rights and complementary assets are available, and market exchanges help resources reveal their dormant values; (2) a firm's membership of an inter-organizational network or a strategic block generally represents an inimitable, not substitutable resource the firm can potentially mobilize; (3) increasing information circulation accelerates the speed of emergence of creative destructions.

Artificial intelligence is composed of two branches. One explores ways to replicate human capabilities; and the other is about how to increase human capabilities for the purpose of making better decisions through utilizing modern technology (Markoff, 2016). An importance factor that affects how AI can help with socio-economic growth is how AI can positively influence innovation and knowledge creation (Aghion et al., 2017). Because knowledge creation is such a process that either regroups what is known or generates something intellectually new, AI can provide its support in both fronts; that is why AI promotes significant economic growth (Agrawal et al., 2018). To possibly understand the significance of the current push for artificial intelligence and to estimate the potential outcomes of such push, an important task is to reveal how AI impacts innovation in general and technological innovation in particular. Relevant literature search reveals that studies on how AI impacts technological innovation are still in the stage of infancy, and their focuses are mainly on how to define relevant concepts. That is where this book (specifically, Chap. 5) comes into being. It addresses many questions regarding how AI and technological innovation are related to each other and how AI influences technological innovation. And, it contributes to the literature mainly in the following two aspects: (1) at the height of theory, this book explores the inherent mechanism underneath how AI affects technological innovation from the perspective of knowledge creation, the spillover effects of knowledge and technology, the capability of learning and absorption and investments in R&D and talents; (2) based on the panel data of manufacturing sectors from China, this book empirically analyzes the effect, degree, and sector heterogeneity of AI on technological innovation, while compares China's manufacture sectors.

In terms of how to understand the meaning of the inconsistent literature on market sensing, considering how important the capabilities of market sensing and market reaching are to a firm, this book (specifically, Chap. 6) contributes to three literature areas: the concept of market-sensing capabilities and related studies, profit opportunities within a stagnant industry, and the development of customer value propositions (CVPs). In particular, contributing to the first literature area, this book demonstrates that market-sensing capability actually empowers a company to identify and to better understand target customers; it helps lower the average cost of business operation, while increase expected profits. As for the literature on the profitability in stagnant industries, different from the existing works on specific industries, this book establishes results with broad-range applicability to many industries that are absent of market-level growth. As for the literature on the formulation and the effectiveness of CVPs, most studies are oriented toward case-specific analysis, while producing nothing about the effectiveness of CVPs except a few remotely related publications. Enriching these literature areas, this book looks at, among others, how market knowledge can assist the creation of effective CVPs, why a creative comprehension of market invitations is fundamentally important in the creation of effective CVPs, and under what conditions an adopted CVP becomes effective. In short, this book augments the literature in the following three ways: (1) it clears inconsistencies in relevant empirical findings, (2) it offers conclusions generally applicable to various markets when stated conditions are met, and (3) it points to the importance of market knowledge and its innovative understanding in the formulation of effective CVPs.

Regarding the literature on corporate governance, this book (specifically, Chap. 7) presents a systemic theory on how various decision-making units of a firm work together, interact with each other, and how stakeholders with inconsistent objectives put in their efforts to accomplish their, respectively, different, or even divergent goals. It first figuratively develops a preliminary understanding of relevant empirical discoveries by using the systemic yoyo model; and then it turns its attention to the establishment of a simple analytic model for studying the price behaviors of different investment projects. By employing these different models, this book shows that even though the boards, dominated by long-term, large shareholders, prefer long-term, value-building projects, CEOs' successes on short-term projects bear such a consequence that is favorable to the CEOs. In particular, such short-term successes help CEOs acquire additional trust from and control over the boards. More interestingly, this book proves that the number of short-term projects a CEO likes to take on is less than the number the board would like him to take on. That is, in practice, no matter how much the large shareholders worry about the possibilities that the CEO could expropriate their investment funds or spend the funds on his private benefits of control, and how much they do to prevent their worries from becoming true, the CEO still has substantial control right (gained over time) and discretion to allocate funds in ways he chooses.

1.3.2 Contributions to the Literature of Decision-Making

For managers and entrepreneurs to understand what is happening in the present world of business, where avalanche changes have been happening, this book (specifically, Chap. 8) develops a general theory based on the rigor of game theory and the logical reasoning of systems science. On top of this development, the book provides explanations for why markets have been changing faster, customers become less patient than ever before, and what the most important organizational element is for a firm to successfully ride waves of transient competitive advantages.

To understand why sustainable competitive advantages are a concept of the past, this book employs Bjerknes' Circulation Theorem to develop a systemic view of how local, regional, and then world economies evolve with time. That naturally explains what makes present competitive advantages feel like transient. To identify the most important organizational characteristic for a firm to have in order to succeed in the present world of business, this book shows that it is internal stability of the firm in terms of a long-term unwavering ambition and major investment in creating a common identity, culture, and commitment to leadership development in individual employees. Such internal stability equips the firm with the essential organizational culture for necessary changes to take place.

The development of this theory enriches the literatures of how to survive in a fast-changing market, evolution of business organizations, adaptability in a challenging environment and downstream market competition, respectively.

To help equip decision-making managers and entrepreneurs to transit into the era of fast-changing world of business, where market competition is increasingly intensifying due to the globalization of international economies and unification of international finances, this book (specifically, Chap. 9) uncovers four necessary conditions for a firm to satisfy to prepare itself to successfully ride waves of transient competitive advantages. After establishing the underlying connections among the four conditions by employing the logic of systemic thinking, the case of a legendary company is analyzed to validate the theory established in this book. This work contributes to the literature in three different perspectives, first, the readiness for a firm to embrace changes; second, knowledge, interactions, and networks; and third, strategies that lead to competitive advantages and improved performance.

Considering that competition is one spirited characteristic of the market economy and continuously finding a new profitable market niche, an entrepreneurial behavior that makes competition increasingly intensive, are the key for success in running business enterprises, this book (specifically, Chap. 10) investigates (1) the characteristics of market competition, and (2) the problem of sales associates' compensation (or sales force compensation). By using the rigor and language of game theory, this book shows when market competition will intensify, under what conditions the existing loyal consumer base of an established firm will start to deteriorate, and how a firm should motivate and compensate its sales force to achieve additional success. Other than making theoretical advances, the established results in this book can be directly applied to design new strategies to deal with market competition in order for firms to optimize their profits.

What is developed contributes to the literature of market competition and that of sales associates' compensation (or sales force compensation). To the former, conclusions in this book add additional insights of very different kinds and carry that literature many steps forward. In particular, this book shows the following main results, among others, regarding how a firm can potentially double its expected profits by being strategic; when all incumbent firms could potentially double their profits; under exactly what conditions the market competition will intensify; and when the existing loyal consumer base of an established firm will start to deteriorate. As for the literature of sales associates' compensation, this book establishes the following results, among others, regarding how sales associates' compensation should be aligned with the profit maximization of the firm; how by revealing private cost information of individual sales associates within the firm increases the expected incomes of the associates; and how the firm should assign incentive weights to each sales associate in order to maximize its profits.

To potentially help front-line managers and entrepreneurs handle the fierce world-wide competition, this book (specifically, Chap. 11) reveals the main strategic tactics that underlie the innovative activities of a manufacturing firm and demonstrates how such a firm's organizational culture, corporate structure, and leadership influence its degree of innovativeness. Regarding strategic tactics, this book determines the effect of strategies on innovation by examining why a firm needs to have clearly stated missions and a long-term, unwavering ambition. Then, it categorizes the 16 strategy variables, as recognized in the previous literature, into either primary or secondary strengths behind the innovativeness of a manufacturing firm. Here, a factor is seen as secondary, if it emerges as a natural consequence of the primary factors. As for the second outcome on how a firm's organizational culture, corporate structure and leadership influence its degree of innovativeness, this book analyzes the reason why mission and ambition stand for two important binding forces of any organizational culture, examines the significance of culture as a primary determinant of innovativeness, and discusses why total quality management is one prudent execution of the goal of an organization. To analyze the impact of leadership on innovation, this book demonstrates why a commitment of the leadership is of utmost importance to achieve successful innovation. And, it shows that "ownership structure" represents one of the predominant factors that influence the innovativeness of a firm, while other structure related factors, such as "formal structure," "flexible structure," "centralization of decision-making," "empowerment of employees," and "interaction between firm's units," are all of less importance and are merely pragmatic applications of the long term, unwavering ambition.

Regarding the effort of establishing a general theory that relates international business activities and the performance of firms, this book (specifically, Chap. 12) integrates the findings reported in the literature, while developing a series of general conclusions. Expectedly, what is achieved here can provide useful guidelines for practical applications and future research.

One of the most important contributions this book makes to the existing international business literature is the introduction and application of systems science (especially, the systemic yoyo model) to the study of international activities and how such activities affect the involved firms in terms of their economic performance. In addition to creating a brand-new perspective of looking at the international business activities, the employment of the systemic logic of reasoning and the methodology of systems science makes it more intuitive, specifiable, predictable, and repeatable for decision makers to determine what kinds of international activities—export, import, or both, their firms should be engaged in. By utilizing the systemic yoyo model, front-line managers and entrepreneurs will be able to make their important decisions in a timelier and more reliable fashion. These advantages of course have tremendous practical implications, considering the fact that competitive advantages in the present business world are no longer sustainable, and have been becoming transient (McGrath, 2013).

In terms of the literature, this work contributes to the empirical studies based on transaction level data on exports and imports and those of theoretical investigations. To the former area of the literature, this book confirms many of the empirically observed patterns. Although some of these results developed herein had also been derived by certain theoretical investigations (Melitz & Redding, 2014; Neary, 2010), the results presented in this book do not suffer from the same methodological deficiencies as the previous theoretical works do. In particular, for a constructed model to function properly, the modeler has to make a few basic assumptions, although they are not true in real life. For example, to investigate the impact of trade on intra-industry reallocations and aggregate industry productivity, Melitz (2003) assumes, among others, that (1) the collection of all goods (indexed by ω) considered by a representative consumer is a continuum; and (2) there is a continuum of firms, each of which produces a different variety ω of product. Evidently, the total number of goods considered by any consumer has to be a natural number, while the same is true for the number of firms that produce the products a consumer is interested in consuming. The reason for Melitz and others to introduce these and or similar assumptions is to fit the situation of concern into the framework of the calculus-based methodology. In comparison, the conclusions developed in this chapter does not suffer from these methodological deficiencies.

1.3.3 Contributions to the Literature of Interacting Economic Forces

To study the question of child labor and its efficiency under the assumption that the rotten members of the family are the parents instead of the kids (Bommier & Dubois,

2004; Lin, 2009), this book (specifically, Chap. 13) considers three independent variables—child labor, formal schooling, and level of maturity, and introduces the rule of the government. By comparing the strengths and weaknesses of the models employed by different scholars, this book adopts the two-time period approach, during the first of which the children are little and cannot live on their own without support from certain adults, such as parents or caretakers. And during the second time period, the children are now adults and live independently from their parents and caretakers.

The empirical literature on child labor has been inconsistent, for example, Canagarajah and Coulombe (1997) state in their study of Ghana that "poverty is significantly correlated with the decision to send children to school, and there is a significant negative relationship between going to school and working." To the contrary, Weiner (1991, p. 195) reports, "In India the proprietors of large businesses have not opposed child-labor laws ... one of the complaints of managers of large firms is that their labor force is not sufficiently educated, that too many workers are unable to read manuals or follow the simple instructions written on machines." To clear up these and other inconsistent discoveries about the effects of child labor, this book theoretically confirms some of the known conclusions established empirically, strengthen a few weakly-stated results derived earlier by different scholars without considering child's disutility of work from period 1 and levels of maturity. For example, this book shows that (1) a ban on child labor is not Pareto improving, and (2) if the laissez faire levels of child labor or formal schooling are not zero, then it leads to the rotten parents' effect, as so named by Bommier and Dubois (2004). In other words, when the condition in (3) holds true, the parents will rationally sacrifice the childhood utility of their children by making them work and study beyond their limits. They anticipate that doing so will result in higher future earnings of the children, and consequently larger transfers from the children.

Thaler (1989) calls for a better explanation for the stable wage differentials existing inter-industrially over time and across national borders, although many attempts have been tried unsatisfactorily without assuming something difficult to accept. To answer the call, this book (specifically, Chap. 14) develops another theory for the said phenomenon without repeating the previous works by introducing unnecessary assumptions for anyone to accept, be the person an economist or a random person waking on the street.

Comparing to studies of the past in this area, the main contribution of this book is its success with the development of models and analyses that evolve naturally without based on any empirically confirmed hypotheses. And, the maximization of the established models is achieved through using the simple Lagrange method and some elementary knowledge of differential equations. To this end, we like to point out that although the previous volume of this monograph series has clearly shown that not all firms maximize their profits, the present world of business is indeed composed of mostly such firms that maximize the returns of their major stakeholders.

A second contribution this book makes is how the understanding of why additional workers are hired is expanded as a new dimension of profit making. By analyzing the major differences between perfect and imperfect capital markets, this book uncovers some of the invisible differences between firms, and consequently between industries. These subtle differences lead firms and industries to varied opportunities, causing relevant business entities to behave differently in terms of wage setting and other practical aspects of daily operations.

To examine the financial crises that are caused or created purposefully by certain group(s) of people in order to acquire economic and political gains, this book (specifically, Chap. 15) employs the concepts of observability and controllability of economic systems to develop some very important observations. For example, it is shown that in the most general circumstance, each economic system is vulnerable to external influences. And, domestic monetary and fiscal policies can only effectively impact a portion of the domestic economy with visible consequences. What is worse is that an offender of a particular economy can concentrate its might on a specifically chosen attack point so that it is not entirely visible to the government of the target economy. That inevitably makes self-defense of the target economy more challenging.

By using the systemic intuition of the yoyo model and the Bernanke–Gertler model of the fundamental value of capital, this book also demonstrates theoretically how financial crises could be caused and/or created purposefully by certain group (s) of people in order to acquire economic and political gains through the use of movements of money across national borders. Because of the present-day globalization of the world economy, national and regional economies have been closely intertwined with each other. Hence, when one nation or geographic region suffers from economic and financial crises, the consequent damaging effects and adverse impacts tend to spread internationally. In particular, the discussion in this book indicates that when a large amount of foreign investments gathers in one place over either a long period or a short period of time and then leaves suddenly and massively, that local economy will suffer through a positive bubble, caused by the increased money supply as a consequence of the foreign investments, and then a following negative, disastrous burst, caused by the sudden dry-out of the money supply. And because a large number of economic activities are either unexpectedly delayed or totally impossible to complete, the local investors can no longer continuously collect their originally expected dividends for many time periods to come. If such situations are seen differently, this result indicates that foreign investments can be potentially employed as a weapon of mass destruction, if they leave strategically and suddenly, no matter whether they come quickly in a short period of time or slowly over a relatively longer period of time.

As for the question of how policy makers of a nation could possibly design a measure to counter sudden and purposeful leaves of foreign investments in order to avoid the undesirable disastrous consequences, this book (specifically, Chap. 16) establishes a control theory model for the general economic system, on which one can readily design measures to regulate the economy by employing relevant methods of the control theory. The complexity and dynamics of any real economy tend to make the estimates of the model's parameters inaccurate or change without any advanced notice. So, it is necessary under such circumstances to introduce effective strategies into the theoretical model so that the controlled variables could approach the target values accurately in order to guarantee the stability of the economic system. Based on this kind of thinking, on the basis of the feedback control method, this book symbolically formulates the problem of designing regulatory policies and establishes a feedback control model for the economic system. It provides proofs and symbolic reasonings for how well this developed theory could perform in practice. Then, by using examples, this book confirms the feasibility and applicability of the developed theory.

Beyond what are outlined above, the primary contribution of this book is the long list of managerial recommendations that can be easily implemented in real-life situations. Especially, all theoretical results of this book are true in general, which distinguishes this work from the existing literature, wherein speculations are involved in the analyses of data and anecdotes, mining of data, and suggestions (in place of concrete recommendations) are offered. The improved results, as derived in this book, stem from the logic reasoning of systems science and the adopted approach of holistic thinking. In particular, the methodology adopted here overcomes the methodological deficiencies of prior data- and/or anecdote-based conclusions that interfere with the possibility to generalize empirical discoveries beyond the limitations of data or anecdotes used. Methodological weaknesses of empirical studies arise due to problems in the measurement of variables and the analysis of collected data (Becheikh et al., 2006). The former is concerned with uncertainty in measurement (Czichos et al., 2011), and the latter with drawbacks of data analysis and data mining (Liu & Lin, 2006).

1.4 Organization of Contents in This Volume

This book advances a unified general theory for as many applied economic and business issues as posed previously by applying the logic of systemic thinking and systems scientific methodology in two different ways. One is to employ such logic of reasoning to resolve a good number of unsettled problems and fill gaps existing in the literature. The other is to help mobilize various available methodologies to investigate issues of concern in order to take advantage of the strengths of these different approaches. Beyond this Chap. 1 that introduces the reader to the rest of this volume with all the necessary background information, the entire book consists of additional three parts and 15 chapters.

The first additional part addresses a list of issues related to the creation and capture of value. In particular, this part consists of six chapters. Chapter 2 looks at the supply-chain ecosystem of a business firm and how the innovative comprehension of a market signal brings forward challenges to the upstream supplies and downstream complementors. Chapter 3 presents a general theory on how to beneficially develop synergies for producers and consumers, and multi-sided markets. Chapter 4 examines the value potentials out of innovations and recourses, market forbearance, supply-chain and strategic blocks, networks, and convenient platforms.

Chapter 5 studies the relationship between artificial intelligence and technological innovations, and the mechanism underneath how the former stimulates the latter. Then, some real-life data are used to empirically reconfirm the validity of the conclusions derived earlier in this chapter. Chapter 6 investigates a firm's market-sensing and market-reaching capabilities, and customer value propositions, as a tool for market reaching, can be made effective. Chapter 7 pays a revisit to the agency problem. Beyond showing why such problem forever exists, it looks at how a firm's CEO and board of directors interact through the interactive dynamics of long-term and short-term projects.

Part III studies the issues related to managerial decision-making in modern business world. This part consists of five chapters. In particular, Chap. 8 looks at a firm's competitive advantages—either sustainable or transient, and how the market moves faster and customers become less patient than ever before. Chapter 9 examines the necessary steps that are needed for a firm to adapt to the new era of the business world by sorting through competitions the firm faces both internally and externally. Then, a real-life case study is employed to reinforce the established conclusions. Chapter 10 investigates the question of how to deal with indecisive customers by employing pricing strategies and by elevating the competitiveness of sales associates. Chapter 11 studies the adoption of appropriate strategies and necessary organizational supports needed to implement the adopted strategies in order for a firm to survive, to grow, and to succeed in the present, intense-competition filled market place. Chapter 12 considers the question of how a firm could decide to stay domestic or to go international, and how international trades could potentially improve the performance of the firm.

Part IV focuses on the management of large-scale business forces and how they interact with each other. In particular, this part contains four chapters. Chapter 13 looks at some important issues related to child labor—a widely studied topic, as a phenomenon opposite to what is considered in Becker's rotten kid theorem, where instead of rotten kids, the parents are rotten. Chapter 14 develops a general theory to explain the stably and internationally existing inter-industrial wage differentials, which has been observed since over half a century ago. Chapter 15 shows why any economy is vulnerable to foreign attacks due to the reason that the economy can always be decomposed into four parts, three of which are either uncontrollable or unobservable or both. Then, it lists one possible way for a currency war to take place. Chapter 16 introduces a few possible methods for a nation to defend its economy against currency attacks.

All in all, other than employing the logic of systemic thinking and the methodology of systems science to establish generally-true conclusions in applied economic and business areas, this book also shows that in terms of the employment of various methodologies, a systemic approach is needed so that all available tools of analysis and reasoning can be utilized systemically according to the characteristics of the problems of concern.

Because of the particular way the conclusions in this book are established, we expect that scholars, interested in studying topics in applied economic and business areas, and managers and entrepreneurs, who are involved in actual decision-making in their daily works, will find this book timely and beneficial in their works. And to make this book friendly to readers, we tried our best to develop each chapter as self-contained as possible so that readers do not need to flip through the pages to look up relevant concepts or results.

Acknowledgment Various specialists, scholars, colleagues, and friends had contributed more or less to the composition of the chapters in this book. I like to use this opportunity to send them my heartfelt thanks for various opportunities for me to collaborate with these highly inspirational professionals over the past years. The following are the details on how these collaborators contributed to each of the chapters of this volume.

Chapter 1 Jeffrey Yi-Lin Forrest (Slippery Rock University).

Chapter 2 Jeffrey Yi-Lin Forrest (Slippery Rock University).

Chapter 3 Jeffrey Yi-Lin Forrest (Slippery Rock University), Qiang Bu (Pennsylvania State University Hersey).

Chapter 4 Jeffrey Yi-Lin Forrest (Slippery Rock University), Joachim Wagner (Leuphana University, Germany), Melanie Anderson (Slippery Rock University), John Lipinski (Indiana University), Yong Liu (Jiangnan University, China), Xiaoguang Tian (Purdue University Fort Wayne).

Chapter 5 Jeffrey Yi-Lin Forrest, Lawrence Shao, Theresa A. Wajda (Slippery Rock University), Bailey C. Forrest (Google), Yong Liu (Jiangnan University, China), Michael Y. Hu (Kent State University), Dale Shao (Marshall University), Jun Liu (Nanjing University of Information Science & Technology), Zhen Li (Texas Woman's University), Brian W. Sloboda (University of Phoenix).

Chapter 6 Jeffrey Yi-Lin Forrest (Slippery Rock University), Kangping Wu (Tsinghua University), Baek-kyoo Joo (Slippery Rock University), Li Yan (Université du Québec en Outaouais, Canada), Kosin **Isariyawongse** (Edinboro University).

Chapter 7 Jeffrey Yi-Lin Forrest (Slippery Rock University), Ashkan Hafezalkotob (Islamic Azad University, Iran), Louie Ren (University of Houston – Victoria), Yong Liu (Jiangnan University), Pavani Tallapally (Slippery Rock University).

Chapter 8 Jeffrey Yi-Lin Forrest (Slippery Rock University), Lawrence Shao (Slippery Rock University), Jun Liu (Nanjing University of Information Science & Technology), Brian W. Sloboda (University of Phoenix), Dale Shao (Marshall University).

Chapter 9 Jeffrey Yi-Lin Forrest (Slippery Rock University), Zaiwu Gong (Nanjing University of Information Science and Technology), Erkan Köse (Nuh Naci Yazgan University, Turkey), Diane D. Galbraith (Slippery Rock University),Oğuzhan A. Arık (Nuh Naci Yazgan University, Turkey).

Chapter 10 Jeffrey Yi-Lin Forrest (Slippery Rock University), Joachim Wagner (Leuphana University, Germany), Jennifer Nightingale (Slippery Rock University), Huan Guo (Jianghan University, China), Jennifer Roy (Waynesburg University).

Chapter 11 Jeffrey Yi-Lin Forrest (Slippery Rock University), Davood Darvishi (Payame Noor University, Iran), Abdou K. Jallow (Slippery Rock University), Zhen Li (Texas Woman's University).

Chapter 12 Jeffrey Yi-Lin Forrest (Slippery Rock University), Kurt Schimmel (Slippery Rock University), Fen Wang (Central Washington University), Ashkan Hafezalkotob (Islamic Azad University, Iran), Jian Liu (Nanjing University of Science and Technology).

Chapter 13 Jeffrey Yi-Lin Forrest (Slippery Rock University), Zaiwu Gong (Nanjing University of Information Science and Technology), Rhonda S. Clark (Slippery Rock University), Reneta Barneva (The State University of New York at Fredonia).

Chapter 14 Jeffrey Yi-Lin Forrest (Slippery Rock University), Davood Darvishi (Payame Noor University, Iran), Rhonda S. Clark (Slippery Rock University), Mojtaba Seyedian (The State University of New York at Fredonia), Jun Liu (Nanjing University of Information Science & Technology).

Chapter 14 Appendix Jeffrey Yi-Lin Forrest (Slippery Rock University), Lawrence Shao (Slippery Rock University), Shynara Sarkambayeva (Jumadilova) (Satbayev University), Dale Shao (Marshall University), Sunita Mondal (Slippery Rock University).

Chapter 15 Jeffrey Yi-Lin Forrest (Slippery Rock University), Tufan Tiglioglu (Alvernia University),Yong Liu (Jiangnan University), Donald Mong (Slippery Rock University), Marta Cardin (Ca' Foscari University of Venice, Italy).

Chapter 16 Jeffrey Yi-Lin Forrest (Slippery Rock University), Zaiwu Gong (Nanjing University of Information Science and Technology), Zhen Li (Texas Woman's University), Shynara Sarkambayeva (Jumadilova) (Satbayev University, Kazakhstan), John Golden (Slippery Rock University).

Chapter 17 Jeffrey Yi-Lin Forrest (Slippery Rock University), Dillon Z. Forrest (Steady, LLC), Bruce Orvis (Slippery Rock University).

References

Adner, R., Oxley, J. E., & Silverman, B. S. (Eds.). (2013). *Collaboration and competition in business ecosystems*. Emerald.

Aghion, P., Jones, B. F., & Jones, C. I. (2017). Artificial intelligence and economic growth. NBER Working Paper No. 23928.

Agrawal, A. K., Gans, J. S., & Goldfarb, A. (2018). Prediction, judgment and complexity: A theory of decision making and artificial intelligence. NBER Working Paper No. 24243.

Alshanty, A. M., & Emeagwali, O. L. (2019). Market-sensing capability, knowledge creation and innovation. *Journal of Innovation & Knowledge, 4*(3), 171–178.

Amit, R., & Zott, C. (2001). Value creation in e-business. *Strategic Management Journal, 22*(6/7), 493–520.

Ardyan, E. (2016). Market sensing capability and SMEs performance. *DLSU Business & Economics Review, 25*(2), 79–97.

Barney, J. B. (1991). Firm resources and sustained competitive advantage. *Journal of Management, 17*(1), 99–120.

Becheikh, N., Landry, R., & Amara, N. (2006). Lessons from innovation empirical studies in the manufacturing sector: A systematic review of the literature from 1993 to 2003. *Technovation, 26*(5), 644–664.

Becker, G. S. (1974). A theory of social interactions. *Journal of Political Economy, 82*(6), 1063–1093.

Bernard, A. B., & Jensen, J. B. (1995). Exporters, jobs, and wages in U.S. manufacturing: 1976–1987. *Brookings Papers on Economic Activity, Microeconomics* (pp. 67–119).

Bjerknes, V. (1898). Uber einen hydrodynamischen Fundamentalsatz und seine Anwendung besonders auf die Mechanik der Atmosphare und des Weltmeeres. *Kongliga Svenska Vetenskaps-Academiens Nya Handlingar, 31*, 1–35.

Bommier, A., & Dubois, P. (2004). Rotten parents and child labor. *Journal of Political Economy, 112*(1), 240–248.

Canagarajah, R., & Coulombe, H. (1997). *Child labor and schooling in Ghana. Human development technical report (Africa region)*. World Bank.

Czichos, H., Saito, T., & Smith, L. (Eds.). (2011). *Springer handbook of metrology and testing* (2nd ed.). Springer.

Day, G. S. (1994). The capabilities of market-driven organizations. *Journal of Marketing, 58*(4), 37–52.

Drucker, P. F. (1954). *The practice of management*. Harper & Row.

EC (European Commission). (2018). *Artificial intelligence: An European perspective*. Retrieved April 16, 2019, from http://publications.jrc.ec.europa.eu/repository/bitstream/JRC113826/ai-flagship-report-online.pdf

Einstein, A. (1997). *The collected papers of Albert Einstein: The Berlin years* (Vol. 8). Princeton University Press.

Eisenhardt, K., & Martin, J. (2000). Dynamic capabilities: What are they? *Strategic Management Journal, 21*(10/11), 1105–1121.

Forrest, J. Y. L. (2013). *A systemic perspective on cognition and mathematics*. CRC Press.

Forrest, J. Y. L. (2014). *A systems perspective on financial systems*. CRC Press.

Forrest, J. Y. L. (2018). *General systems theory: Foundation, intuition and applications in business decision making*. Springer.

Forrest, J. Y. L., Buttermore, J., & Wajda, T. A. (2017). At Nash equilibrium when new market competitions appear? *Kybernetes: The International of Cybernetics, Systems and Management Science, 46*(2), 256–271.

Forrest, J. Y. L., & Liu, Y. (2022). *Value in business: A holistic, systems-based approach to creating and achieving value*. Springer.

Forrest, J. Y. L., Nicholls, J., Schimmel, K., & Liu, S. F. (2020). *Managerial decision making: A holistic approach*. Springer.

Forrest, J. Y. L., & Tallapally, P. (2018). Customers are less patient, sustainable advantage becomes transient and the key for firms to succeed in fast changing markets. *Journal of Business, Economics and Technology, 21*(1), 1–14.

Forrest, J. Y. L., & Tao, L. X. (2014). *Investment and employment opportunities in China*. CRC Press.

Forrester Research Report. (2000). Global eCommerce approaches hypergrowth. April 2000.

Government of Japan. (2015). Retrieved April 16, 2019, from https://www8.cao.go.jp/cstp/kihonkeikaku/5basicplan_en.pdf

Hein, E., Detzer, D., & Dodig, N. (Eds.). (2016). *Financialisation and the financial and economic crises: Country studies*. Edward Elgar Publishing.

Hitt, M. A., & Ireland, R. D. (2017). The intersection of entrepreneurship and strategic management research. In D. L. Sexton, H. Landstrom, & C. Jones (Eds.), *The Blackwell handbook of entrepreneurship* (pp. 45–63). Blackwell.

Kahneman, D., Knetsh, J., & Thaler, R. (1986). Fairness as a constraint on profit seeking: Entitlements in the market. *The American Economic Review, 76*(4), 728–741.

Kenny, A. (2012). *A new history of western philosophy*. Oxford University Press.

Kline, M. (1972). *Mathematical thought from ancient to modern times*. Oxford University Press.

Klir, G. (1985). *Architecture of systems problem solving*. Plenum Press.

Klir, G. (2001). *Facets of systems science*. Springer.

Lemoussu, S., Chaudemar, J. C., & Vingerhoeds, R. A. (2018). Systems engineering and project management process modeling in the aeronautics context: Case study of SMEs. *International Journal of Mechanical and Mechatronics Engineering, 12*(2), 88–96.

Lin, Y. (1999). *General systems theory: A mathematical approach*. Plenum and Kluwer Academic Publishers.

Lin, Y. (2007). Systemic yoyo model and applications in Newton's, Kepler's laws, etc. *Kybernetes: International Journal of Systems and Cybernetics, 36*(3/4), 484–516.

Lin, Y. (2009). *Systemic yoyos: Some impacts of the second dimension*. Auerbach Publications.

Lin, Y., & Forrest, B. (2011). *Systemic structure behind human organizations: From civilizations to individuals*. Springer.

Lin, Y., & OuYang, S. C. (2010). *Irregularities and prediction of major disasters*. CRC Press.

Lindblom, A., Olkkonen, R., Mitronen, L., & Kajalo, S. (2008). Market-sensing capability and business performance of retail entrepreneurs. *Contemporary Management Research, 4*(3), 219–236.

Liu, S. F., & Lin, Y. (2006). *Grey information: Theory and practical applications*. Springer.

Markoff, J. (2016). *Machines of loving grace: The quest for common ground between humans and robots*. HarperCollins.

McGrath, R. G. (2013). *The end of competitive advantage: How to keep your strategy moving as fast as your business*. Harvard Business Review Press.

Melitz, M. J. (2003). The impact of trade on intra-industry reallocations and aggregate industry productivity. *Econometrica, 71*, 1695–1725.
Melitz, M. J., & Redding, S. J. (2014). Heterogeneous firms and trade. *Handbook of International Economics, 4*, 1–54.
Neary, J. P. (2010). Two and a half theories of trade. *The World Economy, 33*(1), 1–19.
OWH. (2016a). *Preparing for the future of artificial intelligence*. Retrieved April 20, 2019, from https://obamawhitehouse.archives.gov/sites/default/files/whitehouse_files/microsites/ostp/NSTC/preparing_for_the_future_of_ai.pdf
OWH. (2016b). *The national artificial intelligence research and development strategic plan*. Retrieved April 16, 2016, from https://www.nitrd.gov/PUBS/national_ai_rd_strategic_plan.pdf
Payne, A., & Frow, P. (2005). A strategic framework for customer relationship management. *Journal of Marketing, 69*(4), 167–176.
Payne, A., Frow, P., & Eggert, A. (2017). The customer value proposition: evolution, development, and application in marketing. *Journal of the Academy of Marketing Science, 45*, 467–489.
Penrose, E. T. (1959). *The theory of the growth of the firm*. John Wiley & Sons.
Porter, M. E. (1985). *Competitive advantage: Creating and sustaining superior performance*. Free Press.
Qu, Y. (1985). *The songs of the South: An anthology of ancient Chinese poems by Qu Yuan and Other Poets (translated by David Haykes)*. Penguin Classics.
Santalo, J., & Becerra, M. (2008). Competition from specialized firms and the diversification-performance linkage. *Journal of Finance, 63*(2), 851–883.
Shannon, C. E. (1949). *The mathematical theory of communication*. Illinois University Press.
Slichter, S. (1950). Notes on the structure of wages. *The Review of Economics and Statistics, 32*(1), 80–91.
Smith, A. (1776). *The Wealth of Nations, books I-III (1986 printing)*. Penguin Books.
Solow, R. M. (1979). Another possible source of wage stickiness. *Journal of Macroeconomics, 1*(1), 79–82.
Soros, G. (1998). *The crisis of global capitalism: Open society endangered*. Public Affairs.
Stigler, G. J. (1958). The economics of scale. *The Journal of Law and Economics, 1*, 54–71.
Stock, G. N., Greis, N. P., & Fischer, W. A. (2002). Firm size and dynamic technological innovation. *Technovation, 22*, 537–549.
Sugiyarti, G., & Ardyan, E. (2017). Market sensing capability and product innovation advantages in emerging markets: The case of market entry quality and marketing performance of Batick Industry in Indonesia. *DLSU Business & Economics Review, 27*(1), 175–189.
Thaler, R. (1989). Interindustry wage differentials. *Journal of Economic Perspectives, 3*, 181–193.
von Bertalanffy, L. (1968). *General systems theory*. George Braziller.
Wagner, J. (2016). A survey of empirical studies using transaction level data on exports and imports. *Review of World Economics, 152*, 215–225.
Wang, R. X., & Hu, G. H. (2005). *International finance*. Press of Wuhan University of Science and Technology.
Webster, F. E. (2002). *Market-driven management: How to define, develop and deliver customer value* (2nd ed.). Wiley.
Weiner, M. (1991). *The child and the State in India*. Princeton University Press.
Wu, Y., & Lin, Y. (2002). *Beyond nonstructural quantitative analysis: Blown-ups, spinning currents and modern science*. World Scientific.
Xi, J. P. (2017). Retrieved April 16, 2019, from http://www.gov.cn/zhuanti/2017-10/27/content_5234876.htm
Ye, G. L., Priem, R. L., & Alshwer, A. A. (2012). Achieving demand-side synergy from strategic diversification: How combining mundane assets can leverage consumer utilities. *Organization Science, 23*(1), 207–224.
Ying, Y. R., & Forrest, J. Y. L. (2015). *Capital account liberation: Methods and applications*. CRC Press.

Part II
Value Creation and Capture

Chapter 2
The Ecosystem of a Firm

Jeffrey Yi-Lin Forrest, Yong Liu, Theresa A. Wajda, Erkan Köse, and Oguzhan Arik

Abstract This chapter, which is mainly based on (Forrest et al., Dependence of a firm's performance on its ecosystem's upstream/downstream challenges. In: Proceedings of the 2019 Annual Meeting of National Association of Business, Economics and Technology. National Association of Business, Economics and Technology, pp. 83–100, 2019a; Forrest et al., How challenges and successes of a firm depend on its input-output ecosystem. In: Proceedings of the 2019 Annual Conference of Decision Sciences Institute. Decision Sciences Institute, pp. 2381–2402, 2019b), investigates holistically the supply-chain ecosystem of a focal firm, when the firm innovatively deciphers a market invitation and attempts to profitably answer the market call. It establishes a series of general conclusions regarding the firms' environmental challenges. In particular, it shows, among other results, that (1) challenges, faced by either upstream component(s) or downstream complement(s), place, respectively, a cap on how much "value" the firm can create and how much it can capture; (2) challenges upstream components face help build performance advantage for the focal firm over its competitors; however, if the firm's challenges are mostly on its upstream suppliers, then the performance advantage's lifespan will be greatly shortened; (3) an innovative firm has to consider the availability and development of appropriate complements in its introduction of innovative products; (4) when contracting with upstream suppliers, a focal firm has to deal with technological uncertainty and suppliers' behavioral uncertainty

Jeffrey Yi-Lin Forrest (Department of Accounting Economics Finance, Slippery Rock University, Slippery Rock, PA USA; Email: jeffrey.forrest@sru.edu), Yong Liu (School of Business, Jiangnan University, Wuxi, Jiangsu, China; Email: clly1985528@163.com), Theresa A. Wajda (Department of Management and Marketing, Slippery Rock University, Slippery Rock, PA USA; Email: theresa.wajda@sru.edu), Erkan Köse (Industrial Engineering Department, Nuh Naci Yazgan University, Kayseri, Turkey; Email: erkankose93@gmail.com), and Oguzhan Arik (Industrial Engineering Department, Nuh Naci Yazgan University, Kayseri, Turkey; Email: oaarik@nny.edu.tr) are equally contributed to this chapter.

J. Y.-L. Forrest, *Systemic Principles of Applied Economic Philosophies II*,
Translational Systems Sciences 39, https://doi.org/10.1007/978-981-99-7939-4_2

with the former affects the firm's ability to create value and the latter impacts its ability to capture value.

Thus, the more capable a focal firm is at identifying challenges, the more adept this firm will be in creating and sustaining marketplace advantage as well as imposing greater challenges on its ecosystem. Upon the conclusion of relevant analyses, practical managerial significance of this chapter and open questions for future research are given.

Keywords Downstream complements · Problem solving · Supply-chain ecosystem · Technological uncertainty · Upstream components · Value system · Vertical interdependence

2.1 Introduction

When a firm comprehends a market signal innovatively, it has positioned itself in an advantageous situation to develop a significant competitive advantage over its competitors. However, to materialize such an advantage, other than internal reasons the firm has to analyze how other players in its supply-chain ecosystem (Adner et al., 2013) could affect its fortune. For example, the difficult daily commuting problem, confronting those individuals who live in a suburban area and commute to work inside a major U.S. metropolitan, necessarily invites politicians and entrepreneurs alike to come up with a solution. One possible resolution to this challenge, for example, is to design, produce, and offer flying cars (Lemoussu et al., 2018) to these frustrated commuters. To manufacture realistically such cars, a firm has to have appropriate components supplied to it in its assembling of the imagined product. However, the value created for commuters is not practically realizable until the appropriate road conditions and air traffic controls, as key complements, are constructed and installed in order for such cars to move and fly around freely and orderly. So, a natural question arises: When a firm innovatively deciphers a market invitation for innovation, how will the consequent design of the firm's new product (s) post challenges to other players within its ecosystem? Speaking differently, the question can be rephrased as follows: how will the consequent success of the firm depend on the success of other players in its ecosystem?

This chapter, which is mainly based on Forrest et al. (2019a, b), seeks to address this theoretically and practically important question by randomly selecting a firm as the firm of our focus of discussion. To accomplish this end, the chapter first distinguishes suppliers and complementors so that suppliers provide their outputs for the focal firm to integrate in its effort to offer a complete product to its customers and complementors facilitate necessary conditions for customers to fully utilize the product. Then, the chapter develops the following main conclusions among others:

- The upper limits of value the focal firm can create and capture are, respectively, constrained by the challenges facing its upstream components and downstream complementors;

- The performance advantage of a focal firm over its competitors is positively correlated to the level of challenges the firm's suppliers face and negatively to that of the firm's complementors;
- To successfully ride waves of transient competitive advantages, a firm has to introduce such innovative products that suppliers can possibly provide necessary components and complementors can readily facilitate needed complements; and
- When contracting with upstream suppliers, a firm has to deal with technological and behavioral uncertainty, where the former affects the firm's creation of value, and the latter impacts the firm's capture of value.

The remainder of this chapter is organized as follows. Section 2.2 provides a literature review while showing how this chapter contributes to the established knowledge. Section 2.3 introduces the well-known dishpan experiment and other necessary background information to make this chapter as self-contained as possible. Section 2.4 constructs the supply-chain ecosystem of an arbitrarily chosen business firm. Section 2.5 studies the relationship between market success and challenges a firm faces. Sections 2.6 and 2.7 address challenges facing either upstream firms or downstream enterprises. After looking at two kinds of upstream uncertainties in Sect. 2.8, Sect. 2.9 concludes the presentation with managerial recommendations and unsettled problems for future research.

2.2 Literature Review

Due to the power of systems thinking and methodology, this chapter contributes to an array of different literatures, simultaneously covering business ecosystems, value capture and creation, competitive advantage, and customer adoption of innovation, firm uncertainties (contractual, behavioral and technological), as well as technology life cycle. In this section, we review relevant works in each of these discrete literatures.

In the literature of ecosystems, Adner et al. (2013) publish a collection of papers addressing how system players collaborate and compete with each other. Refuting the common beliefs that knowledge ecosystems in technology hotspots leads to business ecosystems in which there are competitive advantages for each of the players in the ecosystem, Clarysse et al. (2014) find a particular case where a structured knowledge ecosystem is concentrated around only a number of central players. The result is an imagined business ecosystem that is nearly non-existent. When a business ecosystem includes well-established companies and new ventures, Zahra and Nambisan (2012) claim that success of that ecosystem requires collaboration and competition that demands strategic thinking to leverage a firm's resources and capabilities. Kapoor and Agarwal (2017) study how platform firms in a business ecosystem orchestrate the ecosystem's functioning by providing platforms and setting the rules for participation by complementor firms. They develop a reason for how the ecosystem's structural and evolutionary features may shape the extent to which participating complementor firms can sustain their superior performance. Instead of using technical interdependencies, Hellström et al. (2015) explore how firms in an energy business ecosystem collaborate by using a business model lens, pointing to the importance of locating the factors that drive the business models of collaborating firms to facilitate system transitions and change in the logic of an industry. Attour and Lazaric (2018) emphasize that transformation of a knowledge ecosystem can lead to the emergence of a technological platform that provides the resources required especially for firm startup. By conceptualizing the construct of ecosystems, Adner (2017) offers an examination of the relationship between ecosystems and a host of other constructs, such as business models, platforms, coopetition, multisided markets, networks, technology systems, supply chains, and value networks.

In the literature on value creation and capture, Chemmanur et al. (2014) analyze how entrepreneurial firms differ when they are corporate venture capital (CVC) based or independent venture capital (IVC) based in terms of their innovativeness. What is found is that CVC-backed firms are more innovative, although they are younger, riskier, and less profitable than those backed by IVC. Kagermann (2015) discusses the impact, challenges, and opportunities of digitization and finds that the two key instruments for greater value creation in the Age of Industry 4.0 are platform-based cooperation and a dual innovation strategy. By looking at how the usage of big data analytics (BDA) affects value creation, Chen et al. (2015) conceptualize BDA use as an information processing capability that brings competitive advantage to organizations and identify paths through which factors influence the actual usage of BDA.

Regarding performance and competitive advantages, Yadav et al. (2017) look at the association between a firm's environmental efforts and the sustainability of its competitive advantage through analyzing how changes in the firm's environmental performance affect the persistence of its profitability growth. These authors find that environmental resources permit superior financial performing firms to maintain their competitive advantage, while complementing poorly performing firm's efforts to recover. This chapter empirically supports the proposition that economic value can be created through benefiting the environment. Prajogo and Oke (2016) examine the effect of human capital (HC) on service innovation advantage (SIA) and business performance (BP), and how external environmental factors play a role. These authors show that HC is positively correlated to the creation of value or SIA which in turn results in rent generation for firms, and that the effect of SIA on BP is influenced by environmental factors such that it is strengthened by dynamic environments and weakened by competitive environments. Chang et al. (2016) consider the inconsistent relationship between supply-chain integration (SCI) and firm performance by proposing that the inconsistency may be associated with selection bias, failure to consider the mediating routes of how SCI affects financial performance, and lack of investigation of moderators. Their findings confirm the early claim that each dimension of SCI indeed improves financial performance.

In terms of market adaptation of innovation, Oliveira et al. (2016) aim to identify determinants of mobile payment adoption by proposing a new model. These researchers find that compatibility, perceived technology security, performance expectations, innovativeness, and social influence have significant effects on consumer adoption. This work provides a basis for further refinement of individual models of acceptance. Bilgicer et al. (2015) study the role of social contagion in customer adoption of new sales channels by focusing on two aspects of social contagion (i.e., local contagion and homophily), as they influence a consumer's preference for either an internet channel or a brick-and-mortar store. Bilgicer et al. find that social contagion does indeed play a major role with long-term versus short-term customers being less inclined to consider alternate sales channels. By recognizing the importance of downstream activities of the innovation process, specifically marketing and commercialization, Brem and Viardot (2015) consider the adoption of innovations by the market by providing conceptual insights and manners that appear to stimulate and facilitate the adoption of every kind of innovation. Laukkanen (2016) posits that all innovations meet consumer resistance and overcoming this unfriendliness needs to occur prior to product adoption. He examines how five adoption barriers—usage, value, risk, tradition, and image—and three consumer demographics—gender, age, and income—influence consumer adoption versus rejection decisions in internet and mobile banking. Laukkanen finds that value is the strongest barrier, while image slows adoption; and that both gender and age significantly predict adoption and rejection decisions.

As for the literature of various uncertainties, Hendrikse et al. (2015) provide empirical evidence that somewhat supports the following hypotheses: (1) general trust of the franchisor reduces the franchisor's perception of relational risk and hence the necessity to control the network relationship by more complete contract planning, and (2) knowledge-based trust increases information sharing between the partners and hence the knowledge base for specifying more detailed contracts. To better understand how contractual and relational governance interact, Cao and Lumineau (2015) conduct a qualitative review and meta-analysis of the existing literature. Some findings uncovered by these researchers include the following: (1) Contractual governance is positively related to trust and relational norms, (2) There are two sides to relational governance, (3) Contracts, trust, and relational norms jointly improve satisfaction and relationship performance while jointly reducing opportunism, and (4) Contractual and relational governance can complement or substitute for each other in certain situations. Hallberg (2015) argues that uncertain governance choices are subject to specific decision-biases and potentially corrective functions of current organization as well as asymmetries in actors' access to decision-supporting systems. Specifically, Hallberg maintains that with overestimated unbiased rationality and asymmetric access to decision-supporting systems, transaction cost economics runs the risk of underestimating the degree of vertical integration in actual firms. By looking through the lens of the relational view, Bstieler and Hemmert (2015) disentangle the effects of relational and contractual governance on collaboration outcomes by using survey data from South Korea. They find that the strength of prior business ties enhances relational governance and contributes to knowledge acquisition and collaboration satisfaction. And even though the impact of contractual governance is weaker than relational governance, when both governance mechanisms are applied simultaneously, the positive returns on collaboration satisfaction diminish.

Mondragon and Mondragon (2018) investigate the role of systems integrators at managing complex products with modular architectures under technological uncertainty in the automotive supply chain. They show that systems integrators in low technological uncertainty have to be able to redesign their architectures due to the implementation of unknown technologies in key individual components, and for complex product and architectures under high technological uncertainty, the most important source of innovation still lies in the specialization of individual activities. Addressing inconsistent empirical findings regarding the relationship between supply-chain integration (SCI) and performance, Huang et al. (2014) develop a SCI model that includes buyer-supplier-supplier relationships and propose a contingency framework for reexamining the SCI-supplier performance relationship under demand and technological uncertainties. These scholars find that although SCI seems to have a significant positive effect on the suppliers' performance, this positive relationship can be weakened by demand uncertainty and strengthened by technological uncertainty. Considering the challenge facing the commercialization of an emerging technology that employs an immature production process, Roca et al. (2017) unpack how the characteristics of a technology may influence the options for regulatory intervention. These scholars propose a generalizable framework for regulating emerging process-based technologies in safety-critical industries. By employing the industrial economics and knowledge-based perspective, Burton and Galvin (2018) hypothesize how the combined effects of product architecture type, product complexity and the rate of product component change may influence task, knowledge and firm boundaries. They suggest that whether mirroring or misting is an efficient strategic choice is influenced by the characteristics of both the product architecture and the rate of technological change at the product component level, as well as changes across time as products evolve.

By drawing on effectuation theory, Jiang and Tornikoski (2018) theorize how founder teams' perceptions of uncertainty and behavioral logics develop during new venture creation processes, suggesting a possible evolution from a causal conditional relationship between perceived uncertainty and behavioral logics to an integrative relationship. Through integrating transaction cost economics and justice theory, Trada and Goyal (2017) examine the impact of perceived unfairness on distributor opportunism and uncover the dual effects of perceived unfairness on opportunism: directly enhancing opportunism and aggravating (positively moderating) the effects of economic forces on opportunism. By theoretically clarifying from a transaction cost economics point of view under what circumstances multinational companies (MNCs) should outsource their innovation functions, Yeo and Saboori-Deilami (2017) show that heterogeneity between the home and host country affects the autonomy of the innovation at the host country. This autonomy in turn leads to higher transaction cost, which turns out to be the main determinant of the decision on whether or not to outsource the innovation function. Bruneel et al. (2017) empirically show that technology complexity within new technology-based firms negatively influences the level of inter-organizational trust in key partner relationships, while both relationship and partner characteristics moderate the technology complexity-trust relationship.

Regarding technology life cycle, addressing the fact that previous studies have not considered the dynamic and idiosyncratic aspects of a technology's progression. Lee et al. (2017) propose a stochastic technology life cycle analysis to trace the phases of a technology's progression based on patent citations, thus leading to the identification of the patterns of technology life cycles at the individual patent level. Due to the significance of discussions on the patterns of technological innovation in terms of the efficient distribution of national R&D resources and the establishment of corporate managerial strategies. Byun et al. (2018) calculate and analyze technology cycle time (TCT) by technological area based on patent data. Contrast to the common belief that firms should match their organizational form to the prevailing nature of technology. Helfat et al. (2016) provide a new explanation for why vertically integrated and specialized firms may continue to coexist as industries evolve and why these firms may rationally choose to stay integrated and bear the sunk costs of developing integrative capabilities as well as the ongoing costs of maintaining them, even when they lose money during some time periods due to competition from lower cost specialized firms.

This chapter contributes to the literature in various ways. First, it introduces systems science into the investigation of the asymmetrical distribution of challenges across the ecosystem of a firm. Second, it establishes generally true propositions, leading to reliable applications, without suffering from the constraints and limitations of anecdotal and data analysis (or data mining). In other words, the results established in this chapter are universally true within the system of our cohesive theory constructed on top of a few basic assumptions and logical reasoning.

2.3 The Dishpan Experiment

To make this chapter as self-contained as possible, let us briefly look at the yoyo model for the general system. For relevant details, see volume one of this monograph. And for relevant justifications of this model, see Lin (2009).

What this model says is that each entity in the universe, be it physical or intellectual, and be it a tangible or intangible object, a living being, an organization, a market, or an economy, can be *intuitively* seen as a realization of a certain multi-dimensional spinning yoyo, around which there are an eddy and a meridian field. This systemic structure stays in a spinning motion as depicted in Fig. 2.1a. If it stops its spin, it will no longer exist as an identifiable system. What Fig. 2.1b demonstrates is that some of the outputs of the yoyo field actually return back into the yoyo body after having been emitted out from the body. And, what Fig. 2.1c shows is that due to the interaction between the eddy field, which spins perpendicularly to the axis of spin, of the model, and the meridian field, which rotates parallel to the axis of spin, things that are either new to the yoyo body or returning to the input side travel along a spiral trajectory.

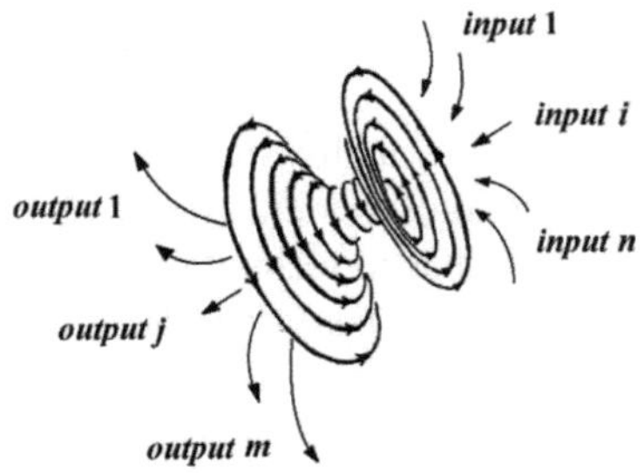

(a) The abstract yoyo structure underneath each system

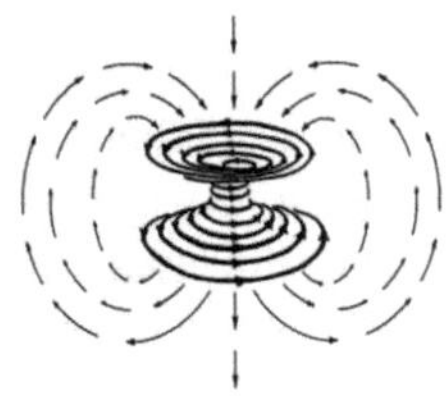

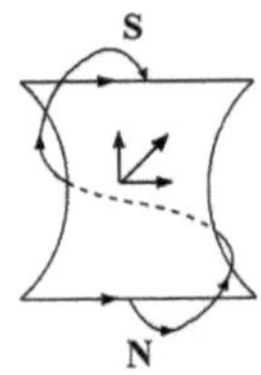

(b) The meridian field shown in dotted curves (c) Typical trajectory of how matters return

Fig. 2.1 The yoyo model of the general system. (**a**) The abstract yoyo structure underneath each system. (**b**) The meridian field shown in dotted curves. (**c**) Typical trajectory of how matters return

Comparing to the construction of Euclidean spaces (or Cartesian coordinate systems), one can tell that this yoyo model is more widely existing in the universe than the fictitious crossings of real-number lines. In particular, the phenomena of spin exist in all levels of the physical existence, in business interactions, and in political struggles.

This yoyo model of general systems includes the following key components: input, output, spin, and axis of spin. The first two components—input and output—are easy to understand, because each viable business entity has to take in things, such as investments, information, materials for production, etc., and give off things, such as products, after-sale service, etc. Next, let us spend a little time and effort to comprehend the key terms—spin and axis of spin—by thinking about a business firm.

First, each business organization, such as a firm, is an objectively existing system that is made up of such objects as people and some physical elements, where some specific relations between the objects help the collection of the objects emerge into an organic whole or system or a firm. For example, without the specific setup of organizational whole (relationships), a university of higher education will not exist even though the people, the buildings, the equipment, etc., are all around. Second, there are many ways to see why each business organization spins about an invisible axis. In particular, as is well-known in management science, each firm has its own particular organizational culture; differences in organizational cultures lead to varied levels of productivity (Forrest et al., 2020). Now, the basic components of an organizational culture change over time. These changes constitute the evolution of the firm and are caused by the need for the firm to survive and to succeed through inventing and importing ideas from other organizations and consequently modifying or eliminating some of the existing ones.

The concept of spin beneath the systemic yoyo structure of the firm comes from what ideas to invent, which external ideas to import, and which existing ones to eliminate. If idea A will likely make the firm more prosperous with a higher level of productivity, while idea B will likely make the firm stay as it has been, then these ideas will form a spin in the organizational culture. Specifically, some members of the firm might like additional productivity so that their personal goals can be materialized in the process of creating the additional productivity, while some other members might like to keep things as they have been so that what they have occupied, such as income, prestige, social status, etc., will not be adversely affected. These two groups of employees will fight against each other to push for their agendas so that theoretically, ideas A and B actually "spin" around each other. For one moment, A is ahead; for the next moment B is leading. And at yet another moment no side is ahead when the power struggle might very well reach a state that is similar to the initial state of affairs. In this particular incidence, the abstract axis of spin is invisible because no one is willing to openly admit his underlying purpose for pushing for a specific idea (either A or B or other ones).

In order to understand how the yoyo model (Fig. 2.1) can be applied to the studies of evolution and development of systems, organizations, etc., the rest of this section will look at the well-known dishpan experiment.

Dave Fultz, University of Chicago, and his colleagues in late 1950s (Fultz et al., 1959) constructed the following experiment: they partially filled a cylindrical vessel with water, placed it on a rotating turntable, and subjected to heating near the periphery and cooling near the center. The bottom of the container is intended to simulate one hemisphere of the earth's surface, the water the air above this hemisphere, the rotation of the turntable simulates the earth's rotation, the heating and cooling simulate the excess external heating of the atmosphere in low latitudes and the excess cooling in high latitudes.

In order to observe flow patterns at the upper surface of the water, which was intended to simulate atmospheric motion at high elevations, Fultz and his colleagues sprinkled some aluminum powder. A special camera that effectively rotated with the turntable took time exposures so that a moving aluminum particle would appear as a streak and sometimes each exposure ended with a flash, which could add an arrowhead to the forward end of each streak. The turntable generally rotated counter clockwise, as does the earth when viewed from above the North Pole.

Even though everything in the experiment was arranged with perfect symmetry about the axis of rotation, such as no impurities added in the water, the bottom of the container was kept flat, etc., Fultz and his colleagues observed more than they had bargained for. First, both expected flow patterns (as shown in Fig. 2.2a, b) appeared, and the choice depended on the speed of the turntable's rotation and the intensity of the heating. Briefly, with fixed heating, a transition from circular symmetry (Fig. 2.2a) to the more chaotic pattern (Fig. 2.2b) would take place as the rotation

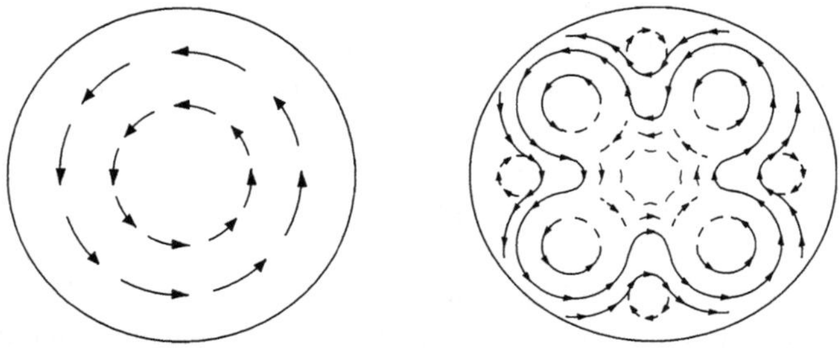

(a) Symmetric flow at the upper surface (b) Asymmetric flow at the upper surface

Fig. 2.2 Patterns observed in Fultz's dishpan experiment. (**a**) Symmetric flow at the upper surface. (**b**) Asymmetric flow at the upper surface

increased past a critical value. With a sufficiently rapid, but fixed rate of rotation, a similar transition would occur when the heating reached a critical strength, while another transition from that in Fig. 2.2b back to symmetry in Fig. 2.2a would occur when the heating reached a still higher critical strength.

A few years before the previous dishpan experiment was conducted in Chicago, Raymond Hide, Cambridge University, did a similar experiment in England (Hide, 1953). Instead of a dishpan, Hide used two concentric cylinders with a fluid placed in the ring-shaped region between the cylinders. He discovered similar transitions between symmetric and asymmetric flow patterns. In this experiment, the asymmetric flow was often regular and consisted of a chain of apparently identical waves, which would travel around the ring-shaped region without changing their shapes. What's more remarkable about what Hide found is that a chain of identical waves would appear. However, as they traveled along, they would alter their shapes in unison in a regular periodic fashion and after many rotations of the turntable, they would regain their original shape and then repeat the cycle (Fig. 2.3).

What's important about these experiments is that structures, such as jet streams, traveling vortices, and fronts appear to be basic features in rotating heated fluids, and are not peculiar to atmospheres only.

To make our logical reasoning valid for the rest of this book, we assume that each and every firm in the business world exists for the purpose of satisfying a particular market niche through generating a positive cash flow. The positive cash flow can be

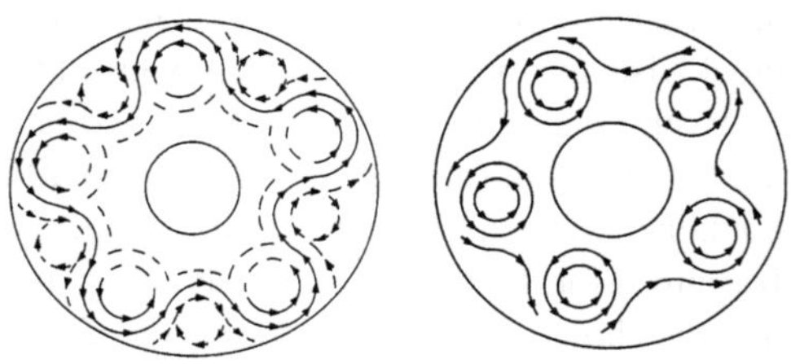

(a) One flow pattern (b) Another flow pattern

Fig. 2.3 Streak patterns of the flow at the upper surface of Hide's dishpan experiment. (**a**) is followed by (**b**) after eight rotations; and (**b**) is followed by (**a**) after another eight rotations. (**a**) One flow pattern. (**b**) Another flow pattern

a result of profits from the marketplace, or investments from various investors, or both.

By a *value system*, we mean (Porter, 1985) such associated activities that jointly transform raw materials into products or services for end users. These activities are usually performed by various firms with end users known as *consumers*. In contrast, intermediate, B2B purchasers in a value system are referred to as *customers* instead of consumers. When a firm delivers its products and/or services to both customers and consumers simultaneously, for the sake of convenience of communication, we will just refer to both of these users as customers.

Assume that value creation is the principal objective of any business enterprise, where the outputs are more valuable than the sum of the inputs. It consists of two components: creating value for customers as well as creating value for shareholders. The former helps sell products and services, while the latter, in the form of a rising stock price, insures the future availability of investment capital to fund the operations or to help with the positive cash flow of the enterprise. The *value creation* of a value system is determined by the expected benefits that consumers will receive from their purchases, as represented by their willingness-to-pay (WTP). Due to the lack of perfect price discrimination, consumers generally maintain a consumer surplus, because consumers' spending with payments into the value system is mostly less than the aggregate WTP.

After value has been created, the business enterprise whose efforts led to the value creation needs to capture the value in order to achieve its financial goal of first surviving and then thriving in the economic world. For example, value is created when farmers plant and grow crops; however, these farmers have to capture their created value by harvesting and selling their crops. Value capture by an individual firm is usually determined by its ownership of resources and power status within the value system, as well as by the firm's cost structure and negotiating skill in relation to other firms in the value system (Bowman & Ambrosini, 2001; Priem, 2007).

2.4 A Firm's Supply-Chain Ecosystem and Its Systemic Intuition

The success of our focal firm primarily depends on how well other firms are doing in its input–output environment because of their economic interdependence, where the inputs of one firm are the outputs of some other firms. That is, by using the flow of inputs and outputs we can talk about the ecosystem within which the focal firm resides with other firms seen as either upstream components or downstream complements of the system (Adner & Kapoor, 2010). In particular, suppliers represent some of the upstream components of the focal firm; customers, supporters, and assistants who help to make the product of the focal firm usable by consumers are the downstream complements. Supporters and assistants are called complementors because although they are outside the focal firm's direct supply chain they need to

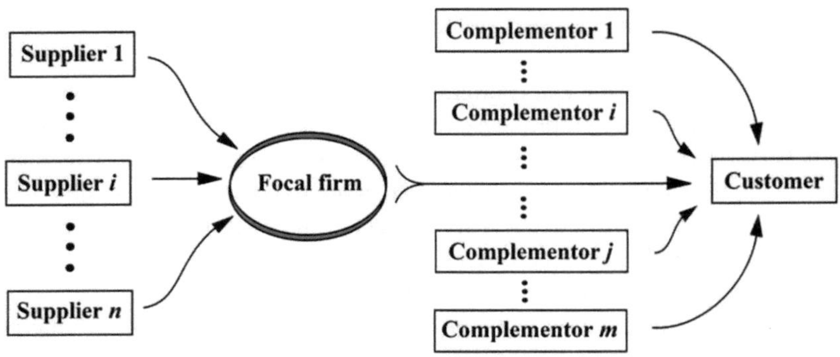

Fig. 2.4 The ecosystem of any focal firm

invest and develop new infrastructure to make the focal firm's product practically usable by the ultimate consumer. Governments, regulators, etc., are examples of complementors that help to build and to regularly maintain, for instance, the roads necessary for transporting products, or the specification of new safety procedures, etc. With this explanation in place, we can see that the set of components of the focal firm also includes upstream complementors that help to make the outputs of the suppliers usable by the focal firm.

Figure 2.4 depicts the systemic structure of this ecosystem, where the focal firm utilizes the inputs, which will be called components, from n supplies and delivers its outputs to customers with the support and assistance of m complementors, $m, n = 1, 2, 3, \ldots$ These support and assistance are called complements. As shown in Fig. 2.4, only first-tier components and complements are given, although this structure in real life should be extended forward and backward along the chain of value creation to include actors of other tiers, such as suppliers' suppliers, customers' customers, complementors' complementors, etc. And when the full range of all players of different tiers is included in the ecosystem, one actually develops a practical situation of linked systems (Lin & Ma, 1987). (To make the figure intuitively clear, all upstream complementors of the focal firm are omitted.) In other words, the ecosystem of the focal firm possesses the characteristics of the yoyo model in Fig. 2.1a, where the firm's internal working is around how its employees with adequate organizational supports can innovatively integrate the components from suppliers in order to deliver its functional product(s) to its customers. Note that similar systemic constructs such as this one has also attracted the attention of academics and practitioners (Adner, 2006; Iansiti & Levien, 2004; Intel Corporation, 2004; SAP Corporation, 2006).

A collection T is said to be a partially ordered set, if there is an order relation $\leq$ defined on T such that it satisfies the property of reflexivity (for any $x \in T$, $x \leq x$), that of transitivity (for $x, y, z \in T$, $x \leq y$ and $y \leq z$ imply $x \leq z$), and that of antisymmetry (for $x, y \in X$, $x \leq y$ and $y \leq x$ imply $x = y$). If any $x, y \in X$ can be compared by $\leq$, then the order relation $\leq$ is said to be complete. Then, the type of the ordered pair $(T, \leq)$ is referred to as the order type of T or $\leq$ (Kuratowski & Mostowski, 1976), denoted by a Greek letter.

By modeling each firm in the ecosystem of the focal firm and the market as a system, and a mapping ℓ_{ts} from an upstream supplier firm S_s to a downstream customer firm S_t as the linkage of how S_s's component m_s is applied in S_t's product m_t, we have the following result.

Theorem 2.1 Assume that T is a given partially ordered set of type α and that S is an α-type hierarchy of systems over T, satisfying that each state S_t is a nontrivial system, for $t \in T$. Then S can be made into a linked hierarchy by a family $\{\ell_{ts}: t, s \leq T, s \geq t\}$ of linkage mappings of S.

The proof of this result is very technical and is left to the Appendix.

One interpretation of this theorem of systems science can be given as follows: When the focal firm receives a market invitation for innovation, meaning that the partially ordered set T has a set of minimal elements (representing the various market demands related to the invitation), then each and every firm within the ecosystem of the focal firm will be challenged one way or another to provide a resolution to their respective challenges in order to jointly answer the market call. Although the initial market invitation might not be answered perfectly, some combinations of individual firms' resolutions to their respective challenges would provide at least a partial solution to the market demand.

2.5 Market Success and Challenges A Firm Faces

Based on the ecosystem of the focal firm constructed previously, this section establishes a few fundamental conclusions about the focal firm in terms of its market success, the values it creates and captures, and the magnitude of challenges it faces in the marketplace.

Proposition 2.1 If the focal firm plans to answer a market invitation for new innovation, then the success for it to meet the relevant challenges depends often on those of other firms within the supply-chain ecosystem to meet their respective challenges, arising from the focal firm's plan.

In fact, this result follows from how the ecosystem of the focal firm is constructed, as shown in Fig. 2.4. In particular, this ecosystem organically relates the firm's performance with not only the challenges the firm faces (Christensen, 1997; Henderson & Clark, 1990), but also those that confront the external partners. For instance, to meet a challenge, the focal firm may very well need to acquire certain special upstream components, which may in turn represent challenges to the relevant suppliers and their corresponding complementors. At the same time, a solution to the challenge, as identified by the focal firm, may likely require downstream complementors to successfully meet their corresponding challenges in order for the focal firm's new product to be fully usable by the customers. In other words, this ecosystem, as a systemic model of the environment of the focal firm, explicitly explains how the network of challenges centered on that particular challenge the focal firm faces needs to be successfully resolved by different actors in the ecosystem in order for the ecosystem to create value.

On the practical front, there are many real-life instances that support the conclusion of Proposition 2.1. For example, direct current (DC) generation technologies declined because of unconquerable bottlenecks in the development of DC distribution technology (Hughes, 1983), while in the semiconductor lithography industry optical lithography dominates all non-optical approaches as a consequence of the fact that suppliers, customers, and complementors played roles in meeting their respective challenges in optical lithography technology (Henderson, 1995). On a more personal level, when a colleague had to convert her house to gas heating from its original 100% electric home, although the conversion was possible and done successfully without any trouble, the system became louder than before. Apparently, the duct work in electrical homes is not directly (1–1) compatible with that of gas-heated homes. The duct work of the former homes is narrow so that the newly installed gas system pushes more air through a smaller space, and hence, lending itself to a noisier output.

When the focal firm answers a market invitation for additional innovation, it most likely creates challenges for the upstream components and downstream complements, depending on the innovation the firm plans to embark on. The following result tells how the value the firm creates from its answer to the market call is affected by these subsequent challenges confronting the members of the firm's ecosystem.

Proposition 2.2 The value the focal firm can *create,* when it answers a market invitation, is bounded from above by the upstream component challenges, and that it can capture is bounded from below by the downstream complement challenges.

In fact, the first conclusion follows from the fact that the focal firm's ability to actually make a product that is expected to be competitive in the marketplace is constrained by the challenges the upstream components faces. The second conclusion is a consequence of the fact that how much of the full benefit of the focal firm's offering the customer can enjoy from consumption is influenced by the downstream complements.

By the magnitude of a challenge the focal firm faces, it means how much the challenge requires the current approach of problem solving of the firm to change. In other words, the magnitude of a challenge to the focal firm corresponds to the degree to which this firm is charged with changing its approach to problem solving.

Proposition 2.3 When the focal firm is challenged by the marketplace, the magnitude of the challenge is positively correlated to that of changes required for the firm's ecosystem to undergo in order for the firm to successfully meet the challenge.

When the focal firm confronts a challenge in the marketplace, it has to make certain necessary changes in its adopted way of problem solving in order to come up with a resolution beneficially. Now, the required changes necessary to produce the desired resolution could be in:

- The discovery of market trends, the consequent design of brand-new ideas, and the development of competitive products (Henderson & Clark, 1990; Tushman & Anderson, 1986), or
- The identification of how some environmental elements can be integrated into firms' internal structures (Brusoni et al., 2001; McGrath, 2013; Takeishi, 2002), or
- The determination of how to scale up the production and delivery of identified solutions (Argote, 1999; Hatch & Mowery, 1998).

However, for the ecosystem's purpose of creating value, the focal firm's current approach of problem solving has achieved a dynamic equilibrium with those of the other players in the ecosystem. In other words, in their effort of achieving the common goal of value creation, all players in the ecosystem are in a state of mutual forbearance. That is, the players, be they firms, complementors or consumers, mitigate the overall challenge of creating and capturing value by dividing the series of necessary activities into bundles, each of which is manageable by one player according to its strength (Bernheim & Whinston, 1990). They cede efforts in less efficient areas to other more capable players, while in exchange the latter do the same in areas where the former are more efficient (Li & Greenwood, 2004). The players' codependence gradually makes the ecosystem stable in their concerted effort of value creation and value capture (Yu & Cannella Jr., 2012). Eventually, the association of the players becomes strengthened (Fuentelsaz & Gómez, 2006) and the network of adopted approaches of problem solving by different players reaches equilibrium (Haveman & Nonnemaker, 2000). Therefore, when the focal firm is forced to make changes in its adopted approach of problem solving, the stability and equilibrium of this network has to be broken; and at the same time, the greater the change the focal firm has to make, the greater alteration the entire ecosystem will have to make in order for the system to reach another equilibrium.

In terms of the systemic yoyo model, the situation implied by the setup of Proposition 2.3 can be depicted in Fig. 2.5, where one linear branch of the supply chain is shown as the horizontal curve with the arrows indicating the direction of movement of inputs and outputs of the firms along the chain, and the vertical arrowed curves stand for the combined eddy field of the individual eddy fields of the firms along the supply chain. When a certain amount of value is created and captured by the firms, an equilibrium and stability between the vertical and horizontal fields are established. However, when the focal firm faces a challenge from the marketplace, it means that its outputs need to be altered, which in turn implies that components from suppliers different from before will be needed. That consequently means that the suppliers' outputs have to be different from before. At the same time, the outputs of the downstream firms will in turn be changed accordingly. Such a domino effect quickly rises upward affecting all the suppliers and the suppliers' suppliers as well as downward exerting demands for downstream firms to alter their offers accordingly. So, once again, this analysis indicates that the more a change is

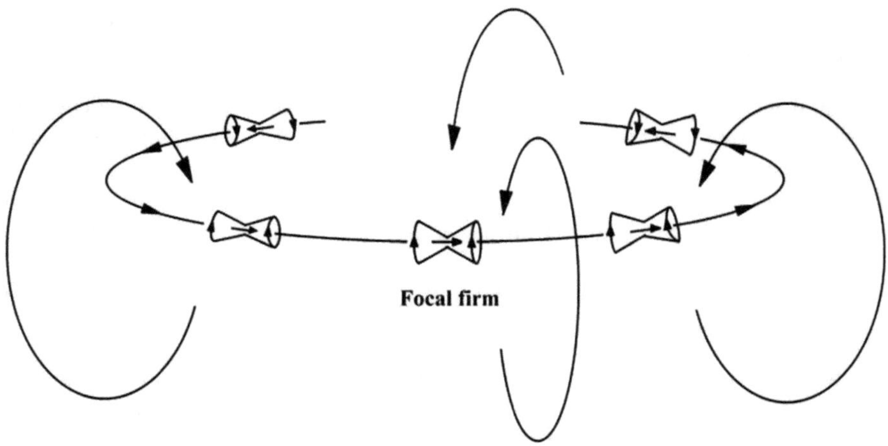

Fig. 2.5 One linear branch of the supply chain within the ecosystem of the focal firm

required of the focal firm, the greater change the entire ecosystem will have to go through.

2.6 Challenges Facing Upstream Firms

For an arbitrarily chosen focal firm, it forms jointly with other firms within its input–output environment such an ecosystem that the inputs of one firm are the outputs of some other firms, Fig. 2.6. So, the firms in this ecosystem can be classified as either upstream components or downstream complements of the focal firm (Adner & Kapoor, 2010). Here, suppliers represent some of the upstream components of the focal firm; customers, supporters, and assistants, called complementors, who help make the product of the focal firm usable by consumers are the downstream complements. Although they are outside the focal firm's direct supply chain, the complementors need to invest and develop new infrastructure to make the focal firm's product usable by the ultimate consumer. From this explanation we see that the set of components of the focal firm also includes upstream complementors that help to make the outputs of the suppliers usable by the focal firm.

In this section, we look at how the focal firm challenges the upstream of the ecosystem if the firm aspires to be a market leader. Generally, innovative ideas of the focal firm are often objectified into actual products through necessary changes in components, while the focal firm needs to originally integrate these new components into its desired offer (Brusoni et al., 2001; Iansiti, 1998). Here, the origin of the innovative ideas really comes from an epoch-making understanding of the market cue, as what Proposition 4.3 in the first volume of this book series describes, where due to the human desire to live in increasingly better conditions.

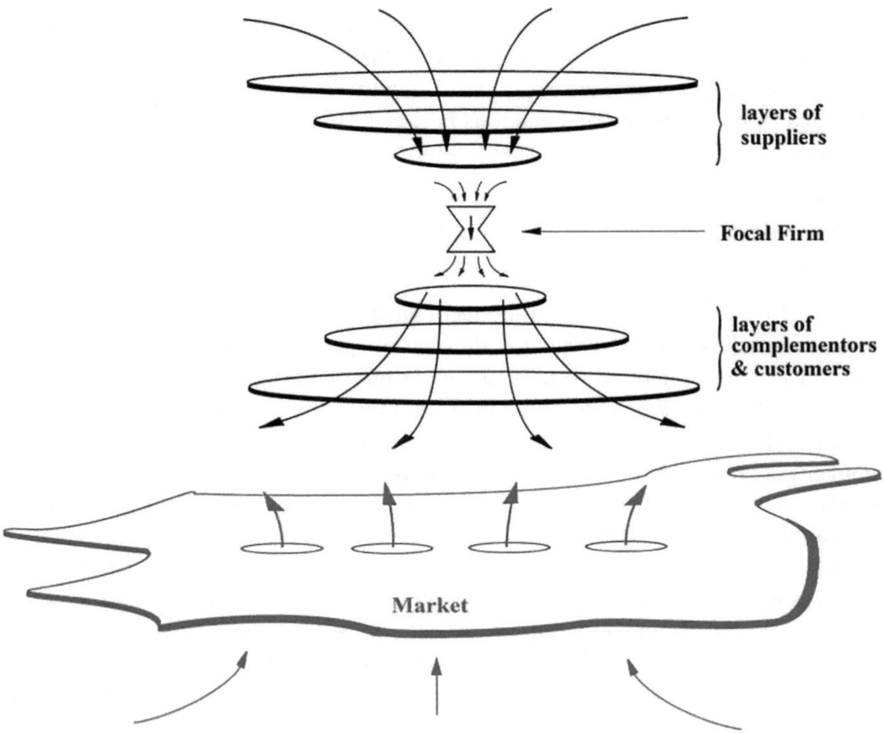

Fig. 2.6 The yoyo structure of the focal firm's ecosystem

Proposition 2.4 The performance advantage the focal firm enjoys over its competitors is positively correlated to the magnitude of challenges the upstream components face.

By considering a linear branch of the supply chain in the focal firm's ecosystem, it can be readily seen that when an innovation of the focal firm requires corresponding innovations in the upstream components and/or complements, the development challenges of the firm increases. In such a case, the firm has to overcome additional obstacles in specifying, sourcing, and integrating new components into its newly designed products. These obstacles generally challenge the firm to revamp its existing production as well as organizational routines or to totally replace these routines by new ones. Hence, challenges of the components increase the scale and scope of the firm's learning and doing, and consequently the performance advantage the firm gains over its rivals from progressing along its learning curve.

Additionally, the increased coordination with upstream suppliers (Dyer & Singh, 1998) and more frequent travels through the cycles of learning, design, and production that accompany challenging components (Clark & Fujimoto, 1991) benefit the focal firm through greater experiences with new knowledges, different ways of creating innovative designs, and forever improving procedures of operation and production, Such benefits enjoyed by the focal firm help to reduce the ease for later rivals to imitate this progress (Lippman & Rumelt, 1982; Rivkin, 2000) and consequently the offers. For example, such difficulty in imitating innovations, which emerged from extensive collaborations between Toyota and its suppliers, has been well documented by Dyer and Hatch (2006).

Proposition 2.5 If the focal firm creates challenges, when it answers a market call for additional innovation, mostly onto the upstream suppliers, then the firm will enjoy a much shortened period of performance advantage.

This conclusion follows from the fact that the actual learning experience of the focal firm will be mainly located at the step of specifying what necessary components it needs to relatively readily assemble into its designed product(s). In other words, the key developments within the focal firm's effort to produce its new offer to the market are undertaken by the upstream suppliers. So, once the required developments are done, the components will also be available for the firm's rivals. These rivals can then free ride on the learning, discovery, and investments of the focal firm to offer their similar products. That will definitely shorten the focal firm's period of exclusivity in the market or the firm's performance advantage. This analysis also explains why Proposition 2.5 does not contradict the conclusion in Proposition 2.4.

Systemically, the input–output mechanism of the challenge the focal firm brings on its ecosystem can be depicted in Fig. 2.7a, where the amount of inputs and that of outputs need to be at equilibrium in order for the yoyo structure of the firm to stay healthy and viable for the long run. So, when the challenge places most of its burden on the mechanism of inputs while that of outputs stays unaffected, the viability of the yoyo structure of the challenge on the ecosystem cannot last too long, because the input–output mechanism will be so congested that it has to stop working (Fig. 2.7b).

As a corollary of Proposition 2.5, we have the following result conveniently.

Proposition 2.6 The performance advantage the focal firm enjoys in the marketplace can be lengthened, if the firm is innovative in its effort to assemble components internally.

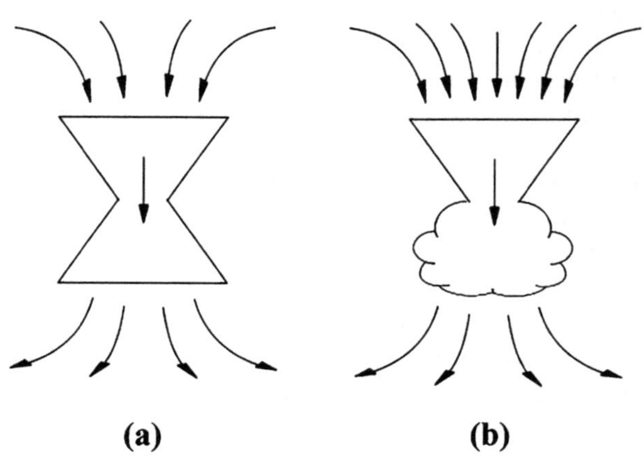

Fig. 2.7 The input–output mechanism: (**a**) in balance; (**b**) unbalanced

Empirically, this conclusion is supported by Brusoni and Prencipe (2001) and Hoetker (2006) when they demonstrate the increasing need in the present world of technological advances for the focal firm to possess its greater organizational and learning capabilities in its role as a system integrator when specialist component suppliers appear. At the same time, such capabilities generally take good amount of time and great effort to acquire (McGrath, 2013).

2.7 Challenges Downstream Enterprises Face

Compared to upstream suppliers, whose outputs enable the focal firm to practically produce its innovative offer and present it to the market, the actual value of the offer for customers is only created through the availability of appropriate complements. For example, the ability for flying cars (Lemoussu et al., 2018) to create value for users is realistically hampered until the appropriate road conditions and air traffic controls, as key complements, are constructed and installed in order for such cars to move and fly around freely. As a matter of fact, many innovative products rely on the availability of appropriate complements to expose their full value to users. So, in this section, we look at how what is learned by the focal firm and what it innovatively designs post challenges on the downstream complementors, Fig. 2.8. This figure actually also provides an explanation for why different firms receive the market invitation differently. In particular, the market calls—the upward moving arrows of the market—for additional competition and new innovation are partially shielded off

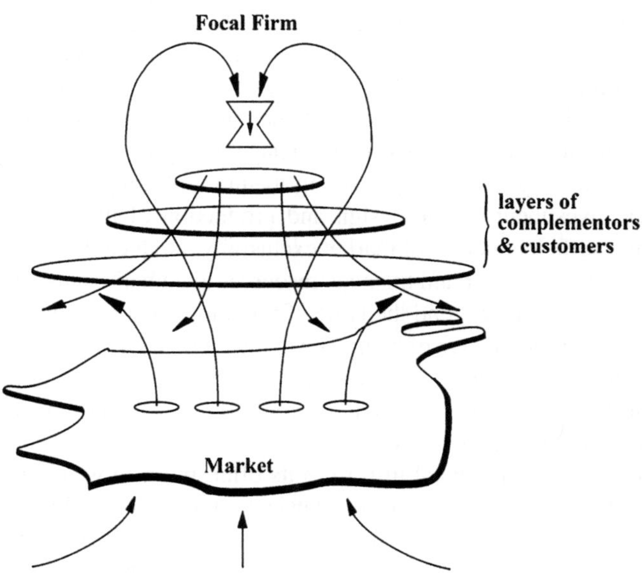

Fig. 2.8 Interaction between focal firm's innovation and challenges of complementors

by the downward moving field of the ecosystem of the firm, while different firms have their individually different systemic yoyo fields in terms of their spinning directions, strengths, etc.

Proposition 2.7 The development of complements can directly affect customers' adoption of the focal firm's innovative offer. That is, each innovative offer of the focal firm generally only constitutes an incomplete innovation.

In fact, it suffices to list particular cases to support the conclusion in this proposition. To this end, the evolution of modern technology has many times experienced imbalances in the development pace of complementary innovations, which created "reverse salients" (Hughes, 1983). In the personal computer industry, for example, the value of various products developed by suppliers had been constrained by complements (Ethiraj, 2007). Similarly, over 100 years ago, the railroad and printing industries delayed their adoption of electricity due to the challenges that were unconquerable at the time in complements (Goldfarb, 2005). Please note that Proposition 2.7 was initially suggested by Rosenberg (1972, p. 21).

Intuitively, this conclusion can be readily seen from Fig. 2.8. In particular, for the focal firm to deliver its offer to the market, appropriate layers of complementors and customers have to be in place first in order for the firm's outputs to reach the field of the market.

Proposition 2.8 The performance advantage the focal firm enjoys from its innovative offer is negatively correlated to the magnitude of the challenges complementors face.

That is because when complementors confront with great challenges, delays will appear inevitably in the availability of appropriate complements needed for customers to fully enjoy the value of the innovative offer of the focal firm. Such delays consequently reduce the timely value creation of the offer, because the lack of appropriate complements slows down the adoption rate of the offer. Other than giving rivals additional time to catch up with the innovative design and production of the offer before the market takes off, the delays also prevent the focal firm from greatly expanding its production, perfecting its initial offering, and recuperating its earlier heavy investment on the design and production of the offer. Without the advantage of a sufficient period of market exclusivity, the focal firm will not be able to muster enough manpower and financial resources to embark on its next innovative frontiers. In other words, beyond the issue of imitation, later entrants will not suffer from much of the disadvantage of being late to the market. By lowering the adoption rate of the innovative offer of the focal firm and by stripping away the necessary resources for the firm to look beyond the current offer, no matter how innovative the focal offer is, greater challenges complementors face in reality not only reduce the performance advantage the focal firm from its offer, but also wear away the firm's capability to successfully ride waves of transient competitive advantages.

Hence, this analysis also implies the following result, considering that the present world of business is in the era of transient competitive advantages (McGrath, 2013).

Proposition 2.9 If the focal firm plans to successfully ride waves of transient competitive advantages, its innovative designs of products have to consider whether or not downstream complementors can readily develop appropriate complements.

2.8 Upstream Uncertainties of a Supply-Chain Ecosystem

From the discussions in the previous two sections, it can be seen quite clearly that the focal firm is closely associated with the upstream suppliers and the downstream complementors and customers. So, it is natural for us to look at how such vertical interdependence that threads through the ecosystem of the firm can possibly be managed. The yoyo structure of the focal firm's ecosystem and its relation with the market are depicted in Fig. 2.6, where the sustainability of the focal firm really depends on the outputs of the upstream suppliers and the accommodation of downstream customers and complementors.

So far in this chapter we have looked at how an initial receipt of a market invitation for innovation by the focal firm starts a chain of associated challenges, some of which confront upstream suppliers while others confront downstream complementors. In particular, from the recognized market invitation, the focal firm first designs and then attempts to produce its innovative offer. However, to present a particular offer to answer the market invitation and a value-creating solution to customers, the firm has to combine its innovative design and effort of new production with specifically needed supplies. This will most likely post challenges to upstream suppliers, and unambiguously necessary complements, which generally presents challenges to downstream complementors, to facilitate the indispensable conditions for customers to enjoy the full potential of the focal offer. Our established propositions indicate that the distribution of the associated challenges across the ecosystem is an essential driver behind the outcomes of all firms involved. In this section, we will investigate how vertical integration can actually play the role of a governance strategy to manage such interdependence among all the parties of the ecosystem.

Proposition 2.10 When dealing with upstream suppliers, the focal firm has to face two types of uncertainties—technological and suppliers' behavioral uncertainty, both of which play a rule on the firm's performance advantage. And, the technological uncertainty affects the firm's ability to create value, while suppliers' behavioral uncertainty impacts the firm's ability to capture value.

In fact, when the focal firm contracts with upstream suppliers for special purpose components that involve high levels of development challenges, the suppliers do not really know whether or not they can discover appropriate solutions to their development challenges, and if successful with such discoveries, then when they will be able to actually deliver the contracted products (Clark, 1985). This scenario represents the technological uncertainty the focal firm has to face. Evidently, resolution of the technological uncertainty decides the focal firm's value creation: if the suppliers cannot provide the needed components, then the focal firm will not be able to bring its imagined product to the market to satisfy the demand of customers. In this case, Proposition 2.4 implies that the greater technological uncertainty the focal firm faces, the greater performance advantage it can enjoy over its competitors.

At the same time, the performance advantage of the focal firm, as a consequent of successful resolutions of technological uncertainties confronting upstream suppliers (Proposition 2.4), may realistically entice these suppliers to behave opportunistically due to suddenly increased demands from the competitors of the focal firm. That is, the focal firm has to deal with suppliers' behavioral uncertainty regarding whether or not and when (some of) the suppliers will behave opportunistically (Jap & Anderson, 2003; Sutcliffe & Zaheer, 1998). If (some of) the suppliers renegotiate the contract terms opportunistically with the focal firm because of the increasing demand for their products, then the focal firm will not be able to appropriate its originally expected rents. As implied by Proposition 2.5, suppliers' opportunistic behavior will then greatly shorten the lifespan of the exclusive performance advantage of the focal firm.

Systemically speaking, technological uncertainty appears with the situation of whether or not the desired inputs of the focal firm (Fig. 2.6) can be adequately fed by the large arrowed input curves that trespass through the layers of the upstream suppliers; and it might take a long time and a lot of effort to construct some of these needed curves. And suppliers' behavioral uncertainty exists because in the location of the focal firm in Fig. 2.6, most of the firm's rivals can fit too.

2.9 A Few Final Words

To succeed in the present world of business, a firm has to ride waves of transient competitive advantages, as anecdotally confirmed by McGrath (2013). Accomplishing this end means that the firm needs to constantly monitor and decipher market clues in innovative ways. At the same time, the firm needs to know how to deal with uncertainties that appear within the interactions with upstream suppliers and downstream complementors. As claimed by Adner and Kapoor (2010) and as shown in this chapter, challenges facing an original design, consequent production and eventual offer to the market are often situated inside both a focal firm and outside in the firm's ecosystem. That makes this chapter go beyond the literature of innovative firms' internal and environmental challenges by theoretically establishing a series of generally true conclusions.

By holistically looking at the supply-chain ecosystem of a focal firm that has been successful with its creative understanding of the market signal, this chapter provides a systemic framework by focusing on input–output threads located throughout the supply chain. Within this framework, the chapter shows that the focal firm's innovative idea introduced to answer the market invitation generally posts challenges to upstream suppliers and downstream complementors. It illustrates that suppliers' resolutions to component challenges help the focal firm to produce its ideal product, and that complementors' success with their challenges facilitates the necessary conditions for the focal offer to reach customers with full potential of value creation.

This chapter examines how a focal firm's creative understanding of a market invitation can challenge both suppliers and complementors simultaneously with asymmetrical levels of effects on the performance of the focal firm. Specially, the following main results, among others, are established:

- Upstream component challenges and downstream complement difficulties can, respectively, constrain the values a focal firm can create and capture; and
- When a focal firm is more capable to learn and to act accordingly, that firm's ecosystem will experience greater challenges.

As for the focal firm's performance advantage over its competitors, it is shown that it is positively correlated to the level of the firm's upstream component challenges, and negatively correlated to that of downstream complement challenges. Among other results, the following are shown:

- To ride waves of transient competitive advantages successfully, a firm has to introduce innovative products, to which suppliers can certainly provide necessary solutions while complementors can readily develop appropriate complements.
- When contracting with upstream suppliers, the focal firm has to deal with two kinds of uncertainties: technological uncertainty, and suppliers' behavioral uncertainty, each of which affects the performance advantage of the focal firm.

By utilizing holistic thinking and logical reasoning, this chapter is able to investigate the dynamics of the supply-chain ecosystem of a focal firm and produce different while more insightful understandings than those in the literature (e.g. Anderson & Tushman, 1990; Cusumano et al., 1992; Utterback & Abernathy, 1975) on the distribution of challenges, appearance of uncertainties, and performance of a focal firm.

The general results developed in this chapter provide practical managerial guidelines on how to manage challenges, originated from attempts of answering market calls, in innovative fashions. In particular, we have the following recommendations:

- A firm's investment in speeding up the commercialization cycles when pursuing first mover advantage has to carefully consider whether or not other firms in the firm's ecosystem can promptly meet their respective challenges.
- When introducing an innovative product to answer a market invitation, the more upstream suppliers and the less downstream complementors are challenged, the greater value the product is expected to create and capture.
- If a perceived innovative product posts challenges, downstream complementors will likely have difficulty in meeting the market's need in a timely manner. Consequently, the innovative product needs to be modified to ease the expected difficulty confronting complementors.
- Investing in internal capability to assemble components into innovative products will help lengthen a firm's performance advantage in the marketplace.

- When investing jointly with suppliers in introducing a new technology, a firm needs to prepare for the increasing potential of suppliers' behavioral uncertainty.

To summarize what is accomplished in this chapter in one sentence, we have the following: a firm can estimate the levels of relative challenges across its ecosystem well in advance of the commercialization of its innovative idea.

As for the limitations of this chapter, the first one stems from the assumption of why a firm in the business world exists, because not all firms aim at generating positive cash flows. Firms, developed for reasons beyond generating positive cash flows, can behave in different ways than what is described in this chapter. Second, although this chapter looks at the distribution of challenges across the ecosystem of a focal firm, it did not consider the innovation challenges the focal firm faces in its core activities, especially when they are somewhat correlated with challenges external to the firm. Third, in the relationship among the players within the ecosystem of a focal firm, the history and nature of specific exchanges also need to be considered in order to reveal their possible effects on the relationship (Argyres & Liebeskind, 2002). Fourth, this chapter stays within the context of a single supply chain. However, in real-life supply chains, as systems, also interact with each other. That interaction of a higher systemic level could very possibly affect the distribution of challenges within each of the interacting supply chains. In other words, this chapter only presents a baseline structure on top of which other factors and considerations need to be overlaid. Fifth, this chapter assumes explicitly that all other variables, such as strategies employed and their interactions, the specific nature of innovative change, demand uncertainty, modes of cross-firm coordination, etc., are held constant. So, each of these other variables needs to be jointly considered either individually or collectively.

Corresponding to these listed and other unlisted limitations, future studies should incorporate additional contingencies and antecedents in order to produce more practical useful insights than what have been established in this chapter.

Appendix: Proof of Theorem 2.1

Let each collection of elements (or things) be referred to as a set. Given two sets X and Y, f is a function or mapping from X to Y, provided that f represents a rule that spells out how each element x in X (or written as $x \in X$) is paired with an element y in Y (or $y \in Y$), written as $f: X \to Y$, and the pairing between x and y is symbolically written as $f(x) = y$.

If S is a (general) system (Lin, 1999), then S is an ordered pair (M,R) of sets, where R is a set of some relations of the elements in the set M. Each element in M is called an object of S, and M and R are called the object set and the relation set of S, respectively. A system $S = (M,R)$ is said to be trivial if $M = \varnothing$.

Given two systems $S_i = (M_i, R_i)$, $i = 1, 2$, and a mapping h: $M_1 \to M_2$, by using transfinite induction, define two classes $\widehat{M}_i$, $i = 1, 2$, and a class mapping $\widehat{h}$: $\widehat{M}_1 \to \widehat{M}_2$ with the following properties:

$$\widehat{M}_i = \bigcup_{n \in \mathbf{ON}} M_i^n, i = 1, 2,$$

where **ON** stands for the collection of all ordinals, and for each $x = (x_0, x_1, \ldots, x_\alpha, \ldots) \in \widehat{M}_1$,

$$\widehat{h}(x) = (h(x_0), h(x_1), \ldots, h(x_\alpha), \ldots).$$

For each relation $r \in R_1$, let $\widehat{h}(r) = \left\{\widehat{h}(x) : x \in r\right\}$ be a relation on M_2 with length $n(r)$. Without confusion, h will also be used to indicate the class mapping $\widehat{h}$ and h is now seen as a mapping from system S_1 into system S_2, denoted h: $S_1 \to S_2$.

If two systems S_1 and S_2 are the same or equal, that is, $M_1 = M_2$ and $R_1 = R_2$, and a mapping $h : M_1 \to M_2$ satisfies $h(x) = x$, for any $x \in M_1$, then we say that this mapping h is the identity mapping from S_1 to S_2, written as id_{S_1}.

Assume that $(T, \leq)$ is a partially ordered set with order type α (Lin, 1999), where the symbol $\leq$ stands for the order relation between elements of T. An α-type hierarchy S of systems over the partially ordered set $(T, \leq)$ is defined as a function defined on T such that for each $t \in T$, $S(t) = S_t = (M_t, R_t)$ is a system, called the state of the α-type hierarchy S at the moment t. Without causing confusion, we omit the words "over the partially ordered set $(T, \leq)$."

Given an α-type hierarchy S of systems, assume that ℓ_{tr}: $S_r \to S_t$ is a mapping from the state system S_r into the state system S_t, for any $r, t \in T$ with $r \geq t$, such that

$$\ell_{ts} = \ell_{tr} \circ \ell_{rs} \text{ and } \ell_{tt} = \text{id}_{S_t},$$

where r, s, t are arbitrary elements in T satisfying $s \geq r \geq t$, and $\text{id}_{S_t} = \text{id}_{M_t}$ is the identity mapping on the set M_t. This collection $\{\ell_{ts}: t, s \in T, s \geq t\}$ is referred to as a family of linkage mappings of the α-type hierarchy S, and each ℓ_{ts} a linkage mapping from the state system S_s into the state system S_t.

An α-type hierarchy of systems S, denoted $\{S, \ell_{ts}, T\}$ or $\{S(t), \ell_{ts}, T\}$, is referred to as a linked α-type hierarchy (of systems) if a family $\{\ell_{ts}: t, s \in T, s \geq t\}$ of linkage mappings is given or can be constructed based on given conditions.

Now, for the given nontrivial α-type hierarchy S of systems in Theorem 2.1, assume that $S_t = (M_t, R_t)$, for each $t \in T$. From the Axiom of Choice (Lin, 1999), it follows that there exists a choice function C: $T \to \bigcup\{M_t : t \in T\}$ such that $C(t) \in M_t$ for each $t \in T$. A family $\{\ell_{ts}: t,s \in T, s \geq t\}$ of linkage mappings of S can now be defined as follows. For any $s, t \in T$ with $s > t$, let

$$\ell_{ts}(x) = C(t),$$

for all $x \in M_s$ and $\ell_{tt} = \mathrm{id}_{M_t}$. This ends the proof of Theorem 2.1.

References

Adner, R. (2006). Match your innovation strategy to your innovation ecosystem. *Harvard Business Review, 84*(4), 98–107.

Adner, R. (2017). Ecosystem as structure: An actionable construct for strategy. *Journal of Management, 43*(1), 39–58.

Adner, R., & Kapoor, R. (2010). Value creation in innovation ecosystems: How the structure of technological interdependence affects firm performance in new technological generations. *Strategic Management Journal, 31*(3), 306–333.

Adner, R., Oxley, J. E., & Silverman, B. S. (Eds.). (2013). *Collaboration and competition in business ecosystems*. Bingley.

Anderson, P. C., & Tushman, M. L. (1990). Technological discontinuities and dominant designs. *Administrative Science Quarterly, 35*(4), 604–633.

Argote, L. (1999). *Organizational learning: Creating, retaining and transferring knowledge.* Kluwer.

Argyres, N. S., & Liebeskind, J. P. (2002). Governance inseparability and the evolution of the biotechnology industry. *Journal of Economic Behavior and Organization, 47*, 197–219.

Attour, A., & Lazaric, N. (2018). From knowledge to business ecosystems: Emergence of an entrepreneurial activity during knowledge replication. *Small Business Economics, 54*, 575–587. https://doi.org/10.1007/s11187-018-0035-3

Bernheim, B. D., & Whinston, M. D. (1990). Multimarket contact and collusive behavior. *RAND Journal of Economics, 21*, 1–26.

Bilgicer, T., Jedidi, K., Lehmann, D. R., & Neslin, S. A. (2015). Social contagion and customer adoption of new sales channels. *Journal of Retailing, 91*(2), 254–271.

Bowman, C., & Ambrosini, V. (2001). "Value" in the resource-based view of the firm: A contribution to the debate. *Academy of Management Review, 26*, 501–502.

Brem, A., & Viardot, É. (2015). Adoption of innovation: Balancing internal and external stakeholders in the marketing of innovation. In A. Brem & É. Viardot (Eds.), *Adoption of innovation* (pp. 1–10). Springer.

Bruneel, J., Spithoven, A., & Clarysse, B. (2017). Interorganizational trust and technology complexity: Evidence for new technology-based firms. *Journal of Small Business Management, 55*(S1), 256–274.

Brusoni, S., & Prencipe, A. (2001). Unpacking the black box of modularity: technologies, products and organizations. *Industrial and Corporate Change, 10*, 179–205.

Brusoni, S., Prencipe, A., & Pavitt, K. (2001). Knowledge specialization, organizational coupling, and the boundaries of the firm: Why do firms know more than they make? *Administrative Science Quarterly, 46*, 597–621.

Bstieler, L., & Hemmert, M. (2015). The effectiveness of relational and contractual governance in new product development collaborations: Evidence from Korea. *Technovation, 45-46*, 29–39.

Burton, N., & Galvin, P. (2018). When do product architectures mirror organisational architectures? The combined role of product complexity and the rate of technological change. *Technology Analysis & Strategic Management, 30*(9), 1057–1069.

Byun, J. G., Sung, T. F., & Park, H. W. (2018). Technological innovation strategy: how do technology life cycles change by technological area. *Technology Analysis & Strategic Management, 30*(1), 98–112.

Cao, Z., & Lumineau, F. (2015). Revisiting the interplay between contractual and relational governance: A qualitative and meta-analytic investigation. *Journal of Operations Management, 33-34*, 15–42.

Chang, W., Ellinger, A. E., Kim, K., & Franke, G. R. (2016). Supply chain integration and firm financial performance: A meta-analysis of positional advantage mediation and moderating factors. *European Management Journal, 34*(3), 282–295.

Chemmanur, T. J., Loutskina, E., & Tian, X. (2014). Corporate venture capital, value creation, and innovation. *The Review of Financial Studies, 27*(8), 2434–2473.

Chen, D. Q., Preston, D. S., & Swink, M. (2015). How the use of big data analytics affects value creation in supply chain management. *Journal of Management Information Systems, 32*(4), 4–39.

Christensen, C. M. (1997). *Innovator's dilemma: When new technologies cause great firms to fail*. Harvard Business School Press.

Clark, K. B. (1985). The interaction of design hierarchies and market concepts in technological evolution. *Research Policy, 14*, 235–251.

Clark, K. B., & Fujimoto, T. (1991). *Product development performance*. Harvard Business School Press.

Clarysse, B., Wright, M., Bruneel, J., & Mahajan, A. (2014). Creating value in ecosystems: Crossing the chasm between knowledge and business ecosystems. *Research Policy, 43*(7), 1164–1176.

Cusumano, M., Mylonadis, Y., & Rosenbloom, R. (1992). Strategic maneuvering and mass market dynamics: The triumph of VHS over Beta. *The Business History Review, 66*(1), 51–94.

Dyer, J. H., & Hatch, N. W. (2006). Relation-specific capabilities and barriers to knowledge transfers: creating advantage through network relationships. *Strategic Management Journal, 27*(8), 701–719.

Dyer, J. H., & Singh, H. (1998). The relational view: Cooperative strategy and sources of inter-organizational competitive advantage. *Academy of Management Review, 23*(4), 660–679.

Ethiraj, S. K. (2007). Allocation of inventive effort in complex product systems. *Strategic Management Journal, 28*(6), 563–584.

Forrest, J. Y.-L., Liu, Y., Wajda, T. A., Köse, E., & Arik, O. A. (2019a). Dependence of a firm's performance on its ecosystem's upstream/downstream challenges. In *Proceedings of the 2019 Annual Meeting of National Association of Business, Economics and Technology* (pp. 83–100). National Association of Business, Economics and Technology.

Forrest, J. Y.-L., Liu, Y., Wajda, T. A., Köse, E., & Arik, O. A. (2019b). How challenges and successes of a firm depend on its input-output ecosystem. In *Proceedings of the 2019 Annual Conference of Decision Sciences Institute* (pp. 2381–2402). Decision Sciences Institute.

Forrest, J. Y. L., Nicholls, J., Schimmel, K., & Liu, S. F. (2020). *Managerial decision making: A holistic approach*. Springer.

Fuentelsaz, L., & Gómez, J. (2006). Multipoint competition, strategic similarity and entry into geographic markets. *Strategic Management Journal, 27*(5), 477–499.

Fultz, D., Long, R. R., Owens, G. V., Bohan, W., Kaylor, R., & Weil, J. (1959). Studies of thermal convection in a rotating cylinder with some implications for large-scale atmospheric motion. In *Meteorological monographs* (Vol. 21). American Meteorological Society.

Goldfarb, B. (2005). Diffusion of general-purpose technologies: understanding patterns in the electrification of US manufacturing 1880-1930. *Industrial and Corporate Change, 14*(5), 745–773.

Hallberg, N. L. (2015). Uncertainty, judgment, and the theory of the firm. *Journal of Institutional Economics, 11*(3), 623–650.

Hatch, N. W., & Mowery, D. C. (1998). Process innovation and learning by doing in semiconductor manufacturing. *Management Science, 44*(11), 1461–1477.

Haveman, H. A., & Nonnemaker, L. (2000). Competition in multiple geographic markets: The impact on growth and market entry. *Administrative Science Quarterly, 45*(2), 232–267.

Helfat, C. E., Campo-Rembado, M. A., Helfat, C. E., & Campo-Rembado, M. A. (2016). Integrative capabilities, vertical integration, and innovation over successive technology lifecycles. *Organization Science, 27*(2), 233–504.

Hellström, M., Tsvetkova, A., Gustafsson, M., & Wikström, K. (2015). Collaboration mechanisms for business models in distributed energy ecosystems. *Journal of Cleaner Production, 102*(1), 226–236.

Henderson, R. M. (1995). Of life cycles real and imaginary: the unexpectedly long old age of optical lithography. *Research Policy, 24*(4), 631–643.

Henderson, R. M., & Clark, K. B. (1990). Architectural innovation: the reconfiguration of existing product technologies and the failure of established firms. *Administrative Science Quarterly, 35*(1), 9–30.

Hendrikse, G., Hippmann, P., & Windsperger, J. (2015). Trust, transaction costs and contractual incompleteness in franchising. *Small Business Economics, 44*(4), 867–888.

Hide, R. (1953). Some experiments on thermal convection in a rotating liquid. *Quarterly Journal of the Royal Meteorological Society, 79*, 161.

Hoetker, G. (2006). Do modular products lead to modular organizations? *Strategic Management Journal, 27*(6), 501–518.

Huang, M. C., Yen, G. F., & Liu, T. C. (2014). Reexamining supply chain integration and the supplier's performance relationships under uncertainty. *Supply Chain Management: An International Journal, 19*(1), 64–78.

Hughes, T. P. (1983). *Networks of power: Electrification in western society 1880-1930*. Johns Hopkins University Press.

Iansiti, M. (1998). *Technology integration: Making critical choices in a dynamic world*. Harvard Business School Press.

Iansiti, M., & Levien, R. (2004). *The keystone advantage: What the new dynamics of business ecosystems mean for strategy, innovation, and sustainability*. Harvard Business School Press.

Intel Corporation. (2004). *Intel sees unified platform and ecosystem as key to enabling the digital home*. Press release 17 February.

Jap, S. D., & Anderson, E. (2003). Safeguarding interorganizational performance and continuity under expost opportunism. *Management Science, 49*(12), 1684–1701.

Jiang, Y., & Tornikoski, E. T. (2018). Perceived uncertainty and behavioral logic: Temporality and unanticipated consequences in the new venture creation process. *Journal of Business Venturing, 34*, 23–40. https://doi.org/10.1016/j.jbusvent.2018.06.002

Kagermann, H. (2015). Change through digitization: Value creation in the age of industry 4.0. In H. Albach, H. Meffert, A. Pinkwart, & R. Reichwald (Eds.), *Management of permanent change* (pp. 23–48). Springer.

Kapoor, R., & Agarwal, S. (2017). Sustaining superior performance in business ecosystems: Evidence from application software developers in the iOS and android smartphone ecosystems. *Organization Science, 28*(3), 379–595.

Kuratowski, K., & Mostowski, A. (1976). *Set theory: With an introduction to descriptive set theory*. North-Holland.

Laukkanen, T. (2016). Consumer adoption versus rejection decisions in seemingly similar service innovations: The case of the Internet and mobile banking. *Journal of Business Research, 69*(7), 2432–2439.

Lee, C. Y., Kim, J., Noh, M. S., Woo, H. G., & Gang, K. W. (2017). Patterns of technology life cycles: Stochastic analysis based on patent citations. *Technology Analysis & Strategic Management, 29*(1), 53–67.

Lemoussu, S., Chaudemar, J. C., & Vingerhoeds, R. A. (2018). Systems engineering and project management process modeling in the aeronautics context: Case study of SMEs. *International Journal of Mechanical and Mechatronics Engineering, 12*(2), 88–96.

Li, S. X., & Greenwood, R. (2004). The effect of within industry diversification on firm performance: Synergy creation, multi-market contact and market structuration. *Strategic Management Journal, 25*(12), 1131–1153.

Lin, Y. (1999). *General systems theory: A mathematical approach*. Plenum and Kluwer Academic Publishers.

Lin, Y. (2009). *Systemic yoyos: Some impacts of the second dimension*. Auerbach Publications.

Lin, Y., & Ma, Y. H. (1987). Some properties of linked time systems. *International Journal of General Systems, 13*(2), 125–134.

Lippman, S. A., & Rumelt, R. P. (1982). Uncertain imitability: An analysis of interfirm differences in efficiency under competition. *Bell Journal of Economics, 13*(2), 418–438.

McGrath, R. G. (2013). *The end of competitive advantage: How to keep your strategy moving as fast as your business*. Harvard Business Review Press.

Mondragon, A. E. C., & Mondragon, C. E. C. (2018). Managing complex, modular products: How technological uncertainty affects the role of systems integrators in the automotive supply chain. *International Journal of Production Research, 52*, 6954–6970. https://doi.org/10.1080/00207543.2018.1424362

Oliveira, T., Thomas, M., Baptista, G., & Campos, F. (2016). Mobile payment: Understanding the determinants of customer adoption and intention to recommend the technology. *Computers in Human Behavior, 61*, 404–414.

Porter, M. E. (1985). *Competitive advantage: Creating and sustaining superior performance*. Free Press.

Prajogo, D. I., & Oke, A. (2016). Human capital, service innovation advantage, and business performance: The moderating roles of dynamic and competitive environments. *International Journal of Operations & Production Management, 36*(9), 974–994.

Priem, R. L. (2007). A consumer perspective on value creation. *Academy of Management Review, 32*, 219–235.

Rivkin, J. W. (2000). Imitation of complex strategies. *Management Science, 46*(6), 824–844.

Roca, J. B., Vaishnav, P., Morgan, M. G., Mendonça, J., & Erica Fuchs, E. (2017). When risks cannot be seen: Regulating uncertainty in emerging technologies. *Research Policy, 46*(7), 1215–1233.

Rosenberg, N. (1972). Factors affecting the diffusion of technology. *Explorations in Economic History, 10*(1), 3–33.

SAP Corporation. (2006). *SAP ecosystem unites to bring innovation to chemicals industry*. Press release, 8 May.

Sutcliffe, K. M., & Zaheer, A. (1998). Uncertainty in the transaction environment: An empirical test. *Strategic Management Journal, 19*(1), 1–23.

Takeishi, A. (2002). Knowledge partitioning in the interfirm division of labor: The case of automotive product development. *Organization Science, 13*(3), 321–338.

Trada, S., & Goyal, V. (2017). The dual effects of perceived unfairness on opportunism in channel relationships. *Industrial Marketing Management, 64*(July), 135–146.

Tushman, M., & Anderson, P. (1986). Technological discontinuities and organizational environments. *Administrative Science Quarterly, 31*(3), 439–465.

Utterback, J. M., & Abernathy, W. J. (1975). A dynamic model of process and product innovation. *Omega, 3*(6), 639–656.

Yadav, P. L., Han, S. H., & Kim, H. (2017). Sustaining competitive advantage through corporate environmental performance. *Business Strategy and the Environment, 26*(3), 345–357.

Yeo, C. S., & Saboori-Deilami, V. (2017). Strategic challenges of outsourcing innovation in global market. *Asia Pacific Journal of Innovation and Entrepreneurship, 11*(1), 5–16.

Yu, T., & Cannella, A. A., Jr. (2012). A comprehensive review of multimarket competition research. *Journal of Management, 39*, 76–109.

Zahra, S. A., & Nambisan, S. (2012). Entrepreneurship and strategic thinking in business ecosystems. *Business Horizons, 55*(3), 219–229.

Chapter 3
Beneficially Developed Synergistic Innovations

Jeffrey Yi-Lin Forrest, Yaoguo Dang, Larry McCarthy, Sifeng Liu, and Yong Liu

Abstract This chapter, which is mainly based on (Forrest et al., Conditions under which synergistic innovations appear. In: Proceedings of the 2019 Annual Conference of Decision Sciences Institute. Decision Sciences Institute, pp. 2061–2080, 2019a; Forrest et al., Simultaneous consumer utilities, multi-sided markets and consumer synergies. In: Proceedings of the 2019 Annual Meeting of National Association of Business, Economics and Technology. National Association of Business, Economics and Technology, pp. 101–121, 2019b), investigates the issues related to the following questions, among others: (1) how can producer-side synergies be created by employing the strategy of economies of scope? (2) How can demand-side synergies be developed by making use of simultaneous consumer utilities and multi-sided markets? And (3) When can simultaneous consumer utilities be produced by collocating products and/or services?

Due to the specific approach taken, this chapter is able to describe how resources interact with each other and how simultaneous consumer utilities, two-sided markets and consumers' willingness to pay react to each other. It first looks at how such economic entities and basic concepts as business firm, resource, innovation, diversification, synergy, segment of consumers, etc., can be, respectively, modeled as interacting systems. It then addresses the previously listed questions and related ones by establishing a series of generally-true propositions through examining how relevant systems exert forces on each other. Because of the systemic certainty contained in the discussions offered here, this chapter is able to provide practically

Jeffrey Yi-Lin Forrest (Department of Accounting Economics Finance, Slippery Rock University, Slippery Rock, PA, USA; Email: Jeffrey.forrest@sru.edu), Yaoguo Dang (College of Economics and Management, Nanjing University of Aeronautics and Astronautics, Nanaking, China; Email: iamdangyg@163.com), Larry McCarthy (Department of Accounting Economics Finance, Slippery Rock University, Slippery Rock, PA, USA; Email: larry.mccarthy@sru.edu), Sifeng Liu (College of Economics and Management, Nanjing University of Aeronautics and Astronautics, Nanaking, China; Email: sfliu@nuaa.edu.cn), and Yong Liu (School of Business, Jiangnan University, Wuxi, Jiangsu, China; Email: clly1985528@163.com) are equally contributed to this chapter.

J. Y.-L. Forrest, *Systemic Principles of Applied Economic Philosophies II*,
Translational Systems Sciences 39, https://doi.org/10.1007/978-981-99-7939-4_3

useful guidance for managers, entrepreneurs and retailers to create values for consumers and capture values for their companies.

Keywords Entrepreneurial judgment · Entry deterrence price · Inconsistent resources · Multi-sided markets · Saturated market · Simultaneous consumer utilities · Synergistic innovation

3.1 Introduction

Recent researches in strategic management suggest and demonstrate the need for firms to develop the necessary organizational culture and capability to effectively ride waves of transient competitive advantages (e.g., McGrath, 2013). To meet this need successfully, a firm can strategically look either (1) inwardly at its nascent, heterogeneous resources and dynamic capabilities or (2) outwardly at product markets and consumer demands. In particular, task (1) helps the firm see what values it can create for consumers (e.g., Barney, 1991; Eisenhardt & Martin, 2000), while task (2) can potentially reveal where consumer synergies are located and what can then be potentially developed (Drucker, 1954). No matter whether to look inwardly or outwardly, the essence is for the firm to find potentials of different competitive advantages (Porter, 1985; Santalo & Becerra, 2008; Ye et al., 2012). One way to achieve this end is for the firm to create economies of scope by diversification at either the producer side (Porter, 1985; Santalo & Becerra, 2008) or the demand side (Ye et al., 2012) or both. If a firm adopts this approach, then the firm has to address the following natural questions:

1. How can producer-side synergies be created when using the strategy of economies of scope?
2. How can demand-side synergies be developed by making use of simultaneous consumer utilities and multi-sided markets, after all it is consumers who determine the success of companies (Penrose, 1959)?
3. What are the most fundamental decisions a retailer can make in terms of its offers to consumers?
4. How can collocating products and/or services lead to simultaneous consumer utilities?
5. When can the firm develop a positively correlated multi-sided market?

Aiming at addressing these questions, this chapter, which is mainly based on Forrest et al. (2019a, b), establishes a cohesive theory on how to potentially develop synergistically innovative ideas at either the producer side or the demand side by developing simultaneous consumer utilities, two-sided markets, and addressing related issues. This theoretical development relies 100 percent on logical reasoning, systems thinking, and the intuitive yoyo model (Lin, 2009) without analyzing any set of data or anecdotes, while producing general conclusions and widely employable recommendations. Because data mining and anecdotal analysis can only help uncover potential facts due to their constraints inherently existing in the available data and/or anecdotes and limitations of the relevant analysis tools, results, and conclusions established in this chapter are more reliable and practically useful than those based on data and anecdotes.

The rest of this chapter is organized as follows. Section 3.2 reviews the relevant literature and demonstrates the contributions of this chapter. Section 3.3 develops insights on synergistic innovation of the producer side. Section 3.4 looks at similar issues on the demand side. Section 3.5 studies how different sides of the market can be created by collocating products. And this chapter is concluded in Sect. 3.6.

3.2 Literature Review

Because this chapter contributes simultaneously to the literatures of entrepreneurship, innovation, and strategy, this section will look at these literatures individually and show where this work's contributions lie in each case.

For the literature of entrepreneurship, Penrose (1959) notes that companies grow when they attend to the needs of consumers; Priem and Butler (2001a), Kor et al. (2007), and McMullen (2015) maintain that subjective entrepreneurial judgment is important to firm success and that resources gain economic value through customers' usage of them. And, a resource can be utilized in multiple different ways that can differentially increase the magnitude and scale of internal activities of a firm and create additional values for consumers externally (e.g., Augier & Teece, 2008; Kor et al., 2007). While Sirmon et al. (2008) and others investigate how internal resources can be bundled to produce efficiency inside a firm, Ye et al. (2012) consider how consumer preferences can be bundled outside a firm to produce simultaneous consumer utilities and two-sided market effects. Their work indicates that the entrepreneurial alertness to external opportunities, the so-called pure entrepreneurial judgment (Kirzner, 1973, 2018), can come before making any investment and can exist without any intimate knowledge of available resources.

In comparison, this chapter emphasizes on the creation of consumer synergies through collocation of commonly available products and/or services, one aspect of pure entrepreneurial judgment. By doing so, it contributes to the entrepreneurship literature by establishing the following main results, among others, that can be generally applied in real-life scenarios: (1) A retailer's location and the depth and breadth of offers represent the most important, most fundamental, as well as mutually constraining tactical decisions of the retailing firm. (2) If two offers of a firm facilitate beneficial interactions of two consumer segments, then that firm establishes a positively correlated two-sided or multi-sided market. And (3) when a firm conducts its business within a saturated market, its demand-side advantage established through collocating commonly available goods can be sustainable, if the marginal profit from the advantage is not more than the entry cost of a new competitor.

For the literature of innovation, Smith (1776) acknowledges over 200 years ago the importance of innovation. The topic of innovation of the producer side has been well investigated through the years by many scholars (Aas et al., 2015; Adner & Levinthal, 2001; Damanpour, 1991; Visnjic et al., 2016). In the business world, innovation is characterized as the introduction of original products and processes (Becheikh et al., 2006) that enable firms to competitively enter or create new markets (Smith & Tushman, 2005). And it has been treated by many as one major factor of long-term performance (Kanter, 2001). Veugelers and Cassiman (1999) find that high levels of perceived risks and costs and low appropriation determine the innovation sourcing strategy while not discouraging innovation from taking place. In particular, these authors find that small firms tend to restrict their innovation efforts to exclusive makes or simply buy strategies and large firms tend to acquire knowledge both internally and externally when implementing their innovation strategies. The fast development of internet-based technologies forces firms to become forever more competitive and innovative than before (Buffington, 2016; Caputo et al., 2016; Zollo et al., 2016).

Contributing to this activity area of research, this chapter establishes the following general result: (1) by adding to a successful set X of resources or replacing some resources in X by other resources, a firm can potentially create to positive synergies; (2) under the influence of a particular factor, such as location, circumstance, etc., if one of a firm's collocated offers that are necessary to consumers meets a competitive market demand, while other offers provide convenience, then the firm provides simultaneous consumer utilities.

For the literature of strategies, resource-based approaches tend to look inwardly, while looking outwardly leads to the recognition that consumer demand need to be addressed seriously. The former inward scrutinization addresses issues related to how heterogeneous resources and dynamic capabilities of firms can create value for consumers (e.g., Barney, 1991; Eisenhardt & Martin, 2000; Nason & Wiklund, 2018) through bundling internal resources in different ways (e.g., Sirmon et al., 2008). Because the concept of resources offers a framework for integrating multiple, dissimilar resources to explain their synergistic, differential effects on firms' performance and the contingencies associated with each effect (Fang et al., 2011), resource-based approaches greatly contribute to the knowledge of strategies (e.g., Lockett et al., 2009). As for the approach of looking outwardly into the environment, Barney (2001) and Priem and Butler (2001a, 2001b) recognize that after all it is consumers that determine the success of firms (Drucker, 1954; Penrose, 1959). Along this line of thinking, scholars examine various strategic issues, such as how market demand affects technological innovations and competitive advantages (e.g., Adner & Zemsky, 2006; Tripsas, 2008); how consumer-focused strategies can lead to value creation and capture (e.g., Adner & Snow, 2010; Gans et al., 2008; Priem, 2007); and how consumers influence entrepreneurial innovation (Sawhney et al., 2005; Shah & Tripsas, 2007). In particular, Ye et al. (2012) study how bundled preferences of consumers can be employed as a basis for developing firms' strategies in an effort that is parallel to the recent producer-focused synergy studies on economies of scope (e.g., Crossland & Smith, 2002; Gary, 2005; Tanriverdi & Venkatraman, 2005).

By attending to both the demand side and the producer side of the strategy literature, this chapter establishes the following main results, among others, that hold true generally: (1) if a firm makes its resources available to all business units in its attempt to produce an economy of scope, the firm will then be able to innovate synergistically. (2) Mobilizing inconsistent resources generally produce negative synergies. (3) If a set of core resources is behind a firm's portfolio of offers, the firm should continuously focus on exploiting its existing competitive advantages instead of developing new advantages. And, (4) when a firm operates a two-sided market with its collocated assortment of goods, if there are few attractors compared to the number of attractees, then that firm can charge the attractees higher prices than the market norm.

Other than the contributions listed above, what is more important is that this chapter holistically incorporates the demand side into the studies of strategic management, entrepreneurship, and innovation. At the same time, by using logical reasoning, which is similar to what is well-tested method in science and mathematics, this chapter integrates different streams of research into an organic whole, while moving beyond empirically confirming and anecdotally prescribing to the fact that subjective entrepreneurial judgment or managerial ability are important variables for strategic success (e.g., Foss et al., 2007; Holcomb et al., 2009; McMullen, 2015; Ye et al., 2012). On top of that, a theoretical foundation is developed so that strategic relatedness in providing simultaneous consumer utilities of the demand side (Sakhartov & Folta, 2014; Ye et al., 2012) and resource-based relatedness in diversification of the supply side (Farjoun, 1998; Kim & Finkelstein, 2009; Villasalero, 2017) can be identified.

By using the systemic yoyo model, this chapter develops a theoretical foundation that is employable to the identification of strategies that lead to simultaneous consumer utilities of the demand side (Sakhartov & Folta, 2014; Ye et al., 2012). And, it theorizes some of the fundamental properties of two-sided markets uncovered previously by Rochet and Tirole (2006), Sun and Tse (2009), Ye et al. (2012), and others, either empirically or anecdotally. (For a similar but different approach, see Azevedo & Leshno, 2016). At the end, this chapter provides specific, while generally applicable, recommendations for managers and entrepreneurs to explore and to identify demand-side potentials in their efforts of developing economies of scope.

To make logical reasoning in this chapter move forward smoothly, assume that each business firm exists for the purpose of satisfying a particular market niche through generating a positive cash flow, which can be profits from the marketplace, or investments from various investors, or both. In other words, the firm has to actively pursue after certain endeavors in order to meet some market demand(s).

By consumers, it means the end users of products and/or services, while customers the intermediate users. When a product/service is used by both end and intermediate users, these users are collectively known as customers. By resource, it means an asset of a firm, be it tangible or not (Harmancioglu et al., 2009), which that firm can use to design and implement its strategies (Barney & Arikan, 2001). In other words, a resource stands for something, be it physical, financial, intellectual, or organizational, the firm can mobilize to accomplish its business goals. And, a resource can generally provide alternative services that differentially increase either the efficiency inside the firm or consumer value creation outside the firm.

3.3 Synergies Beneficially Necessary to Producers

By synergistic innovation, it stands generally for such an innovative strategy of the focal firm that systemically deploys and redeploys known elements that exist either within or outside that firm to produce additionally economic benefits. In particular, known elements can be resources—either tangible or intangible, established management routines, production processes, consumer preferences, market demands, etc.; and the word "systemically" means that the focal firm can develop a meaningful system or a set of systems that organically combine the known elements to produce new products with much improved functionalities, and/or new services that meet a forever evolving market demand or consumer preference. The following are some good examples of synergistic innovations in action on either producer side or consumer side.

- Different combinations of known technological processes can produce positive synergy (Crossland & Smith, 2002).
- When knowledge across business units of the focal firm is shared, benefits from transferred skills can be anticipated (Hitt et al., 2001).
- When economies of scope and skill transfers are combined, the social network of the focal firm can greatly contribute to that firm's innovativeness (Tsai, 2001).
- Evolving consumer tastes stimulate firms to embark on technological development and innovation (Adner & Zemsky, 2006).
- The benefits consumers enjoy when their knowledge learned from using one product can literally reduce or eliminate the learning time required to use another product (Priem, 2007; Tanriverdi & Lee, 2008).
- The appearance of a disruptive technology can help reveal a new dimension or confirm an existing dimension of consumer preferences for various industries (Adner & Snow, 2010).

This section establishes relevant concepts and elementary properties regarding synergistic innovations at the producer side (Priem & Butler, 2001a, 2001b). The concept of synergistic potential arising from resource relatedness has been introduced since at least the early 1970s (e.g., Palich et al., 2000; Rumelt, 1974) when Rumelt noted that firms, which diversify through employing respectively related resources, generally outclass those firms, which also diversify, but only doing so by utilizing unrelated resources.

3.3.1 Availability of Resources

By synergistic innovation at the producer side, it means that the focal firm designs and employs an innovative strategy that systemically deploys available resources in such a way that the firm can produce an economy of scope in terms of products and/or services. By producer synergy, it means that through product diversification as a way to widen a firm's stock of assets and skills, the firm is able to expand the perimeter of its value activities (Porter, 1985, p. 380). By synergistic potential arising from resource relatedness, it means the potential of producing new products and/or services, which helps increase the economy of scope of a firm, by innovatively mobilizing related resources. When a mobilization of certain resources leads to positive economic benefits, then we say that the resources create a positive synergy. Otherwise, we say that the mobilization produces a negative synergy.

Proposition 3.1 Assume that the focal firm endeavors to produce an economy of scope. Then, it can potentially develop synergistic innovations from its effort of diversification, if it is able to repeatedly deploy its resources, be they tangible or intangible, by making them available to all business units.

To see why this proposition holds true, let us model the firm of concern as a system $S = (M, R)$ such that the object set M consists of the resources the firm controls and each relation r in the relation set R stands for a product produced by mobilizing a subset of the resources in M. Now, the given assumption means that freedom and encouragement are given for the employees of the firm to establish possible associations among elements in any subset of M, where each element in M can be repeatedly used in as many associations as possible. That of course implies that a potential of designing and producing many additional products and/or services appear. This logical reasoning is well depicted in Fig. 3.1a, b, where the rectangle stands for the object set M. In Fig. 3.1a, A and B are the two existing products of the firm, which are produced, respectively, by associating resources in their enclosed areas. When employees are encouraged to associate resources any way imaginable, additional enclosed areas, such C and D in Fig. 3.1b, can be produced.

This proposition can be shown rigorously by using the following theorem of systems science, where S is said to be a multi-leveled system, if at least one of its objects is also a system, … For the rigorous definition of this concept, see the appendix of this chapter. And, for any set X, the symbol $|X|$ stands for the cardinality

(a) Existing collocations of resources (b) Creating additional collocations

Fig. 3.1 Additional collocations of resources are stimulated. (**a**) Existing collocations of resources. (**b**) Creating additional collocations

of *X*. For a system *S*, *m* is referred to as a fundamental object in *S*, if *m* is no longer a system in the form of an ordered pair $m = (M_m, R_m)$ of some set M_m of objects and some set R_m of related defined on M_m.

Theorem 3.1 Let $S = (M, R)$ be a multi-leveled system and *M*(*S*) the set of all fundamental objects in *S*. If the following four conditions hold true, then $|M| < |M(S)|$.

- The object set *M* and that of each object system of *S* are finite;
- Each object that appears in any relation in the system *S* or an object system of *S* only appears once in that relation; and
- *S* has at least one chain of object systems of more than one level and each object system on the chain contains more than one object.

For a detailed, extremely technical proof of this result, see the Appendix.

Now, let us model the focal firm with business units strictly defined and resources divided according to the unit divisions as a system $S = (M, R)$, where each object *m* in *M* stands for the bundle of resources available only to a particular business unit and each relation *r* in *R* as a product or service of the firm. Then the set *M*(*S*) of all fundamental objects of the system *S* stands for the totality of resources the firm has control over. Now, the conclusion of Theorem 3.1 says that $|M| < |M(S)|$, which means that the number of available resources is greater than that of business units. Therefore, there are more ways to define relations (products) on *M(S)* than on *M*. That proves Proposition 3.1.

In terms of the literature, comparing to Proposition 3.1, a more specific conclusion is given by strategic management scholars. For example, it has been argued (e.g., Porter, 1985) that positive synergies from diversification can emerge if a firm is able to share tangible functions and intangibles, such as knowledge and skills, among business units.

3.3.2 *Consistent and Inconsistent Resources*

Assume that the focal firm has been successful with its competitive advantage A, while the changing business environment recently provides signals for the firm to pursue its next competitive advantage B. As what has been frequently happened, the development of the new advantage B generally demands the mobilization of some resources away from the maintenance of advantage A (McGrath, 2013). In such a situation, A and B are seen as two opposing advantages or opposing goals of the firm. Then, the following result describes when a mobilization of certain resources can lead to negative synergies.

Proposition 3.2 Let X and Y be mutually exclusive sets of resources the focal firm employs to maintain advantage A and to develop B, respectively. Then, mobilizing a resource in X and one in Y will generally produce negative synergy(-ies).

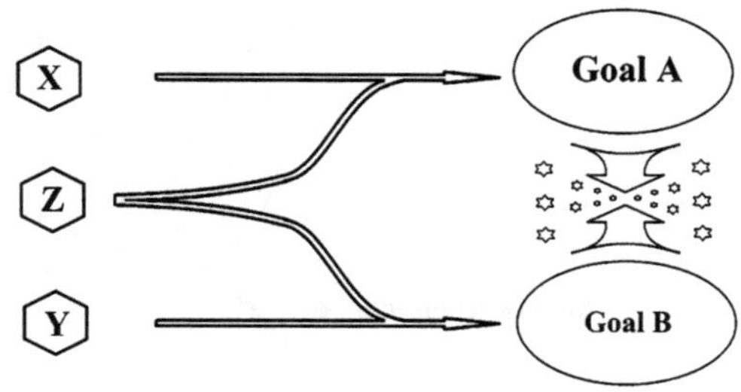

Fig. 3.2 How resources are divided corresponding to business goals A and B

To illustrate how two business goals (or advantages) of the focal firm could be opposing to each other, let us consider the following situation (McGrath, 2013):

- A = the goal of implementing the strategy of exploiting the competitive advantages proven successful over time; and
- B = the goal of implementing the strategy of constantly designing and developing new competitive advantages.

Based on this illustration it can be seen that the set of resources employed to materialize goal A and the set of those used for goal B are not the same. All the involved resources can be written into three mutually disjoint sets X, Y, and Z, other than X and Y, as defined in the proposition, set Z includes all those resources that are needed for materializing both business goals A and B, Fig. 3.2. The elements in set Z could include such commonly deployable resources in multiple directions as strong relationships that lead to information sharing, risk taking, and adoption of innovations (Dutta et al., 1999). Now, it is ready to see that a joint mobilization of the special resources in X and those in Y generally leads to undesirable effects or negative synergies.

Two resources x and y are said to be inconsistent resources, if mobilizing these resources jointly leads to negative synergy. For example, any resource from set X and any resource from set Y in Proposition 3.2 will be inconsistent, because jointly they lead to undesirable outcome(s). Now, in terms of when a mobilization of certain resources can potentially lead to positive synergies, we have the following conclusion, where X represents the set of resources that have been used to generate a positive synergy in the focal firm's effort to create an economy of scope.

Proposition 3.3 The focal firm can potentially produce positive synergy(-ies), if one or more additional resources, which are consistent with the ones already available in X, become available.

This result holds true, because altering set X is generally the way for the focal firm to produce additional versions of the product initially developed on X with varying degrees of functionality. Systemically, either adding another set of consistent resource into X or replacing some resources in X by another set of consistent resources mean that the new resources will alter the yoyo structure that underlies the original association of the resources in X in terms of spinning strength, the orientation of the spinning axis, the area the spin field covers, etc. The resultant yoyo

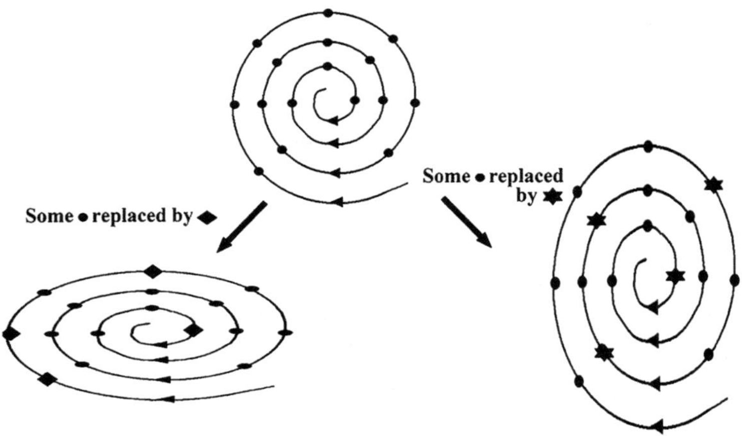

Fig. 3.3 Altering an existing systemic field by changing its composition

structure of the updated set X of course means a different product or service, which is either very different from or somehow related to the original one. Depicting this situation, Fig. 3.3 also demonstrates why the condition that the set of new resources used to alter X has to be consistent with the remaining resources in X, otherwise, the resultant yoyo body can be potentially broken into pieces, as what Proposition 3.2 shows. In Fig. 3.3, the original X evolves into either X' or X", where some of the round dots are replaced by diamonds in the former case, while by starts in the latter case.

Proposition 3.4 If the collection of the focal firm's competitive advantages is jointly supported by a set of core resources, then there is a good chance for the firm to continuously exploit its established competitive advantages instead of constantly developing new ones.

This result is a corollary of the previous propositions. In particular, if there is a set of core resources that underlies a firm's collection of competitive advantages, the superior value of those resources will be widely acknowledged by the stakeholders of the firm if not yet the case already. So, there has been or will be a developed momentum for the firm to continue its current state of affairs based on the following first law on state of motion.

First law on state of motion (Lin, 2009): Each imaginable and existing entity in the universe is a spinning yoyo of a certain dimension. Located on the outskirt of the yoyo is a spin field. Without being affected by another yoyo structure, each particle in the said entity's yoyo structure continues its movement in its orbital state of motion.

The scenario outlined in this proposition can be seen from a different angle: after putting in tremendous amounts of time and efforts in trying various combinations of resources to get a business operation going, the founders of the firm, as systems themselves with life cycles, can be most likely tired both mentally and physically.

That explains why under such circumstances, there is a good chance for the firm to continuously exploit its established competitive advantages instead of constantly developing new advantages, unless new stimuli, either from competitors or from the changing market condition, appears to redirect the attention and energy of the founders and/or their successors.

3.4 Potential Synergies for Consumers

Since over 50 years ago when Penrose (1959) noted that when paying attention to the needs of consumers, companies grow, studies in strategic management have advocated for paying additional attention to the demand side in decision-making (e.g., Adner & Zemsky, 2006; Priem, 2007). Riding on this trend of thoughts, this section investigates the concepts and elementary properties of synergistic innovations at the demand side (Ye et al., 2012) by placing end users of products and services in the square center.

3.4.1 Possibilities to Raise Fees

Similar to how the concept of producer synergy is defined earlier in the previous section we have the following (Ye et al., 2012): By consumer synergy, it stands for an increased value created for consumers and captured by a firm through employing combination(s) of products and/or services that jointly expand consumer utilities beyond the sum of the consumer utilities offered individually by the products and/or services. For illustration purpose, let us look at an excellent example constructed by Ye et al. (2012).

A state university in northern USA has a population of over 29,000 students, most of whom are unmarried undergraduates living on tight budgets. As most of the rental properties around the campus do not offer laundry facilities, self-service, coin-operated laundromats near the university compete for the students' business. Another successful kind of college-town business, attractive mostly to college women, is indoor tanning. Instead of offering these services separately, two entrepreneurs provide their independent, single-location businesses, each of which jointly provide coin-operated self-service laundry facility and indoor tanning service. Such business combination creates consumer synergies from diversification of commonly available assets—same or similar equipment—without much reduction in the overhead costs (from completely different sets of equipment) and labor costs (the combined business types require considerably different production and customer service skills). However, this business combination creates tremendous amount of demand-side synergies due to the following reasons:

1. Students can start washing their clothes and then tan their skin simultaneously, saving the otherwise unproductive and costly waiting time; and
2. Students are provided with a place for the potential of establishing relationships because the location of combined services provides opportunities for both males and females to meet, where women's greater participation in the tanning service attracts a larger number of men to the laundry service.

Consequently, the created consumer (or demand-side) synergies help, respectively, support higher fees collected from the laundry service than other standalone stores and maintain competitive prices for the much-increased demand for the tanning service. In other words, a greater value is, respectively, created for consumers and captured by business providers because of the resultant consumer synergies from product-and-service diversification.

In general, if two or more market demands can be met simultaneously, such as the situation described in reason (1) above, while saving valuable resources for consumers, such as time and/or money, then we say that the diversification effort of meeting different market demands has created a simultaneous consumer utility effect. If two services, each of which attracts a different segment of consumers, although the segments might be overlapping, are collocated so that the increased traffic flow due to the joint offer of services from one segment of consumers attracts an increasing traffic flow from the other segment of consumers, while the latter does not have any adverse effect on the former, as described in reason (2.) above, then we say that the diversification of services has created a two-sided market effect.

Proposition 3.5 Along with appropriately bundled products and/or services, higher fees can be charged for a product or service than the market norm, if the bundle (s) produce certain simultaneous consumer utility effects.

First, when a simultaneous consumer utility effect is created by collocating diverse products and/or services, by definition it means that consumers have saved some of their valuable resources. That saving generally is convertible into consumers' willingness to pay more than what is expected on the average in the marketplace. When a two-sided market effect is developed by collocating diverse products and/or services, the alternatively reinforcing effects on the traffic flows of the different segments of consumers make the demand for the joint offer of products and/or services rise. That in turn supports rising prices.

Systemically speaking, each simultaneous consumer utility effect can be described by employing the yoyo model shown in Fig. 3.4. In this systemic depiction, three market demands A, B, and C can be satisfied by either three different business entities X, Y, and Z separately or by one business firm whose yoyo field encompasses all those of the three entities X, Y, and Z. The idea is kind like, but not exactly the same as that of one-stop shopping. The reason why consumers are willing to pay extra is demonstrated by the fact that the conflict zones existing in areas between the yoyo fields X, Y, and Z no longer exist, if these small yoyo fields can be combined into a much larger field that encompasses those of X, Y, and Z.

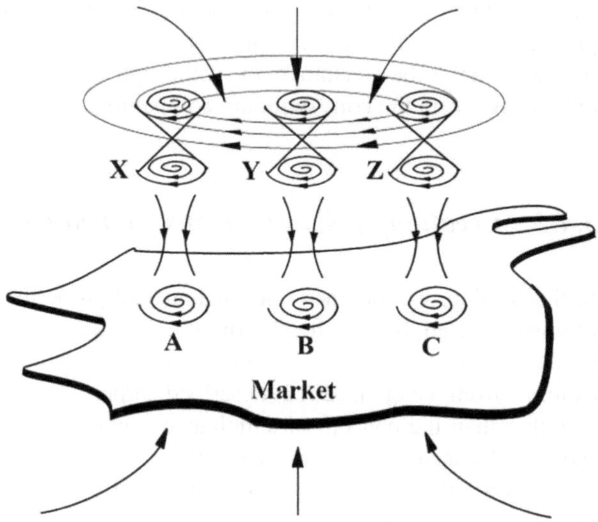

Fig. 3.4 Meeting three market demands simultaneously

Proposition 3.6 Along with appropriately bundled products and/or services, higher fees can be charged for a product or service than the market norm, if the bundle (s) produce a two-sided market effect.

For two-sided market effects, the concept can be intuitively seen systemically in Fig. 3.5. In this systemic intuition two different market segments A and B of consumers are identified, where consumers in B are closely attached to those in A who at the same time are particularly attracted to the service provided by firm X while can also take advantage of the service of Y. From such a realization of potentially creating a two-sided market through diversified offers of products

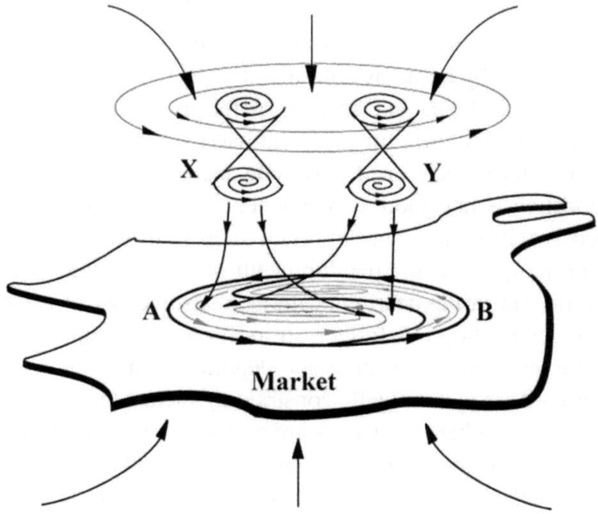

Fig. 3.5 How a two-sided market effect appears

and/or services, the business ideas of both X and Y are combined into one business practice, whose yoyo field encompasses those of both X and Y. This new business firm will attract the consumers in A, through which those consumers in B are also pulled over from the corresponding competitors.

3.4.2 Creation of Simultaneous Consumer Utilities

In this section, we look at some fundamental properties of simultaneous consumer utilities, created by the focal firm through offering a collocated assortment of products and/or services to consumers. For illustration, one can simply look at the example from Ye et al. (2012) described earlier.

Other than the concept of simultaneous consumer utilities, there is also that of sequential consumer utilities. The former, as described in the previous example, means when the consumer saves time by performing two or more activities at the same time, while the latter describes when consumers benefit from making a series of purchases sequentially without spending much additional time from one store to another, say, in a shopping mall. This section will only focus on the concept of simultaneous consumer utility and relevant consumer synergies.

Because our focus in this section is on how the focal firm could potentially create simultaneous consumer utilities through offering a collocated assortment of products and/or services, let us first look at the strategic significance of the firm's depth and breadth of its assortment of products/services.

Proposition 3.7 For each retailer, the following represent two mutually constraining tactical decisions beyond their ultimate importance to business success:

1. The location; and
2. The depth and breadth of its assortment of products/services offered to consumers

A retailer's location affects shopping time and other related costs (e.g., travel) that are generally borne by consumers when they shop for desired goods and/or services, while the depth and breadth of the assortment of products/services offered at a particular location provides the basis for consumers to evaluate the worth of their time and other related costs (Betancourt & Gautschi, 1990). In other words, if a location is not good, convenience and savings on time and other shopping-related costs will dictate consumers to shop at nearby stores for their desired goods and services; and if the depth/breadth of the product/service assortment offered is not sufficient in the nearby locations, consumer will be happy to spend extra time and money to shop in a further off location to save time and increase their simultaneous utilities. That is, location and depth/breadth of the assortment of products/services offered are two mutually constraining factors that the value of one determines that of the other, where the values are best assessed by consumers (Moreau & Dahl, 2005).

Consumers make their patronage choices among retailers by evaluating trade-offs of retailers' depth—such as that offered by specialty stores, breadth—such as that offered by general stores, and convenience—such as that offered by convenience store (Messinger & Narasimhan, 1997). Therefore, consumers' demand for benefits and maximization of their overall utilities drives the demand for particular product combinations in a retailer's assortment, which in turn determines which location is considered convenient. That explains why both location and the depth/breadth of the assortment of products/services to be offered to consumers represent the two most important, most fundamental tactical decisions of retailers.

Systemically, a retailer's choice of the depth/breadth of its assortment of products/services offered to consumers stands for the material foundation for the yoyo field of the retailer to exist, while the location represents how conveniently the yoyo field can absorb necessary inputs (e.g., consumers). Only when these two elements coexist, the yoyo field of the retailer can possibly "spin" and "spin" viciously.

Evidently, it can be seen that collocating two randomly selected products and/or services might not naturally result in simultaneous consumer utility. For example, the attempt of Sears, Roebuck and Company to provide consumers a one-stop shop of hard goods, soft goods, insurance services, and financial services was unsuccessful (Sobel, 1999). So, a natural question is: Under what condition(s) will the collocation of two or more products and/or services result in simultaneous consumer utility, which in turn leads to consumer synergies? To this end, we have the following result.

Proposition 3.8 If the focal firm offers its customers collocated products and/or services that satisfy the conditions below, then the firm is able to produce simultaneous consumer utilities.

- Each collocated product/service is necessary to consumers under the influence of a particular factor, such as location, circumstance;
- One of those collocated meets a competitive market demand; and
- Other collocated ones provide convenience.

Because one of the collocated products and/or services is assumed to meet a competitive market demand, when a consumer decides to go with that focal firm to satisfy his need or demand, the customer's decision will be further strengthened and backed by all the other collocated products and/or services due to the convenience they provide. Hence, jointly this assortment of products and/or services results in simultaneous consumer utilities.

Next, let us use examples to illustrate how Proposition 3.8 can be employed practically, where in each case, we need to identify the products and/or services that are collocated, the group of consumers, that particular factor, a product or service that meets a competitive market demand, and what convenience other collocated products and/or services provide. First, let us look at successful collocations, where consumers receive simultaneous utilities and business firms capture values through pricing decisions designed to maximize profitability across product types collocated.

- For the previous case of collocated laundry/indoor tanning services, the tanning part serves as the service in Proposition 3.8 that meets a competitive market demand of mostly female college students, while the laundry service provides convenience—for both washing clothes and meeting opposite genders. The particular factor is the specific location—the vicinity of a large university campus of mostly unmarried undergraduate students.

- For the case of combined gasoline station and convenience store, consumers are mostly drivers of automobiles and the particular factor is the fact that all cars need to be fueled regularly. Providing gasoline satisfies a competitive market demand, and the store provides convenience items which consumers can readily obtain when their vehicles are being filled with gasoline.
- For the case of collocated coffee shop and bookstore, the group of consumers contains all coffee drinkers, the factor is the fact that a lot of people are addicted to coffee. In this case, the competitive market demand is coffee drinks, and the book store provides a convenience for consumers to avoid rough outdoor climates and a comfortable environment to enhance the enjoyment of drinking coffee, as well as staying update with current affairs.
- For the case of major car dealers, such as general motors (GM), each of them collocates the service of selling cars with that of purchase financing. The group of consumers includes all potential drivers, and the particular factor is the reality that in America life can be quite difficult if a person does not have a car. The service of selling cars meets a competitive market demand, while the financing service provides convenience for car buyers and flexibility for the dealer to provide discounts on its automobiles.
- For the case of online retailers, such as amazon.com, the collocated assortment of products consists of those on sale through the internet, the group of consumers includes everybody who has internet access, and the particular factor is the fact that the majority of the population currently has connection to the internet. The competitive market demand is the retail of almost everything needed in life, and the convenience is that the internet connection eliminates all the travel costs and consumers can purchase a variety of needed items at the same time without stepping even one step out of his front door. (Note: amazon.com is only a case of one-stop shopping with nearly simultaneous consumer utility, because for cases of true simultaneous utilities the consumer saves time by performing two activities at the same time.)

Next, let us revisit the unsuccessful collocation attempt of Sears, Roebuck and Company, as mentioned earlier. In this case, the company collocated the retailing of hard and soft goods and the offer of insurance and financial services, while we cannot identify a clear core product(s) or service(s) that meet a competitive market demand with others providing convenience at the same time.

3.5 Sides of Market Created by Collocating Products

This section consists of two subsections. The first subsection looks at two-sided markets, created by the focal firm through offering collocated assortments of products and/or services to consumers; doing so helps cross-market-segment externalities to increase the corresponding consumer utilities. And, the second subsection examines the relationship between the ownership of the collocated assets and market success and when the strategy of collocating commonly available products and/or services can be potentially successful.

3.5.1 A Market with Various Sides

By a two-sided market, it means that there are externalities across different participating segments of consumers (cf. Sun & Tse, 2009). In other words, the participations on both sides of a two-sided market are either positively or negatively correlated to each other. For example, New York Stock Exchange (NYSE) is a positively (correlated) two-sided market, where the more stocks are listed, the more investors are drawn to the exchange; and the more investors frequent NYSE, the more companies list their stocks on the exchange. And, the interaction between consumers and advertisements might stand for a negatively (correlated) two-sided market depending on how consumers react to advertisements. On the other hand, not all markets are two-sided. For example, a typical product market is not two-sided, because increasing supply does not necessarily increase the demand, although increasing demand tends to result in rising supply.

Also, practical experiences indicate that collocating randomly selected products and/or services might not naturally result in a two-sided market effect. And many real-life cases support this conclusion. For example, pets.com tried to develop a two-sided market by linking pet owners and suppliers of pet products. However, its heavy investments did not create sufficient benefits for consumers to cover relevant costs. So, the expensive venture failed (Evans & Schmalensee, 2007). Hence, a natural question is: Under what condition(s) will the collocation of two or more products and/or services result in a two-sided market effect, which consequently leads to consumer synergies?

To potentially address this question, let us first look at the systemic structure of a two-sided market (Fig. 3.6), where the focal firm establishes a "platform" (the large, multi-layered spin field encompassing those of N and M) by offering two (or more) market segments of consumers, as indicated by N and M, its particularly collocated assortment of products and/or services. Through that platform, value is created by that firm through facilitating interactions between mutually interdependent market segments of customers, while that firm captures this value by collecting fees from at least some of the participating consumers. If the two sides of a two-sided market are positively correlated, then participants on either side of the market receive more

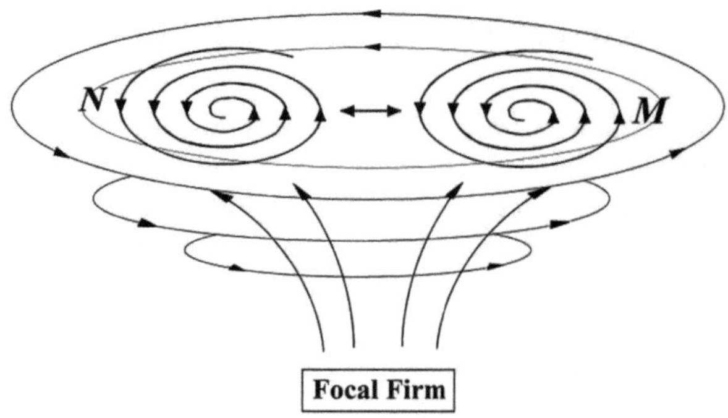

Fig. 3.6 The systemic structure of a two-sided market

value when membership increases on the other side (Rochet & Tirole, 2006). Based on this systemic intuition, we have the following result.

Proposition 3.9 If the focal firm provides consumers with collocated products and/or services that satisfy the following conditions, then the firm will, if not yet, be successful in terms of establishing a platform for a positively correlated two-sided or multi-sided market.

- Two collocated products and/or services facilitate beneficial interactions of at least two market segments; and
- Other collocated products and/or services make the interactions efficient or convenient.

To see why this proposition holds true, let A and B be the two assumed products and/or services in the collocated assortment of goods that focal firm offers to consumers. Assume that the particular market segments of consumers between which A and B facilitate beneficial interactions are *N* and *M*. Then, as depicted in Fig. 3.6, when all other collocated products and/or services help make these interactions efficient or convenient, a spin field (or platform) that encompasses the yoyo fields of *N* and *M* emerges. That means that the focal firm has successfully established a positively correlated two-sided market with *N* being one side and *M* the other. Note that in this systemic modeling, the fields of *N* and *M* must be converging fields that spin in the same direction; otherwise, the platform field cannot be emerging as claimed above.

Next, let us use examples to illustrate how Proposition 3.9 can be employed practically, where in each case, we need to identify the products and/or services that are collocated, the two particular products and/or services and the corresponding market segments of consumers that will be stimulated to interact beneficially, and whether or not the rest of the collocated products and/or services are supportive.

- For the previous case of collocated laundry/indoor tanning services, evidently it is the laundry service and the indoor tanning that stimulate the following two market segments of consumers—female and male college students—to interact beneficially. In this case, the two particular services exert their functionalities only

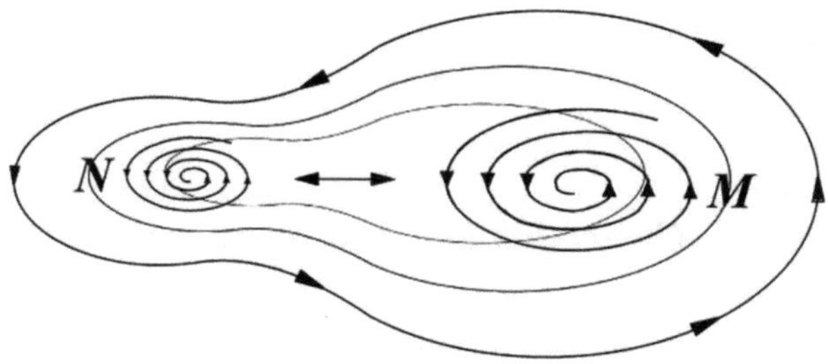

Fig. 3.7 The general systemic structure of a two-sided market

implicitly, where the focal firm only needs to attract as many female consumers to the indoor tanning service as possible and then the rest of the two-sided market will play out naturally with least amount of effort from the focal firm.

- For the case of online retailers, such as amazon.com, the collocated assortment of products and services are those on sale through the internet and an online platform. The online platform provides a means for sellers and buyers to interact beneficially so that the more sellers list the more buyers appear, and vice versa.
- Online dating services represent another case of two-sided markets, where the focal firm operates an online platform for the male and female sides of the dating market to join.
- Organizations, be they local, national, or international, that work to develop community projects generally establish two-sided markets by offering such events as showcases, designed to join entrepreneurs and venture capitalists.

In the systemic structure of a two-sided market in Fig. 3.6, the yoyo pools of *N* and *M* do not have to be similar sizes. Instead, in real life the general structure should look like the one depicted in Fig. 3.7, where the pool of one side of the market is smaller than the other side due to the reason that customers on different sides may enjoy different marginal utilities from participating in the platform. In other words, the presence of an additional participant, say, on side *M* may have a much greater positive effect on the utility of the other side *N*. In such a case, participants, say, on side *N* with lower marginal utility for participation are called attractors, and those on the other side, say, *M*, with higher marginal utility are attractees (Ye et al., 2012). Such designation of participants of a two-sided market naturally leads to the following pricing strategy.

Proposition 3.10 Assume that the focal firm operates a multi-sided market through offering a collocated assortment of products and/or services. If the number of attractors is a lot smaller than that of attractees, then that firm can offer a competitive discount to attractors with the lost revenue compensated by making attractees bear higher prices.

The marketing intuition behind this result is straightforward. When more attractors participate in a two-sided market with the said characteristics due to competitively discounted prices, a lot more attractees will be on board. That jointly generates increased demand for the platform. Therefore, more economic value for the focal firm that operates the two-sided market is captured. For related discussions, see Rochet and Tirole (2003), Armstrong (2006), and Jullien (2005).

3.5.2 Ownership and Market Success

Discussions in the previous sections show that market-side strategic innovations, based on collocations of commonly available products and/or services that deliver simultaneous utilities and/or serves two-sided markets with mutual attraction of different market segments of consumers, can create value for consumers and capture value for the focal firm that offers a collocated assortment of goods. It is definitely the virtuosity of an entrepreneur who innovatively associates some seemingly unrelated assets into an assortment that produces for consumers novel synergistic benefits that accrue from consumer perceptions and needs. So, a natural question arises (Ye et al., 2012): Can the products and/or services in a collocated assortment, which provides consumer synergies through simultaneous utilities, two-sided markets, or both, be offered individually by different business firms?

Proposition 3.11 Assume that the focal firm plans to offer simultaneous consumer utilities by operating a multi-sided market through collocating products and services. If the collocated products and services are commonly available, then the firm needs to offer all these products and services by itself.

Without loss of generality, assume that only two products are collocated in this given situation. Then, the reason why this result holds true in general is the following: Let us reason by contradiction. Assume that these two collocated products are individually offered by two separate firms with N being one side of the imagined two-sided market and M the other (Fig. 3.7). Because each of the separate firms has to generate a positive cash flow from the marketplace, the stability of the resultant platform—the large field encompassing the fields of N and M in Fig. 3.7—is not guaranteed as an operating organic whole or a connected system (Lin, 1999). That means that in practice the attraction between N and M does not exist steadily. In other words, the firm that attracts side N of the imagined two-sided market can easily join hands with another firm that has been attracting a consumer segment M' that is similar to M, because the products and/or services collocated are assumed to be commonly available. The systemic significance of common availability means that in the ocean of all the yoyo fields of the commonly available products and services each local field X can readily find another local field Y to temporarily form for a platform for a short-lived two-sided market, because in that ocean of yoyo fields, each individual yoyo pool is constantly fighting for survival and growth.

In terms of the literature, various studies also suggest that common ownership is efficient in different contexts. In particular, Williamson (1979) argues that collocation requires investment to cover the sunk costs so that post-contract opportunism represents a real moral hazard for separate firms. Ye et al. (2012) see the need to determine what consumer subsidies one firm must offer so that the other firm can reap the rewards of greater overall willingness to pay and then a mutually agreeable procedure for settling relevant revenues and costs must be negotiated between the separate firms. And with the changing consumer preference renegotiation will become a constant issue of concern. That will lead most likely to moral hazards and recurring contracting costs, a resolution of which, based on Williamson (1979) and Alchian and Woodward (1987), is a common ownership. Even if opportunism and contracting costs are non-existent, common ownership may still be preferred over markets or contracting, because the acquired experiences through the sole ownership provides the knowledge for better coordination of value-creating assets (Conner & Prahalad, 1996). In short, the very concept of collocating products and/or services for the purpose of delivering consumer synergies implicitly indicates that both flexibility for what to collocate and responsiveness to changing market demands are the basics of success and are only afforded by a common ownership.

Considering the nature of the products and services—common availability—to be collocated to produce consumer synergies in a resultant two-sided market, another natural, yet also practically important question arises (Ye et al., 2012): Can the focal firm's innovative and successful collocation of commonly available products and/or services provide a sustainable advantage for that firm?

If we employ the resource-based theory (Kozlenkova et al., 2014) to look at this question, the answer does not look promising, because the following two conclusions have been developed by Barney and Hesterly (2012):

- If a firm possesses such resources that few other firms have due to various constraints, then it is likely for that firm to develop a sustainable competitive advantage. And
- If a resource(s) is simultaneously valuable, rare, and exploitable by a firm, then the resource(s) can generate a sustainable competitive advantage for that firm.

Here, the assumed common availability implies that the products and/or services to be collocated are neither rare nor difficult for any firm to acquire. So, when proven successful, imitators would possibly follow the readily shown path to business success, leading to intensified competition and consequent competitive parity (Powell, 1992). However, the key technical detail in this reasoning is that the statement "if condition A holds true, then conclusion B follows" does not implies anything about what happens to A if B holds true. In the context of our current discussion, this means that although the products and/or services to be collocated are commonly available, it does not necessarily mean that the established consumer synergies and two-sided markets cannot be sustainable.

So, to address our question just given above, let us next turn our attention to the concept of managers' willingness to compete (Madhok et al., 2010) in their strategic decision-making, the essence of which is a choice about how to effectively allocate the limited resources (Grant, 2008; Lin, 2009). Indeed, in real life, beyond the ability to enter a market, no firm actually has the willingness and necessary resources to enter every market or most markets it is technically able to due to various reasons, such as that of forbearance (Bernheim & Whinston, 1990). In particular, firms yield their competition against their stronger competitors in those markets where they are less efficient, while in exchange the latter do the same in markets where the former are more efficient (Li & Greenwood, 2004). For example, Madhok et al. (2010) analyze a two-firm, two-product case and show that when one firm with limited resources has a comparative advantage for both products compared with the other firm, the former chooses to manufacture the product where it has the greater advantage while voluntarily abandoning the other market to the latter. In other words, many firms that have the ability to compete in multiple markets choose to do so in only one or a few while avoiding others so that their competitive advantages may actually be sustainable due to the choices of whom to compete with. Or speaking differently, the focal firm with limited availability of resources generally abandons less attractive markets and chooses to compete in such market(s) that allows it to capture the greatest value (Adner & Snow, 2010).

Proposition 3.12 Assume that the focal firm conducts its business within a saturated market, and that its demand-side advantage is established through collocating commonly available products and/or services and conducting a resultant multiple-sided market. Then the advantage can be sustainable, if the margin of profits due to the advantage is not more than the entry cost of a new competitor.

In fact, in a saturated market (Wagner et al., 2007), there is not much consumer movement; and incumbent firms provide an over-abundant supply of goods to a stable consumer base of a whole spectrum of heterogeneous preferences. That generally means that the margin of profit for the incumbent firms is thin (Forrest et al., 2017). Therefore, if the focal firm's collocation of commonly available products and/or services indeed provides a demand-side advantage in a saturated market, then that firm must have attracted people away from the established consumer base of the incumbent firms due to these people's simultaneous enjoyment/need of the other products and/or services within the collocated assortment. Such a group of consumers can only be a portion of the saturated market. And once the consumer segment of the focal firm, as the first mover, is well served, the cost of entering that segment is drastically increased for potential competitors up to the new entry deterrence price (Lieberman & Montgomery, 1988). That is, in this case, the first mover can obtain better margin of profits compared to other incumbent firms. Secondly, the assumed multiple-sided market the focal firm is operating serves as an isolating mechanism that benefits that firm as the first mover. The cross-segment externalities of the multiple-sided market within the saturated market are especially difficult for a competitor to penetrate, because the potential competitor must entice a critical mass of participants away from the established platform in order to be profitable.

Systemically speaking, the conditions that the firm conducts its business within a saturated market and that the margin of profits due to the advantage is not more than the entry cost of a new competitor, as assumed in Proposition 3.12, are necessary for this conclusion to hold true, as conclusions in Chapter 4 of volume 1 indicate. Since discussions in that chapter are very technical, all details are omitted here.

3.6 A Few Final Words

The present world of market economies has been turbulent. For a firm to survive and grow successfully in such turbulence world, it has to continuously look for potentials of different competitive advantages (McGrath, 2013). Diversification at either the producer side (Porter, 1985; Santalo & Becerra, 2008) or the demand side (Ye et al., 2012) or both represents one possible way to satisfy this desperate need. If a firm adopts this approach of diversification, then the firm faces the challenge of how to develop the necessary ideas for diversification. To address this challenge, this chapter establishes a series of both theoretically and practically significant results.

Because of the particular approach taken here, this chapter is able to develop urgently needed conclusions generally useful for managerial problem solving and decision-making (Lockett et al., 2008) and to address some key issues in strategic management. It provides a completely different approach to business success from what is suggested by Baker and Nelson (2005)—apply combinations of available resources to new problems and opportunities.

In particular, for managers, entrepreneurs, and retailers who focus on the demand side, this chapter shows by considering collocations of commonly available products and/or services that other than an intimate understanding of consumers' needs and the creativity to envision a novel collocation of commonly available resources (Ye et al., 2012), superior consumer benefits can be created by offering consumer groups utilities that they were not previously aware. In particular, this chapter shows when consumers are willing to pay extra for their needs (Propositions 3.5 and 3.6). And, this chapter provides specific ways to collocate commonly available products and/or services by targeting different segments of consumers, while sufficiently consider how the served segments of consumers could potentially interact with each other to produce simultaneous consumer utilities (Proposition 3.8) and two-sided market effects (Proposition 3.9). For example, it is found that when the magnitudes of the sides of a two-sided market are significantly different, offering competitive marketing strategies on the attractors can greatly increase the overall consumer participation in the two-sided market, while the costs of marketing can be at least partially compensated by the attractees (Proposition 3.10). And, it demonstrates why all the commonly available products and/or services in a collocated assortment need to be offered by the same ownership (Proposition 3.11).

Beyond theoretical results, this chapter also provides practically applicable recommendations. For example, when strategically planning for collocations of commonly available products and/or services, a manager/entrepreneur should always keep in mind the potential of complementary consumer benefits (Propositions 3.5, 3.6 and 3.8), where consumer interactions can create another dimension of growth and satisfaction and where a two-sided or even multi-sided market can emerge (Propositions 3.9, 3.10, and 3.11). And, when a two- or multi-sided market is established, appropriate pricings can be introduced to target attractors and attractees (Proposition 3.10) in order to help with value capture. Additionally, the demand-side advantage can actually be sustained, providing a real-life support of the concept of first mover advantage (Lieberman & Montgomery, 1988).

For retailers, this chapter shows why their locations and the depths and breadths of their assortments of products/services are important for their success. However, when determining particular locations and the depths and breadths of their assortments, these three variables need to be considered holistically, because they are also interrelated and define each other (Proposition 3.7).

For managers and entrepreneurs who like to promote their corporate growth and improve performance through economies of scope, beyond explaining why such an approach will help (Proposition 3.6), this chapter also shows the need to constantly look out for newly emerging competitions (Proposition 3.12). Additionally, it emphasizes on how to possibly create synergistic innovations by

- Making their limited resources available to all business units within their companies,
- Discovering what new ideas could be introduced through combining different resources,
- Naturally formulating a portfolio of diversified products and/or services,
- Staying alert about when their firms could likely become exploiters of existing competitive advantages instead of explorers of new advantages in the turbulent consumers' markets, and
- Avoiding negative synergies by not jointly mobilizing inconsistent resources.

As for the limitations of this chapter, one stems from the assumption on why a firm exists. In the business world, firms conduct their business very differently from each other contingent upon why/how they are established. That means that conclusions derived in this chapter do not universally apply to every actual situation. Although this chapter's attention is on how both conceptually and practically the focal firm can synergistically collocate commonly available products and/or services in its effort to create economies of scope, if did not consider the limitations a firm is subject to. These limitations and related issues surely help point to future research problems in order to develop additional, more in-depth practically useful conclusions and recommendations beyond what is presented here.

Appendix: Proof of Theorem 3.1

Given a system $S_0 = (M_0, R_0)$, another system $S_n = (M_n, R_n)$ is said to be an nth-level object system of system S_0, provided that there are systems

$$S_i = (M_i, R_i), \text{for } i = 1, 2, \ldots, n\text{–}1,$$

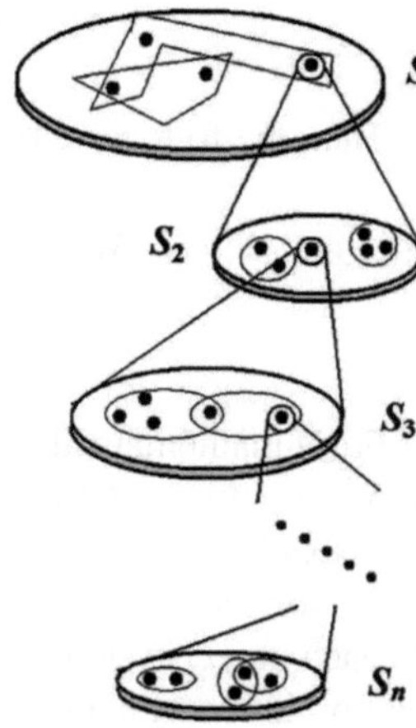

Fig. 3.8 A chain of object system

such that S_i is an object in M_{i-1}, $1 \leq i \leq n$. In this case, each element in M_n is referred to as an nth-level object of system S_0. When the system S_0 has at least one nth-level object system, for $n = 1, 2, \ldots$, then the system is referred to as a multi-leveled (or multi-level) system.

A chain of object systems of S_0 is a sequence $\{S_i = (M_i, R_i) : i < \alpha\}$, for some ordinal number α, of different-level object systems of S_0, such that for each pair $i, j < \alpha$ satisfying $i < j$, there exists an integer $n = n(i, j)$, a function of i and j, such that S_j is an nth-level object system of S_i, Fig. 3.8, where each oval area stands for a system with its objects indicated by dots and relations by enclosed regions. Then the following result (Lin, 1999, p. 193) is true:

(∗) Each chain of object systems of S must be finite.

Now, we define the set $M(S)$ of all fundamental objects as follows: First, let us rewrite the system $S = (M, R)$ as $S = (M_0, R_0)$ for the sake of notational convenience. Define

$$^*M_0 = \{x \in M_0 : x \text{ is not a system}\}$$

and

$$\tilde{M}_0 = \bigcup\{M_x : x = (M_x, R_x) \in M_0 - {}^*M_0\}$$

Assume that for a natural number n, two sequences $\{^*M_i : i = 0, 1, 2, \ldots, n\}$ and $\{\tilde{M}_i : i = 0, 1, 2, \ldots, n\}$ have been defined, satisfying that

$$^*M_i = \{x \in \tilde{M}_{i-1} : x \text{ is not a system}\}$$

and

$$\tilde{M}_i = \bigcup \{M_x : x = (M_x, R_x) \in \tilde{M}_{i-1} - {}^*M_i\}.$$

Then the following two sets can be defined for the index number $i + 1$,

$$^*M_{i+1} = \{x \in \tilde{M}_i : x \text{ is not a system}\} \text{ and } \tilde{M}_{i+1} = \bigcup \{M_x : x = (M_x, R_x) \in \tilde{M}_i - {}^*M_{i+1}\}.$$

From mathematical induction, it follows that a sequence $\{^*M_i : i \in \omega\}$ is defined. Now, by letting $M(S) = \bigcup \{^*M_i : i \in \omega\}$, result (*) above guarantees that $M(S)$ consists of all fundamental objects in system S.

As for the conclusion that $|M| < |M(S)|$, it follows from the assumptions that (1) each object system of S has a finite object set, (2) each object that appears in any relation in the system S or an object system of S only appears once in that relation, and (3) S has at least one chain of object systems of more than one level and each object system on the chain contains more than one object. Here, conditions (1) and (2) are necessary for producing the resultant inequality by limiting our counting cardinalities $|M|$ and $|M(S)|$ within the realm of natural numbers.

References

Aas, T. H., Breunig, K. J., Hydle, K. M., & Pedersen, P. E. (2015). Innovation management practices in production-intensive service firms. *International Journal of Innovation Management, 19*(5), 1550055. https://doi.org/10.1142/S1363919615500553

Adner, R., & Levinthal, D. (2001). Demand heterogeneity and technology evolution: Implications for product and process innovation. *Management Science, 47*(5), 611–628.

Adner, R., & Snow, D. (2010). Old technology responses to new technology threats: Demand heterogeneity and graceful technology retreats. *Industrial and Corporate Change, 19*(5), 1655–1675.

Adner, R., & Zemsky, P. (2006). A demand-based perspective on sustainable competitive advantage. *Strategic Management Journal, 27*(3), 215–239.

Alchian, A. A., & Woodward, S. (1987). Reflections on the theory of the firm. *Journal of Institutional and Theoretical Economics, 143*(1), 110–136.

Armstrong, M. (2006). Competition in two-sided markets. *RAND Journal of Economics, 37*(3), 668–691.

Augier, M., & Teece, D. J. (2008). Strategy as evolution with design: The foundations of dynamic capabilities and the role of managers in the economic system. *Organization Studies, 29*(8–9), 1187–1208.

Azevedo, E. M., & Leshno, J. D. (2016). A supply and demand framework for two-sided matching markets. *Journal of Political Economy, 124*(5), 1235–1268.

Baker, T., & Nelson, R. E. (2005). Creating something from nothing: Resource construction through entrepreneurial bricolage. *Administrative Science Quarterly, 50*(3), 329–366.

Barney, J. (1991). Firm resources and sustained competitive advantage. *Journal of Management, 17*(1), 99–120.

Barney, J. (2001). Is the resource-based "view" a useful perspective for strategic management research? Yes! *Academy of Management Review, 26*(1), 41–56.

Barney, J., & Arikan, A. (2001). The resource-based view: Origins and implications. In M. Hitt, R. Freeman, & J. Harrison (Eds.), *Handbook of strategic management* (pp. 124–185). Blackwell.

Barney, J., & Hesterly, W. (2012). *Strategic management and competitive advantage: Concepts and cases* (4th ed.). Pearson.

Becheikh, N., Landry, R., & Amara, N. (2006). Lessons from innovation empirical studies in the manufacturing sector: A systematic review of the literature from 1993 to 2003. *Technovation, 26*(5), 644–664.

Bernheim, B. D., & Whinston, M. D. (1990). Multimarket contact and collusive behavior. *RAND Journal of Economics, 21*(1), 1–26.

Betancourt, R., & Gautschi, D. (1990). Demand complementarities, household production, and retail assortments. *Marketing Science, 9*(2), 146–161.

Buffington, J. (2016). The future of manufacturing: An end to mass production. In J. Buffington (Ed.), *Frictionless markets* (pp. 49–65). Springer.

Caputo, A., Marzi, G., & Pellegrini, M. M. (2016). The internet of things in manufacturing innovation processes: Development and application of a conceptual framework. *Business Process Management Journal, 22*(2), 383–402.

Conner, K. R., & Prahalad, C. K. (1996). A resource-based theory of the firm: Knowledge versus opportunism. *Organization Science, 7*(5), 477–501.

Crossland, P., & Smith, F. I. (2002). Value creation in fine arts: A system dynamics model of converse demand and information cascades. *Strategic Management Journal, 23*(5), 417–434.

Damanpour, F. (1991). Organizational innovation: A meta-analysis of effects of determinants and moderators. *The Academy of Management Journal, 34*(3), 555–590.

Drucker, P. F. (1954). *The practice of management*. Harper & Row.

Dutta, S., Narasimhan, O., & Rajiv, S. (1999). Success in high-technology markets: Is marketing capability critical? *Marketing Science, 18*(4), 547–568.

Eisenhardt, K., & Martin, J. (2000). Dynamic capabilities: What are they? *Strategic Management Journal, 21*(10/11), 1105–1121.

Evans, D. S., & Schmalensee, R. (2007). *Catalyst code: The strategies behind the world's most dynamic companies*. Harvard Business School Press.

Fang, E., Palmatier, R., & Grewal, R. (2011). Effects of customer and innovation asset configuration strategies on firm performance. *Journal of Marketing Research, 48*(3), 587–602.

Farjoun, M. (1998). The independent and joint effects of the skill and physical bases of relatedness in diversification. *Strategic Management Journal, 19*(7), 611–630.

Forrest, J. Y. L., Buttermore, J., & Wajda, T. A. (2017). At Nash equilibrium when new market competitions appear? *Kybernetes: The International of Cybernetics, Systems and Management Science, 46*(2), 256–271.

Forrest, J. Y.-L., Dang, Y. G., McCarthy, L., Liu, S. F., & Liu, Y. (2019a). Conditions under which synergistic innovations appear. In *Proceedings of the 2019 Annual Conference of Decision Sciences Institute* (pp. 2061–2080). Decision Sciences Institute.

Forrest, J. Y.-L., Dang, Y. G., McCarthy, L., Liu, S. F., & Liu, Y. (2019b). Simultaneous consumer utilities, multi-sided markets and consumer synergies. In *Proceedings of the 2019 Annual Meeting of National Association of Business, Economics and Technology* (pp. 101–121). National Association of Business, Economics and Technology.

Foss, K., Foss, N. J., Klein, P. G., & Klein, S. K. (2007). The entrepreneurial organization of heterogeneous capital. *Journal of Management Studies, 44*(7), 1165–1186.

Gans, J. S., MacDonald, G., & Ryall, M. D. (2008). *The two sides of competition and their implications for strategy. Working paper*. Melbourne Business School. Retrieved from https://works.bepress.com/michael_ryall/15/

Gary, M. S. (2005). Implementation strategy and performance outcomes in related diversification. *Strategic Management Journal, 26*(7), 634–664.

Grant, R. M. (2008). *Contemporary strategy analysis: Concepts, techniques, applications* (6th ed.). Blackwell Publishing.

Harmancioglu, N., Droge, C., & Calantone, R. (2009). Strategic fit to resources versus NPD execution proficiencies: What are their roles in determining success? *Journal of the Academy of Marketing Science, 37*(3), 266–282.

Hitt, M. A., Bierman, L., Shimizu, K., & Kochhar, R. (2001). Direct and moderating effects of human capital on strategy and performance in professional service firms: A resource-based perspective. *The Academy of Management Journal, 44*(1), 13–28.

Holcomb, T. R., Holmes, R. M., Jr., & Connelly, B. L. (2009). Making the most of what you have: Managerial ability as a source of resource value creation. *Strategic Management Journal, 30*(5), 457–485.

Jullien, B. (2005). Two-sided markets and electronic intermediaries. *CESifo Economic Studies, 51*(2-3), 233–260.

Kanter, R. M. (2001). *Evolve! Succeeding in the digital culture of tomorrow*. Harvard Business School Press.

Kim, J. Y., & Finkelstein, S. (2009). The effects of strategic and market complementarity on acquisition performance: Evidence from the U.S. commercial banking industry, 1989–2001. *Strategic Management Journal, 30*(6), 617–646.

Kirzner, I. M. (1973). *Competition and entrepreneurship*. University of Chicago Press.

Kirzner, I. M. (2018). The ethics of pure entrepreneurship: An Austrian economics perspective. *The Review of Austrian Economics, 32*, 89–99. https://doi.org/10.1007/s11138-017-0412-1

Kor, Y. Y., Mahoney, J. T., & Michael, S. C. (2007). Resources, capabilities and entrepreneurial perceptions. *Journal of Management Studies, 44*(7), 1187–1212.

Kozlenkova, I. V., Samaha, S. A., & Palmatier, R. W. (2014). Resource-based theory in marketing. *Journal of the Academy of Marketing Science, 42*, 1–21.

Li, S. X., & Greenwood, R. (2004). The effect of within industry diversification on firm performance: Synergy creation, multi-market contact and market structuration. *Strategic Management Journal, 25*(12), 1131–1153.

Lieberman, M. B., & Montgomery, D. B. (1988). First-mover advantages. *Strategic Management Journal, 9*, 41–58.

Lin, Y. (1999). *General systems theory: A mathematical approach*. Kluwer Academic/Plenum Publishers.

Lin, Y. (2009). *Systemic yoyos: Some impacts of the second dimension*. CRC Press (an imprint of Taylor and Francis).

Lockett, A., O'Shea, R. P., & Wright, M. (2008). The development of the RBV: Reflections from Birger Wernerfelt. *Organization Studies, 29*(8–9), 1125–1141.

Lockett, A., Thompson, S., & Morgenstern, U. (2009). The development of the resource-based view of the firm: A critical appraisal. *International Journal of Management Reviews, 11*(1), 9–28.

Madhok, A., Li, S., & Priem, R. L. (2010). The resource-based view revisited: Comparative firm advantage, willingness-based isolating mechanisms and competitive heterogeneity. *European Management Review, 7*(2), 91–100.

McGrath, R. G. (2013). *The end of competitive advantage: How to keep your strategy moving as fast as your business*. Harvard Business Review Press.

McMullen, J. S. (2015). Entrepreneurial judgment as empathic accuracy: A sequential decision-making approach to entrepreneurial action. *Journal of Institutional Economics, 11*(3), 651–681.

Messinger, P. R., & Narasimhan, C. (1997). A model of retail formats based on consumers' economizing on shopping time. *Marketing Science, 16*(1), 1–23.

Moreau, C. P., & Dahl, D. W. (2005). Designing the solution: The impact of constraints on consumers' creativity. *Journal of Consumer Research, 32*(1), 13–23.

Nason, R. S., & Wiklund, J. (2018). An assessment of resource-based theorizing on firm growth and suggestions for the future. *Journal of Management, 44*(1), 32–60.

Palich, L. E., Cardinal, L. B., & Miller, C. C. (2000). Curvilinearity in the diversification-performance linkage: An examination of over three decades of research. *Strategic Management Journal, 21*(2), 155–174.

Penrose, E. T. (1959). *The theory of the growth of the firm*. John Wiley & Sons.

Porter, M. E. (1985). *Competitive advantage: Creating and sustaining superior performance*. Free Press.

Powell, T. C. (1992). Strategic planning as competitive advantage. *Strategic Management Journal, 13*(7), 551–558.

Priem, R. L. (2007). A consumer perspective on value creation. *The Academy of Management Review, 32*(1), 219–235.

Priem, R. L., & Butler, J. E. (2001a). Is the resource-based "view" a useful perspective for strategic management research? *The Academy of Management Review, 26*(1), 22–40.

Priem, R. L., & Butler, J. E. (2001b). Tautology in the resource-based view and the implications of externally determined resource value: Further comments. *The Academy of Management Review, 26*(1), 57–66.

Rochet, J. C., & Tirole, J. (2003). Platform competition in two-sided markets. *Journal of the European Economic Association, 1*(4), 990–1029.

Rochet, J. C., & Tirole, J. (2006). Two-sided markets: A progress report. *RAND Journal of Economics, 37*(3), 645–667.

Rumelt, R. P. (1974). *Strategy, structure, and economic performance*. Harvard University Press.

Sakhartov, A. V., & Folta, T. B. (2014). Getting beyond relatedness as a driver of corporate value. *Strategic Management Journal, 36*(13), 1939–1959.

Santalo, J., & Becerra, M. (2008). Competition from specialized firms and the diversification-performance linkage. *Journal of Finance, 63*(2), 851–883.

Sawhney, M., Verona, G., & Prandelli, E. (2005). Collaborating to create: The internet as a platform for customer engagement in product innovation. *Journal of Interactive Marketing, 19*(4), 4–17.

Shah, S. K., & Tripsas, M. (2007). The accidental entrepreneur: The emergent and collective process of user entrepreneurship. *Strategic Entrepreneurship Journal, 1*(1–2), 123–140.

Sirmon, D. G., Gove, S., & Hitt, M. A. (2008). Resource management in dyadic competitive rivalry: The effects of resource bundling and deployment. *The Academy of Management Journal, 51*(5), 919–935.

Smith, A. (1776). *The wealth of nations, books I-III (1986 printing)*. Penguin Books.

Smith, W. K., & Tushman, M. L. (2005). Managing strategic contradictions: A top management model for man-aging innovation streams. *Organization Science, 16*(5), 522–536.

Sobel, R. (1999). *When giants stumble: Classic business blunders and how to avoid them.* Prentice Hall.

Sun, M., & Tse, E. (2009). The resource-based view of competitive advantage in two-sided markets. *Journal of Management Studies, 46*(1), 45–64.

Tanriverdi, H., & Lee, C. H. (2008). Within-industry diversification and firm performance in the presence of network externalities: Evidence for the software industry. *The Academy of Management Journal, 51*(2), 381–397.

Tanriverdi, H., & Venkatraman, N. (2005). Knowledge relatedness and the performance of multibusiness firms. *Strategic Management Journal, 26*(2), 97–119.

Tripsas, M. (2008). Customer preference discontinuities: A trigger for radical technological change. *Managerial and Decision Economics, 29*(2–3), 79–97.

Tsai, W. (2001). Knowledge transfer in intraorganizational networks: Effects of network position and absorptive capacity on business unit innovation and performance. *The Academy of Management Journal, 44*(5), 996–1004.

Veugelers, R., & Cassiman, B. (1999). Make and buy in innovation strategies: Evidence from Belgian manufacturing firms. *Research Policy, 28*(1), 63–80.

Villasalero, M. (2017). A resource-based analysis of realized knowledge relatedness in diversified firms. *Journal of Business Research, 71*(Feb), 114–124.

Visnjic, I., Wiengarten, F., & Neely, A. (2016). Only the brave: Product innovation, service business model innovation, and their impact on performance. *Journal of Product Innovation Management, 33*(1), 36–52.

Wagner, P., Olsen, J., & Thach, L. (2007). *Wine marketing & sales: Success strategies for a saturated market* (2nd ed.). Board and Bench Publishing.

Williamson, O. E. (1979). Transaction cost economics: The governance of contractual relations. *Journal of Law and Economics, 22*(2), 233–261.

Ye, G. L., Priem, R. L., & Alshwer, A. A. (2012). Achieving demand-side synergy from strategic diversification: How combining mundane assets can leverage consumer utilities. *Organization Science, 23*(1), 207–224.

Zollo, L., Marzi, G., Boccardi, A., & Ciappei, C. (2016). Gli effetti della Stampa 3D sulla competitivita aziendale. Il caso delle imprese orafe del distretto di Arezzo. *Piccola Impresa/Small Business, 2*(2), 80–100.

Chapter 4
Innovations and Resources

Jeffrey Yi-Lin Forrest, Sailau Baizakov, Yong Liu, Yohannes G. Haile, John Golden, Abel Gyan, Yaya Sissoko, and Qiaoxing Li

Abstract In the present, rapidly changing world of business, various unprecedented kinds of markets have been developed or still been emerging accompanying the evolutionary development of modern technology. And, various types of players, both conventional and nonconventional, have been actively engaged in the activities of these developed and emerging markets. Facing these new markets and unconventional players, decision-making managers and entrepreneurs, as well as scholars of the academic world, have been simultaneously challenged in unparallel ways. To meet these timely challenges, this chapter, which is mainly based on Forrest et al. (Adv Syst Sci Appl 20(3):50–72, 2020a) and Forrest et al. (J Business Econ Stud 24(1):33–53, 2020b), examines potentials of value creation and value capture at the firm level from several diverse vantage points.

First, to possibly develop deeper insights than what has been achieved in the literature, this chapter employs systems methodology and such a logical reasoning that is similar to the one commonly used in mathematics and natural science, which starts from a several basic axioms with results established along with new concepts introduced. Second, this chapter looks at issues of concern, respectively, from the angles of market competition, innovation, resource, inter-organizational network, and close association between sellers and buyers. Then, some practically reliable

Jeffrey Yi-Lin Forrest (Department of Accounting Economics Finance, Slippery Rock University, Slippery Rock, PA, USA; Email: Jeffrey.forrest@sru.edu), Sailau Baizakov (Institute of Mathematics and Mathematical Modeling, Almaty, Kazakhstan; Email: Baizakov37@mail.ru), Yong Liu (School of Business, Jiangnan University, Wuxi, Jiangsu, China; Email: clly1985528@163.com), Yohannes G. Haile (Black School of Business and School of Engineering, Pennsylvania State University Behrend, Erie, PA, USA; Email: yxh313@psu.edu), John Golden (Department of Accounting Economics Finance, Slippery Rock University, Slippery Rock, PA, USA; Email: John.golden@sru.edu), Abel Gyan (Department of Information Technology Management, Slippery Rock University, Slippery Rock, PA, USA; Email: Abel.gyan@sru.edu), Yaya Sissoko (Department of Economics, Indiana University of Pennsylvania, Indiana, PA, USA; Email: ysissoko@iup.edu), and Qiaoxing Li (Key Laboratory for Cloud Computing and Complex System of Guangxi Universities, Guilin University of Electronic Technology, Guilin, China; Email: qxli@gzu.edu.cn) are equally contributed to this chapter.

J. Y.-L. Forrest, *Systemic Principles of Applied Economic Philosophies II*, Translational Systems Sciences 39, https://doi.org/10.1007/978-981-99-7939-4_4

general recommendations are provided to conclude this chapter along with a few topics and directions for future research.

Keywords Creative destruction · Firm-level trust · Globalization · Opportunism · Platform · Schumpeterian rents · Small-numbers situations · Strategic alliance · Systemic hole · Virtual markets

4.1 Introduction

Globalization, be it economic or not, has created new ways for wealth creation (Forrester Research Report, 2000). For example, virtual markets have appeared to process direct seller-and-buyer transactions remotely. That has greatly changed the conventional way of market competition and provided boundless opportunities for entrepreneurs. Such a stimulating era of business has made once accustomed form and rule of competition changed in order for businesses and individuals to adapt to emerging formats of decision-making and inter-organizational interactions. It has attracted the attention of scholars, front-line managers, and entrepreneurs (Hitt & Ireland, 2017), leading to enhanced information acquisition, knowledge development, and sharing of know-hows (Amit & Zott, 2001). A comparison of what is realistically happening and how the literature of scholarly works expands shows that most studies on value creation and capture provide managerial suggestions of limited validity instead of general recommendations due to their various empirical constraints. Hence the following theoretically important question arises naturally:

> Based on original, empirical studies on issues and matters of value, which consist of a dominating part of the literature, can generally true conclusions be established so that they do not suffer from the inherent constraints of data- and anecdote-based analyses?

This question is very important epistemologically, because addressing it will definitely help introduce new methodologies into studies of business-related topics and issues that can be employed widely to develop useful conclusions instead of the suggestions as currently done. At the same time, this question is also practically significant due to the fact that competitive advantages, at least some of which were once sustainable, have become mostly transient, short-lived. That is, the business world is currently in the era of transient competitive advantages; consumer preferences evolve rapidly and become less patient (Forrest & Tallapally, 2018; McGrath, 2013).

This current chapter, which is mainly based on Forrest et al. (2020a, b), will address this important question by developing a series of formal propositions on the basis of logical reasoning and systems thinking (Lin, 2009) through considering, respectively, innovations, resources, the market state of mutual forbearance, inter-organizational networks, platforms that directly connect sellers and buyers, and how information flows affect the emergence of creative destruction. In particular, among others, this chapter establishes the following generally-true conclusions:

- With free competition, innovation can effectively help create value if protective property rights and complementary assets are available. Within such a market of free competition, exchanges help resources reveal their dormant values.
- Mobility of resources is positively proportional to the capable value creation.
- Market mutual forbearance among the incumbent firms helps the incumbents gain improved profitability until the state of mutual forbearance is disrupted.
- A firm's membership of an inter-organizational network or a strategic block generally represents an inimitable, not substitutable resource the firm can potentially mobilize.

The rest of the chapter is organized as follows. Section 4.2 provides a review of related literatures, points to the contribution of this chapter, and summarizes the key concepts that will be dealt with in the rest of this chapter. Section 4.3 examines value potentials out of either innovations or resources. Section 4.4 looks at how values can potentially emerge out of market forbearance and network structures of the market. Section 4.5 focuses on several value-related issues of business networks, convenient platforms, and creative destructions. Section 4.6 concludes this chapter with practical recommendations for managers, entrepreneurs, and retailers.

4.2 The Literature and Preparation

This section consists of two subsections. The first one provides a review on related literatures, while discussing what contributions this paper makes respective to what has been known. The second subsection prepares for a smooth logical flow of thinking for the rest of this chapter.

4.2.1 Literature Review

Innovation's importance in wealth creation has been recognized since at least the time of Adam Smith (1776). Ever since then, although the concept of innovation has been massively investigated by many scholars, relevant research has mainly focused on what factors determine the innovativeness of a firm (Ahuja et al., 2009; Becheikh et al., 2006). Within the presently phenomenal progresses in scientific and technological innovations, Baizakov et al. (2019) examine the dynamics of an economic entity by exploring the connection of income and expenses. On the backdrop of this huge literature, the current chapter presents a brand-new approach of reasoning and analysis. Because of this adopted new approach, this chapter is able to establish a much clearer relationship between protective property rights, complementary assets, and innovation's effectiveness in value creation.

As for resources and related studies, the role played by organizational resources in firms' success is first recognized by Penrose (1959). Gradually, scholars apply the concept of resources to logically illustrate synergistic and differential effects of various factors on firms' performance (Fang et al., 2011). So, starting in the 1980s, the so-called resource-based view of the firm begins to catch people's attention (Kozlenkova et al., 2014; Porter, 1979; Wernerfelt, 1984). For example, although non-financial performance of insurance companies is statistically significantly affected by resources, Ombaka et al. (2015) find that the effect of resources on firm performance indicators is mixed. By analyzing capability-performance relationship through the point of view of resources, Cacciolatti and Lee (2016) are able to elucidate how different types of marketing capabilities help improve firm performance. Contributing to this literature, the current chapter shows that a firm's capabilities are also resources of the firm, how latent values of resources can be made visible, how value can be created out of resources, and under what conditions resources are unmatched and not readily substitutable.

In the business world, firms are mostly members of networks (or systems) of various business organizations and exchange associations instead of atomistic actors that compete with each other, as what the major part of the literature shows (Galaskiewicz & Zaheer, 1999; Granovetter, 1985; Gulati, 1998). When firms are individually a part of some strategic networks, other than having access to information, resources, markets, and technologies, they also have advantages of learning, knowledge sharing, and economies of scale and scope. Such advantages collectively help lift these firms onto higher levels of performance and market influence (Gulati et al., 2000). In particular, regarding networks of business entities, Harrigan (1985) and Kogut (1988) look at how interfirm partnerships are formed; Baum and Dutton (1996) investigate firms' behaviors and consequent performances; Forsgren (2016) further explores Uppsala model of the general internationalization process; and Öberg (2018) inspects the concept of innovation and a few relevant topics, among others. Furthering this literature, among other results, the current chapter establishes (1) why firms in the position of systemic holes in a supply-demand network represent control and profitability; (2) why expanding market influence helps a network of business organizations improve its member firms' levels of profitability; and (3) why firms can benefit enormously from creating and maintaining platforms that directly connect sellers and buyers.

As for the relationship between information and wealth creation, literature searches did not provide much information. The small body of the relevant literature can be grouped into the following two groups—one on the relationship between an organization's interior and exterior and the other on information and business successes. In particular, by an organization's interior, it means the knowledge on the organization's characteristics; by an organizational exterior, it stands for the state of sharing and exchange of information, knowledge, and goods with the outside world. By using the database of Standard & Poor's (S&P) 500 of the time period from 1996 to 2009, Datta (2016) suggests that at the micro-firm level there were an optimum recombination of exterior sourcing and technology distinctness. Uzuegbunam et al. (2018) investigate the association between national culture and global connectedness with the creative destruction process at the macro-level of nations. This chapter develops hypotheses about a nation's adoption of creatively destroying technologies based on the cultural dimensions of uncertainty avoidance and cultural tightness (vs. looseness), and about global connectedness dimensions of depth and breadth. These authors find significance for interaction between tightness and dimensions of global connectedness by using the data of agricultural biotechnology adoptions in 58 nations.

As for the literature on information and business successes, by using the data from an in-depth interview with seven providers and consumers of electric cars, Stryja and Satzger (2018) suggest to design and use particular information systems so that potential consumers are able to test new innovations before they make their purchase decisions of the consequent products. By surveying the literature, Li and Nguyen (2017) review the related studies on when firms engage in collaboration opportunities that involve information, and what critical elements are for business success. This chapter highlights works in various angles, including economies of scale, knowledge sharing, market size and volatility, selection of strategic partners, intellectual property rights, spillover effects, collaboration costs, trust and commitment, opportunism, and overall collaboration strategies.

Enriching this literature on information and wealth creation, this chapter establishes the general fact that increasing information circulation accelerates the speed of emergence of creative destructions. By joining this result and Theorem 4.1, this chapter shows that market information and shown consumer demand jointly stimulate entrepreneurs to produce their market offers based on their individually disparate circumstances and varied cognitive aptitudes. Various incremental and disruptive innovations appear collectively on top of market information, consumer demands, and correspondingly varied entrepreneurs' efforts.

4.2.2 Preparation for Understanding Value Potentials

This subsection aims at achieving two objectives: (1) it introduces the necessary terminologies to make the logical reasoning in the rest of this chapter flow seamlessly and to make this chapter as self-contained as possible. (2) It establishes a theorem to serve as the building block of the conclusions derived in this chapter.

First, this chapter assumes that each business firm considered herein exists for the purpose of satisfying a particular market niche with its operation financially maintained by a positive cash flow as a consequence of its business conducts. Although in the past such positive cash flows backed firms' performance and profits (Sobel, 1999), that is no longer the case in recent times, where positive cash flows can be assured through investment inflows based on promises or potentials (Li & Ma, 2015). For example, within the landscape of global e-commerce, online retailers have focused on pumping up their future promises and potentials so that they can continuously attract sufficient amounts of venture capitals by emphasizing increasing their market shares instead of solely on making profits. Insomuch, some well-known retailers have been losing money one year after another since their inception.

By value in this chapter, it stands for the benefit offered by a product, service or good to an economic agent, even though it is defined differently by competing schools of economics. Value in fact has been widely studied in various disciplines, such as computer science, economics, investment, marketing, mathematics, music, philosophy, semiotics, etc. Because the related literatures are enormous, we omit a review of the studies here. By value creation, it stands for a process a firm goes through to offer its output that is valuable to an economic agent. Such a process consists of two components: creating value either for consumers or for shareholders. When consumers are the target, value(s) are created to satisfy certain market demands. When shareholders are the end purpose, the process aims at attracting future investment capital. Opposite to the concept of value creation is that of value capture. It stands for the value a firm realizes by implementing a value creation process that satisfies market demand(s).

By consumers, we mean the end users of products, services, or goods; and, by customers those firms that employ those products, service, or goods as inputs to produce their outputs. By resource, it stands for an asset of a firm that it can mobilize to introduce and implement its business strategies (Barney & Arikan, 2001; Harmancioglu et al., 2009). That is, a resource of a firm is anything that the firm can employ to realize its business objectives; it can take a physical, financial, intellectual, or organizational form. Beyond resources, it is innovative mobilization of resources that practically provides a firm with alternative facilities that differentially improve its internal efficiency and create value externally for consumers or customers. By advantage (or competitive advantage), it represents a special way for a firm to mobilize its resources, such as a strategy or particular way of operation, production, or management, so that the firm is able to generate more value than other firms, considered marginal or just break even, in its market (Peteraf & Barney, 2003).

Here, the term *virtual market* means such a setting whereby internet infrastructure helps facilitate business transactions and business deals. The internet infrastructure is a worldwide electronic network. It helps create virtual communities and unconventional commercial arrangements (Hagel III & Armstrong, 1997); it enables knowledge and know-hows to be widely shared among firms and instantly avails product information to consumers.

Several additional characteristics of virtual markets include:

- Convenient connectivity (Dutta & Segev, 1999),
- Easy completion of transactions (Balakrishnan et al., 1999),
- Self-serving platform for cross-regional and inter-organizational networks to form (Shapiro & Varian, 1999), and
- A provider of free or low-priced information (Evans & Wurster, 1999).

Entrepreneurial startups and corporate ventures have been—and still are—successfully riding the quick emergence of virtual markets while creating tremendous amount of new wealth (Amit & Zott, 2001).

Next, the following game-theoretic result, which generalizes the results in Forrest et al. (2017), plays the role of foundation for the discussion in the rest of this chapter.

Theorem 4.1 If the market described below is in Nash equilibrium, then the following are equivalent:

1. At least one new firm enters the market competitively and profitably with their versions of substitute offer.
2. There is a consumer surplus of switchers who make purchase decisions based on which supplier's price is lower.

The market considered in Theorem 4.1 is assumed to satisfy the following conditions. It is served by a fixed number of firms with their horizontally differentiated offers. Its operation is only affected by market forces, such as demand and supply, and consumers' forever evolving preferences and tastes. In other words, this market is perfectly competitive without any outside interference. As a consequence of interacting forces between the systems of values and beliefs of individual consumers and the missions of the incumbent firms, each of these firms has a base of loyal customers. These loyal customers only consider the offers of their favored firms unless the prices of the offers are more than their reservation prices. Different from loyal customers, there are those customers in the marketplace who make purchases based on which firm's unit-value price is lower. These customers are collectively known as switchers. And, the firms' strategies of pricing are known to all involved companies who respond by playing Nash equilibria through untainted self-analyses.

Proof. What is assumed in this theorem implies that the said market is in a state of mutual forbearance (Bernheim & Whinston, 1990). The incumbent firms alleviate their rivalries by partitioning the market according to their strengths so that they surrender dominance to their stronger competitors in marketplaces where they are less efficient (Li & Greenwood, 2004). The codependence of these firms gradually decreases the rates of market entry and exit (Fuentelsaz & Gómez, 2006; Yu & Cannella Jr., 2012), while reducing interfirm hostility (Haveman & Nonnemaker, 2000). Due to this state of mutual forbearance, let us consider the aggregate of the incumbent firms as one imaginary firm with α being its market share in percentage. So, $\beta = 1 - \alpha$ denotes the percentage size of the consumer surplus.

Let us assume that that there are n incumbent firms and that all relevant boundary conditions are normalized such that incumbent firms' individual selling prices, production costs, loyal customers' reservation values within the said market, lower and upper boundary conditions, and magnitudes of loyal-customer bases are all, respectively, normalized to P_i $(0 \leq P_i, \leq 1)$, 0, 1, 0, 1, and α/n, $i = 1, 2, \ldots, n$.

Proof of 1) $\Rightarrow$ 2). Assume that by randomizing its price over the interval from production cost to loyal customers' reservation value, or [0,1] after applying normalization, a firm enters into the said market of n incumbent firms, which are collectively seen as one aggregate firm. So, the consumer surplus must satisfy $\beta = 1 - \alpha > 0$.

Proof of 2) $\Rightarrow$ 1). Assume that the consumer surplus satisfies $\beta = 1 - \alpha > 0$. Firstly, let α_0 be a real number so that $\beta = 1 - \alpha > \alpha_0 > 0$ and $\alpha = \ell\alpha_0$, where ℓ is a natural number. Secondly, let us imagine that the aggregate firm is divided into ℓ many identical (imaginary) "firms," named i, $i = 1, 2, \ldots, \ell$. Each of these firms provides consumers with an identical product and enjoys the market share $\alpha_0 = \alpha/\ell$ of loyal consumers. These firms compete over the switchers with adjustable prices. And thirdly, these ℓ imaginary firms do not have any symmetric pure strategy Nash equilibrium.

For the rest of this proof, it suffices to show that there is one firm that will be expected to profit by entering this market through uniformly randomizing its price strategy over the interval [0,1]. To this end, let $F(P)$ be the price distribution of Firm j, one of the imaginary firms of the aggregate firm. The aggregate firm or equivalently each of the ℓ imaginary forms sets its price after considering the price of the entering firm and those of all other imaginary firms. Hence, the profits for Firm j from its loyal consumers is $\alpha_0 P$ and those from its share of the switchers is $\prod_{i \neq j}^{\ell}(1-P)[1-F(P)]\beta P = \beta P(1-P)[1-F(P)]^{\ell-1}$. Hence, the profit Π Firm j generates when the firm sells its product at price P is

$$\alpha_0 P + \beta P(1-P)[1-F(P)]^{\ell-1}$$

and the objective of Firm j is to maximize the following by choosing its price distribution $F(P)$

$$E(\Pi) = \int_{-\infty}^{+\infty} \left\{\alpha_0 P + \beta P(1-P)[1-F(P)]^{\ell-1}\right\} dF(P)$$

$$= \int_{0}^{1} \left\{\alpha_0 P + \beta P(1-P)[1-F(P)]^{\ell-1}\right\} dF(P)$$

where $E(\Pi)$ stands for Firm j's expected profit for all possible prices. The reason why the upper and lower limits of the integral are changed, respectively, from $+\infty$ and $-\infty$ to 1 and 0 is because when $P < 0$ or when $P > 1$, the profits are zero.

The equilibrium indifference condition of Firm j is

$$\alpha_0 \times P + \beta \times P(1-P)[1-F(P)]^{\ell-1} = \alpha_0 \times 1. \tag{4.1}$$

So, for the ℓ imaginary firms, solving Eq. (4.1) leads to their symmetric equilibrium pricing strategy as follows:

$$F(P) = 1 - \left(\frac{\alpha_0}{\beta P}\right)^{\frac{1}{\ell-1}}. \tag{4.2}$$

From $\beta > \alpha_0$, it follows that $\alpha_0/\beta < 1$. So, for any Price P, satisfying $1 \geq P \geq \alpha_0/\beta$, Eq. (4.2) is well-defined as a probability distribution. This end implies that for the ℓ imaginary firms, or equivalently, the aggregate firm, the lowest allowed price is α_0/β.

To complete this proof, it suffices to show that the entrant actually expects to make profits in this new market. To this end because $\lim_{P\to 1^-} F(P) = 1 - (\alpha_0/\beta)^{1/(\ell-1)} \neq F(1) = 1$, the cumulative price distribution function $F(P)$ has a jump discontinuity at the reservation value $P = 1$, where the amount of jump is $(\alpha_0/\beta)^{1/(\ell-1)}$. That is, $F(P)$ has a mass point of size $(\alpha_0/\beta)^{1/(\ell-1)}$ at the reservation price $P = 1$. So, the expected profit of the entrant is the following:

$$E(\Pi) = \int_0^{\alpha_0/\beta} \beta P dP + \int_{\alpha_0/\beta}^{+\infty} \beta P[1 - F(P)]^{\ell} dP \tag{4.3}$$

$$= \int_0^{\alpha_0/\beta} \beta P dP + \int_{\alpha_0/\beta}^{1} \beta P[1 - F(P)]^{\ell} dP + \beta\left(\frac{\alpha_0}{\beta}\right)^{\ell/(\ell-1)} \tag{4.4}$$

where the first term in the right-hand side of Eq. (4.3) stands for the expected profit of the entrant when it charges the lowest price in the marketplace and captures the entire consumer surplus, and the second term is the entrant's expected profit when it is in direct competition with the ℓ incumbent firms.

It can be readily shown that all the terms on the left-hand side of Eq. (4.4) are positive. So, it implies that if the consumer surplus $\beta = 1 - \alpha > 0$, there will be at least one entrant into the said market to compete with the incumbent firms.

4.3 Potential Values out of Innovations and Resources

This section consists of two parts with the first focusing on the systemic modeling of the concept of innovations, while the second part looks at how property rights, latent potentials of resources and transaction efficiencies affect the creation and capture of values.

4.3.1 Systemic Modeling of the Concept of Innovations

The concept of product is defined differently in management and marketing from that in economics, for related references, see discussions below, let us first define this concept for our discussions in this chapter. By product, it means such a thing or process, either tangible (physical) or intangible (non-physical), which is produced by a firm to meet a market demand. For example, an iPhone is a tangible and physical product that consumers can use to make their lives more enjoyable and convenient. An annuity established with an insurance company is an intangible product through which the company makes its promises that consumers can count on when certain prescribed situations appear. Services like self-serving laundry facilities, indoor tanning salons, represent such products that consumers can utilize through using the facilities and salons. Investment recommendations of financial firms are also products, known as informational goods; they are produced by relevant firms through a "manufacturing" process, consisting of gathering, organizing, and analyzing facts and data. In general, complementary products are bundled together to promote consumer utilities, attract additional customers and improve sales.

To keep everybody on the same pace, the concept of innovation is defined as follows in a parallel fashion to that defined for the manufacturing sector (Forrest et al., 2018): By innovation, it means some activities, related to the production or offering of a product or a bundle of products, which lead to extraordinarily added value for a firm in comparison to other activities that other firms in the same economic sector simultaneously embark on. The phrase "the production or offering of a product" of course includes the related R&D efforts and actual design of one or several original products that causes extraordinarily added value for the firm of concern. In other words, each innovation consists of pertinent activities that lead to the eventual introduction of original product(s). These activities can, for example, be a redesign of the business model currently in use, works devoted to adequately comprehending market signals, efforts directed to acquiring new knowledge, energies purposefully spent in converting newly acquired know-hows to actual production, etc.

Conversely, the phrase "offering of a bundle of products" is overwhelmingly dissimilar. It means to collect several somehow relevant products together in one deliverable package to consumers. The key here is that the products that are bundled together do not need to be special or original in terms of their characteristics and functionalities. The creativity and innovative thinking behind a bundle of products, be they mundane or original, lie in the potential and/or actual developments of simultaneous consumer utilities and multi-sided markets (Ye et al., 2012). When consumers enjoy their consumptions from using several products concurrently, they experience a moment of simultaneous consumer utilities; and when different markets are served and pulled together, a so-called multi-sided market is created.

The emphasis on the comparatively added value in the previous definition of innovation implicitly assures this concept to include different aspects of applications. For instance, the emphasized added value suggests that

- Over time creativity can possibly emerge;
- Both current and predicted market demands that are comprehended internally and accepted externally will help promote creativity;
- By adopting needed business processes, expected values are created and captured;
- This particular definition of innovation implies not only inventions but also translations of them into market offers to meet identified demands;
- It maintains potentials open for newness and originality of market offers and relevant business process(es); and

- It integrates covertly potentials of technological changes, adoption of different processes and consequent outcomes.

This definition of innovation reflects the essence that innovation is a driving force behind the creation and capture of new and exceptional value, and that it emerges in various situations and in disparate ways, such as design and production of new market offers, novel procedures of production, measures of improved efficiency, creation of new markets, discovery of new sources of supply, and reformation of industries, as claimed by Schumpeter (1934). Being able to charging high rents represents one of the benefits of the originality and scarcity brought forward by innovations. That entices and stimulates entrepreneurial spirits, even though these elevated rents gradually weaken as the initial originality turn into humdrum industry exercises and the scarcity disappears. That is why creative destruction emerges (Schumpeter, 1942): The early menaces endured by entrepreneurs pave the way for the appearance of consequent originality and scarcity, while as knowledge accumulates and information spreads over time and distance, the know-hows underlying entrepreneurial initiatives become commonly known.

4.3.2 Property Rights, Potentials of Resources, and Transaction Efficiency

Discussions above imply that each innovation is identifiable to some resolute activities formulated to satisfy a recognized market demand, no matter whether the demand is large or small. Technology plays its role in innovation by providing improvements, such as making various operations more efficient, making more relevant discoveries, lowering the operational expenditure, etc. Based on discretely dissimilar identifications of market demands, entrepreneurs embark their individually different innovations, leading to a spectrum of different market offers. The joint effort of these entrepreneurs transforms existing markets, creates new markets, and develops unprecedented industries. That fundamentally drives the continuous development of the economy.

Proposition 4.1 In an open, competitive economy, (1) both complementary assets and the effectiveness of protective property rights positively affect an innovation's potential of value creation; (2) exchanges enabled by different markets assist the latent values of resources to be practically materialized.

The truthfulness of the first result follows directly from the discussions above. In particular, being open and competitive encourages entrepreneurial spirit. With emboldened entrepreneurial spirit, effective protection of property rights and mobilizability of complementary assets will jointly provoke fervent people to innovate for the purpose of satisfying market demands.

In terms of the literature, Teece (1987) provides a related, anecdote-based discussion.

The second conclusion is a consequence of Theorem 4.1. In particular, the assumed market in that theorem encourages consumers to develop their consumption preferences increasingly more sophisticated. Such endless progression in consumer preferences and tastes inexorably expands the consumer surplus in the marketplace. That, as indicated by Theorem 4.1, then increases the market competition among the incumbent firms, although they might be in a state of mutual forbearance. This logical reasoning illustrates how latent values of resources are developed and materialized through creative competitions of resources available to individual entrepreneurs.

See Moran and Ghoshal (1999) for associated empirical studies. For what economic variables could potentially influence a firm's innovativeness, see Becheikh et al. (2006), Forrest, Nicholls, et al. (2020), Hitt and Ireland (2017).

Transaction is defined by Williamson (1983) as a trade that a product is transferred from one owner to another across a technologically distinguishable interface such that a round of production and delivery finishes and another round begins. Transaction cost is defined by Demsetz (2003) as the cost of a completed trade, where the term "trade" means the commonly known buying/selling, or emotional interactions between people, informal gift exchanges of different parties, etc. For the particular purpose of this chapter, the current chapter will not establish results from Cheung (1992) definition of transaction costs, even though Cheung's definition covers a much broader range of scenarios than Demsetz's.

As rules that are commonly accepted and followed by members in a society, institutions indirectly determine the scale of transaction costs. Various factors generally determine transaction costs (Williamson, 1979). Examples of such factors include frequency of trading, specificity, asymmetry of information, uncertainties, bounded rationality, opportunistic behaviors in small-numbers situations, and others. That is why when companies are able to facilitate low transaction costs, they can tactfully improve their performance and growth (North, 1992). A firm is said to have transaction efficiency, if it is able to lower its transaction costs more than its competitors can. The result below follows naturally:

Proposition 4.2 A firm can create value for consumers and capture value from the market by improving transaction efficiency. In other words, transaction efficiency represents a source of value for both consumers and producer firms.

Theorem 4.1 readily implies this proposition, because transaction efficiency reduces a firm's selling price. That assists the firm to keep its existent loyal consumers and capture the entire market segment of switchers. In other words, by using transaction efficiency, the firm creates value for consumers and simultaneously captures value for itself.

For empirical studies on how firms recognize the need to lower costs, risks associated with coordination and transaction, and how information technology can lessen costs and risks, see Clemons and Row (1992). For anecdotes on how a networked environment, such as the internet, can help decrease transaction costs, see Dyer (1997).

Proposition 4.2 and discussions above jointly imply that a firm can create and capture value by reducing asymmetry of information, involved uncertainty, complexity, boundedness of rationality, and bargaining behavior in small-numbers situations. That is, by economizing transaction costs with innovation, firms will be able to squeeze values out of their business transactions.

Additionally, by improving their reputation, trusts, and transactional experiences, e.g., frequent transactions, firms will be able to reduce their costs of distinctive exchanges with each other. That is, improving their reputation, trusts, and transactional experiences will help increase a firm's transaction efficiency.

4.3.3 Potential Values Out of Resources

By resource, it means an asset, either tangible or intangible (Harmancioglu et al., 2009), a firm can employ to design and apply its strategies in order to realize its business objective (Barney & Arikan, 2001). In other words, a resource is such a thing, be it physical, or financial, or intellectual, or organizational, that a firm can employ to materialize its business objective. By capability, it generally represents a process, mostly information based, that allows a firm to holistically mobilize its available resources to reach its objective (Makadok, 2001).

Proposition 4.3 Each firm-specific capability represents a unique resource of the firm.

By combining all the discussions above, a firm can be uniquely identified with its system of firm-specific resources. Although the resources of the firm can be mostly also available to other firms, they are related to each other within the firm purposefully for particular business objectives. This identification between a firm and its unique system of resources can naturally lead to the well-known resource-based view or theory (RBV) of the firm (Kozlenkova et al., 2014) based on the recognition of the following three basic and intuitive axioms, for related details, see Forrest et al. (2019).

Axiom 4.1 (Resource Heterogeneity): No matter which industry a firm is a part of, the firm owns its unique system of resources.

Axiom 4.2 (Resource Immobility): Due to practical difficulties of trading resources between firms and formulating similar associations among available resources within individual firms, differences in the systemness of firms' available resources endure over time.

Axiom 4.3 (Different Levels of Efficiency): Different firms enjoy their individually different levels of performance, no matter whether the firms belong to the same industry or not.

A resource is seen as valuable to a firm (Barney, 1997), if it enables the firm to introduce and to implement a particular strategy that helps increase that firm's performance beyond what would be the case without the resource. By combining the RBV and the concept of value creation, the result below follows:

Proposition 4.4 A firm's ability to mobilize its valuable and rare resources represents its ability to create value.

The scarcity of the firm's valuable resources naturally leads to this proposition, if the firm is able to mobilize these resources. It is because only when the firm has an ability to employ the said resources, the scarcity and valuableness of the resources will jointly assist the firm to create certain advantages over other firms until such a time when the scarcity disappears.

Proposition 4.5 If a firm has control over some valuable and rare resources, while its business goal is consistent with that of its stakeholders, then the firm can potentially create value by utilizing the particular resources.

In fact, the if condition implies that the management of the firm is able to effectively exploit its valuable and rare resources. Hence, this firm is capable of creating value by mobilizing these resources, as jointly indicated by Propositions 4.3 and 4.4.

Proposition 4.6 A firm's ability to fully work with its capabilities of marketing, research and development (R&D), and operations can potentially lead to value creation.

To see the truthfulness of this proposition, let us look at the capabilities of marketing, research and development (R&D), and operation, individually one by one. First, for each firm, it presents itself to the world by revealing what the firm is, what demands of the product market the firm can satisfy, and how the firm plans to change to accomplish its goal (Kotler & Keller, 2016). In other words, the marketing capability helps a firm acquire the knowledge and forecast about its current and future competitions (Jaworski & Kohli, 1993). Speaking differently, marketing capability helps a firm orient its effort and activities of innovation and operation, and adequately presents the firm to the market, while showing what the firm can do to satisfy market demands.

Secondly, the R&D capability of a firm translates the market information, innovatively acquired from using the marketing capability, into the terms specific to the firm. Such specific terms direct the firm with its design and production of new or original products that potentially satisfy consumers' incessantly changing demand. At the same time, this capability prevents competitors from imitating the firm's new products (Irwin & Klenow, 1994). When a firm has a strong and reputable track record of R&D achievements, the firm will be able to boost its image and form favorable consumer expectations.

Thirdly, the operational capability of a firm practically realizes the market information and knowledge, acquired through marketing and R&D capability, into deliverable products.

By combining all these three capabilities together, one can see that only when the marketing capability is able to acquire novel information and knowledge from the market, it will make it possible for the R&D capability to introduce the state-of-the-art designs of new and original products, which will give the operational capability a chance to adopt appropriate and accommodating procedures. Through the joint working of these three capabilities, a firm's chain of activities becomes practically mobile and imperfectly imitable. Within such a situation, the firm is perfectly positioned to create value few rivals can compete with. In other words, Proposition 4.6 follows directly from Propositions 4.3 and 4.4 jointly.

For related discussions based on anecdotes and empirical data, see McGrath (2013) and Hayes et al. (1988).

In short, previous discussion implies from the view point of the RBV that holistically organizing specialized valuable and scarce resources into a functional system is necessary to create value. In other words, only when a firm is able to identify itself with its unique system of resources, it will be able to possibly generate value(s) by systemically mobilizing its valuable and rare resources. For empirical studies that are relevant to this conclusion, please consult with Amit and Schoemaker (1993), Barney (1991), Peteraf (1993), and Wernerfelt (1984).

If the concept of time is introduced into those of resource and capability, that is, treating each resource or capability as a function of time, the resultant will naturally be a general resource-based theory of firm evolution. The scarcity of a resource is realistically time dependent. For example, the present value of $100 million investment is a function of time. A resource, which might be initially inimitable, gradually becomes widely available as time passes. By joining what is discussed here with Proposition 4.3, it can be seen that each real-life capability (and each resource) is truly time-dependent (or a function of time). Hence, the dynamic capability, as so named by Teece et al. (1997), is a specialized scenario of the concept of capability defined in this chapter. In other words, studies of dynamic capabilities can be reframed within what is presented in this book and the concept of time does not need to be explicitly mentioned in most of the general discussions of resources and capabilities. With this understanding, the resource-based theory, as established in this book, can be employed to address many important questions, such as

- How can values be declared and necessitated?
- How can competitive advantages be made sustainable (Barney, 1991; McGrath, 2013)? And
- How are resources, which are seen valuable at certain moments of time, developed over time?

Considering each resource (or capability) as a function of time is more than a simple mind exercise. Indeed, doing so is engrained in how a firm's business operations are mostly managerial and organizational processes, targeting the formation of coordination, integration of knowledge and resources, realization of a revitalization, or completion of a transformation (Eisenhardt & Martin, 2000; Teece et al., 1997), or collective learning (Lei et al., 1996). Only such resources and capabilities that are seen as functions of time can realistically help firms with their value creation and capture through Schumpeterian rents (Teece et al., 1997). In particular, when resources and capabilities are time dependent, they play their roles in strategic decision-making, knowledge acquirement, product development, how-to skill creation, social network formation, and others.

Proposition 4.7 Because of the appearance of virtual markets, each created value becomes short-lived, and unprecedented opportunities for value creation and capture appear.

This proposition follows from the fact that virtual markets reside on the Internet; and other than being widely available, the Internet also provides conveniently and readily accomplishable exchanges between buyers and sellers. Additionally, the Internet is available 24/7 for entrepreneurs to uncover new resources, to explore potential substitutes, and to exploit existing resources in inventive ways through timely information and knowledge sharing either freely or at very low prices. Such affordability and convenience quicken the circulation of knowledge and know-hows, some of which used to be difficult to acquire. That elucidates why each created value becomes short-lived.

Additionally, Proposition 4.1(2) also provides a reason on why virtual markets offer unprecedented opportunities for value creation and value capture.

4.4 Market Forbearance and Network Structures

In the presently globalizing economy, at the time when firms compete autonomously with each other for advantages and profits, they are also players in inter-organizational networks. By being parts of such networks, firms team up in partnership (Galaskiewicz & Zaheer, 1999). Corresponding to this trend of development, this section examines how values can be potentially created out of market forbearance, supply-chain ecosystems, and strategic blocks.

4.4.1 Potential Values Out of Market Forbearance

By a strategic network, it means a network of various business entities that are connected together by various inter-organizational ties. It is strategically organized to gain certain market advantages for all partner firms (Gulati et al., 2000). For example, a firm is a system with supplies as inputs and products as outputs. So, it is naturally a part of a supply chain, known as the firm's ecosystem (or network), composed of its upstream components and downstream complements (Adner & Kapoor, 2010). In particular, a firm's suppliers represent some of its upstream components; customers, supporters, and assistants who help to make the product of the firm available to consumers are some of the firm's downstream complements. Although supporters and assistants are not exactly any part of the firm's direct supply chain, in the ecosystem of the firm, they need to help provide necessary infrastructure so that the product(s) of the firm can realistically reach their ultimate consumers.

Many firms recognize the role strategic networks play in their access to information, markets, and technologies (Gulati et al., 2000), opportunities of risk sharing, economies of scale and scope (Shapiro & Varian, 1999), knowledge sharing and advanced learning (Dyer & Nobeoka, 2000). The nature of interdependence within each network helps the member firms of the network harvest the ensuing benefits (Blankenburg et al., 1999).

Proposition 4.8 If an oligopolistic industry is in a state of mutual forbearance, then the incumbent firms within the industry will gain improved profitability.

If a state of mutual forbearance exists in an oligopolistic industry, as assumed, the incumbent firms enjoy a wide-ranging influence on the industry's profitability due to their collective dominance in the marketplace relative to upstream components and downstream complements, and deepened levels of collusion, tacit, etc. Because sturdy barriers deter any firm's attempt to enter into the industry, the profitability of the incumbents improves as the state of mutual forbearance strengthens. So, such scenario of profitability can be seen as relatively sustainable until at least some of the incumbents can no longer stay in sync with consumers' forever evolving preferences and tastes (Theorem 4.1). That is when the existing state of mutual forbearance breaks done.

Related to this proposition, Scherer and Ross (1990) and Galaskiewicz and Zaheer (1999) provide empirical evidence. They demonstrate that dense and strong ties among the incumbent firms of an industry or a market could be conducive to oligopolistic coordination, tacit or otherwise. In the banking industry, Podolny (1993) confirms that associations of top-tier banks help their member banks maintain good returns.

Assume that $S = (M, R)$ is a connected system, for details, see Chapter 2 of volume 1 in this monograph series. If an object $m \in M$ satisfies

$$S' = (M - \{m\}, R|(M - \{m\})) = S_1 \oplus S_2 \oplus \ldots \oplus S_k, \qquad ((4.5),)$$

where $S_i = (M_i, R_i)$, $i = 1, 2, \ldots, k$, is a connected system and $M_i \cap M_j = \varnothing$, for $i, j = 1, 2, \ldots, k$, satisfying $i \neq j$, for a whole number $k \geq 2$, then the object m is referred to as a systemic hole (or simply hole) of the original system S. Speaking less symbolically, if removing an object from a connected system makes the system disconnect, then the particular object is a (systemic) hole of the system.

To understand this concept intuitively, assume that $S = (M, R)$ represents the systemic structure of a complete supply chain with the top most upstream players being the providers of raw materials and the bottom most downstream players the consumers or the end users. Specifically, in this systemic model of the supply chain, the object set M consists of all players of the supply chain, such as suppliers, producers, retailers, consumers, etc. And, the relation set R describes how these players are connected with each other through their inputs and outputs. For example, two players m_1 and m_2 are considered associated, provided that m_1's products are supplies of m_2 either directly or indirectly.

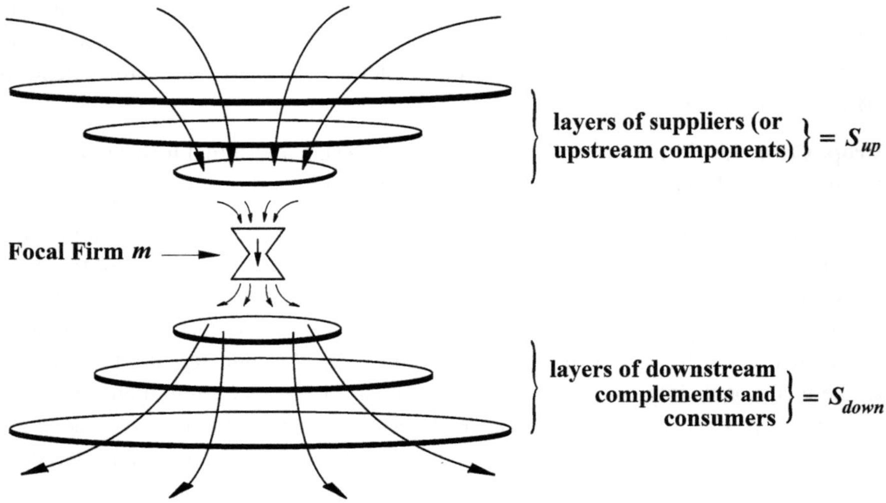

Fig. 4.1 A systemic hole in a supply-chain ecosystem

If a particular player $m \in M$ is a hole in this supply-chain system S, then removing m will make this supply-chain system S break up into two disjoint subsystems as follows, neither of which constitutes a complete supply chain, as follows:

$$S_{up} = \left(M_{up}, R_{up}\right) \text{ and } S_{down} = \left(M_{down}, R_{down}\right), \tag{4.6}$$

where the object set M_{up} is composed of all players that are upstream to m, and the object set M_{down} all players that are downstream to m.

These two sub-supply chains S_{up} and S_{down} are not complete supply chains, because the outputs of S_{up} cannot satisfy the demands of S_{down}, while S_{down} cannot produce its product(s) without the input from S_{up}. In terms of business, if any two trading parties in the customer-supplier network of an industry can only close their transactions by going through a specific focal industrial sector, then this industrial sector is a systemic hole in the entire supply–demand network. Note that a supply–demand network may have several systemic holes. This concept of systemic holes is shown in Fig. 4.1, where m stands for such a hole along with the disjoint subsystems S_{up} and S_{down}, where the large arrows indicate the direction of the input–output flows of the supply chain S.

Proposition 4.9 Each systemic hole within a supply–demand network represents power and profitability for firms that occupy the hole.

To show this proposition, the general supply–demand network is modeled by the connected system $S = (M, R)$. All players in the network are objects in the object set M; all supply-and-demand relationships of the players are elements in the relation set R. Let an object $m \in M$ be a systemic hole in S. Then, the locational advantage of the object m implies that removing m from the supply-and-demand system S will break

S into two subsystems S_{up} and S_{down}, as defined previously, neither of which is functional. In particular, players in S_{up} cannot find the ultimate buyers of its products, while players in S_{down} cannot be served with necessary supplies. In other words, this object $m \in M$ controls the livelihood of all other players in S. Such power of life or death of the object m surely provides a solid foundation for its elevated level of profitability.

Related to this proposition, Burt (1992) empirically finds that those industrial sectors that occupy systemic hole positions are gifted with good returns by taking proportionally over-weighted large stocks of resources.

4.4.2 Potential Values Out of Supply-Chain and Strategic Blocks

As the title of this subsection suggests, we will look at how firms can potentially create values out of their respective supply-chain ecosystems and out of their strategic blocks.

Proposition 4.10 If a supply-chain network is in a state of expanding base of consumers, then firms with memberships within the network can improve their profitability through strengthening their market positions in terms of a broad web of resource flows.

This proposition is really a corollary of Theorem 4.1. In particular, the assumed supply-chain network of expanding consumer base implies that no competitor is taking market territory away from this network (Theorem 4.1). Instead, this network is expanding its market share over time. These facts jointly mean that the market position of each member firm of the network can, at least potentially, enlarge, which in turn potentially boosts the profitability of the firm.

Conversely, for a supply-chain network of a dwindling consumer base, each of its member will unfavorably experience shrinking stock of available resources, leading potentially to a lowering level of profitability. To this end, a good example is the situation of reducing investment in a nation military. The deteriorating capital input will make the national defense industry suffer.

Assume that the industry of concern is modeled as a symbolic system $S = (M, R)$ so that (1) each object $m \in M$ represents the unique systemic expression of a firm within the industry and each firm within the industry has a systemic expression as an object in M; and (2) each relation $r \in R$ describes how relevant firms are related to each other through business exchanges. Based on discussions above, such systemic modeling can be done. For example, each firm can be identified with the unique system of its resources; and the entire industry is then simply the totality of all these firm systems connected to each other by their business connections and dealings.

Assume that this industry system can be written as the following free sum of n partial systems, for details, see Chapter 2 of volume 1,

$$S = \oplus_{i=1}^{n} S_i = S_1 \oplus S_2 \oplus \ldots \oplus S_n \tag{4.7}$$

satisfying that $S_i = (M_i, R_i)$ is connected, $M_i \cap M_j \neq \emptyset$, when $i \neq j$, for $i, j = 1, 2, \ldots, n$. In other words, the industry is composed of n many clusters, each of which includes firms that are strategically associated to each other. In this case, each S_i is called a strategic block within the industry. The terms used here are borrowed from Nohria and Garcia-Pont (1991), who studied the global automobile industry. Speaking in business terms, each S_i represents a strategic alliance of firms, which do not have alliance relationship with other firms in the industry.

Proposition 4.11 Each strategic block within an industry can help its member firms reach a higher level of profitability than the case when a firm is not a part of any strategic block. And, the more influential a strategic block is in the marketplace, the more positive effect on profitability its member firms enjoy.

The first two conclusions are direct consequences of the real-life fact that each strategic block is organized to implements an individually unambiguous strategy with its particular accent in order to gain particular competitive advantages. Because of their individually varying strategies employed, different strategic blocks influence the market differently. That implies varying scales of profitability from one block to another, making firms in different blocks achieve correspondingly different levels of performance. Proposition 4.10 directly implies the third conclusion.

Regarding empirical supports of this proposition, Piskorski and Nohria (1999) find major variations in profitability among firms with membership in different strategic blocks within the venture capital industry. Zaheer and Zaheer (1999) look at the competitive global industry of currency trading through interactions of banking firms. Through organizing alliances into networks, Baum et al. (2000) confirm by using data from Canadian biotechnology industry that startups in biotechnology industry can improve their performance if they purposefully join alliances.

4.5 Business Networks and Convenient Platforms

Continuing previous discussions, this section examines the values of membership in inter-organizational network(s) and in strategic blocks, and the benefits of establishing and maintaining platforms that directly connect sellers and buyers.

4.5.1 Inter-Organizational Networks and Strategic Blocks

This subsection explores the values a firm can potentially enjoy from its memberships in organizational network(s) and in strategic blocks.

Proposition 4.12 The membership of an inter-organizational network and a strategic block generally represents an inimitable, not substitutable resource for the member firms.

The truthfulness of this proposition comes from the purpose of developing inter-organizational networks and organizing strategic blocks and Propositions 4.7, 4.8, 4.9, and 4.10. In particular, the main purpose for firms to join an inter-organizational network includes the maintenance of their levels of profitability and the development and enhancement of their locational advantages in broader network of resource flows. Similar goals are true for firms to join or organize strategic blocks. At the same time, inter-organizational networks and strategic blocks play the role of practical barriers for other firms to enter an industry or to move across the lines of strategic groups. Hence, memberships in either an inter-organizational network or a strategic block create prospects, competitive advantages as well as restrictions for member firms.

Also, this proposition follows from Theorem 4.1, which specifically states that as long as the product market possesses sufficient demand, it signals for new competitions and innovations. However, the same signal is received by firms differently due to their respectively varied capabilities of learning, histories and backgrounds, available resources, etc. These different comprehensions of the market signal naturally motivate entrepreneurial firms to develop their respectively different solutions. Therefore, these firm correspondingly demand relevant innovative supplies from their upstream suppliers and downstream complementors in order to successfully produce their market offers (Adner et al., 2013). These differences in understanding market signals, in available resources and in demands on upstream suppliers and downstream complementors all make the membership in an inter-organizational network and/or strategic block an imperfectly imitable, imperfectly substitutable resource a firm is able to potentially apply.

Regarding the literature relevant to this proposition, Gulati et al. (2000) develop a related but different conclusion. As for applications, with membership in a network and strategic block, Gulati (1999) confirms a firm's access to relationships and information; Zaheer and Zaheer (1997) recognize a firm's access to knowledge, alertness and responsiveness; Westney (1993) sees that a greater number of opportunities becomes available to a firm; and Becheikh et al. (2006) realize that additional capital, goods, services, technology, etc., become readily available to a firm. A firm can mobilize these external resources to augment its competitive position in its industry. Due to their distinctive and history-specific developments, inter-organizational networks and strategic blocks represent resources that are difficult, if not impossible, for others to imitate or substitute (Gulati & Gargiulo, 1999). That once again shows why membership in an inter-organizational network and association with a strategic block are a firm's resources that are inimitable or extremely difficult to imitate by competitors and are not easily substitutable with other resources. This end confirms why memberships in inter-organizational networks and strategic blocks are resources a firm can enjoy and potentially mobilize.

By opportunism, it means a circumstantial advantage taking of an observant policy. Such advantage taking is primarily driven by self-interest(s) without considering any underlying principles and consequences for others. Such behaviors generally and assuredly exist with people either individually or collectively no matter what specific case and context are concerned with (Lin & Forrest, 2011). They take place within and on top of the adopted philosophical beliefs and value systems that prescribe what behaviors are considered acceptable and which are not acceptable, wrong or immoral. This fact provides a way to detect opportunistic behaviors by comparing what is ongoing with the norms, although standard of morality exists in a market of free competition other than laws and regulations on contracts and transaction settlements. This discussion well explains the concept of opportunism and shows no difficulty in defining this concept, as otherwise claimed by Chen et al. (2002).

Proposition 4.13 If an inter-organizational network/strategic block satisfies the following condition, then the firm-level trust in the network/block is mostly enhanced with informational asymmetry reduced and opportunistic behaviors costlier.

- The inter-organizational network consists of firms from different industries;
- The strategic block consists of firms within one industry.

By firm-level trust, it stands for the guarantee that no firm takes the advantage of any other firm's weakness (Barney & Hansen, 1994). Business dealings generally occur within a continuously existing chain of prior associations, either directly or indirectly, and an extensive web of connections. Hence, important resources and necessary origins of referrals are commonly provided through inter-organizational networks and strategic blocks with firms' characters as the basis of each referral. Because it generally takes time to have one's characters recognized while it is only a matter of quick moment to have one's recognized characters destroyed (Lin & Forrest, 2011), firms within an inter-organizational network and a strategic block tend to behave professionally within the boundaries of the norms and principles of these organizations. That is the reason why inter-organizational networks and strategic blocks generally increase firm-level trust and make opportunistic behaviors costly.

Through the membership in such networks and blocks, member firms strengthen their business ties, interact with each other frequently to share respective capabilities and resources and to overcome vulnerabilities. The very nature of such networks and blocks empowers their member firms to acquaint with each other very well. These are the reasons why informational asymmetry of member firms within such networks and blocks is reduced.

Regarding the literature, Gulati et al. (2000) were the first people who established the first draft of this proposition, even though it was phrased very differently.

Based on the previous discussion, it can be seen that when firm-level trust and opportunism cost are elevated, the costs of business transactions get lower. And when informational asymmetry between firms increases, transaction costs also rise.

Speaking differently, market-level worries decrease with any of the following: improving firm-level trust, reducing informational asymmetry, and elevating opportunism cost. Hence, the result below follows naturally:

Proposition 4.14 If an inter-organizational network/strategic block satisfies the conditions in Proposition 4.13, then the network's and block's membership can help a firm boost its ability to create and capture value.

4.5.2 *Platforms that Directly Connect Sellers and Buyers*

By borrowing the ideas behind the concepts of inter-organizational networks across industries and strategic blocks within an industry, the concept of platforms appears. In particular, a platform is such a network with members from the product market that connect competing sellers with contending buyers directly. Figure 4.2 graphically shows a platform within the product market with the focal firm m being a systemic hole. Then, the conclusion below follows naturally.

Proposition 4.15 A firm can capture value handsomely by developing and maintaining a platform that match each customer with multiple suppliers and each supplier with multiple customers until similar platforms become widely available.

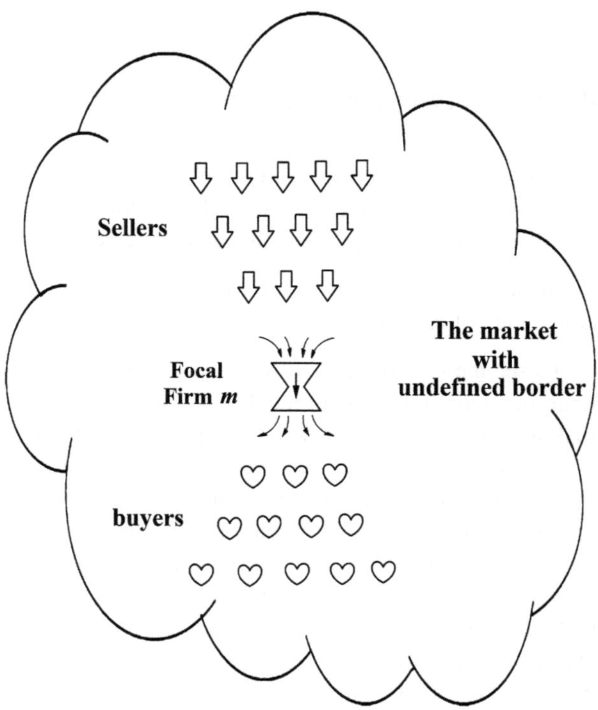

Fig. 4.2 A platform that directly connects sellers and buyers

This proposition is a corollary of the following result developed by Forrest and Anderson (2017): In the product market, finding decided buyers represents a great challenge for sellers due to the wide availability of similar products and substitutes; locating willing takers of bargaining bid prices denotes a major struggle for buyers. In particular, in an afore-described platform that directly matches sellers and buyers, the provided convenience helps all involved parties save hugely in terms of information costs, bargaining costs, policing and enforcement costs, as well as time spent on searches. Hence, any firm that develops and maintains such a platform that connects each bid price to multiple sellers and each offer to multiple buyers has practically created values for both sides of the product market. Additionally, this firm will continuously capture its value until such a time when its service is no longer a systemic hole within the network of sellers and buyers (Proposition 4.9). At that time, all platform providers divide the total value potentially capturable among themselves.

Also, this proposition can follow from Proposition 4.2. Specifically, each platform, which directly connects sellers and buyers in multiplicity, greatly improves the transactions efficiency of the firm that maintains the platform.

Within the present landscape of the business world, priceline.com, among many online business operations, is such a platform as discussed above. It directly connects sellers and buyers by directly forwarding consumers' desired prices to multiple potential sellers. If a willing seller takes a bid price, then business exchange is complete. The item of concern, such as a rental car, reservation of a resort hotel, or a plane ticket, is sold over the Internet (Amit & Zott, 2001).

4.5.3 Creative Destructions

To lay the necessary foundation for the introduction of the general value-chain framework, this section looks at the relationship between the availability and circulation of information and the appearance of creative destructions.

Proposition 4.16 The availability of information is positively correlated to the emergence of creative destructions.

To see the truthfulness of this proposition, let us get a sense of how information underlies economic development. In primitive times of history, humans survived by making use of whatever was immediately available within their vicinities. At those times, each family had to construct and build what it needed to survive. Motivated by the universal desire for better living conditions beyond survival, information on various know-hows began to pass around from one family to another family, from one tribe to another tribe, and from one geographical location to another location. As flows of information were gradually accompanied by those of goods and then those of both goods and talented people, closed circulations of information, knowledge and goods appeared over the land as the traveling talents brought these elements back to where they initially started their travels. People started to place orders over longer and longer distances. Accordingly, family-based workshops were organized to satisfy the rising demands from different families, from different tribes, then from other locations. And increasingly larger quantities of products and goods were produced with improving quality and delivered all over the land. That is, the growing demands and increasing supplies gradually led to the cultivation of the initial seeds of modern commerce, although initially only locally in today's standard.

As circulation spheres of information, knowledge and goods increased to protracted distances, emerging demands from further away places started to appear, forcing the family-based workshops to accelerate their productions. Corresponding to increasing number of orders to be filled and shipped across lands and waters over further and further out distances, new and more efficient technologies for mass production, transportation, and communication were developed. Such technological advancements connected initially isolated and separated local markets together into an economy of growing scale through long-distance shipments of goods and movements of information and knowledge. That is, the disconnected family-based workshops of the earlier times became more related through supply chains, order networks, and delivery routes.

As the circulation of information, knowledge, and goods covered an increasing size of regions, with their much-increased productivity, those small, family-based workshops began to serve their corresponding regional markets. That economic development further elevated consumer demands to a higher level, which reciprocally encouraged the small workshops to advance into large factories backed with advanced technologies. Along the path of such economic developments, industrial development appeared and started to leap forward in gradually larger-scales one by one. These leaps in industrial development further stimulated worldwide spread of information, knowledge, and products (Wen, 2016). The economic history of past several hundred years has revealed the power of accelerating circulations of information, knowledge and goods, while the circulations induced the emergence of business enterprises of the modern form (Sobel, 1999), no matter whether they are global players or small startups. See Forrest et al. (2018) for an in-depth discussion on the evolution of manufacturing firms.

Returning to the argument for the truthfulness of Proposition 4.16, by creative destruction, it means an evolutionary process an organization goes through by unremittingly transforming its internal structure, be it organizational, economic, or cultural, into a new one (Schumpeter, 1942). From this definition and the discussion in the previous paragraphs, one can see that the forces, exerting on the transformation of an organization's internal structure, are originated from newly acquired information and knowledge and the business firm's longing for survival and growth. Therefore, the strengths of these forces rise with the speed of information circulation. That is, the speedier information circulates throughout the land, the more an organization has to transform its internal structure and the higher frequency creative destructions emerge.

E-commerce of the current business landscape represents a lively example of how Proposition 4.16 plays out in real life. The Internet, through which people from different parts of the world can communicate with each other quickly and conveniently, has merged regional economies into a giant world economy, where long-distance deliveries are facilitated by modern transportation tools without much trouble. Simultaneously, supported by the Internet, various virtual markets are developed to directly connect buyers and seller from all over the globe. They have ingeniously *reshaped* and unremittingly transformed the traditional commerce. With freely available (or at very low costs) information and knowledge on the Internet, entrepreneurs, be they on the supply side or the demand side, *now can* innovatively comprehend market signals and create wealth in various unparalleled ways (Ye et al., 2012). They find collaborators through virtual means from different supply chains and different industries, and consumers from different markets over various distances. These unprecedented opportunities provide unconventional means to create and capture values. Hence, Proposition 4.16 implies that as e-commerce further evolves, creative destructions in all areas of life will emerge in rising frequency until such a time when the Internet reaches its full potential.

4.6 A Few Final Words

To succeed in the turbulent business world, firms have to embrace transient competitive advantages in order to create value and to capture value by taking advance of unconventional opportunities (McGrath, 2013). For example, newly emerging virtual markets have provided an increasing number of firms to complete at least portions of their transactions online (Forbes, 2018; Forrester Research Report, 2000). By employing technologies, sellers and buyers can now connect to each other either freely or at very affordable prices through convenient and efficient platforms on which buyers place orders and sellers deliver products (Amit & Zott, 2001). To help understand the speedy changes of the present business world, this chapter accomplishes several goals through examining: (1) how a firm creates potential values out of several different angles – innovation and resource; and (2) how a firm captures potential values from the respective angles of market forbearance, supply-chain network, strategic blocks, inter-organizational networks, and direct seller-buyer platforms. Due to the novel methodology employed here, the established conclusions in this chapter are expected to provide managers and entrepreneurs with a dependable way to make their decisions instead of suggestions of limited validity derived on anecdotes and data.

Specifically, this chapter employs systems methodology and logical reasoning that is parallel to the one widely used in mathematics and physics to study the fast-changing world of business in terms of innovation, resources, networks, and strategic blocks. Regarding innovation, this chapter pinpoints when innovation offers potentials for value creation. In the perspective of resources, it finds when latent values of resources can be practically made visible through value creation. From the angle of networks and strategic blocks, this chapter demonstrates how the market state of mutual forbearance is positively related to sustainably increased profitability, why the systemic hole position of a firm provides the firm with advantages and economic benefits, and how the membership in a strategic block of increasing market influence positively affects the profitability of a firm. In terms of direct association of sellers and buyers, this chapter shows that each firm that creates and maintains convenient platforms will readily create and capture values.

As for practical implications, this chapter can provide general recommendations instead of suggestions for decision makers, such as entrepreneurs, managers, and retailers. In particular, this chapter shows the importance for entrepreneurs to innovatively understand market signals in their individually different ways. Being able to do so will lead firms to their idiosyncratic products (Theorem 4.1).

For managers, they can create additional values out of their resources by encouraging information sharing, such as exchanges of ideas, and sharing resources, and recognizing success, such as widely and openly recognizing employee contributions, offering financial incentives, (Propositions 4.1, 4.3, and 4.16). Policies and relevant procedures need to be implemented to acquire and mobilize their firm-specific resources (Proposition 4.4), while tying managers' interests with those of stakeholders (Proposition 4.5). Marketing efforts, R&D activities, and operational practicalities need to be considered jointly in managerial decision-making (Proposition 4.6). Such collective thoughtfulness will stimulate internal collaboration, leading to more reliable value creation and capture.

For retailers, incessantly try to make transactions more efficient (Proposition 4.2). Take advantage of whatever new convenience technology offers (Proposition 4.7).

To conclude this chapter, it needs to be noted that all conclusions in this chapter are established on the assumption that each firm exists for the purpose of addressing a market niche by generating positive cash flows from the product market. However, in reality firms exist for various reasons beyond what is assumed here. This end will be an important reason for why some applications of the general results developed in this chapter might not work in practice, if the firms of concern exist not for this said purpose. This limitation, along with many other ones not listed here, of this current chapter opens doors for future research.

References

Adner, R., & Kapoor, R. (2010). Value creation in innovation ecosystems: How the structure of technological interdependence affects firm performance in new technological generations. *Strategic Management Journal, 31*(3), 306–333.

Adner, R., Oxley, J. E., & Silverman, B. S. (Eds.). (2013). *Collaboration and competition in business ecosystems*. Bingley.

Ahuja, G., Lampert, C. M., & Tandon, V. (2009). Moving beyond Schumpeter: Management research on the determinants of technological innovations. *The Academy of Management Annals, 2*(1), 1–98.

Amit, R., & Schoemaker, P. (1993). Strategic assets and organizational rent. *Strategic Management Journal, 14*(1), 33–46.

Amit, R., & Zott, C. (2001). Value creation in e-business. *Strategic Management Journal, 22*(6/7), 493–520.

Baizakov, S., Forest, J. Y. L., & Baizakov, N. (2019). Modeling the managements of the economies of developing countries. *Advances in Systems Science and Applications, 19*(2), 101–119. https://doi.org/10.25728/assa.2019.19.2.673

Balakrishnan, A., Kumara, S. R. T., & Sundaresan, S. (1999). Manufacturing in the digital age: Exploiting information technologies for product realization. *Information Systems Frontiers, 1*, 25–50.

Barney, J., & Arikan, A. (2001). The resource-based view: Origins and implications. In M. Hitt, R. Freeman, & J. Harrison (Eds.), *Handbook of strategic management* (pp. 124–185). Blackwell.

Barney, J. B. (1991). Firm resources and sustained competitive advantage. *Journal of Management, 17*, 99–120.

Barney, J. B. (1997). *Gaining and sustaining competitive advantage*. Addison-Wesley.

Barney, J. B., & Hansen, M. H. (1994). Trustworthiness as a form of competitive advantage. *Strategic Management Journal, Winter Special Issue, 15*, 175–190.

Baum, J. A. C., Calabrese, T., & Silverman, B. S. (2000). Don't go it alone: Alliance network composition and startups' performance in Canadian biotechnology. *Strategic Management Journal, 21*(3), 267–294.

Baum, J. A. C., & Dutton, J. (1996). The embeddedness of strategy. In P. Shrivastava, A. S. Huff, & J. E. Dutton (Eds.), *Advances in strategic management* (Vol. 13, pp. 3–40). JAI Press.

Becheikh, N., Landry, R., & Amara, N. (2006). Lessons from innovation empirical studies in the manufacturing sector: A systematic review of the literature from 1993 to 2003. *Technovation, 26*(5), 644–664.

Bernheim, B. D., & Whinston, M. D. (1990). Multimarket contact and collusive behavior. *RAND Journal of Economics, 21*(1), 1–26.

Blankenburg, H. D., Eriksson, K., & Johanson, J. (1999). Creating value through mutual commitment to business network relationships. *Strategic Management Journal, 20*(5), 467–486.

Burt, R. S. (1992). *Structural holes: The social structure of competition*. Harvard University Press.

Cacciolatti, L., & Lee, S. H. (2016). Revisiting the relationship between marketing capabilities and firm performance: The moderating role of market orientation, marketing strategy and organisational power. *Journal of Business Research, 69*(12), 5597–5610.

Chen, C. C., Peng, M. W., & Saparito, P. A. (2002). Individualism, collectivism, and opportunism: A cultural perspective on transaction cost economics. *Journal of Management, 28*(4), 567–583.

Cheung, S. N. S. (1992). On the New Institutional Economics. In L. Werin & H. Wijkander (Eds.), *Contract economics* (pp. 48–65). Blackwell.

Clemons, E. K., & Row, M. C. (1992). Information technology and industrial cooperation: The changing economics of coordination and ownership. *Journal of Management Information Systems, 9*, 9–28.

Datta, A. (2016). Antecedents to radical innovations: A longitudinal look at firms in the information technology industry by aggregation of patents. *International Journal of Innovation Management, 20*(7), 1650068. https://doi.org/10.1142/S1363919616500687

Demsetz, H. (2003). Ownership and the externality problem. In T. L. Anderson & F. S. McChesney (Eds.), *Property rights: Cooperation, conflict, and law*. Princeton.

Dutta, S., & Segev, A. (1999). Business transformation on the Internet. *European Management Journal, 17*, 466–476.

Dyer, J. H. (1997). Effective interfirm collaboration: How firms minimize transaction costs and maximize transaction value. *Strategic Management Journal, 18*(7), 535–556.

Dyer, J. H., & Nobeoka, K. (2000). Creating and managing a high-performance knowledge-sharing network: The Toyota case. *Strategic Management Journal, 21*(3), 345–367.

Eisenhardt, K. M., & Martin, J. A. (2000). Dynamic capabilities: What are they? *Strategic Management Journal, 21*(10-11), 1105–1121.

Evans, P. B., & Wurster, T. S. (1999). *Blown to bits: How the new economics of information transforms strategy*. Harvard Business School Press.

Fang, E., Palmatier, R., & Grewal, R. (2011). Effects of customer and innovation asset configuration strategies on firm performance. *Journal of Marketing Research, 48*(3), 587–602.

Forbes. (2018). *How can businesses adapt to a rapidly changing world?* Retrieved September 17, 2019, from https://www.forbes.com/sites/quora/2018/01/05/how-can-businesses-adapt-to-a-rapidly-changing-world/#4edbc26a5930

Forrest, J. Y.-L., & Anderson, M. (2017). Customers' indecisiveness: A pricing strategy approach. *Pennsylvania Economic Review, 24*(2), 46–64.

Forrest, J. Y.-L., Baizakov, S., Haile, Y. G., Gyan, A., & Liu, Y. (2020). Potentials of value creation and capture based on innovation, resources, strategic networks and blocks. *Advances in Systems Science and Applications, 20*(3), 50–72.

Forrest, J. Y.-L., Buttermore, J., & Wajda, T. (2017). At Nash equilibrium when new market competitions appear? *Kybernetes: The International of Cybernetics, Systems and Management Science, 46*(2), 256–271.

Forrest, J. Y.-L., Liu, Y., Golden, J., Sissoko, Y., & Li, Q. X. (2020a). A reformulated value chain framework useful for different kinds of markets. *The Journal of Business and Economic Studies, 24*(1), 33–53.

Forrest, J. Y. L., Nicholls, N., Schimmel, K., & Liu, S. F. (2020b). *Managerial decision making: A holistic approach*. Springer.

Forrest, J. Y. L., Shao, L., McKinney, R., & Shao, D. (2019). Firm performance and market expansion from the point of view of resources. *International Journal of Business and Systems Research, 15*, 468–490.

Forrest, J. Y.-L., & Tallapally, P. (2018). Customers are less patient, sustainable advantage becomes transient and the key for firms to succeed in fast changing markets. *Journal of Business, Economics and Technology, 21*(1), 1–14.

Forrest, J.Y-L., Tucker, R., Lin, C.C., & Mondal, S. (2018). Impacts of manufacturing firms' culture, structure and leadership on innovation: A systemic approach. In *Proceedings of the 41st Annual Meeting of Northeastern Association of Business, Economics and Technology*, State College, PA.

Forrester Research Report. (2000). *Global eCommerce approaches hypergrowth*. April 2000.

Forsgren, M. (2016). A note on the revisited Uppsala internationalization process model – The implications of business networks and entrepreneurship. *Journal of International Business Studies, 47*(9), 1135–1144.

Fuentelsaz, L., & Gómez, J. (2006). Multipoint competition, strategic similarity and entry into geographic markets. *Strategic Management Journal, 27*(5), 477–499.

Galaskiewicz, J., & Zaheer, A. (1999). Networks of competitive advantage. In S. Andrews & D. Knoke (Eds.), *Research in the sociology of organizations* (pp. 237–261). JAI Press.

Granovetter, M. (1985). Economic action and social structure: A theory of embeddedness. *American Journal of Sociology, 91*, 481–510.

Gulati, R. (1998). Alliances and networks. *Strategic Management Journal, 19*(4), 293–317.

Gulati, R. (1999). Network location and learning: The influence of network resources and firm capabilities on alliance formation. *Strategic Management Journal, 20*(5), 397–420.

Gulati, R., & Gargiulo, M. (1999). Where do interorganizational networks come from? *American Journal of Sociology, 104*(5), 1439–1493.

Gulati, R., Nohria, N., & Zaheer, A. (2000). Strategic networks. *Strategic Management Journal, 21*(3), 203–215.

Hagel, J., III, & Armstrong, A. G. (1997). *Net gain: Expanding markets through virtual communities*. Harvard Business School Press.

Harmancioglu, N., Droge, C., & Calantone, R. (2009). Strategic fit to resources versus NPD execution proficiencies: What are their roles in determining success? *Journal of the Academy of Marketing Science, 37*(3), 266–282.

Harrigan, K. R. (1985). *Strategies for joint ventures*. Lexington Books.

Haveman, H. A., & Nonnemaker, L. (2000). Competition in multiple geographic markets: The impact on growth and market entry. *Administrative Science Quarterly, 45*(2), 232–267.

Hayes, R. H., Wheelwright, S. C., & Clark, K. B. (1988). *Dynamic manufacturing*. The Free Press.
Hitt, M. A., & Ireland, R. D. (2017). The intersection of entrepreneurship and strategic management research. In D. L. Sexton, H. Landstrom, & C. Jones (Eds.), *The Blackwell handbook of entrepreneurship* (pp. 45–63). Blackwell.
Irwin, D. A., & Klenow, P. J. (1994). Learning-by-doing spillovers in the semiconductor industry. *Journal of Political Economy, 102*(6), 1200–1227.
Jaworski, B. J., & Kohli, A. K. (1993). Market orientation: Antecedents and consequences. *Journal of Marketing, 57*(July), 53–70.
Kogut, B. (1988). Joint ventures: Theoretical and empirical perspectives. *Strategic Management Journal, 9*(4), 319–332.
Kotler, P., & Keller, K. L. (2016). *A framework for marketing management* (6th ed.). Pearson.
Kozlenkova, I. V., Samaha, S. A., & Palmatier, R. W. (2014). Resource-based theory in marketing. *Journal of the Academy of Marketing Science, 42*, 1–21.
Lei, D., Hitt, M. A., & Bettis, R. (1996). Dynamic core competences through meta-learning and strategic context. *Journal of Management, 22*, 549–596.
Li, M., & Nguyen, B. (2017). When will firms share information and collaborate to achieve innovation? *The Bottom Line, 30*(1), 65–86. https://doi.org/10.1108/BL-12-2016-0039
Li, S. X., & Greenwood, R. (2004). The effect of within industry diversification on firm performance: Synergy creation, multi-market contact and market structuration. *Strategic Management Journal, 25*(12), 1131–1153.
Li, T., & Ma, J. H. (2015). Complexity analysis of dual-channel game model with different managers' business objectives. *Communications in Nonlinear Science and Numerical Simulation, 20*, 199–208.
Lin, Y. (2009). *Systemic yoyos: Some impacts of the second dimension*. Auerbach Publication, an imprint of Taylor and Francis.
Lin, Y., & Forrest, B. (2011). *Systemic structure behind human organizations: From civilizations to individuals*. Springer.
Makadok, R. (2001). Toward a synthesis of the resource-based and dynamic-capability views of rent creation. *Strategic Management Journal, 22*(5), 387–401.
McGrath, R. G. (2013). *The end of competitive advantage: How to keep your strategy moving as fast as your business*. Harvard Business Review Press.
Moran, P., & Ghoshal, S. (1999). Markets, firms, and the process of economic development. *Academy of Management Review, 24*, 390–412.
Nohria, N., & Garcia-Pont, C. (1991). Global strategic linkages and industry structure. *Strategic Management Journal, Summer Special Issue, 12*, 105–124.
North, D. C. (1992). *Transaction costs, institutions, and economic performance*. ICS Press.
Öberg, C. (2018). The role of business networks for innovation. *Journal of Innovation & Knowledge, 4*, 124–128. https://doi.org/10.1016/j.jik.2017.10.001
Ombaka, B. E., Awino, Z. B., Machuki, V. N., & Wainaina, G. (2015). Exploring resources and performance relationships in commercial enterprises: An empirical perspective. *Journal of Management and Strategy, 6*(4), 12–28.
Penrose, E. T. (1959). *The theory of growth of the firm*. Blackwell.
Peteraf, M. A. (1993). The cornerstones of competitive advantage: A resource-based view. *Strategic Management Journal, 14*(3), 179–191.
Peteraf, M. A., & Barney, J. (2003). Unraveling the resource-based tangle. *Managerial and Decision Economics, 24*(4), 309–323.
Piskorski, M. & Nohria, N. (1999). Allocation to open and closed portfolios. Harvard Business School working paper.
Podolny, J. (1993). A status based model of market competition. *American Journal of Sociology, 98*, 829–872.
Porter, M. E. (1979). How competitive forces shape strategy. *Harvard Business Review, 57*(2), 137–145.

Scherer, F. M., & Ross, D. (1990). *Industrial Market structure and economic performance*. Houghton Mifflin.

Schumpeter, J. A. (1934). *The theory of economic development: An inquiry into profits, capital, credit, interest, and the business cycle*. Harvard University Press.

Schumpeter, J. A. (1942). *Capitalism, socialism, and democracy*. Harper.

Shapiro, C., & Varian, H. R. (1999). *Information rules: A strategic guide to the network economy*. Harvard Business School Press.

Smith, A. (1776). *The wealth of nations, books I-III (1986 printing)*. Penguin Books.

Sobel, R. (1999). *When giants stumble: Classic business blunders and how to avoid them*. Prentice Hall.

Stryja, C., & Satzger, G. (2018). Try before you buy: How to design information systems to enhance consumer willingness to test sustainable innovations. *Journal of Technology Management & Innovation, 13*(1), 19–26. https://doi.org/10.4067/S0718-27242018000100019

Teece, D., Pisano, G., & Shuen, A. (1997). Dynamic capabilities and strategic management. *Strategic Management Journal, 18*(7), 509–533.

Teece, D. J. (1987). Profiting from technological innovations: Implications for integration, collaboration, licensing, and public policy. In D. J. Teece (Ed.), *The competitive challenge: Strategies for industrial innovation and renewal* (pp. 185–219). Ballinger.

Uzuegbunam, I. S., Geringer, J. M., & Oberst, C. (2018). Creative destruction within and across countries: Do culture and connectedness matter. *Academy of Management Proceedings, 2018*(1), 97. https://doi.org/10.5465/AMBPP.2018.97

Wen, Y. (2016). *The making of an economic superpower: Unlocking China's secret of rapid industrialization*. World Scientific.

Wernerfelt, B. (1984). A resource-based view of the firm. *Strategic Management Journal, 5*(2), 171–180.

Westney, D. E. (1993). Cross-Pacific internationalization of R&D by U.S. and Japanese firms. *R&D Management, 23*(2), 171–181.

Williamson, O. E. (1979). Transaction cost economics: The governance of contractual relations. *Journal of Law and Economics, 22*, 233–261.

Williamson, O. E. (1983). Organizational innovation: The transaction cost approach. In J. Ronen (Ed.), *Entrepreneurship* (pp. 101–133). Lexington.

Ye, G. L., Priem, R. L., & Alshwer, A. A. (2012). Achieving demand-side synergy from strategic diversification: How combining mundane assets can leverage consumer utilities. *Organization Science, 23*(1), 207–224.

Yu, T., & Cannella, A. A., Jr. (2012). A comprehensive review of multimarket competition research. *Journal of Management, 39*, 76–109.

Zaheer, A., & Zaheer, S. (1997). Catching the wave: Alertness, responsiveness, and market influence in global electronic networks. *Management Science, 43*(11), 1493–1509.

Zaheer, A. & Zaheer, S. (1999). The structure of global competition: A network approach. Paper presented at the SMJ Special Issue Conference, Northwestern University.

Chapter 5
Artificial Intelligence and Technological Innovation

Jeffrey Yi-Lin Forrest, Yong Liu, Jun Liu, Huihong Chang, and Bohua Yang

Abstract This chapter, which is mainly based on Forrest and Liu (*Value in Business: A Holistic, Systems-Based Approach to Creating and Achieving Value*. Switzerland: Springer; 2022, Chapter 18) and Liu et al. (*Technological Forecasting & Social Change*, 158, 120142; 2020), investigates how artificial intelligence (AI) may impact technological innovation. In the first half, this chapter defines what technological innovation entails and then it establishes a series of general propositions. In the second half, this chapter empirically analyzes the impact of AI on technological innovation based on the industrial robot data provided by the International Federation of Robotics (IFR) and the panel data of China's 14 manufacturing sectors from 2008 to 2017.

The theoretical analysis reveals the working mechanism underlying the effect of AI on technological innovation. In particular, AI stimulates technological innovation through three different channels: (1) it accelerates knowledge creation and creates technology spillover, (2) it advances firms' capacities of learning and absorption, and (3) it boosts investments in R&D and human talents.

The empirical confirmation supports what are revealed above. In particular, our empirical results indicate that under the condition of controlling intensity of R&D investment, FDI, ownership structure, technical imitation, AI significantly promotes technological innovation. And the impact of AI on technological innovation experiences sector heterogeneity: AI has more significant impact on the technological innovation of low-tech sectors. The higher the level of AI, the greater its impact

Jeffrey Yi-Lin Forrest (Department of Accounting Economics Finance, Slippery Rock University, Slippery Rock, PA, USA; Email: Jeffrey.forrest@sru.edu), Yong Liu (School of Business, Jiangnan University, Wuxi, Jiangsu, China; Email: clly1985528@163.com), Jun Liu (School of Management Science and Engineering, Nanjing University of Information Science and Technology, Nanjing, China; Email: liujun@nuist.edu.cn), Huihong Chang (School of Management Science and Engineering, Nanjing University of Information Science and Technology, Nanjing, China; Email: changhuihong@nuist.edu.cn), and Bohua Yang (Business School, Jiangsu Normal University, Tongshan New District, Xuzhou, Jiangsu, China; Email: mathyang@126.com) are equally contributed to this chapter.

J. Y.-L. Forrest, *Systemic Principles of Applied Economic Philosophies II*,
Translational Systems Sciences 39, https://doi.org/10.1007/978-981-99-7939-4_5

on technological innovation. Based on the established conclusions, corresponding suggestions and recommendations for managerial decision-making are provided.

Keywords Big data · Entropy method · "fourth" industrial revolution · Imitation of human capabilities · Intelligent society · Internet of things · Knowledge creation · Smart manufacturing

5.1 Introduction

With the current political and geographical developments in the world, patterns of economic development have been changing quickly in unprecedented ways. In order to respond adequately to the fast-changing environment, many leading nations from around the world have made their strategic adjustments. They have started to zoom in on artificial intelligence (AI) as their next strategic direction. For example, the following two important documents, which plainly put out seven chief stratagems for the advancement of AI in the USA, were published in 2016 by the Obama White House:

- Preparing for the future of artificial intelligence (OWH, 2016a) and
- The National Artificial Intelligence Research and Development Strategic Plan (OWH, 2016b).

Again, on May 10, 2018, the White House (WH, 2018) created the Select Committee on Artificial Intelligence for the purpose of joining the strengths and capabilities of different units of the government to improve the efficiency of federal level investment in AI related areas. By keeping up with such movements started in the USA, in May of 2018, the European Commission (EC, 2018) submitted its corresponding document, entitled "Artificial Intelligence: A European Perspective." It pronounces the EU's place in the international AI competition while presenting a plan for corresponding actions. That plan involves the goal of increasing investment in AI related R&D and ideals on how to update the European system of education and training in order to maintain development strength of European talents. Parallel to the USA and Europe, the Japanese government also assigns great importance to AI and relevant development. In its "Report on the 5th Science and Technology Basic Plan (2016–2020)" (Government of Japan, 2015), the Japanese government recommends to establish at the national level a relatively complete R&D promotion mechanism to center on internet of things, big data, AI and other technologies, and the materialization of a super intelligent society through extending AI to all aspects of life.

As the fastest growing developing nation in the world, the importance of AI also catches China's attention. The term of AI appears in the 2017 Report of the 19th National Congress of the Communist Party of China (Xi, 2017), reflecting the Chinese ambition of keeping up with the international development and to stimulate the economic restructuring by profoundly fusing internet, big data, and AI with the real economy. At the end of 2017, the central government revealed China's "Three-Year Action Plan to Promote the Development of a New Generation of AI Industry 2018–2022" (II - Industrialization and Informationalization, 2017). This document details the jobs and responsibilities related to the development of the next generation of AI in order to promote industrial development and push for "Made in China 2025." It tries to stimulate organic combination of AI technology and the real economy by focusing on the commercialization of new AI technologies through promoting deep fusions of information and manufacturing technologies. In the past few years, China has created great advantages in the world economy in the industrialization of AI with fruitful results. For example, many current Chinese technologies, such as Baidu's face recognition and the speech recognition of iFlytek, are in the international leading positions in their respective market segments. In terms of practical applications, China has also established its great advantages. For instance, China's huge potential market space and large population base have helped its development of advantage in big data supports (Du et al., 2018). Furthermore, AI has been increasingly employed in manufacturing, finance, education, medical care, logistics, and other areas of the economy. It continuously makes people's lives more intelligent than before and the whole society evolves in the direction of intelligence.

According to the "WIPO Technology Trends" released by the World Intellectual Property Organization (WIPO) in 2019, the USA and China are far ahead of other countries in patent applications in AI and related basic research (Amit et al., 2019). And, China has developed significant advantages in emerging deep learning technologies (Tao et al., 2019). In applications of technologies, China also has gained some advantages: Firstly, in terms of face recognition, the application of relevant technology in store face payment, airport flight information retrieval and other life scenarios are continuously improving the user experience and saving user time. Secondly, in the development of automatic storage business, for example, JD Shanghai Operation Center can organize, select, and deliver 200,000 orders every day by using automatic robot with only 4 people in charge. Thirdly, the level of industrial automation is getting increasingly higher. According to data provided by the International Federation of Robotics (IFR), the number of Chinese industrial robots installed in 2018 was 154,032, exceeding the total number of robots installed in Europe and the Americas.

Although the importance of AI has been widely recognized and AI technologies have been increasingly employed, scholarly research on how AI impacts technological innovation is still rare. In particular, the intelligentization of manufacturing leads to a common enabling technology for mechanical product innovations, while it also assists with the innovation of new manufacturing technologies (Zhou, 2012). Such intelligentization will develop the current manufacturing industry into an integrated one, where product design, production, and management are more digitized and intelligentized. And the second machine age, where AI and digitization are prevailingly visible, will realize unprecedented technological progresses (Brynjolfsson & McAfee, 2014).

The subject area of AI is composed of two branches. One branch composes of ways to replicate human capabilities and the other is to increase human capabilities for the purpose of making better decisions through utilizing the power of modern technology (Markoff, 2016). An important factor that affects how AI can help with socioeconomic growth is how AI can positively influence innovation and knowledge creation (Aghion et al., 2017). Because knowledge creation is such a process that either regroups what is known or generates new knowledge, AI can provide its support in both of these fronts; that is why AI promotes significant economic growth (Agrawal et al., 2018).

By glancing through the available literature, it is found that studies on how AI impacts technological innovation are still in the stage of infancy, and their focuses are mainly on how to define relevant concepts. Still open and waiting to be addressed are many questions regarding how AI and technological innovation are related to each other. This is where this chapter, which is mainly based on Forrest and Liu (2022) and Liu et al. (2020), comes into being. It contributes to the literature mainly in the following two aspects:

- At the height of theory this chapter explores the inherent mechanism underneath how AI affects technological innovation from the perspective of knowledge creation, the spillover of knowledge and technology, the capability of learning and absorption and investments in R&D and talents;
- Based on panel data of manufacturing sectors from China, this chapter empirically analyzes the effect, degree, and sector heterogeneity of AI on technological innovation while compares China's manufacture sectors.

The rest of this chapter is organized as follows: Section 5.2 consists of some elementary empirical observations that motivate the study presented in this chapter. Section 5.3 provides the theoretical analysis on how artificial intelligence affects technological innovation by looking at first the basic concepts and then the mechanism through which AI impacts technological innovation. Section 5.4 empirically confirms the main conclusions of the theoretical investigation in the previous section. Section 5.5 concludes this chapter with relevant managerial suggestions and recommendations.

5.2 Elementary Empirical Observations

With the implementation of various policies, artificial intelligence (AI) develops rapidly in China with excellent results derived and breakthroughs in key technologies appearing in many areas. However, due to regional differences in scientific and technological strengths, qualities of talents and infrastructures, the levels of AI development in different regions are also different. From the perspective of input, such as investment inputs, including those inputs of equipment and talents, this chapter measures various aspects of AI. Investment in equipment is the foundation on which AI develops while providing strong support for firms to introduce relevant technologies and to establish networks. To this end, this chapter employs investment in the fixed assets of telecommunication as a proxy variable. Investment in AI talents is an important guarantee for the development of artificial intelligence. Increasing such investment helps improve the level of AI and the capability for enterprises to innovate. This chapter employs the number of software developers as its proxy variable. By borrowing the thinking logic of Shi et al. (2018), this chapter, respectively, uses the products of investments in fixed assets of telecommunication and the numbers of software developers to measure the development levels of individual provinces, while these investments and counts of developers are normalized by using the entropy method. The greater the magnitudes of these products, it implies the higher development levels of the relevant AI. Figure 5.1 reflects figuratively the provincial development levels of AI and regional differences of China, which is generated by using geographic information systems software ARCGIS based on the 2015 AI development index (AI) of individual provinces.

As shown in this figure, the provinces with relatively high levels of development in AI are mostly located along China's east coast, including Liaoning, Beijing, Shandong, Jiangsu, Zhejiang, Henan, Sichuan, and Guangzhou. Other than such remote areas as Gansu, Hainan, Ningxia, and Qinghai, the development levels of AI in the rest of the provinces are similar. The main reason that leads to such uneven distribution in AI development is that the eastern provinces located along the coast have been enjoying high levels of economic development and rich human capital. These provinces have the necessary infrastructure, technology, and capital to support fast development of AI, leading to their relatively high AI levels. Conversely, most of the provinces that show relatively low levels of AI development are located in the

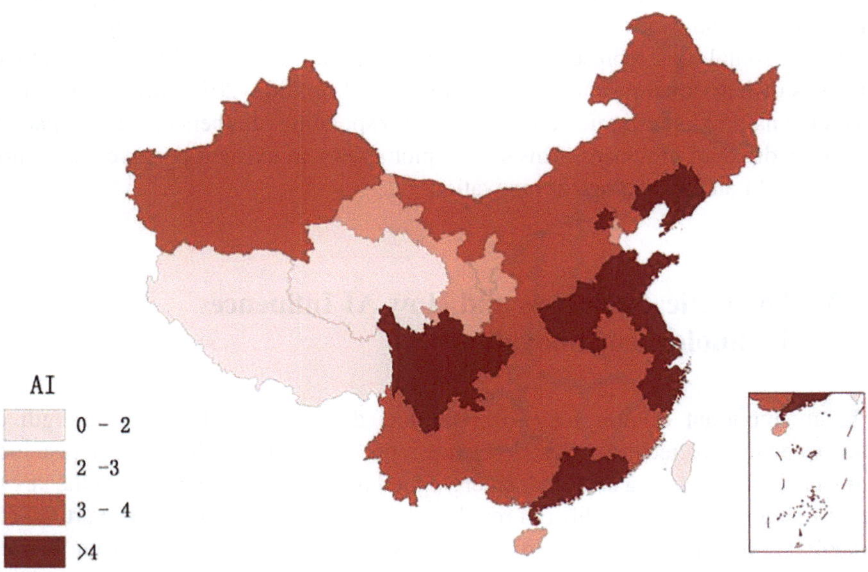

Fig. 5.1 Provincial levels of development of artificial intelligence in 2015

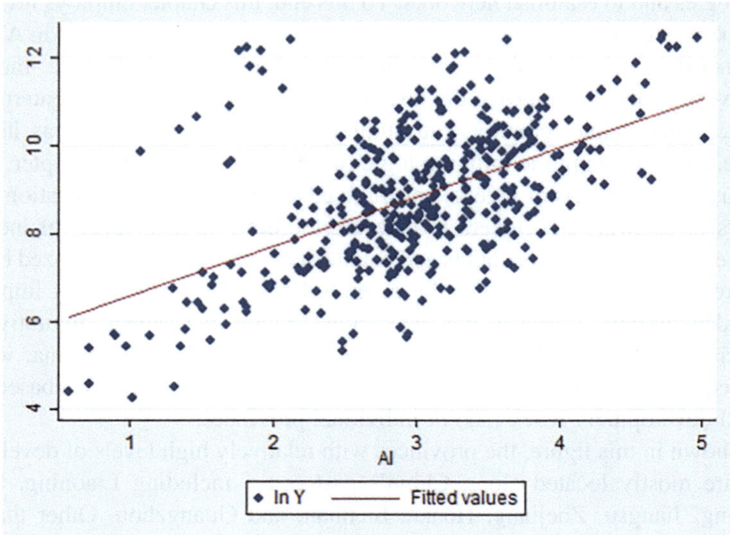

Fig. 5.2 A scatter plot between artificial intelligence and technological innovation

mid-western remote areas with comparatively backward levels of economic development. Business firms there started relatively later and evolve comparatively slower compared to those located in the eastern provinces, causing the AI technologies in these mid-western provinces also relatively more backward.

To reflect intuitively the relationship between the level of AI development and technological innovation, the scatter plot in Fig. 5.2 is produced by using Stata 13.0. The horizontal axis represents the natural logarithmic values of the development indices of individual provinces during the period of 2003–2015, while the vertical axis the natural logarithmic values of the corresponding numbers of granted patents of the individual provinces. This scatter plot shows an existent positive correlation between AI and technological innovation.

5.3 Theoretical Analysis and How AI Influences Technological Innovation

As an important driving force of economic development, the core strength of advancement for technology and science, and the essence behind the appearance of smart manufacturing and other emerging industries, AI has been seen as the key to advancing the "fourth" industrial revolution (Cheng & Peng, 2018). The artificially intelligent technology consists of finer areas (Wang & Yang, 2017), such as deep learning, computer vision, speech recognition, virtual personal assistant, intelligent robots, engine recommendation, etc. In particular, computer vision can identify objects, scenes, and activities out of images and in turn employ these identifications in automated processes of production. It can quickly collect a lot of information, process the information automatically, and complete the monitor of an entire process of production, quality control, product testing, and other tasks. Therefore, it greatly improves the efficiency and automation of production (Acemoglu & Restrepo, 2018). The technology of deep learning can model a specific problem from the real world through utilizing mathematical methods so that similar problems in related fields can be revolved once for all. At the same time of accomplishing realistic applications, the development and application of deep learning expand the applicability range of the entire AI technology, providing technical support for discovering new knowledge (Lecun et al., 2015).

Comparing to ordinary robots, intelligent ones are smarter and can complete complex, high-level works and tasks (Makridakis, 2017), such as quick and convenient modification of the content and method of a job, exploration of optimal decision-making, manufacturing, etc. The wide-range applications and high levels of permeation of these technologies in such areas as computer science, heavy industries, medicine, education, finance, trade, and other areas have been not only substituting people for completing tedious works but also identifying new patterns from vast amounts of data for reference (Trajtenberg, 2018). Additionally, applications of these technologies can affect the process of knowledge creation, that of spillovers and the capability of learning and absorption. The consequent effect on technological innovation is produced mainly through the following channels. That is, AI promotes technological innovation by

- quickening knowledge creation;
- accelerating the spillover of knowledge and technology;
- improving the capability of learning and absorption; and
- increasing investments in R&D and talents.

5.3.1 The Definition of Artificial Intelligence

In various definitions of AI, the following common element is included: AI refers to human-like intelligent activities programmed to perform specific tasks (Russell & Norvig, 2016; Goodfellow et al., 2018). Margaret and Tay (2019) and Coccia (2019a) believe that AI has the ability to think like humans and can be used to perform specific roles and tasks that were originally performed by people in public places and social life. And this ability is constantly increasing, can be comparable to humans, and even better than humans in some cases. For example, the application of deep learning of AI in cancer imaging can help pathologist test and classify cancer in early stages of cancer development, enable patients to receive timely treatment and increase their chances of survival or recovery (Coccia, 2019b). Russell and Norvig (2016) think that AI refers to systems with human attributes, such as learning, speaking, and other cognitive functions. Agrawal et al. (2018) consider that AI includes a series of technologies, including machine learning, deep learning, natural language processing, robots, etc., can be defined as advanced prediction technologies. Jay et al. (2018) maintain that AI is a cognitive science that integrates image processing, natural language processing, robotics, machine learning, and other technologies. The combination of AI with emerging technologies such as the industrial internet of things, big data analysis, and cloud computing, applied to industrial production, can help produce flexible, efficient, and green operating methods while also providing solutions for industrial applications. Iafrate (2018) believes that AI is a technology that can complete complex tasks that originally required human involvement. Its main advantage is that it can analyze and make decisions in milliseconds even in a very complex data analysis environment. Kaplan and Michael (2019) deem that AI has the ability to achieve specific tasks by flexibly learning existing data. He (2018) considers that AI mainly includes two aspects: computational intelligence and perceptual intelligence. Computational intelligence has the ability to quickly calculate and store memory, involving the application of data and algorithms. Perceptual intelligence refers to the perception capabilities of humans, such as vision, hearing, and touch. AI can capture and analyze the information of surroundings and make reasonable responses through various sensors. Christian et al. (2019) consider that AI is becoming more and more important in many areas of economy and society, not only because its technological capabilities are constantly improving, but more importantly, AI can continue to develop independently by adapting to the new environment.

Based on the above researches, this chapter considers that AI is the use of machine learning[1], deep learning,[2] computer vision[3], and other technologies to achieve imitation of human capabilities through programming and algorithmic processing. AI has the ability to learn, reason, perceive, and make decisions independently. It can replace part of human and mental labor and provide users with efficient auxiliary functions, such as data processing and technical analysis, which can greatly improve work and production efficiency.

---

[1] Machine learning is the use of algorithms to analyze data, find, summarize, and learn regularities from data, and then make decisions and predict the development of events in the real world.

[2] Deep learning is a special kind of machine learning. It is to process data by establishing and simulating the human brain for analysis. The method of deep learning breaks through the bottleneck of traditional machine learning and achieves beyond what traditional machine learning algorithms cannot achieve.

[3] Computer vision uses algorithms to identify and detect targets in images or videos and to track and measure targets. It is an application of machine learning in the field of vision.

5.3.2 *Understanding the Meaning of Technological Innovation*

To understand the concept of technological innovation, let us first briefly look at how the concept of innovation has evolved in the literature.

In as early as 1776, Adam Smith (1776) acknowledged in his *The Wealth of Nations* the importance of innovation as an activity that fosters wealth. After then, the topic of innovation has not been thoroughly studied until when Joseph Schumpeter (1934) published his book "The Theory of Economic Development." In this book, Schumpeter claims that innovation represents the driving force of economic development. Innovation, be it about products and services, managerial operations, or processes of production, underlies every competitive advantage as a fundamental guiding principle (Forrest et al., 2019). That is both theoretically and practically why business firms have to address the issue of innovation if they desire to ride successfully waves of transient competitive advantages, expand their existing territories, and enter new markets (Brown & Eisenhardt, 1995; OECD, 1997; Rosenthal, 1992; Stock et al., 2002). Because of its vital importance, innovation has gained a tremendous amount of scholarly attention in recent decades (Becheikh et al., 2006).

In terms of the concept of innovation, Damanpour (1996, p. 694) considers innovation as "a process that includes the generation, development, and implementation of new ideas or behaviors. Further, innovation is conceived as a means of changing an organization, either as a response to changes in the external environment or as a preemptive action to influence the environment. Hence innovation is broadly defined here to encompass a range of types, including new products or services, new process technologies, new organizational structures or administrative systems, or new plans or programs pertaining to organizational members."

Leonard and Swap (1999, p. 7) see innovation as "the embodiment, combination, and/or synthesis of knowledge in novel, relevant, valued new products, processes, or services." From the angle of library and information science, Deiss (2004, pp. 18–19) treats innovation as "things that change the way we can do what we want to do; [those that] have added value to our daily lives . . . new, desired, or needed services that add value for university faculty, students, and other scholars ... Innovation is more significantly about what our target audience can do – about the increased capacity of library users to do what they want and need to do in the way that most benefits their productivity, pleasure, and excellence . . . facilitating the work of our primary constituents in ways that are new and useful to them." Baregheh et al. (2009, p. 1334) maintains that "innovation is the multi-stage process whereby organizations transform ideas into new/improved products, service or processes, in order to advance, compete and differentiate themselves successfully in their marketplace."

Rowley (2011, p. 253) defines the concept as follows: "an innovation is a change, in a product, service, process or, more widely, an organization." And, Kaser (2011) sees innovation not "just about doing things that are new or different" but "about doing things that in the eye of the beholder (the user, patron, or customer) meet a need that may not have been appreciated before ... [and] the things that truly alter and improve how we do things; they may even shift our proverbial paradigms." For firms that produce products or provide services, innovation is mainly materialized through introducing original products, services, and processes (Becheikh et al., 2006) that enable firms to enter competitively or create new markets (Smith & Tushman, 2005). Many scholars treat innovation as one major factor of firms' long-term success (Kanter, 2001).

To explore the meaning of innovation from the perspective of front-line managers, starting in 2011, General Electric (2012) commissioned surveys of senior business executives in countries across the world. To single out the key components of different perspectives on innovation, Jeff Dance (2008) lists thirty plus definitions of innovation and provides his summary as follows: Innovation is something fresh (new, original, or improved) that creates value, where "something" can be a process, product, or service that starts as an idea or thought.

To avoid potential distraction by the huge literature on the concept of innovation, let us next look at the concept of technological innovation in order to make this chapter unfold smoothly.

Based on the previously listed attempts of defining the concept of innovation, the definition of technological innovation by Branscomb (2001), and the concept of innovation in manufacturing sector (Forrest et al., 2019), let us define technological innovation as follows:

> Technological innovation is such a set of activities – which could be just one particular activity or several, occurring either simultaneously or temporally – that leads to a fresh technology (new, original or improved) that produces exceptionally added value to a company when compared to other technology-related activities that take place in the same sector as the one the company belongs to.

Because of the emphasis on the comparatively added value, this definition of technological innovation entails many aspects of the concept. For example, it implies

1. An extraordinary level of creativity has to be involved over time;
2. The creativity has to be internally conceived, driven by environmental forces, either current or predicted, and externally adopted, such as market acceptance;
3. Relevant new processes, either productive or managerial or both, have to be implemented to realize the said value;
4. Intended benefits and advantages are materialized;
5. Other than technology-related inventions, this definition also emphasizes on employing the fresh technology to produce marketable fresh products or processes; and
6. Although not explicitly mentioned, the definition includes the roles of relevant processes and outcomes.

Because technological innovations play an increasingly prominent role in the continuous growth of leading economies, governments have been shifting their attention from science and technology policies to a focus on research and innovation policies (Vaughan, 2013). The previous discussion shows that innovation in general and technological innovation in particular are really a socioeconomic process that leads to observable growth in performance of high priority capabilities and growth in values.

5.3.3 *AI Quickens Knowledge Creation*

The definition of technological innovation, as just introduced above, indicates that such innovation represents either a collection or a process of activities, where the former is the case when the activities take place simultaneously, while the latter is the case when the activities take place sequentially. Additionally, technological innovation contains not only purely social activities, but also creative ones that involve knowledge recognition and integration on which the freshness of a new technology emerges, as confirmed by Weitzman (1998). To this end, knowledge is the core of technological innovation; effective creation of new knowledge is the basis for technological innovation (Chen, 2010). Each technological innovation manifests itself through the emergence of new knowledge and an integration and new and existent knowledge.

Proposition 5.1 Each of the following kinds of knowledge creation can potentially lead to new technological innovation:

- A new way of understanding existing knowledge,
- A creative integration of different areas of knowledge, or
- The production of some original knowledge.

Corresponding to knowledge creation, as described above, the development of AI provides data-collection support for revealing brand new ways to look at the existing knowledge, fast speed support for trying different ways to integrate knowledge, and exploration convenience for uncovering new knowledge. That is, we have

Proposition 5.2 The growth of AI accelerates knowledge creation in the forms listed in Proposition 5.1.

In particular, applications of AI technology have clearly helped business firms to increase their capability of data collection, leading to the rapid development of various tools to deal with big data. Interactions between clouds and devices provide unprecedented supplies and carriers for the creation of new knowledge and promote the explicitization of tacit knowledge, while such knowledge can be stored and used in clouds and terminal devices. That in turn accelerates the speed of data acquisition and improves the accuracy and reliability of the consequent understanding and knowledge.

Because of the development of artificial intelligence, introduced are such advanced analytics tools as the technologies of much improved internet and clouds. For example, the technologies of deep learning and computer vision are able to provide more quickly than ever before a large number of sources of information. That helps create new knowledge and new computational schemes faster than before so that the process of knowledge regrouping accelerates (Agrawal et al., 2018). In other words, what is speeding up is the process that starts from data to information to knowledge creation. For example, when they developed the solid electrolyte new material for lithium ion batteries, Japan's Fujitsu Limited and Chemical RIKEN (or Institute of Physical and Chemical Research) employed related technology of artificial intelligence. This technology helped the scientists control their number of repeated operations and reasonably predict the properties of synthetic compounds. Hence, within a shorter period than expected, the scientists were able to pinpoint out the optimal material combination for high lithium ion conductivity while simultaneously discovered more efficient high lithium ion conductivity. For details on this case, see Fujitsu Limited and Riken (2018).

Additionally, the development of AI promotes the popularization and application of internet and communication methods of platform economies. It breaks down the boundaries of knowledge within and between companies. It accelerates the dissemination and diffusion of knowledge and the process of creating new knowledge through knowledge exchange and integration. This end in turn greatly influences the development of AI (Goldfarb & Trefler, 2018). Therefore, we have

Proposition 5.3 It is through accelerating knowledge creation that technological innovations are positively incited by artificial intelligence.

5.3.4 Spillover Effects of AI

Because of its inevitable spread between various departments of a business firm, the AI technology is promoted simultaneously by all divisions of the firm, leading to the development of inter-departmental technological innovation. With increasingly higher levels of profits, brought forward by AI-based innovations, beneficiary departments will bump up their demands for additional intelligent technologies. After having received the gains from the departments that applied intelligent technologies, the R&D department continues its efforts to improve its firm's technical sophistication and to develop new smart technologies in order to satisfy the new demands. The consequent application of intelligent technologies of a new round once again largely promotes the innovation spillovers for the R&D department. When such a cycle repeats itself, it eventually stimulates a cumulatively cyclic growth of AI and technological innovation.

Proposition 5.4 Artificial intelligence plays an important role in strengthening the following development cycle:

(a) Intelligent technology →
(b) Growth in inter-divisional communication →
(c) Appearance of inter-divisional technological innovation →

(d) Growth in profits →
(e) Demand for more intelligent technology → (a).

At the level of firms, applications of AI technology help reduce the cost of information transfer and sharing between business firms. The formation of knowledge, technology, and information networks makes it more convenient for enterprises to exchange information and sharing know-hows. Hence, the cost of spreading technological innovations across companies is lowered, making inter-firm knowledge and technology spillovers much easier than before. That is subsequently conducive to the diffusion and spread of technological innovations, which further promotes the continuous improvement of technological innovation capabilities of all enterprises involved.

Proposition 5.5 With artificial intelligence, knowledge sharing and technology transfer become easier over time, which makes any attempt to keep trade secrets increasingly difficult.

The development of AI accelerates the interactive integration between mobile internet and internet of things. That in turn encourages enterprises located at different places to join forces in their processes of production by taking advantages of their respective resources (Lv & Han, 2015). When firms are no longer constrained by their geographical locations, they can apply control remotely and organize production over long distance as long as all equipment work normally. And, in a production process, additional requirements can be added at any time and the pre-determined process can be changed adaptively in order to satisfy the varying market conditions. The release from the earlier geographic constraint encourages various talents, firms, and industries to join their efforts and resources on their focal industrial chain. Under the joint effect of finer division of labor, information sharing, resource integration, etc., firms scattered all over the land will be able to achieve cooperatively their common goals of production. Such change in business operation from the past will gradually break the boundaries of traditional corporate organizations, making firms no longer closed entities, instead a modularized production network. Such networks will greatly facilitate communication and cooperation between enterprises. In short, we have the following conclusion, where new philosophies of business include, but not limited to, remote manufacturing, computer-integrated business system, platform economy.

Proposition 5.6 The unprecedented rise of artificial intelligence has led to new philosophies of business by removing physical constraints, such as distance, location, uneven distribution of resources, and others. It in turn stimulates the development of technological innovation.

For related empirical studies, see (Caputo et al., 2016; Holmstrom et al., 2016; Roos, 2015; Wu et al., 2015).

5.3.5 AI Improves Learning and Absorption Capabilities

No matter how innovative a firm is, if it cannot appropriately decipher the market information, it is doomed to fail or to become irrelevant. To this end, there are plenty of examples on how corporate giants fell on hard times. One of the notable recent examples is the case of Eastman Kodak. Historically, this firm operated on a culture of innovation and change. However, it did not take necessary actions when the market signaled it to do so. When faced with the challenge of disruptive technology, filmless photos, Kodak did not take decisive actions to combat the inevitable. For more detailed analysis of this firm, see (Kotter, 2012; McGrath, 2013). To this end, we quote Theorem 4.1 from Chap. 4 below in order to make the logical reasoning in this chapter self-contained.

Theorem 5.1 If the market described below is in Nash equilibrium, then the following are equivalent:

1. At least one new firm enters the market competitively and profitably with their versions of substitute offer.
2. There is a consumer surplus of switchers who make purchase decisions based on which supplier's price is lower.

The market considered in Theorem 5.1 is assumed to satisfy the following conditions. It is served by a fixed number of firms with their horizontally differentiated offers. Its operation is only affected by market forces, such as demand and supply, and consumers' forever evolving preferences and tastes. In other words, this market is perfectly competitive without any outside interference. As a consequence of interacting forces between the systems of values and beliefs of individual consumers and the missions of the incumbent firms, each of these firms has a base of loyal customers. These loyal customers only consider the offers of their favored firms unless the prices of the offers are more than their reservation prices. Different from loyal customers, there are those customers in the marketplace who make purchases based on which firm's unit-value price is lower. These customers are collectively known as switchers. And, the firms' strategies of pricing are known to all involved companies who respond by playing Nash equilibria through untainted self-analyses.

This theorem clearly indicates that appropriately understanding market cues is essential in terms of helping a firm to decide the right thing to do and the right product or service to produce and to develop instead of simply investing more heavily in innovation. In particular, the entering firm needs to understand appropriately the switchers in the theorem. Their indecisiveness of which firm's product they would buy could practically mean that they are not happy with the products available in the market; however, due to the necessity of human living they have to make purchases. That surely opens up a wide door for firms with strong learning and absorption capabilities to explore their appropriate directions to develop their businesses.

Other than knowing what is appropriate to do based on market information, learning and absorption also directly relate to the entry efficiency of external knowledge into an enterprise. That explains why we have the following:

Proposition 5.7 Technological innovation is generally backed by capabilities of learning and absorption of knowledge such that the more a firm is able to learn, the more the firm is able to innovate appropriately.

In terms of learning and absorption, the development of AI can help employees to improve these capabilities. Such development constantly brings forward with more sophisticated equipment and devices. For example, people have been using continuously improved computers to model and simulate intelligent human activities to substitute for parts of the brain works widely employed in traditional production systems. These sophisticated equipment and devices have been becoming reliable and efficient analysis tools for employees to make more effective decisions than ever before due to their capabilities of reasoning, learning, association, and problem solving based on known knowledge (Camerer, 2019). Because of the capabilities of these equipment and devices of constantly improving sophistication, employees' abilities of learning and absorption rise.

Additionally, the development of AI has been practically promoting the learning and absorption capabilities of enterprises. For example, such technologies as deep learning, intelligent image recognition, applications of big data, etc., can help industrial robots to form independent judgements and to take corresponding actions (Lecun et al., 2015; Du et al., 2018). These robots' independent completions of complex tasks, their capability of transforming acquired information into knowledge and taking justified subsequent actions play a very positive role in the innovative activities of enterprises. Summarizing these discussions at the level of employees and that of enterprises, we have

Proposition 5.8 Through cultivating the organizational ability of learning, artificial intelligence directly stimulates technological innovation.

5.3.6 AI Increases Investments in R&D and Talents

For a representative firm, its purpose for having an in-house research and development (R&D), if all possible, is to help the firm to achieve one or more of the following:

- Generate, exploit, and convert knowledge, which is newly found either internally or external, into new products and/or processes (Keizer et al., 2002);
- Acquire, integrate, convert, and exploit new technologies (Debackere et al., 1996);
- Entice cooperative partners (Hall & Bagchi-Sen, 2002); and
- Construct new-technology settings which are very costly and particularly difficult, even impossible, to acquire from competitors (Lee, 1995).

By employing systems methodology, Forrest et al. (2018) show that when a company grows to a certain scale of strength, it will naturally possess R&D capabilities as described above. So, in such a case, it is strategically significant and important for the firm to officially recognize and organize such a division within the company with sufficient financial and administrative supports. To this end, the literature empirically verifies that in-house R&D has been widely accepted as a crucial determinant of a firm's innovativeness (Hall & Bagchi-Sen, 2002; Parthasarthy & Hammond, 2002), Therefore, we have the following:

Proposition 5.9 The chance for a technological innovation to occur can be greatly increased by investing in research and development.

In fact, investment in R&D plays an important role in every aspect of a R&D process. It attracts talents, covers laboratory costs, helps provide test equipment and devices, etc. All these expenditures potentially lift a firm's innovativeness to much elevated levels and lead to the occurrence of technological innovation.

Other than attracting talents, directed investment in scientific and technological talents represents another important component of technological innovation. An effective organization of quality scientific and technological talents with other essential factors can produce a significant impact on the efficiency and capabilities of technological innovation. Within an enterprise, the development of AI potentially leads to additional intelligent industrial robots, high-end intelligent equipment, and a subsequent set of intelligent production processes. Such advances can gradually replace, to a certain degree, human labor, increase productivity, reduce costs, so that enterprises can devote more manpower, material and financial resources into research and development activities, effectively increasing the investment in R&D and talents.

Additionally, enterprises can create and capture higher levels of value by employing artificially intelligent technologies. With rising levels of profits, enterprises will in turn be able to increase their investment in R&D and talents, based on which the rising levels of profits initially came from. That promotes a new round of technological innovation, forming a new virtuous cycle (Proposition 5.4). Hence, we have the following result.

Proposition 5.10 Artificial intelligence can potentially lead to technological innovations through increasing investment in R&D and talents either directly or indirectly.

5.4 Empirical Confirmation

This section attempts to confirm some of the established propositions above by an empirical means.

5.4.1 The Development of Model and Source of Data

As suggested by the literature, other than AI, additional factors, such as the investment intensity in R&D (Patterson & Ambrosini, 2015), foreign direct investment (Feng, 2019), ownership structure (Yi et al., 2017), and technological imitation (Zhang & Li, 2015), also influence technological innovation. For our purpose, these factors are used as control variables in the following measurement model:

$$ln\,\mathrm{Y}_{i,t} = \alpha + \beta_1\, ln\,\mathrm{AI}_{i,t} + \beta_2\, ln\,\mathrm{K}_{i,t} + \beta_3\, ln\,\mathrm{FDI}_{i,t} + \beta_4\, ln\,\mathrm{STATE}_{i,t} + \beta_5\, ln\,\mathrm{TETI}_{i,t} + \varepsilon_{i,t},$$

where the subscripts i and t stand for province i and year t, respectively, AI artificial intelligence, K investment in R&D, FDI foreign direct investment, STATE ownership structure, TETI technical imitation, α is a constant term, β a coefficient of each variable, and ε is a random error.

Specifically, the response variable Y is measured by using the number of patent authorizations as in Carree et al. (2015) in various manufacturing sectors as an indicator of technological innovation. This choice is different from Filippetti et al. (2016) who employ the number of patent applications, Christiansen (1999) who adopts the number of new product developments, and Guan and Gao (2009) who uses the sales of new products. The main explanatory variable AI is measured by the number of industrial robots as in Acemoglu and Restrepo (2018), because AI in manufacturing is mainly realized through industrial robots.

As for the control variables, this section measures

1. “investment in R&D” (K), as in Han et al. (2014), by using the radio of internal expenditures of R&D to the total output value;
2. “foreign direct investment” (FDI) in an industry by using the ratio of the total output value of foreign-funded enterprises to the total output value of that industry (Wang et al., 2010);
3. “ownership structure” (STATE) by using the ratio of the output value of state-owned enterprises in an industry to the total output value of the industry (Sun et al., 2017; Bai, 2011); and
4. “technology imitation” (TETI) by using the proportion of enterprises’ technical transformation costs to the total industrial output value (Wang & Wang, 2019).

By synthesizing the classification standards of the International Federation of Robotics and the China Industrial Statistics, this section is able to examine a set of panel data for the time period 2008–2017 from International Robot Alliance Website, “China Statistical Yearbook,” “China Science and Technology Statistical Yearbook.” The data set reflects 14 manufacturing sectors, covering a wide range from textile and clothing to production and supply of electricity, heat, gas, and water.

5.4.2 Results and Discussion

In terms of the effect of AI on technological innovation, regression analysis is utilized on the available data. The corresponding coefficients are estimated by, respectively, using fixed effects (FE), random effects (RE), feasible generalized least squares (FGLS) method, and the system generalized method of moment (System-GMM). By comparing the resultant estimates, Hausman test suggests that FE produces better results than RE. Because FE and FGLS produce estimates of the same signs, while FGLS can possibly eliminate existing heteroscedasticity and serial correlation (Woodridge, 2002), it means that FGLS is a better method than FE. And, because System-GMM can partially resolve the endogenous problem (Roodman, 2009), and because the signs of the coefficients of *ln*AI, as estimated, respectively, by FGLS and System-GMM, are the same, it becomes clear that this analysis can simply focus on the estimates of System-GMM.

Because the coefficient of AI influence on technological innovation is equal to 0.1945 and passes the test of 5% significance, it means that when all the control variables are fixed, AI positively impacts technological innovation (Propositions 5.4, 5.6, 5.8 and 5.10). In particular, through the application of various related technologies, AI helps increase the flow and sharing of knowledge, boost the capability to learn, absorb, and create knowledge. Consequently, AI accelerates the conversion, development, and utilization of knowledge. In short, AI, through various means, assists a firm to significantly increase its productivity and to liberate resources so that unrestricted resources in turn strengthen R&D efforts and activities, leading to much improved capability of technological innovation.

Regarding the control variables, the relatively large coefficient is that of "investment in R&D." It is positive and equal to 0.7586 while passing the 1% significance test. This fact demonstrates that the amount invested in R&D efforts benefits the innovativeness of a manufacturing firm in the area of technology. In terms of "foreign direct investment," its coefficient is equal to -0.0798 while failing the significance test. Hence, it means that this control variable does not impact technological innovation significantly. As for "ownership structure," its coefficient is equal to -0.4439 and passes the 10% significance test, indicating that "ownership structure" does have a constraining effect on the innovativeness of a manufacturing firm. Specific to the data employed here, this end implies that in the overall Chinese economy, if the segment of state-owned enterprises occupies a large proportion, then the innovativeness of the manufacturing industry will be low. That is because state-owned enterprises tend to affect the industrial allocation efficiency and technical efficiency (Sun et al., 2017). These adversely affected efficiencies will surely impact technological innovation negatively. As for the control variable "technical imitation," its coefficient is equal to -0.0644 and passes the significance test of 5%, demonstrating that such imitation has a notably limiting effect on the technology innovation. That is because although enterprises in the 14 manufacturing industries considered in this section adopted advanced technologies, they still have not effectively digested and absorbed the true essence of the technologies beyond the stage of imitation. In this sense, quick introduction of advanced technologies generally hinders the development of technological innovation. In short, this empirical study reconfirms the results of Propositions 5.1, 5.7, and 5.9.

5.5 A Few Final Words

This chapter examines how AI impacts technological innovation by such a logical reasoning that is parallel to the one widely used in mathematics and natural science (Kline, 1972). It first looks at the concept of technological innovation by referencing back to numerous definitions of innovation and explores how this concept can be defined generally without the need to make periodic alterations. This new definition stresses simultaneously the originality of a technology in terms of its newness, or freshness, or enhancement, and the following creation of value. Starting from this general definition of technological innovation and the specific logical reasoning, a series of generally true propositions are developed. Specifically, this chapter is able to discover the root on which an original technology can potentially appear out of the R&D effort of technological innovation (Proposition 5.1), how AI stimulates technological innovation (Propositions 5.3, 5.6, 5.8, and 5.10). Although this last result is similar to what are derived in Aghion et al. (2017) and Agrawal et al. (2018), the difference is that this chapter explains the mechanism of how AI affects technological innovation in four angles: knowledge creation, knowledge spillover, learning ability, and investment in R&D and talents.

Beyond theoretical discussions, this chapter also empirically tests the promotional effect of AI on technological innovation and finds that the impact of AI on technological innovation experiences industry heterogeneity: Compared with high-tech sectors, AI has a more significant role in promoting technological innovation in low-tech industries, and sectors with higher levels of AI have a greater role in promoting technological innovation. These two points are the highlights of this chapter and enrich the existent literature, including the works of Aghion et al. (2017), Agrawal et al. (2018), and others. Specifically, by controlling "investment in R&D," "foreign direct investment," "ownership structure," and "technology imitation," it is found that advances in AI assist the development of technological innovation. At the same time, the control variable "investment in R&D" indeed benefits the technological innovativeness of a manufacturing firm, while "foreign direct investment" does not impact technological innovation significantly, and other two control variables have constraining effects on the innovativeness of a manufacturing firm. These empirical results reconfirm the results of Propositions 5.1, 5.7, and 5.9.

The theoretical conclusions established in this chapter naturally lead to the following policy suggestions and recommendations:

1. Raise the level of sophistication of AI for the purpose of promoting technological innovativeness of manufacturing enterprises.

First, invest increasingly in the AI effort and activities that result in new service formats, such as cloud computation, management of big data, internet of things, intelligent manufacturing. In its penetration into various industrial sectors, employ AI technology to upgrade and transform traditional industries while encourage the creation of new knowledge and the development of novel technologies.

Second, organize by using AI-based technologies inter-organizational networks and strategic blocks, consisting of government agencies, business firms, research institutes and universities, as platforms for coordinated innovations to occur. Within such networks and blocks, the government can help coordinate joint efforts of industry, academia, and R&D by associating, exchanging, and sharing information and knowledge among innovation entities. Such governmental guidance can either directly or indirectly promote rapid turnover and spread of AI technologies between and among individual business firms and different industries. The consequently shortened R&D periods in turn stimulate the creation and spillover of new knowledge and new technology, which helps raise the capability of technological innovativeness.

Third, considering the present challenges facing Chinese manufacturing firms, it becomes more necessary than ever before that communications between the government, industry, and enterprises need to be promoted. By doing so, China will be enabled to

- uninterruptedly advance its technological innovativeness,
- develop needed mechanisms for producing and discovering talents, and
- effectively coordinate the development of AI industry.

With such capabilities well developed, China will lead the global development of the AI industry and will acquire its dominance within the increasingly severe international competition.

2. Create a mechanical way to encourage the development of AI technology and the AI industry.

Adopt well-designed measures to promote the development of AI technology and the AI industry so that relevant new knowledge can be formed and novel technologies can be created. Well-designed measures need to address the problem of how to smoothly and effectively facilitate exchanges of ideas and information and that of how to coordinate the demands of local, regional, national, and international markets. Addressing these issues holistically will assist business enterprises to engage in innovative activities in order to provide creative offers to different markets of various levels (Theorem 5.1). Successfully doing so fortifies cross-regional and cross-national exchanges and cooperation, which in turn support the introduction of advanced knowledge and technology and promote the healthy development of an AI industry.

Design and implement necessary coping policies, speed up the systematic advancement of the underlying industrial chain of AI, and continuously improve the quality and scale of technological innovation while promoting the sustainability of the economy.

As stated in other parts of this book, the validity of the conclusions established in this chapter is also constrained. For example, AI's impact on technological innovation is analyzed in four different angles: the creation of knowledge, the overflow of knowledge, capabilities of learning and absorption, and investment in R&D efforts. However, if one likes to directly confirm these established conclusions empirically, he/she will find that it is difficult, if not impossible, to design appropriate proxies and to collect adequate data for such variables as "creation of knowledge," "overflow of knowledge," and "capabilities of learning and absorption." This fact opens a wide door for future empirical research.

Conversely, the section of empirical confirmation only considers the panel data of China's manufacturing sector during a particular time period. So, the developed confirmations of this chapter might not hold true if data are from other countries or regions in the world. Hence, similar empirical confirmations can be carried out with data from outside China.

References

Acemoglu, D., & Restrepo, P. (2018). Artificial intelligence, automation and work. NBER working paper no. 24196.

Aghion, P., Jones, B. F., & Jones, C. I. (2017). Artificial intelligence and economic growth. NBER Working Paper No. 23928.

Agrawal, A. K., Gans, J. S., & Goldfarb, A. (2018). Prediction, judgment and complexity: A theory of decision making and artificial intelligence. NBER Working Paper No. 24243.

Amit, K. S., Manvendra, J., Ajith, A., & Pranab, K. (2019). Muhuri, Engineering applications of artificial intelligence: A bibliometric analysis of 30 years (1988-2018). *Engineering Applications of Artificial Intelligence, 85*, 517–532.

Bai, J. H. (2011). Are government R&D subsidies efficient in China! Evidence from large and medium enterprises. *China Economic Quarterly, 10*(04), 1375–1400. https://doi.org/10.4236/ajibm.2014.49056

Baregheh, A., Rowley, J., & Sambrook, S. (2009). Towards a multidisciplinary definition of innovation. *Management Decision, 47*(8), 1323–1339.

Becheikh, N., Landry, R., & Amara, N. (2006). Lessons from innovation empirical studies in the manufacturing sector: A systematic review of the literature from 1993 to 2003. *Technovation, 26*(5), 644–664.

Branscomb, L. M. (2001). Technological innovation. *International Encyclopedia of the Social & Behavioral Sciences*, 15498–15502.

Brown, S. L., & Eisenhardt, K. M. (1995). Product development: Past research, present findings, and future directions. *Academy of Management Review, 20*(2), 343–378.

Brynjolfsson, E., & Mcafee, A. (2014). *The second machine age*. Norton.

Camerer, C. F. (2019). Artificial intelligence and behavioral economics. In A. K. Agrawal, J. Gans, & A. Goldfarb (Eds.), *The economics of artificial intelligence: An Agenda*. University of Chicago Press.

Caputo, A., Marzi, G., & Pellegrini, M. M. (2016). The internet of things in manufacturing innovation processes: Development and application of a conceptual framework. *Business Process Management Journal, 22*(2), 383–402.

Carree, M., Piergiovanni, R., Santarelli, E., et al. (2015). Factors favoring innovation from a regional perspective: A comparison of patents and trademarks. *International Entrepreneurship and Management Journal, 11*(4), 793–810.

Chen, C. J. (2010). The effects of knowledge attribute, alliance characteristics, and absorptive capacity on knowledge transfer performance. *R & D Management, 34*(3), 311–321.
Cheng, C. P., & Peng, H. (2018). The mechanism of artificial intelligence affecting employment and China's countermeasures. *China Soft Science Magazine, 2018*(10), 62–70.
Christian, V., Constantinescu, C., & Popescu, D. (2019). Application potentials of artificial intelligence for the design of innovation processes. *Procedia CIRP, 84*, 810–813.
Christiansen, J. A. (1999). *Competitive innovation management: Techniques to improve innovation performance*. Palgrave MacMillan.
Coccia, M. (2019a). Artificial intelligence technology in cancer imaging: Clinical challenges for detection of lung and breast cancer. *Journal of Social and Administrative Sciences, 6*, 82–98.
Coccia, M. (2019b). Deep learning technology for improving cancer care in society: New directions in cancer imaging driven by artificial intelligence. *Technology in Society, 60*, 101–198.
Damanpour, F. (1996). Organizational complexity and innovation: Developing and testing multiple contingency models. *Management Science, 42*(5), 693–716.
Dance, J. (2008). What is innovation? 30+ definitions lead to one fresh summary. *Fresh Consulting* (blog), May 22, 2008, Retrieved May 2, 2019, from http://freshconsulting.com/what-is-innovation.
Debackere, K., Clarysse, B., & Rappa, M. A. (1996). Dismantling the ivory tower: the influence of networks on innovative output in emerging technologies. *Technological Forecasting and Social Change, 53*, 139–154.
Deiss, K. J. (2004). Innovation and strategy: Risk and choice in shaping user-centered libraries. *Library Trends, 53*(1), 17–32.
Du, C. J., Hu, J., & Chen, W. X. (2018). Development model and countermeasures of China's new generation of artificial intelligence industry. *Economic Review Journal, 04*, 41-47+2.
European Commission (EC) (2018). Artificial intelligence: An European perspective. Retrieved April 16, 2019, from http://publications.jrc.ec.europa.eu/repository/bitstream/JRC113826/ai-flagship-report-online.pdf.
Feng, Y. C. (2019). Effects of environmental regulation and FDI on urban innovation in China: A spatial Durbin econometric analysis. *Journal of Cleaner Production, 235*. https://doi.org/10.1016/j.jclepro.2019.06.184
Filippetti, A., Frenz, M., & Ietto-Gillies, G. (2016). The impact of internationalization on innovation at countries' level: The role of absorptive capacity. *Cambridge Journal of Economics, 41*(2), 413–439.
Forrest, J. Y. L., Lin, C. C., Mondal, S., & Tucker, R. (2019). Environmental forces underneath the innovativeness of manufacturing firms. *Theoretical Economics Letters, 9*, 1353–1382. https://doi.org/10.4236/tel.2019.95088
Forrest, J. Y. L., & Liu, Y. (2022). *Value in business: A holistic, systems-based approach to creating and achieving value*. Springer.
Forrest, J. Y. L., Mondal, S., Tucker, R., & Lin, C.C. (2018). Effects of manufacturing firms' strategies on innovation: A holistic view. Proceedings of the 2018 Annual Conference of NABET, November 1 – 2, 2018, State College, PA., pp. 74–94.
Fujitsu Limited & & Riken (2018). Fujitsu and RIKEN demonstrate AI's utility in material design. Retrieved April 29, 2019, from https://www.fujitsu.com/global/about/resources/news/press-releases/2018/0316-01.html.
General Electric (2012). *GE global innovation barometer: Global Research Report*, 30, http://files.gecompany.com/gecom/innovationbarometer/GE_Global_Innovation_Barometer_Report_January_2012.pdf.
Goldfarb, A., & Trefler, D. (2018). AI and international trade. NBER Working Paper No. 24254.
Goodfellow, I., Bengio, Y., & Courville, A. (2018). *Deep learning*. MIT Press.
Government of Japan (2015). Retrieved April 16, 2019, from https://www8.cao.go.jp/cstp/kihonkeikaku/5basicplan_en.pdf.
Guan, J. C., & Gao, X. (2009). *Exploring the h-index at patent level*. John Wiley & Sons.

Hall, L. A., & Bagchi-Sen, S. (2002). A study of R&D, innovation, and business performance in the Canadian biotechnology industry. *Technovation, 22*, 231–244.

Han, X. F., Hui, N., & Song, W. F. (2014). Can informatization improve the technology innovation efficiency of Chinese industrial sectors. *China Industrial Economics, 2014*(12), 70–82.

He, Z. M. (2018). Overview of artificial intelligence. *Science and Technology Economy Guide, 26*(33), 35.

Holmstrom, J., Holweg, M., Khajavi, S. H., & Partanen, J. (2016). The direct digital manufacturing (r) evolution: Definition of a research agenda. *Operations Management Research, 9*, 1–10.

Iafrate, F. (2018). *Artificial intelligence and big data—The birth of a new intelligence*. ISTE Ltd and John Wiley & Sons.

II - Industrialization and Informationalization (2017). Three-year action plan to promote the development of a new generation of AI industry 2018–2022. Retrieved April 22, 2019, from http://www.miit.gov.cn/n1146285/n1146352/n3054355/n3057497/n3057507/c5979554/content.html.

Jay, L., Davari, H., Singh, J., & Pandhare, V. (2018). Industrial artificial intelligence for industry 4.0-based manufacturing systems. *Manufacturing Letters, 18*, 20–23. 2213-8463.

Kanter, R. M. (2001). *Evolve! Succeeding in the digital culture of tomorrow*. Harvard Business School Press.

Kaplan, A., & Michael, H. (2019). Rulers of the world, Unite! The challenges and opportunities of artificial intelligence. *Business Horizons, 0007-6813*. https://doi.org/10.1016/j.bushor.2019.09.003

Kaser, D. (2011). Editor's notes: Innovation can be fun. *Computers in Libraries, 31*(5), 4.

Keizer, J. A., Dijkstra, L., & Halman, J. I. M. (2002). Explaining innovative efforts of SMEs. An exploratory survey among SMEs in the mechanical and electrical engineering sector in the Netherlands. *Technovation, 22*, 1–13.

Kline, M. (1972). *Mathematical thought from ancient to modern times*. Oxford University Press.

Kotter, J. (2012). Barriers to change: The real reason behind the Kodak downfall. *Forbes*, May 2, 2012, www.forbes.com/sites/johnkotter/2012/05/02/barriers-to-change-the-real-reason-behind-the-kodak-downfall

Lecun, Y., Bengio, Y., & Hinton, G. (2015). Deep learning. *Nature, 521*(7553), 436.

Lee, J. (1995). Small firms' innovation in two technological settings. *Research Policy, 24*, 391–401.

Leonard, D. A., & Swap, W. C. (1999). *When sparks fly: igniting creativity in groups*. Harvard Business School Press.

Liu, J., Chang, H. H., Forrest, J. Y. L., & Yang, B. H. (2020). Influence of artificial intelligence on technological innovation: Evidence from the panel data of china's manufacturing sectors. *Technological Forecasting & Social Change, 158*, 120142. https://doi.org/10.1016/j.techfore.2020.120142

Lv, T., & Han, N. (2015). Intelligent manufacturing: The global trend and Chinese strategy. *Frontiers, 2015*(11), 6–17.

Makridakis, S. (2017). The forthcoming artificial intelligence (AI) revolution: Its impact on society and firms. *Futures, 90*(June), 46–60.

Margaret, A. G., & Tay, K. T. (2019). Artificial intelligence and sustainable development. *The International Journal of Management Education, 18*, 1472–8117.

Markoff, J. (2016). *Machines of loving grace: The quest for common ground between humans and robots*. HarperCollins.

McGrath, R. G. (2013). *The end of competitive advantage: How to keep your strategy moving as fast as your business*. Harvard Business Review Press.

OECD. (1997). *The measurement of scientific and technological activities, proposed guidelines for collecting and interpreting technological innovation data*. Organization for Economic Cooperation and Development.

OWH (2016a). *Preparing for the future of artificial intelligence.* Retrieved April 20, 2019, from https://obamawhitehouse.archives.gov/sites/default/files/whitehouse_files/microsites/ostp/NSTC/preparing_for_the_future_of_ai.pdf.

OWH (2016b). *The national artificial intelligence research and development strategic plan.* Retrieved April 16, 2016, from https://www.nitrd.gov/PUBS/national_ai_rd_strategic_plan.pdf.
Parthasarthy, R., & Hammond, J. (2002). Product innovation input and outcome: moderating effects of the innovation process. *Journal of Engineering and Technology Management, 19*, 75–91.
Patterson, W., & Ambrosini, V. (2015). Configuring absorptive capacity as a key process for research intensive firms. *Technovation, 36-37*, 77–89.
Roodman, D. (2009). How to do Xtabond2: An introduction to difference and system GMM. *Stata Journal, 9*(1), 86–136.
Roos, G. (2015). Servitization as innovation in manufacturing: A review of the literature. In: *The handbook of service innovation* (pp. 403-435). London: Springer.
Rosenthal, S. R. (1992). *Effective product design and development.* Irwin.
Rowley, J. (2011). Should your library have an innovation strategy? *Library Management, 32*(4/5), 251–265.
Russell, S. J., & Norvig, P. (2016). *Artificial intelligence: A modern approach.* Pearson Education Limited.
Schumpeter, J. A. (1934). *The theory of economic development.* Harvard University Press.
Shi, X. A., Li, L. S., Cheng, Z. H., & Liu, J. (2018). Impact analysis of "internet+" on the value-chain improvement of China's manufacturing. *Studies in Science of Science, 36*(08), 1384–1394.
Smith, A. (1776). *The wealth of nations, Books I-III, (1986 printing).* Penguin Books.
Smith, W. K., & Tushman, M. L. (2005). Managing strategic contradictions: A top management model for man-aging innovation streams. *Organization Science, 16*(5), 522–536.
Stock, G. N., Greis, N. P., & Fischer, W. A. (2002). Firm size and dynamic technological innovation. *Technovation, 22*, 537–549.
Sun, Z., Xiao, L. P., & Liu, L. H. (2017). The changes of industrial ownership structure and innovation: Is the state-owned enterprise dominant in favor of innovation? *Nankai Economic Studies, 2017*(06), 3–19.
Tao, X., Zhang, Y., & Ren, X. B. (2019). AI from a global perspective: Trends, impacts, and challenges. *Competitive Intelligence, 15*(03), 2–11.
Trajtenberg, M. (2018). AI as the next GPT: A political-economy perspective. NBER working paper no. 24245.
Vaughan, J. (2013). *Technological innovation: perceptions and definitions.* ALA TechSource, a publishing unit of the American Library Association.
Wang, L. J., & Wang, Q. L. (2019). Study on the relationship of input and output of re-innovation after digesting the introduced technology in high-tech industry: An empirical study based on different industry data. *China Soft Science, 01*, 184–192.
Wang, R., Yan, B., & Deng, W. G. (2010). The impact of FDI on the independent innovation capability of Chinese indigenous industries: From the perspective of industrial linkages. *China Industrial Economics, 11*, 16–25.
Wang, Z. H., & Yang, Z. (2017). Thoughts on artificial intelligence technology research and future intelligent information service system. *Telecommunications Science, 33*(05), 1–11.
Weitzman, M. L. (1998). Recombinant growth. *Quarterly Journal of Economics, 113*(2), 331–360.
WH (2018). Retrieved April 16, 2019, from https://www.fedscoop.com/white-house-artifical-intelligence-committee-kratsios/.
Woodridge, J. M. (2002). *Econometric analysis of cross section and panel data.* The MIT Press.
Wu, D., Rosen, D. W., Wang, L., & Schaefer, D. (2015). Cloud-based design and manufacturing: A new paradigm in digital manufacturing and design innovation. *Computer-Aided Design, 59*, 1–14.
Xi, J. P. (2017). Retrieved April 16, 2019, from http://www.gov.cn/zhuanti/2017-10/27/content_5234876.htm.
Yi, J., Hong, J., & Hsu, W. C. (2017). The role of state ownership and institutions in the innovation performance of emerging market enterprises: Evidence from China. *Technovation, 2017*, S016649721730247X.

Zhang, Y. C., & Li, X. T. (2015). Measurement of technological innovation efficiency and its influencing factors in China's high-tech transformation of traditional industries: An empirical analysis based on the transcendental logarithmic stochastic frontier model. *Technology. Economics, 34*(03), 18-26+111.

Zhou, J. (2012). Digitization and intelligentization of manufacturing. *China Mechanical Engineering, 23*(20), 2398–2400.

Chapter 6
Market-Sensing and Market-Reaching Capabilities

Jeffrey Yi-Lin Forrest, Abdykappar Ashimov, Zaiwu Gong, Louie Ren, Yuriy Borovskiy, Edward Scott, Shahriar Gias, and Gerardo Eloy Soto Ruiz

Abstract This chapter, which is mainly based on Forrest et al. (Review of Economic and Business Studies 13(2):53–76, 2020a) and Forrest et al. (Pennsylvania Economic Review 28(1):17–42, 2021), studies the concepts of market-sensing capabilities and market-reaching capabilities. For the former concept, this chapter studies its impact on a company from the perspective of market competition. Then it looks at, as a case analysis, sources of profits within a slow growth industry. As a second case analysis, results, developed in this chapter, are employed to reveal how a company can formulate effective customer value propositions (CVPs). For the latter concept, the focus is given to CVPs since they represent the key for a startup to be launched and foundation for an existing company to direct its business efforts. However, as of the present day, no systematic theory exists regarding how an effective CVP can be potentially formulated and strategically employed in real life. As a matter of fact, the very concept of CVP is still not properly defined; although the term has been widely used in the literature, it is only nonchalantly tossed around. So, considering CVPs' importance in the area of marketing, this chapter attempts to lie down the first step toward the development of a general theory of customer value propositions.

Jeffrey Yi-Lin Forrest (Department of Accounting Economics Finance, Slippery Rock University, Slippery Rock, PA, USA; Email: Jeffrey.forrest@sru.edu), Abdykappar Ashimov (Center of Parametric Control, Kazakh National Research Technical University named after K. Satpayev, Almaty, Kazakhstan; Email: ashimov37@mail.ru), Zaiwu Gong (College of Management Science and Engineering, Nanjing University of Information Science and Technology, Nanjing, China; Email: zwgong26@163.com), Louie Ren (School of Business Administration, University of Houston—Victoria, Victoria, TX, USA; Email: ren800us@yahoo.com), Yuriy Borovskiy (Center of Parametric Control, Kazakh National Research Technical University named after K. Satpayev, Almaty, Kazakhstan; Email: yuborovskiy@rambler.ru), Edward Scott (Department of Accounting Economics Finance, Slippery Rock University, Slippery Rock, PA, USA; Email: edward.scott@sru.edu), Shahriar Gias (Department of Management and Marketing, Slippery Rock University, Slippery Rock, PA, USA; Email: shahriar.gias@sru.edu), and Gerardo Eloy Soto Ruiz (Marketing Department, Autonomous University of the West, Sinaloa, Mexico; Email: Lic.GerardoSR@hotmail.com) are equally contributed to this chapter.

J. Y.-L. Forrest, *Systemic Principles of Applied Economic Philosophies II*,
Translational Systems Sciences 39, https://doi.org/10.1007/978-981-99-7939-4_6

This chapter shows, among others, that (1) the capability of market sensing permits a company to classify customers into various classes, (2) it lowers operational costs while increasing expected profits, (3) the profit of a company within such an industry that experiences slow growth can grow only through a combination of raising unit price and lowering unit cost, (4) how market knowledge and its innovative understanding can potentially lead to the formulation of effective CVPs, (5) an effective CVP stands for a tool of value creation and capture for a company to employ readily and strategically; (6) when an adopted CVP is effective; and (7) how a company can actually deliver promises by materializing its CVP. At the chapter end, provided are some recommendations for practical applications and additional issues for future research.

Keywords Customer relations · Customer value propositions · General-purpose resources · Margin growth · Market-level growth · Outside-in approach · Profit potentials · Stagnant industries

6.1 Introduction

It is widely recognized that market sensing and market reaching, particularly customer value propositions (CVPs), are important capabilities for a company to effectively organize itself (Webster, 2002), survive and succeed in increasingly fast-evolving markets (Day, 1994; Forrest et al., 2017; McGrath, 2013). It is on specific understandings of market signals and effective CVPs that an enterprise creates values for customers and captures values from the market (Forrest & Liu, 2022; Payne & Frow, 2005). However, the existent literature on CVPs is still mostly on the stage of how to define the concept of CVPs (Payne et al., 2017) while that on market sensing points to inconsistent findings. For example, Ardyan (2016) finds that such capability does not have any positive effect on companies' profitability, and Lindblom et al. (2008) reveal some effect but not significant. In terms of its impacts on the quality of market entry and the creation of knowledge, scholars find the capability has either some positive or quite significant impacts (Sugiyarti & Ardyan, 2017; Alshanty & Emeagwali, 2019). Hence, the objective of this chapter, which is mainly based on Forrest et al. (2020a, 2021), is to address the following natural question while possibly improving the situation in the development of the theory and application of CVPs: What do these inconsistent empirical results on market-sensing mean in theory and in practice?

As discussed above, the objective of this chapter is both theoretically and practically important. For example, for either a manager or an entrepreneur, knowing the future direction of consumer demands is essential for a firm to plan itself strategically. It is especially so for the current landscape of business where once sustainable competitive advantages have become transient (McGrath, 2013). To potentially achieve the objective given above, this chapter attempts to adopt unconventional methodologies. The logic behind this attempt is that the existent literature is frequently empirical, and in many circumstances, inconsistencies and contradictory discoveries are simply results of the tools of analysis employed (Einstein, 1997). Additionally, beyond attempting to accomplish the objective above, this chapter also enables us, as case studies, to look at profit opportunities in stagnant industries without much market growth and show how market knowledge and relevant innovative understanding of the knowledge can assist a company to construct effective CVPs.

The rest of this chapter is organized as follows: Section 6.2 looks at the relevant literature. Section 6.3 explores issues of market-sensing capabilities. Section 6.4 studies why CVPs should be seen as a market-reaching capability. Section 6.5 investigates customer relations and crafts of CVPs, as individual cases. Then, this chapter concludes in Section 6.6.

6.2 Literature Review

This chapter touches on and contributes to three literature areas: the concept of market-sensing capabilities and related studies, profit opportunities within a stagnant industry, and the development of CVPs. First, investigations on market-sensing capabilities have revealed inconsistent findings due to the empirical nature of these works. In particular, it is found (Bharadwaj & Dong, 2014) that for a company to synchronize with market change and deliver superior value to consumers, its learning of the market signals should cover all customers, which is a statistically and practically impossible task, while market-sensing capability is shown (Ardyan, 2016; Lindblom et al., 2008) to have neither positive nor significant effect on the profitability of firms. To link market-sensing capability and firm performance, Bayighomog Likoum et al. (2018) propose an empirically research agenda, and it is confirmed (Alshanty & Emeagwali, 2019) that market-sensing capability does have a positive effect on knowledge creation for small and medium sized enterprises. Contributing to this literature, at the same time when it avoids all constraints of statistics- and anecdote-based approaches, this chapter demonstrates that market-sensing capability actually empowers a company to identify and better understand target customers; it helps lower the average costs of business operation; and it increases expected profits.

As for the studies on the profitability in stagnant industries, our literature search points to only limited number of works. Even so, each of these works examines a particular industry or market. In particular, Ferber and Schlappa (2016) show how brownfield land can be managed more effectively and sustainably by using good practices and a model for the purpose of facing the challenge of stagnant European urban land markets. Tournois (2016) examines how a breakthrough product in the cosmetics market, the BB cream, led to fruitful economic growth. By overviewing the geography of the seaweed hydrocolloid industry, Porse and Rudolph (2017) provide several industry-wide suggestions. By looking at challenges facing small-scale furniture productions in Jepara, Indonesia, Clements et al. (2019) are able to evaluate the association of regional producers. Through focusing on stagnant or low-productivity-growth U.S. industries, Le et al. (2020) inspect the financial development and productivity growth of member firms in these industries. Different from these existing works on specific industries, this chapter is able to establish results with broad-range applicability to many industries that lack market-level growth.

Our literature search found that studies on the formulation of CVPs are mostly oriented toward applications while producing nothing about the effectiveness of CVPs except a few remotely related publications. For example, processes and tools are developed (Osterwalder et al., 2014) to help design and produce products that actually sell and generate sales for companies. Applying such processes and tools to financial planning leads to a framework of CVP development (Lecours, 2017). It is recommended (Wouters et al., 2018) that startups construct two sequential value propositions so that the first one demonstrates superior values created for customer firms and the second one on values that are captured by customer firms. In particular, the first proposition details the innovative offering, and the second one leveraging assistance. By employing the so-called service-dominant logic, four principles are developed (Kowalkowski, 2011) based on the literature for the purpose of guiding a company to uncover market opportunities for itself.

Regarding the few remotely relevant publications on the effectiveness of CVPs, Terho et al. (2012) theorize value-based selling as an operative sales tactic in product markets. Eggert et al. (2018) argue that the literature on value has advanced from an emphasis on exchanges of resources and value in exchange to that on integration of resources and value in use by clearly distinguishing value in exchange and value in use. By recognizing a CVP for the sharing economy business model, Zhang et al. (2019) are able to compare competitive advantages of different CVPs in such economies. By looking at tourist enterprises, Butler et al. (2019) suggest counterparts to the prevalent business models to realize sustainability and to create value for communities. By specifically examining hospitality companies, Shulga and Busser (2019) study in which way and why customers receive willingly these companies' value propositions. Enriching these literatures, this chapter looks at, among others, how market knowledge can assist the creation of effective CVPs, why a creative comprehension of market invitations is fundamentally important in the creation of effective CVPs, and under what conditions an adopted CVP becomes effective.

To summarize, this chapter augments the literature in the following three ways: (1) it clears inconsistencies in relevant empirical findings, (2) it offers conclusions generally applicable to various markets when stated conditions are met, and (3) it points to the importance of market knowledge and its innovative understanding in the formulation of effective CVPs.

In the rest of this chapter, by proposition it stands for one of the following two unrelated situations. First, it means a statement, which is numerically labeled, such as Proposition 1, Proposition 2, ..., that is arguably true based on logical reasoning initiated on some preliminarily true beginnings. In such a statement, there is always an if-condition, either explicitly given or not within the proposition, followed by a conclusion. And the if-condition sometimes can also be written as an assumption. Second, a proposition stands for a particular selling point or offer as well investigated in the scholarly works of and employed practically in the context of marketing. Examples for this end include the unique selling proposition (Reeves, 1961), the emotional selling proposition (Lindstrom, 2005), customer value proposition (Payne et al., 2017), etc.

6.3 Market-Sensing Capabilities

As the title suggests, this section investigates the general characteristics of a firm's market-sensing capability. It consists of two subsections with the first one revealing the essence and practical meanings of such capability. And, the second subsection addresses the question about how a firm could potentially lift its performance in an industry that has no market-level growth.

6.3.1 The Importance of Market-Sensing

To theoretically answer this question, consider an oligopoly market of free competition, served by n companies, where $n = 1, 2, 3, \ldots$ is a natural number. Assume that this market is only operationally affected by the forces of demand and supply, while the demand and supply are functions of consumers' forever-evolving preferences and tastes. Because technology influences the equilibrium between market demand and supply, this assumption indirectly implies that technological advances do impact the market competition.

For the sake of convenience of communication, assume that in the said marketplace the incumbent companies provide their horizontally differentiated offers such that each of them offers only one product. And each incumbent company is fully supported by its loyal customers as long as the company's price is not more than their reservation price. To this end, consumers' forever-evolving preferences and tastes may practically turn once loyal customers into switchers who purchase from the company which offers the best value. The very presence of switchers indicates that some customers in the marketplace are not totally satisfied with any of the available products.

For switchers, the assumption that they make purchases only from the company that offers the best price means the best price per unit value, because in real life no two products in the marketplace are perfectly substitutable for each other. So, to compare the prices of two non-substitutable products, one can simply compare their prices of corresponding unit values. In the rest of this chapter, collectively, the totality of all switchers is referred to as the consumer surplus in the marketplace. So, other than trying to keep their corresponding loyal customers, the incumbent companies compete with each other over the consumer surplus by using pricing strategies.

In terms of the incumbent companies' decision-making, assume that the managers know how others price their products so that they all set their prices to achieve Nash equilibrium. To do this, the managers provide their best responses through pure self-analysis.

The competitive dynamics of this market is well illustrated by Theorem 4.1 from Chap. 4. For the sake of convenience and self-containment of this chapter, let us restate that theorem as follows in non-technical terms for the convenience of the potential audience of this chapter.

Theorem 6.1 In Nash equilibrium, if the proportion of consumer surplus in the oligopoly market defined above is greater than the percentage magnitude of the smallest loyal-consumer base of the incumbent companies, then at least one company can profitably enter the market with its substitute offering so that the expected aggregate profit of all entrants can be potentially greater than that of the incumbent with the smallest base of loyal consumers.

By market-sensing capability, it means such a capability with which a company can acquire an innovative understanding of market signals. Speaking differently, market-sensing capability assists a company to acquire its particular understanding about customers, competitors, the supply-chain ecosystem, and a much broader market environment. This definition of market-sensing capability generalizes that given by Day (1994). It is also different from that given by Lindblom et al. (2008) so that other than sensing the market, this definition is not concerned with employing any innovative understanding of the market to plan for subsequent actions.

Examining this concept of market-sensing capability in light of Theorem 6.1 produces the following result.

Proposition 6.1 If a company possesses a superb market-sensing capability, then it is capable of

1. locating market segments of either not adequately served or unsatisfied customers with currently existing market offers and
2. capturing market insights that help lower average business costs by adopting appropriate technologies, acquiring and deploying resources, etc., to satisfy evolving demands and to take advantage of prospective opportunities.

Conclusion (1) follows directly from Theorem 6.1, where the market surplus is made up of both not adequately served and unsatisfied customers. Because customers' preferences and needs constantly evolve, presently happy customers can become either unsatisfied or not adequately served so that they become switchers. So, if a company possesses a superb market-sensing capability, then it can identify existing and potential switchers. Now, Theorem 6.1 indicates that if switchers can be identified as the next target, then new competitions will germinate accordingly.

For conclusion (2), it means particularly (Theorem 6.1) that if the magnitude of the market surplus is greater than that of an incumbent company's loyal-customer base, then, jointly, the new entrants can potentially make more profits than some of the incumbent companies. For this situation to actually happen in real life, the entrants must have acquired something new, such as knowledge, technology, or managerial routine, that helps greatly lower their average costs of production. Instances of this "something" can be a new technology, a recently managerial breakthrough that drastically increases management efficiency, or a novel capability that helps improve the level of production. That is, with a superb market-sensing capability, a company is able to attain some of these listed resources to lower the average unit cost of its product.

In terms of relevant studies, Slater and Narver (2000) provide a specific case of conclusion (1), and Hult (1998) and Morgan et al. (2009a) derive particular cases of conclusion (2).

6.3.2 Markets that are Short of Market-Level Growth

The purpose of growing profit can generally be achieved by increasing sales revenue or margins or both. Other than the scenario (1), which is very rare in life (Dickson, 1992; Keats & Hitt, 1988) and happens when a market is expanding, for example, the market of personal computers in the 1970s (Sobel, 1999), the following proposition portrays the general profit picture of a company:

Proposition 6.2 When the focal company conducts business in an industry that has no market-level growth, its growth in profit can only be materialized by lifting margins, as actualized by a combination of either raising the unit price or lowering the unit cost.

To demonstrate this proposition, it suffices to show that the focal company cannot successfully improve its sales revenue. In general, sales revenue can be increased either by raising the sales of additional units to current customers or by obtaining new customers or both.

Assume that n companies, $n = 1, 2...$, jointly serve the industry (or market) in which the focal company conducts business with their mutually substitutable offers to their respective bases of loyal customers, if the prices are not more than their reservation prices. For these loyal customers, their demands are generally satisfied by their respective companies. Thus, it is nearly impossible to sell additional units of offered products to these customers except when the price per unit value is lowered substantially and/or the demand increases from these loyal customers.

As for selling additional units, enticing a loyal customer to purchase one additional unit of product is equivalent to acquiring a new customer. To obtain new customers, the incumbent companies need to compete by adjusting their per unit-value prices, because assumed is that they all serve the market with their mutually substitutable offers, including features and functionalities of products and follow-up services.

As noted by various scholars, the present world of business is commonly embraced with transient competitive advantages (McGrath, 2013) and customers' patience becomes much less than before (Forrest & Tallapally, 2018). Therefore, the product market contains an increasing number of discontent and underserved customers, partially due to their quickly changing preferences and tastes. No matter whether these customers were once loyal to their particular companies or not, they become potential new customers of the focal company. And, as adjustable per unit-value prices are used to entice new customers, they also need to be available to loyal customers in order to sustain their loyalty by making them feel they are treated fairly. Assume that the forever advancing technology makes all companies' pricing strategies known to each other. Hence, to possibly attract new customers, all competing companies play the Nash equilibrium through pure self-analysis.

By continuing the proof of Theorem 4.1 in Chap. 4, the following game-theoretical analysis shows that each incumbent company expects to make the same amount of profit as if it only sells to its loyal customers with the price at their reservation value, although it tries to attract as many new customers as possible. Therefore, this conclusion and the analysis above jointly imply that the focal company cannot expect to raise its sales revenue by increasing unit sales to either current customers, or acquiring new customers, or a combination of both. For establishing this conclusion, as part of the argument for Proposition 6.2, the following looks at game-theoretical details.

In the previous set-up, all competing companies are identical, because their individually different boundary conditions can be normalized as in the proof of Theorem 4.1. Therefore, there is no pure strategy Nash equilibrium (Narasimhan, 1988; Forrest et al., 2017), for details, see Chap. 4 and all the symbols used below are the same as those in the proof of Theorem 4.1. In order to compute for a symmetric mixed strategy Nash equilibrium, let $F_i(P)$ be the price distribution of company i, $i \in \{1, 2, \ldots, n\}$. Then, company i's objective is to maximize the following function by choosing appropriate F_i:

$$\begin{aligned} E(\Pi_i) &= \int_{-\infty}^{\infty} \left\{ uP + \prod_{j \neq i}^{m} [1 - F_k(P)] vP \right\} dF_i(P) \\ &= \int_0^1 \left\{ uP + \prod_{j \neq i}^{m} [1 - F_k(P)] vP \right\} dF_i(P) \end{aligned} \tag{6.1}$$

where $E(\Pi_i)$ stands for company i's expected profit for all possible pricing strategies, and all other symbols are the same as those defined and normalized in the proof of Theorem 4.1. The reason why the upper and lower limits of the integral are changed, respectively, from the initial $+\infty$ and $-\infty$ to 1 and 0 is that when $P < 0$ (= the cost of production) or when $P > 1$ (= reservation price), the profits are zero.

Company i can readily earn its expected amount of profit u by charging its loyal customers the reservation price, which is normalized to 1. However, Theorem 6.1 implies that it cannot simply do so; otherwise, new competitions might invade its market territory. That is, to potentially maximize its profit and to protect its market territory, each incumbent company has to adjust price P to absorb as many switchers as possible as new customers so that the consumer surplus can be potentially exhausted. Also, no company is motivated and incentivized to price its product below $u/(u + v)$, because doing so will yield less profit than u despite of attracting all market surplus, because $uP + vP \geq u \rightarrow P \geq u/(u + v)$. Solving the following equilibrium indifference condition for company i

$$u \times P + \prod_{j \neq i}^{n} [1 - F_k(P)] v \times P = u \times 1, \frac{u}{u+v} \leq P \leq 1, i = 1, 2, \ldots, n, \tag{6.2}$$

produces the following symmetric equilibrium price distribution:

$$F(P) = F_i(P) = F_j(P) = 1 - \left[\frac{(1-P)u}{P(1-nu)}\right]^{\frac{1}{n-1}}, \frac{u}{u+v} \leq P \leq 1, \tag{6.3}$$

So that $F(u/(u + v)) = 0$ and $F(1) = 1$. So, the expected profit of each incumbent company is equal to

$$\begin{aligned} E(\Pi) &= \int_{-\infty}^{+\infty} \left\{ uP + \prod_{j \neq i}^{m} [1 - F_k(P)] vP \right\} dF(P) \\ &= \int_{\frac{x}{x+y}}^{1} u dF(P) = uF(P)|_{\frac{u}{u+v}}^{1} = u. \end{aligned} \tag{6.4}$$

In other words, in Nash equilibrium of the symmetric mixed strategy, the expected profit of each incumbent company does not vary and is equal to that it can readily earn from its loyal customers, although these incumbents try to obtain as many new customers as possible.

Proposition 6.3 When a company does business in such an industry that experiences no market-level growth, its growth in profit from expanding sales revenue and that from margins, two basic components that drive a company's profit, do not ordinarily appear simultaneously.

To see the argument for this proposition, first examine what resource stands for. Specifically, it represents an asset a company possesses, which is either tangible or not (Harmancioglu et al., 2009) and can be employed to carry out the strategies adopted by the company (Barney & Arikan, 2001). In other words, a resource is a thing that a company can mobilize to achieve its corporate objectives through implementing its adopted strategies. It can take different forms, which can be, for example, physical, financial, informational, intellectual, or organizational.

Without loss of generality, each company can be identified with its unique system of resources (Barney & Hesterly, 2012; Peteraf & Barney, 2003), consisting of a set resources and a set of relations that associate the resources in ways that are unique to the company. Such identification is unique, because, for instance, among other factors each company has its own unique set of human resources and particular ways to utilize these human resources. Therefore, the assumption given in the proposition indicates that

1. If a company desires to either maintain the current level of or improve its sales revenue, it has to increase the number of units of product sold to existing customers and/or to acquire new customers. For details, see the argument and analysis of Proposition 6.2.
2. If the company plans to improve its margins, it has to raise the price for each unit sold, lower unit cost, or use a combination of these options.

For the accomplishment of item (1), Proposition 6.2 implies that other than lifting sales revenue, the situation will be more about maintaining the level of the sales revenue. So, the company has to assign specific resources to the exploitation of the market value of their existing offers. As for the accomplishment of item (2), the company's resources need to be classified into two classes: (i) one useful for the exploration of incremental improvements of the existing market offers and (ii) the other for the production of completely new offers that feature more use values to customers than the currently available ones. Note that resources tenaciously adopted to accomplish (i) and those for (ii) do not generally work well together (McGrath, 2013), since they aim at achieving inconsistent goals. At the same time, there are common resources that can be either deployed easily or needed to realize different business goals. Examples of such common resources include, but not limited to, networks that lead to information sharing, risk taking, and adoption of innovations (Dutta et al., 1999).

Let the set of resources that lead to the realization of goal (i) and the set of those that help with that of goal (ii) be denoted as X and Y, respectively. Assume that the sets X and Y do not include any general-purpose resources so that X and Y are mutually exclusive. Then when resources from X and those from Y interact, they will likely produce unwanted outcomes. In other words, the profit generated from sales revenue and that from margins do not generally increase simultaneously, because resources in X and those in Y tend to produce neutralizing or adverse effect(s). Figure 6.1 depicts the situation discussed here, where the collection of resources exclusively developed for business goal (i) and that for (ii) do not overlap. Additionally, resources available for general purposes can be deployed repeatedly to attend varying, even inconsistent purposes.

In terms of the literature, various scholars, such as Markman and Gartner (2002) and Steffens et al. (2009), have confirmed different specific versions of the general result stated in Proposition 6.3.

What is stated in Proposition 6.3 raises the following practical challenges to decision-making managers:

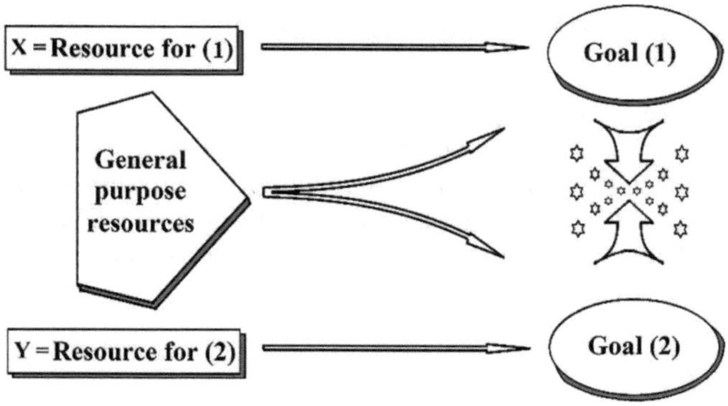

Fig. 6.1 Separation of available resources

- What could and should they do when it becomes clear that the current competitive advantage is eroding, especially, when the situation is only clear to themselves?
- How could and should their organizations be restructured in such a way that they can concurrently uncouple the current advantage and mobilize resources, either existing or newly acquired, into the development of the next perceived advantage?

To illustrate these challenges, let us examine the well-known American media-services provider and production company, named Netflix. As a co-founder, chairman and CEO of Netflix during the mid-2000s, Wilmot Reed Hastings recognized from the success of YouTube that the preferred method for users to access contents would be streaming so that Netflix's DVD business would soon be obsolete and no longer be the core of the company's future.

Based on this creative realization of the market trend, which was most advanced in time among all rivals, Qwickster, a spinoff of Netflix, was formed to continuously exploit the company's successful DVD services by maximizing the underlying cash flow for the duration of the expected decline of these services. At the same time, the leadership of Netflix looked to the future. Its job was to manage rapid development of and access to digital content. To minimize potentially adverse effects between the exploitation of the continuing DVD services and the exploration of newly discovered opportunities, Netflix operated intelligently into two independent business directions.

In terms of Proposition 6.3 and business operational processes, Netflix decision makes practical sense. However, because no one else at the time in the marketplace saw the coming of the expected new era, many customers became enraged by the switch. They were infuriated by the potential that they might have to double their effort when they desired to access contents in both formats and in two different places. Additionally, cable television, satellite dish services, and other content providers experienced growing wary of Netflix's disruptive nature. See McGrath (2013) for more in-depth discussion of this case study.

6.4 CVPs: A Market-Reaching Capability

This section studies market-reaching capability by focusing on customer value propositions (CVPs). It is made up of two subsections. The first one explains why CVPs are an effective tool for a firm to use in its efforts of value creation and value capture. The second subsection inspects the effectiveness of a CVP through examining three different issues—value- and differentiation-based CVPs, jointly created CVPs and making adopted CVPs effective internally.

6.4.1 CVPs: A Tool for Value Creation and Capture

By a CVP, it means a business tool (Payne et al., 2017) that an organization employs to strategically facilitate communication regarding its ability to share resources and offer a superior value package to targeted customers. A CVP is said to be effective to a company, provided that by fulfilling the promises of the CVP the company captures additional net profit when compared to before the CVP is developed and implemented by the company.

To study the effectiveness of a CVP, let us first imagine that a focal company develops and implements a CVP within an oligopoly market of free competition. Assume that the market of concern is a system that is closed from or free of any interference from its environmental factors other than forces of supply and demand. That is, the market's free competition is not influenced in any way by factors of any foreign market beyond supply and demand. Assume that there is a fixed number of incumbent companies that serve the focal market with their horizontally differentiated offerings.

To make the setting here as close to real-life situation as possible, assume that each incumbent company has successfully developed a base of loyal consumers; each of these loyal consumers makes purchases only from the company she is loyal to if the company's price is not more than her reservation price. Opposite to loyal consumers, there are also consumers in the marketplace who purchase only from one of those companies that offer the lowest price. The existence of these switchers reflects how consumer's preference and taste evolve unremittingly over time so that once satisfied consumers might very well become discontent. Collectively, this chapter will refer to these switchers as the consumer surplus in the marketplace.

In terms of CVPs, Theorem 6.1 means that seeing the existence of a good magnitude of consumer surplus, a visible market invitation for new innovations and additional competition, companies, incumbent or not, need to creatively formulate the knowledge regarding what the switchers truly look for. For example, their indeterminacy from whom they make their purchases can be seen as a sure sign that these consumers are not pleased with the available offers in the marketplace. However, due to whatever reason, such as necessities of living, these people have to make purchases from one incumbent or another. Hence, companies in such a situation need to mobilize their learning and absorption capabilities to formulate their appropriate CVPs in order to clear their directions of next phase of development.

The definition of CVPs, as initially phrased by Payne et al. (2017), characterizes the concept from four different angles: (i) a CVP is a communication device, (ii) it promises resource sharing, (iii) it identifies targeted customers, and (iv) it pinpoints to the superior value of a company's offer from those of competitors. The first angle shows the functionality of a CVP that brings to the targeted customers the aware of the value a particular offer provides, along with such a message about how the customers can help improve the economic, functional, emotional, and symbolic features of the offer. The said value that is to be communicated here is initially within the imagination of the supplier, as focused on in early studies (e.g., Kowalkowski, 2011), surely needs to be passed on to consumers, as noted by Rintamaki et al. (2007) in the retailing realm. Beyond delivering underlining value to targeted customers, this definition of CVP also stresses the involvement of customers in collaborations. Since a company's effort of creating value can be greatly enhanced by the first-hand consumer knowledge, how to communicate customer value has been seen as a priority of research by marketers (Marketing Science Institute, 2010, 2014).

Let us now pay our attention to how the concept of CVPs can be naturally and intuitively seen through the lens of systems thinking and logic. The importance of such lens or intuition cannot be overlooked if we examine knowledge exploration historically. For example, all currently widely employed statistics-based and calculus-based methods in the business area are 100% developed on the intuition of the Cartesian coordinate system (Kline, 1972), although the majority of published works in business disciplines avoid mentioning the geometric intuitions underlying their methods employed. For our purposes here, the systems thinking and logic will help us reason logically based on an intuitively visible "playground," as in the cases of how statistics-based and calculus-based methods are developed in the first place (Forrest, 2018, pp. 187–191).

As discussed in Chap. 1, by system, it means a whole composed of some objects and some relations that associate the objects in specific ways. In real life, such a whole emerges exactly due to specified relations (Lin, 1999). Hence, it is readily for anyone to see that business entities are systems, and that studies in economics and business are mostly about the evolutions, structures, and interactions of different economic systems (e.g., Porter, 1985). To help effectively investigate the evolution and interaction of systems (or organizations or structures), Lin (2009) introduces the yoyo model as an aid of intuition for researchers to figuratively imagine what might be happening. In particular, one can intuitively see the general input–output system as a multi-dimensional spinning entity. If that entity is imagined in the 3-dimensional space we live in, it would possess the structure shown in Fig. 6.2, as introduced in Chap. 1, quoted here for the sake of convenience. The input side sucks in "*things,*" such as information, investment, human talents, etc., in order to maintain the existence of the system. After having "processed" the "*things*" through the "neck,"

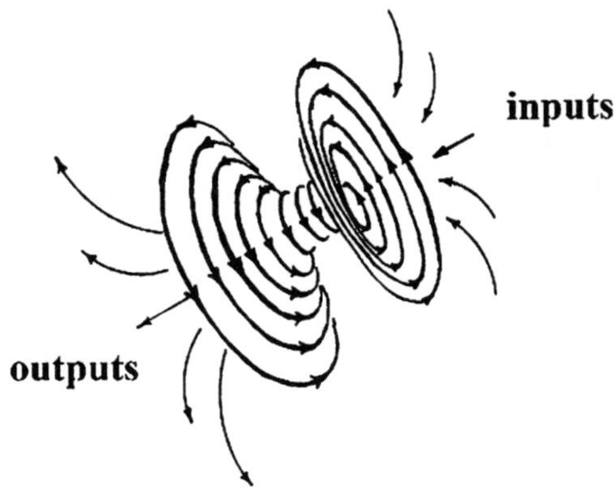

Fig. 6.2 Systemic intuition of a general input–output system

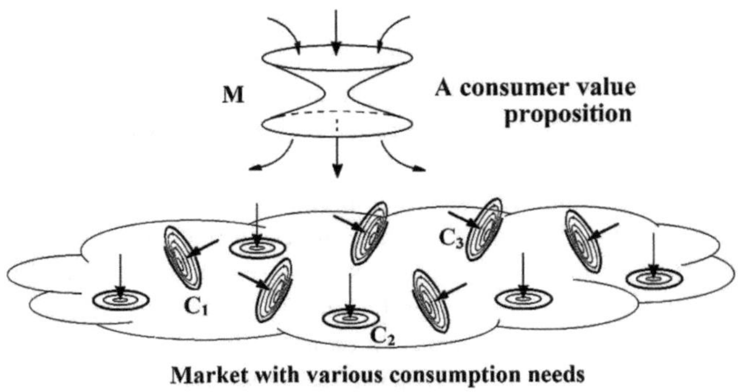

Fig. 6.3 An intuitive depiction of the concept of CVP

the entity gives off outputs, such as physical offers, services, informational goods, etc. The name "yoyo" comes from the general shape of this intuitive structure.

Now, if the concept of CVPs is seen through the lens of this yoyo model, a systemic intuition for this concept naturally emerges as that shown in Figure 6.3. In particular, the focal company is labeled and modeled by the yoyo structure M, which is also identified with the customer value proposition the company adopts. The input–output arrowed flows indicate the communication of the company with the customers in the marketplace, shown as small yoyo fields from the marketplace. Because of the alignment of their input–output flows with each other, the fields C_1, C_2, and C_3 are among the targeted customers of company M. The idea of resource sharing is implied by the fact that the input–output arrowed flows of company M, associated with those of targeted customers, help strengthen the flows of the yoyo fields of these customers. And the idea of superior value is depicted by the alignment of the yoyo field M with those of the targeted customers.

Other than the need for such an intuition, as discussed earlier, one benefit of exploiting such systemic modeling and intuition is that the model helps naturally combine disassociated discoveries into one organic whole of understanding. For example, the listed angles as emphasized by the concept of CVP have been in the past only occasionally while not concurrently dealt with by different studies (Ballantyne et al., 2011; Rintamaki et al., 2007). But now, with this yoyo model, they are all naturally and collectively shown in the systemic intuition given in Fig. 6.3.

The theoretical and practical importance of this systemic modeling of the concept of CVPs is the following, as shown by the discussions above:

Proposition 6.4 CVP provides not only a tool for a company to strategically create value for its targeted customers but also an approach for the company to tactically utilize to capture value.

6.4.2 *The Effectiveness of a CVP*

With the concept of CVP modeled systemically, the question of whether or not a specific CVP is practically effective can be naturally addressed. Once again, the effectiveness here means that a specific CVP actually produces additional profit, after deducting all the costs of developing and implementing the CVP, for a company beyond the case without the CVP.

6.4.2.1 Value- and Differentiation-Based CVPs

The following result outlines conditions under which an adopted CVP, which is developed to deliver superior value for customers and differentiation from competitors, is effective.

Proposition 6.5 If, as its marketing effort, a company formulates such a CVP that describes how it delivers superior value to the marketplace and how it differentiates itself from competitors, then the CVP's effectiveness is closely dependent on

- The magnitude of the market segment of customers who are discontented with the available offers in the marketplace;
- The potential for the proposed value to meet the demands of the discontented (or targeted) customers; and
- The efficiency the company communicates the particular CVP.

To see the truthfulness of this result, let us examine the listed conditions one by one. For the first condition, only with the existence of an appropriately large market segment of discontented customers, a company that aims at this market segment will have the potential of providing its offer at a high enough, as well as competitive enough, price over the cost to achieve appropriate profitability and growth (Theorem 6.1). Additionally, to catch the attention of the currently discontented customers, the adopted CVP of course has to contain the promise of delivering their expected benefits (the second condition) and only when the promised benefits of the CVP are efficiently communicated with the targeted customers (the third condition), the initial potential and promise will turn into a massive number of actual purchases. That is, only when promised benefits are well communicated along with competitive pricing and the existence of a sufficiently large segment of discontented customers, they can produce the desired level of profit and growth for the company. Systemically speaking, an effective CVP, as depicted in Fig. 6.3 as the yoyo body M, must be able to realistically line up with a solid base of many customer yoyo fields, such as the Cs in Fig. 6.3, in the marketplace in order to sustain itself and to potentially help the company to grow its level of profits.

To see how promises and relevant communications help a company succeed in the real-life business world, one only needs to look at IBM's past dominance in the area of general business computers until the Digital Equipment Corporation (DEC) appeared (Lanning & Michaels, 1988). In particular, IBM's computers were not superior products when compared to those offered by some other companies. At the same time, IBM's price was not competitive, either. However, IBM's earlier dominance relied on its reliability (promised value) and clear communication (the third condition) of this benefit to the targeted large clientele of customers (the first condition). However, when the promised benefits dissipated with the advancement of technology, in particular, when reliability became a nonissue, IBM's dominance in general business computers ended due to the reason that the company could not provide the emerging market demand for interconnectivity among offices and production facilities.

Next, let us look at an application of Proposition 6.5 to such an economic sector that its customers and market demands are more or less well-defined. Examples of such economic sectors include those that deliver necessities to satisfy the very basics of human living. For a company within such an economic sector, if it desires to generate extraordinary profits, it needs to develop and implement such a CVP that focuses on the delivery and efficient communication of distinguishingly superior value to customers, such as organic foods, green products, etc. To practically achieve this, the company needs to understand and stay in sync with customers' perspectives (Berry et al., 2002; Molineux, 2002; Smith & Wheeler, 2002) and use experiences (Lanning, 1998). To illustrate this end, let us, for example, consider a New Jersey-based commerce bank that attempted to make banking experiences fun so that customers would like to visit the bank's branch locations repeatedly. When a new branch just opened, fun-filled events, highlighting comedians, acrobats, foods, caricaturists, and others, were organized for an entire week as a way to advertise itself to the community and to attract potential customers. While both adults and children were attracted to the events, the bank was able to effectively communicate its superior value to customers—opening seven days a week and most branches operating until 8 pm each weekday, very different from other banks. Conversely, such efforts may not work out successfully. For example, Tandy Corp. tried in the 1990s to increase the profitability of its superstores in the area of consumer electronics by increasing the interaction between staff and customers. Although an approach similar to Disney's was employed, the effort did not work out successfully. See Morgan and Rao (2003) for the relevant details of these two examples.

From these two examples of very different outcomes, one has to wonder what is making the difference. Do the examples imply that Proposition 6.5 does not hold true generally? The answer to this question is NO. One important reason for the second example to not work out as expected is that there are not a segment of well-defined customers and clear demands in the economic sector of consumer electronics. In other words, consumer electronics is not among the necessities of human living. More generally, this economic sector does not have a well-defined market segment of discontented customers, condition 1 in Proposition 6.5.

6.4.2.2 Jointly Created CVPs

A CVP is said to be co-created by a company (or supplier) and customers, if both the company and customers, at least some of them, are involved in the development of the CVP so that the reciprocal benefits, potentially offered to and from the company and some customers, are known to the company and the customers. A co-created CVP generally addresses concerns of different stakeholders from both supply and demand sides, such as a company' resources, capabilities, and investors, and consumers' specific desires—social and environmental preferences. Such approach to developing CVPs, known as an outside-in approach (Day, 2011), can have not only the potential of developing an effective CVP but also practically establish and fortify an intimate relationship between a company and its major customers (Ballantyne, 2003). A good example of such an intimate relationship is the important associations between upstream suppliers and downstream complements in a supply-chain ecosystem (Adner et al., 2013).

Proposition 6.6 If a company (as a supplier) co-creates a CVP with some of its downstream customer firms so that the company's outputs are supplies of the latter firms, then the CVP's effectiveness to the supplier closely depends on one of the following two conditions:

- Collectively, the customer firms occupy a sufficiently large magnitude of dissatisfied customers with the offers currently available in the marketplace;
- The developed CVP is also attractive to other customer firms so that all interested customer firms collectively occupy a sufficiently large magnitude of dissatisfied customers with offers currently available in the marketplace.

Theorem 6.1 quite readily implies this proposition. Specifically, the supplier's economic fortune is clearly and closely dependent on how well its downstream customer firms do, which is also indicated by the definition of co-created CVPs. And, how well the downstream customer firms do can only be assured by the existence of a sufficiently large market segment of discontented customers with the offers available in the market (Proposition 6.5). Likewise, this same logic also holds true for the second condition with the following key point: the market's depth or the purchasing power is sufficient to support the supply-chain ecosystem, within which the particular supplier is in some sense the upper most player, Fig. 6.4. In

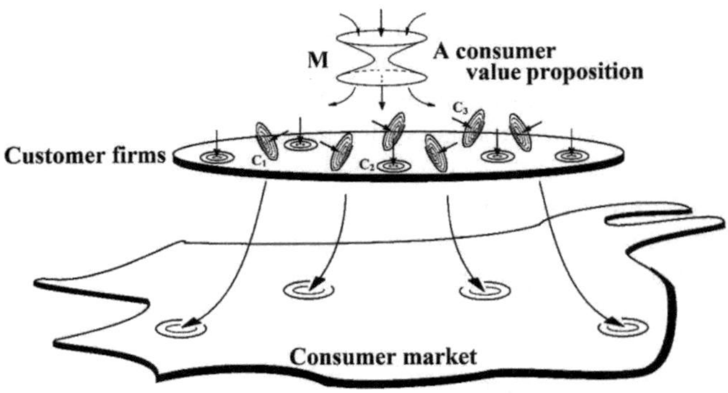

Fig. 6.4 Consumer market depth of a CVP

particular, the firms the particular CVP M attracts, such as those labeled as C_1, C_2, and C_3, have to be well supported by a large number of consumers in the ultimate product market. Without such a sufficiently large number of such consumers, the focal supplier firm cannot be financially sustained. This recognition about the market condition of course has to be considered naturally in the development of the co-created CVP M.

In terms of practical applications, collectively Propositions 6.4 and 6.5 emphasize that if a company wants its adopted CVP to be effective (or brings in the desired, elevated level of profit), it has to clearly communicate to the targeted customers its differentially promised delivery of superior value. Other than producing strong reverberation with the customers, the communication also needs to stress what benefits the targeted customers can expect to receive along with their related costs (Anderson et al., 2006; Rintamaki et al., 2007; Ulaga & Eggert, 2006). As the very principle underneath the concept of co-created CVPs, the company needs to distribute the created value appropriately across customer relations (Payne et al., 2017).

Another key consideration for the development of a CVP is that the underlying supply-chain ecosystem has to have the necessary context and capability to implement the eventually developed CVP. Without such consideration, it will be extremely difficult for a focal company to deliver the promised superior value, because the delivery of value depends on how well the entire supply-chain ecosystem can meet challenges brought on by the focal company and how the ecosystem's complementors can adequately afford the necessary infrastructure (Adner et al., 2013). For example, Theranos, a now-defunct health technology company, offers an excellent illustration to what is just discussed (Carreyrou, 2018). In particular, as the founder and CEO of the company since its inception in 2003, Elizabeth Holmes formulated her CVP for the company and the targeted consumers: with small amounts of blood pricked from fingertips, the company's small and automated devices can perform blood testing rapidly. The very idea Theranos effectively communicated was that the company had revolutionized blood testing that needed surprisingly small amounts of blood to produce a large number of test results. Since the promises, as described in the CVP and communicated to customers, were not truly delivered, the company started to fall in 2015. Various investigations into the company and its conducts exposed qualms about the company's CVP and whether or not Holmes misled investors and the government.

The US SEC in 2018 charged the company and Elizabeth Holmes of using false or exaggerated claims to mislead investors. And, Holmes was barred from serving any public company for ten years as an officer or director. The company's communication was extremely effective and successful during its rise from 2003 to 2014. It obtained the support of such influential people as Henry Kissinger, Hillary Clinton, George Shultz, and many others. However, the delivery of promised superior value did not materialize due to the reason that the imagined small, automated device was never successfully developed.

Other than pointing to where Theranos failed, this example also illustrates the importance of co-created CVPs with upstream suppliers in order to successfully build the vitally important device, for example. In other words, in the B2B market, the competitive environment really forces companies to develop their effective CVPs jointly with their upstream suppliers and downstream complementors. The reason is, as revealed by the case of Theranos, a creative understanding of a market invitation generally challenges suppliers technically to provide innovative supplies, and complementors to design and construct infrastructures that never existed before.

6.4.2.3 Making Adopted CVPs Effective Internally

As indicated above, such as the definition of CVPs, one reason a company desires to have an effective CVP is that it can attract prospects and retain customers by means of sharing resources and of delivering better value than any of the current and potential rivals. To actually accomplish this goal in real life, the company must introduce nontraditional operation processes (Davenport, 1993; McGrath, 2013) beyond established practice within the organization's domain and control. These new processes will need reconfiguration and rearrangement of related tasks and resources to deliver the promises contained in the adopted CVP. Naturally, the actual operation of these new processes will require the investment of resources, such as personnel, knowledge, networks, etc. Without such investment, the implemented new processes will not successfully commingle as new capabilities for the organization (Forrest et al., 2019).

For a CVP to be effective for a company, the company has to be capable of inculcating a market invitation into its organization and culture for the purpose of eventual introduction of new and innovative offers, such as products, services, or informational goods (Forrest et al., 2017). That is, an effective CVP directly reconfigures a company's business processes, organizational structure and culture that in turn contribute overtly to resource sharing and to the creation of promised superior value.

Each company represents a live system with different operational processes working simultaneously and interactively. An effective CVP assists a company with its design and introduction of innovatively new operational processes. To see how such an assistance practically works out, let us concentrate on a few macro-level processes underneath business tasks, which are basic, common as well as critical for achieving the goal of sharing resources and delivering superior value. To this end, the discussion above and the dependence of a firm's success on its supply-chain ecosystem (Adner et al., 2013) jointly imply that a company needs to successfully accomplish the following tasks:

1. Specify customer solution(s), either new or revamped, to meet the signaled market demand(s);
2. Acquire adequate supplies and make the desired offers; and
3. Fortify current networks of various stakeholders, such as customer firms and end users, and develop new associations.

Congruently, the company needs to create and manage the following three essential macro-level operating processes:

- management of customer solutions,
- management of the supply-chain ecosystem, and
- management of customer relations.

The first operating process emphasizes on innovatively interpreting the consumer surplus existing in the product marketplace and inventively advance answers to meet the market demand (Theorem 6.1). It is in this process, a potentially effective CVP is developed and adopted. Each advanced answer can be realistically challenging downstream complementors in terms of materialistically providing necessary infrastructures to help push the solution to reach the end users. The second operating process deals with the concrete production of the desired offer(s). It involves the effort of acquiring necessary supplies and that of bringing together supplies into imagined customer solution(s). The former step here can potentially represent technological challenges to upstream suppliers, while the latter step can be relatively easier because the relevant how-to information should have been considered in the step of advancing inventive answer(s). The third operating process handles various aspects of communication with customers identified when the CVP is initially developed and adopted. It also addresses potential prospects, such as the creation of market knowledge, maintenance and further development of customer relations, shaping market perception of the organization and its offers.

In real life, each of these macro-level operating processes consists of several micro-level processes (Day, 1994). In particular, each of these macro-level processes contains such next-level subordinate processes as human resource management, technology development, financial supervision, etc. The reason why these latter processes are seen as subordinate to the three macro-level ones is because when seen as independent processes, they only play their respective supporting roles for the macro-level processes.

Proposition 6.7 If a company desires to make its adopted CVP effective, it needs to saturate its managers' minds with the promises of the CVP, as well as to mobilize their supports toward adopting the relevant operating processes, necessary for the ultimate delivery of promises, no matter how unusual these processes might be.

Based on the definition of a CVP's effectiveness, for an adopted CVP to be effective to a company, the CVP needs to have a capability to help the company improve its efficiency with some parts of the afore-described macro-level operating processes. Specifically, the improvement needs to be visible with a reduction in costs, or an increase in productivity, or the production of new/original market offers, or a combination of these enhancements. However, as an input–output system, the very being and operation of a company tend to stay within the influence of the inertia of its past trajectory of development, as shown by the First Law on State of Motion, see Chap. 3 of this volume or Lin (2009). That is, for a meaningful improvement to appear in any part of the company's operating processes, the management of the company has to be acted upon by external force(s). To this end, the given setting of the proposition—a CVP has been adopted and the company wants to make it effective—means that there are indeed some market forces that have been acting on the managers of the company. These forces can be on developing market trend in terms of consumer preferences, a new advancement in technology, competitive pressures from rival companies, etc. Therefore, to materially promote necessary changes in the operation of the company, as indicated by the company's desire of making its CVP effective, managers at all levels have to both support and participate in the development and actual introduction of changes to the existent operating processes or of brand-new ones. That sanctions this proposition's conclusion.

6.5 Case Studies: Customer Relations and Crafts of CVPs

All propositions in the previous sections are derived on the bases of the rigor of game theory and the logical reasoning that is parallel to the one widely used in natural science and mathematics (Kline, 1972). The rigor plays the role of a solid foundation for the construction of the propositions, while the particular logical reasoning helps avoid limitations of data- and anecdote-based approaches. That explains the reason why these established propositions represent generally true conclusions unless the correspondingly stated assumptions are not satisfied. Contrary to this end, because the technique of hypothesis testing is widely employed in the literature, relevant empirical studies can provide only managerial suggestions. As a matter of fact, hypothesis testing stands for a statistics-based approach, very useful in terms of uncovering potential facts but not proving any fact (Forrest et al., 2020b).

This section, as an application, examines how the propositions developed earlier in this chapter can help establish results on how customer relationship management capability and profitability and the formulation of effective CVPs are related to one another. By the capability of customer relationship management (CRM) or CRM capability for short, it represents a company's capability that it enables the company to influence and control customer-level profits through

1. clearly classifying customers and prospects according to their profit potentials,
2. developing individually appropriate relationship with each echelon of customers and prospects, and
3. sustaining developed customer relations so that they are optimal based on the assessed profit potentials of the respective customer echelons.

This definition of CRM capabilities expresses the realization that beyond individual business transactions, it is these relationships that lead to profits for companies and satisfaction for customers (Verhoef, 2003), and that customers and potentials are not similarly attractive for a company to meet their needs profitably (Niraj et al., 2001).

Proposition 6.8 A company's CRM capability is positively correlated to the company's ability to generate profits from the growth of both sales' revenue and margins.

Let us see why this proposition is true from two angles: (1) sales revenue growth and (2) margin growth. As for (1), a company's CRM capability helps orient the company's effort toward the understanding of how customers and prospects can contribute to the overall profitability picture differently (Reinartz et al., 2005), before any of these people is converted into a switcher (Theorem 6.1). Hence, when a company is more capable of working with customer relationships, it will more adequately classify customers and prospects into multi-layered echelons of attractiveness so that it will be able to develop and manage relationships with the echelons corresponding to their individually varied levels of attractiveness. Specifically, at the high extreme on the attractiveness spectrum, a company will like to devote its valuable resources on the instigation and conservation of relationships with high-potential prospects and high-revenue-producing customers. And at the low extreme of the spectrum, without putting in any additional effort a company simply employs prices to enlarge its market territory by targeting switchers of the market (Theorem 6.1). Hence, one can expect that companies with stronger CRM capabilities generate more profits or at least maintain their profitability from customers of all different echelons of attractiveness.

At this junction, it is worth pointing out that there are such companies (Ryals, 2005) that only pay attention to and devote their efforts on high-potential prospects and highly profitable customers. For these companies, they tend to have fewer customers and generate less profits (Reinartz et al., 2005). To this end, one very good case that vibrantly demonstrates how such narrow-minded attempts can and do lead to disastrous outcomes is the story of Pan American World Airways (Sobel, 1999). In particular, the airline company mostly concentrated on lucrative international air traffic while ignoring the domestic market. Hence, when it suffered from skyrocketing energy prices and terrorist attacks, the company was wiped out as a major player in the air-travel industry. The very reason why such efforts of concentrating on high profile prospects and customers led to disastrous failures is the difficulty or impossibility of maintaining such relationships over relatively long periods of time, during which customers' needs and preferences evolve constantly.

Regarding (2), margin growth, a strong CRM capability assists a company to fine-tune its effort on how to position resources on the instigation and upkeep of appropriate relationships with prospects and customers of different echelons of attractiveness. When its knowledge and experience on prospects and customers of different attractiveness increase, a company is able to lower its service costs gradually over time (Reinartz & Kumar, 2000) while obtaining a rising level of customer retention and more experienced users of its market offers. All these improved operational efficiencies further lower the company's service cost over time (Ryals, 2005). Therefore, it can be seen that strongly CRM capable companies are generally able to increase their margins by continually lowering their service costs, as a result of appropriately allocating resources to prospects and customer of different attractiveness levels. Such allocation of resources consequently raises the level of satisfaction of customers in different echelons of attractiveness. When suitable relationships are upheld with those customers whose purchases are not affected merely by prices, companies with strong CRM capabilities are able to charge higher prices for their products (Cao & Gruca, 2005). So, Proposition 6.8 is supported.

In terms of the literature, this result is inconsistent with Morgan et al. (2009b). Specifically, these scholars hypothesized and empirically confirmed that a company's revenue growth rate is a decreasing function of the company's CRM capability, while its margin growth rate is an increasing function.

Market knowledge is a concept closely related to that of CRM capabilities. It refers to knowledge about market demand in terms of who customers and prospects are, what their needs in life are, what problems they face, whom competitors are, and what features their offers possess.

Proposition 6.9 As a market-based resource, market knowledge can be used to craft effective CVPs.

Indeed, market knowledge is a resource based on market(s), because the very existence of such knowledge depends on that of some market(s). To see why such knowledge can be employed to formulate effective CVPs, let us, respectively, treat a focal company and its customers and prospects as input–output systems in such a way that the mission of the company represents its CVP and market demands the desired inputs of the customers and prospects. Then when the CVP is communicated to the market, the communication helps associate the company's input–output flows with those of targeted customers and prospects in the market. In this systemic modeling, resource sharing is echoed in affiliated input–output flows of the company and the targeted customers and prospects. The concept of superior value is reflected in the alignment of these harmonious input–output flows, for details, see Fig. 6.5.

This systemic intuition demonstrates that if an adopted CVP is effective to a company, then the input–output flows of the company need to align with those of a sufficient number of customers and prospects. And, the company's market knowledge is intuitively seen as how the company understands the patterns of its rivals' input–output flows relative to the market and how the input–output flows of customers and prospects respond to the marketing efforts of these companies.

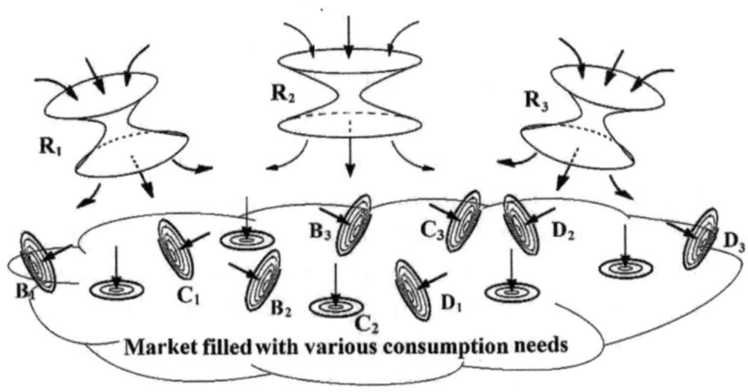

Fig. 6.5 Rivals and their market territories

Intuitively, in Fig. 6.5 three of the rivals of the focal company are shown as the input–output flows R_1, R_2, and R_3, respectively. The market territory of R_1 includes B_1, B_2, and B_3; that of R_2 contains C_1, C_2, and C_3; and that of R_3 has D_1, D_2, and D_3. In such setting, the focal company's market knowledge covers how R_1 and Bs associate with each other, that between R_2 and Cs, that between R_3 and Ds, and how these semi-separate territories interact with one another. When we say that the focal company possesses such market knowledge, it represents that this company knows how its rivals interact with their associates and customers and how these interactions do not meet the expectations of customers. Such knowledge can readily assist the focal company to discover market niche(s) that it can possibly fill based on its available resources and capabilities, and the niche(s) demonstrate which customers are not adequately satisfied by its rivals, how large such consumer surplus (Theorem 6.1) is, and what these discontent customers are longing for.

Discussions above collectively elucidate the reason why market knowledge is such a resource that it is market-based and that the focal company can utilize to formulate its effective CVP(s).

In terms of the relevant literature, Proposition 6.9 is different from what is confirmed by Kozlenkova et al. (2014) and also dissimilar to the statement that market knowledge is a resource for crafting CVPs (Payne et al., 2017). As a matter of fact, if one does not consider the effectiveness of CVPs, he can formulate CVPs without using any market information. Although Proposition 6.9 is different from these mentioned works, this chapter still likes to use this opportunity to honor these scholars: It is their pioneering work that eventually led to the development of this proposition.

Proposition 6.10 In terms of the formulation of effective CVPs, creative comprehension of market invitations is the key element.

Theorem 6.1 readily implies this conclusion. In particular, the market normally gestures the call for additional competition and innovation by showing a large consumer surplus. For the case when $n = 1$, that is when the market is monopolistic, rather than switchers in Theorem 6.1, the level of customer dissatisfaction and the magnitude of discontent customers are employed as signs of market invitation for new competition and innovation. In this case, a large host of producers potentially appear to answer the market call, depending on the relevant profit potential. Specifically, after sensing the market call and great profit potential, entrepreneurs with different background knowledge and experience proactively introduce their individually different versions of market offers to possibly satisfy the recognized customer demand. Hence, a different way to uncover a market opportunity is to discover where a producer surplus appears. In other words, for a CVP to be effective, it has to be an offspring of pioneering and wide-ranging understanding of market signals.

To help further comprehend this proposition, a real-life case of business from Ye et al. (2012) comes to mind.

In the northern part of the USA, there is a state university of over 29,000 students. They are mostly unmarried undergraduates and live on tight budgets. Because these students are young and physically active, most rental properties do not offer easily damaged laundry facilities to their student tenants. To fill this market need, many standalone laundromats appeared near the campus and compete for students' business by offering self-servicing, coin-operated laundry machines. And because of the limited amount of outdoor sunlight, as caused by the long and cold winters of the region, another successful business, targeting appearance-conscious college women, is indoor tanning salons.

Different from the laundromat services, which do not really differentiate themselves from each other than some minor variations, such as locations, indoor tanning salons compete for business by providing competitive prices and indoor experiences. That is, these two kinds of business, respectively, serve their individually different market needs, while customers move freely from one service location to another or depending on who is more competitive.

Recognizing innovatively the large magnitude of a consumer surplus (Theorem 6.1), two entrepreneurs creatively launched their independent coin-operated self-service laundry facility combined with indoor tanning service at one single location under the same roof. The innovativeness of this new business can be seen in the following two ways:

1. It saves students their otherwise unproductive and costly waiting time by concurrently completing two tasks—clothes washing and skin tanning.
2. It provides a natural opportunity and location for male and female students to develop relationships. Specifically, the apparent savings of time from doing two unrelated errands simultaneously attract greater participation of women in the business installment in general and the tanning service in particular. Such a greater number of women in the facility entices to the laundry service a much larger number of men who do not have any preference as to which laundromat to use.

As a consequence of this creative understanding of the market signal, the joined business is able to amass higher fees from the laundry service than other standalone laundromats. And, it endures the market competition of the tanning service.

Specifically, the female demand for the tanning service rises as a consequence of the heavy flow of male users of the laundry facility.

6.6 A Few Final Words

Consequent to the recognition of the importance of market-sensing and market-reaching in terms of company performance (Day, 1994; Forrest et al., 2017; Marketing Science Institute, 2010; McGrath, 2013), a number of scholars have contributed to the study of the concept of market-sensing and that of CVPs. However, the efforts on the former have led to inconsistent conclusions, while the latter is only seriously defined recently by Payne et al. (2017) without the needed theory of CVPs developed to offer practically applicable results. Hence, there is a need to clear the inconsistencies related to market-sensing and a need to fill the gap in the literature of CVPs.

To this end, this chapter takes the approach of going beyond the methodology commonly used in the literature and uses game theory and the logical reasoning that is widely used in mathematics (Kline, 1972) while attempting to develop such a theory of CVPs as called for by Payne et al. (2017). One major hurdle in doing so successfully is the adoption of a novel methodology that has the potential of providing the power of logical reasoning while avoiding the constraints of statistics-based and calculus-based methods. The adopted methodology in this research is systems science and the systemic yoyo model.

Because of the adoption of such an unconventional methodology, this chapter establishes generally true facts instead of hypotheses, including

- A superb market-sensing capability implies an ability to create vitally important market knowledge and increase its expected profits. Such consequences are generally achieved by adopting appropriate technologies, by acquiring and deploying resources (Propositions 6.1 and 6.2).
- Within a stagnant industry that lacks market-level growth, a superb market-sensing capability points to potential profit growth through raising margins (Proposition 6.2).
- An effective CVP can be materialistically drafted out of market knowledge and innovative understanding of the knowledge (Propositions 6.9 and 6.10).
- The effectiveness of a co-created CVP depends on the width of the ultimate market (Proposition 6.6).
- With sufficient internal managerial support, a company can practically deliver the promises of its adopted CVP (Proposition 6.7).

As commonly practiced in business operations (Duan et al., 2019; McGrath, 2013), implementing best practices and data-driven decision makings have been widely employed. However, no matter how good the practices had been recorded and how effectively decisions been data driven, the consequences of implementing the practices and decisions can be and have been often widely different from what were expected (Forrest et al., 2020b). This business reality richly reveals the practical significance of this chapter because the developed conclusions produce general recommendations instead of suggestions for decision-making managers and entrepreneurs. Specifically, the recommendations below for general managerial purposes can follow readily from the established results in this chapter.

- To achieve better performance, a company has to attain and advance its market-sensing capability. With such capability, the company is able to know under-served customers, dissatisfied ones with currently available market offers, and appropriate technology that can potentially improve productivity (Proposition 6.1);
- When the potential of market-level growth is absent, a company needs to either raise the price and/or lower the cost of each unit sold (Proposition 6.2) while not giving much effort to improving the sales revenue (Proposition 6.3);
- To succeed in the marketplace, a company needs to manage customer relationships in such a way that resources are deployed corresponding to the levels of attractiveness of customers and prospects (Proposition 6.8); and
- To formulate effective CVPs, companies need to make joint use of their market knowledge and innovatively understanding of that knowledge (Propositions 6.9 and 6.10).
- Each ambitious company that wishes to flourish in the marketplace needs to bring its adopted CVP into line with what the market surplus signals (Theorem 6.1 and Proposition 6.8).
- To successfully achieve this alignment, the company's management needs to scrupulously evaluate the depth and width of the identified market segment (Proposition 6.5 and 6.6).
- And, it needs to beseech full-hearted managerial backing of all levels (Proposition 6.7).

Behind all results established in this chapter is the following implicit assumption: each company, considered here, is financially solvent, because of the positive cash flows from the product market as a consequence of its meeting market demand (s) with its particular offer(s). However, this assumption in today's world of business is no longer generally true. So, as future research attempts, results parallel to those developed in this chapter need to be considered for companies that exist for other purposes, such as producing promising futures, expanding market territories, or others (Li & Ma, 2015).

References

Adner, R., Oxley, J. E., & Silverman, B. S. (Eds.). (2013). *Collaboration and competition in business ecosystems*. Emerald.

Alshanty, A. M., & Emeagwali, O. L. (2019). Market-sensing capability, knowledge creation and innovation. *Journal of Innovation & Knowledge, 4*(3), 171–178.

Anderson, J., Narus, J., & Van Rossum, W. (2006). Customer value propositions in business markets. *Harvard Business Review, 84*(3), 91–99.

Ardyan, E. (2016). Market sensing capability and SMEs performance. *DLSU Business & Economics Review, 25*(2), 79–97.

Ballantyne, D. (2003). A relationship-mediated theory of internal marketing. *European Journal of Marketing, 37*(9), 1242–1260.

Ballantyne, D., Frow, P., Varey, R. J., & Payne, A. (2011). Value propositions as communication practice. *Industrial Marketing Management, 40*(2), 202–210.

Barney, J., & Arikan, A. (2001). The resource-based view: Origins and implications. In M. Hitt, R. Freeman, & J. Harrison (Eds.), *Handbook of strategic management* (pp. 124–185). Blackwell.

Barney, J., & Hesterly, W. (2012). *Strategic management and competitive advantage: Concepts and cases* (4th ed.). Pearson.

Bayighomog Likoum, S. W., Shamout, M. D., Harazneh, I., et al. (2018). Market-sensing capability, innovativeness, brand management systems, market dynamism, competitive intensity, and performance. *Journal of the Knowledge Economy*. https://doi.org/10.1007/s13132-018-0561-x

Berry, L. L., Carbone, L. P., & Haeckel, S. H. (2002). Managing the total customer experience. *Sloan Management Review, 43*(3), 85–89.

Bharadwaj, N., & Dong, Y. X. (2014). Toward further understanding the market-sensing capability–value creation relationship. *Journal of Product Innovation Management, 31*(4), 799–813.

Butler, R. W., Adam, R., & Szromek, A. R. (2019). Incorporating the value proposition for society with business models of health tourism enterprises. *Sustainability, 11*(23), 6711. https://doi.org/10.3390/su11236711

Cao, Y., & Gruca, T. S. (2005). Reducing adverse selection through customer relationship management. *Journal of Marketing, 69*(4), 219–229.

Carreyrou, J. (2018). *Bad Blood: Secrets and lies in a Silicon Valley startup*. Alfred A. Knopf.

Clements, C., Alwang, J., & Achdiawan, R. (2019). Value chain approaches in a stagnant industry: The case of furniture production in Jepara, Indonesia. *Bulletin of Indonesian Economic Studies, 55*(3), 341–365.

Davenport, T. H. (1993). *Process Innovation: Reengineering Work Through Information Technology*. Harvard Business School Press.

Day, G. S. (1994). The capabilities of market-driven organizations. *Journal of marketing, 58*(4), 37–52.

Day, G. S. (2011). Closing the marketing capabilities gap. *Journal of Marketing, 75*(4), 183–195.

Dickson, P. R. (1992). Toward a theory of competitive rationality. *Journal of Marketing, 56*(1), 69–84.

Duan, Y. Q., Edwards, J. S., & Dwivedi, Y. K. (2019). Artificial intelligence for decision making in the era of Big Data – evolution, challenges and research agenda. *International Journal of Information Management, 48*(October), 63–71.

Dutta, S., Narasimhan, O., & Rajiv, S. (1999). Success in high-technology markets: Is marketing capability critical? *Marketing Science, 18*(4), 547–568.

Eggert, A., Ulaga, W., Frow, P., & Payne, A. (2018). Conceptualizing and communicating value in business markets: From value in exchange to value in use. *Industrial Marketing Management, 69*(February), 80–90.

Einstein, A. (1997). In R. Schulmann et al. (Eds.), *The collected papers of Albert Einstein: The Berlin years* (Vol. 8). Princeton University Press.

Ferber, U., & Schlappa, H. (2016). Managing brownfield land in stagnant land markets. In W. J. V. Neil & H. Schlappa (Eds.), *Future Directions for the European Shrinking City* (pp. 138–154). Routledge.

Forrest, J. Y.-L. (2018). *General systems theory: foundation, intuition and applications in business decision making*. Springer.

Forrest, J. Y.-L., Ashimov, A., Ren, L., Gias, S., & Borovskiy, Y. (2021). Conditions under which adopted consumer value propositions are effective. *Pennsylvania Economic Review, 28*(1), 17–42.

Forrest, J. Y.-L., Buttermore, J., & Wajda, T. A. (2017). At Nash equilibrium when new market competitions appear? *Kybernetes, 46*(2), 256–271.

Forrest, J. Y.-L., Gong, Z. W., Scott, E., & Soto Ruiz, G. E. (2020a). Market-sensing capabilities, profitability within stagnant industries and crafting of customer value propositions. *Review of Economic and Business Studies, 13*(2), 53–76.

Forrest, J. Y. L., & Liu, Y. (2022). *Value in business: A holistic, systems-based approach to creating and achieving value*. Springer.

Forrest, J. Y.-L., Liu, Y., Swift, E., & Karimi, T. (2019). Exploitation, exploration, development and decay of resources: A systemic view. *Proceedings of the 2019 annual conference of Pennsylvania Economic Association*, 139-165.

Forrest, J. Y.-L., Nicholls, J., Schimmel, K., & Liu, S. F. (2020b). *Managerial decision making: A holistic approach*. Springer.

Forrest, J. Y.-L., & Tallapally, P. (2018). Customers are less patient, sustainable advantage becomes transient and the key for firms to succeed in fast changing markets. *Journal of Business, Economics and Technology, 21*(1), 1–14.

Harmancioglu, N., Droge, C., & Calantone, R. (2009). Strategic fit to resources versus NPD execution proficiencies: What are their roles in determining success? *Journal of the Academy of Marketing Science, 37*(3), 266–282.

Hult, G. T. (1998). Managing the international strategic sourcing process as a market-driven organizational learning system. *Decision Sciences, 29*(winter), 193–216.

Keats, B. W., & Hitt, M. A. (1988). A causal model of linkages among environmental dimensions, macro organizational characteristics, and performance. *Academy of Management Journal, 31*(3), 570–598.

Kline, M. (1972). *Mathematical Thought from Ancient to Modern Times*. Oxford University Press.

Kowalkowski, C. (2011). Dynamics of value propositions: Insights from service-dominant logic. *European Journal of Marketing, 45*(1/2), 277–294.

Kozlenkova, I., Samaha, S., & Palmatier, R. (2014). Resource-based theory in marketing. *Journal of the Academy of Marketing Science, 42*(1), 1–21.

Lanning, M. (1998). *Delivering profitable value*. Perseus Publishing.

Lanning, M., & Michaels, E. (1988). A business is a value delivery system. *McKinsey Staff Paper* No. 41, July.

Le, N., Nguyen, H. M., & Schultz, E. (2020). Financial development and productivity growth in stagnant industries. SSRN: Retrieved May 4, 2020, from https://ssrn.com/abstract=3275778.

Lecours, M. (2017). Developing a framework to craft a value proposition. *Journal of Financial Planning, 30*(3), 23–25.

Li, T., & Ma, J. H. (2015). Complexity analysis of dual-channel game model with different managers' business objectives. *Communications in Nonlinear Science and Numerical Simulation, 20*, 199–208.

Lin, Y. (1999). *General Systems Theory: A Mathematical Approach*. Plenum and Kluwer Academic Publishers.

Lin, Y. (2009). *Systemic Yoyos: Some impacts of the second dimension*. Auerbach Publication, an imprint of Taylor and Francis.

Lindblom, A., Olkkonen, R., Mitronen, L., & Kajalo, S. (2008). Market-sensing capability and business performance of retail entrepreneurs. *Contemporary Management Research, 4*(3), 219–236.

Lindstrom, M. (2005). *Brand sense: Build powerful brands through touch, taste, smell, sight, and sound*. Free Press.

Marketing Science Institute. (2010). *MSI research priorities 2010–12*. MSI.

Marketing Science Institute. (2014). *MSI research priorities 2014–16*. MSI.

Markman, G. D., & Gartner, W. B. (2002). Is extraordinary growth profitable? A study of Inc. 500 high-growth companies. *Entrepreneurship: Theory and Practice, 27*(1), 65–75.

McGrath, R. G. (2013). *The end of competitive advantage: How to keep your strategy moving as fast as your business*. Harvard Business Review Press.

Molineux, P. (2002). *Exploiting CRM: Connecting with customers*. Hodder & Stoughton.

Morgan, I., & Rao, J. (2003). Making routine customer experiences fun. *Sloan Management Review, 45*(1), 93–95.

Morgan, N., Slotegraaf, R., & Vorhies, D. (2009a). Linking marketing capabilities with profit growth. *International Journal of Research in Marketing, 26*(4), 284–293.

Morgan, N. A., Vorhies, D. W., & Mason, C. (2009b). Market orientation, marketing capabilities, and firm performance. *Strategic Management Journal, 30*(8), 909–920.

Narasimhan, C. (1988). Competitive promotional strategies. *Journal of Business, 61*(4), 427–429.

Niraj, R., Gupta, M., & Narasimhan, C. (2001). Customer profitability in a supply chain. *Journal of Marketing, 65*(3), 1–16.

Osterwalder, A., Pigneur, Y., Bernarda, G., & Smith, A. (2014). *Value proposition design: How to create products and services customers want*. Wiley.

Payne, A., & Frow, P. (2005). A strategic framework for customer relationship management. *Journal of Marketing, 69*(4), 167–176.

Payne, A., Frow, P., & Eggert, A. (2017). The customer value proposition: evolution, development, and application in marketing. *Journal of the Academy of Marketing Science, 45*, 467–489.

Peteraf, M., & Barney, J. (2003). Unraveling the resource-based tangle. *Managerial and Decision Economics, 24*(4), 309–323.

Porse, H., & Rudolph, B. (2017). The seaweed hydrocolloid industry: 2016 updates, requirements, and outlook. *Journal of Applied Phycology, 29*, 2187–2200.

Porter, M. E. (1985). *Competitive Advantage: Creating and Sustaining Superior Performance*. Free Press.

Reeves, R. (1961). *Reality in advertising*. Alfred A. Knopf.

Reinartz, W., & Kumar, V. (2000). The CRM process: Its measurement and impact on performance. *Journal of Marketing Research, 64*(4), 17–35.

Reinartz, W., Thomas, J., & Kumar, V. (2005). Balancing customer acquisition and retention resources to maximize customer profitability. *Journal of Marketing, 69*(1), 63–79.

Rintamaki, T., Kuusela, H., & Mitronen, L. (2007). Identifying competitive customer value propositions in retailing. *Managing Service Quality, 17*(6), 621–634.

Ryals, L. (2005). Making customer relationship management work: The measurement and profitable management of customer relationships. *Journal of Marketing, 69*(4), 252–261.

Shulga, L. V., & Busser, J. A. (2019). Customer acceptance of four types of hospitality value propositions. *International Journal of Hospitality Management*, October, https://doi.org/10.1016/j.ijhm.2019.102388.

Slater, S. F., & Narver, J. C. (2000). Intelligence generation and superior customer value. *Journal of the Academy of Marketing Science, 28*(1), 120–127.

Smith, S., & Wheeler, J. (2002). *Managing the customer experience: Turning customers into advocates*. Financial Times Prentice Hall.

Sobel, R. (1999). *When giants stumble: Classic business blunders and how to avoid them*. Prentice Hall.

Steffens, P., Davidsson, P., & Fitzsimmons, J. (2009). Performance configurations over time: Implications for growth- and profit-oriented strategies. *Entrepreneurship Theory and Practice, 33*(1), 125–148.

Sugiyarti, G., & Ardyan, E. (2017). Market sensing capability and product innovation advantages in emerging markets: The case of market entry quality and marketing performance of Batick Industry in Indonesia. *DLSU Business & Economics Review, 27*(1), 175–189.

Terho, H., Haas, H., Eggert, A., & Ulaga, W. (2012). 'It's almost like taking the sales out of selling'—Towards a conceptualization of value-based selling in business markets. *Industrial Marketing Management, 41*(1), 174–185.

Tournois, L. (2016). When markets stagnate: Finding new territory through reverse innovation. *Journal of Business Strategy, 37*(6), 18–27.

Ulaga, W., & Eggert, A. (2006). Value-based differentiation in business relationships: Gaining and sustaining key supplier status. *Journal of Marketing, 70*(1), 119–136.

Verhoef, P. C. (2003). Understanding the effect of customer relationship management efforts on customer retention and customer share development. *Journal of Marketing, 67*(4), 30–45.

Webster, F. E. (2002). *Market-driven management: How to define, develop and deliver customer value* (2nd ed.). Wiley.

Wouters, M., Anderson, J. C., & Kirchberger, M. (2018). New technology startups seeking pilot customers: Crafting a pair of value propositions. *California Management Review, 60*(4), 101–124.

Ye, G. L., Priem, R. L., & Alshwer, A. A. (2012). Achieving demand-side synergy from strategic diversification: How combining mundane assets can leverage consumer utilities. *Organization Science, 23*(1), 207–224.

Zhang, T. C., Gu, H. M., & Jahromi, M. F. (2019). What makes the sharing economy successful? An empirical examination of competitive customer value propositions. *Computers in Human Behavior, 95*(June), 275–283.

Chapter 7
Agency Problem, Managerial Control, and Projects' Interactions

Jeffrey Yi-Lin Forrest and Sifeng Liu

Abstract This chapter, which is mainly based on Lin and Liu (Kybernetes: The International Journal of Cybernetics, Systems and Management Science 40(9–10): 1354–372, 2011), examines several issues related to corporate governance, where firms need capital to fund their ventures or provide founders with cash-out opportunities, while suppliers of finance want to be assured that they get a return on their investment. It studies in terms of value the mutual restrictions and interactions between a firm's board of directors, which is assumed to be dominated by long-term, large shareholders, and the CEO, who is not a long-term, large shareholder. Other than showing why the agency problem exists forever in real life, this chapter answers a series of open questions, such as (a) why investors leave their money to managers who have enormous discretion on how to expropriate much of it for their personal gain; (b) if these investors want to control a profitable or potentially profitable firm through their financing, why they don't simply go out and start their own firms because they have the financial resources; (b) how CEOs and their boards, dominated by large, long-term shareholders, agree on which projects, long-term or short-term, to devote their limited energy and labor efforts to.

Keywords Agency problem · Corporate governance · Fundamental share-value · Nonpecuniary benefits · Price behaviors · Short-term equity performance · Venture capital

---

Jeffrey Yi-Lin Forrest (Department of Accounting Economics Finance, Slippery Rock University, Slippery Rock, PA, USA; Email: Jeffrey.forrest@sru.edu) and Sifeng Liu (School of Economics and Management, Nanjing University of Aeronautics and Astronautics, Nanjing, China; Email: sfliu@nuaa.edu.cn) are equally contributed to this chapter.

J. Y.-L. Forrest, *Systemic Principles of Applied Economic Philosophies II*,
Translational Systems Sciences 39, https://doi.org/10.1007/978-981-99-7939-4_7

7.1 Introduction

In terms of corporate governance, there is clearly a need to holistically understand how various decision-making units of a firm work together, interact with each other, and how stakeholders with inconsistent objectives put in their efforts to accomplish their, respectively, different, or even divergent goals. This chapter represents one of the first steps devoted to materializing this important effort in the area of corporate governance.

Before developing a specific analytic model, this chapter, which is mainly based on Lin and Liu (2011), first establishes a systems foundation based on the systemic yoyo model (Lin, 2008) to understand some of the relevant empirical discoveries. On such a qualitative foundation, an explanation is provided for, among others:

1. Why an elaborate legal system is needed for venture capital to flow smoothly and why certain governments around the world are willing to go extra miles to establish such a legal system.
2. Why the agency problem, existing between the large shareholders and the CEO, cannot be resolved completely and the best one can do about this problem is to reduce its severity.
3. Why outside financers still leave their money to managers in all market economies from around the world even with the knowledge of the unsolvable agency problem.
4. Why there are boards of directors in the first place.

With these new and deepened understandings about the mutual interactions and restrictions between the board of directors and the CEO, this chapter then turns its attention to establish a simple analytic model, on which it studies the price behaviors of different investment projects, the dynamics between long-term and short-term projects and assets, and the power struggle between the board and the CEO. The developed analytical reasoning indicates that when assets are undervalued, the mispricing of the long-term asset in equilibrium is worse than that of the short-term asset. When the assets are overpriced, the mispricing of the short-term asset in equilibrium is worse than that of the long-term asset. With this result in place, an explanation is given to explain why CEOs would prefer, among different kinds of projects, undervalued short-term investment projects.

In terms of CEOs' choices of long-term and short-term projects, it is found that even though the boards, dominated by long-term, large shareholders, prefer long-term, value-building projects, CEOs' successes on short-term projects have a consequence favorable to the CEOs. In particular, such short-term successes help CEOs acquire additional trust from and control over the boards. More interestingly, this chapter is able to prove that the number of short-term projects a CEO likes to take on is less than the number the board would like him to take on. That is, in practice, no matter how much the large shareholders worry about the possibilities that the CEO could expropriate their investment funds or spend the funds on his private benefits of control, and how much they do to prevent their worries from becoming true, the

CEO still has substantial control right (gained over time) and discretion to allocate funds in ways he chooses.

In terms of the methodology employed here, similar to what is done in previous chapters, the current chapter also models each corporation and each supplier of finance as an abstract economic yoyo, where the input side takes in investments of various kinds from available sources, while the output side applies and spends what is invested in various ways. More specifically, if a yoyo field models a corporation, then its input side absorbs funds, talents, etc., from various sources, such as banks, mutual funds, pension plans, insurance companies, individual investors, etc. And part of the materials spit out of the output side contains such a portion of the corporation's profits that it is returned to the investors as capital gains or dividends. If a yoyo represents an investor, be it large or small, then the input side stands for ways and amounts he could get his return on his investments, and the output side contains opportunities of future finance provided to each particular corporation. Hopefully, such a systemic modeling can help shed new lights on the understanding of corporate governance so that rich economies can be marginally improved and major institutional changes can be stimulated in places where they need to be made.

The rest of this chapter is organized as follows: Section 7.2 provides a literature review and some needed preparation for the ensuing discussions. Section 7.3 establishes a systemic foundation for understanding several phenomena related to corporate governance. Section 7.4 investigates a firm's ownership, large stakeholders and how the price of investment projects involves. Section 7.5 looks at the dynamical interactions of long- and short-term projects. The chapter concludes in Sect. 7.6.

7.2 The Rotten Kid Theorem

To set the conclusions of this chapter on a solid footing, and to make this chapter as self-contained as possible, this section prepares the reader with relevant details of Becker's rotten kid theorem.

In general, people and firms interact with each other for different reasons and purposes. From these varied reasons and purposes, conflicting interests appear. Hence, a very important question arises as follows: how can some of the people with different personalities and preferences (or firms with conflicting objectives) be kept together to work toward a common purpose? To address this question, Becker (1974), in *A Theory of Social Interactions*, published the following rotten kid theorem.

Theorem 7.1 (Becker's (1974) Rotten Kid Theorem). If a family has a head who cares about all other members so much that he transfers his resources to them automatically, then any redistribution of the head's income among members of the household would not affect the consumption of any member, as long as the head continues to contribute to all. Additionally, other members are also motivated to maximize the family income and consumption, even if their welfare depends on their own consumption alone.

In other words, what this theorem suggests is that family members, even those who are selfish, will contribute to efforts to raise family income, if there is a benevolent head that voluntarily bequeaths gifts to other members periodically. The importance of this theorem has been well described by Bergstrom (1989, p. 1138):

> If it is generally correct, the Rotten Kid theorem must be one of the most remarkable and important results in the theory of incentives. For it tells us that a sufficiently benevolent household head would *automatically* internalize all the external effects that family members have on each other. Benevolent parents of intelligent, though selfish, children can breathe easier. In the family there will be no free riders or principal agent problems. Elaborate incentive schemes and detection devices are unnecessary. All that is needed is to explain the Rotten Kid theorem to each family member and they will all (except possibly for a few irrational lapses) behave in the common interest. Not only would this be remarkable good news for parents, it would suggest a promising way of avoiding the incentive problems that bedevil firms and other social organizations. Shouldn't it be possible to find group incentive structures similar to those of families with benevolent heads?

In short, the rotten kid theorem can streamline a family, firm, or any organization. To witness this end, various implications and applications of this theorem appear in studies of family altruism and asset transfers (Becker, 1991; Bhalotra, 2004; Altonji et al., 1997), moral hazard (see Ghaudhuri et al., 2005, and references therein), the effects on consumption and savings of public debts, social security, and other governmental transfers among generations (Barro, 1974), patterns of parental bequests (Menchik, 1980; Becker, 1991), child labor and labor supplies (Baland & Robinson, 2000; Bommier & Dubois, 2004; Fernandes, 2000), foreign aids (Federio, 2004), and intergenerational education and culture transmissions (Patacchini & Zenou, 2004), among countless others.

Due to the theorem's wide-ranging importance, Bergstrom (1989) emphasizes that it is worthwhile to find the limits of generality for theorems with strong and interesting conclusions, the rotten kid theorem included. Subsequently, he constructed three examples, each of which shows where this theorem could go wrong. Along the same idea, after developing a two-time-period model for the study of child labor, which encompasses the human capital dimension, Baland and Robinson (2000) show that the rotten kid theorem does not hold true when parental savings are at a corner. Additionally, Bommier and Dubois (2004) use a similar model to reveal that a child's disutility, a dimension overlooked by previous researchers, considerably affects the validity of this important theorem. To summarize, the validity of the rotten kid theorem is conditional; there is a need to find conditions under which this important theorem holds true. By continuing and expanding what was achieved in Bergstrom (1989), Lin and Forrest (2008) establish the following result:

Theorem 7.2 Lin and Forrest (2008). Becker's rotten kid theorem holds true if and only if the distribution of the benevolent head's resources is not in conflict with the consumption preferences of any selfish member.

This theorem makes Becker's result become more tangible and easier to be applied in various theoretical and applied situations. And some of the conclusions derived in the rest of this chapter can be seen as direct consequences of Theorem 7.2.

7.3 A Systemic Foundation for Understanding Corporate Governance

This section provides a systemic foundation for understanding and justifying a series of empirical discoveries regarding corporate governance. It consists of two subsections. The first one demonstrates why the well-known agency problem exists in real life forever. And the second subsection investigates why investors leave their money with managers who have enormous discretion on how to expropriate the investments for their personal gains and how fights for managerial control take place at the level of board of directors.

7.3.1 Forever Existence of Agency Problem

From Alchian (1950) and Stigler (1958), the following evolutionary theory naturally follows:

> No one should worry about corporate governance reform, because in the long run market competition would force firms to minimize costs. And as part of this cost minimization, firms would be able to adopt appropriate rules and to raise external capital at the lowest cost.

By considering the landscape of the realistic business world, it is clear that firms and investors coexist side by side and interact with each other. Due to differences in their abilities and availabilities of their resources, some of these firms and investors will be destroyed and some will combine into greater business entities with enhanced capabilities to absorb additional investors' funds and to explore additional opportunities. To potentially maintain the peace of society and the stability of the economy, governments help prevent abusive competitions and maximize cash flows, which indirectly assists the government to collect the most amount of taxes. To materially achieve this goal, regulatory bodies are introduced to benefit firms and investors of various sizes so that they would not be easily crushed and that, when necessary, firms would still be able to attract capitals for their needs of business ventures from all potential sources.

If one identifies each firm and every investor as a spinning yoyo field (Lin, 2008) that interacts with each other, then what is seen in the previous paragraph is evidently true in general. In other words, even though market competition is a powerful force that pushes toward economic efficiency, it alone is not sufficient to solve the problem of corporate governance. That is, the aforementioned evolutionary theory holds true only conditionally in such a sense that the field of competition must be level for all competitors (yoyos) to participate in (spin). To this end, countries like the USA, Britain, Germany, and Japan have well introduced sophisticated laws to protect investors.

For a publicly traded firm, because financers generally are either too small or not qualified or not informed enough to make detailed operational decisions, they rely on the manager to run the firm. Consequently, the manager ends up with substantial control rights and discretion to allocate funds as he chooses. He can expropriate the funds (Zingales, 1994) or spend the funds on his private benefits of control, such as building an empire for himself (Owen, 1991), spending on consumption perquisites (Burrough & Helyar, 1990), expanding the firm irrationally, pursuing pet projects that do not benefit the investors (Jensen, 1986), etc. And worst of all, managers can expropriate investors by staying on the job even if they are no longer competent enough to run the firm (Shleifer & Vishny, 1989). To prevent any of these possibilities of how the manager could misuse the investors' investments—an agency problem—the systemic yoyo model suggests that one possible solution would be make sure to place the manager's personal yoyo in the same spin field of the yoyos of all of the investors—earn a return for his finance or effort in the firm. That is, tie the financial interests of the manager with those of the financers (Jensen & Meckling, 1976).

One method of tying the manager's interest with those of the investors is to employ incentive contracts, which have been in use since at least the time of Berle and Means (1932). However, evidence (Yermack, 1997) exists, showing that incentive contracts create enormous opportunities for self-dealing for managers, as indicated by the enclosed areas in Fig. 7.1. This figure suggests, as how the arrows in enclosed areas point to opposite directions, that no solution exists to solve this agency problem completely; as long as the manager is not the same as the numeraire investor, an abstract investor representing the common characteristics and desires of all financers together, there will be conflicts.

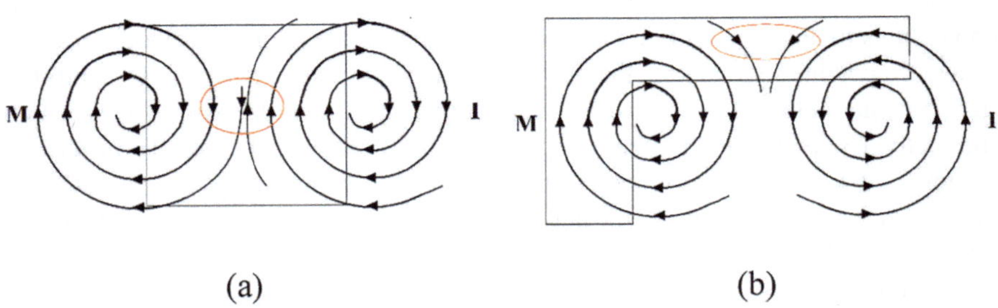

Fig. 7.1 Conflicts of interests between the manager M and the numeraire investor I (**a**) Direct and head-to-head conflicts; (**b**) Moderate degree of conflicts

The reason why the yoyos M and I in Fig. 7.1 are convergent is that the manager M and the investor I both want to grab more of the financial return and many other privileges. In Fig. 7.1a, both yoyos M and I tend to combine into a greater yoyo due to their harmonic spinning direction. In Fig. 7.1b, the yoyos M and I will try to destroy each other without the slightest chance to combine due to their opposite spinning directions.

At the same time, the dishpan experiment, see Chap. 2 for relevant details, shows that as long as the manager is not the same as the only investor, the agency problem will appear in one form or another. In particular, individual investors have a single goal: earn a return on their investment. However, the manager in general has more goals to achieve and more benefits, such as any of the aforementioned private benefits and perquisites of control, to enjoy beyond simply making an earning or return on his labor effort and talent for being the manager. This analysis and the previous systemic yoyo modeling jointly imply the following conclusion in terms of corporate governance.

Proposition 7.1 If there exist investors who are not the decision-making manager, there will be an unsolvable agency problem. The best one can do is to reduce its severity.

If the yoyos in Fig. 7.1 are observed from the other side (look at them from inside the page outward), the spin fields M and I are then shown as in Fig. 7.2. Because the yoyo fields are all divergent when seen in this angle, they do not tend to combine into a greater yoyo as in the case of Fig. 7.1a, unless M (or I) is much more powerful than I (or M) (Fig. 7.2a). Once again, the yoyo interactions in Fig. 7.2b will never combine relatively peacefully due to their opposite spinning directions unless one of them is destroyed completely by the other. That is, if the relationship between the board of directors and the CEO is as depicted in Figs. 7.1a and 7.2a, the firm has a chance to grow into a successful business venture. If the relationship between the board and the CEO turns out like the one shown in Figs. 7.1b and 7.2b, then the firm is heading to its eventual destruction, unless the CEO is replaced or some of the main shareholders or creditors give up their controlling influence.

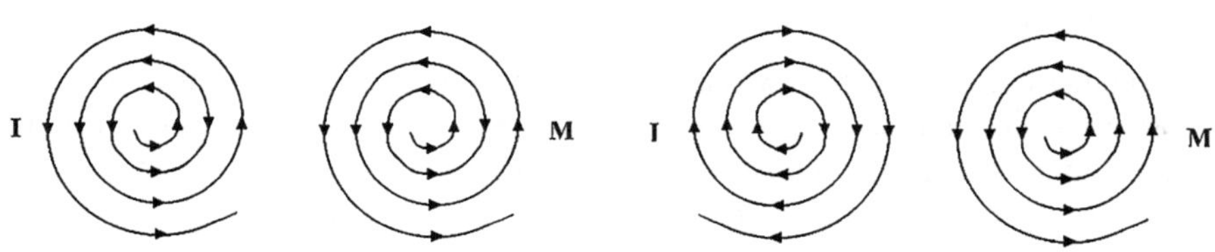

(a) (b)

Fig. 7.2 Conflicting ideas of how to manage the firm between the manager M and investor I (**a**) How head-to-head conflicts look differently; (**b**) How moderate degree of conflicts manifests differently

7.3.2 Boards of Directors and Fights for Managerial Control

Proposition 7.1 above points directly to the following question: Why do investors leave their money to managers who have enormous discretion on how to expropriate much of it for their personal gain (Shleifer & Vishny, 1997)? What is puzzling is that outside finance occurs in all market economies and on an enormous scale in the developed ones, such as those in the USA, Britain, Germany, and Japan.

To address this question, the systemic yoyo model provides the answer. Specifically, because eddy motions exist in pairs (because movements in opposite directions coexist), one can see that when there is an opportunity, there will be risks and there will be risk takers. Among them, some are prudent, others are not and are gullible and get taken. The reason why in developed market economies, enormous outside finance exists (also explaining why these economies are more developed than others) is because the societal structures (yoyos), such as the local and national governments, underlying the economic yoyos of the developed economies spin in the same directions and angles as the yoyos of these economies. In particular, the fiscal welfare of the governments is closely tied to the cash flows in the economies through taxation. So, to make all the yoyos of large scales, such as different levels of the governments and firms, do well financially, the governments introduced laws to protect investors. Because of these laws, many small investors, as the tiny particles evolving about in the spin fields of the underlying yoyos, become gullible and get taken either sometimes or most of the time. Conversely, the laws established are not simply for protecting investors whose financial gains in general do not contribute much to the fiscal welfare of the governments, but also for playing the magic role of monitoring the behaviors of firms. Every time investors get taken, some noise will be made and heard, which very likely brings additional monetary awards to the governments through the use of the legal system.

Proposition 7.2 The general reason why investors leave their money to managers to potentially grow their investments is the existence of a stable government hierarchy that directly benefits from keeping the managers behave appropriately, although the managers have enormous discretion on how to expropriate the investments for their personal gains.

Another outcome of the laws and regulations introduced by governments is that most firms are required to have a board that meets a list of requirements: it must contain at least a certain number of directors, meet with some specified regularity, have various committees, contain a proportion of the membership independent from the management, etc. As for why such boards are required in the first place, as challenged by Hermalin and Weisbach (2003), the systemic yoyo model suggests that a firm's board exists as the concentrated area of interests of all involved parties, including the firm's management, investors, and creditors, specifically those large shareholders and significant creditors. The board serves as the "narrow" neck of the economic yoyo of the firm. It connects the activities of the firm with all the parties whose interests are tied to the success of the firm. Without the neck (or the board), the firm would not exist both financially and physically. The existence of a functioning board induces investors to trust the manager with their money, where the directors of the board both individually and collectively help the firm to attract investments from different sources.

Proposition 7.3 When a firm has a quality board of directors, it makes it easier for investors to trust the company (or the manager) with their money.

Through the use of law protections, large investors provide external financing in exchange for their control rights of the firm (Hart, 1995). A natural question at this junction is: If these investors want to control a profitable or potentially profitable firm through their financing, why don't they simply go out and start their own firms because they have the financial resources? The systemic yoyo model suggests that starting a new firm (a yoyo) and succeeding in the competition with other existing firms in the same economic sector through absorbing other firms (yoyos) and destroying those which cannot be absorbed, while causing fierce competition, is more difficult than simply controlling a firm that has been most or will potentially be most successful in its economic sector.

The most important legal right investors, as shareholders of a firm, have is that of voting on important corporate matters and in elections of the board of directors, which in turn has monitoring rights over the manager (Manne, 1965). As expected from the systemic yoyo model, the manager could effectively interfere with the voting process in his favor (Pound, 1988) if control rights, such as votes, are split among many shareholders (yoyos that are too small compared to that of the manager). So, to break the imbalance in sizes, some investors with a collectively large cash flow at stake gain more effective control rights by being large. There are several forms that concentration can take, such as large shareholders, takeovers, and large creditors. When some investors own a substantial percentage of shares, they would have the incentive and strength to monitor, put pressure on, or oust the management through proxy fight or a takeover, or gain the outright control of the firm (Shleifer & Vishny, 1986) with 51% or more ownership. When large shareholders are less common, hostile takeovers, as a mechanism for consolidating ownership, emerge (Jensen & Ruback, 1983). In a hostile takeover, a bidder makes a tender offer to the dispersed shareholders of the target firm. If the shareholders accept the offer, the bidder acquires control of the target firm. Takeovers are considered a mechanism in the USA used to effectively control managerial discretion (Easterbrook & Fischel, 1991). Similar to large shareholders, significant creditors are also potentially active investors, who want the returns on their investments materialized. These creditors' power comes from the control rights when firms default or violate debt covenants (Smith & Warner, 1979) and future lending needs of the firms. So, the creditors control substantial cash flow rights and the ability to interfere with the firms' major decision-making.

Even if shareholders elect the board, directors do not necessarily represent their interests. In the USA, boards, especially those dominated by outside directors, sometimes remove top managers after poor performance (Weisbach, 1988). Using the systemic yoyo model, this end is quite clear. When the board of a firm is dominated by outside directors, the board would likely be controlled by large shareholders or creditors. Because the large shareholders and creditors may not qualify or be informed enough to judge and monitor the performance of the manager, they are more likely to place on the board their spokesperson and representatives from outside the firm. These outside directors are employed to counter the power and influence of the manager. Otherwise, more directors from inside the firm or interlocking directors, which means the managers of firms serving on each other's boards, would dominate the board. This result explains:

1. Why the board composition, as measured by the insider–outsider ratio, is not correlated with firm's performance (MacAvoy et al., 1983)
2. Why the size of a board is negatively related to the firm's financial performance (Lipton & Lorsch, 1992; Jensen, 1993; Yermack, 1996), because the dishpan experiment indicates that the larger a spin field, the more likely for chaotic movements within the field to exist. That is, the greater the board sizes, the less effective the board.
3. With higher proportions of outside directors, why smaller boards tend to make arguably better decisions concerning acquisitions (Shivdasani, 1993), poison pills (Brickley et al., 1994), executive compensation (Core et al., 1999), and CEO replacement (Denis & Denis, 1995).

7.4 Ownership, Large Stakeholders, and Projects' Price Behavior

This section investigates how the ownership and large stakeholders of a firm play a role in the political structure of the firm and how short- and long-term projects dynamically interact with each other. For this purpose, this section consists of two subsections with the first one focusing on the former topic and the second on the latter one.

7.4.1 A Firm's Ownership and Large Stakeholders

Based on our analysis in Sect. 7.1, it should be logical to expect that for most companies from around the world, their ownership should not be completely dispersed, and instead it should be concentrated in the hands of families and wealthy investors. This end is verified by Eisenberg (1976) for developed economies. In the USA, large shareholders, especially over 50 percent majority ownership, are relatively uncommon, probably due to legal restrictions on high concentrations of ownership and exercise of control by banks, mutual funds, insurance companies, and other institutions (Roe, 1994). Even so, ownership is not completely dispersed and also concentrated by families and wealthy investors (Eisenberg, 1976; Shleifer

& Vishny, 1986). DeLong (1991) points to a significant governance role played by J. P. Morgan Partners in the companies J. P. Morgan invested in the early twentieth century. More recently, U.S. banks play a major governance role in bankruptcies, where they change managers and directors (Gilson, 1990).

In Germany, large commercial banks through proxy voting arrangements often control over a quarter of the votes in major companies and also have smaller but significant cash flow stakes as direct shareholders or creditors (Franks & Mayer, 1994). It is estimated that about 80 percent of the large German companies have an over 25 percent nonbank large shareholder (Gorton & Schmid, 1996), where bank and nonbank block holders improve the performance of German companies. In smaller German companies, the norm is family control through majority ownership or pyramids (Franks & Mayer, 1994). In Japan, although ownership is not nearly as concentrated as in Germany, large cross-holdings as well as shareholdings by major banks are the norm (Prowse, 1990). Yafeh and Yosha (1996) find that large shareholders reduce discretionary spending by Japanese managers. In France, cross-ownership and so-called core investors are common (OECD, 1995). In most of Europe, Latin America, East Asia, and Africa, corporations typically have controlling owners, who are often founders or their offspring. The effectiveness of large shareholders is closely tied to their ability to defend their rights and put a lighter burden on the legal system than smaller investors might, if they tried to enforce their rights.

Large shareholders and investors, to protect their investment, guarantee their return, and prevent the managers from expropriating funds and spending on their private benefits of control, would monitor the managers' moves and decision-making closely. To study analytically how the board of a publicly traded company and the CEO interact, let us focus our attention on such a problem as how the CEO chooses between long-term and short-term projects (assets). In this chapter, projects and assets are used interchangeably, because for investors, they mainly care about when mispricings of their holdings disappear so that they can close their positions with profits. By short-term projects, they mean such projects that they cannot stay mispriced for long. Otherwise, these projects would be called long-term.

Assume that the board is effectively controlled by large, long-term shareholders. The controlling interest wants long-term growth, even though it could mean that they sometimes have to suffer from certain occasional temporary losses. And assume that the CEO is not a long-term, large shareholder of the company. That is, there is a conflict of interest here between the board and the CEO. In particular, the board desires the CEO to devote all his talent and labor effort to work on the existing long-term projects and initiate new ones so that the market value of the company would grow steadily over time. Conversely, the CEO needs short-term equity performance, because poor equity performance raises the likelihood of replacement by the board or through a hostile takeover. In either case, the CEO loses his job and all privileges of control. Kaplan and Minton (1994) show that companies with large shareholders or a principal banking relationship are more likely to replace managers in response to poor performance than companies without them. Shivdasani (1993) shows that large outside shareholders increase the likelihood that a company is taken over, whereas

Denis and Serrano (1996) show that if a takeover is defeated, management turnover is higher in poorly performing companies that have block holders.

7.4.2 Price Behaviors of Investment Projects

To address the problem of the CEO's choices between long-term and short-term projects, let us first look at the mispricings of both of these different investment projects. Throughout this chapter, assume that there is no discount of future over time.

Assume that a short-term asset is traded at p_s ($<v_s$) a share in time period 1, where v_s is the fundamental share-value of the asset. In this period, an investor buys $n(p_s)$ shares at the market price p_s a share. His total cost of the investment is $I_s = n(p_s)p_s$. Because this asset is a short-term investment, the mispricing disappears in period 2 and the trading price now equals the fundamental value v_s. So, the profit from this short-term asset is

$$n(p_s)v_s - I_sR = \frac{I_s v_s}{p_s} - I_sR = I_s\left(\frac{v_s}{p_s} - R\right), \tag{7.1}$$

where $R > 1$ is the gross interest spent on the total investment amount I_s.

Assume that for a long-term asset, the same investor buys in period 1 $n(p_L)$ shares at p_L a share, satisfying $p_L < v_L$, where v_L is the fundamental share-value of the asset. So, the total cost to the investor is $I_L = n(p_L)p_L$. Because the asset is a long-term investment, its mispricing does not disappear until period 3, when the total profit is

$$n(p_L)p_L - I_LR^2.$$

Discounting this amount to period 2 provides

$$\frac{1}{R}\left[(p_L)p_L - I_LR^2\right] = \frac{1}{R}\left[\frac{I_L v_L}{p_L} - I_LR^2\right] = I_L\left[\frac{v_L}{I_LR} - R\right]. \tag{7.2}$$

If the investor wants to produce the same return on his investments from the short-term and long-term assets, we have from Eqs. 7.1 and 7.2 that

$$I_s\left[\frac{v_s}{p_s} - R\right] = I_L\left[\frac{v_L}{p_LR} - R\right].$$

From the assumption that $I_s = I_L$, meaning that the investor allocated the same amount of funds to each opportunity, we have

$$\frac{v_s}{p_s} = \frac{v_L}{p_L} \cdot \frac{1}{R}, R > 1. \tag{7.3}$$

That is, for the investor to put his money with the long-term asset in period 1, this asset must be more mispriced than the short-term asset. Although this result is the same as that obtained by Shleifer and Vishny (1990), where they employed a different model, the results in the following paragraphs are opposite of those predicted by these authors.

Similar to the analysis above, the mispricings between short-term and long-term assets can be compared for three additional different cases:

1. Both the long-term and short-term assets are traded in period 1 at a per-share price $p_i > v_i$, for $i = s, L$.
2. The investor is risk averse and the long-term asset is riskier than the short-term investment, and the trading prices satisfy $p_i < v_i$, for $i = s, L$.
3. The same situation as in case 2 holds true, except that the trading prices satisfy $p_i > v_i$, for $i = s, L$.

For case 1, an equation similar to Eq. 7.3 holds true. However, this new equation means something completely opposite of that of Eq. 7.3. In particular, for this current situation, Eq. 7.3 implies that for the investor to put his money in the short-term asset, the asset must be more mispriced than the long-term asset. This end confirms the practical experience that going short can make a quicker and more handsome profit in a relatively short period of time than going long (Soros, 1998).

For case 2, the following holds true:

$$\frac{v_s}{p_s} < \frac{v_L}{p_L} \cdot \frac{1}{R_L}, R_L > 1, \tag{7.4}$$

where R_L is the long-term gross interest rate. For case 3, we have

$$\frac{v_L}{p_L} \cdot \frac{1}{R_L} = \frac{v_s}{p_s} + (R_L - R_s) > \frac{v_s}{p_s}, R_s > 1, \tag{7.5}$$

where $R_s < R_L$ stands for the short-term gross interest rate.

Summarizing what we have obtained, it can be seen that

Proposition 7.4 (1) When assets are undervalued, the mispricing of the long-term asset in equilibrium is worse than that of the short-term asset. (2) When the assets are overvalued, the mispricing of the short-term asset in equilibrium is worse than that of the long-term asset. (3) When a risky long-term asset is involved, the mispricings of the long-term asset are even worse if both assets are undervalued, and the mispricing of the safer short-term asset is worse if both assets are overvalued, than when risk-free assets are considered.

Because it takes a longer time for fundamental uncertainties to resolve, CEOs are typically averse to severely underpricing their long-term equity. Considering their job security, they also try to avoid overvalued short-term projects and all long-term projects, even though some of these projects could be detrimentally important to the long-term health and growth of their companies. Combining this reasoning with the fact that CEOs' compensation depends typically in part on short-term equity performance,

Proposition 7.5 A CEO, who is not a large, long-term shareholder of the firm he works for, generally prefers undervalued short-term projects.

Based on this conclusion, the following natural question arises: how do CEOs and their boards, dominated by large, long-term shareholders, agree on which projects, long-term or short-term, to devote their limited energy and labor efforts to? The next section will study this problem.

7.5 Dynamical Interactions of Long- and Short-Term Projects

To study the interactions between the CEO and the board of directors of a publicly traded company, assumed earlier is that the controlling shareholder directors care about near-term earnings of the company for the stability of their investment portfolio. However, their focus is more about how to improve the long-term, healthy growth, even if they have to temporarily suffer some short-term financial setbacks. At the same time, the board newly hired a CEO who is not a large, long-term shareholder of the company.

7.5.1 Modeling the Interaction

Because of the somewhat contradicting desires of the board, the controlling shareholder directors either implicitly or explicitly allow the CEO to embark on both long-term and short-term projects for the company. In the following, a simple model is established to describe the effect of the CEO's taking on short-term projects on the value of the company in the eyes of these shareholder directors.

Suppose that there are two time periods $t = 1, 2$. In period 1, the CEO puts in his labor and time to work on various projects, both long-term and short-term. As developed in Conyon and Read (2006), in this period, the value of the company is

$$y = a + e + \varepsilon, \tag{7.6}$$

where a stands for the CEO's level of ability, e his labor effort, and ε a normally distributed random error with mean zero. That is, investors in the (stock) market value the company in terms of the CEO's ability, effort, and a random noise that is not influenced by the variables a and e.

Because the CEO does not want to lose his job, he has to work on his company's short-term equity performance, even though he is aware of the fact that the particular shareholder directors like him to focus as much of his labor effort as possible on the long-term growth of the company. So, to the board, the real cost for the CEO to take on short-term projects is the opportunity costs of his effort, assuming that the capital markets are perfect. That is, investment capital is not a problem. When needed, the company can always take out loans. Time and labor effort not spent on long-term projects may well result in lost long-term growth opportunities. That is, the CEO's total labor effort e is split into two parts: e_s and e_L, where e_s with subscript s stands for the effort the CEO spends on short-term projects and e_L with the subscript L on long-term projects. So, the value of the company, as seen in the eyes of the controlling shareholder directors, becomes

$$y = a + e_L + \varepsilon, \tag{7.7}$$

where $e_L = e - e_s$ with $(-e_s)$ representing the opportunity costs for the CEO's working on short-term projects.

One of the reasons why the board allows the CEO to work on short-term projects is that such projects generally can realize their value in a short period. So, they provide an opportunity for the board to observe the CEO further, and such projects give the CEO a chance to harness his ability through working with people in the company new to him, exploring new knowledge and possibilities, etc. In general, through taking on numerous short-term projects, the CEO is expected to become more effective in his work and decision-making. Let the change in the CEO's ability in period 1 gained solely from taking on short-term projects be

$$h_1 = f(a_0)n, \text{ satisfying } f(a_0) > 0 \text{ and } f'(a_0) > 0,$$

where n stands for the number of short-term projects the CEO initiates and manages in period 1, and a_0 his endowed initial level of ability, which the board knows from records and references. Because h_1 is an increasing function in n, assumed is that taking on various short-term projects can only enrich the CEO's knowledge base and make him more able to manage and initiate additional projects, both short- and long-term. Therefore, the ability of the CEO in period 1 is given by $a_0 + h_1$, and the company's value in period 1 is given, as seen by the controlling shareholder directors, as follows:

$$y = a_0 + h_1 + e_L + \varepsilon. \tag{7.8}$$

That is, in period 1, the CEO decides on the number n of short-term projects to initiate and manage and how much labor effort $e_s = e - e_L$ to devote to these short-term projects so that he maximizes his personal utility function:

$$U = E(w) + \beta(E(y) + E(b)) - e_s n, \tag{7.9}$$

where $E(w)$ is the CEO's expected wage from the company, which is determined by the board in period 2, and $E(b)$ (≥ 0) his expected nonpecuniary benefits gained from these short-term projects, such as recognition locally, reputation within the industry of the company, etc., defined by

$$E(b) = b(a_0)e_s n, \text{ satisfying } 1 > b(a_0) > 0 \text{ and } b'(a_0) > 0.$$

$E(y)$ stands for the expected value of his company in period 1, as seen by the controlling shareholder directors, and $\beta \in (0, 1)$ is a parameter measuring the degree the CEO cares about how well his company does under his leadership. Here, $(-e_s n)$ stands for the CEO's disutility of initiating and managing short-term projects.

In period 2, based on the observed value of the company

$$y^* = y(n^*, e_s^*) = a_0 + h_1^* + e_L^*,$$

the board decides on how much compensation w to pay the CEO, where the y^*-value is uniquely determined by n^* and e_s^*. Here, * stands for observed values. Based on the idea of Nash bargaining, the board and the CEO negotiate a specific amount w of compensation to pay the CEO by solving

$$V = (y^* - w) \times w^\alpha = \{(a_0 + h_1^* + e_L^*) - w\} \times w^\alpha, \tag{7.10}$$

where $\alpha \in (0,+\infty)$ represents the bargaining power of the CEO over the board. For instance, when $\alpha \approx 0$, the board has almost 100 percent bargaining power over the CEO. Conversely, when $\alpha \to \infty$, the CEO has a dominating influence over the board.

7.5.2 Analysis of the Model

To solve our theoretical model, let us begin by considering the negotiation between the board and the CEO in period 2. The negotiation results in the maximization of V in Eq. 7.10 with respect to w subject to the constraint $w \leq a_0 + h_1^* + e_L^*$. Denote the solution to this problem by $\widehat{w}$. Then, we have

$$\widehat{w} = \frac{\alpha}{1+\alpha} y^*. \tag{7.11}$$

At the extremes, we have, respectively, $\alpha \approx 0$ and $\alpha \to \infty$. When $\alpha \approx 0$, that is, when the board has nearly total control over the CEO, the board pays the CEO almost none of his contributions to the value of the company. According to

Theorems 7.1 and 7.2, at such an extreme, the CEO would not voluntarily try to maximize the value of the company. This is, of course, not what the board wants to happen. Conversely, if the CEO has a dominating influence over the board, $\alpha \to \infty$, the board will pay the CEO nearly the entirety of his contributions to the value of the company. Because this circumstance does not fit well with the setup of the situation considered in this chapter, where large, long-term shareholders control the board, this extreme is unlikely to occur. So, what is left open is interesting: Eq. 7.11 implies the following:

Proposition 7.6 Beyond trying to create value for the company, the CEO is motivated to gain as much control over the board as possible, while the board wants to stay as independent from the CEO as possible.

The first conclusion follows from $\widehat{w} \to y^*$, when $\alpha \to \infty$. And the second conclusion is a consequence of the fact that the board wants to neither have total control over the CEO (or $\alpha \nrightarrow 0^+$) nor be controlled by the CEO (or $\alpha \nrightarrow \infty$).

Now, in period 1, anticipating the compensation $\widehat{w}$ in Eq. 7.11, the CEO chooses n- and e_s-values. The CEO's indirect utility is given by

$$U = U(n, e_s) = \left(\frac{\alpha}{1+\alpha} + \beta\right) E(y) + \beta E(b) - e_s n. \tag{7.12}$$

Assume that n and e_s (or e) are variables independent of each other. Then, the first-order conditions with respect to n and e are given, respectively, by

$$\left(\frac{\alpha}{1+\alpha} + \beta\right) f(a_0) + \beta b(a_0) e_s - e_s = 0 \tag{7.13}$$

and

$$\left(\frac{\alpha}{1+\alpha} + \beta\right) + \beta b(a_0)\left(1 - \frac{\partial e_L}{\partial e}\right) n - \left(1 - \frac{\partial e_L}{\partial e}\right) n = 0. \tag{7.14}$$

That is, in period 1, the CEO chooses the total number n^* of short-term projects to initiate and to manage, and his overall level $e^* = e_L^* + e_s^*$ of labor effort to work on his job as the CEO of his company, with e_L^* amount spent on the long-term projects and e_s^* on the short-term projects, where

$$n^* = \frac{\frac{\alpha}{1+\alpha} + \beta}{\left(1 - \frac{\partial e_L}{\partial e}\right)(1 - \beta b(a_0))} \tag{7.15}$$

and

$$e_s^* = \frac{\left(\frac{\alpha}{1+\alpha} + \beta\right) f(a_0)}{1 - \beta b(a_0)}. \tag{7.16}$$

If the CEO exerts roughly a fixed amount of labor effort e_L on the initiation and management of long-term projects, then he would initiate and manage as many as

$$n^* = \frac{\frac{\alpha}{1+\alpha} + \beta}{1 - \beta b(a_0)} \tag{7.17}$$

short-term projects.

Proposition 7.7 The higher the level the CEO's initial ability a_0 is, the more short-term projects he would initiate and manage and the more labor effort, correspondingly, he will devote to these projects.

The conclusion follows directly from Eqs. 7.15, 7.17, and 7.16.

Additional to what is stated in Proposition 7.7, the CEO's supplementary effort spent on the short-term projects helps him gain those nonpecuniary benefits $b = \beta b(a_0) e_s n$, which he can use to gain more bargaining power over the board. At the same time, the CEO's increased number of successful short-term projects raises his level of ability by as much as $h_1 = f(a_0)n$. So, he becomes more effective in his management duties, and consequently, we have

Proposition 7.8 With an increasing number of successful short-term projects, the CEO will help raise the company's value as a consequence of his increased commitment to short-term projects.

Additionally, Eq. 7.15 implies that only when the marginal increase in the total labor effort e from working on all projects is greater than the marginal increase in the labor effort e_L spent on the long-term projects (meaning the CEO tried to use some of his personal time to work on short-term projects) does the CEO take on short-term projects. Because taking on additional short-term projects generally means that the amount of time spent on the management of existing long-term projects decreases, that is, $\partial e_L / \partial e < 1$, Eq. 7.15 implies that in general, the CEO would take on short-term projects.

7.5.3 *Power Struggle Between the Board and the CEO*

The fact that the CEO has been hired by the board means that the majority of the directors feel that the CEO could do a good job to satisfy their needs. That is, starting on the first day when the CEO begins to work for the company as the executive officer, he has a certain amount of bargaining power over the board. Equation 7.11 implies that it is natural for the CEO to try to gain more bargaining power through whatever is necessary and workable, as long as he is able to make a positive contribution to increase the value of the company. To achieve this end, Eq. 7.8 indicates that the CEO would take on as many short-term projects as possible while keeping his effort level e_L on long-term projects as steady as possible.

From Eqs. 7.15 and 7.16, we obtain

$$\operatorname{sign}\left(\frac{\partial n^*}{\partial \alpha}\right) = \operatorname{sign}\left(1 - \frac{\partial e_L}{\partial e}\right) \tag{7.18}$$

and

$$\frac{\partial e_s^*}{\partial \alpha} = \frac{f(a_0)}{(1-\beta b(a_0))(1+\alpha)^2} > 0. \tag{7.19}$$

Proposition 7.9 The more bargaining power the CEO has over the board, the more his ideas on short-term projects will be implemented, and the more time and higher-quality service the CEO will spend on and render to managing short-term projects.

These conclusions follow directly from Eqs. 7.18 and 7.19.

Conversely, from Eqs. 7.15 and 7.16, we obtain

$$\frac{\partial \alpha}{\partial n^*} = \frac{A}{(An^* - \beta - 1)^2} \tag{7.20}$$

and

$$\frac{\partial \alpha}{\partial e_s^*} = \frac{B}{(Be_s^* - \beta - 1)^2}, \tag{7.21}$$

where $A = (1 - \partial e_L/\partial e)(1 - \beta b(a_0))$ and $B = (1 - \beta b(a_0))/f(a_0)$. That is, Eqs. 7.20 and 7.21 imply that

Proposition 7.10 By taking on short-term projects and spending extra labor effort on them, the CEO could potentially increase his bargaining power over the board.

Because labor effort spent on short-term projects has a direct impact on how much bargaining power the CEO has over the board, it is now reasonable to assume that the effort level e_L (respectively, e and e_s) is a function of n such that $\partial e_L/\partial n < 0$ and $\partial^2 e_L/\partial \alpha^2 > 0$. Intuitively, this assumption means that the more short-term projects the CEO takes on, the less time he has available for his long-term projects. And when he takes on even more short-term projects, his time spent on long-term projects will asymptotically approach a minimal level required to take care of long-term projects.

Now, let us look at the relationship between the optimal value n of short-term projects taken by the CEO from the standpoint of the board and the value from the standpoint of the CEO. The board wants to maximize its expected value in Eq. 7.8. So, the board's optimal n value satisfies

$$\frac{\partial E(y)}{\partial n} = f(a_0) + \frac{\partial e_L}{\partial n} = 0. \tag{7.22}$$

And at this n-value,

$$\begin{aligned}\frac{\partial U}{\partial n} &= \left(\frac{\alpha}{1+\alpha}\beta\right)\left(f(a_0) + \frac{\partial e_L}{\partial n}\right) + (\beta b(a_0) - 1)\left(e_s + n\frac{\partial e_s}{\partial n}\right) \\ &= (\beta b(a_0) - 1)\left(e_s + n\frac{\partial e_s}{\partial n}\right)\end{aligned} \tag{7.23}$$

Based on the same reasoning for the assumption that $\partial e_L/\partial n < 0$ applies here, we have $\partial e_s/\partial n > 0$. So, Eq. 7.23 implies that $\partial U/\partial n < 0$. That is, the CEO's personal optimal n-value is less than the board's optimal n-value. Here, the following result has been shown.

Proposition 7.11 The number of short-term projects the CEO likes to take on is less than the number the board would like him to take on.

This result is comforting to both the CEO and the board. It means that the CEO can simply work on as many short-term projects as he pleases without the need to worry that his attempt and hard work might offend some of the large, long-term shareholder directors. At the same time, Eqs. 7.20 and 7.21 spell out the fact that as long as the CEO is successful with his short-term projects while keeping all long-term projects on track, the board would put more trust in him and automatically give him more bargaining power.

7.6 A Few Final Words

Corporate governance has been well investigated by many scholars due to its close tie to a firm's performance (e.g., Alchian, 1950; Hermalin & Weisbach, 2003; Shleifer & Vishny, 1989, 1997; Stigler, 1958). However, there are still many unsettled problems to be resolved (e.g., Shleifer & Vishny, 1997) and many empirical discoveries to be understood (e.g., Brickley et al., 1994; Core et al., 1999; Denis & Denis, 1995; Jensen, 1993; Lipton & Lorsch, 1992; MacAvoy et al., 1983; Shivdasani, 1993; Yermack, 1996) at the height of abstract theory. Therefore, there is a need to attack these unsettled problems and elevate relevant empirical discoveries to the level of general knowledge by introducing an adequate methodology.

To potentially accomplish this end, this chapter introduces the logic of systems thinking into the investigation of corporate governance. After laying down a systemic foundation for describing the overall situation of corporate governance, the chapter is able to show

- when and how the unsolvable agency problem always exists in real life (Proposition 7.1),
- under what conditions investors will be willing to leave their money to managers to potentially grow their investments, even though these managers have enormous discretion on how to expropriate the investments for their personal gains (Propositions 7.2 and 7.3),
- how the prices of short-term and long-term projects behave (Proposition 7.4),

In terms of the interaction between the CEO and the board of directors, this chapter demonstrates, among others, that

- Other than attempting to create value, the CEO is motivated to gain as much control over the board as possible, while the board likes to stay independent from the CEO (Proposition 7.6).
- The number of short-term projects the CEO would initiate and manage is positively correlated to the CEO's ability, while his successes with short-term projects can help raise his company's value and his bargaining power over the board (Propositions 7.7, 7.8, and 7.10),
- The CEO does not need to worry in general how many short-term projects he initiates and manages (Proposition 7.11).

Any time when acting and reacting interactions exist, the logic of systems thinking and the yoyo model can be employed, because the existence of such interactions means an eddy motion as implied in Newton's second law of motion (Lin, 2007). Therefore, one can reasonably expect that he will be able to revisit many or most of the basic concepts in economics beyond those of corporate governance in the light of spinning yoyos and through the methodological lens of systems science. Consequently, he will be able to explain the results, at least some of them, obtained in behavioral economics and behavioral finance. More specifically, for example, we should now be more equipped than before to analyze the anomaly existing between utility maximization, as economists do all the time to produce their often-surprising inferences on people's desires and consumption behaviors, and experienced utility, as each one of us, as consumers and decision makers, goes through on a daily basis (Kahneman & Thaler, 2006). For some of such attempts, see volume one of this book. As another example, we can look at the connection between economics and corporate culture (Hermalin, 2001) from a different angle with nonlinearity involved.

References

Alchian, A. (1950). Uncertainty, evolution, and economic theory. *Journal of Political Economy, 58*(3), 211–221.

Altonji, J. G., Hayashi, F., & Kotlikoff, L. J. (1997). Parental altruism and inter vivos transfers: Theory and evidence. *Journal of Political Economy, 105*(6), 1121–1166.

Baland, J. M., & Robinson, J. (2000). Is child labor inefficient? *Journal of Political Economy, 108*(4), 663–679.

Barro, R. J. (1974). Are government bonds new wealth? *Journal of Political Economy, 82*(6), 1095–1117.

Becker, G. (1974). A theory of social interactions. *Journal of Political Economy, 82*(6), 1063–1093.

Becker, G. (1991). *A treatise of the family*. Harvard University Press.

Bergstrom, T. (1989). A fresh look at the rotten kid theorem and other household mysteries. *Journal of Political Economy, 97*(5), 1138–1159.

Berle, A., & Means, G. (1932). *The modern corporation and private property*. Macmillan.

Bhalotra, S. (2004). Parent altruism, cash transfers and child poverty. Discussion Paper 4/562, Department of Economics, University of Bristol, UK.

Bommier, A., & Dubois, P. (2004). Rotten parents and child labor. *Journal of Political Economy, 112*(1), 240–248.

Brickley, J., Coles, J., & Terry, R. (1994). Outside directors and the adoption of poison pills. *Journal of Financial Economics, 35*(3), 371–390.

Burrough, B., & Helyar, J. (1990). *Barbarians at the gate: The Fall of RJR Nabisco*. Harper & Row.

Conyon, M., & Read, L. (2006). A model of the supply of executives for outside directorships. *Journal of Corporate Finance, 12*(3), 645–659.

Core, J., Holthausen, R., & Larcker, D. (1999). Corporate governance, chief executive officer compensation, and firm performance. *Journal of Financial Economics, 51*(3), 371–406.

DeLong, B. (1991). Did Morgan's men add values? An economist's perspective on financial capitalism. In P. Temin (Ed.), *Inside the business enterprise: Historical perspectives on the use of information* (pp. 205–250). Chicago University Press.

Denis, D., & Denis, D. (1995). Performance changes following top-management dismissals. *The Journal of Finance, 50*(4), 1029–1057.

Denis, D., & Serrano, J. (1996). Active investors and management turnover following unsuccessful control contests. *Journal of Financial Economics, 40*(2), 239–266.

Easterbrook, F., & Fischel, D. (1991). *The economic structure of corporate law*. Harvard University Press.

Eisenberg, M. (1976). *The structure of the corporation: A legal analysis*. Little, Brown and Co.

Federio, G. (2004). Samaritans, rotten kids and policy conditionality. Working Paper 0409004, Development and Comp Systems.

Fernandes, A. (2000). Altruism with endogenous labor supply. Papers 0002, Centro de Estudios Monetarios Y. Financieros.

Franks, J., & Mayer, C. (1994). The ownership and control of German corporation. Manuscript, London Business School.

Ghaudhuri, A., Gangadharan, L., & Maitra, P. (2005). An experimental analysis of group size and risk sharing. Research Paper 955, Department of Economics, University of Melbourne, Melbourne Victoria, Australia.

Gilson, S. (1990). Bankruptcy, boards, banks, and block holders. *Journal of Financial Economics, 27*(2), 355–387.

Gorton, G., & Schmid, F. (1996). Universal banking and the performance of German firms. Working Paper 5453, National Bureau of Economic Research, Cambridge, MA.

Hart, O. (1995). *Firms, contracts, and financial structure*. Oxford University Press.

Hermalin, B. (2001). Economics and corporate culture. In S. Cartwright et al. (Eds.), *The international handbook of organizational culture and climate* (pp. 217–262). John Wiley & Sons.

Hermalin, B., & Weisbach, M. (2003). Boards of directors as an endogenously determined institution: A survey of the economic literature. *ERBNY Economic Policy Review*. April 7–26.

Jensen, M. (1986). Agency costs of free cash flow, corporate finance, and takeovers. *The American Economic Review, 76*(2), 323–329.

Jensen, M., & Meckling, W. (1976). Theory of the firm: Managerial behavior, agency costs, and ownership structure. *Journal of Financial Economics, 3*(4), 305–360.

Jensen, M. C. (1993). The modern industrial revolution, exit, and the failure of internal control systems. *The Journal of Finance, 48*(3), 831–880.

Jensen, M. C., & Ruback, R. S. (1983). The market for corporate control: The scientific evidence. *Journal of Financial Economics, 11*(1-4), 5–50.

Kahneman, D., & Thaler, R. (2006). Utility maximization and experienced utility. *Journal of Economic Perspectives, 20*(1), 221–234.

Kaplan, S. N., & Minton, B. A. (1994). Appointments of outsiders to Japanese boards: Departments and implications for managers. *Journal of Financial Economics, 36*(2), 225–258.

Lin, Y. (2007). Systemic yoyo model and applications in Newton's, Kepler's laws, etc. *Kybernetes: International Journal of Systems and Cybernetics, 36*(3/4), 484–516.

Lin, Y. (2008). *Systemic Yoyos: Impacts of the second dimension*. Auerbach Publications, an imprint of Taylor and Francis.

Lin, Y., & Forrest, D. (2008). Economic yoyos and Becker's rotten kid theorem. *Kybernetes: International Journal of Systems and Cybernetics, 37*(2), 297–314.

Lin, Y., & Liu, S. F. (2011). Small and large projects: Their dynamics and which ones to take. *Kybernetes: The International Journal of Cybernetics, Systems and Management Science, 40*(9-10), 1354–1372.

Lipton, M., & Lorsch, J. W. (1992). A modest proposal for improved corporate governance. *Business Lawyer, 48*(1), 59–77.

MacAvoy, P., Cantor, S., Dana, J., & Peck, S. (1983). All proposals for increased control of the corporation by board of directors: An economic analysis. In *Statement of the business roundtable on the American Law Institute's proposed "Principles of Corporate Governance and Structure: Restatement and Recommendation*." New York: Business Roundtable.

Manne, H. G. (1965). Mergers and the market for corporate control. *Journal of Political Economy, 73*(2), 110–126.

Menchik, P. L. (1980). Primogeniture, equal sharing, and the U.S. distribution of wealth. *The Quarterly Journal of Economics, 94*(2), 299–316.

OECD (Organization for Economic Cooperation and Development) (1995). Corporate governance environments in OECD countries. February 1.

Owen, T. (1991). *The Corporation under Russian Law, 1800–1917: A Study in Tsarist Economic Policy*. Cambridge University Press.

Patacchini, E., & Zenou, Y. (2004). *Intergenerational education transmission: Neighborhood quality and/or parents' involvement? Working Paper 631 (2004)*. IUI, Research Institute of Industrial Economics.

Pound, J. (1988). Proxy contests and the efficiency of shareholder oversight. *Journal of Financial Economics, 20*(Jan-Mar), 237–265.

Prowse, S. D. (1990). Institutional investment patterns and corporate financial behavior in the United States and Japan. *Journal of Financial Economics, 27*(1), 43–66.

Roe, M. (1994). *Strong managers, weak owners: The political roots of American Corporate Finance*. Princeton University Press.

Shivdasani, A. (1993). Board composition, ownership structure, and hostile takeovers. *Journal of Accounting and Economics, 16*(1-3), 167–198.

Shleifer, A., & Vishny, R. W. (1986). Large shareholders and corporate control. *Journal of Political Economy, 94*(3), 461–488.

Shleifer, A., & Vishny, R. W. (1989). Management entrenchment: The case of manager-specific investments. *Journal of Financial Economics, 25*(1), 123–139.

Shleifer, A., & Vishny, R.W. (1990). Equilibrium short horizons of investors and firms. *The American Economic Review, Papers and Proceedings of the 102nd Annual Meeting of the American Economic Association,* 80(2), 148-153.
Shleifer, A., & Vishny, R. W. (1997). A survey of corporate governance. *The Journal of Finance, 52*(2), 737–783.
Smith, C. W., & Warner, J. B. (1979). On financial contracting: An analysis of bond covenants. *Journal of Financial Economics, 7*(2), 117–161.
Soros, G. (1998). *The crisis of global capitalism: Open society endangered.* Public Affairs.
Stigler, G. J. (1958). The economics of scale. *The Journal of Law and Economics, 1*, 54–71.
Weisbach, M. S. (1988). Outside directors and CEO turnover. *Journal of Financial Economics, 20*(Jan-Mar), 431–460.
Yafeh, Y., & Yosha, O. (1996). Large shareholders and banks: Who monitors and how? Manuscript, Hebrew University, Jerusalem, Israel.
Yermack, D. (1996). Higher market valuation of companies with a small board of directors. *Journal of Financial Economics, 40*(2), 185–211.
Yermack, D. (1997). Good timing: CEO stock option awards and company news announcements. *The Journal of Finance, 52*(2), 449–476.
Zingales, L. (1994). The value of the voting right: A study of the Milan stock exchange experience. *The Review of Financial Studies, 7*(1), 125–148.

Part III
Managerial Decisions in Modern Business World

Chapter 8
Sustainable and Transient Competitive Advantages

Jeffrey Yi-Lin Forrest and Pavani Tallapally

Abstract By relying on game theory and relevant methods of reasoning of systems science, this chapter, which is mainly based on Forrest (General Systems Theory: Foundation, Intuition and Applications in Business Decision Making. Switzerland: Springer, 2019, Chapter 17) and Forrest and Tallapally (Journal of Business, Economics and Technology, 21(1):1–14, 2018), presents some main results on how firms compete for customers who switch from the product of one company to another by adjusting prices; how their expected profits stay stagnant; why their bases of loyal customers deteriorate while customers become less patient than ever before. In particular, derived results, among others, include: (1) In a developed marketplace, risk neutrality would lead to stagnation in profits and irrational decision on pricing; (2) when the competition of the market grows with more new firms entering the market, the loyal-customer base of the incumbent firms deteriorates over time; and (3) systemic models are developed to explain why competitive advantages of the past seem to be sustainable, while present competitive advantages transient. On top of these results, the rest of the chapter provides deductive explanations for

1. Why markets have been changing faster;
2. Why customers are less patient than ever before, and
3. What the most important organizational element is in order for firms to successfully surf through waves of transient competitive advantages one after another.

Additionally, this chapter also provides a practically useful intuition for making sound and quick managerial decisions.

Keywords Fleeting opportunities · Market entry timing · Online retail · Organizational inefficiency · Price per unit value · Stagnation in profits

Jeffrey Yi-Lin Forrest (Department of Accounting Economics Finance, Slippery Rock University, Slippery Rock, PA, USA; Email: Jeffrey.forrest@sru.edu) and Pavani Tallapally (Department of Accounting Economics Finance, Slippery Rock University, Slippery Rock, PA, USA; Email: pavani.tallapally@sru.edu) are equally contributed to this chapter.

J. Y.-L. Forrest, *Systemic Principles of Applied Economic Philosophies II*,
Translational Systems Sciences 39, https://doi.org/10.1007/978-981-99-7939-4_8

8.1 Introduction

With the blossoming of online retail businesses, traditional, storefront-based retails get hit big time. Currently, a massive number of retail stores are closing and a huge number of employees are laid off from the retail industry..., as the news goes. That is only a snapshot of the avalanche changes in the present business world, where markets change faster, competitive advantages of companies become much shorter lived, and business entities are reconfigured as more cohesive wholes than before.

Looking at the dramatic development in the business world, other than mustering comprehensive conjectures about what is underneath the fast-changing practices behind magnificent successes and devastating failures based on anecdotes and data mining, a natural question for decision-making managers and entrepreneurs arises:

> Can a general theory be developed, from which managers and entrepreneurs can plausibly and deductively explain what is happening with reliability?

To address this question theoretically, this chapter, which is mainly based on Forrest (2019) and Forrest and Tallapally (2018), is able to also examine such issues as how firms compete for customers who switch from the product of one company to another by adjusting prices; how their expected profits stay stagnant; why their bases of loyal customers deteriorate, while customers become less patient than ever before. By doing so, this chapter establishes the following results, among others, by employing the intuition of systemic thinking and the rigor of game theory: (1) Within an oligopoly market, in the Nash equilibrium, when the competition of the market grows with an increasing number of firms entering the market, the base of loyal customers for each incumbent firm will gradually diminish; (2) in a developed marketplace, risk neutrality would lead to stagnation in profits and irrational decision on pricing; and (3) systemic models are developed to explain why competitive advantages of the past seem to be sustainable, while present competitive advantages transient.

Based on these results, derived deductively are natural explanations for why markets have been changing faster, customers become less patient than ever before, and what the most important organizational element is for a firm to successfully ride waves of transient competitive advantages.

To understand why the idea of sustainable competitive advantages is a concept of the past, this chapter employs Bjerknes' circulation theorem to develop a systemic view of how local, regional, and then world economies evolve with time. That naturally explains deductively what makes present competitive advantages feel like transient. To identify the most important organizational characteristic for a firm to succeed in the present world of business, this chapter shows that it is internal stability of the firm in terms of a long-term unwavering ambition and major investment in creating a common identity, culture, and commitment to leadership development in individual employees. Such internal stability equips the firm with the essential organizational culture for necessary changes to take place.

The rest of this chapter is organized as follows: Section 8.2 provides a review of the related literature. Section 8.3 investigates such a market that is coordinately monopolized and how a stagnation in profits can be expected and explains why market movement has been accelerating, while consumers become less patient. Section 8.4 looks at market competitions in terms of sustainable or transient advantages. Section 8.5 identifies an important organizational lifeforce. Then, this chapter is concluded in Sect. 8.6.

8.2 Literature Review

Chan and Chan (2010) maintain that in the fast-changing fashion market, being flexible and adaptive is a key for survival. So, they study supplier selection to support supply chain strategies with quick responses. They present an example of solving the problem in the apparel industry by using the analytical hierarchy process. Based on their previous conclusions that technology strategy variables tend to predominate as predictors of survival in the fast-changing rigid disk drive industry, Christensen et al. (1998) test the hypothesis that the technological strategies and market strategies of a new entrant are highly interrelated and that their joint effect plays an important role in a firm's chance of survival.

Because organizations evolve through periods of incremental or evolutionary development punctuated by discontinuous or revolutionary changes, Tushman and O'Reilly III (1996) consider it a challenge for managers to adapt the culture and strategy of their organizations to its current environment while not undermining the companies' ability to adjust to radical changes in that environment. Day (1994) studies how businesses can achieve and sustain their market-driven orientation, while finding that the emerging capabilities approach to strategic management offers ways to design change programs that will enhance a market orientation with increased capabilities in market sensing and customer linking. By contrasting two distinct business cases Day and Schoemaker (2016) assess the managerial implications of sensing, seizing, and transforming, critical capabilities for successful organizational adaptation. Among other results, these authors develop an embryonic contingency model to illustrate why the relative importance of dynamic capabilities varies across firms.

Kaharuddin et al. (2017) investigate and measure the transient competitive advantage readiness among hotels, cafes, and fashion retail industry in Bandung, Indonesia. Contradicting Porter's views, Bashir and Verma (2017) highlight how business model innovation can serve as a competitive advantage by reviewing and analyzing the literature on competitive advantage. Leavy (2016) considers what dynamic capabilities will be needed to compete in a world of transient advantage, like modern China, with its complicated and quickly changing demand pattern, hyper-competition, shifting industry boundaries, and discontinuities in the regulatory context.

By reviewing the literature on adaptability, Koller (2016) introduces the concept of adaptive advantage and addresses the problem of its implementation in an organization by looking at innovation culture, decision-making style, and accumulated experience of a sample of "old" and innovative firms. Purkayastha and Sharma (2016) inductively analyze the unique decisions of three firms that develop a competitive advantage by shaping their business model. The authors emphasize on the criticality of business model as a higher-level construct formed from multiple structural and strategic decisions that, eventually, become a source of competitive advantage.

Guo et al. (2012) address the role of downstream market competition under symbiotic production and demonstrate that incorporating different types of competition in product markets will partially eliminate the inefficiency as caused by double marginalization. Chang et al. (2015) consider the effect of market competition on the relationship between corporate governance and capital structure dynamics. Debruyne and Reibstein (2005) investigate when incumbents should enter into new market niches created by technological innovation. Their results demonstrate that incumbents are more likely to respond to innovations in their industry when their counterparts do so. Because a new product (attacker) entering into a competitive market is likely to provoke responses from some or all of the existing products (defenders), Kumar and Sudharshan (1988) investigate the development of optimal defensive strategies based on an understanding of the possible reactions of all the defenders to an optimal attack. Similar results are also obtained by (Hauser & Shugan, 1983), where different consumer response models and a different equilibrium assumption are used.

So, comparing what this chapter develops and the literature, the results established herein enrich the relevant knowledge at the height of theoretical abstraction with a much wider range of applicability. Moreover, beyond these contributions, the general question this chapter attempts to address is to show that other than inductive reasoning, deductive reasoning needs to be employed to produce scientifically sound theories and conclusions. Here, inductive reasoning is the exclusively used logic of thinking in the literature in areas related to the discussions of this chapter, where anecdotes and data mining are employed to draw general conclusions. However, it is well known in science that such conclusions are generally not reliable. To this end, this chapter establishes a theoretical model for how a marketplace develops and evolves by using concepts, theories, and laboratory observations of systems science, and a theoretical result by employing game theory. After that, this chapter shows how empirical conclusions, drawn previously and inductively on anecdotes and data mining by various scholars, can be deductively established or improved. Scientifically speaking, such theoretical conclusions are more reliable than those conjectured based on anecdotes and data mining.

8.3 Coordinated Monopoly and Expected Stagnation in Profits

This section studies a specific, while commonly existent, market condition, where the market of concern is occupied by a few incumbent firms. Although these firms compete with each other, they are also situated in a state of mutual forbearance. This section consists of two subsections. The first one sets up the basics of the particular market and shows how several key parameters can be normalized so that the symbiotic and mutual interactive firms can be compared. The second subsection explores the scenario of how the incumbent firms evolve with stagnant levels of profits while exploiting their loyal consumers.

8.3.1 Basic Assumptions

Consider an oligopoly market with m incumbent firms, named 1, 2, . . ., m. These firms offer the market with mutually substitutable products, although the products are different in terms of quality and follow-up services. Without loss of generality, assume that each firm produces only one product. Assume that these firms have decisively controlled their respective shares of the market with individually solid bases of loyal consumers; consequently, these firms have become risk neutral and plan to continuously reap in their respective profits by securely defending their established turfs. As in a real-life market, assume that there are customers in the marketplace who make their purchases based on whose price is the lowest. So, these customers will be called switchers; they are not loyal to any of the incumbent firms. To attract the business of these switchers, the incumbent firms adjust their selling prices. In other words, assume that the incumbent firms produce their products that are horizontally differentiated at constant marginal costs.

Assume that the managements of the m incumbent firms are well aware of the pricing strategies of the other firms and have established their best responses by playing the Nash equilibrium through pure self-analyses. Because of all these assumptions, in this chapter, such a market will be referred to as coordinately monopolized (by these incumbent firms).

Proposition 8.1 In the market described above, the average price P_i of firm i can be normalized into an equivalent price α_i, satisfying $0 \le \alpha_i \le 1$, while the corresponding cost and maximum expected selling price are, respectively, normalized to 0 and 1.

Proof For firm i (=1, 2, . . ., m), the price P_i of its product, on the average, satisfies $C_i \le P_i \le M_i$, where C_i stands for the cost of production and M_i the maximum expected selling price (or the reservation price). Then the actual average selling price can be written as follows:

$$P_i = C_i + \alpha_i(M_i - C_i), i = 1, 2, \ldots, m \tag{8.1}$$

for some parameter α_i from the interval [0,1]. In other words, no offer, on the average, is sold at a price below its cost. Now, instead of competing against each other by using the absolute terms of the selling prices P_i, the factories compete by adjusting the parameters α_i, $i = 1, 2, \ldots, m$, to see who is more competitive in terms of unit value of their offers.

To understand the meaning of the parameters α_i, $i = 1, 2, \ldots, m$, let us use the price per unit value. In particular, although the offers of the incumbent firms are considered horizontally differentiated or mutually substitutable, in real life they still entail individually different features and functionalities, such as differences in appearance, in craftmanship, and in quality of service. For example, the conventional walkie-talkies and modern iPhones can be seen as substitutable products if used in the limited situations for which the former was designed. Because the latter possesses much more values and functionalities beyond the said limited use scope of the former, each iPhone is much higher priced than that of a walkie-talkie. Now, if one compares the price per unit value (or unit value) of a walkie-talkie to that of an iPhone, he will most likely find that the unit-value price of an iPhone is cheaper than that of a walkie-talkie. So, in real life, a consumer can compare two products by using their price per unit value.

Without loss of generality, in the rest of this chapter, each firm's price P_i will be normalized as outlined in Proposition 8.1. And the normalized price α_i will still be written as P_i.

Evidently, each of the m incumbent firms is generally limited by its unique set of constraints (or boundary conditions). Such conditions for the individual firms are realistically caused by differences in resources available to the firms and their factories. Each firm can utilize its resources, which are defined as tangible or intangible assets (Harmancioglu et al., 2009), to design and implement its business strategies (Barney & Arikan, 2001). For example, each firm has its unique set of missions, organizational culture, history, administrative structure, capital-flow pattern, and managerial style. Symbolically, assume that for the m firms, the factors involved in the production and marketing of their offers are $f_1, f_2, f_3, \ldots$ Then, for firm i (= 1, 2, 3, . . ., n), the magnitude N_i of its base of loyal customers reflects how available resources are mobilized in ways that are accepted both internally and externally, which is where individuals' systems of values and beliefs are involved. So, the magnitude N_i must be naturally constrained by its lower boundary condition $L_i(f_1, f_2, f_3, \ldots)$ and upper boundary condition $U_i(f_1, f_2, f_3, \ldots)$ as follows:

$$L_i(f_1, f_2, f_3, \ldots) \leq N_i \leq U_i(f_1, f_2, f_3, \ldots). \tag{8.2}$$

Therefore, for firm i, $i = 1, 2, \ldots, m$, there is a unique number β_i in the interval [0,1] satisfying

$$N_i = L_i(f_1, f_2, f_3, \ldots) + \beta_i[U_i(f_1, f_2, f_3, \ldots) - L_i(f_1, f_2, f_3, \ldots)]. \tag{8.3}$$

Similar to the previous analysis of Proposition 8.1, it can be concluded that the magnitude N_i of the base of firm i's loyal customers, for fixed $f_1, f_2, f_3, \ldots$, can be normalized to the parameter β_i ($\in[0, 1]$). That is, the result below holds true.

Proposition 8.2 For the m incumbent firms, their lower and upper boundary conditions can be normalized to 0 and 1, respectively. And, the magnitudes of their bases of loyal customers can be normalized to parameters that take values between 0 and 1 inclusively.

In the rest of this chapter, for firm i (= 1, 2, ..., m), let the magnitude of its loyal customers be denoted as β_i, satisfying $0 \leq \beta_i \leq 1$, its price distribution be $F_i(P)$. And, let the magnitude of the market segment of switchers be denoted as β such that $\beta = 1 - \sum_{i=1}^{m} \beta_i$ and $0 \leq \beta \leq 1$.

Theorem 8.1 In Nash equilibrium, a symmetric mixed strategy exists for the m incumbent firms in the aforementioned market, if and only if the magnitudes of the loyal-customer bases of the firms are equal to each other.

Proof With the normalizations described in Propositions 8.1 and 8.2 in place, the m firms only need to compete against each other by using prices. With some genuine argument, it can be shown (Narasimhan, 1988; Varian, 1980) that there is no pure strategy portfolio for the m-player game presented here. Then, firm k's profit from its loyal customers are $\beta_k P$ and those from its share of the switchers are $\prod_{i=1, i\neq k}^{n}[1 - F_i(P)]\beta P$. Hence, the objective function for firm k is to maximize the following expected profit by adjusting $F_k(P)$:

$$E(\Pi_k) = \int_{-\infty}^{+\infty} \left\{\beta_k P + \prod\nolimits_{i=1, i\neq k}^{n}[1 - F_i(P)]\beta P\right\} dF_k(P), \tag{8.4}$$

where Π_k is firm k's profit, and $E(\Pi_k)$ its expected profit. The Nash equilibrium indifference condition for firm k is

$$\beta_k P + \prod\nolimits_{i=1, i\neq k}^{n}[1 - F_i(P)]\beta P = \beta_k, k = 1, 2, \ldots, n. \tag{8.5}$$

Equation 8.5 implies the following system of equations:

$$\{[1 - F_1(P)] \ldots [1 - F_{k-1}(P)][1 - F_{k+1}(P)] \ldots [1 - F_n(P)]\beta P = \beta_k(1 - P), \tag{8.6}$$

for any $k = 1, 2, \ldots, n$. Let $k = i$ and $j = 1, 2, \ldots, n$, respectively, $i \neq j$. Then dividing the ith equation by the jth equation from Eq. 8.6 produces

$$\frac{1-F_j(P)}{1-F_i(P)}=\frac{\beta_i}{\beta_j}, \text{or } 1-F_j(P)=\frac{\beta_i}{\beta_j}[1-F_i(P)]. \tag{8.7}$$

By letting $i=1$, Eq. 8.7 leads to

$$1-F_j(P)=\frac{\beta_1}{\beta_j}[1-F_1(P)], j=2,3, \ldots, n. \tag{8.8}$$

Now, Eq. 8.8 implies that $F_i(P) = F_j(P)$, if and only if $\beta_i = \beta_j$, for all $i, j = 1, 2, \ldots, n$.

8.3.2 Coordinated Monopoly and Profit Stagnation

This section looks at the general case when the oligopoly and coordinately monopolized market is served by m incumbent firms, as described in the previous section.

Based on what is established in Theorem 8.1 and the systemic intuition by using the dishpan experiment, assume that the size of the loyal consumer base of each firm is a constant α such that these consumers only purchase the product of their respective firms provided that the price is not more than their reservation value, which is again set to 1. Let the segment of all switchers, who switch from one firm to another totally depending on the price, in the market be of the size β. Then the following equation holds true:

$$m\alpha+\beta=1, \tag{8.9}$$

where both α and β are normalized as described earlier.

Theorem 8.2 In the symmetric Nash equilibrium of this coordinately monopolized market, each of these m firms' expected profits stays constant and is equal to α although each of them tries to attract as many switchers as possible, while each of these firms exploits its loyal consumers by charging them an as high price as possible.

The systemic intuition behind this result is clear: imagine the market of concern as the entire spinning dish in the dishpan experiment, while each of the m firms as one of the local eddy leaves so that there are a total of m local eddies in the spinning dish. Hence, no matter how hard each of the local eddy spins in order to pull more of the fluid particles into its field, some of the fluid particles always tend to wonder around the spin field of the dish without actually becoming part of any of the local eddies. In other words, as soon as such a pattern of fluid movement as in the dishpan experiment is formed and becomes stabilized, it will be difficult or impossible for the local eddies to grow any larger.

Proof By continuing the proof of Theorem 8.1, the objective function of firm i is

$$\max_{F_i(P)} E(\Pi_i) = \int_0^1 \left\{\alpha P + \prod\nolimits_{j \neq i}^{m} [1 - F_k(P)]\beta P\right\} dF_i(P). \tag{8.10}$$

Firm i can earn α by charging the reservation value 1, because all the firm's loyal consumers will purchase its product at that price. However, to potentially maximize profits, each firm likes to adjust the price P in order to take in as many of the switchers as possible. At the same time each firm does not have any incentive to price its product below the price of $\alpha/(\alpha + \beta)$, because any price below $\alpha/(\alpha + \beta)$ will yield profits less than α despite of attracting all the switchers, where

$$\alpha P + \beta P \geq \alpha \rightarrow P \geq \frac{\alpha}{\alpha + \beta}.$$

The equilibrium indifference condition for firm i is

$$\alpha \times P + \prod\nolimits_{j \neq i}^{m} [1 - F_j(P)]\beta \times P = \alpha \times 1, \ \frac{\alpha}{\alpha + \beta} \leq P \leq 1, \tag{8.11}$$

for $i, j = 1, 2, \ldots, m$, and $i \neq j$. So, the symmetric equilibrium price distribution is the following continuous function:

$$F(P) = F_i(P) = F_j(P) = 1 - \left[\frac{(1 - P)\alpha}{P(1 - m\alpha)}\right]^{\frac{1}{m-1}}, \ \frac{\alpha}{\alpha + \beta} \leq P \leq 1, \tag{8.12}$$

satisfying the boundary conditions:

$$F\left(\frac{\alpha}{\alpha + \beta}\right) = 0 \text{ and } F(1) = 1. \tag{8.13}$$

In this unique mixed strategy Nash equilibrium, there is no mass point of prices that the firms charge with positive probability. Hence, each firm's expected profits are

$$\begin{aligned} E(\Pi) &= \int_{-\infty}^{+\infty} \left\{\alpha P + \prod\nolimits_{j \neq i}^{m} [1 - F_k(P)]\beta P\right\} dF(P) \\ &= \int_{\frac{\alpha}{\alpha+\beta}}^{1} \alpha dF(P) \\ &= \alpha F(P)\Big|_{\frac{\alpha}{\alpha+\beta}}^{1} = \alpha. \end{aligned} \tag{8.14}$$

That is, in the symmetric mixed strategy Nash equilibrium, each firm's expected profits do not change although each of the firms tries to attract as many switchers as possible, while each of these firms exploits its loyal consumers by charging them as high price as possible.

8.3.3 Accelerated Market Movement and Less Patient Consumers

Because of the advent of the internet in particular and the knowledge-based economy in general, decreases in protective trade regulations and advances in technology, consumers and markets are changing faster than ever. And, customers are becoming increasingly less patient with service providers and product suppliers than before. As a consequence, the advantages that made many commercial companies iconic, such as the 163-year-old Alliance Boots (UK), have evaporated. Therefore, many companies now seek to be quicker, more decisive, and more candid so that they address any negative news immediately. They spend more time thinking about the future than any time in the past. To capture opportunities and act as an organic whole, many companies seek to break down internal structural solos while creating courageous leaders who are fully engaged in capturing opportunities and moving away from strategies and practices that are no longer appropriate for the future (McGrath, 2013, p. ix). Therefore, two natural questions arise: (i) What makes markets change faster and customers less patient than ever? (ii) What makes past sustainable competitive advantages presently transient?

The answers to these two questions are closely related. Let us address first one first. To this end, let us revisit the oligopoly market described above and derive the following result, where the technical proof is given in the appendix of this chapter.

Theorem 8.3 In the Nash equilibrium, when the competition of the afore-described market grows with an increasing number of firms entering the market, the base of loyal customers for each incumbent firm will gradually diminish.

This theorem provides an answer to the first question posed in the beginning of Sect. 8.4: What have made markets change faster and customers less patient than ever? In particular, because of the growing globalization of the world commerce, consumer markets, which were once regional and tightly controlled by local firms, are becoming international with increasing number of firms from different corners of the world competing for the same customers. In terms of the systemic yoyo model, initially, the world consisted exclusively of local markets, as indicated by the small eddy leaves in Fig. 8.1a, where the overall circular pool stands for the world market. Because the international commerce did not exist or the scale was very small so that it can be ignored, the overall circular dish in Fig. 8.1a does not spin. That is, the businesses of the world are not functioning as a system. Next, with the advancement of modern transportation and communication technology, the world becomes more connected through international transfers of goods, information, and knowledge, the originally disconnected regional markets become connected as shown in Fig. 8.1b. The counterclockwise spin of the overall dish models the fact that goods, information, and knowledge are now traveling throughout the world, while originally local firms, the local eddies that also rotate round with the overall dish, are also serving the entire world market. Such much-increased sources of

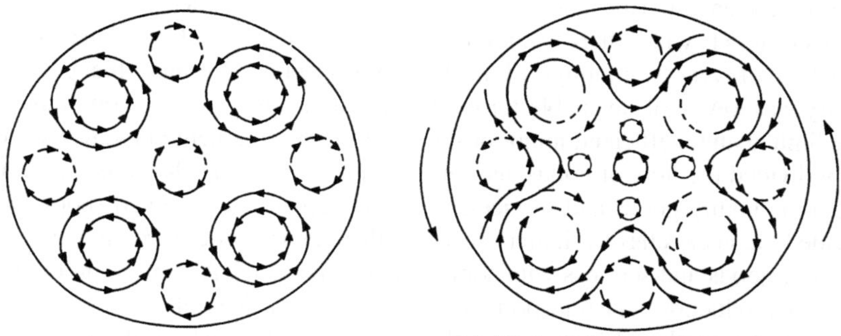

(a) Regional markets (b) Globalizing world markets

Fig. 8.1 The world full of regional markets. (**a**) Regional markets. (**b**) Globalizing world markets

suppliers of goods and services make customers spoiled so that they become less patient than ever before with anything unsatisfactory.

8.4 Competitive Advantages: Sustainable or Transient

In this section, let us answer the second question of Sect. 8.4 in two parts:

- Why do competitive advantages of the past seem sustainable? And
- What makes present competitive advantages feel like transient?

To address the first part, let us start by looking at Bjerknes' circulation theorem (1898) (Hess, 1959). This theorem shows that nonlinearity mathematically stands (mostly) for singularities and in terms of physics it represents eddy motions. Such motions are a problem of structural evolutions, a natural consequence of uneven evolutions of materials. For the technical details of this discussion, please see the appendix of this chapter.

Additionally, this theorem reveals the commonly existing and practically significant eddy effects of fluid motions and implies that uneven eddy motions are the most common form of movements observed in the universe. Because uneven densities create twisting forces, fields of spinning currents are naturally created. Such fields do not have uniformity in terms of types of currents. Clockwise and counterclockwise eddies always co-exist, leading to destructions of the initial smooth, if any, fields of currents. What is important is that the concept of uneven eddy evolutions reveals that forces exist in the structures of evolving objects and do not independently exist outside of the objects.

Now, let us look at the question we are addressing: Why do competitive advantages of companies in the past seem sustainable?

At the early times, people lived in more primitive conditions than the present time. Due to the existing natural conditions and available resources within the environment and societies, some people and households started to exchange their surplus of goods with others for improving the quality of their lives. That led to the formation of very beginnings of business transactions. Because the population density was low, tools available for production, transportation, and communication were limited and inefficient, minor obstacles of the environment in today's standard easily divided the flow of goods and services into small-scale shops. Because other than some luxury goods and services, these individual and separated shops mostly provided the necessities for human survival, they naturally delivered mostly identical set of goods and services with some minor differences. As time went on, better tools for production and transportation and better practices of management were designed and employed in various individual shops. The natural desire for better living conditions paved the way for inventions of new tools, discovery of new methods of production, and introduction of more efficient ways of management to pass around the land through word of mouth and through improving technology of communication. So, a circulation of information and people with special abilities and resources started to form. As the circulation started to appear, Bjerknes' circulation theorem guarantees the appearance of abstract eddy motions over the land consisting of migration of people, spread of knowledge and information, and transportation of goods. That explains how local and then regional markets were initially formed and why all markets have conditions and barriers against new entrants. That is, over time incumbent firms have naturally established their respective competitive advantages as part of the conditions and barriers that help the firms to exploit their market shares while preventing competitions from new entrants. That explains why competitive advantages of the past seem to be sustainable, and indeed, they were for the most part sustainable. Consequently, most of strategy frameworks and tools in use were based on the single dominant notion: The purpose of designing and adopting strategies is to achieve a sustainable competitive advantage.

At this junction, there is a natural need to justify the scientific validity for us to employ the Bjerknes' circulation theorem as in the previous paragraph, because in theory this theorem holds true only for fluids. Firstly, when the systemic yoyo model is initially introduced earlier, we have given a relevant explanation for how and why each human organization is a spinning pool of fluid, consisting of flows of such fluids as energy, information, materials, etc., that circulate within the inside of, go into, and are given off from the organization. Secondly, the systemic yoyo model of systems naturally leads to the realization that the universe is a huge ocean of eddies, which changes and evolves constantly. That is, we can study the totality of the physically existing world as fluids. Thirdly, as described in the previous paragraph, people in the land helped circulate information, knowledge, goods, etc., all of which are studied by using continuous or differentiable functions in social sciences in general and economics in particular. When these aspects of a market are modeled by such functions, they are generally seen in physics and mathematics as flows of fluids and are widely known as flow functions. Specifically, in the formation of an economy, these commonly shared aspects (or fluids) make the land to have operational markets, where individual persons are simply local "impurities" of the fluids;

and each of the "impurities" carries some concentrated amount of "energy," information, knowledge, etc.

Secondly, let us see what makes present competitive advantages feel like transient. Recent frequently occurring breakthroughs and fast advances in communication technology, management methodologies, and manufacturing capabilities have made important know-how information more widely available, helped remove many insurmountable barriers of the past for the general public. In other words, such detailed information as for how to start up a competitive company, how to run a firm efficiently, and how to improve and market product beautifully have helped companies, either incumbent or new coming, to compete with each other on an unprecedented, equally leveled ground due to the fast advancement of communication technology. In addition, with the development of modern engineering technology, manufacturing an imagined product, which combines all the best-selling functionalities of relevant products, has become doable and much less costly than before. So, the secrets behind most of the so-called sustainable competitive advantages of the past have become common knowledge, while as soon as a new advantage leads to success, the underlying ideas become public information in no time. That is exactly the reason why newer competitive advantages have to be frequently introduced and evolved into fresh formats quickly.

In terms of the systemic yoyo model, the evolution of an economy, just as described in the previous paragraphs, can be shown most closely and vividly by using the dishpan experiment, Fig. 8.2. When the movement of the fluid within a rotational dish is under enough pressure created by either the sufficient speed of rotation or sufficient difference in temperature between the center and the periphery of the dish, the pattern of uniform movement in Fig. 8.2a will develop into the chaos in Fig. 8.2b. The number of local eddy leaves is determined either by the rotational speed or by the temperature difference or both and increases with the speed and the temperature difference.

Of course, for our situation in hands, the pattern in Fig. 8.2a needs to be replaced by that in Fig. 8.1a, because different from the perfect symmetry in the setup of the

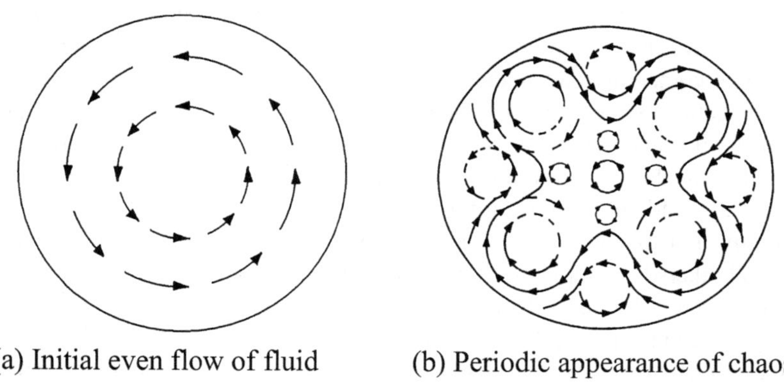

(a) Initial even flow of fluid (b) Periodic appearance of chaos

Fig. 8.2 The dishpan experiment. (**a**) Initial even flow of fluid. (**b**) Periodic appearance of chaos

dishpan experiment, the initial distribution of local markets (and economies) is not even or symmetric. Instead, it is dictated by natural conditions and availability of resources. Additionally, the symmetrical distribution of local eddy leaves in Fig. 8.2b will not be so symmetrical for our model of the world economy, either. Now, if we look at this model closely, we can see that as the pressure increases, caused by either the spinning speed or the "temperature" difference between the center and periphery of the dish, the number of eddy leaves will grow larger. Therefore, competitive advantages have to become temporary and transient in order for the incumbent eddy leaves to maintain their quality of livelihood. That is, in order to win in volatile and fast-moving environments, decision-making managers and entrepreneurs need to learn and master the skills of how to discover and exploit short-lived opportunities with speed and decisiveness. They need to realize the fact that the deeply ingrained structures and systems that they used to reply on to extract maximum value from a competitive advantage are actually liabilities, which are outdated and even dangerous, in the current fast-moving competitive environment.

8.5 An Organizational Lifeforce

Recent business practice, such as Fuji (film)'s story (Kunii et al., 1999; Inagaka & Osawa, 2012), suggests that simply managing well, developing quality products, and building up well-recognized brands are insufficient to remain on top in the increasingly heated global competition of the world economy. It seems that what is working in the face of rapid change is to invest in new competitive advantages while pulling resources from declining ones. Although no one gets it right every time and sometimes the moves are painful, companies cannot afford to be trapped by their past.

Historically, each iconic company found itself successfully in a favorable position in a well-defined industry and then optimally exploited a long-term competitive advantage. However, many of such storied organizations are either gone or no longer relevant today. Their downfall is the outcome of practices designed on the concept of sustainable competitive advantage. The deeply ingrained organizational structures and management systems, as designed to extract maximum value from a competitive advantage, become liabilities when the competition of the business world requires instead the capability to surf through waves of fleeting opportunities. To compete in these volatile and uncertain environments, companies have to conduct their business differently. For example, such big-name companies as DuPont, 3M, Nokia, Intel, IBM, and others have all realized that traditional approaches were not keeping pace with the speed of the markets in which they were competing (McGrath, 2013).

As proved in the previous section, competitive advantages come and go in waves. So, the job of strategists is to discover and take strategic initiatives by launching ever-new waves (MacMillan, 1982). To this end, MacMillan (1988) and D'Aveni and Gunther (1994) introduced the concept of hyper-competition to characterize markets in which firms' competitive advantages would be quickly competed away. And in practice, successful firms look candidly at what happened, figure out how to do what they attempted to do better the next time, and move on. They move from one wave of competitive advantages to another without staying with one wave too long because it will become exhausting, and they always look for the next one. Just like great surfers, after having ridden a wave either successfully or not, they get back on their boards to challenge the next tidal wave. In other words, transient competitive advantages of the present business world have been replacing most of the sustainable advantages of the past.

To adapt to the new environment of transient competitive advantages, companies have to design and apply new and different strategies on where to compete, how to compete, and how to win by constantly looking into the future. Central to this end is to reconfigure and renew advantages internally. It is through the reconfiguration process that assets, people, and capabilities make the transition from one advantage to another. Without such dynamism in the structures and processes of the organization, the firm will likely suffer from difficulties as soon as its competitors are competing in the next wave of transient advantages (McGrath, 2013).

By studying the best performing companies with a market capitalization of over $1 billion U.S. dollars as of the end of 2009 in 2010, ten such companies stood out for the time period of 2000–2009 (McGrath, 2013). These companies successfully coped with and then thrived amidst the challenge of moving from one advantage to the next, while their leadership promoted common key themes that came out of compelling strategy diagnoses. What is common to these outlier firms is their public commitment to world-class ambition, coupled with a clear sense of strategic direction. For example, at Infosys the leaders talk about Infosys 1.0 (basically labor arbitrage), Infosys 2.0 (global expansion into services), and then the emergence of Infosys 3.0 (McGrath, 2013).

Each of these companies grounded its strategies in the firm's stretch ambition, while the ambition provided an aiming point for the people directly or indirectly related to the company. Moreover, the ambition turned out to be important to long-term ongoing reconfiguration of the firm and is essential for preventing the company and its people from becoming complacent and content in pursuing yesterday's advantages.

Other than long-term, unwavering ambitions of being the world-class, the outlier firms also stabilize their organizations by investing in the creation of a common identity, culture, and commitment to leadership development. They wage significant attention to values, culture, and alignment in order to create the right cultural foundation that allows changes to happen. As confirmed by Bob Best, CEO of Atmos energy, "Culture is the foundation for all success. This has been a very important process to the long-term health and success of our company." For details, see (Senn-Delaney Leadership Consulting Group, 2023).

In terms of the systemic yoyo model, what is unearthed above inductively based on anecdotes can be derived deductively as follows: Having a long-term, unwavering ambition is equivalent to fixing the direction of the axis of spin for the underlying yoyo structure of the firm, Fig. 8.3. When the direction of the axis is

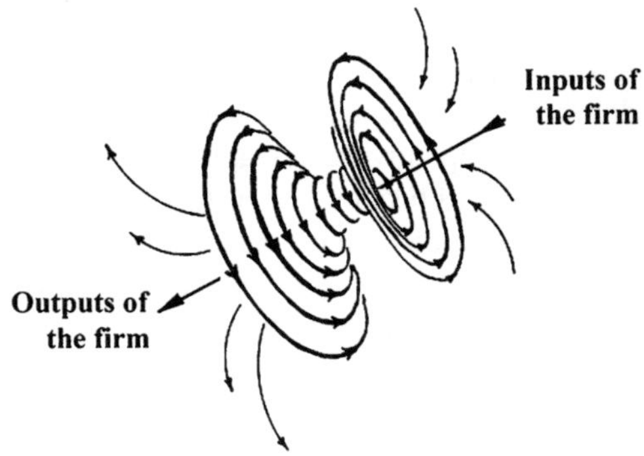

Fig. 8.3 A underlying yoyo structure with its axial direction fixed

fixed, supported, and promoted by the leadership, all layers of the eddy pool that spins around the axis will be able to focus their attention on interacting with their neighboring environments. That is, all employees located on different layers of the eddy pool can direct their attention to what is important for their divisions without the need to worry about potential change in the organization's business direction.

In terms of creating a common identity and culture for a firm to be health and prosperous, its importance is well spelled out by the following theoretical result, whose reasoning is in the appendix of this chapter:

Theorem 8.4 (Forrest & Orvis, 2016). Inefficiency always exists in the organizational system of any firm that has at least one full-time employee whose personal value is not in total agreement with the organization's mission, where the concept of organizational efficiency is defined as how well its employees help reach the defined mission of the organization.

From how personal systems of values and beliefs are formed (Forrest & Orvis, 2016), the details of which are given in the appendix of this chapter for the completeness of this presentation, it follows that finding employees with identical personal values are practically impossible. Moreover, personal systems of values and beliefs evolve with time and changes of the environment within which people live. So, initially similar values and beliefs tend to diverge over time. Additionally, suppose that a firm can find all the employees who have the desirable identical personal systems of values and beliefs, then what is observed in the dishpan experiment suggests that differences among the personal systems of values and beliefs will inevitably appear within the smooth operation of the organization. In particular, within the current context, one can naturally imagine that the entire dishpan stands for the mission of the organization of concern and the spin of the dishpan the operation of the organization, while individual employees' personal systems of values and beliefs are drops of the water inside the dishpan. Therefore, this dishpan experiment indicates that although the organization of concern can find and hire supposedly employees of identical personal systems of values and beliefs, this initial uniformity in individual personal values and beliefs will soon be destroyed by the smooth operation of the organization. Speaking in terms of the daily language, interactions and conflicts of employees' interests of the organization materialistically destroy the uniformity that exists in personal systems of values and beliefs. Therefore, Theorem 8.4 implies that organizational inefficiency starts to appear.

By pondering over Theorem 8.4 in more details from various angles and based on the discussion in the previous paragraph, one can readily see that organizational inefficiency always naturally exists within the operation of any firm (Theorem 8.4). So, for the firm to perform well while riding through one wave to next of competitive advantages, the firm has to behave as an organic whole with its unique identity, culture, and commitment to leadership development (that potentially lead to the discovery of new competitive advantages by individual employees). Without doing so, Theorem 8.4 implies that over time, no matter how successful a firm can presently be, internally mounting inefficiencies will eventually destroy the very foundation of the firm.

Summarizing the previous discussions in this section, a key organizational element for a firm to ride successfully transient-advantage waves is its internal stability. Here, the word "stability" is characterized by the fixed direction of the axis of the underlying yoyo structure of the firm (a long-term stretch ambition); that direction is supported and promoted by the leadership; and major investment is made around the fixed direction in order to create a common identity, culture, and commitment to leadership development in individual employees. More specifically, the particularly chosen direction of the axis aims at cultivating the necessary organizational cultural foundation through emphasizing on values, culture, and alignment so that changes can readily occur when needed. This end is similar to how human mind works (Lin & Forrest, 2011), while the term "human mind" is replaced by the "mind of a firm."

8.6 A Few Final Words

This chapter develops a general theory on what makes markets change faster and customers less patient than ever before, how firms compete for customers who switch from the product of one company to another by adjusting prices; how their expected profits stay stagnant; why their bases of loyal customers deteriorate, while customers become less patient than ever before. Then, deductively, instead of inductively based on anecdotes and data mining, as exclusively used in the relevant literature, this general theory is employed to establish the following main conclusions, among others:

1. In a developed marketplace, risk neutrality would lead to stagnation in profits and irrational decision on pricing;
2. When the severity of market competition grows with more new firms entering the market, the loyal-customer base of the incumbent firms deteriorates over time;

3. Systemic models are developed to explain why competitive advantages of the past seem to be sustainable, while present competitive advantages transient.

Based on these game-theoretic results, the rest of the chapter provides deductive explanations for

- Why markets have been changing faster;
- Why customers are less patient than ever before, and
- What the most important organizational element is in order for firms to successfully surf through waves of transient competitive advantages one after another.

Additionally, this chapter shows why internal stability is the key for a firm to ride successfully the waves of transient competitive advantages with a long-term stretch ambition, supported and promoted by the leadership with major investment in cultivating common identity, culture, and commitment to leadership development in individual employees. Therefore, an organizational culture is established to emphasize on values, culture, and alignment so that changes can be readily made when the market demands such.

In terms of market entry timing, this work clears up a few indecisive conclusions established by empirical studies of the literature. For example, it is theoretically shown that (i) as long as the market contains sufficient consumer surplus, new competition will naturally appear no matter what particular contingencies and antecedents are prevalent and (ii) established business entities should not be early movers of any new market until some first movers have demonstrated the existence and depth of the market.

All the results established in this chapter are developed on the intuition of the systemic yoyo model by looking at the market as a spinning yoyo field and by observing the dynamics of the internal movement of the "fluid" in Fig. 8.4. However, the well-known dishpan experiment suggests that when either the rotational speed of the dish or the temperature difference between the periphery and the center of the dish increases, the number of the local eddy pools will grow and the asymmetric pattern of flow will eventually return to that shown in Fig. 8.5 with time. So, what

Fig. 8.4 Asymmetric flow observed in Fultz et al.'s (1959) dishpan experiment

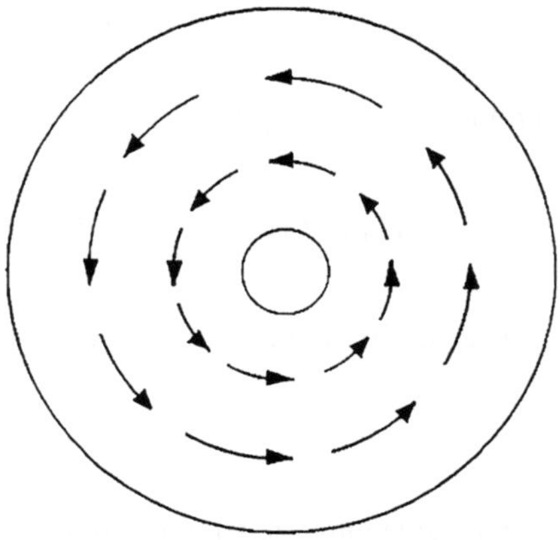

Fig. 8.5 Systemic bird's-eye view of the market of concern

could be potentially more thought provoking than what have been established in this chapter is to investigate the following open questions and related issues:

Question 8.1 How would the existing firms adjust themselves if the established market starts to shrink and eventually disappear, as the flow pattern in Fig. 8.4 starts to transform back into the one shown in Fig. 8.5 with time?

In other words, all the results, presented in this chapter, attempt to capture momentary "photographic" shots of the dynamics of an evolutionary process. In comparison, the most significant results will be those that portrait not only momentary shots but also reveal the laws underlying the evolution of the development process: germination—growth—maturity—disappearance. Results of this nature would fit the description of post-modern science, as well described in (Lin, 2009).

Appendix: Technical Details Relevant to this Chapter

The Proof of Theorem 8.3 This market does not have any pure strategy Nash equilibrium and nonsymmetrical mixed strategy Nash equilibrium, for details, see Narasimhan (1988) and Varian (1980).

Let $F_i(P)$ stand for the price distribution of firm i, $\in\{1,2,\ldots,m\}$, which compete with each to attract switchers. The assumption that an increasing number of firms enter the market implies that the consumer surplus satisfies $\beta = 1 - \alpha > 0$. Assume that there are n new firms that enter the market by uniformly randomizing its price P over the interval [0,1], where their cost bases are also assumed to be constant and set to zero and the reservation value for a loyal consumer to make purchase from his firm is 1. Then, the profits of incumbent Firm i are given by

$$\alpha P + \beta P(1-P)^n \prod_{j \neq i}^{m} [1 - F_j(P)]$$

and the objective function of incumbent Firm i is

$$\max_{F_i(P)} E(\Pi_i) = \int_0^1 \left\{ \alpha P + \beta P(1-P)^n \prod_{j \neq i}^{m} [1 - F_j(P)] \right\} dF_i(P).$$

The equilibrium indifference condition for incumbent Firm i is

$$\alpha \times P + \beta \times P(1-P)^n \prod_{j \neq i}^{m} [1 - F_j(P)] = \alpha \times 1.$$

So, the symmetric equilibrium price strategy of each incumbent firm i, $i = 1, 2, \ldots, m$, is

$$\begin{aligned} F(P) = F_i(P) &= 1 - P^{\frac{-1}{m-1}}(1-P)^{-\frac{n-1}{m-1}}\left(\frac{\alpha}{\beta}\right)^{\frac{1}{m-1}} \\ &= P^{\frac{-1}{m-1}}(1-P)^{-\frac{n-1}{m-1}} h(P), \end{aligned}$$

where $h(P) = P^{\frac{1}{m-1}}(1-P)^{\frac{n-1}{m-1}} - \left(\frac{\alpha}{\beta}\right)^{\frac{1}{m-1}}$.

For this strategy $F(P)$ to be valid, we must have $F(P) = 0$, for $P \leq \underline{P}$, $F(P) = 1$, for $P \geq \overline{P}$, and $F(P) \geq 0$, for $\underline{P} \leq P \leq \overline{P}$, where $\underline{P}$ and $\overline{P}$ are some fixed price levels such that $0 \leq \underline{P} < \overline{P} \leq 1$.

For such price levels $\underline{P}$ and $\overline{P}$ to exist, $h(P)$ must satisfy the following: $h(P) \geq 0$, for $\underline{P} \leq P \leq \overline{P}$, where $\underline{P}$ and $\overline{P}$ are some fixed price levels such that $0 \leq \underline{P} < \overline{P} \leq 1$, and that $h(0) < 0$ and $h(1) < 0$. Since

$$h'(P) = \frac{1}{m-1} P^{\frac{1}{m-1}}(1-P)^{\frac{n-1}{m-1}}\left[P^{-1} - (n-1)(1-P)^{-1}\right],$$

it can be shown that $h(P)$ reaches its maximum at $P = 1/n$. That is, in order for the previously mentioned price levels $\underline{P}$ and $\overline{P}$ to exist, $h(P)$ must satisfy $h\left(\frac{1}{n}\right) > 0$, which means

$$\frac{\alpha}{\beta} < \frac{1}{n}\left(1 - \frac{1}{n}\right)^{n-1} = \left(1 - \frac{1}{n}\right)^n \left(1 - \frac{1}{n}\right)\frac{1}{n}.$$

So, when $n \to \infty$, $\alpha/\beta \to (1/e) \times 1 \times 0 = 0$. This end means that the base of loyal customers for each incumbent firm gradually diminishes when an increasing number of new firms enter the market.

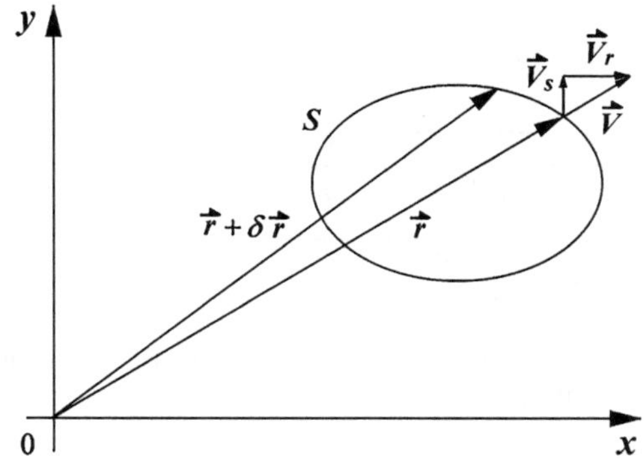

Fig. 8.6 The definition of a closed circulation

Relevant Technical Details of Bjerknes' Circulation Theorem In particular, at the end of the nineteenth century, V. Bjerknes (1898) discovered the eddy effects due to changes in the density of the media in the movements of the atmosphere and ocean.

By circulation, it means a closed contour in a fluid. Mathematically, each circulation Γ is defined as the line integral about the contour of the component of the velocity vector locally tangent to the contour. In symbols, if $\vec{V}$ stands for the speed of a moving fluid, *S* an arbitrary closed curve, $\delta\vec{r}$ the vector difference of two neighboring points of the curve *S* (Fig. 8.6), then a circulation Γ is defined as follows:

$$\Gamma = \oint_S \vec{V}\delta\vec{r}. \tag{8.15}$$

Through some ingenious manipulations (Wu & Lin, 2002), the following well-known Bjerknes' circulation theorem is obtained:

$$\frac{d\vec{V}}{dt} = \iint_\sigma \nabla\left(\frac{1}{\rho}\right) \times (-\nabla p)\cdot\delta\sigma - 2\Omega\frac{d\sigma}{dt}, \tag{8.16}$$

where σ is the projection area on the equator plane of the area enclosed by the closed curve *S*, *p* the atmospheric pressure, ρ the density of the atmosphere, and Ω the earth's rotational angular speed.

The left-hand side of Eq. 8.16 represents the acceleration of the moving fluid, which according to Newton's second law of motion is equivalent to the force acting on the fluid. On the right-hand side, the first term is called a solenoid term in meteorology, originating from the interaction of the *p*- and ρ-planes due to uneven density ρ so that a twisting force is created. Consequently, materials' movements must be rotational with the rotating direction determined by the equal *p*- and ρ-plane

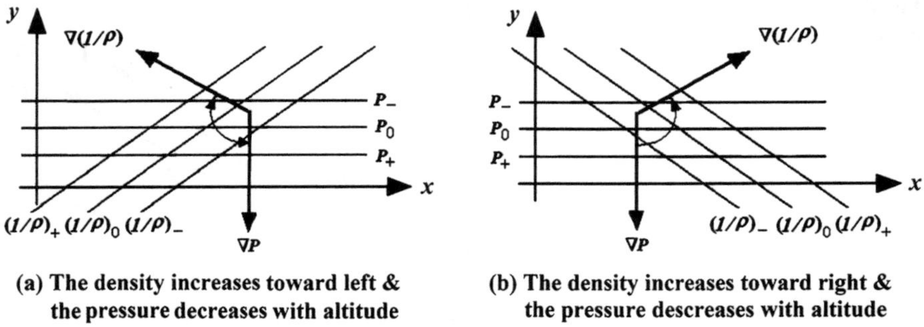

Fig. 8.7 Solenoid circulations. (**a**) The density increases toward left & the pressure decreases with altitude (**b**) The density increases toward right & the pressure decreases with altitude

distributions (Fig. 8.7). The second term in Equation (8.16) comes from the rotation of the earth.

The Proof of Theorem 8.4 This proof is based on (Forrest & Orvis, 2016) and done by contradiction. That is, assume that there is such a fully efficient organization, which satisfies the conditions of the theorem, while the organization's mission is not in total agreement with the personal value of full-time employee k.

Let Y be a variable measuring one aspect of employee k's personal value such that the utility of k increases with Y, while the work efficiency of k in terms of helping to realize the mission of the organization decreases with Y. Symbolically, we have

$$U_k = U_k(X_k, Y), \tag{8.17}$$

satisfying

$$\frac{\partial U_k}{\partial X_k} > 0 \text{ and } \frac{\partial U_k}{\partial Y} > 0, \tag{8.18}$$

where U_k is the utility of k, X_k the total consumption of k, and the production function of the organization is

$$P = P(X_c, U_k, \ldots), \tag{8.19}$$

satisfying

$$\frac{\partial P}{\partial X_c} > 0, \frac{\partial P}{\partial U_k} > 0, \ldots, \tag{8.20}$$

where X_c represents the expenditure of the organization, including the monetary expenses on all employees except k, and the dots the abbreviation of all the utilities of all other employees. The fact that employees' utilities enter into the organization's production function means that the organization keeps its employees' welfare as part of its objectives of operation. Now, the monetary bonus that measures the work efficiency of k is expressed by

$$h_k = h_k(Y), \text{satisfying } \frac{dh_k}{dY} < 0. \tag{8.21}$$

Note: In real life, such a variable Y might only exist implicitly and cannot be measured readily. However, its negative effect on the quality and efficiency generally can be clearly seen. So, we simply assume without loss of generality that Y can be measured in determining the monetary bonus.

To the organization, its resources are distributed to its employees to maximize its production function P in Eq. (8.19) subject to the following constraint:

$$X_c + X_k = X_c + (I_k + h_k), \tag{8.22}$$

where I_k is k's income from his work at the organization.

This maximization problem leads to the following contradiction:

$$\partial X_k / \partial Y > 0 \text{ and } \partial X_k / \partial Y = dh_k / dY < 0.$$

That implies that the assumption that the organization that satisfies the conditions of the theorem is fully efficient is incorrect.

The Formation of Personal Systems of Values and Beliefs By personal values, it means the underlying assumptions and values of philosophy or the value system of a person, which consists of the person's beliefs about how the world functions and the person's moral codes with which the person is recognized with particular identity and integrity.

Now, when each person is seen as a spinning systemic yoyo, each human being lives in a vast ocean of spinning fields of other people, physical objects, abstract thoughts, and myriad of other things and matters. Soon after a person is born, the person starts to interact with the world or some yoyo fields. These interactions with people, physical objects, abstract thoughts, and the myriad of other things and matters shape the person's philosophical assumptions and values, similar to how a civilization formulates its value system (Lin & Forrest, 2011). Because of the subtle differences between the interactions experienced by one person from those by another person, each person has his own set of very specific philosophical assumptions and values. These assumptions and values dictate the behaviors and decision-making of the person for the rest of his life. Although differences may be "subtle" when seen from the angle of the magnificent scale of the entire ocean of spin fields, they are generally major to the individuals involved, causing important differences in the relevant personal value systems. Note: This argument for the formation of personal values is based on (Forrest & Orvis, 2016). For more related details, please refer this reference.

References

Barney, J. B., & Arikan, A. (2001). The resource-based view: Origins and implications. In M. Hitt, R. Freeman, & J. Harrison (Eds.), *Handbook of strategic management* (pp. 124–185). Blackwell.

Bashir, M., & Verma, R. (2017). Why business model innovation is the new competitive advantage. *IUP Journal of Business Strategy; Hyderabad, 14*(1), 7–17.

Bjerknes, V. (1898). Uber einen hydrodynamischen Fundamentalsatz und seine Anwendung besonders auf die Mechanik der Atmosphare und des Weltmeeres. *Kongl Sven. Vetensk. Akad. Handlingar, 31*, 1–35.

Chan, F. T. S., & Chan, H. K. (2010). An AHP model for selection of suppliers in the fast changing fashion market. *The International Journal of Advanced Manufacturing Technology, 51*(9), 1195–1207.

Chang, Y. K., Chen, Y. L., Chou, R. K., & Huang, T. H. (2015). Corporate governance, product market competition and dynamic capital structure. *International Review of Economics & Finance, 38*, 44–55.

Christensen, C. M., Suárez, F. F., & Utterback, J. M. (1998). Strategies for survival in fast-changing industries. *Management Science, 44*, S207–S220.

D'Aveni, R. A., & Gunther, R. E. (1994). *Hypercompetition: Managing the dynamics of strategic maneuvering*. The Free Press.

Day, G. S. (1994). The capabilities of market-driven organizations. *Journal of Marketing, 58*(4), 37–52.

Day, G. S., & Schoemaker, P. J. H. (2016). Adapting to fast-changing markets and technologies. *California Management Review, 58*(4), 59–77.

Debruyne, M., & Reibstein, D. J. (2005). Competitor see, competitor do: Incumbent entry in new market niches. *Marketing Science, 24*(1), 55–66.

Forrest, J. Y. L. (2019). *General systems theory: Foundation, intuition and applications in business decision making*. Springer.

Forrest, J. Y. L., & Orvis, B. (2016). Principles of management efficiency and organizational inefficiency. *Kybernetes: The International Journal of Cybernetics, Systems and Management Sciences, 45*(8), 1308–1322.

Forrest, J. Y. L., & Tallapally, P. (2018). Customers are less patient, sustainable advantage becomes transient and the key for firms to succeed in fast changing markets. *Journal of Business, Economics and Technology, 21*(1), 1–14.

Fultz, D., Long, R. R., Owens, G. V., Bohan, W., Kaylor, R., & Weil, J. (1959). Studies of Thermal Convection in a Rotating Cylinder with Some Implications for Large-Scale Atmospheric Motion. *Meteorol. Monographs (American Meteorological Society), 21*, 4.

Guo, W. C., Lai, F. C., Liu, C. J., & Mai, C. C. (2012). Symbiotic production and downstream market competition. *Atlantic Economic Journal, 40*(3), 329–340.

Harmancioglu, N., Droge, C., & Calantone, R. (2009). Strategic fit to resources versus NPD execution proficiencies: What are their roles in determining success? *Journal of the Academy of Marketing Science, 37*(3), 266–282.

Hauser, J. R., & Shugan, S. M. (1983). Defensive marketing strategies. *Marketing Science, 2*(4), 319–360.

Hess, S. L. (1959). *Introduction to theoretical meteorology*. Holt, Rinehart and Winston.

Inagaka, K., & Osawa, J. (2012). Fujifilm thrived by changing focus. *Wall Street Journal*, January 20.

Kaharuddin, A., Handaru, A. W., Sardan, W., & Mohammed, H. A. A. (2017). Transient competitive advantage readiness: findings from hotels, cafés, and fashion retails in Bandung, Indonesia. *International Journal of Business and Globalisation, 18*, 3. https://doi.org/10.1504/IJBG.2017.083240

Koller, M. R. T. (2016). Exploring adaptability in organizations: Where adaptive advantage comes from and what it is based upon. *Journal of Organizational Change Management, 29*(6), 837–854.

Kumar, K. R., & Sudharshan, D. (1988). Defensive marketing strategies: An equilibrium analysis based on decoupled response function models. *Management Science, 34*(7), 805–815.

Kunii, I. M., Smith, G., & Gross, N. (1999). Fuji: Beyond films. *Business Week*, November 21, 132-138.

Leavy, B. (2016). The next wave of global disruption and the role of China's entrepreneurs. *Strategy & Leadership, 44*(3), 27–37.

Lin, Y. (2009). *Systemic Yoyos: Some impacts of the second dimension.* Auerbach Publication, an imprint of Taylor and Francis.

Lin, Y., & Forrest, B. (2011). *Systemic structure behind human organizations: From civilizations to individuals*. Springer.

MacMillan, I. C. (1982). Seizing competitive initiative. *Journal of Business Strategy, 2*(4), 43.

MacMillan, I. C. (1988). Controlling competitive dynamics by taking strategic initiative. *Academy of Management Executive, 2*(2), 111–118.

McGrath, R. G. (2013). *The End of Competitive Advantage: How to Keep Your Strategy Moving As Fast as Your Business.* Harvard Business Review Press.

Narasimhan, C. (1988). Competitive promotional strategies. *Journal of Business, 61*(4), 427–429.

Purkayastha, A., & Sharma, S. (2016). Gaining competitive advantage through the right business model: Analysis based on case studies. *Journal of Strategy and Management, 9*(2), 138–155.

Senn-Delaney Leadership Consulting Group. Interview with Atmos Energy CEO Bob Best. www.senndelaney.com/bobbestarticle.html, assessed on April 23, 2023.

Tushman, M. L., & O'Reilly, C. A., III. (1996). The ambidextrous organizations: Managing evolutionary and revolutionary change. *California Management Review, 38*(4), 8–30.

Varian, H. R. (1980). A model of sales. *American Economic Review, 70*(4), 651–659.

Wu, Y., & Lin, Y. (2002). *Beyond nonstructural quantitative analysis: Blown-ups, spinning currents and modern science*. World Scientific.

Chapter 9
Successful Adaption to the Present Era

Jeffrey Yi-Lin Forrest and Jennifer Nightingale

Abstract To help equip decision-making managers and entrepreneurs to transit into the era of fast strategic changes, this chapter, which is mainly based on Forrest and Nightingale (Successfully transition into the era of transient competitive advantages. *Proceedings of 2017 NABET Annual Conference*, October 26 – 27, 2017, State College, PA., 57–79; 2017), establishes a specific set of procedural steps for a firm to smoothly and successfully adapt to the new norm of the business world, where the firm's once sustainable competitive advantages have become transient. To accomplish this goal, this chapter develops generally true conclusions on the basis of the established result about when new competitions naturally appear within the marketplace and why competitions within any business organization always exist inevitably.

By combining with published conclusions derived on anecdotal analyses and inductive reasoning, this chapter advances the systemic reasons for why a list of time-honored steps will practically work, and how firms can successfully surf through waves of transient competitive advantages with improving performance.

Keywords Arenas · Competitive advantage · Culture of innovative spirits · Digital revolution · Disengagement · State of mutual forbearance

9.1 Introduction

In theory, change is good. However, change is difficult for most people to cope with. Generally, change means uncertainty and uncertainty brings forward unexpected risks; such uncertainty and unexpected risks challenge the established status quo,

---

Jeffrey Yi-Lin Forrest (Department of Accounting Economics Finance, Slippery Rock University, Slippery Rock, PA, USA; Email: Jeffrey.forrest@sru.edu) and Jennifer Nightingale (Department of Information Technology and Management, Slippery Rock University, Slippery Rock, PA, USA; Email: Jennifer.nightingale@sru.edu) are equally contributed to this chapter.

J. Y.-L. Forrest, *Systemic Principles of Applied Economic Philosophies II*, Translational Systems Sciences 39, https://doi.org/10.1007/978-981-99-7939-4_9

while they can easily appear and do occur. Nevertheless, the modern world of business is changing fast and evolving faster than ever before. And, competition in the marketplace is increasingly intensifying due to the globalization of international economies and unification of international finances. With these accelerating change and development, once sustainable competitive advantages have become transient, short-lived (McGrath, 2013). In other words, if a business organization does not or cannot transform itself along with the shifting landscape of the business world, it will be obsolete and become history in no time.

In the 1980s, Michael Porter (1985) defined competitive advantage as a function of either providing comparable buyer value more efficiently than competitors (low cost) or performing activities at comparable cost but in unique ways that create more buyer value than competitors and, therefore, command a premium price (differentiation). His theory has been one of the most commonly used by managers and entrepreneurs over the past few decades to assist them in finding a way to conceptualize the firm that would expose the underpinnings of competitive advantage and its sustainability.

Looking at the long list of once-storied business organizations that are either gone or no longer relevant, a natural question arises: Are there necessary steps that a firm needs to go through in order for the firm to ready itself potentially for successfully riding waves of transient competitive advantages? To address this question, this chapter, which is mainly based on Forrest and Nightingale (2017), discusses four conditions that are necessary for a firm to satisfy in order to prepare itself for successfully riding waves of transient competitive advantages by applying theoretical results and by relying on what McGrath (2013) developed inductively. After establishing the underlying connections among the four conditions by employing the logic of systemic thinking, the case of a legendary company is analyzed to validate the established theory of this chapter.

The rest of this chapter is organized as follows: Section 9.2 provides a review of the relevant literature. Section 9.3 presents two theoretical results and their systemic intuition that lay down the foundation for the discussions of the following sections. Section 9.4 is the main section of this chapter that details the steps needed for a firm to adapt to the present era of transient competitive advantages. Section 9.5 analyzes a case of a legendary company by focusing on a nearly two-century old firm, known as W. R. Grace. Section 9.6 concludes the presentation of this chapter.

9.2 Literature Review

The literature related to what is developed in this chapter can be viewed from three different perspectives: (i) the readiness for a firm to embrace change, (ii) knowledge, interactions, and networks, (iii) strategies that lead to competitive advantages and performance.

For perspective (i), from the angle of strategic management, a new paradigm is introduced by Duez (2012) based on the thought of economic proximity.

Considering the relationship between corporate social responsibility and firm performance, Saeidi et al. (2015) identify sustainable competitive advantage, reputation, and customer satisfaction as three probable mediators. These authors find that corporate social responsibility indirectly promotes firm performance through enhanced reputation and related competitive advantages that improve the level of customer satisfaction. In the context of China-like emerging economies, from a strategic process perspective, the concept of a firm's dynamic capability is defined (Li & Liu, 2014) as the firm's potential to systematically solve problems so that each such capability is formed by the firm's propensity to sense opportunities and threats, to make timely decisions, and to implement strategic decisions and changes efficiently to ensure the right direction. Based on this concept, the relationship between dynamic capabilities and competitive advantages can be established, where Li and Liu also explore the role environmental dynamism plays by using a sample of 217 enterprises from China.

In terms of perspective (ii), it is found (Moustaghfir, 2012) that firms can acquire competitive advantages by using knowledge assets and that organizational capabilities have the potential to yield long-term superior performance. The effort to simultaneously restrain rivalries and increasing competitive advantages on profits seems to be negative (Makadok, 2010). When **the** video games industry is employed as an ideal laboratory, the consequences of hyper-competition and implications of either maintaining competitive advantages or developing temporary advantages can be well investigated (Carpenter et al., 2014)**. Because the majority of the knowledge about** competitive advantages draws mostly upon the experience of Western firms, Peng et al. (2001) uses the massive Japanese investment in an effort to replicate *keiretsu* (interfirm) networks in Asia since the 1980s to shed new light on the sources of competitive advantages. These authors develop a multilevel perspective by focusing on how competitive advantage is preserved and strengthened for firms, networks, and nations involved.

Regarding perspective (iii), by basing on the literature of corporate innovation, social innovation, and corporate social innovation, Herrera (2015) uses case studies to build a framework that describes such factors that lead to successful corporate social innovation, and, such social innovation in turn can potentially create opportunities for co-creation, thereby leading to shared value and enhancing competitive advantage. Fronmueller (1996) uses a sample of large firms to test the relationship between backward vertical integration and low cost and that between forward vertical integration with differentiation-based competitive advantage. Peterson (2013) addresses the question of whether deploying compliance and ethics programs would assist U.S. organizations in implementing internal mechanisms necessary to achieve a competitive advantage from the law. By looking at exporting manufacturers, Leonidou et al. (2015) examine the external and internal determinants of green export strategy and its effects on export competitive advantage and performance. Their result confirms the instrumental role of both external forces (i.e., foreign environmental public concern and competitive intensity) and internal factors (i.e., the green sensitivity of the top management and organizational green culture) in crafting an environmentally friendly export strategy of business.

By comparing what this chapter presents and the literature, it can be readily seen that this chapter enriches the relevant knowledge with new conclusions at the height of theoretical abstraction and a potential of much wider range of practical applications.

9.3 Competitions a Company Faces both Internally and Externally

To lay down the theoretical foundation for the rest of this chapter, this section introduces two generally true results. First, let us look at market competitions that are external to any incumbent firm of an established market. In particular, the following is Theorem 4.1 cited from Chap. 4 for the convenience of the presentation here.

Theorem 9.1 If the market described below is in Nash equilibrium, then the following are equivalent:

1) At least one new firm enters the market competitively and profitably with their versions of substitute offer.
2) There is a consumer surplus of switchers who make purchase decisions based on which supplier's price is lower.

The market considered in Theorem 9.1 is assumed to satisfy the following conditions. It is served by a fixed number of firms with their horizontally differentiated offers. Its operation is only affected by market forces, such as demand and supply, and consumers' forever evolving preferences and tastes. In other words, this market is perfectly competitive without any outside interference. As a consequence of interacting forces between the systems of values and beliefs of individual consumers and the missions of the incumbent firms, each of these firms has a base of loyal customers. These loyal customers only consider the offers of their favored firms unless the prices of the offers are more than their reservation prices. Different from loyal customers, there are those customers in the marketplace who make purchases based on which firm's unit-value price is lower. These customers are collectively known as switchers. And, the firms' strategies of pricing are known to all involved companies who respond by playing Nash equilibria through untainted self-analyses.

Speaking differently, all the assumed conditions of the market mean that the market is in a state of mutual forbearance. That is, the incumbent firms mitigate rivalry by dividing up the market in proportion to their respective strengths (Bernheim & Whinston, 1990). They cede dominance to their stronger competitors in those market segments where they are less efficient, while in exchange the latter do the same in segments where the former are more efficient (Li & Greenwood, 2004). The codependence of these incumbent firms motivates them to de-escalate rivalry (Yu & Cannella Jr., 2012). So, the rates of entry and exit in the market

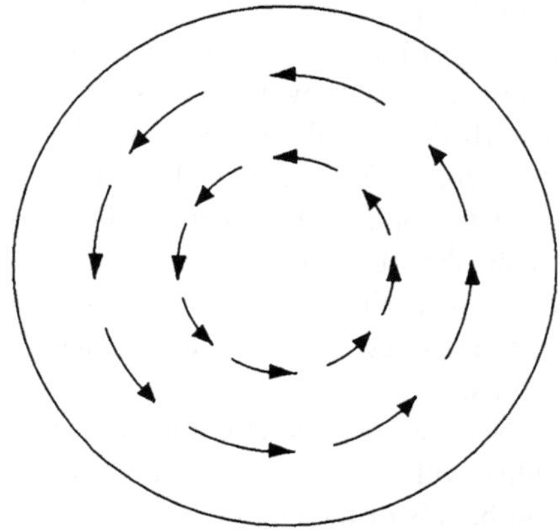

Fig. 9.1 The systemic birds-eye view of the market

decrease (Fuentelsaz & Gómez, 2006), and interfirm hostility declines (Haveman & Nonnemaker, 2000). At the same time, these assumed market conditions generally mean that the technology involved and the relevant business operations have been standardized. So, for a new firm to enter such a market with profit potential, it is reasonable to assume that this firm has come up with a more efficient technology and/or operation that can greatly reduce the overall business expenditure.

To see the systemic intuition of this result, let us fathom the marketplace as an abstract yoyo field, and we look at the multi-dimensional yoyo body at a distance from above either the convergent input side or the divergent output side, while imagine that everything here takes place in our 3-dimensional space. In other words, graphically we are looking at the market of concern as the pool of spinning fluid in Fig. 9.1.

Now, the dishpan experiment (Chap. 2) guarantees that when this pool spins at a sufficient speed or experiences sufficient difference in temperature between the center and the periphery, the pattern of uniform movement in Fig. 9.1 will develop into the chaos, shown in Fig. 9.2. The number of local eddy leaves is determined either by the rotational speed or by the temperature difference or both and increases

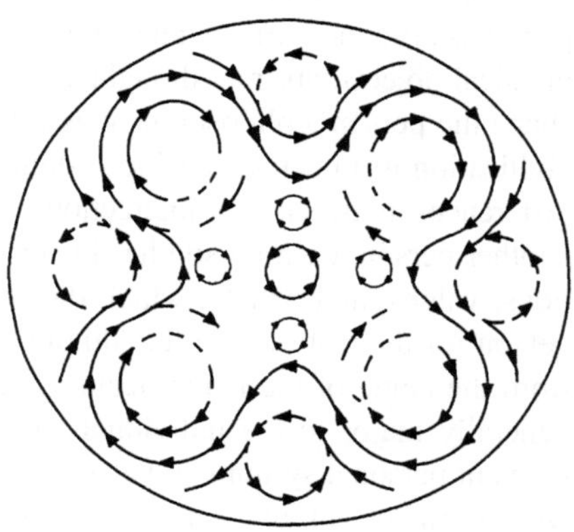

Fig. 9.2 Asymmetric flow observed in Fultz's dishpan experiment

with the speed and the temperature difference. This systemic modeling and laboratory experiment suggest that the fluid nowhere within this spinning pool can avoid being disturbed by the flows, be they either orderly or chaotically. And being disturbed regionally means that a local flow pattern will appear inevitably.

Theorem 9.1 indicates that although the *m* incumbent firms are risk neutral and want to continuously reap in their respective profits by securely defending their established turfs, they still have to fight over the price switchers of the marketplace in order to eliminate or reduce the magnitude of the switcher segment. Otherwise, new competition(s) will inevitably enter the market with the potential of making good profits.

Next, let us look at competitions that materially exist within any organizational entity with at least two employees as reflected by the individual systems of values and beliefs of the employees.

Generally, no matter which business entity is concerned with, there are competitions in terms of how the organization should be managed, how the detailed operations should be carried out, and how employees' efforts and devotions need to be directed. And each stakeholder of the organization always seems to have ideas about how things can improve.

One reason why abundant competitive situations exist is because each person, as a living being that is severely limited by its sense organs, looks at the world with a pair of colored eyes. The word "color" in the literature is also known by such terms as personal values and/or philosophical assumptions about the world (Lin & Forrest, 2011; Villalobos & Vargas, 2015; Terán et al., 2015). In other words, because philosophical assumptions and value-belief systems vary from one person to another, from one people to another, from one culture to another, . . ., the same physical world becomes extremely beautiful and multi-colored when people individually try to describe what they see and what the world is really about.

By underlying assumptions and values of philosophy, we mean the value-belief system of a person that consists of his beliefs about how the world functions and his moral codes with which he is recognized with his particular identity and integrity (Lin & Forrest, 2011). The systemic yoyo model implies that each human being lives in a vast ocean of spinning yoyo fields, which are those of other people, physical objects, abstract thoughts, and myriad of other things and matters. Soon after a person is born, he starts to interact with the world. It is these interactions with people, physical objects, abstract thoughts, and the myriad of other things and matters that shape the person's philosophical assumptions, values, and beliefs, similar to how a civilization formulates its value system (Lin & Forrest, 2011). Because of the subtle differences between the interactions experienced by one person from those by another person, each person has his own set of very specific philosophical assumptions, values, and beliefs, which dictate the behaviors and decision-making of the person for the rest of his life. Although the differences may be "subtle" when seen from the angle of the magnificent scale of the entire ocean of spin fields, they are generally major to the individuals involved, causing important differences in the relevant personal systems of values and beliefs. That actually explains why children who grow up in the same household may have quite different personalities, characteristics, and thinking processes. And that explains why different people have different underlying philosophical assumptions, values, and beliefs (the value-belief systems), because firstly no two people grow up within a perfectly identical environment, and secondly with age people's philosophical assumptions, values, and beliefs evolve according to their, respectively, changing environments. For a more in-depth discussion, see (Forrest & Orvis, 2016).

Proposition 9.1 Competitions always exist within any organizational system that has at least two employees.

Intuitively, this result holds true, because no two employees share the same system of values and beliefs, and any two employees will look at many aspects of the organizational system differently. That difference between their value-belief systems naturally leads to competitive consequences of the two employees. For a technical proof of this result, please go to the appendix of this chapter.

9.4 Necessary Steps Needed for a Company to Adapt to the New Era

Based on the theoretical results presented in previous section, this section contains the main theory of this chapter and develops a detailed procedure with particular steps necessary for a firm to acclimate to and succeed in the era of transient competitive advantages.

To lay down the common ground as our reference point for discussion, Section 9.4.1 describes the elementary characteristics of our focal firm that operates within the old strategic framework of sustainable competitive advantages. Then we look at the steps necessary for the firm to ride successfully the waves of ephemeral advantages in Sect. 9.4.2 by emphasizing on the critical significance of having a long-term, unwavering ambition, the importance of having stable relationships both internally and externally, the absolute need to stay strategically agile, and the necessity of making innovation the norm of the firm's business operation.

9.4.1 Evolution of the Focal Firm

Historically, the firm—our focal firm—was initially a family workshop that produced whatever the family needed and then some additional products desired by the neighbors. With increasing demand from outside the family, some unskilled and uneducated labors of the neighborhood families were hired during their idling times and off seasons from their land works. Over time, the family-based workshop evolved into a factory with the original raw labors transformed into skilled, organized, full-time factory workers. As the average income of the population grew, the increasing purchasing power of the market gradually transformed the family-controlled factory of primitive technologies into a prospering, powerful modern industrial organization. For an excellent presentation on how business firms evolve over time, see (Wen, 2016).

In its successful evolution, the firm has excelled in every stage of development in terms of its organizational structure and culture, and its competition with other players within the same industry. The firm recognizes that its success has been heavily relied on finding a favorable position in a defined industry and then exploiting its long-term competitive advantages, while using innovations, although they are separate from the firm's core activities, to create new business opportunities. Since advantages are long-term and sustainable, as soon as the firm has achieved a solid position within its industry, it optimizes its people, assets, and systems around its advantages, which promotes people who are good at running big businesses, operates with greater efficiency, and minimizes costs. The management structure directs resources and talents to strong core businesses, which are associated with high performance. In other words, the firm optimizes its systems and processes around a set of sustainable advantages.

For decades, due to various barriers of entry, such as colossal expenses, technological sophistication, regulatory limitations, etc., this business model has been working wonders, and the firm has dominated the market. That further ratifies the firm's beliefs that each industry consists of enduring and stable competitive forces and the interactive pattern of these forces can be extrapolated into the future with sustainable benefits.

However, in recent years, the constraints that held this business model in place have eroded. Boundaries between industries have become blurred, the mass market fragmented, ample varieties of the same product introduced. Additionally, the advent of internet has facilitated an explosion of seemingly infinite possibilities for meeting the demand of consumers. This relaxation of constraints has fundamentally undermined the established business mode. Furthermore, many firms' advantages have become standards in the industry, such as online package tracking, making it difficult for the firm to maintain a competitive advantage for any desirable length of time. And the most important dynamic the firm experiences is no longer intra-industrial competition but rather regular invasions of players from other industries. So, the firm realizes that traditional approaches to strategy and innovation are no longer keeping pace with the speed of change of the markets in which it is competing. Nonetheless, the advantages' past sustainability has led to the build-up of inertia and power along the lines of the existing business model. It has allowed people to fall into routines and habits of mind, resulting in the conditions for turf wars and organizational rigidity. While innovation has become more restricted, the firm has fostered denial reactions rather than proactive designs of strategic next steps. Because of its preference for equilibrium and stability, many shifts in the marketplace have met by the firm's leaders denying that these shifts mean anything negative for them.

The accelerating speed of change of the new economy has made the firm face situations in which advantages are copied or imitated quickly and technology changes rapidly, while customers seek other alternatives. Such new market dynamics make the firm believe that it does not have time to implement management tools and feels understaffed so that it consequently is sticking increasingly to tools it has already had experience with. Ironically, at the same time, despite a lot of innovations in management tools and approaches, the firm is increasing its reliance on strategy tools that it had inherited from the past. As the sustainable competitive advantages of the past are replaced with transient ones, the deeply ingrained structures and systems designed to extract maximum value from each competitive advantage have turned out to be liabilities when the environment requires instead the capability to surf through waves of short-lived opportunities. Evidently, to compete in such more volatile and uncertain environments, the firm needs to do things and conduct its business differently.

Because of the digital revolution, instead of within-industry competition being the most significant competitive threat, the firm faces competitions from other industries, and even from different business models. So, in order to adequately analyze what is really going on at the level that decisions need to be made, the firm has to conduct its analysis at a more granular level of arenas (McGrath, 2013) that reflects the connection between market segment, offer, and geographic location and connects customers and solutions beyond the conventional description of offerings that are near substitutes for one another. In other words, the firm needs to analyze how to meet corresponding challenges of particular rivals in specific geographic locations with appropriate technologies.

The firm faces with the necessity to produce the outcomes that particular customers seek and alternative ways those outcomes may be met in order to continue its success. It is because the most substantial threats to the firm's advantages can potentially appear in nonobvious locations. In other words, the firm has to learn to leverage such ephemeral matters as deep customer relationships and the capability to design irreplaceable experiences across multiple arenas, because advantages based on product features, new technologies, the "better mousetrap," etc., are shown to be less durable than once believed. In fact, short-term advantages only provide a snapshot of a firm's strengths and weaknesses, as well as the competitive "battle-field" they are moving toward (Maxwell, 2010). The firm will have to focus on creating capabilities and skills that will be relevant to whatever arenas it happens to find itself operating in. And it may even have to be more relaxed about traditional protections and barriers to entry because competition will devolve around highly intangible and emotional factors.

Instead of focusing on its relative position with respect to other players in the same industry, its market share, and traditional kinds of competitive threats, such as product introduction, pricing, promotions, and so on, the firm has to spend additional time and energy to think about creating products and services in multiple industries in order to succeed with the concept of arenas. For example, the firm needs to consider establishing a cash management account, as Merrill Lunch did in the 1980s when no money-center bank realized what was going on, or move into telephone operating systems and online video, as Google did recently, or edge into health care, as retailers, such as Walmart, are doing. The idea is that the firm needs to aim at producing outcomes that are arena based instead of industry based.

9.4.2 Necessary Steps for Successful Transitions

When companies' competitive advantages were sustainable in the past, the emphasis of strategic decision-making was to invest in capabilities that help spot industry trends and design the corresponding strategy so that decent payoffs can be obtained. The underlying assumptions behind this practice, which had been taken as gospel, were that each industry is relatively stable, consists of relatively enduring and stable competitive forces, and that the interactive pattern of these forces can be extrapolated into the future. From that derived were the beliefs that industry matters most and that when the existing forces are deeply understood, one can create a road map for other decisions that will last for at least some time. In other words, the major assumption was that the world of the near future, such as five years from now, was, to some extent, comprehensible today.

However, with the world economy increasingly globalized, the sustainable competitive advantages of the past have become transient, market conditions evolve much, much faster, and customers become less and less patient than ever before. So, a real challenge all successful companies face today is how to adjust themselves to effectively ride evolutionary waves of competitive advantages, where each wave consists of the following phases: launch, ramp-up, exploitation, and disengagement. In particular, during the launch phase, new opportunities are identified, resources reallocated, and a team of people with different expertise is assembled to create something new. This phase emphasizes on innovation and consequent discovery of new development directions. During the ramp-up phase, if an opportunity gets traction, then the newly developed advantage starts to expand from the initial few segments into more and more market areas. The business gains ground; systems and processes for getting the business to scale are implemented; the initial experiments become full-scaled market introductions. If the ramp-up phase is successful, the company will enjoy a period of exploitation when the business is doing well and generating good profits. During this phase, the firm establishes a clear, advantageous differentiation from competitors, its market share and profitability expand with attractive prices and profit margins. When an advantage is exhausted, the profitable opportunity will undergo a process of erosion. By disengaging, the firm disposes of its assets and other capabilities that are no longer relevant to its future. Here, disengagement is not the same as business failure. As a matter of fact, disengagement starts to take place when the business is still profitable (McGrath, 2013).

McGrath (2013) looks at every company that is publicly traded globally with a market capitalization of over $1 billion U.S. dollars as of the end of 2009, which totals 4,793 firms. Then she examines the number of these firms that had been able to grow revenues by at least 5% annually for the proceeding five years from 2004 to 2009, where 5% was the least whole percentage number above the global gross domestic product growth ($\approx$ 4%) during this time period (Mahanta, 2012). As a result, she identifies ten growth outliers. Based on what is summarized by McGrath from studying these ten growth outliers and based on what is established in the previous section, one can see that for the purpose of preparing a firm to effectively ride evolutionary waves of transient competitive advantages, the firm needs to follow the steps below:

- Aim at realizing a long-term, unwavering ambition;
- Stabilize relationships;
- Foster strategic agility; and
- Make innovation the norm.

We will next dive into details of these steps in the following sub-subsections.

9.4.2.1 Long-Term and Unwavering Ambitions

The first and foremost step for the firm to become successful in riding waves of transient competitive advantages is to establish a long-term, unwavering public commitment to the ambition of becoming world class, the best of the world, and such ambition is embraced, endorsed, and sought after by the leadership of the firm. With such an outsized ambition (relative to competitors) in place, the leadership will have to naturally set the bar high while have a clear sense of strategic direction in every endeavor. It will also promote common key themes that are the results of compelling strategy diagnoses in its attempt to steer the firm's development in the desired direction.

Here, the leadership commitment is the key. As a matter of fact, leadership is one of the most salient aspects of the organizational context. It is the process of social influence in which one person or a small group of people can enlist the aid and support of others in the accomplishment of a common task (Chemers, 2001), or ultimately it is about creating a way for people to work together and to make something extraordinary happen (Kouzes & Posner, 2007). When the firm desires to be the best, its selected leaders will most likely possess the following key traits and demonstrate a pattern of motives (Kirkpatrick & Locke, 1991; McClelland, 1975): drive (a broad term which includes achievement, motivation, ambition, energy, tenacity, and initiative), motivation (the desire to lead but not to seek power as an end in itself), honesty, integrity, self-confidence (which is associated with emotional stability), cognitive ability, and knowledge of the business. For a systematic analysis on the concept of leadership, see (Lin & Forrest, 2011).

As for why leadership is important in terms of the systemic yoyo model, it is because leadership stands for one's capability to adjust his underlying field structure so that many other neighboring fields will spin in similar fashions without much difficult readjustment. In particular, if one can utilize a process of social influence to obtain aids and supports of others in accomplishing a common task (Chemers, 2001), it implies that there has appeared a big whirlpool (the ambition). This pool may initially be conceptual and physically invisible. However, it does cover a large territory, within which many smaller fields (individual people) are located. Now, the leader is the person who can realign all the individual eddy fields in such a way that the conceptual large field becomes a visible reality. In this systemic modeling, the initially invisible large field is the expected something extraordinary (Lin & Forrest, 2011).

To showcase the firm's achievements to the world, not surprisingly, references to awards and recognitions need to be literally festooned on its corporate website. The key here is that whatever venture the firm is engaged in and whichever strategy the firm employs are grounded in a compelling ambition. That provides an aiming point for the employees within the firm to work toward and a comforting point for customers outside the firm to buy the products and use the service the firm produces and provides.

Notice that the ultimate ambition of the firm needs to be stretch so that its attainment and maintenance cannot be easily accomplished. For example, being the "world class, the best" represents a dynamic state that can only be attained and maintained through continuous effort and trying. This end is important to long-term reconfiguration of the firm and will help prevent the firm from becoming complacent and content to pursue yesterday's advantages. At the same time, what are important are particular mechanisms that will keep complacency at bay, such as moving people around within the company in order to facilitate their looking at the business in different ways from different vantage points.

Accompanying the stretch ambition, the firm needs to invest in creating an organizational identity, culture, and commitment to leadership development by paying considerable attention to values, codes, and alignment (Proposition 9.1). The ambition plays the role of the conceptual starting point for all activities, while the investment aims at establishing a practically useful foundation for materializing the goal by providing trainings, because the necessary cultural foundation will allow the firm to make changes when it needs to. A desirable culture is the foundation of success for the firm, represents a very important process to the long-term health and success of the company.

As implied by Proposition 9.1, in order for the firm to move from one set of advantages to another, the firm has to consciously set out to educate and up-skill its people. To make this end practically possible, the firm has to hire employees based on their ability to learn new things, or their learnability. And to avoid having to fire people when competitive conditions shift, the firm must continuously train and develop its people. In other words, when the firm is ambitious with the goal of becoming the best, it has to prepare itself to ride with the tide of market waves. To make this possible, training people to be able to move from one advantage to another becomes a cost of doing business. It is just as important a bill to pay as the one the firm pays to keep the lights on and computers running. Investing in employees' capacity to move around eliminates a tremendous barrier to change and emphasizes the creation of transition capability.

9.4.2.2 Stability of Relationships

The second most important step for the firm to successfully ride waves of transient competitive advantages is to maintain an endogenous stability in terms of the firm's ambition and relevant strategy statements no matter how chaotic the external world can be or how the firm is in the midst of major change. In other words, the firm needs to be so sufficiently stable endogenously that it does not internalize any chaos from its environment and does not alter its pre-determined, conceptual path of development even when the internal affairs are difficult due to either changes in adopted strategies, or disengaging from old advantages and launching new advantages.

In terms of systemic thinking, the yoyo field of the firm is always located within the conflicts of much large yoyo fields (of other entities in the environment). If we model the field of the firm as *m* in Fig. 9.3, then for the scenario in Fig. 9.3a, small yoyo *m* will be pushed upward by the meridian fields of *N* and *M* along the direction of X → Y. If the meridian field Y of *N* is much stronger than that of *M*, then the majority of the yoyo structure of *m* will be pulled into the field of *N*. Conversely, if the meridian field of *M* is much stronger, then the majority of the yoyo structure of *m* will be pulled into the field of *M*. If the meridian fields Y of both *N* and *M* are roughly the same strength, then the existing yoyo structure *m* will be torn apart into pieces, some of which will be absorbed by either *N* or *M*. For the situation in Fig. 9.3b, the meridian field u of *m* is pushed upward by the meridian field X of *N*, and the meridian field v of *m* is attracted downward due to the fact that the same

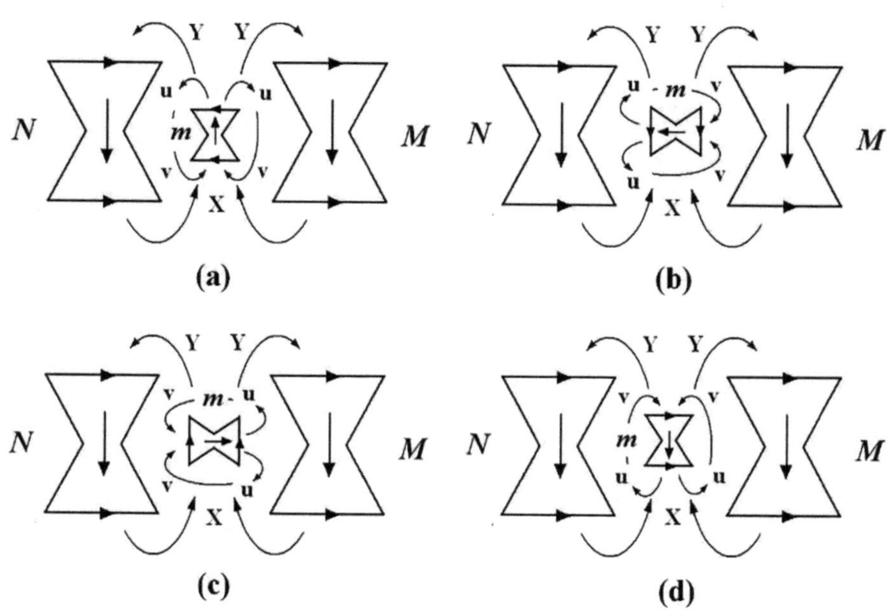

Fig. 9.3 The fate of yoyo *m* within the conflict between *N* and *M*, whose meridian and eddy fields spin harmonically. Cases **(a)**–**(d)** provide, respectively, different positions of *m* within the meridian fields of *N* and *M*

polarities repel and opposite attract. So, yoyo *m* will spin clockwise in order to reposition itself as in that of Fig. 9.3a. If when it reaches the top of the combined meridian field of *N* and *M*, it is still in a position as shown in Fig. 9.3b, then it will be absorbed by *N*; if at that moment, it is positioned like in Fig. 9.3a, then it will be destroyed as described in the analysis of Fig. 9.3a.

For the scenario in Fig. 9.3c, once again due to the property that the like polarities repel and opposite attract, the small yoyo *m* will experience counterclockwise spin in its general upward movement. If at the top of the combined meridian field of *N* and *M*, yoyo *m* is still in its position as in Fig. 9.3c, then it will be absorbed into *M*; if it is poisoned as in Fig. 9.3a, it then will be destroyed by the meridian fields of *N* and *M*. For the situation in Fig. 9.3d, yoyo *m* experiences an extreme instability due to its positioning of the polarities. If the field intensity of *N* and *M* working on *m* are the same, the general upward movement of *m* will be sped up. If one of meridian fields of *N* and *M* is stronger, then yoyo *m* will be lifted further upward on that side, causing *m* to spin either clockwise (if the meridian field of *N* is stronger) or counterclockwise (if the meridian field of *M* is stronger). In either case, *m* will be repositioned in one of the situations as in Fig. 9.3b or c.

Similarly, the survival of the much smaller yoyo field *m* within the interaction between two relatively greater yoyos *N* and *M* as shown in Figs. 9.4 and 9.5 can be analyzed. These figures depict the three most general scenarios of how the much greater yoyos *N* and *M* can be interacting with each other.

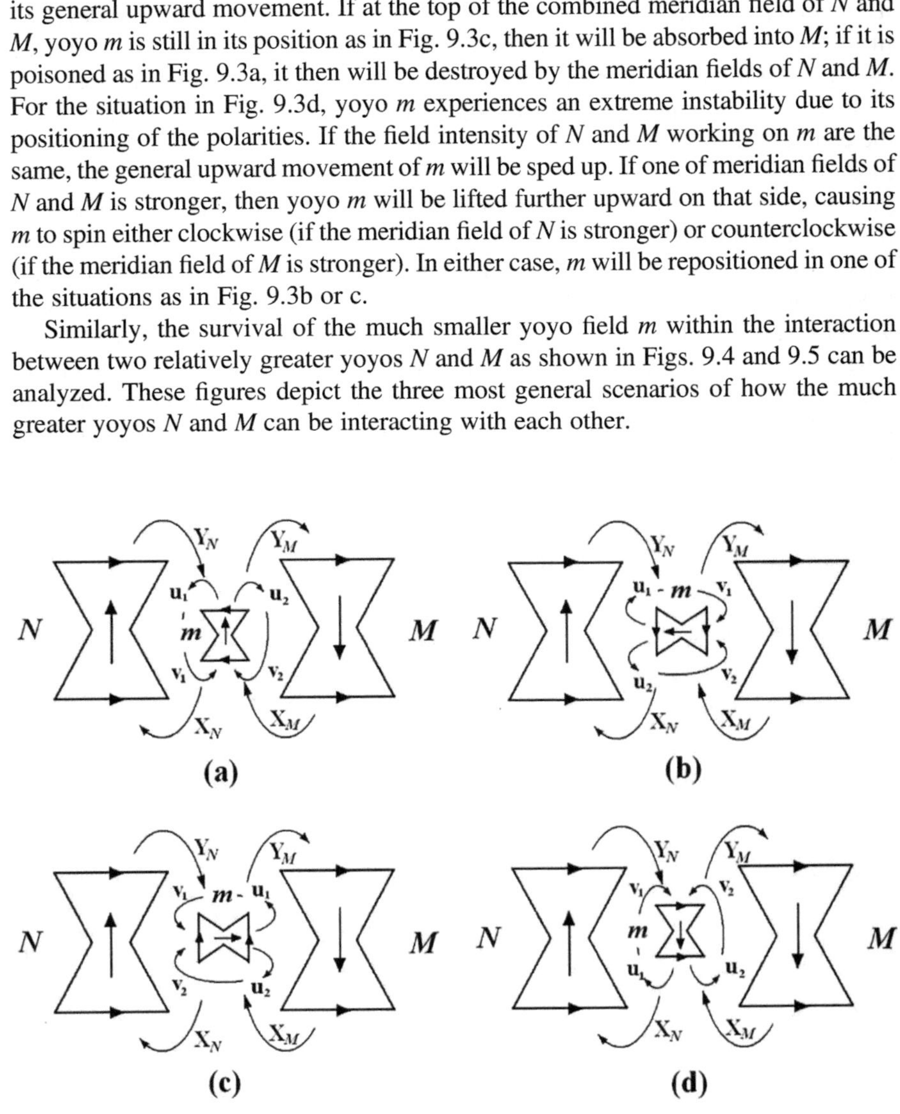

Fig. 9.4 The fate of yoyo *m* within the conflict between *N* and *M*, whose meridian fields spin in opposite directions while eddy fields harmonically. Cases **(a)**–**(d)** provide, respectively, different positions of *m* within the meridian fields of *N* and *M*

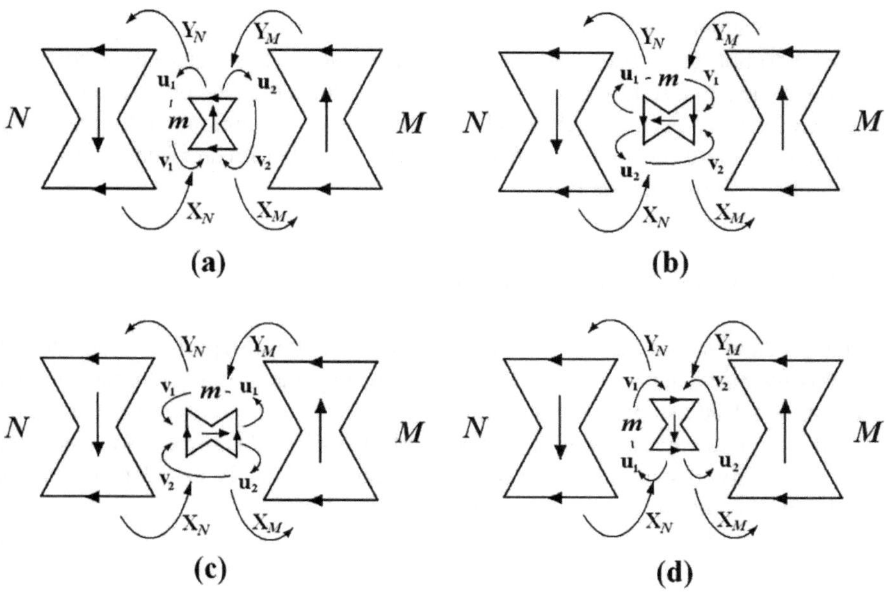

Fig. 9.5 The fate of yoyo *m* within the conflict between *N* and *M*, whose meridian fields spin in opposite directions while eddy fields harmonically. Cases **(a)**–**(d)** provide, respectively, different positions of *m* within the meridian fields of *N* and *M*

To materialize the established stretch ambition, the firm has to first stay viable as a system (or endogenous stability). So, these systemic analyses imply that to achieve the needed endogenous stability, which is fundamental for the firm to stay as a viable system, the executive team of the firm needs to create a tremendous force for stability by sticking to the pre-determined simple strategic priorities, by building culture and developing talent, and by leveraging a few core capabilities. And to maintain the operational consistency and stability in the leadership, the most senior executive of the firm needs to be promoted from an internal position. Otherwise the needed consistency and stability in leadership will be most likely interrupted by white knights and outside-the-industry saviors. And because achievements of the firm can only be consequences of collectively works of all stakeholders, the most senior leaders need to generally be kept in low profiles instead of being high-profile public figures, although they need to be respected, acknowledged for their contributions, and somewhat visible in the press.

The analyses of Figs. 9.3, 9.4, and 9.5 also indicate that to stay viable within the turbulent conflicts of *N* and *M*, the firm *m* has to keep its input–output flows stable. That implies that the firm has to maintain extremely stable relationships with its clients and ecosystem partners; otherwise, these relationships will be difficult to re-establish as indicated by Theorem 9.1. In other words, the firm changes in an evolutionary manner as its customers' preferences and needs change and that in fact aligns the interests of the firm's clients and service firms rather than pitting them against one another. The fact that some outputs of the yoyo field in Fig. 2.1(a) of Chap. 2 do not return back into the system as inputs means that when it becomes obviously clear that some employees can no longer be redeployed or retrained, then a parting of the ways is necessary. And when this is the only option, the firm needs to well manage these separations so that those who are either fired or laid off maintain good relationships with the firm.

9.4.2.3 Necessary Agility with Business Strategies

In the previous sub-subsection, we discussed the important step of creating internal stability over time in terms of the firm's vision, management strategy, organizational culture, and leadership. However, equally important to these established internal systems and structures are well-developed and sophisticated approaches to fostering strategic agility to sparking changes routinely and consistently in order to avoid as much downsizing, restructuring, or sell-offs as possible.

Instead of having processes for major downsizing, dramatic restructuring, and otherwise getting out of declining areas in a big way in the face of ephemeral competitive advantages, the firm needs to embed changes in its normal routines, reallocate resources flexibly and on an ongoing basis. The firm needs to redeploy resources and shift emphases by accepting industry evolution, especially regarding technology, and by embracing the changes in order to enter new markets instead of cutting costs, divesting, and taking sudden, wrenching exits. In particular, the firm needs to use industry changes as opportunities to disengage and exit old businesses and enter new market segments with higher growth potential and to integrate their old technologies into new waves instead of divesting completely. By accepting the evolution of its industries, the firm needs to choose to upgrade for the purpose of moving up the value chain.

When exiting an area, the firm needs to follow an evolutionary path by slowing down the allocation of resources to the area. So, instead of chopping off the area, it lives its life and the related activities find their way to insignificance in a period of time. At the same time, the relevant leadership and talent are repurposed for other efforts and people are assigned to other responsibilities. To achieve such desirable outcome, the budgeting and the allocation of major resources need to be fast, flexible, and have to be managed centrally in order not to be held hostage by powerful executives. (In many companies, resources are trapped (or held "hostage") at the divisional or business unit level. When one area of the business is under pressure or an opportunity falls between units, it is generally difficult for a company to respond effectively because incumbent executives regard change as a threat.) To successfully ride waves of transient competitive advantages, the firm has to centrally coordinate its decision-making with respect to major strategic challenges while giving considerable latitude for action at the business unit level.

In terms of the systemic yoyo model, what previous sub-subsection discussed is how to keep the yoyo field of the firm as solid as possible so that it can readily change its orientations and positions with the evolving environment. In this

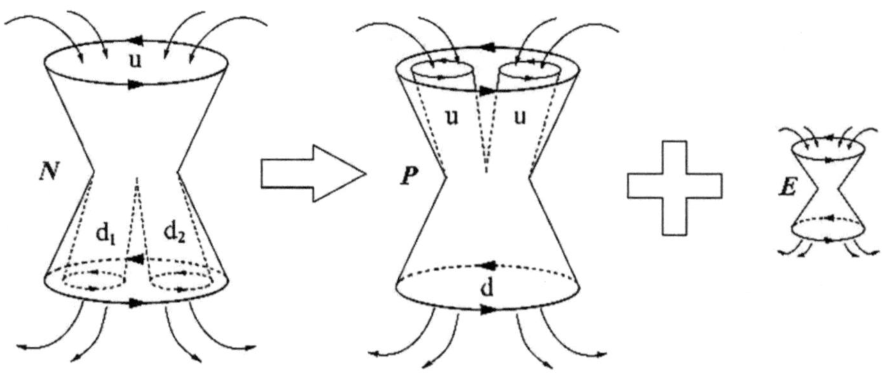

Fig. 9.6 A profitable business area is disengaged

sub-subsection, we look at how the yoyo field of the firm *N* needs to be managed so that a profitable, but eroding, business area can be disengaged with resources reallocated. Fig. 9.6 shows how the process of disengagement takes place. In particular, the firm is the yoyo field *N* in the scenario in Fig. 9.6, where the competitive advantage of business area d_2 is eroding although it is still profitable. By isolating d_2 out from the rest of the operation, d_2 is split out from the yoyo field of the original yoyo field *N* of the firm into the independent yoyo field *E*, while the firm's allocation of resources is divided into two portions labeled by u. One of these portions represents resources available for exploring new opportunities.

The evolution from the original yoyo field *N* into *P* + *E* can be detailed as follows. One of the d-quarks in *N* is split off and becomes *E* (Lin & He, 2010). Without loss of generality, assume that d_2-quark is split off from *N*. When d_2-quark leaves *N*, it takes a piece of the u-quark with it. Right before the piece of the u-quark leaves *N* (Fig. 9.7a), the original even flow of materials in the black-hole side of *N* is greatly affected. In particular, into area A in Fig. 9.7a no more material is supplied so that a relative vacuum is created, while due to conflicts in spinning directions, area B is jammed with extra materials. At the same time, when the original spinning flows

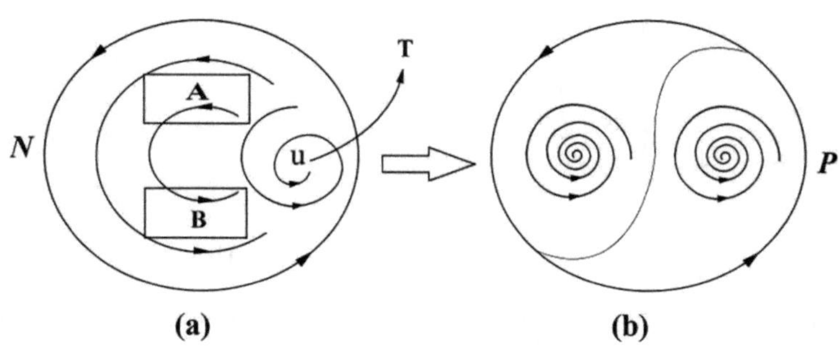

Fig. 9.7 The mechanism for the formation of two converging sub-eddies (**a**) Right before the u-quark leaves *N* (**b**) After the u-quark leaves *N*

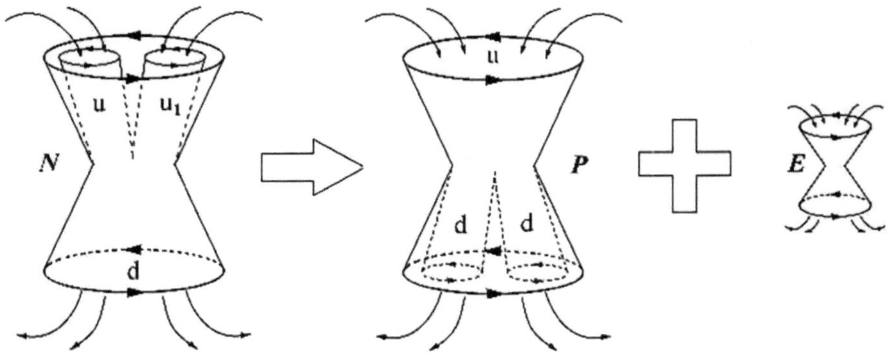

Fig. 9.8 A non-profitable resource allocation is disengaged

plus the accumulated strength of pushing in area B throws the newly formed regional u-quark out of the eddy field of *N* along the direction of the arrow T, the congestion in area B and the vacuum in area A establish a new u-quark on the left-hand side to these areas. So, the flow pattern in Fig. 9.7b, as shown from above the black-hole side of the original yoyo *N*, is formed, where the local eddy motion on the right-hand side is the residual pool left behind by the departed u-quark in Fig. 9.7a.

Similarly, we can analyze the scenario that an opportunity during a ramp-up phase gets some traction, but not sufficient enough for the firm to bring the newly developed opportunity up to scale. In this case, the firm can conveniently spin off the opportunity into an independent entity while still use its outputs as those of the firm.

In particular, Fig. 9.8 shows the process of the split of the firm *N* into *P* and *E*, where the u_1-quark is split off to become *E*, while the original d-quark in *N* evolves into the structure of 2 d-quarks in *P*. The appearance of the 2 d-quarks in P is analyzed in Fig. 9.9 similar to that is done with Fig. 9.7. All the details are omitted here.

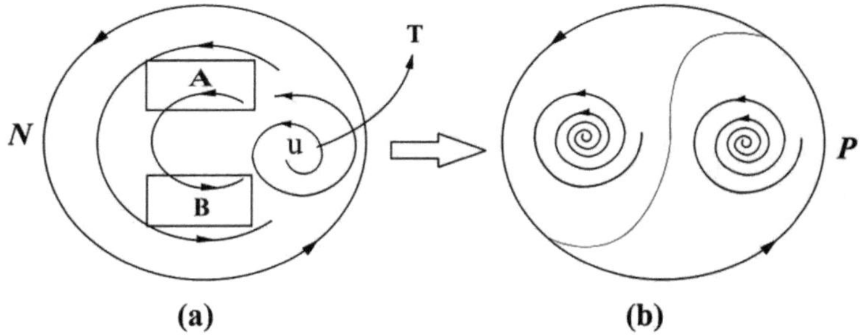

Fig. 9.9 The mechanism for the formation of two diverging sub-eddies (**a**) Right before the u-quark leaves *N* (**b**) After the u-quark leaves *N*

9.4.2.4 Innovation: The Norm of the Present Business World

As discussed in Sect. 9.4.2.1, having the stretch ambition of becoming "world class and the best of the world" means that the firm has to keep up with the most recent developments in the industries it competes in and find ways to lead in at least some of the developments. In other words, the firm needs to make considerable investments in flexibility and innovation.

In terms of flexibility, it means the capability for the firm to readily adopt new procedures and systems that will increase the situation at hands. For example, if the traditional annual budgeting processes and efficiency-oriented values no longer work efficiently, then the firm needs to enthusiastically modify the processes and values, even if this may lead to a small degree of sub-optimization. To reflect the unwavering commitment to the established ambition, the firm needs to go as far as to create a corresponding award system in which the employees who best exemplify the firm's values are rewarded.

The key principle behind flexibility is that the adjusted pace of operations allows the firm to be extremely responsive to changes in the environment and to catch the need to make changes and adapt earlier than other companies. To practically implement this principle, of course, the firm has to deal with a major barrier to effective change, the fear and sense of career risk that often lead managers to cling onto eroding businesses long after they should have moved on.

In terms of innovation, it represents the firm's attempt to lead in at least some of the developments in the industries it competes in. So, rather than being an episodic, on-again, off-again endeavor, innovation has to be continuous, mainstream, and part of everyone's job. To candidly echo the culture of innovative spirits, innovation and opportunity recognition processes need to appear unequivocally and unendingly on the firm's website, be featured in its recruitment materials, and reinforced by investment. In particular, the firm needs to proudly list how much it is investing in new activities, such as R&D, international expansion, etc.

Because the connotation of innovation in our context stands for creating new ways to lead industrial developments, the effort has to be companywide, and the firm needs to correspondingly have well-established processes for managing the entire innovation pipeline that cuts across business units. For example, if the firm decides to pursue growth strategies, it can introduce firstly ways for users to have easy access from everywhere; secondly a media platform for user interactions that adds information from users to other data that can be found on the firm's site to make the site and the firm's products and services more valuable; thirdly, individualized information that focuses on developing offerings for specific individuals and parties based on their interests and needs; and finally, open network partnerships, which seek to offer businesses solutions to their problems. Within each of these areas, managers need to regularly identify where they think the next set of promising opportunities will be and how resources can be dedicated to the opportunities that appear most compelling. At the same time, the firm's leaders need to continually monitor the usage of key services and their impact on relations with key partners to determine when a service need no longer to be offered.

For example, the senior executive team of the firm can task each division every year to articulate one or two big things they are going to do that will dramatically and in real time move their business forward, and then go public with that declaration. That is, the firm is continuously thinking of new things as part of everybody's day job.

To summarize, conclusions derived in this sub-subsection are natural consequences of the theory developed in the previous sub-subsections. It ties different aspects of the firm into practical details in terms of flexibility and innovation.

9.5 The Analysis of a Legendary Company

In this section, let us look at a case of success where the company of our focus has stood the test of time for nearly two hundred years. Although our chosen company does not satisfy the criteria used in McGrath's (2013) study, when she selected her outlier companies, it does present us a perfect business organization that repeatedly went through all the necessary steps for it to be successful in riding the waves of transient competitive advantages, as listed in the previous section, even when other named companies still treated competitive advantages as sustainable.

By clicking the internet link https://grace.com/en-us/Pages/About-Grace.aspx (accessed on July 22, 2017), we see the following message: A Global Leader in Specialty Chemicals and Materials. Under this title, we read: "Grace Catalysts Technologies and Grace Materials Technologies provide innovative products, technologies and services that improve the products and processes of our customer partners around the world." That is then followed with vision, purpose, and values as follows.

- Vision: Grace strives to be a premier specialty chemical and materials company. We provide innovative technologies and value-added products and services around the world to enhance the quality of life.
- Purpose: We are dedicated to our customers. They trust us to provide products, knowledge, technologies, services, and the people to make their products work better.
- Values: (1) Teamwork**:** Treat each other with respect. Work safely and effectively with each other to win in the marketplace. Communicate openly and candidly; (2) Performance**:** Provide products and services that will make our customers successful; (3) Integrity**:** Maintain and expect the highest level of ethical behavior; (4) Speed**:** Work with a sense of urgency to meet our customers' needs. Move quickly to seize opportunities in the marketplace. Anticipate market shifts and respond before our competitors; and (5) Innovation**:** Encourage people to constantly look for new ways to create value.

By clicking the link entitled "Our History," we find that the past of the company can be traced back to as far as 1832, nearly two hundred years ago. During the past two centuries, this business entity has taken different forms, gone through many evolutionary vicissitudes, and successfully ridden the tidal waves of shifting competitive advantages. That is, this business entity, among very few of similar business organizations, has splendidly stood the test of time.

In the rest of this section, let us look at the development history starting with William Russell Grace who founded W. R. Grace & Co. in Peru in 1854. Although the history of our focus organization traces back to Davison, Kettlewell & Co. in Baltimore, Maryland, of 1832, it is W. R. Grace that eventually took over the business of the former in W. R. Grace's business evolution.

9.5.1 The Start of Everything

William Russell Grace left Ireland during the potato famine of the 1840s and bounced around the world as a sailor. In 1851 he shipped out to Calleo, Peru, then in the midst of a boom in the guano trade, and after a brief apprenticeship W. R. entered that business. However, harvesting and sale of bird droppings for fertilizer was only one of his many interests. He was bold in vision and daring in execution. He would go wherever profits were to be made purchasing or founding projects and then discarding them when they lost their glow. In 1854, when it suited his needs, he organized W. R. Grace & Co. as the vehicle through which most of his efforts would be channeled.

W. R. owned and ran Peruvian textile mills and sugar estates, a rubber industry in a Brazilian jungle, and a nitrate business in the Chilean desert. There were Grace constructed railroads in the Andes, and he introduced American agricultural and electrical equipment to the west coast of South America. He was involved in a scheme to dig a canal across Nicaragua that preceded the Panama Canal. When Peruvian finance was in shambles, W. R. and his brother, Michael, were asked to help reorganize it and put the country back on its feet.

Although deeply involved in South America, W. R. pursued holdings in other parts of the world. He founded Grace Brothers & Co. of London and then went on to the Far East. Within two decades, he had accumulated trading interests that stretched from Peru to Tokyo, from the Baring Sea to the Straits of Magellan. In 1865, W. R. relocated to New York to become the mayor of the city. Afterwards, he returned to the business world and started some companies in the USA.

9.5.2 The Transitional Time

W. R. suffered a stroke in 1898 and died in 1904 when his nephew Edward Eyre was serving as the president of the business organization. In 1936, W. R. Grace was still heavily involved in South America trade and in a wide variety of businesses. It owned and operated sugar plantations in Peru, refineries, a chapter plant, and a facility that produced caustic soda, chlorine, and muriatic acid. The company made rum from molasses at Cartavio in Peru. There were tin, wolfram, lead, zinc mines, and textile mills in Colombia, Peru, and Chile. And oilseed operation, a coffee plantation in Guatemala. A trading business in East Indian Coffee and cocoa. The ship agency operates in 30 or so ports. Cotton mills. Woolen mills. And much more.

Other than handling the company's business, the Grace bank was known as the savviest financial institution in its special niche. The Grace Line was one of America's most renowned carriers, taking cargoes and passengers to and from the USA to ports along the west coast of Latin America. Panagra was the major air carrier from the USA to points south. A popular radio program of the time, *Nights in Latin America*, spun visions of the exotic southern continent, along with playing native music. In 1936 there were several coffee roasters near Hanover Square, where W. R. moved his New York Headquarters in 1885, which provided the district with an aroma.

The Grace offices were populated mostly by men who had served for many years in one or more of the Grace casas in Peru, Ecuador, Chile, and Bolivia. As was the case with all new hires, after graduating from Yale, Peter Grace began in the mail room. With the obligation of following the company's rigorous training regimen, Peter moved from one division to another, from New York to Peru, Chile, and beyond in order for him to become a generalist and develop the necessary commitment to business. In 1940, as Peter was involved with the company's burgeoning South American trade, he traveled to Chile and met Raul Simon, who headed the company's Chilean operations. Before working for the Grace, Simon had served in government, worked as a journalist, and authored a few books. In other words, Simon was one of the very few Grace executives who could be considered an intellectual. In his conversations with Peter, Simon predicted that the USA would enter the European war then raging. Latin American countries would sell a great deal of raw materials to the USA and come out of war quite prosperous, which would prove their undoing. Simon believed that demagogues would come to power throughout Latin America, promising the people endless prosperity. In time all foreign investments would be taken over, while inflation would destroy values. He convinced Peter that the company would have to leave South America before this happened.

As predicted by Simon, the South American trade was enormously profitable. In 1938, the last full prewar year, W. R. Grace had revenues of \$1.7 million; in 1941, they came to \$9.1 million and reached just under \$12 million in 1945. That year, Peter became the president of W. R. Grace.

9.5.3 *Peter Grace: The Leader of the Third Generation*

During the war Peter Grace developed a three-part plan. In addition to taking the company out of South America, he needed to unearth other businesses for it to enter. Instead of starting companies, it made more sense to make purchases, because the company lacked requisite expertise and knowledge to operate anything but those Latin American enterprises and would need managers and technicians from the acquired companies. The third part of the strategy was to transform W. R. Grace into a public company in order to ease the task of raising funds and have stock options to keep and attract talents for managing the acquired businesses.

The implementation of the plan had to be slow because the board still did not take Peter seriously, see him as a menace to their dividend payments, and consider W. R. Grace as the family preserve. Additionally, the program had to be carried out carefully so as not to upset the existing operations. As board members retired or died, Peter would replace them with new people who agreed with his vision for the company. In 1952, just before the diversification started and when Peter got into a car accident and spent three months in the hospital, Andrew Shea, the number two man of the company, went after Peter and tried to get him fired. Shea was one of the Latin American hands and felt he had to save the old company. After surviving the challenge, Peter got W. R. Grace listed on the New York Stock Exchange in early 1953 while perfecting his plans for diversification.

From three promising areas, petroleum, chemicals, and electronics, chemicals was chosen because of the scale of the area and the existence of many niches, some of which resembled several of W. R. Grace's old businesses. Through using his connections, Peter acquired the proper talent, although he had to make some bright young men without much experience in chemicals to be executives. Because petrochemicals were considered most promising, Peter acquired Davison Chemical by late 1953, then Dewey & Almy, and then on to more deals in chemicals. By 1957, chemicals grew to 55% of the company's assets from 3% in 1950, making W. R. Grace one of the ten largest chemical companies in America. At the same time period, revenues rose from $265 million to $460 million and earnings from $8.5 million to $15.5 million.

Starting in early 1960s, Peter started to lose his sense of direction, while by then he had accumulated sufficient power to do anything he wanted to do. Other than notoriously shortened attention span, Peter attempted to micromanage and displayed a compulsive concern with information.

In terms of disengagement, the Grace Bank was sold in 1965; Panagra sold in 1967; the Grace Line in 1969. Then in that year, a Peruvian military junta started expropriating foreign properties. Disgusted, Peter ordered the wholesale divestiture of all South American companies often at prices below what they should have fetched.

By then Peter was more secure in his position and was prepared to act boldly and to purchase companies in industries he found interesting. From this period onward to 1990, Peter purchased massively in food industry, restaurants, specialty department stores, petroleum firms and drilling companies, health care industry, etc. Because many of these purchases mandated borrowing, by the end of 1985, the company's long-term debt reached $1.6 billion. The need to cut back on the debt and failures of several aspects of the new W. R. Grace motivated Peter to exit from the failed ventures smoothly. By the year 1991, specialty retailers and restaurants were sold off. For a more detailed account on what had gone wrong with Peter Grace's later career, see (Sobel, 1999).

9.5.4 More Recent State of Company Affairs

In 1992, due to Peter's illness, J. P. Bolduc became the president and chief operating officer of the company. After relocating to Boca Raton, Bolduc restructured the company, sold off additional properties, and gave W. R. Grace a more focused appearance than it had before. And as of this writing this focused appearance has continued.

In the following, let us fast forward from 1995 to 2016 and focus on major events of business expansions only.

After J. Peter Grace died in 1995, Albert J. Costello became the next leader of the Grace organization. In this year, Grace acquired Cormix Construction Chemicals and expanded market penetration in the UK, Middle East, and Asia Pacific. In 1996, while disposing several noncore businesses, Grace built its first packaging and silica products plant in Malaysia and expanded construction products business into India and Vietnam. In 1997, Grace introduced Procor™ fluid-applied waterproofing, a liquid alternative to sheet membrane waterproofing. In 1998, Grace merged its Cryovac packaging business with Sealed Air Corporation, making the business organization a global specialty chemicals company, focusing on catalysts and silica products, specialty construction chemicals and building materials, and container protection products. And in this year, Paul J. Norris became the CEO. In 1999, Grace formed the Performance Chemicals unit, comprising construction chemicals and materials, and Darex Container Products. In 2000, Grace continued successful bolt-on acquisition strategy with the Crosfield Groups' hydro-processing business, the International Protective Coatings firestop products and systems business, the LUDOX® colloidal silicas business, and the Hampshire Polymers business. In 2001, Grace Performance Chemicals acquired Pieri SA's construction chemicals business, while Grace Davison Catalysts entered into a joint venture, Advanced Refining Technologies, for hydro-processing catalysts with Chevron Products Company. And Grace Davison Silicas acquired The Separations Group, as well as the precipitated silicas business of Akzo-PQ Silica. In 2002, Grace Davison Catalysts acquired the catalyst manufacturing assets of Borealis A/S, while Advanced Refining Technologies acquired an exclusive license for the hydro-processing catalyst technology of Japan Energy Corporation. Grace Performance Chemicals acquired Addiment, Inc., a leading supplier of specialty chemicals to the concrete paver and masonry industries. In 2003, Grace Davison Silica Products acquired MODcol Corporation, a manufacturer of preparative chromatography columns and provider of custom column packing services. Silica Products strengthened its European presence with its acquisition of the high performance liquid chromatography business of Argonaut Technologies. And Grace Performance Chemicals acquired certain assets of Tricosal Beton-Chemie GmbH & Co., a leading supplier of specialty chemicals and materials to the European construction industry. In November, Fred Festa became the President and Chief Operating Officer of W. R. Grace & Co.

In 2005, Grace acquired Midland Dexter Venezuela, S. A., a supplier of coatings and sealants for rigid packaging in the local and export markets of Latin America; Perstorp Peramin Ab, a concrete admixture business in Sweden; The assets of Single-Site Catalysts, LLC, a supplier of organometallic catalysts; and Flexit Laboratories Pvt. Ltd., an Indian chromatography company, through Grace subsidiary, Alltech Associates Applied Science Limited (UK). It opened a new office in Shanghai and a technical service center in Beijing and reached an agreement for the Kuwait Catalyst Company to manufacture Advanced Refining Technologies catalysts for the petroleum refining industry in the Arabian Gulf region. In 2006, Grace opened a manufacturing facility in Tennessee to produce products for residential and commercial construction, a new Discovery Sciences technical center in Shanghai and a marketing office in Moscow. The company acquired a catalyst components business and custom catalyst assets in order to expand existing polyolefin catalysts manufacturing capabilities. In 2007, Grace Davison opened a new facility in Surat, India, focused on manufacturing columns and cartridges for chromatography applications. Grace expanded its R&D capabilities in Europe with the official opening of an innovation center in Poznan, Poland, and opened a new facility manufacturing cement processing additives and concrete admixtures in the Hoc Mon District of Ho Chi Minh City, Vietnam. In 2009, Grace opened a Customer Centre of Excellence near Barcelona, Spain and a manufacturing facility in Chennai, India for the production of specialty chemicals used in commercial, infrastructure, and residential construction. In 2010, Grace acquired Wuhan Meilixin New Building Materials Co., Ltd., a manufacturer of waterproofing products located in China, and Synthetech, Inc., a manufacturer of fine chemicals specializing in organic synthesis, biocatalysis, and chiral technologies.

In 2011, Grace opened a cement additives and concrete admixtures facility near Delhi, India, received a three-year, $3 million grant from the U.S. Department of Energy to develop advanced post-combustion technologies for capturing carbon dioxide (CO_2) from coal-fired power plants. Gregory E. Poling became Grace's President and Chief Operating Officer. In 2012, Grace succeeded (jointly with Formac Pharmaceuticals) with human clinical trial demonstrating the novel use of silica for drug delivery. It acquired the assets of Noblestar Catalysts Co., Ltd., a manufacturer of fluid catalytic cracking (FCC) catalysts, catalyst intermediates and related products used in the petroleum refining industry and located in Qingdao, China, and signed a multi-year agreement with Braskem to develop process technologies and catalyst solutions to produce green chemicals. In 2013, Advanced Refining Technologies LLC® (ART) signed an agreement with Chevron Lummus Global (CLG) for the exclusive right to sell CLG's hydrocracking and lubes hydro-processing catalysts to CLG's licensees and other petroleum refiners for unit refills. Grace acquired Chemind Construction Products, located in Brisbane, Australia, and the assets of the Polypropylene Licensing and Catalysts business of The Dow Chemical Company, and entered into a joint venture with Al Dahra Agricultural Company to build and operate the first fluid catalytic cracking (FCC) catalysts and additives plant in the Middle East. In 2016, Grace separated into two independent public companies, where Catalysts Technologies and Materials Technologies remained in Grace while a new entity, named GCP Applied Technologies, Inc., focusing on Construction Products and Darex Packaging Technologies businesses. On July 1, Grace acquired the BASF Polyolefin Catalysts business with production facilities in Pasadena, Texas and Tarragona, Spain, making Grace the #1 worldwide in polyolefin catalysts.

9.6 A Few Final Words

Without directly relying on anecdotes and data, this chapter develops a systemic theory about how a firm can successfully transit into the present, new era of transient competitive advantages. Beyond listing the necessary steps for the desired transition, this chapter also provides the logical reason based on systems science on why these steps are practically important and how they are fundamentally connected.

Because conclusions presented in this chapter are not subject to the limitations of anecdotal analysis, statistical confirmation, and data mining, managers and entrepreneurs can practically employ the managerial guidelines, derived in this chapter, for their various decision-making purposes. The theoretical and practical value of the conclusions of this chapter cannot be overemphasized, considering the fact that with the globalization of the world economy, the once sustainable competitive advantages of the business world have become transient so that new managerial decisions need to be made under ever increasingly tight time constraints and high pressures (McGrath, 2013).

Appendix: Technical Details

The Proof of Proposition 9.1 By contradiction, consider a fully efficient organization that satisfies given condition, where the organization's mission is not in total agreement with the personal value of employee k. Let Y be a variable measuring one aspect of employee k's personal value such that

$$U_k = U_k(X_k, Y), \tag{9.1}$$

satisfying

$$\frac{\partial U_k}{\partial X_k} > 0 \text{ and } \frac{\partial U_k}{\partial Y} > 0,$$

where U_k is the utility of k, X_k the total consumption of k, and the production function of the organization is

$$P = P(X_c, U_k, \ldots), \tag{9.2}$$

satisfying

$$\frac{\partial P}{\partial X_c} > 0, \frac{\partial P}{\partial U_k} > 0, \ldots,$$

where X_c represents the expenditure of the organization except that spent on k, and the dots all the utilities of all other employees. The monetary bonus that measures the work efficiency of k is expressed by

$$h_k = h_k(Y), \tag{9.3}$$

satisfying

$$\frac{dh_k}{dY} < 0.$$

In real life, although this variable Y might only exist implicitly and cannot be measured readily, its negative effect on the quality and efficiency generally can be clearly seen. So, we simply assume without loss of generality that Y can be measured in determining the monetary bonus. The organization's resources are distributed to its employees to maximize its production function P in Eq. 9.2 subject to the following constraint:

$$X_c + X_k = X_c + (I_k + h_k), \tag{9.4}$$

where I_k is k's income from his work at the organization. Maximizing the production function in Eq. 9.2 subject to the constraint in Eq. 9.4 leads to the contradiction:

$$\partial X_k / \partial Y > 0 \text{ and } \partial X_k / \partial Y = dh_k / dY < 0.$$

That implies that the assumption that the organization that satisfies the conditions of the proposition is fully efficient is incorrect.

References

Bernheim, B. D., & Whinston, M. D. (1990). Multimarket contact and collusive behavior. *RAND Journal of Economics, 21*, 1–26.

Carpenter, M., Daidj, N., & Moreno, C. (2014). Game console manufacturers: The end of sustainable competitive advantage? *Communications & Strategies.*, 2nd Quarter, *94*, 39–60.

Chemers, M. M. (2001). Cognitive, social, and emotional intelligence of transformational leadership: Efficacy and effectiveness. In R. E. Riggio, S. E. Murphy, & F. J. Pirozzolo (Eds.), *Multiple intelligences and leadership* (pp. 139–160). Lawrence Erlbaum.

Duez, P. (2012). From competitive advantage to differential advantage: A new model of strategic management. *Proceedings of the 6th International Management Conference "Approaches in Organizational Management"*, November 15–16, 2012, Bucharest, Romania, pp. 9-24.

Forrest, J. Y. L., & Nightingale, J. (2017). Successfully transition into the era of transient competitive advantages. *Proceedings of 2017 NABET Annual Conference*, October 26 – 27, 2017, State College, PA., 57-79.

Forrest, J. Y. L., & Orvis, B. (2016). Principles of management efficiency and organizational inefficiency. *Kybernetes: The International Journal of Cybernetics, Systems and Management Sciences, 45*(8), 1308–1322.

Fronmueller, M. P. (1996). The competitive advantage potential of vertical integration. *Omega, 24*(6), 715–726.

Fuentelsaz, L., & Gómez, J. (2006). Multipoint competition, strategic similarity and entry into geographic markets. *Strategic Management Journal, 27*(5), 477–499.

Haveman, H. A., & Nonnemaker, L. (2000). Competition in multiple geographic markets: The impact on growth and market entry. *Administrative Science Quarterly, 45*(2), 232–267.

Herrera, M. E. B. (2015). Creating competitive advantage by institutionalizing corporate social innovation. *Journal of Business Research, 68*(7), 1468–1474.

Kirkpatrick, S., & Locke, E. (1991). Leadership: Do traits matter? *Academy of Management Executive, 5*(2), 48–60.

Kouzes, J., & Posner, B. (2007). *The leadership challenge*. Jossey Bass.

Leonidou, L. C., Fotiadis, T. A., Christodoulides, P., Spyropoulou, S., & Katsikeas, C. S. (2015). Environmentally friendly export business strategy: Its determinants and effects on competitive advantage and performance. *International Business Review, 24*(5), 798–811.

Li, D. Y., & Liu, J. (2014). Dynamic capabilities, environmental dynamism, and competitive advantage: Evidence from China. *Journal of Business Research, 67*(1), 2793–2799.

Li, S. X., & Greenwood, R. (2004). The effect of within industry diversification on firm performance: Synergy creation, multi-market contact and market structuration. *Strategic Management Journal, 25*, 1131–1153.

Lin, Y., & Forrest, B. (2011). *Systemic structure behind human organizations: From civilizations to individuals*. Springer.

Lin, Y., & He, X. Y. (2010). Particle yoyos and their quark structures. *Kybernetes: The International Journal of Cybernetics, Systems and Management Sciences, 39*(2), 204–217.

Mahanta, V. (2012). How Aditya Puri has managed to pull off 30% plus growth for HDFC Bank. *Economic Times, 29*, 2012.

Makadok, R. (2010). The interaction effect of rivalry restraint and competitive advantage on profit: Why the whole is less than the sum of the parts. *Management Science, 56*(2), 356–372.

Maxwell, S. (2010). Competitive advantage research: Why you need it now. Retrieved September 30, 2017, from https://labs.openviewpartners.com.

McClelland, D. (1975). *Power: The inner experience*. John Wiley & Sons.

McGrath, R. G. (2013). *The end of competitive advantage: How to keep your strategy moving as fast as your business*. Harvard Business Review Press.

Moustaghfir, K. (2012). Explicating knowledge-based competitive advantage. *International Journal of Synergy and Research, 1*(1), 23–38.

Peng, M. W., Lee, S. H., & Tan, J. J. (2001). The *keiretsu* in Asia: Implications for multilevel theories of competitive advantage. *Journal of International Management, 7*(4), 253–276.

Peterson, E. A. (2013). Compliance and ethics programs: competitive advantage through the law. *Journal of Management & Governance, 17*(4), 1027–1045.

Porter, M. E. (1985). *Competitive advantage: Creating and sustaining superior performance*. Free Press.

Saeidi, S. P., Sofian, S., Saeidi, P., Saeidi, S. P., & Saaeidi, S. A. (2015). How does corporate social responsibility contribute to firm financial performance? The mediating role of competitive advantage, reputation, and customer satisfaction. *Journal of Business Research, 68*(2), 341–350.

Sobel, R. (1999). *When giants stumble: Classic business blunders and how to avoid them.* Prentice Hall.

Terán, O., Sibertin-Blanc, C., & Gaudou, B. (2015). The influence of moral sensitivity on organizational cooperation. *Kybernetes, 44*(6/7), 1067–1081.

Villalobos, J., & Vargas, M. (2015). Towards a simple dynamical model of citizens' perception. *Kybernetes, 44*(6/7), 1134–1145.

Wen, Y. (2016). *The making of an economic superpower: Unlocking China's secret of rapid industrialization.* World Scientific.

Yu, T., & Cannella, A. A., Jr. (2012). A comprehensive review of multimarket competition research. *Journal of Management, 39*, 76–109.

Chapter 10
Indecisive Customers and Sales Associates with Elevated Competitiveness

Jeffrey Yi-Lin Forrest, Melanie Anderson, and Larry McCarthy

Abstract This chapter, which is mainly based on Forrest and Anderson (Customers' indecisiveness: A pricing strategy approach, *Pennsylvania Economic Association 2017 Conference Proceedings*, 80–95, 2017) and Forrest and McCarthy (Sales associates' compensations: A game theoretic approach. *Pennsylvania Economic Association 2017 Conference Proceedings*, 52–64, 2017), investigates (a) the characteristics of market competition by employing the thinking logic of systems science, and (b) the problem of sales associates' compensation (or sales force compensation). The importance of these topics is manifested in the fact that competition is one spirited characteristic of the market economy and continuously finding a new profitable market niche, an entrepreneurial behavior that makes competition increasingly intensive, is the key for success in running business enterprises. Rigorous deductions are provided in the language of game theory. Among other results, this chapter shows when market competition will intensify, under what conditions the existing loyal consumer base of an established firm will start to deteriorate, and how a firm should motivate and compensate its sales force to achieve additional success. The established results and the reasoning employed in this chapter can be directly applied to design new strategies for competition between firms in order for them to optimize their profits.

Keywords Consumer satisfaction · Cournot competition · Dynamics of market competition · Exit strategies · Purchase decision-making · Sales force · Symmetric mixed strategy

---

Jeffrey Yi-Lin Forrest (Department of Accounting Economics Finance, Slippery Rock University, Slippery Rock, PA, USA; Email: Jeffrey.forrest@sru.edu), Melanie Anderson (Department of Accounting Economics Finance, Slippery Rock University, Slippery Rock, PA, USA; Email: melanie.anderson@sru.edu), and Larry McCarthy (Department of Accounting Economics Finance, Slippery Rock University, Slippery Rock, PA, USA; Email: larry.mccarthy@sru.edu) are equally contributed to this chapter.

J. Y.-L. Forrest, *Systemic Principles of Applied Economic Philosophies II*,
Translational Systems Sciences 39, https://doi.org/10.1007/978-981-99-7939-4_10

10.1 Introduction

One characteristic of the market economy is the constant competition that widely exists in the marketplace. To continuously find a new profitable market niche, entrepreneurial behaviors that make competition increasingly intensive are the key for success in running business enterprises. So, two natural questions arise as follows for anyone who dreams to acquire success in the business world:

- What characterizes a market that begets new opportunities or competition?
- How should a firm motivate and compensate its sales force in order to win market competitions against its rivals?

To this end, this chapter, which is mainly based on Forrest and Anderson (2017) and Forrest and McCarthy (2017), attempts to address these questions by investigating a condition under which market competition will intensify, how the existing loyal consumer base of an established firm will start to deteriorate, and how a firm can gain an upper hand in the market competition internally by looking at how a firm's sales associates should be appropriately compensated (or the problem of sales force compensation).

These questions have been active areas of research with a great potential of direct applications in real life. And what is presented in this chapter attempts to address these questions from a specific angle. In particular, we will develop several main results, among others, regarding the following issues:

1. When the consumer surplus of the market, which is the totality of all price switchers, is sufficiently large, market competition will intensify with additional profits to be made;
2. When the number of competing firms increases, the number of loyal customers will decline and eventually approach zero; and
3. How different pricing strategies could be employed to potentially double expected profits.
4. How the competitive spirits of a firm's sales associates can be lifted to a different height.

The rest of this chapter is organized as follows: Section 10.2 offers a literature review and documents the contribution of this chapter. Section 10.3 provides an effective way to deal with indecisive customers. This section consists of three subsections that, respectively, examine the situation of strategic firms and provide a pricing strategy that can produce higher levels of expected profits. Section 10.4 considers how the competitive spirit of sales associates can be lifted. It consists of four subsections, respectively, establishing an abstract maximization problem for the sales associates' compensation of concern, studying the amounts of sales of individual associates at Cournot equilibrium, looking at the associates' payoffs at Cournot equilibrium, and investigating the relationship between the associates' private cost information and expected incomes, and specifically formulating how associates' incentive weights should be determined at the firm level. And, Section 10.5 concludes the presentation of this chapter.

10.2 Literature Review

The relevant literature can be seen in two different lights: market competition and sales associates' compensation (or sales force compensation). For the former literature, for example, Belu and Caragin (2008) analyze possibilities that a company has when considering to enter a foreign market, and the importance of such a decision that involves market assessment and analysis. Kopalle and Lehmann (2006) develop a two-period model to determine consumer satisfaction in the first period formed on the gap that exists between the actual quality and expectations; that satisfaction in turn impacts the sales of the second period. Siebert (2015) investigates the optimal entry strategies for firms to use when entering into new or empty markets by considering how many products of different qualities the firms should introduce. Guo et al. (2012) address the role of downstream market competition under symbiotic production and demonstrate that incorporating different types of competition in product markets will partially eliminate the inefficiency caused by double marginalization. Chang et al. (2015) consider the effect of market competition on the relationship between corporate governance and capital structure dynamics. Debruyne and Reibstein (2005) investigate when incumbent firms should enter into new market niches created by technological innovations and advances. Kumar and Sudharshan (1988) investigate the development of optimal defensive strategies based on an understanding of the possible reactions of all the defenders to an optimal attack. Similar results are also obtained by Hauser and Shugan (1983), where different consumer response models and a different equilibrium assumption are used.

In comparison with the literature, conclusions in this chapter add additional insights of very different kinds to the existing literature on market competition and carry that knowledge many steps forward. In particular, this chapter shows the following main results, among others, regarding how a firm can potentially double its expected profits by being strategic; when all incumbent firms could potentially double their profits; under exactly what conditions the market competition will intensify; and when the existing loyal consumer base of an established firm will start to deteriorate.

As for sales associates' compensation (or sales force compensation), it represents an area of research with a great potential of direct applications in real life. A good number of scholars have contributed to this area of research. For example, Basu et al. (1985) develop a theory of sales force compensation plans, where the sales of a product depend not only on the sales associates' effort but also on the uncertainty in the selling environment. Joseph and Thevaranjan (1998) analyze a framework that simultaneously examines the role of *both* monitoring and incentives in the design of sales force control systems. Lal and Srinivasan (1993) modify the agency theory approach for understanding salesforce compensation plans by incorporating the intra-temporal nature of the sales person's effort-rate decision. Inderst and Ottaviani (2009) analyze the implications of the inherent conflict between two tasks performed by direct marketing agents: prospecting for customers and advising on the product's "suitability" for the specific needs of customers. Sheth and Sharma (2008) examine the evolution of sales organizations as a result of the shift from product- to service-focused commerce that took place in the past three decades.

Misra and Nair (2011) present an empirical framework to analyze real-world sales force compensation schemes, and report on a multi-million-dollar, multi-year project involving a large contact lens manufacturer in the USA. Frenzen et al. (2010) develop and empirically test a framework of important drivers of price delegation to sales people based on agency-theoretic research and investigate the impact of price delegation on firm performance. Chan et al. (2014a, b) examine how compensation systems impact peer effects and competition in collocated sales teams by using department store sales data and show that compensation systems influence worker incentives to help and compete with peers within the same firm, which in turn changes the capability of the firm to compete with rivals.

Lo et al. (2011) use data on individual sales associate compensation contracts to show that firms design their pay plans to both discriminatingly select (i.e., attract and retain) sales people and provide them with the right level of incentives. Daljord et al. (2016) focus on the constraints faced by firms in fine-tuning contracts to the full heterogeneity distribution of their employees and explore the implication of these constraints for the provision of incentives within the firm. Chung et al. (2013) estimate a dynamic structural model of sales force response to a bonus-based compensation plan. Kräkel and Schöttner (2016) explain when the compensation plans that are most common in practice, such as fixed salaries, quota-based bonuses, commissions, or a combination thereof, are optimal.

In comparison, conclusions in this chapter add additional results of very different kinds to the existing literature on sales force compensation and carry that knowledge many steps forward. In particular, the following major conclusions are established:

- How sales associates' compensation should be aligned with the profit maximization of the firm;
- How by revealing private cost information of individual sales associates within the firm increases the expected incomes of the associates; and
- Specifically, how the firm should assign incentive weights to each sales associate in order to maximize its profits.

Additionally, another main contribution of this chapter is that it shows vividly how the relevant reasoning and intuitive thinking in marketing research can be based on systems science in general and systemic yoyo model in particular.

10.3 An Effective Way to Deal with Indecisive Customers

As suggested by the title, this section studies the question of how to deal with indecisive customers. It consists of three subsections. The first one examines a special case when only one firm is strategic; the second subsection studies the case when all incumbent firms are strategic; and the third subsection looks at a particular pricing strategy that can produce higher levels of expected profits.

10.3.1 When Merely One Firm is Strategic

This section first studies the existence of either pure or mixed strategy equilibrium and introduces a pricing strategy that can potentially double a firm's expected profit.

10.3.1.1 Existence of Equilibria of Either Pure or Mixed Strategies

In terms of customer behaviors, indecisiveness is a commonly seen phenomenon (McWilliams, 2004; Mittal et al., 2008; Shin et al., 2012), where customers do not seem to know exactly what they want in the eyes of the sales people. This end in fact can be fundamentally explained by using the concept of personal systems of values and beliefs (Forrest & Orvis, 2016), where the indecisiveness is rooted in the differences in personal values and beliefs. Such differences in turn lead to varied perceptions about how goods could be used and services enjoyed because generally no good or service perfectly matches an existing personal system of values and beliefs, and the consequent perception.

At the same time, the systemic yoyo model provides another explanation. Specifically, when the yoyo field of the customer is obligated to absorb whatever necessary from the environment in order to fill an existing void, since the field is located within a vast, dynamic ocean of different yoyo pools, the customer is not exactly sure what he needs in the first place and then he is not sure where he could acquire whatever that might fit the need about which he is uncertain about.

From the previous two paragraphs, it follows that when a customer is indecisive in his purchase decision-making, there generally is a whole host of reasons for his indecisiveness. So, corresponding to different situations, appropriate sales' approaches need to be taken by the sales associates in order to complete successful sales. In the following let us focus on the logical reasoning underneath pricing strategies. That is, we assume that the indecisiveness of a potential purchase reflects the fact that the particular customer is a price switcher who makes purchase decisions based on the best price available to him in terms of per unit-value, for a related study, see Homburg et al. (2012). To this end, we assume that the oligopoly market of our concern has m firms, named $1, 2, \ldots, m$, which provide horizontally differentiated products at constant marginal costs, which we set to zero without loss of generality.

Assume that each Firm k has a market share α of the loyal customers such that these customers only purchase the product of Firm k provided that the price is no more than their reservation value, which is set to 1. Let $\beta = 1 - m\alpha$ be the portion of the switchers who base their purchase decisions on which price is lower. The risk-neutral managements of these m firms are well aware of the pricing strategies of the other firms and have established their best responses by playing the Nash equilibrium through pure self-analyses. For how the marginal costs of production and the market shares of the loyal customers of the firms can be assumed as above without loss of generality, see Chap. 8 for relevant discussions.

Lemma 10.1 The game the incumbent firms play does not have any pure strategy equilibrium, where each firm's available strategy is the selling price of the firm's product.

Proof For any pure strategy portfolio $(x_1, x_2, \ldots, x_m)$, if there is a unique index $i \in \{1, 2, \ldots, m\}$ such that

$$x_i < x_j, \text{ for } j \in \{1, 2, \ldots, m\} \text{ and } j \neq i, \tag{10.1}$$

then Firm i has successfully attracted all the price switchers and can therefore slightly raise its price x_i to bring in additional profits as long as the new price still satisfies the condition in Eq. 10.1, while all other firms maintain their respective strategy unchanged. So, the pure strategy portfolio $(x_1, x_2, \ldots, x_m)$ is not a Nash equilibrium.

If the set

$$I = \left\{ i \in \{1, 2, \ldots, m\} : x_i = \min_{j=1}^{m} \{x_j\} \right\} \tag{10.2}$$

has cardinality $|I|$ great than 1, then the Firms k, $k \in I$, have absorbed all the price switchers. Due to the fact that everything in this scenario is set up symmetrically, we can see that each of these firms would have taken in $\beta/|I|$ portion of the switcher segment of the market. So, Firm k's profits, $k \in I$, are $\alpha x_k + (\beta/|I|)x_k$. So, one of these firms, say Firm k, can lower its price slightly to x_k', satisfying

$$\frac{x_k'}{x_k} > \frac{\alpha + \beta / \mid I \mid}{\alpha + \beta}, \tag{10.3}$$

to bring in additional profits by attracting all the switchers. That is, the pure strategy portfolio $(x_1, x_2, \ldots, x_m)$ is not a Nash equilibrium. Similar argument can be used to show that even when not all firms $k \in I$ share the same portion of the price switchers, then the Firm with the fewest price switchers could slightly lower its price to increasing its profits by attracting all the price switchers. That is, once again, the pure strategy portfolio $(x_1, x_2, \ldots, x_m)$ is not a Nash equilibrium.

Lastly, if for any $i \in \{1, 2, \ldots, m\}$, $x_i = 1$, then Firm j, for any chosen $j \in \{1, 2, \ldots, m\}$, can slightly lower its price from the reservation value 1 to anywhere in the

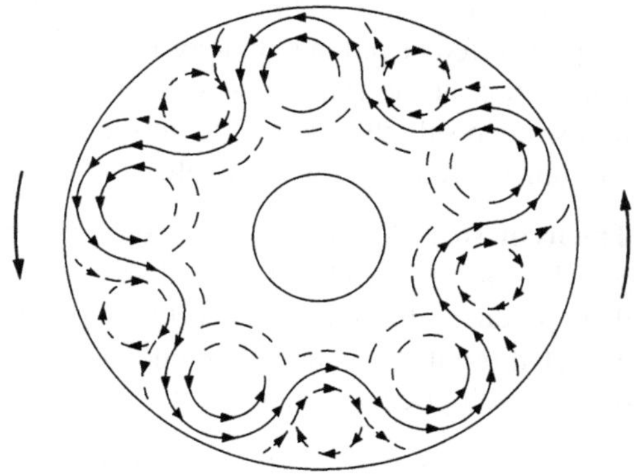

Fig. 10.1 A spinning field in equilibrium

interval ($\alpha/(\alpha + \beta)$, 1) to produce more profits by taking in the entire segment of the switchers. So, (1, 1, . . ., 1) is not a Nash equilibrium, either. That is, the game we are looking at does not have any pure strategy Nash equilibrium.

To make this chapter as self-contained as possible, let us cite Theorem 8.2 as follows:

Lemma 10.2 (Zhou et al., 2015). The game the incumbent firms play does have a symmetric mixed strategy Nash equilibrium. And, in this symmetric Nash equilibrium, each of the existing firms' expected profits stay constant and are equal to α although the firms try to attract as many switchers as possible.

From the angle of the systemic yoyo model, Lemmas 10.1 and 10.2 are quite intuitively clear. In particular, let us imagine the market as the entire spinning yoyo field in Fig. 10.1, while each of the m firms is one of the local eddy leaves so that the m local eddies in the spinning dish have reached their balance in their movements. Hence, no matter how hard each of the local eddy spins in order to pull more of the fluid particles into its field, some of the fluid particles always tend to wonder around the large field without actually becoming part of any of the local eddies. In other words, as soon as such a pattern of fluid movement as the one shown in Fig. 10.1 is formed and becomes stabilized, it will be difficult or impossible for the local eddies to grow any larger. (Note: The pattern shown in Fig. 10.1 was initially discovered by Raymond Hide (1953) of Cambridge University, England, and then by Dave Fultz and his colleagues of University of Chicago (1959). The evolution of the pattern has been well observed and studied by scholars in fluid dynamics and meteorology.)

10.3.1.2 A Pricing Strategy That Potentially Doubles the Expected Profit

What Lemma 10.1 indicates is that if an identical pricing strategy is employed by all firms, the competition will intensify while the consequent profits do not increase. So, a natural question is: While holding on to the intensifying competition, can a firm adopt a different pricing strategy that is additional to the one already used in the competition at the same time so that it can increase its profits? According to the following result the answer to this question is YES, it can be done when the consumer surplus β is big enough.

Theorem 10.1 Assume that the consumer surplus β of the market place satisfies $\beta = 1 - m\alpha \geq \alpha$, and that other than Firm i no other existing firms plan to market their products differently. Then the particular Firm i could potentially double its expected profits by uniformly randomizing its price P over the interval [0, 1] when dealing with price switchers.

Proof What is given here implies that Firm i now employs two separate and unrelated pricing strategies: one, which is that shown in the proof of Lemma 10.1, for its loyal customers, and the other for price switchers. So, for the sake of communication convenience, let us theoretically treat Firm i as two separate firms, named Firm i and Firm ia, where the former stands for the original Firm i that employs the firm's originally adopted pricing strategies, while the latter deals only with price switchers by uniformly randomizing its price P over the interval [0,1].

From $\beta = 1 - m\alpha \geq \alpha$, it follows that $\alpha/\beta \leq 1$. So, for any price P, satisfying $\alpha/\beta \leq P \leq 1$, the following function $F(P)$:

$$F(P) = 1 - \left(\frac{\alpha}{\beta P}\right)^{\frac{1}{m-1}}, \tag{10.4}$$

represents a well-defined strategy for each of the m existing firms, which satisfies the following equilibrium indifference condition of Firm k, $k = 1, 2, \ldots, m$,

$$\alpha \times P + \beta \times P \prod\nolimits_{j \neq k}^{m} (1-P)\left[1 - F_j(P)\right] = \alpha \times 1, \tag{10.5}$$

which implies that for the m existing firms, their lowest allowed price is α/β.

Next, we show that the expected profits of Firm i are still α, the same as that before adopting the new pricing strategy for price switchers. In fact, from Eq. 10.5 we have

$$\begin{aligned} E_i(\Pi) &= \int_{\alpha/\beta}^{1} \left\{\alpha \times P + \beta \times P(1-P) \prod\nolimits_{j \neq i}^{m} [1 - F(P)]\right\} dF(P) + \alpha \times \left(\frac{\alpha}{\beta}\right)^{\frac{1}{m-1}} \\ &= \int_{\alpha/\beta}^{1} \alpha dF(P) + \alpha \left(\frac{\alpha}{\beta}\right)^{\frac{1}{m-1}} = \alpha. \end{aligned} \tag{10.6}$$

For the rest of this proof, it suffices based on Eq. 10.6 to show that there is such an opportunity that Firm *ia* could expect to make at least as much profits as α. To this end, because

$$\lim_{P \to 1^-} F(P) = 1 - (\alpha/\beta)^{\frac{1}{m-1}} \neq F(1) = 1,$$

the cumulative price distribution function *F*(*P*) has a jump discontinuity at the reservation value $P = 1$, where the amount of jump is $(\alpha/\beta)^{\frac{1}{m-1}}$. So, the expected profits of Firm *ia* are the following:

$$\begin{aligned} E_{\text{ia}}(\Pi) &= \int_0^{\alpha/\beta} \beta P dP + \int_{\alpha/\beta}^{+\infty} \beta P[1 - F(P)]^m dP \\ &= \int_0^{\alpha/\beta} \beta P dP + \int_{\alpha/\beta}^{1} \beta P[1 - F(P)]^m dP + \beta\left(\frac{\alpha}{\beta}\right)^{\frac{m}{m-1}} \\ &= \begin{cases} \dfrac{-m}{2(m-2)}\dfrac{\alpha^2}{\beta} + \dfrac{m-1}{m-2}\dfrac{\alpha^{\frac{m}{m-1}}}{\beta^{\frac{1}{m-1}}} + \beta\left(\dfrac{\alpha}{\beta}\right)^{\frac{m}{m-1}}, & \text{if } m \geq 3 \\ \dfrac{\alpha^2}{2\beta} - \dfrac{\alpha^2}{\beta} \ln \dfrac{\alpha}{\beta} + \beta\left(\dfrac{\alpha}{\beta}\right)^{\frac{m}{m-1}}, & \text{if } m = 2 \end{cases} \end{aligned}$$

And because

$$\frac{\partial}{\partial \alpha}[E_{ia}(\Pi) - \alpha] > 0$$

and when $\alpha = 1/(m + 1) = \beta$, $E_{ia}(\Pi) - \alpha > 0$, it follows that there is $\alpha_{\Pi}^* \in (0, 1/(m+1))$ such that when $\alpha \geq \alpha_{\Pi}^*$, $E_{ia}(\Pi) > \alpha$.

What Theorem 10.1 indicates is that when confronting with indecisive customers, first find out what is beneath the purchase indecisiveness. If it is the price (in terms of per unit-value), then the firm could use such a sales' strategy that it materially randomizes the selling price uniformly over the interval [0,1], where 0 stands for the cost and 1 the reservation price charged to loyal customers. By doing so, the firm could potentially achieve two advantages in the market place:

1. Increase its consumer base; and
2. Grow its baseline of profits.

At the same time, Theorem 10.1 and its proof imply that if the consumer surplus β is not taken care of by the existing firms, potentially new competitions will enter the market. In particular, Firm *ia*, introduced in the proof of Theorem 10.1, can be a completely different firm not related to Firm *i*. When such a situation occurs, it means a new firm enters into the market to compete with the existing firms while expecting to potentially make more profits than any of the existing firms.

10.3.2 When Every Firm is Strategic

This section looks at the situation that every incumbent firm knows the need to be flexible with their pricing. And, it shows when the base of loyal customers for each firm will gradually diminish.

10.3.2.1 The Strategy of Flexible Pricing

Although the situation described in Theorem 10.1 would not appear in real life according to the structure of the spinning field in Fig. 10.1, where all the eddy leaves move and behave in concert, this result still naturally leads to the belief that many of the existing firms, if not all, would like to adopt a similar strategy as Firm i in that theorem. To this end, we have the following result.

Theorem 10.2 A sufficient and necessary condition for each existing Firm i, $i = 1, 2, \ldots, m$, to increase its expected profits by uniformly randomizing its price P over the interval [0, 1] when dealing with price switchers, while still employing its mixed pricing strategy at the Nash equilibrium with the loyal customers, is that the consumer surplus β and the market share α of Firm i satisfy the condition

$$m^m \alpha < (m-1)^{m-1}\beta. \tag{10.7}$$

Proof ($\Longrightarrow$) Assume that Firm i, $i = 1, 2, \ldots, m$, can increase its expected profits by uniformly randomizing its price P over the interval [0, 1] when dealing with price switchers. Just as what is done in the proof of Theorem 10.1, let us conceptually slip Firm i into two firms, named Firm i and Firm ia, where the former is run as before without adopting the pricing strategy of uniformly randomizing its price P over the interval [0,1] when dealing with price switchers, while the latter deals with price switchers only by uniformly randomizing its price P over the interval [0, 1].

The profits of Firm i are given by

$$\alpha P + \beta P(1-P)^m \prod\nolimits_{j \neq i}^{m} [1 - F_j(P)]$$

and the objective function of Firm i is

$$\max_{F_i(P)} E(\Pi_i) = \int_0^1 \left\{ \alpha P + \beta P(1-P)^m \prod\nolimits_{j \neq i}^{m} [1 - F_j(P)] \right\} dF_i(P).$$

The equilibrium indifference condition for Firm i is

$$\alpha \times P + \beta \times P(1-P)^m \prod\nolimits_{j \neq i}^{m} [1 - F_j(P)] = \alpha \times 1. \tag{10.8}$$

So, the symmetric equilibrium price strategy of each Firm i, $i = 1, 2, \ldots, m$, is

$$F(P) = F_i(P) = 1 - \frac{1}{1-P}\left(\frac{\alpha}{\beta P}\right)^{\frac{1}{m-1}}. \tag{10.9}$$

For this strategy to be valid, we must have $F(P) = 0$, for $P \leq \underline{P}$, $F(P) = 1$, for $P \geq \overline{P}$, and $F(P) \geq 0$, for $\underline{P} \leq P \leq \overline{P}$, where $\underline{P}$ and $\overline{P}$ are some fixed price levels such that $0 \leq \underline{P} < \overline{P} \leq 1$.

Next, let us see when such price levels $\underline{P}$ and $\overline{P}$ can exist. To this end, define

$$h(P) = (1-P)P^{\frac{1}{m-1}} - \left(\frac{\alpha}{\beta}\right)^{\frac{1}{m-1}}$$

so that

$$F(P) = \frac{h(P)}{(1-P)P^{\frac{1}{m-1}}}.$$

Then it can be readily checked that $F(P)$ is well defined if and only if $h(P) \geq 0$, for $\underline{P} \leq P \leq \overline{P}$, where $\underline{P}$ and $\overline{P}$ are some fixed price levels such that $0 \leq \underline{P} < \overline{P} \leq 1$, and that $h(0) < 0$ and $h(1) < 0$. Since

$$h'(P) = \frac{P^{\frac{1}{m-1}}}{m-1}\left(P^{-1} - m\right),$$

it can be shown that $h(P)$ reaches its maximum at $P = 1/m$. That is, in order for the previously mentioned price levels $\underline{P}$ and $\overline{P}$ to exist, $h(P)$ must satisfy

$$h\left(\frac{1}{m}\right) = \frac{m-1}{m^{1+\frac{1}{m-1}}} - \left(\frac{\alpha}{\beta}\right)^{\frac{1}{m-1}} > 0. \tag{10.10}$$

That is, Eq. 10.7 holds true.

($\Leftarrow$) Assume that Eq. 10.7 holds true. Then the reasoning in the previous proof can be deducted backward to show that there are price levels $\underline{P}$ and $\overline{P}$, satisfying $0 \leq \underline{P} < \overline{P} \leq 1$, such that $F(P)$, as defined in Eq. 10.9, is a valid symmetric pricing strategy for the existing firms i, $i = 1, 2, \ldots, m$, and that $F(P)$ satisfies the Nash equilibrium indifference condition in Eq. 10.8. In other words, each Firm i, $i = 1, 2, \ldots, m$, can be conceptually run as two firms with Firm i employing the mixed strategy $F(P)$ while the shadow Firm ia deals with price switchers only by uniformly randomizing its price over the interval [0,1].

Now, for Firm i, its expected profits $E(\Pi_i)$ are

$$\begin{aligned} E(\Pi_i) &= \int_0^1 \left\{\alpha P + \beta P(1-P)^m \prod_{j\neq i}^m [1-F_j(P)]\right\} dF_i(P) \\ &= \int_{\underline{P}}^{\overline{P}} \left\{\alpha P + \beta P(1-P)^m \prod_{j\neq i}^m [1-F_j(P)]\right\} dF_i(P) \\ &= \int_{\underline{P}}^{\overline{P}} \alpha dF_i(P) \\ &= \alpha F_i(P)|_{P=\underline{P}}^{\overline{P}} = \alpha \end{aligned} \tag{10.11}$$

and the profits $E(\Pi_{ia})$ of Firm ia are

$$\begin{aligned} E(\Pi_{ia}) &= \int_0^{\underline{P}} (1-P)^{m-1}\beta P dP + \int_{\underline{P}}^{\overline{P}} (1-P)^{m-1}[1-F(P)]^m \beta P dP + \\ &+ \int_{\overline{P}}^1 (1-P)^{m-1}\beta P dP, \end{aligned} \tag{10.12}$$

where the first and third terms, respectively, represent the expected profits of Firm ia, when its price is lower than or higher than that of Forms j, $j = 1, 2, \ldots, m$, and the second term is the expected profits of Firm ia when it is in direct competition with all other firms, be they real or shadow.

Because the first term in Eq. 10.12 is given by

$$\int_0^{\underline{P}} (1-P)^{m-1}\beta P dP = \beta \left[\frac{e^{m\ln(1-P)}(mp+1)}{m^2+m}\right]_{P=0}^{\underline{P}} > 0$$

while the second term in Eq. 10.11 is non-negative and the third term is 0, because no price switchers exist in that price interval, we conclude that $E(\Pi_{ia}) > 0$. So, from Eqs. 10.11 and 10.12, we can conclude that each existing firm can increase its expected profits by uniformly randomizing its price P over the interval [0,1] when dealing with price switchers, while still employing its symmetric mixed pricing strategy at the Nash equilibrium with the loyal customers.

10.3.2.2 Market Competition and Bases of Loyal Customers

Directly from Theorem 10.2, we have

Corollary 10.1 When the competition of a market grows with an increasing number of firms entering the market, the base of loyal customers for each firm will gradually diminish.

Proof It follows from Theorem 10.2 that the consumer surplus β and the market share α of Firm i satisfy the condition

$$\frac{\alpha}{\beta} < \left(1 - \frac{1}{m}\right)^m \frac{1}{m-1} \to \frac{1}{e} \times 0 = 0, \text{ for } m \to \infty.$$

That is, the ratio $\alpha/\beta \to 0$, as $m \to \infty$.

Before we move on to the next result, let us first take a closer look at Eq. 10.7. If $m = 2$, then $(\alpha/\beta)_{m=2} < 1/4$; if $m = 3$, then $(\alpha/\beta)_{m=3} < \frac{4}{27}$; if $m = 4$, then $(\alpha/\beta)_{m=4} < 27/256$; ... And in general, we can prove that $(m-1)^{m-1}/m^m$ is a decreasing function in m. So, if we look at the market with the concept of evolution in mind, where the market could be either expanding or shrinking, then the dynamics of market competition is described by Theorems 10.1 and 10.2 very well. For example, if the market is expanding quickly, then that means that the size β of consumer surplus segment increases quickly when compared to the magnitude of α, the base of loyal customers of an existing firm. So, the existing firms would have to expand their consumer bases by employing competitive pricing strategies; otherwise, Theorem 10.1 implies that new firms would enter the market to grab the segment of consumer surplus. And, as more firms enter the market, Corollary 10.1 implies that the consumer bases of the existing firms would dwindle, while the traditional pricing strategies would have to be replaced by new strategies.

The systemic intuition for this scenario is given in Fig. 10.2. Different from the model in Fig. 10.1, the expanding spinning field in Fig. 10.2 does not have a solid periphery. Instead various elements from the neighborhood, which is relatively motionless when compared to the center of the field, constantly join into the field, making the field grow bigger. Another strikingly different characteristic is that the eddy leaves in Fig. 10.2 spin in directions opposite those in Fig. 10.1 due to the effect of the relatively motionless neighborhood. Now, if the existing eddy leaves do not

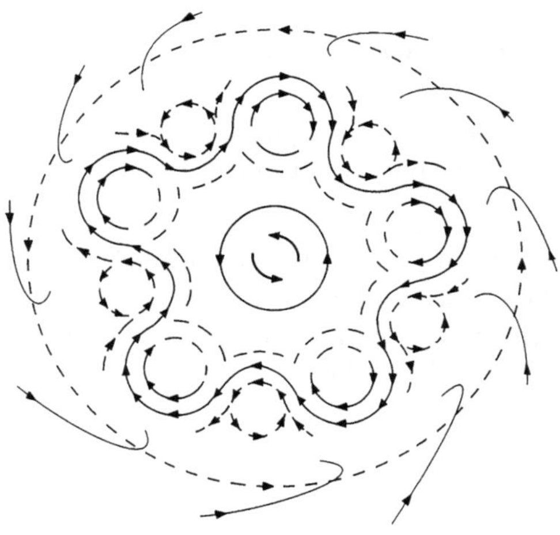

Fig. 10.2 Yoyo field model for an expanding market

grow bigger, more eddy leaves have to appear with the expansion of the overall field in order to have the overall field occupied due to uneven distribution of forces.

On the other hand, if the market shrinks, it initially means that the segment of consumer surplus disappears gradually first, followed by the decline of the loyal consumer bases of the existing firms. That means that as soon as the segment of consumer surplus shows clear signs of contraction, the existing firms need to investigate their exit strategies from the market and explore new market options. To this end, the research on personal values and beliefs (Forrest & Orvis, 2016) comes into play nicely: Those employees with personal systems of values and beliefs not in total agreement with their firm's mission would potentially discover new market directions for the firm, because their perceptions of the world, which are different from that of the firm, might help the firm to uncover one or several new markets with enough consumer surplus for the firm to enter with the potential of making more profits than any of the existing firms within the newly discovered market. This discussion actually shows that organizational inefficiencies (Forrest & Orvis, 2016), which exist at different time moments throughout the development of an organization, might not be all bad in the growth of the organization in terms of evolutions and developments.

10.3.3 A Pricing Strategy That Can Produce Higher Expected Profits

This section studies which price strategy leads to higher expected profits. It consists of two subsections. The first one analyzes a particular case that the market of concern is served by only two incumbent firms, while the second subsection introduces the concept of shadow companies and then compares each incumbent firm with its shadow.

10.3.3.1 A Case Analysis

This subsection analyzes a particular case when the assumed market of concern is served by only two incumbent firms.

Example 10.1 Let us look at the special case of $m = 2$ when Eq. 10.7 becomes $4\alpha < \beta$, where each Firm i is divided theoretically into the real Firm i and the shadow Firm ia as described in the proof of Theorem 10.2. In particular, Firm i deals only with its loyal customers by employing the mixed strategy $F(P)$ in Eq. 10.9, which is simplified as follows:

$$F(P) = 1 - \frac{\alpha}{\beta} \cdot \frac{1}{(1-P)P}, 0 < \underline{P} \leq P \leq \overline{P} < 1,$$

while the shadow Firm *ia* deals with price switchers only by uniformly randomizing its price over the interval [0, 1].

By solving *F*(*P*) = 0, we get $\underline{P} = \left(1 - \sqrt{1 - 4\alpha/\beta}\right)/2$. And because *F*(*P*) reaches its maximum at *P* = 1/2, we have $\overline{P} = 1/2$. Since *F*(*P*) has a mass point of size $4\alpha/\beta$ at $\overline{P} = 1/2$, the expected price of Firm *i* is

$$\begin{aligned} E_i(P) &= \int_{\underline{P}}^{\overline{P}} P \times dF(P) + \frac{1}{2} \times \frac{4\alpha}{\beta} = \frac{1 - \sqrt{1 - \frac{4\alpha}{\beta}}}{2} - \frac{\alpha}{\beta} ln \frac{1 - \sqrt{1 - \frac{4\alpha}{\beta}}}{1 + \sqrt{1 - \frac{4\alpha}{\beta}}} + \frac{2\alpha}{\beta} \\ &= \frac{1}{2} - \left[\frac{4\alpha}{\beta} - \sqrt{1 - \frac{4\alpha}{\beta}}\right] - \frac{\alpha}{\beta} ln \frac{1 - \sqrt{1 - \frac{4\alpha}{\beta}}}{1 + \sqrt{1 - \frac{4\alpha}{\beta}}}, \end{aligned}$$

where the second term on the left hand side is positive and could be very close to 0 if $4\alpha \precsim \beta$.

Define the following auxiliary function:

$$H(x) = x - \sqrt{1 - x}, 0 < x < 1,$$

then *H*(*x*) is an increasing function satisfying

$$\lim_{x \to 1^-} H(x) = 1 \text{ and } \lim_{x \to 0^+} H(x) = -1.$$

So, there is a unique $x \in (0, 1)$ such that *H*(*x*) = 0, which leads to $x = \left(-1 + \sqrt{5}\right)/2$. In other words, we have

$$\frac{-1 + \sqrt{5}}{2} \leq \frac{4\alpha}{\beta} < 1 \rightarrow E_i(P) > E_{ia}(P) = 1/2.$$

The expected profits of Firm *ia* are

$$
\begin{aligned}
E(\Pi_{ia}) &= \int_0^{\underline{P}} (1-P)\beta P dP + \int_{\underline{P}}^{\overline{P}} (1-P)[1-F(P)]^2 \beta P dP \\
&\quad + \left(1-\frac{1}{2}\right)\frac{\beta}{2}\left(\frac{4\alpha}{\beta}\right)^2 \\
&= \int_0^{\underline{P}} (1-P)\beta P dP + \frac{\alpha^2}{\beta}\int_{\underline{P}}^{\overline{P}} \frac{1}{(1-P)P} dP + \frac{\beta}{4}\left(\frac{4\alpha}{\beta}\right)^2 \\
&= \frac{\beta}{6}\left(\frac{1-\sqrt{1-\frac{4\alpha}{\beta}}}{2}\right)^2\left(2+\sqrt{1-\frac{4\alpha}{\beta}}\right) - \frac{\alpha^2}{\beta} ln \frac{1-\sqrt{1-\frac{4\alpha}{\beta}}}{1+\sqrt{1-\frac{4\alpha}{\beta}}} \\
&\quad + \frac{\beta}{4}\left(\frac{4\alpha}{\beta}\right)^2 \\
&= \alpha\left\{\frac{2}{3(4\alpha/\beta)}\left(\frac{1-\sqrt{1-\frac{4\alpha}{\beta}}}{2}\right)^2\left(2+\sqrt{1-\frac{4\alpha}{\beta}}\right)\right. \\
&\quad \left. - \frac{\alpha}{\beta} ln \frac{1-\sqrt{1-\frac{4\alpha}{\beta}}}{1+\sqrt{1-\frac{4\alpha}{\beta}}} + \frac{4\alpha}{\beta}\right\}
\end{aligned}
$$

where

$$\frac{-1+\sqrt{5}}{2} \leq \frac{4\alpha}{\beta} < 1$$

such that

$$E(\Pi_{ia})|_{4\alpha/\beta=\left(-1+\sqrt{5}\right)/2} = 0.94409\alpha$$

and

$$\lim_{4\alpha/\beta \to 1^+} E(\Pi_{ia}) \to 4\alpha/3.$$

So, the continuity of $E(\Pi_{ia})$ in α/β implies that there is $\frac{-1+\sqrt{5}}{2} \leq P^* < 1$ such that $E(\Pi_{ia}) > \alpha$ when $P^* \leq \frac{4\alpha}{\beta} < 1$.

10.3.3.2 Comparison Between a Firm and Its Shadow

What is analyzed in Example 10.1 implies that there is an interval $[P^*, 1) \subset [\underline{P}, 1) = [(-1 + \sqrt{5})/2, 1)$ such that when $4\alpha/\beta \in [P^*, 1)$, the expected price $E_i(P)$ of Firm i is greater than the expected price $E_{ia}(P) = 1/2$ of the shadow Firm ia, while the expected profits $E(\Pi_i)$ of Firm i is less than that of the shadow Firm ia $E(\Pi_{ia})$. In other words, what is confirmed in Example 10.1 is that when the two existing firms occupy consumer bases of a good size, they might become content with what they could make from their loyal customers; and the sufficiently large segment of consumer surplus would conveniently encourage new competitions to foray into the market with the potential of making more profits than any of the existing firms. As for the general case of $m \geq 3$, let us see how to establish Theorem 10.3 below.

Lemma 10.3 The upper limit $\overline{P}$, $0 \leq \underline{P} < \overline{P} \leq 1$, for the pricing strategy

$$F(P) = 1 - \frac{1}{1-P}\left(\frac{\alpha}{\beta P}\right)^{\frac{1}{m-1}},$$

$0 \leq \underline{P} \leq P \leq \overline{P} \leq 1$, as given in Eq. 10.9, is equal to $1/m$. And, $F(P)$ has a mass point of the following size at $\overline{P} = 1/m$,

$$\frac{m^{\frac{m}{m-1}}}{m-1}\left(\frac{\alpha}{\beta}\right)^{\frac{1}{m-1}}. \tag{10.13}$$

Proof It is ready to show that

$$F'(P) = \left(\frac{\alpha}{\beta}\right)^{\frac{1}{m-1}} \frac{1 - mP}{(m-1)(1-P)^2 P^{\frac{1}{m-1}+1}}, \tag{10.14}$$

satisfying $F'\left(\frac{1}{m}\right) = 0$, $F'(P) > 0$, for $\underline{P} \leq P < 1/m$, and $F'(P) < 0$, for $\frac{1}{m} < P < 1$. Therefore, $F\left(\frac{1}{m}\right)$ reaches a local maximum so that we know $\overline{P} = 1/m$. And because

$$F\left(\frac{1}{m}\right) = 1 - \frac{m^{\frac{m}{m-1}}}{m-1}\left(\frac{\alpha}{\beta}\right)^{\frac{1}{m-1}},$$

the pricing strategy $F(P)$ has a mass point of size given in Eq. 10.13 at $\overline{P} = 1/m$.

Lemma 10.4 The lower bound $\underline{P}$, as given in Lemma 10.3, satisfies the following properties:

$$\frac{d\underline{P}}{d(\alpha/\beta)} > 0, \lim_{\alpha/\beta \to 0^+} \underline{P} = 0, \text{and} \lim_{\alpha/\beta \to \left((m-1)^{m-1}/m^m\right)^-} \underline{P} = \frac{1}{m}.$$

Proof The lower bound $\underline{P}$ satisfies the equation $F(P) = 0$. So, we have

$$\underline{P}^{\frac{1}{m-1}} - \underline{P}^{1+\frac{1}{m-1}} = \left(\frac{\alpha}{\beta}\right)^{\frac{1}{m-1}}. \tag{10.15}$$

Differentiating this equation with respect to α/β produces

$$\frac{d\underline{P}}{d(\alpha/\beta)} \cdot \underline{P}^{\frac{1}{m-1}} \left(\underline{P}^{-1} - m\right) = \left(\frac{\alpha}{\beta}\right)^{\frac{1}{m-1}-1}.$$

Because $\underline{P}^{\frac{1}{m-1}} > 0$, $\left(\frac{\alpha}{\beta}\right)^{\frac{1}{m-1}-1} > 0$, and $\underline{P} < 1/m$ (so that $\underline{P}^{-1} - m > 0$), we get $\frac{d\underline{P}}{d(\alpha/\beta)} > 0$.

By rewriting Eq. 10.15, we have

$$\underline{P}^{\frac{1}{m-1}}(1 - \underline{P}) = \left(\frac{\alpha}{\beta}\right)^{\frac{1}{m-1}}, \tag{10.16}$$

So, we obtain

$$\lim_{\alpha/\beta \to 0^+} \underline{P} = \lim_{\alpha/\beta \to 0^+} \underline{P}^{\frac{1}{m-1}} = \lim_{\alpha/\beta \to 0^+} \left(\frac{\alpha}{\beta}\right)^{\frac{1}{m-1}} = 0.$$

And, Eq. 10.16 implies that when $\alpha/\beta \to ((m-1)^{m-1}/m^m)^-$, we have

$$(m\underline{P})^{\frac{1}{m-1}}(1 - \underline{P}) = 1 - \frac{1}{m}$$

so that $\underline{P} = 1/m$. That is, we have shown

$$\lim_{\alpha/\beta \to \left((m-1)^{m-1}/m^m\right)^-} \underline{P} = \frac{1}{m}.$$

Hence, Lemma 10.3 implies that the expected price of Firm i is

$$
\begin{aligned}
E_i(P) &= \int_{\underline{P}}^{1/m} P \times F'(P)dP + \frac{1}{m} \times \frac{m^{\frac{m}{m-1}}}{m-1}\left(\frac{\alpha}{\beta}\right)^{\frac{1}{m-1}} \\
&= PF(P)|_{\underline{P}}^{1/m} - \int_{\underline{P}}^{1/m} F(P)dP + \frac{1}{m} \times \frac{m^{\frac{m}{m-1}}}{m-1}\left(\frac{\alpha}{\beta}\right)^{\frac{1}{m-1}} \\
&= 1 - \frac{1}{m} + \underline{P} + \int_{\underline{P}}^{\frac{1}{m}} [1 - F(P)]dP,
\end{aligned}
$$

which, according to Lemma 10.4, is greater than the expected price $E_{ia}(P) = 1/2$ of the shadow Firm *ia*.

For the expected profits of Firm *ia*, we have

$$
\begin{aligned}
E(\Pi_{ia}) &= \int_1^{\underline{P}} (1-P)^{m-1} \beta P dP + \int_{\underline{P}}^{1/m} (1-P)^{m-1}[1-F(P)]^m \beta P dP + \\
&\quad + \alpha \cdot \frac{m^{\frac{m}{m-1}}}{m-1}\left(\frac{\alpha}{\beta}\right)^{\frac{1}{m-1}}
\end{aligned}
$$

Because

$$
\frac{\partial E(\Pi_{ia})}{\partial\left(\frac{\alpha}{\beta}\right)} > 0,
$$

$$
\lim_{\alpha/\beta \to \left((m-1)^{m-1}/m^m\right)^-} \underline{P} = \tfrac{1}{m}, \text{ (Lemma 10.4)},
$$

and

$$
E(\Pi_{ia}) \to \int_1^{1/m} (1-P)^{m-1} \beta P dP + \alpha, \text{ when } \frac{\alpha}{\beta} \to \left(\frac{(m-1)^{m-1}}{m^m}\right)^-,
$$

it follows that there is a γ satisfying $0 < \gamma < (m-1)^{m-1}/m^m$ such that the expected profits $E(\Pi_{ia})$ of the shadow Firm *ia* is greater than the expected profits α of Firm *i*, when $\gamma < \alpha/\beta < (m-1)^{m-1}/m^m$. That is, by combining Example 10.1 and the discussion above we have shown the following general results:

Theorem 10.3 If each existing Firm i, $i = 1, 2, \ldots, m$, increases its expected profits by uniformly randomizing its price P over the interval [0, 1] when dealing with price switchers, while still employing its mixed pricing strategy at the Nash equilibrium with the loyal customers, then there is γ satisfying $0 < \gamma < (m-1)^{m-1}/m^m$ such that the expected price $E_i(P)$ of Firm i is greater than the expected price $E_{ia}(P) = 1/2$ of the shadow Firm *ia*, while the expected profits $E(\Pi_i)$ of Firm i is less than that of the shadow Firm *ia* $E(\Pi_{ia})$.

10.4 Lifting the Competitive Spirit of Sales Associates

This section investigates how a firm can employ compensation as a tool to lift the competitive spirit of its sales associates. If consists of four subsections. The first subsection describes the problem of compensation of sales associates. The second subsection looks at the levels of sales at Cournot equilibrium. The third subsection examines the payoffs of the sales associates, while the fourth subsection deals with the costs, expected incomes, and incentives of the sales associates.

10.4.1 The Compensation of Sales Associates

Forrest et al. (2017) show that the dynamics of market competition affects firms that exist within the market or the intention for firms to enter the market both externally and internally in terms of pricing strategies. In other words, although the existing firms might not grow their expected profits by participating in market competition through adjusting their prices, they still have to compete in order to prevent new competition from entering the market by sufficiently reducing the magnitude of the consumer surplus. So, a natural question arises for the managers of individual firms: How could each incumbent firm encourage its sales associates to sell more?

To this end, Forrest and Orvis (2016) indicate that sales associates' compensation has to be aligned with the associates' personal value systems in order to promote organizational efficiency. So, when dealing with the problem of sales associates' compensation, let us assume that the goal of the associates is to provide quality service to consumers while maximize their personal incomes, and that the mission of the company is the same: maximize its profits by providing quality products to as many satisfied consumers as possible, which is where the concept of the firm's natural endowments is involved. In order to make the goal of maximizing personal incomes and the goal of optimizing the company profits consistent, let us consider aligning sales associates' compensation with the company's profits. (Note: Our model discussed in this section is inspired by Bagnoli & Watts, 2015).

To address the problem of sales associates' compensation, let us assume that the firm of concern has two sales associates, named 1 and 2. The portion of the variable compensation beyond the fixed base salary of associate i is proportional to

$$P_i = \pi_i + \lambda_i S_i, i = 1, 2, \quad (10.17)$$

where π_i stands for the portion of the firm's profits realized by associate i, S_i associate i's completed sales, and $\lambda_i > 0$ the parameter the firm chooses to maximize its expected profits.

The fixed base salary for the associates is employed to encourage associate i to work together with the other associate as a team so that when necessary, one will be willing to provide the needed support to the other in order for the latter to complete a successful sale. The first term π_i in Eq. 10.17 is employed to encourage associate i to generate as much profits as possible, while the second term is used to stimulate more sales, because after all in practice the firm can only observe the number of completed sales and the amount of profits generated without any effective way to measure the efforts of associates (Joseph & Thevaranjan, 1998). Based on Forrest et al. (2017), increasing sales are important in terms of bringing in additional profits with the potential of more than doubling the profits. And together, the sum of these two terms encourages the associates to complete as many and as profitable sales as possible. Here, the parameter λ_i is contractually determined by the firm at the start of the employment cycle of associate i and is used to get rid of the problem of free riders.

In this model we introduced the information/decision structure to investigate the impact of associates' efforts in the product market on the profit-sharing decision of the firm. One feature of this model is that the firm offers its associates contracts that depend on both of the firm's profits and revenues, delegates sales choices and reward the associates based on revenues and profits as a means of pre-committing to sell more and generate more profits than would be optimal without delegation and pre-commitment. The firm adopts such contracts to specifically change the marginal benefit/marginal cost calculation of its associates in order to motivate them to sell more and to generate more profits. The second feature is the assumption that the incentive contracts chosen by the firm are observable by all parties. This observability of the contracts simplifies the analysis without changing the qualitative nature of the results, for details, see (Kockesen & Ok, 2004; Kockesen, 2007).

In the second stage of employment, given the incentive weights λ_i, $i = 1, 2$, chosen by the firm, each associate engages in Cournot competition in his sales efforts by choosing the sales level q_i in the product market, $i = 1, 2$, that maximizes his expected payoffs conditional on all information available to him. We assume that the risk-neutral associates make their sales decisions to maximize their own expected payoffs.

Assume that the demand curve of the firm is

$$p = \alpha - q_i - q_j, i, j = 1, 2, i \neq j, \tag{10.18}$$

where α is the intercept of the firm's demand curve. Because both associates work for the same firm, we assume that they sell identical or completely substitutable products. Both associates know this demand curve; and each of them only knows their own marginal costs c_i of sales, assuming that there are no fixed costs of sales. Here, we introduce the private information c_i to consider the reservation utility of associate i.

To complete the description of the model, we assume that the firm and the associates have common priors such that all variables are drawn from known distributions with finite and positive means and variances. We also assume that the marginal costs c_i and c_j are independent so that the distribution of c_i given c_j is independent of c_j, for $i, j = 1, 2, i \neq j$. To ensure interior solutions in the second stage of the game, the firm's demand function satisfies the condition that the value of the intercept exceeds the largest value of each associate's marginal costs. We seek a perfect Bayes-Nash equilibrium of the model and begin by solving the second stage of the game, in which the associates compete in the product market.

So, associate i solves the following maximization problem:

$$\max_{q_i} E[\pi_i + \lambda_i S_i | \phi_i], \tag{10.19}$$

where ϕ_i represents the information associate i has about c_i and c_j at the time of his sales' choice, π_i= the profits generated by associate i = (price − marginal cost of associate i) $\times q_i$, and S_i= the revenue produced by associate i = price $\times q_i$.

10.4.2 Level of Sales at Cournot Equilibrium

The maximization problem in Eq. 10.19 can be rewritten as follows:

$$\max_{q_i} E\left[(1+\lambda_i)(\alpha - q_i - q_j)q_i - c_i q_i | \phi_i\right]. \tag{10.20}$$

The first-order condition of this maximization problem is

$$q_i = E\left[\frac{1}{2}(\alpha - q_j) - \frac{c_i}{2(1+\lambda_i)}\middle| \phi_i\right]. \tag{10.21}$$

If both associates know both c_i and c_j, then the associates play a game of complete information. To find the Nash equilibrium at this second stage, we solve the following system of first-order conditions:

$$\begin{cases} q_i = \frac{1}{2}(\alpha - q_j) - \frac{c_i}{2(1+\lambda_i)} \\ q_j = \frac{1}{2}(\alpha - q_i) - \frac{c_j}{2(1+\lambda_j)} \end{cases}$$

and obtain

$$q_i(c_i, c_j) = \frac{1}{3}\left(\alpha - \frac{2c_i}{1+\lambda_i} + \frac{c_j}{1+\lambda_j}\right), \tag{10.22}$$

where $q_i(c_i, c_j)$ stands for the amount of sale of associate i if he knows both c_i and c_j.

If associate i knows c_i only while associate j knows both c_i and c_j, then the associates play such a game that associate i only knows his own private information c_i while associate j has the complete information. To find the Nash equilibrium at this second stage, we solve the following system of first-order conditions by substituting the second equation into the first one:

$$\begin{cases} q_i = \frac{1}{2}\left(\alpha - E\left[q_j|c_i\right]\right) - \frac{c_i}{2(1+\lambda_i)} \\ q_j = \frac{1}{2}\left(\alpha - q_i\right) - \frac{c_j}{2(1+\lambda_j)} \end{cases}$$

and obtain

$$q_i\left(c_i, \text{not } c_j\right) = \frac{1}{3}\left(\alpha - \frac{2c_i}{1+\lambda_i} + \frac{E\left[c_j\right]}{1+\lambda_j}\right), \tag{10.23}$$

where and $q_i(c_i, \text{not } c_j)$ stands for the sale of associate i if he knows c_i but not c_j.

If associate i knows both c_i and c_j while associate j knows c_j, then the associates play such a game that associate i has the complete information while associate j only knows his own private information c_j. To find the Nash equilibrium at this second stage, we solve the following system of first-order conditions:

$$\begin{cases} q_i = \frac{1}{2}\left(\alpha - q_j\right) - \frac{c_i}{2(1+\lambda_i)} \\ q_j = \frac{1}{2}\left(\alpha - E\left[q_i|c_j\right]\right) - \frac{c_j}{2(1+\lambda_j)} \end{cases},$$

where $q_i = q_i(\text{not } c_i, c_j)$ represents the amount of sale of associate i if associate j does not knows c_i while associate i knows both c_i and c_j, and $q_j = q_j(c_j, \text{not } c_i)$ the amount of sale of associate j if associate j does not knows c_i, and the formula of the latter is given by Eq. 10.23 by using symmetry. Substituting this expression for $q_j(c_j, \text{not } c_i)$ into the first equation of this system, we obtain

$$q_i\left(\text{not } c_i, c_j\right) = \frac{1}{3}\left(\alpha - \frac{E[c_i]}{2(1+\lambda_i)} + \frac{E\left[c_j\right]}{1+\lambda_j}\right) - \frac{c_i}{2(1+\lambda_i)}. \tag{10.24}$$

If both associates only know their own private information c_i and c_j, respectively, then to find the Nash equilibrium at this second stage, we solve the following system of first-order conditions:

$$\begin{cases} q_i = \frac{1}{2}\left(\alpha - E\left[q_j|c_i\right]\right) - \frac{c_i}{2(1+\lambda_i)} \\ q_j = \frac{1}{2}\left(\alpha - E\left[q_i|c_j\right]\right) - \frac{c_j}{2(1+\lambda_j)} \end{cases}$$

where $q_k = q_k(\text{not } c_k, \text{not } c_\ell)$, $k, \ell = 1, 2, k \neq \ell$, stands for the amount of sale of associate k if he only knows his own private information c_k. Because $E[q_j|c_i] = E[q_j(\text{not } c_j, \text{not } c_i)|c_i] = E[q_j(\text{not } c_j, c_i)]$, the symmetry between associates i and j and Eq. 10.24 lead to the following:

$$\begin{aligned} E\left[q_j|c_i\right] &= E\left[q_j(\text{not } c_j, c_i)\right] \\ &= E\left[\frac{1}{3}\left(2\alpha - \frac{E\left[c_j\right]}{1+\lambda_j} + \frac{E\left[c_i\right]}{1+\lambda_i}\right) - \frac{c_j}{2(1+\lambda_j)}\right] \\ &= \frac{1}{3}\left(2\alpha - \frac{5E\left[c_j\right]}{2(1+\lambda_j)} + \frac{E\left[c_i\right]}{1+\lambda_i}\right). \end{aligned}$$

Therefore, we have

$$q_k(\text{not } c_k, \text{not } c_k) = \frac{1}{6}\left(2\alpha - \frac{E\left[c_i\right] + 3c_i}{1+\lambda_i} + \frac{2E\left[c_j\right]}{1+\lambda_j}\right). \tag{10.25}$$

Proposition 10.1 At Cournot equilibrium, the amount of associate i's sales is an increasing function of λ_i and decreasing function of λ_j.

Proof The result follows readily from Eqs. 10.22–10.25, where each term with denominator $(1 + \lambda_i)$ is negative, while each term with denominator $(1 + \lambda_j)$ is positive.

What this proposition says is that when the firm's demand curve is given in Eq. 10.18, the efforts and achievements of associates i and j are limiting and constraining each other. It is just as what is depicted in Fig. 10.3, where the spin field represents the operation of the firm of our concern, and when one of the associates, say A_i, grows larger, then the out of proportional growth of A_i will definitely affect the development of A_j. In other words, assigning incentives to revenues generated by individual associates really helps boost sales. In particular, assume that associate i is provided with an incentive weight $\lambda_i > 0$ while associate j is not (that is, $\lambda_j = 0$). Then, the revenue incentive would cause associate i to sell more than that of associate j, even when associate j attempts to maximize his profits.

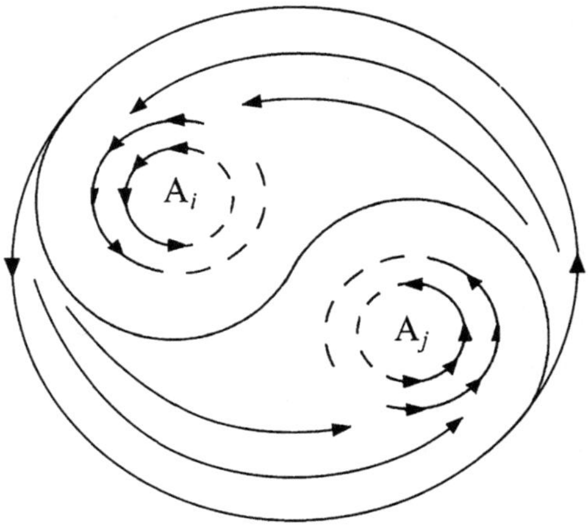

Fig. 10.3 Competition between sales associates within a firm

And the demand curve in Eq. 10.18 implies that associate j would have to accommodate the effects of the incentives by reducing his amount of sales. As a result, associate i's sales would be disproportionally larger than those of associate j.

10.4.3 Payoffs of Sales Associates at Cournot Equilibrium

Based on what has been established in the previous sections, we have

Theorem 10.4 At Cournot equilibrium, the equilibrium payoffs to associate i are proportional to

$$P_i = (1 + \lambda_i)q_i^2, \tag{10.26}$$

and the equilibrium profits of the firm are

$$\Pi = \pi_i + \pi_j = q_i^2 + q_j^2, \tag{10.27}$$

where $\pi_i = q_i^2$, for $i = 1, 2$.

Proof From Eq. 10.17, it follows that

$$P_i = E[\pi_i + \lambda_i S_i|\phi_i] = (1 + \lambda_i)E\left[q_i\left(p - \frac{c_i}{1 + \lambda_i}\right)\middle|\phi_i\right]. \tag{10.28}$$

For the case when associates i and j know both c_i and c_j, from Eq. 10.22, we have

$$P_i(c_i, c_j) = \pi_i + \lambda_i S_i = (1 + \lambda_i)q_i\left(p - \frac{c_i}{1 + \lambda_i}\right)$$

where $p - \frac{c_i}{1+\lambda_i} = q_i$. So, we have $P_i = (1 + \lambda_i)q_i^2$.

For the case when associate i only knows c_i while associate j knows both c_j and c_j, we have from Eq. 10.28 that

$$\begin{aligned}
P_i(c_i, \text{not } c_j) &= (1 + \lambda_i)q_i(c_i, \text{not } c_j)E\left[p - \frac{c_i}{1 + \lambda_i}\middle|c_i\right] \\
&= (1 + \lambda_i)q_i(c_i, \text{not } c_j)\left(\alpha - q_i(c_i, \text{not } c_j) - E\left[q_j \text{not } c_j, c_i|c_i\right] - \frac{E[c_i]}{1 + \lambda_i}\right) \\
&= (1 + \lambda_i)\left[q_i(c_i, \text{not } c_j)\right]^2
\end{aligned}$$

For the case when associate i knows both c_i and c_j while associate j only knows, we have from Eqs. 10.28 and 10.24

$$
\begin{aligned}
P_i(\text{not } c_i, c_j) &= (1+\lambda_i)E\left[q_i(\text{not } c_i, c_j)\left(\alpha - q_i(\text{not } c_i, c_j) - q_j(c_j, \text{not } c_i)\right.\right.\\
&\qquad \left.\left. - \frac{c_i}{1+\lambda_i}\right)|\phi_i\right]\\
&= (1+\lambda_i)q_i(\text{not } c_i, c_j)\left(\alpha - q_i(\text{not } c_i, c_j) - q_j(c_j, \text{not } c_i) - \frac{c_i}{1+\lambda_i}\right)\\
&= (1+\lambda_i)\left[q_i(\text{not } c_i, c_j)\right]^2
\end{aligned}
$$

For the case when associates i and j only knows their own individual c_i and c_j, respectively, we have from Eqs. 10.28 and 10.25 the following:

$$
\begin{aligned}
P_i(\text{not } c_i, \text{not } c_j) &= (1+\lambda_i)q_i(\text{not } c_i, \text{not } c_j)\cdot\\
&\quad \cdot\left(\alpha - q_i(\text{not } c_i, \text{not } c_j) - E\left[q_j(\text{not } c_i, \text{not } c_j)|c_i\right] - \frac{c_i}{1+\lambda_i}\right)\\
&= (1+\lambda_i)\left[q_i(\text{not } c_i, \text{not } c_j)\right]^2
\end{aligned}
$$

So, what is produced above proves Eq. 10.26.

For the equilibrium profits of the firm $\Pi = \pi_i + \pi_j$, where because

$$
\begin{aligned}
P_i(d_i, d_j) &= (1+\lambda_i)\left[q_i(d_i, d_j)\right]^2\\
&= \left[q_i(d_i, d_j)\right]^2 + \lambda_i\left[q_i(d_i, d_j)\right]^2\\
&= \pi_i + \lambda_i S_i
\end{aligned}
$$

for any $d_i \in \{c_i, \text{not } c_i\}$ and $d_j \in \{c_j, \text{not } c_j\}$. If we treat the last two expressions as polynomials in variable λ_i, then comparing the corresponding coefficients leads to $\pi_i = [q_i(d_i, d_j)]^2$. Therefore, Eq. 10.27 is established.

10.4.4 Costs, Expected Incomes, and Incentives of Sales Associates

In terms of the relationship between private cost information of the associates and their individual incomes, we have

Theorem 10.5 When the associates i and j are Cournot competitors, making the private cost information c_i known to associate j does expectedly increase the incomes of i ($= 1, 2, i \neq j$).

Intuitively speaking, when the firm makes the associates' private information not that private among its members, it actually encourages competition between its sales associates. For example, when the firm spends more on associate A_i in Fig. 10.3, it means the area of A_i half is greater than that of A_j half. That naturally puts pressure on associate A_j. Now, for A_j, he has two choices: being squeezed out of his job or measuring up to the challenge. If A_j chooses the former choice, then he will be simply replaced by another sales associate, which is an optimal personnel decision for the firm. That is, no matter who particular A_j is, the systemic field structure in Fig. 10.3 always exists in terms of A_i and A_j individually. On the other hand, A_j does not want his existence to cost too much to the firm, either; otherwise, he runs the risk of being let go or facing a tougher challenge of a newly hired more capable colleague. For related studies, see (Chan et al., 2014a, b).

Proof For the situation in hands, it suffices to show that

$$E\left[P_i\left(c_i, \text{not } c_j\right)\right] > E\left[P_i\left(\text{not } c_i, \text{not } c_j\right)\right] \tag{10.29}$$

and

$$E\left[P_i\left(c_i, c_j\right)\right] > E\left[P_i\left(\text{not } c_i, c_j\right)\right], \tag{10.30}$$

for $i = 1, 2$. That is, what Eqs. 10.29 and 10.30 imply is that no matter whether or not associate j's cost information c_j is known to associate i, making his own cost information c_i known to j expectedly leads to greater amount of profits for associate i. According to Theorem 10.4, instead of Eqs. 10.29 and 10.30, it suffices to show

$$E\left[\left(q_i\left(c_i, \text{not } c_j\right)\right)^2\right] > E\left[\left(q_i\left(\text{not } c_i, \text{not } c_j\right)\right)^2\right] \tag{10.31}$$

and

$$E\left[\left(q_i\left(c_i, c_j\right)\right)^2\right] > E\left[\left(q_i\left(\text{not } c_i, c_j\right)\right)^2\right], \tag{10.32}$$

for $i = 1, 2$. To this end, we have

$$
\begin{aligned}
& E\left[\left(q_i\left(c_i, \text{not } c_j\right)\right)^2\right] - E\left[\left(q_i\left(\text{not } c_i, \text{not } c_j\right)\right)^2\right] = \\
= \; & E\left[\left(q_i\left(c_i, \text{not } c_j\right)\right)^2 - \left(q_i\left(\text{not } c_i, \text{not } c_j\right)\right)^2\right] \\
= \; & \frac{1}{9}\left\{X^2 - 4X\frac{E[c_i]}{1+\lambda_i} + \frac{4E\left[c_i^2\right]}{(1+\lambda_i)^2}\right\} \\
& -\frac{1}{36}\left\{4X^2 - 4X\frac{E[c_i]}{1+\lambda_i} + \frac{7E[c_i]^2}{(1+\lambda_i)^2} - 12X\frac{E[c_i]}{1+\lambda_i} + \frac{9E\left[c_i^2\right]}{(1+\lambda_i)^2}\right\} \\
= \; & \frac{1}{2(1+\lambda_i)^2}\left\{E\left[c_i^2\right] - E[c_i]^2\right\} = \frac{1}{2(1+\lambda_i)^2}\text{var}[c_i] > 0,
\end{aligned}
$$

where $X = \alpha + E[c_j]/(1 + \lambda_i)$. That is, Eq. 10.31 holds true. For Eq. 10.32, we have

$$
\begin{aligned}
E\left[\left(q_i\left(c_i, c_j\right)\right)^2\right] - E\left[\left(q_i\left(\text{not } c_i, c_j\right)\right)^2\right] & = E\left[\left(q_i\left(c_i, c_j\right)\right)^2 - \left(q_i\left(\text{not } c_i, c_j\right)\right)^2\right] \\
& = \frac{1}{9}\left\{\frac{\text{var}\left[c_j\right]}{\left(1+\lambda_j\right)^2} + \frac{7\text{var}\left[c_i\right]}{4(1+\lambda_i)^2}\right\} > 0.
\end{aligned}
$$

That is, Eq. 10.32 holds true.

What is implied by Theorem 10.5 is that no matter whether individual sales associates like or not, the firm needs to make sure somehow its associates know about other associate's cost information in order to stimulate more profits and more revenue.

Next, let us look at the firm's decision on the incentive weights λ_i, $i = 1, 2$, at the first stage of the game. At this stage, the firm chooses λ_i, $i = 1, 2$, to maximize its expected profits,

$$
E[\Pi] = E[\pi_i] + E[\pi_i] = E\left[\left(q_i\left(d_i, d_j\right)\right)^2\right] + E\left[\left(q_j\left(d_j, d_i\right)\right)^2\right]
$$

by taking into account of how the sales associates subsequently find it optimal to compete in the firm's product market. In particular, the firm solves the following maximization problem:

$$
\max_{\lambda_i\left(d_i, d_j\right), \lambda_i\left(d_i, d_j\right)} E\left[\left(q_i\left(d_i, d_j\right)\right)^2 + \left(q_j\left(d_j, d_i\right)\right)^2\right],
$$

for $d_i = c_i$ and $d_j = c_j$, because as the employer the firm knows exactly how much each sales' associate would costs itself. The first-order conditions are

$$2q_i(c_i, c_j)\frac{\partial q_i(c_i, c_j)}{\partial \lambda_i} + 2q_j(c_j, c_i)\frac{\partial q_j(c_j, c_i)}{\partial \lambda_i} = 0 \tag{10.33}$$

and

$$2q_i(c_i, c_j)\frac{\partial q_i(c_i, c_j)}{\partial \lambda_j} + 2q_j(c_j, c_i)\frac{\partial q_j(c_j, c_i)}{\partial \lambda_j} = 0. \tag{10.34}$$

Now, Eqs. 10.33 and 10.34 reduce to the following system of equations:

$$\begin{cases} \alpha - \dfrac{5c_i}{1+\lambda_i} + \dfrac{4c_j}{1+\lambda_j} = 0 \\ \alpha - \dfrac{5c_j}{1+\lambda_j} + \dfrac{4c_i}{1+\lambda_i} = 0. \end{cases}.$$

By solving this system, we establish the following result:

Theorem 10.6 At the Bayes-Nash equilibrium, the firm would define its incentive weights by $\lambda_i = c_i/\alpha - 1$, $i = 1, 2$.

What Theorem 10.6 indicates is that when an associate costs more to the firm than other associates, the firm expects him to generate a greater level of revenue by providing a greater incentive weight to him. Systemically, this result is clear: If the A_i half in Fig. 10.3 costs more to maintain within the overall spin field, then the A_i half in the 3-dimensional structure in Fig. 2.1a in Chap. 2, which is reproduced here for the convenience of the reader, has to give out more to balance its structural stability.

Although the results in this section are established for two sales associates, if we are willing to get caught with tedious symbolic computations, we will be able to develop the same results for *m* many sales associates with their individual incentive weights.

10.5 A Few Final Words

This chapter looks at an issue that is closely related to the very survival of a firm about how to compete with other firms by either finding the market characteristics that beget new opportunities and competition or lifting the competitive spirit of a retail firm's sales associates. It establishes several interesting results, among others:

- A condition under which market competition will intensify,
- How the existing loyal consumer base of an established firm will start to deteriorate,

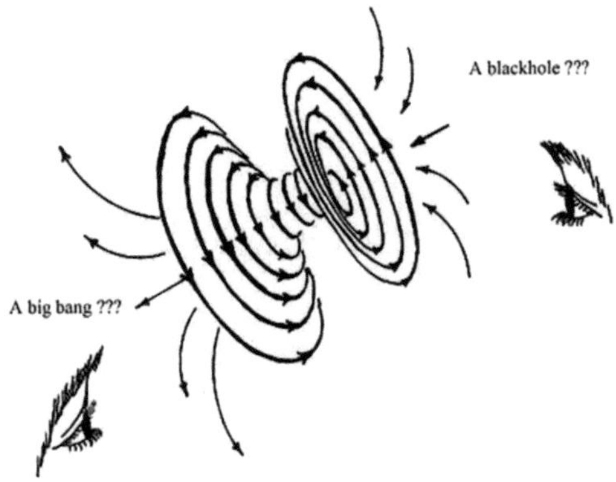

Figure 2.1(a) from Chap. 2. The eddy motion model of the general system

- Why firms should somehow make private cost information of their sales associates known to their respective members,
- What incentive weights a firm should give to its individual sales associates in order to optimize its profits.

At the same time, this chapter shows the importance of systemic thinking and the yoyo model in visualizing the dynamics of market competition. In particular, the yoyo model, different from that of Cartesian coordinate system, as widely employed the mathematics and natural sciences, provides another platform for scholars and decision-making managers to logically think and to visually imagine before they can rigorously prove what they first see and feel intuitively.

At the conclusion of this chapter, it needs to be pointed that what is done in this chapter about sales associates' compensation cannot be directly generalized to other situations of workers' compensation. For example, when individuals' performance is highly dependent on the collaboration and support of others, such as the situation with a basketball team, then what is established above needs to be reconsidered and enriched with relevant details (Antonietti, 2006). The major difference involved here is the following: The sales associates considered in this chapter are treated mostly as isolated individuals, whose achievements are not heavily dependent on other sales associates' support (that is, the conflict of interest in terms of individual performance is minimal), while for an athlete on the basketball team, his performance is highly correlated to a host of factors, including, but not limited to,

- How much the coach allows him to play or communication between the coach and the athlete (Rosca, 2010);
- Rivalries between team mates on and off the court (Tiago et al., 2016; Arai et al., 2014);
- Team mates collaborations (Jane, 2015);
- Commercial endorsements (Fizel et al., 2008);
- How well the athlete could stay healthy.

In particular, the basic setup in Eqs. 10.17 and 10.18 needs to be altered when studying a different setup of employees' performance. In other words, although the presentation in this chapter is limited in terms of how widely it can be applied in real life, it is expected to open up a wide area of study of workers' compensation for different employment scenarios.

References

Antonietti, R. (2006). Human capital, sport performance, and salary determination of professional athletes. *SSRN Electronic Journal*. https://doi.org/10.2139/ssrn.888535

Arai, A., Ko, Y. J., & Ross, S. (2014). Branding athletes: Exploration and conceptualization of athlete brand image. *Sport Management Review, 17*(2), 97–106.

Bagnoli, M., & Watts, S. G. (2015). Delegating disclosure and production choices. *The Accounting Review, 90*(3), 835–857.

Basu, A., Lal, R., Srinivasan, V., & Staelin, R. (1985). Salesforce compensation plans: An agency theoretic perspective. *Marketing Science, 4*, 267–291.

Belu, M., & Caragin, A. R. (2008). Strategies of entering new markets. *The Romanian Economic Journal, 11*(27), 1–16.

Chan, T. Y., Li, J., & Piece, L. (2014a). Compensation and peer effects in competing sales teams. *Management Science, 60*(8), 1965–1984.

Chan, T. Y., Li, J., & Pierce, L. (2014b). Learning from peers: Knowledge transfer and sales force productivity growth. *Marketing Science, 33*(4), 463–484.

Chang, Y. K., Chen, Y. L., Chou, R. K., & Huang, T. H. (2015). Corporate governance, product market competition and dynamic capital structure. *International Review of Economics & Finance, 38*, 44–55.

Chung, D. J., Steenburgh, T., & Sudhir, K. (2013). Do bonuses enhance sales productivity? A dynamic structural analysis of bonus-based compensation plans. *Marketing Science, 33*(2), 165–187.

Daljord, Ø., Misra, S., & Nair, H. S. (2016). Homogeneous contracts for heterogeneous agents: Aligning sales force composition and compensation. *Journal of Marketing Research, 53*(2), 161–182.

Debruyne, M., & Reibstein, D. J. (2005). Competitor see, competitor do: Incumbent entry in new market niches. *Marketing Science, 24*(1), 55–66.

Fizel, J., McNeil, C., & Smaby, T. (2008). Athlete endorsement contracts: The impact of conventional stars. *International Advances in Economic Research, 14*(2), 247–256.

Forrest, J. Y. L., Amatucci, F., & Markman, G. D. (2017). Dynamics of the firm population within an established market, Proceedings of the 48th Annual Meeting of the Decision Sciences Institute, Washington, DC., November 18 – 20, 2017.

Forrest, J. Y. L., & Anderson, M. (2017). Customers' indecisiveness: A pricing strategy approach, *Pennsylvania Economic Association 2017 Conference Proceedings*, 80-95.

Forrest, J. Y. L., & McCarthy, L. (2017). Sales associates' compensations: A game theoretic approach. *Pennsylvania Economic Association 2017 Conference Proceedings*, 52-64.

Forrest, J. Y. L., & Orvis, B. (2016). Principles of management efficiency and organizational inefficiency. *Kybernetes: The International Journal of Cybernetics, Systems and Management Sciences, 45*(8), 1308–1322.

Frenzen, H., Hansen, A. K., Krafft, M., Mantrala, M. K., & Schmidt, S. (2010). Delegation of pricing authority to the sales force: An agency-theoretic perspective of its determinants and impact on performance. *International Journal of Research in Marketing, 27*(1), 58–68.

Fultz, D., Long, R.R., G.V. Owens, , Bohan, W., Kaylor, R., & Weil, J. (1959). Studies of thermal convection in a rotating cylinder with some implications for large-scale atmospheric motion. Meteorol. Monographs (American Meteorological Society), 21, 4.

Guo, W. C., Lai, F. C., Liu, C. J., & Mai, C. C. (2012). Symbiotic production and downstream market competition. *Atlantic Economic Journal, 40*(3), 329–340.

Hauser, J. R., & Shugan, S. M. (1983). Defensive marketing strategies. *Marketing Science., 2*(4), 319–360.

Hide, R. (1953). Some experiments on thermal convection in a rotating liquid. *Quarterly Journal of the Royal Meteorological Society, 79*(339), 161–161.

Homburg, C., Jensen, O., & Hahn, A. (2012). How to organize pricing? Vertical delegation and horizontal dispersion of pricing authority. *Journal of Marketing, 76*(5), 49–69.

Inderst, R., & Ottaviani, M. (2009). Misselling through Agents. *The American Economic Review, 99*(3), 883–908.

Jane, W. J. (2015). Peer effects and individual performance. *Journal of Sports Economics, 16*(5), 531–539.

Joseph, K., & Thevaranjan, A. (1998). Monitoring and Incentives in Sales Organizations: An Agency-Theoretic Perspective. *Marketing Science, 17*(2), 107–123.

Kockesen, L. (2007). Unobservable contracts as precommitments. *Economic Theory, 31*(3), 539–552.

Kockesen, L., & Ok, E. (2004). Strategic delegation by unobservable incentive contracts. *Review of Economic Studies, 71*(2), 397–424.

Kopalle, P. K., & Lehmann, D. R. (2006). Setting quality expectations when entering a market: What should the promise be? *Marketing Science, 25*(1), 8–24.

Kräkel, M., & Schöttner, A. (2016). Optimal sales force compensation. *Journal of Economic Behavior & Organization, 126*, 179–195.

Kumar, K. R., & Sudharshan, D. (1988). Defensive marketing strategies: An equilibrium analysis based on decoupled response function models. *Management Science, 34*(7), 805–815.

Lal, R., & Srinivasan, V. (1993). Compensation Plans for Single- and Multi-product Salesforces: An Application of the Holmstrom-Milgrom Model. *Management Science, 39*(7), 777–793.

Lo, D., Ghosh, M., & Lafontaine, F. (2011). The incentive and selection roles of sales force compensation contracts. *Journal of Marketing Research, 4*(4), 781–798.

McWilliams, G. (2004). Minding the store: Analyzing consumers, best buy decides not all are welcome. *The Wall Street Journal, 8*, A1.

Misra, S., & Nair, H. S. (2011). A structural model of sales-force compensation dynamics: Estimation and field implementation. *Quantitative Marketing and Economics, 9*(3), 211–257.

Mittal, V., Sarkees, M., & Murshed, F. (2008). The right way to manage unprofitable consumers. *Harvard Business Review*, April, 2-10.

Rosca, V. (2010). The coach-athlete communication process: Towards a better human resources management in sport. *Management Research and Practice, 2*(3), 275–283.

Sheth, J. N., & Sharma, A. (2008). The impact of the product to service shift in industrial markets and the evolution of the sales organization. *Industrial Marketing Management, 37*(3), 260–269.

Shin, J., Sudhir, K., & Yoon, D. H. (2012). When to "fire" consumers: Consumer cost-based pricing. *Management Science, 58*(5), 932–947.

Siebert, R. (2015). Entering new markets in the presence of competition: Price discrimination versus cannibalization. *Journal of Economics and Management Strategies, 24*(2), 369–389.

Tiago, T., Tiago, F., Faria, S. D., & Couto, J. P. (2016). Who is the better player? Off-field battle on Facebook and Twitter. *Business Horizons, 59*(2), 175–183.

Zhou, B., Mela, C. F., & Amaldoss, W. (2015). Do firms endowed with greater strategic capability earn higher profits? *Journal of Marketing Research, 52*(June), 325–336.

Chapter 11
Appropriate Strategies and Necessary Organizational Supports

Jeffrey Yi-Lin Forrest, Sunita Mondal, Reg Tucker, and Canchu Lin

Abstract Many factors that influence the innovativeness of a firm has been identified by a good number of scholars due to the importance of innovation in value creation and capture. This chapter, which is mainly based on Forrest et al. (Proceedings of the 2018 annual conference of NABET, November 1–2, 2018, State College, PA, 2018) and Forrest et al. (Proceedings of the 2018 annual conference of NABET, November 1–2, 2018, State College, PA, 2018), introduces the concepts of primary determinants and secondary determinants of the innovativeness of a manufacturing firm. And then, the chapter (a) broadly analyzes the 16 most influential strategy-related factors, classified empirically in the literature, for the purpose of identifying the ones that symbolize the primary determinants of the firm's innovativeness, and (b) identifies the primary organizational factors that contribute to the innovativeness of a manufacturing firm, and distinguishes the secondary factors which naturally appear with the primary ones.

To achieve goal (a), this chapter presents a general systemic theory that underlines the importance for a firm to have clearly stated missions along with a long term, unwavering ambition. It categorizes the 16 variables, pertaining to the overall strategic orientation and growth and operational strategies, as part of primary or secondary factors that influence the innovativeness of a firm. For goal (b), the chapter studies the impact of the general characteristics of firms' culture on innovation in manufacturing based on general organizational culture by using a cost–benefit analysis approach. In particular, the impact of leadership at the firm level on innovation are demonstrated. In the conclusion section, pragmatic and efficient recommendations for managerial decision-making are formulated, highlighting the real-life applicability and contribution of this scholarly research.

Jeffrey Yi-Lin Forrest (Department of Accounting Economics Finance, Slippery Rock University, Slippery Rock, PA, USA; Email: Jeffrey.forrest@sru.edu), Sunita Mondal (Department of Accounting Economics Finance, Slippery Rock University, Slippery Rock, PA, USA; Email: sunita.mondal@sru.edu), Reg Tucker (Stephenson Department of Entrepreneurship and Information Systems, Louisiana State University, Baton Rouge, LA, USA; Email: regtucker@lsu.edu), and Canchu Lin (School of Business, SUNY Farmingdale State College, Farmingdale, NY, USA; Email: linc@farmingdale.edu) are equally contributed to this chapter.

J. Y.-L. Forrest, *Systemic Principles of Applied Economic Philosophies II*,
Translational Systems Sciences 39, https://doi.org/10.1007/978-981-99-7939-4_11

Keywords Ambition · Centralized system · First movers · Informal leaders · Innovation · Knowledge acquisition · Mission · Market territory · Organizational culture

11.1 Introduction

This chapter, which is mainly based on Forrest et al. (2018a) and Forrest et al. (2018b), addresses the following questions: What are the main strategic tactics that underlie the innovative activities of a manufacturing firm? And, how do the culture, structure, and leadership of a manufacturing firm influence the firm's degree of innovativeness?

The theoretical and practical significance of these questions has been acknowledged since the time of Adam Smith (1776) when he treated innovation as a critical factor in enhancing wealth. Owing to the fierce world-wide competition in manufacturing, innovation is inevitable for manufacturing companies' survival and healthy growth (Stock et al., 2002). Hence it is compelling for managers, entrepreneurs, and scholars alike to find answers to these questions, given that organizational culture, structure, leadership, and what strategy to employ represent the crucial foundation of an organization.

In the present time, innovation is increasingly inevitable for every company that wishes to remain competitive, develop comparative advantages, and gain entry into profitable markets (Stock et al., 2002). That explains why the topic these questions represent has remained one of the most popular and hottest ones investigated over many decades by researchers, managers of firms, and policy makers. Previous studies have empirically examined the impact of culture, structure, and leadership on innovation (Darroch & McNaughton, 2002; Francois et al., 2002; Jung et al., 2003; Keizer et al., 2002; Koberg et al., 1996; Souitaris, 2002; Veugelers & Cassiman, 1999). However, these studies, with innovation as the outcome variable and various factors as explanatory variables, suffered from methodological limitations so that the consequent estimates are mostly unreliable. In order to avoid this and related issues, this chapter adopts the systems-scientific approach to better understand how a manufacturing firm can become more innovative and how the firm's culture, structure, and leadership affect its innovativeness.

Regarding the first question, a number of researchers have taken empirical approaches to investigate the impact of 16 strategic variables on innovation (Rothwell, 1992). However, due to the methodological limitations of the chosen approaches, these previous researchers fail to reach a consensus so that different scholars established different degrees of association between these 16 variables and innovation (Souitaris, 2002). Hence, in determining the effect of different strategies on innovation, researchers have encountered a challenge: can a different methodology be employed to examining the impact of strategies on innovation in order to better understand the innovation process so that the derived conclusions can be reliably employed to improve our understanding of the phenomenon? To this end, this chapter analyzes the first question by determining the effect of strategies on innovation. It first establishes a general theory regarding the reasons as to why a firm need to have clearly stated missions and a long-term, unwavering ambition. Additionally, utilizing the intuition of systemic yoyo model, this chapter categorizes the 16 strategy variables, as recognized in the previous literature, into either primary or secondary strengths behind the innovativeness of a manufacturing firm. Here, a factor is seen as secondary, if it emerges as a natural consequence of the primary factors.

As for the second question, this chapter explores how organizational culture is established, and analyzes the reason why mission and ambition stand for two important binding forces of any organizational culture. Additionally, this chapter theoretically examines the significance of the culture of an organization as a primary determinant of innovation, and discusses why total quality management is one prudent execution of the goal of an organization. In order to analyze the impact of leadership on innovation, this chapter first develops a systemic model to explain the meaning of leadership. Then this model is used to demonstrate why a commitment to leadership is of utmost importance to achieve successful innovation. It establishes that leadership factors, such as "presence of a project leader," "CEO's characteristics," "CEO change," and "CEO's qualification and experience," are minor factors, whereas having a long-term, firm ambition is of primary importance.

Delving into the general characteristics of manufacturing firms, this chapter confirms that variables, such as "firm size" and "past performance," are indexes of firm's innovativeness. However, these are secondary factors in comparison to the mission and global strategies of a firm. On the other hand, "age of the firm" and "ownership structure" are predominant factors. By systemically modeling the structure of a manufacturing firm, it is found that such structure related factors, such as "formal structure," "flexible structure," "centralization of decision-making," "empowerment of employees," and "interaction between firm's units," are all of less importance and are merely pragmatic applications of the long-term, unwavering ambition.

Beyond what is outlined above, the primary contribution of this chapter is the set of managerial recommendations that can be easily implemented in real-life situations. Especially, all theoretical results of this chapter are true in general, which distinguishes this work from the existing literature, wherein speculations are involved in the analysis of data, mining of data, and mere suggestions (in place of concrete recommendations) are offered. The improved results, as derived in this chapter, stem from the logical reasoning of systems science and the adopted approach of holistic thinking. In particular, the methodology adopted here overcomes the methodological deficiencies of prior data- and/or anecdote-based conclusions that interfere with generalizations. Methodological weaknesses of empirical studies arise due to problems in the measurement of variables and the analysis of the collected data (Becheikh et al., 2006). The former is concerned with uncertainty in measurement (Czichos et al., 2011), and the latter with drawbacks of data analysis and data mining (Liu & Lin, 2006).

The rest of this chapter is organized as follows: Sect. 11.2 reviews the relevant literature and points out the contributions this chapter makes in comparison with the literature. Section 11.3 looks at the concept of innovation and why the mission stands for the start of all business endeavors of a firm. Section 11.4 analyzes the impact of firms' strategic orientation on innovation, considers growth strategies, and studies operational strategies. Section 11.5 considers the impact of a firm's culture on innovation by first determining how the firm's organizational culture is developed and why mission and ambition are two strong consolidating forces that underlie the firm's organizational structure. Section 11.6 explores the effects of a firm's general characteristics on its innovativeness and the impact of the firm's structure. Section 11.7 determines the effect of a firm's leadership on its innovativeness by first discussing what leadership means, and then explaining why leadership is the bottom line for success. Section 11.8 specifies managerial recommendations, as formulated based on the discussions in this chapter, that can be reliably applied in real life. Lastly, Sect. 11.9 concludes the chapter with some key comments.

11.2 Literature Review

Since this chapter (a) analyzes the strategies that affect the degree of innovation for manufacturing firms, and (b) studies the impact of the culture, structure, and leadership of a manufacturing firm on its innovativeness, this literature review section reports previous studies in four different, but associated fields. The first field relates to prior works where independent variables are employed to explain the outcome variable *innovation*; the second focuses on competitive advantages, where cultivating a competitive advantage is based on innovations; the third focuses on identifying organizational factors that explain the outcome variable innovation, and the fourth reports on innovation centered competitive advantage.

In terms of the literature pertaining to innovation, as far back as two centuries ago, Adam Smith (1776) recognized the crucial role innovation plays in economic activity and in promoting wealth. Given the importance of innovation in the manufacturing sector, the topic has been thoroughly researched for years by multiple scholars (cf., Aas et al., 2015). Innovation has been identified as a critical factor to enhance the success and wealth of manufacturing firms (Adner & Levinthal, 2001) as well as being vital for firms' survival and growth (Visnjic et al., 2016). The definition of innovation in the practical business world pertains to an introduction of original products and processes (Becheikh et al., 2006) that strengthens the competitiveness of manufacturing firms in order to infiltrate existing markets or create new markets (Smith & Tushman, 2005).'

Innovation is regarded as one of the primary contributors to long-term performance (Kanter, 2001). For instance, Damanpour (1987) and others studied managerial innovations and bureaucratic processes following technical advancements.

Product innovation and processes have been studied by Utterback and Abernathy (1975). Topics associated with incremental and radical innovations are discussed by Ettlie et al. (1984). Veugelers and Cassiman (1999) confirm the findings that high risks and costs and less allocation do not dissuade innovation, but it helps to determine how the innovation sourcing strategy is chosen. Additionally, they report that small firms have a higher chance of confining their innovation strategy to an exclusive make or buy strategy, while larger firms are more apt to combining both internal and external knowledge acquisition in their innovation strategy. Amara and Landry (2005) explored information sources utilized by firms for product improvement and identifying processes that affect the uniqueness of innovation. Their study identified that firms in manufacturing have preference for adopting a mix of research sources in development or product improvement. Becheikh et al. (2006) link innovation in products and processes to the environment in manufacturing, with innovation in product receiving greater importance.

Alegre and Chiva (2008) analyze how the capacity of acquiring organizational knowledge impacts the innovation of firms in manufacturing. Lin et al. (2013) explore the connection between green products and whether innovation in such green products can enhance performance of firms. They establish the positive correlation between innovation in green products and a firm's performance, with enhanced achievements for manufacturing firms. De Massis et al. (2015) demonstrate that in terms of innovation strategies and organization of innovation processes, there exists difference between family businesses and commercial firms. In particular, their findings indicate family businesses in manufacturing target incremental innovations of products utilizing external sources, whereas commercial firms employ a primarily closed approach to focus on breakthrough and radical innovation.

With the expansion of globalization and increased adoption of internet-based technologies, manufacturing firms are under the pressure to remain more competitive and innovative than ever before (Zollo et al., 2016). This in turn urges the need for new manufacturing philosophies (Holmstrom et al., 2016). The consequent new philosophical principles had led to the reformulations of the concepts of manufacturing and innovation in the manufacturing sector (Wu et al., 2015). The most notable reformulations are Industry 4.0 and China's manufacturing 2025 (Li, 2018).

As for the literature regarding competitive advantages, Porter (1985) defined such an advantage as a function of either offering lower cost options to consumers compared to rival firms, or manufacturing output at comparable cost but in unique ways that generates higher valuation for buyers thus justifying a premium price (product differentiation). Towards this end, Makadok (2010) observes a negative impact on simultaneously limiting firms' rivalry and enhancing competitive advantage, on the firms' profitability. Peng et al. (2001) attempt to identify the factors which develop competitive advantages, using huge Japanese investment in order to replicate *keiretsu* (interfirm) networks in Asia since the 1980s. Duez (2012) develops a new paradigm for strategic management thoughts from the school of economic proximity.

With respect to emerging economies such as China, Li and Liu (2014) define a firm's dynamic capability as the likelihood for the firm to solve problems systematically, formed by its propensity to sense opportunities and threats, to undertake timely decisions, and to implement strategic decisions and changes efficiently to ensure the right path. Herrera (2015) constructs a framework that determines successful corporate social innovation, which encourages co-creation, thereby leading to shared value and increasing competitive advantage provided innovation is integrated into strategy and operations. Leonidou et al. (2015) analyze both the external and internal determinants of green export business strategy and its impact on export competitive advantage and performance. Their result affirms the major role of both external forces (i.e., foreign environmental public concern and competitive intensity) and internal factors (i.e., top management green sensitivity and organizational green culture) in organizing an environmentally friendly export business strategy. Forrest and Nightingale (2017) authenticate a practical procedure for a smooth transition of a firm into a period of agile strategic changes in face of their transitory competitive advantage. They establish the systemic reasons behind a list of time-honored steps assisting firms to combat fleeting periods of competitive advantage, by linking previously published conclusions based on anecdotes and data mining.

In contrast to the review above, this chapter contributes to the literature in a variety of ways. First, it develops a general systemic theory of organizational philosophical and value systems and culture and demonstrates that it is essential for a manufacturing firm to have clearly established missions and a long-term, unwavering ambition. Second, this chapter holistically evaluates 16 strategy-related factors, which have been empirically identified in the literature, and classifies them, respectively, into primary and secondary forces behind the innovativeness of a firm. Third, it establishes the positive impact of leadership on a firm's innovation, by first establishing the concept of leadership. Fourth, this chapter shows how a firm's organizational culture essentially affects its innovation. Fifth, in order to identify the impact of a firm's general characteristics on innovation, this chapter builds an analytical model which has expansive applications for many issues. Sixth, a systematic modeling is derived to identify the effect of a firm's structure on innovation. Seventh, the chapter develops practically effective recommendations for managerial decision-making at the firm level.

Lastly, the most relevant contribution this chapter makes is that in contrast to the previously, widely employed approaches of empirical analysis, this chapter adopts systems science as the methodology and logic of reasoning that assure the practical applicability of the conclusions reached in this chapter. Additionally, this chapter establishes connections between a firm's size and its degree of innovation, as, respectively, claimed by Schumpeter in 1934 and 1942, that are not in conflict with what previous scholars had determined (Damanpour, 1992; Stock et al., 2002).

11.3 Adoption of Appropriate Strategies

As suggested by the title, this section first examines the concept of innovation and then it establishes that both the venture an organization is engaged in and the strategy the organization employs need to be grounded in the clearly stated mission.

11.3.1 The Concept of Innovation

Owing to the increased importance of innovation in the manufacturing sector, many previous studies have analyzed the concept from different angles (Becheikh et al., 2006; Schumpeter, 1934), while related issues have been emphasized by the Organization for Economic Cooperation and Development (OECD, 1997). With the ever-changing business world, the concept of innovation has been adapting to the changes as well.

In the context of the unfolding Industry 4.0 and China's manufacturing 2025, new dimensions are included in the concept of innovation, as an ongoing process of assimilation of new information. For the results of this chapter to have an enduring impact, we will consider the concept of innovation in its most general form, as noted below:

> Innovation in the manufacturing sector is such a set of activities—which may be just one particular activity or several—that leads to exceptional value added to the company in comparison to other activities that take place in the same sector.

Due to the generic form of the definition and prominence on comparative value added, this definition of innovation encompasses many aspects. As the examples below indicate, any pragmatic adoption of exceptional value added means that

1. An exceptional level and/or quality of ingenuity has to be involved;
2. The ingenuity has to be both internally perceived and externally approved;
3. Appropriate new processes have to be established in order to develop and advance the new or improved products or services onto the market to realize the potential value;
4. Expected benefits are realized;
5. Apart from inventions this definition also asserts on the translation of inventions into profitable new or improved products or processes;
6. The definition permits the likelihood of relative newness; and
7. Although not explicitly mentioned, the definition includes possible roles of relevant processes and outcomes.

An important distinction from past definitions of innovation in manufacturing is that this definition precludes activities that are aimed at making companies survive with respect to their rivals within the industry. As an example, in the competition between Montgomery Ward and Sears, the former diagnosed and invested in resources and capabilities and retaliated against Sears to lessen competition.

However, the approach that it took led Montgomery Ward in a wrong direction. This clarifies the reason behind Montgomery Ward's disappearance from the market place (Sobel, 1999) and signifies the importance of our definition of exceptional value added in the manufacturing sector.

Keeping in mind the importance of our definition of innovation in the manufacturing sector, a correspondence between the study of disaster predictions and that of innovation in manufacturing can be established. A particular event turns into a disaster and incurs huge potential losses is because of the degree of uncertainty in its occurrence (Lin & OuYang, 2010). Likewise, the rationale behind why innovation creates exceptional value added is the fact that it was unexpected by the market, and the market failed to anticipate the significance of it (Christensen et al., 2004).

11.3.2 The Mission, Where Everything Else Starts

This subsection discusses the reasons behind the existence of persistent competitions among employees within any organization. These competitions mainly stem from dispute among employees as to the direction and management of the organization. Differences also exist amid employees on the execution of detailed operations, and proper channeling of employees' effort and loyalty. Every stakeholder of the organization wants to contribute toward the improvement of the firm and have ideas regarding that how.

Because of the unique vision each individual has, there are plenty of competitive scenarios arising within organizations. Due to the fact that each person grows and develops in non-identical environment, and since with age, individuals' views toward the world change in response to their evolving environments, this offers an explanation as to why people's views differ. For a detailed discussion, refer to Forrest and Orvis (2016).

Proposition 11.1 For any organization that has at least two employees, it definitively experiences employee competitions that are world-view-based.

This proposition follows from the fact that every individual has a unique set of values and beliefs, and hence there always exist contradictions or inconsistencies in opinions within an organization. As a result, any two given employees will have different perspectives on some aspects of the organization. This in turn leads to a competitive environment within the organization, and in most cases one of the involved employees turns out to be more vocal in establishing his opinion, while the other remains reticent.

This proposition signifies the importance for any business organization to state its missions distinctly. Failing to do so will severely disrupt its regular operations, due to inconsistent individual beliefs. Particularly, in quest of long-term survival strategy, every successful business requires a clearly stated and strictly practiced mission.

If a company wishes to maintain a leadership position in face of increased competition, it has to indulge in innovation and devote attention to developing a mission that authorizes a long term, determined commitment to remaining a world class leader, emerging as the best in the world. In order to put this in practice, the leadership in an organization have to commit to setting very high standards, and must develop a transparent sense of strategic direction, through promoting common key themes.

It is of utmost importance that a clearly stated and strictly followed mission is implemented. This ensures that current leaders of the organization are able to strengthen individual employees' efforts and unify their beliefs. The discrepancies in individuals' beliefs disappear in reaching for the bigger goal of encompassing company's position as a world leader. However, these differences surface when all employees in a company, regardless of their positions, are encouraged to engage in innovative activities.

The commitment of the leadership is the fundamental factor here. Leadership is the most conspicuous aspect of an organization, with strong leadership being central in the system, and a slight variation of such leadership is likely to create shock waves throughout the entire system. In particular, each business organization can be viewed as a centralized system (Hall & Fagen, 1956) and the following theorem explains how the leadership can effectively influence the direction of development of the company.

Theorem 11.1 (Lin, 1988). Assume ZFC. Suppose that $S = (M,R)$ is a system such that $|M|$, the cardinality of M, $\geq c$, where c is the cardinality of the set of all real numbers, and that each object in S is a system with finite object set. If there exists such an element that belongs to at least c objects in M, there then exists a partial system B of S with an object set of cardinality $\geq c$ and B forms a centralized system.

For all the technical details of this theorem and related proof, see Lin (1988). For the purpose of our discussion, let us analyze one particular interpretation of this result. In any organization, at least one center will appear, considering that the business organization is explored as a system, such that various parts of the organization are linked by different relationships, and some special elements prevail within the system such that each of these elements travels through a variety of different parts of the organization. Hence, as long as the leadership of the organization believes, supports, and seeks after the goal of realizing the established mission through implementing clear strategic direction in every endeavor and through promoting common key themes, then a focused effort will consequently appear. Concurrently, given that resources are mostly not distributed proportionately within an organization, each unit of development battle over the control of resources and influence in the decision-making process. In the process of power struggle, this theorem implies that many potential directions of development along with their spin fields will be either placed in the backburner or eliminated without damaging the underlying structure of the organization, leading to a uniform motion in the organization's spin field (in the language of the yoyo model).

In accordance with Theorem 11.1, we conclude that the leadership commitment represents the process of social influence in which the leader or a small group of leaders can gather the help and support of others in the accomplishment of a common task (Chemers, 2001). Kouzes and Posner (2007) conclude that leadership commitment is eventually aimed at creating a harmonious way for individuals to work toward the achievement of an extraordinary goal. In contrast, when the organization desires to be the best, its selected leaders will most likely possess the corresponding key traits and demonstrate a pattern of motives (Kirkpatrick & Locke, 1991; Lin & Forrest, 2011; McClelland, 1975):

- A burning desire, energy, tenacity, and initiative to achieve, known as drive;
- A desire to lead without seeking power as an end in itself, known as motivation;
- Honesty and integrity, which help to rally supporters;
- Self-confidence, which is associated with emotional stability;
- Cognitive ability, which provides the necessary vision for the future; and
- Knowledge of the business.

In terms of the systemic yoyo model, the reason why leadership is important is because it stands for the organization's ability to adjust its underlying field structure so that all or most of the individual employees' fields will spin in cohesive fashions without much difficult readjustment. In particular, if the leadership can utilize its social influence to obtain aids and supports of other stakeholders of the company in accomplishing a common task (Chemers, 2001), it implies that there has appeared a big whirlpool (the ambition). This pool can initially be conceptual only and hard to perceive. However, it does cover a majority of the larger territory of the organizational pool, within which many smaller fields (individual employees and divisions) are located. Now, an effective leader is such a person who can realign all the individual eddy fields in such a way that the conceptual large field becomes a visible reality. In this systemic modeling, the initially invisible large field is the particular something that is expected to be extraordinary (Lin & Forrest, 2011).

What is important is that irrespective of what venture the organization is engaged in or which strategy the organization employs, they need to be grounded in the clearly stated mission. Such consistent, conceptual, and practical orientation provides a common goal for all employees to work toward and a comforting point for customers to enjoy the firm's offer(s).

11.4 Evaluation of Identified Strategic Factors

Previous literature has examined the economic factors responsible for innovativeness in manufacturing sector, both from an internal and external viewpoint of the concerned companies (Becheikh et al., 2006). In this section, we take a holistic approach to evaluate the strategic factors recognized in the literature from the height of systems science to identify the primary determinants of innovativeness in the manufacturing sector. The significance of such discussion is to identify the strategic factors that consistently contribute to innovation so that relevant strategies can be isolated from a plethora of strategies available to firms in the manufacturing sector.

11.4.1 Clearly Defined Strategic Orientation

This subsection discusses a firm's global strategies on innovation from three distinct approaches: a clearly defined strategy, corporate diversification strategy, and market territory strategy.

Souitaris (2002) empirically indicates that well-developed strategies are more applicable to improving innovation in specialized supplier industries, such as small mechanical and instrumental engineering, and not as much in other industries. In spite of the fact that this is a single study that empirically analyzes this issue, we can still derive the following definitive answer in terms of the association between a clearly defined strategic orientation and the innovativeness of the firm:

Proposition 11.2 For a manufacturing firm, a clearly defined strategic orientation and the innovativeness of the firm are positively correlated to each other.

The logic behind this result is similar to that of why a clearly stated mission can help a business organization to unify individual employees' beliefs, which are diverse and often conflicting, into a set of accepted and reinforced assumptions and values for the organization. In real life, different approaches are generally available for reaching certain pre-determined outcomes with some of the approaches leading to additional benefits while others not. In other words, in practical applications, beyond obtaining the pre-determined outcomes, one needs to adopt approaches, if all possible, that also carry such a value that introduces future products and processes. Hence, a clearly defined strategic orientation has to align well with the company's mission so that when it produces the pre-determined outcomes, adopted approaches also contribute to the realization of the organization's mission.

As for the corporate strategy of diversification, it entails whether a company concentrates its efforts on the production of its specialized products or diversifies what it does. If "diversification" means to reach simultaneously into different markets with varied lines of products, then the systemic yoyo model points to that such diversification has to slit the integrity of the company's technology, work force, and resources into pieces in order to compete in each of the chosen markets. Speaking differently, the original systemic whole of the company, consisting of the technological strength, labor talent, and plenty supply of resources, needs to be weakened in every aspect. That actually explains why empirical results show a significant negative relationship between diversification strategies and innovation (Ahuja & Katila, 2001; Hitt et al., 1996). Regarding the operations of production, specialization, which is the opposite of diversification, can nurture innovativeness by increasing the number of competing units in the search of solutions to specific problems (Robertson & Langlois, 1995). And diversification is often accompanied by various controls that can discourage technological activity (Galende & De la Fuente, 2003). And controls, such as financial controls, are likely to lead to risk averseness and near-sightedness, which in turn demoralize innovativeness (Francois et al., 2002). Completely opposite of this, strategic controls motivate long-term accomplishments by increasing managerial and leadership commitment to innovation (Hitt et al., 1996).

If "diversification" stands for strengthening the functionalities of the company's existing products so that the products will appease customers from different markets, then promoting diversification will stimulate the company's innovativeness.

By combining these discussions, we systemically establish the following results:

Proposition 11.3 Diversification is negatively associated with the innovativeness of a company, if the company employs its diversification strategy to reach as many different markets as possible by producing correspondingly adequate products for each potential market.

Proposition 11.4 Diversification is positively associated the innovativeness of a company, if the company utilizes its diversification strategy to continuously improve the functionalities of its existing products to attract customers from as many different markets as possible.

Note that the second conclusion above does not contradict the case of Eastman Kodak's market failure. It is because in this Kodak case, the company did not muster its resources and capabilities to improve the functionalities of its products in order to attract consumers from as many different markets as possible. Instead, the company continuously fortified its market territory (McGrath, 2013). To this end, Theorem 4.1 of Chap. 4, which is restated below for the convenience of the reader, provides the reason for Kodak's downfall, where the forever changing consumer preferences and tastes help increase the magnitude of the market switchers. That in turn encourages new competition while weakening Kodak's base of royal consumers.

Theorem 11.2 If the market described below is in Nash equilibrium, then the following are equivalent:

1. At least one new firm enters the market competitively and profitably with their versions of substitute offer.
2. There is a consumer surplus of switchers who make purchase decisions based on which supplier's price is lower.

The market considered in Theorem 11.2 is assumed to satisfy the following conditions. It is served by a fixed number of firms with their horizontally differentiated offers. Its operation is only affected by market forces, such as demand and supply, and consumers' forever evolving preferences and tastes. In other words, this market is perfectly competitive without any outside interference. As a consequence of interacting forces between the systems of values and beliefs of individual consumers and the missions of the incumbent firms, each of these firms has a base of loyal customers. These loyal customers only consider the offers of their favored firms unless the prices of the offers are more than their reservation prices. Different from loyal customers, there are those customers in the marketplace who make purchases based on which firm's unit-value price is lower. These customers are collectively known as switchers. And, the firms' strategies of pricing are known to all involved companies who respond by playing Nash equilibria through untainted self-analyses.

Regarding the strategy of market territory, one needs to address the following two questions (Landry et al., 2002):

1. Should a company confine itself to a local market or go beyond the regional border? And
2. Should a company grow by building alliances, such as subcontracting, mergers, and acquisitions?

In terms of the first question, Galende and De la Fuente (2003) and Landry et al. (2002) show empirically that internationalization has significant positive effect on the innovativeness of a company. To this end, we can establish the following theoretical results by making use of the literature on international trade and firm performance, assuming that all other conditions remain constant:

Proposition 11.5 In the current era of transient competitive advantages, those firms that are involved in import-export two-way trades are expected to be most innovative, followed by firms that only import, then firms that only export, and finally firms that conduct their businesses only domestically.

Empirically, Wagner (2013) confirm that the probability for two-way trading firms to survive is the highest, followed by import only firms, then export only firms, and finally domestic only firms. And this discovery is also theoretically shown by Forrest et al. (2019). Now, the current era of transient competitive advantages implies that innovation in products or processes or both is the only important factor underneath the chance of firms' survival (McGrath, 2013). Therefore, Proposition 11.5 follows.

In terms of the systemic yoyo model, to remain competitive in the international market, the constantly enhanced learning from the great number of competitors and customers makes the company continuously innovate (Veugelers & Cassiman, 1999).

Regarding the second question above, where a company grows by building alliances with outside firms, Fig. 11.1 provides a systemic yoyo intuition. This figure presents four possible field interaction patterns with field *N* being the yoyo structure of our focal firm and *M* that of an external firm *N* likes to subcontract to or acquire or merge with. The reason that the focal firm is modeled as a convergent field *N* is because the firm wants to grow its capability. That implies that the firm has to attract an increasing amount of resources and new technology.

Out of these four scenarios, only the first Case (a) offers a comparatively smooth relationship. All other cases represent either trouble or major disruption in business operations due to various reasons, such as inconsistency in inward/outward spins of the fields or harmonicities of the fields. Figure 11.2 explains why the relationship in Case (a) can be relatively smooth. In particular, in this case the convergent and

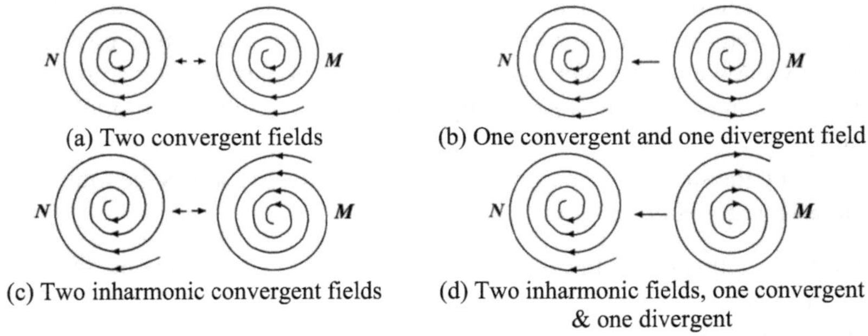

Fig. 11.1 Possible interactions between two different firms. (**a**) Two convergent fields. (**b**) One convergent and one divergent field. (**c**) Two inharmonic convergent fields. (**d**) Two inharmonic fields, one convergent and one divergent

Fig. 11.2 Relatively smooth combination of two convergent/harmonic fields

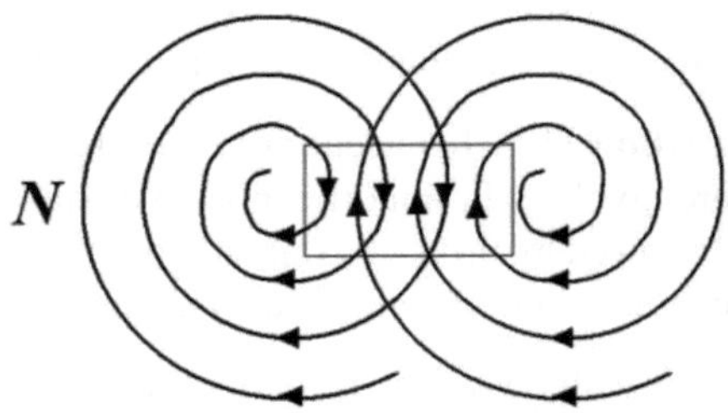

harmonic fields are in the process of merging into one unified field, although the area in the rectangle stands for the area of most conflicts.

This systemic intuition also explains why the relevant empirical studies are split between a positively and a negatively significant association between external growth and innovation. In particular, if Case (a) in Fig. 11.2 is the situation of concern, then a positive relationship appears, where new technologies of the external firm help boost the innovativeness of the firm (Belderbos, 2001). And, when an acquisition causes drops in productivity, a negative relationship appears due to disruptions in the acquiring firm's established routines and the complexity of post-acquisition management (Ahuja & Katila, 2001; Hitt et al., 1996).

11.4.2 The Aim of Growth

This subsection considers the following variables, as identified by the literature as determinants of the innovativeness of a firm: "differentiation strategy," "cost reduction strategy," and "protection mechanism."

For "differentiation strategy," Theorem 11.2 guaranteed its effectiveness on innovation, because only by trying to be different a manufacturing firm can potentially breakdown the vicious price competition prevailing in the market. By striving to differentiate itself from others, a firm is urged to innovate and to increase its pace of innovation in order to stay ahead of competitors and establish a greater competitive advantage. This theoretical conclusion is consistent with the results of various empirical studies, such as Debackere et al. (1996), Galende and De la Fuente (2003), and Zahra (1993).

For "cost reduction strategy," Theorem 11.2 explicitly indicates that implementing this strategy into a company's business operation will make the company unable to maintain its adopted technology and operational routines at their optimal conditions. That will of course unfavorably disturb innovative activities, causing the company to maintain its market presence through imitating the market leaders. This logical conclusion is consistent with the empirical findings of Zahra (1993) and Porter (1980).

In fact, rather than embracing any cost reduction strategy, the systemic yoyo model suggests that the company should instead consider improving the efficiency of its production and business operation in order to increase its productivity while minimize costs. Only when the yoyo field of the company spins more viciously, the company is able to strengthen the flow of all kinds of inputs, such as profits and investments, while exerting greater power in the marketplace.

For the variable "protection mechanism," no matter whether it is through patents, technology complexity, industrial secrecy, keeping key personnel, maintaining a lead time over competitors or any other mechanism, it is about the protection of the integrity of the company's yoyo field against invasions by other companies' fields. Therefore, the importance of this variable on product and process innovation is quite clear: Self-protection stimulates at least some competitors to innovate more than otherwise the case. Such consequence in turn enhances every firm's appropriation of its innovation benefits (Veugelers & Cassiman, 1999), which then encourages these firms with additional wills and resources to innovate more (Malerba et al., 1997).

Summarizing the discussions of this subsection, the variable "differentiation strategy" is a dominating determinant on the innovativeness of manufacturing firms, while the variable "protection mechanism" represents only a part of the effort of maintaining and exploiting the achieved differentiation. The recent fast evolution of the communication technology implies that protecting existing innovation is becoming more difficult than ever. Hence, the focus of a focal firm need to be on continuous innovation rather than spending disproportionally on protection. As for the variable "cost reduction strategy," a firm need to increase its productivity while minimize costs by innovation, such as developing more efficient processes of production and routines of business operation.

11.4.3 Operational Procedures

This subsection analyzes the following set of variables: "R&D assets and strategies," "monitoring of competitors," "marketing strategies," "personnel qualification/

experience," "HR strategies," "advanced equipment/technologies", "degree of capacity utilization," 'financial autonomy," "turnover/profit," "budget/funds availability."

Having an in-house research and development (R&D) is generally for one or more of the following reasons:

- Create, exploit, and transform new how-to knowledge into new market offers and/or processes of operation or production (Keizer et al., 2002);
- Acquire, assimilate, transform, and exploit new technologies (Debackere et al., 1996);
- Establish collaborative partnerships (Hall & Bagchi-Sen, 2002); and
- Develop new technology settings, very costly and/or particularly difficult, even impossible, to acquire from other firms (Li, 2018).

Speaking systemically, Fig. 11.3 depicts an in-house R&D, where the largest spinning base models the systemic structure of a company. The small yoyo bodies A, B, and C stand for the fields of new knowledge, new technologies, and newly located collaborative partners. And the broad scale attraction of all the tiny yoyos describes the setting of a new technology which is unique to the company.

This model indicates that when a company possesses a certain scale of strength, as described by the spin intensity of the underlying yoyo field of the company, it will logically develop its R&D capabilities. Hence, the mission and global strategies of the company will help officially recognize and organize such a division with sufficient supports. Speaking differently, although the variable "in-house R&D" has been widely accepted as crucial for innovation in the empirical literature (Hall & Bagchi-Sen, 2002), it represents only a specific aspect of materializing the company's mission and implementing global strategies. In short, in terms of innovation, in-house R&D is only a secondary determinant.

Consequent to this yoyo model of in-house R&D in Fig. 11.3, Theorem 11.2 also implies that innovation really originates from market demands, followed by innovative ideas on how to meet the demands, and then introduction of technologies for materializing the ideas. These three stages of development follow one another in a circle, Fig. 11.4, so that technologies also help uncover the market demands. That is, the systemic model in Fig. 11.3 and Theorem 11.2 jointly carried the technology-push theory of innovation to a much higher level. Here, this theory maintains that new products and services stem from results of basic research and

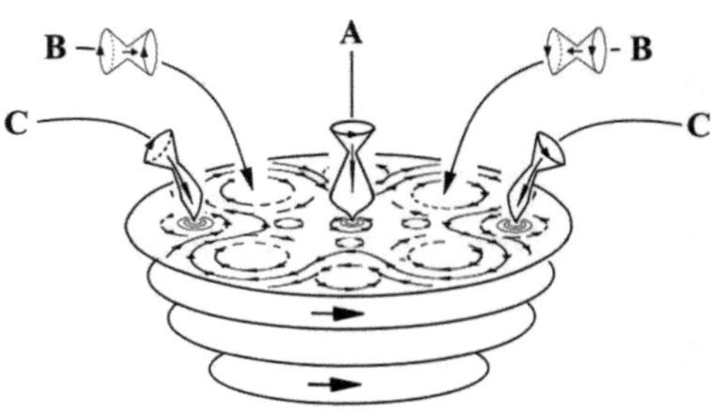

Fig. 11.3 A holistic expression of an in-house R&D

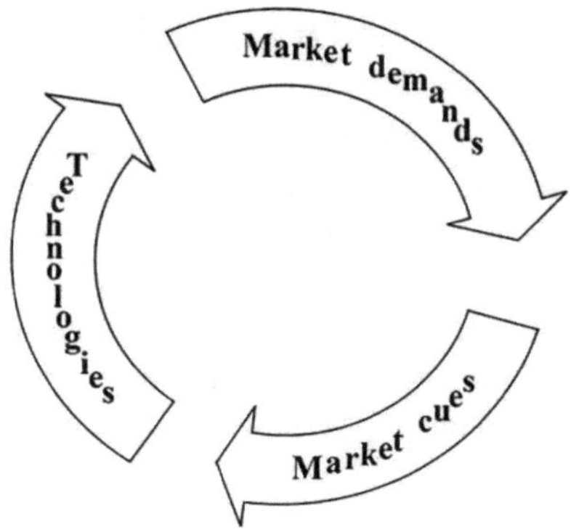

Fig. 11.4 Relationship between market demands, market cues, and technologies

industrial R&D, followed linearly by firms that define, design, produce and market their innovations. Additionally, the systemic model in Fig. 11.3 and Theorem 11.2 jointly generalizes the demand/market pull theory. This theory states that ideas for solutions also originate in the market (Landry et al., 2002). Various empirical studies, such as Darroch and McNaughton (2002) and Souitaris (2002), positively confirm this new theory developed here.

Similarly, theoretical analyses indicate that such variables as "monitoring of competitors," "marketing strategies," "personnel qualification/experience," "HR strategies," "advanced equipment/technologies," and "degree of capacity utilization," are all beneficial and supportive to innovation (Francois et al., 2002; Freel, 2003; Souitaris, 2002). However, they are only secondary when compared to the variables of mission and global strategies of the firm.

As for the variables "financial autonomy," "turnover/profit," and "budget/funds availability", the coexistence of the local eddy pools in Fig. 11.3 reveals their importance on innovation. Because these regional smaller pools do not spin in the same direction, when compared to each other, for innovative activities to take place in one or more of the local areas, each of the pools has to function independently without experiencing adverse effects from others that spin differently. In other words, both financial autonomy and budget/funds availability are very important for the local eddies to function innovatively. Additionally, profitability incentivizes continuous investment in what seem to be working, such as developing in-house R&D, innovating internally, etc. The literature (Souitaris, 2002) well supports empirically all these theoretical conclusions.

Summarizing the discussions in this subsection, one can conclude that all operational strategies analyzed here exert positive influence on the innovativeness of a manufacturing firm. However, they are only secondary when compared to the variables of mission and global strategies of the firm.

11.5 The Organizational Culture of a Firm

This section first looks at the formation of the philosophical systems of values and beliefs of individuals and organizations. And then, it examines what organizational study incorporates and why organizational mission and ambition represent two forces which overcome discrepancies existing in the philosophical values and beliefs of individuals. Established on such a general theory of organizational culture, this section studies the following variables: "resistance to change," "total quality management (TQM)/continuous improvement," and "culture of support for innovation."

11.5.1 How the Organizational Culture Is Formed

To answer this question, let us first analyze the formation if an individual's values and beliefs of philosophy. Such values and beliefs constitute the person's value-belief system that reflects how the individual sees the world and how the world functions. It contains the individual's moral codes, identity and integrity by which his behaviors are evaluated by himself. For relevant discussions. See Chap. 5 of Volume 1.

The systemic yoyo model of systems signifies that each individual resides in a huge ocean of spinning fields or yoyo bodies of various systems. That ocean includes the yoyo fields of other individuals, physical objects, abstract thoughts, and countless other things and matters. Right from birth, a person begins to interact with the world or the yoyo fields of other systems. It is these interactions with different people, physical objects, abstract thoughts, and the countless other things and matter that influence the person's philosophical assumptions (or beliefs) and values. Due to the differences between the interactions experienced by one person from those of another, each person has his set of unique values and beliefs. These values and beliefs determine the behaviors and decision-making of the person for the rest of his life. In spite of the differences in personal experiences that are "negligible" when viewed from the angle of the magnificent scale of the entire ocean of spin fields, they are generally major to the individuals involved. Hence, important differences prevail between the relevant personal systems of values and beliefs. This end explains why children growing up within the same household generally have very different personalities, characteristics, and thinking processes.

When a new life begins, due to the existing disability and resources of limited availability within the environment, the new born slowly develops his elementary beliefs and primary values. Based on these values and beliefs, he transmits signals, such as crying initially, to acquire what is needed, reasons and explains whatever inexplicable, develops approaches to overcome hardships, and establishes methods to manage personal affairs. As the person grows older, he becomes increasingly capable both physically and mentally. So, the person is able to utilize advanced tools, develop abstract thoughts, and apply intelligent methods to deal with personal and interpersonal affairs.

The logical drive for improved living conditions, increased control of elements of the environment and better recognition from others (due to the greater strength of suction and emission power of the yoyo field of the person) enables the person to invent new tools to tackle issues with the environment, discover new methods to reason, and incorporate more efficient ways to deal with various affairs through interactions with the environment. Hence, a circulation of information, knowledge, money, natural resources, etc., begins to form both within and around the person. As such a circulation begins to appear, Bjerknes' (1898) circulation theorem guarantees the appearance within the mind of the person of abstract eddy motions, consisting of the presence of new acquaintances, expansion of knowledge, improvement of old skills, acquirement of new skills, and accumulation of wealth. That is, with age, the person gradually forms his underlying values of philosophy and beliefs on how the world functions, what types of behaviors are acceptable, how a person need to interact with others and the environment in order to accomplish desired outcomes.

As his yoyo field gradually matures over time, the person becomes more able to fight off systems of different beliefs and values that potentially present the danger of destroying the yoyo structure of his own value-belief system. Simultaneously, the person enriches his philosophical beliefs and values and redefines his identities throughout life by slowly and consciously modifying some of the established beliefs and values and by introducing new ones. Here, the person's basic system reflects the fundamental structure and evolution of his yoyo field. Although the system changes and evolves with time and environment, its basic characteristics will stay the same throughout the lifespan of the yoyo structure of the person.

Proposition 11.6 Each person has his unique underlying system of philosophical values and beliefs. That is, different persons have dissimilar value-belief systems.

This result naturally follows from that individuals grow up within different environments, and that no two individuals live and work within a perfectly identical, while changing environment, with which their philosophical values and beliefs evolve respectively. See Lin and Forrest (2011) and Chap. 5 in Volume 1 for related discussions regarding the four human endowments—self-awareness, imagination, conscience, free will—and related concepts.

With the discussion above regarding the development of personal value-belief systems, we can analyze how organizational systems of values and beliefs are devised. In particular, for each working organization in the business world, its value-belief system is generally mirrored in its mission statements, which are collectively expressed by various leaders, both official and informal. Hence, such organizational system of values and beliefs is an integration of all the commonly acknowledged aspects of the individual value-belief systems of the employees of the company. Its evolution also follows a similar path as outlined above for individuals.

Regarding the culture of the organization, it involves values and ideals, norms, institutions, modes of thinking, and the higher intellectual, artistic, moral qualities to which successive generations in the organization have devoted much attention (Lin

& Forrest, 2011). Hence, the so-called organizational culture is just another manifestation of the system of organizational values and beliefs, as reflected in the day-to-day operations of the organization's business and as clearly spelled out in the mission statement.

Correlating the concept of organizational culture and firms' performance, McGrath (2013) reports that the ten best performing firms in the world invest primarily within their respective organizations in creating a common identity, culture, and alignment to establish the appropriate cultural foundation that permits changes. This result is confirmed by Bob Best, CEO of Atmos energy, "Culture is the foundation for all success. This has been a very important process to the long-term health and success of our company," (Senn-Delaney Leadership Consulting Group, n.d.).

11.5.2 Mission and Ambition That Underlie the Organizational Culture

In general, there exist disagreements amongst employees on the direction and management of their organization, on the particulars on implementation of operations, or how to best direct employees' efforts and commitments, as implicitly indicated by Proposition 11.5. Every stakeholder of an organization generally has a fair idea regarding improvement. One of the reasons for the existence of such disagreements is that each individual has a unique perspective of the world according to his value-belief system. This difference in one's philosophical values and beliefs and those of others has the ability to make the same physical world appear very different. Since no two individuals grow up within an identical environment, and because individuals' philosophical values and beliefs tend to change and adapt with age, different individuals end up with different underlying systems of philosophical values and beliefs. For a further in-depth discussion, see Forrest and Orvis (2016).

Proposition 11.7 Philosophical and value-belief-based differences exist within any organization that has at least two employees.

This result follows naturally from how individuals' systems of philosophical values and beliefs are formed initially and evolve over time. So, the fact that no two individuals can practically have an identical set of philosophical values and beliefs—Proposition 11.6—implies that inconsistencies in opinions regarding the organization always exist. Consequently, any two selected employees look at many aspects of the organization differently, leading to competitive consequences of the two employees, although in most circumstances one of them stays quiet.

Propositions 11.6 and 11.7 jointly imply the necessity for a viable business organization to clearly state its missions; otherwise, its daily operations will be torn apart by the inconsistent individual employees' systems of philosophical values

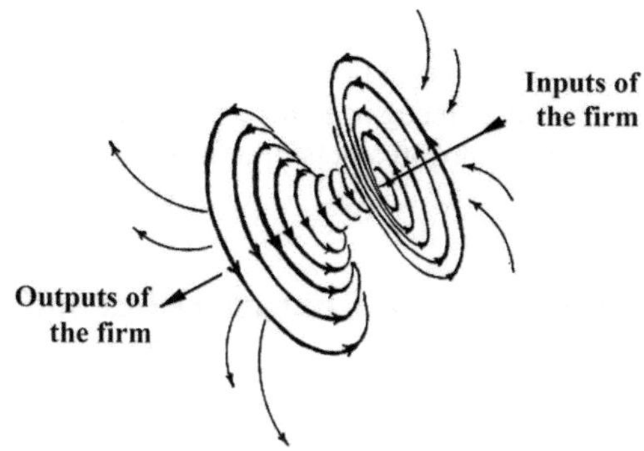

Fig. 11.5 A systemic structure with the axial direction fixed

and beliefs. Specifically, for the minimal business desire of survival, each firm that intend to be long-lasting needs to have a clearly stated and strictly practiced mission. Moreover, if a company wishes to be a business leader that successfully rides waves of transient competitive advantages, which generally has to be innovation based, then it has to develop such a mission that it clearly establishes a long-term, unwavering public commitment to the ambition of becoming world class, the best of the world. In practice, such ambition needs to be embraced, endorsed, and sought after by the leadership of the firm through setting the bar high while having a clear sense of strategic direction in every endeavor, and through promoting common key themes.

In terms of the systemic yoyo model, this discussion means that the established long-term, unwavering ambition specifies the direction of the axis of spin for the underlying yoyo structure of the firm, Fig. 11.5 that is Fig. 8.3 from Chap. 8. When such determination is supported and promoted by the leadership throughout the organization, all layers of the eddy pool (or the culture of the organization) that spins around the axis can now focus their efforts on how to interact with the environment and with each other. Speaking differently, when the needed culture is carefully developed and nurtured, employees at different positions can focus on what is important for the organization instead of worrying about what they are personally interested, adversely affected as the consequence of potential changes in the business direction of the organization. In fact, Proposition 11.7 signifies theoretically the importance of creating and maintaining a common identity and culture for a firm to be healthy and prosperous.

In short, the previous discussions lead naturally to the following generally reliable conclusions, as empirically confirmed by Francois et al. (2002), Veugelers and Cassiman (1999), and Jung et al. (2003), respectively:

1. Organizational culture is a significant determinant of the innovativeness of any firm;
2. Total quality management, as a mechanism of quality control and realization of the culture of continuous improvement, practically implements the long-term, unwavering business ambition of an organization;

3. Any resistance to change is against the ambition and culture, and the spirit of innovation of a firm; and
4. A widely recognized perception of support for innovation is positively correlated to the innovativeness of a firm.

11.6 General Characteristics and Structure of a Firm

This section analyzes such variables that describe the general characteristics of a firm as "size of the firm," "age of the firm," "ownership structure," and "past performance."

11.6.1 The Size of a Firm

An analytical analysis on how a firm's size is determined by the market is provided in the appendix of this chapter. That analysis of the relationship between the manufacturer's total profit and number of employees hired implies the following:

1. As claimed by Schumpeter (1934), entrepreneurs and start-ups represent the foremost source of new ideas and technologies (because Eq. (11.3) says the importance of being the initiator of a new product). That also explains why first movers tend to have their particular advantages (Lieberman & Montgomery, 1988).
2. Additional profits will be generated by increasing the number of employees if the ratio of the per employee revenue over per employee cost ($p_{\mathrm{p}}^{W}/p_{\mathrm{s}}^{W}$) stays constant or decreases, as indicated by the second term of Eq. (11.3). Since market cost (p_{p}^{W}) per employee goes higher over time due to market competition, to keep this ratio constant or decrease, the expected average revenue ($\$p_{\mathrm{s}}^{W}$) per employee has to at least keep up with the increase in the per employee cost (p_{p}^{W}). That can be practically influenced by many factors (MacPherson, 1994). This fact implies that in general innovation activity increases more than proportionally with firm size, as maintained by Schumpeter (1942). In other words, the effects of size on innovation as claimed by Schumpeter in 1934 and 1942, respectively, are not contradictory as many scholars had thought (c.f., Damanpour, 1992; Stock et al., 2002).
3. Market competition is an essential force behind a company's size and innovation activities, since generating extra profits is behind the need of hiring additional employees.

As for the effects of firm's age, ownership structure, and past performance on the innovativeness of a firm, the systemic yoyo model suggests that these variables are only indicative of some aspects of the company. The current state of the company's innovativeness is categorically determined by the present might of spin of the underlying yoyo field, explaining why relevant empirical studies have produced mixed results, neither positive nor negative. For instance, Sørensen and Stuart (2000) exhibit that through age a firm accumulates necessary experience and knowledge on innovation, a positive relationship between a firm's age and its innovativeness. In the contrary, Freel (2003) discovers that age can be a barrier to innovation, since procedures and routines in place resist the integration of external advances. To this end, the systemic yoyo modeling implies that such contradictory findings in fact reflect natural existences in nature, because each firm is a form of life, where age does not have such bearing on the vigor or innovativeness of the firm.

In the same vein, empirical results on how ownership structure affects innovation are also mixed. For example, Michie and Sheehan (2003) find a positive correlation between foreign ownership and the innovativeness of a firm, while Martinez-Ros (1999) reveal that this relationship is instead negative.

As for how the past performance and the innovativeness of a firm are related, the systemic logic suggests that these variables be positively correlated if the past can be extrapolated linearly into the future when the good past performance was innovation dependent. The historical innovation dependence reinforces the certainty that the firm's established competitive position, market share, and great profits are results of its innovativeness (Zahra, 1993).

In short, "firm size" and good "past performance" are indicators of innovativeness of the firm, while "age of the firm" and "ownership structure" are not. Even so, these variables as "firm size" and good "past performance" are merely secondary to the variables of the "mission" and "global strategies" of the firm. In particular, "firm size" and good "past performance" indicate how well the firm had been able to appropriately understand market cues and how adequately the firm had taken appropriate actions.

11.6.2 The Structure of a Firm

Continuing the discussion above, variables that are pertinent to the firm's structure, such as "formal structure," "flexible structure," "centralization of decision-making," "empowerment of employees," and "interaction between firm's units," can be shown to be all secondary. They represent practical implementations of the long-term, unwavering ambition.

Especially, the effects of "formal structure" and "centralization of decision-making" on innovativeness of a firm are not decisively positive or negative; instead, they are dependent on the size of the firm. If a firm is young and comparatively small without any bureaucratic hierarchy, then its systemic yoyo structure can be adequately modeled by the uniform eddy field shown in Fig. 11.6, where information, energy, knowledge, and all other components of the organization, are "spinning" in a uniform motion. In this instance, both formalism and centralization jointly allow the

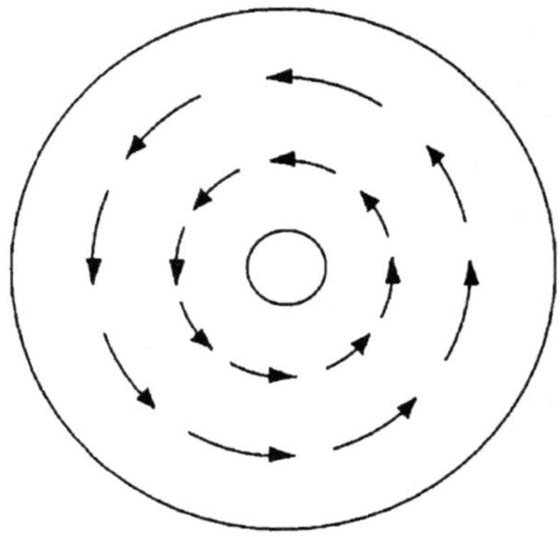

Fig. 11.6 The uniform eddy field of a young firm

young firm to focus its efforts and limited resources on what is crucial for the survival and growth of the firm by not specifying roles of individuals and by lowering ambiguity. That helps improve effectiveness, morale, and innovativeness. For related discussions, see Koberg et al. (1996).

If a firm is well-established, then its systemic yoyo structure can be effectively modeled by the eddy field in either Fig. 11.7a or Fig. 11.7b. In these systemic models, each eddy leaf stands for a unit within the firm. When decision-making is decentralized, as shown in Fig. 11.7a where decentralization is portrayed by the absence of a central circle, then each division is able to function as a relatively independent small, young firm so that it can easily focus its efforts and limited resources on what is essential for the survival and growth of the division. So, the inevitably emerging competition and coordination between the divisions will actually help stimulate and promote the innovativeness of the overall firm to a higher level. On the other hand, if decision-making is centralized, as shown in Fig. 11.7b where the centralization is depicted by the central circle, then other than responding to the changing environment—the outer edge of the dishpan in Fig. 11.7b, each division—an eddy leaf in Fig. 11.7b—has to follow the mandates of the central decision-making body. That is, the wide spectrum of activities the firm is involved in

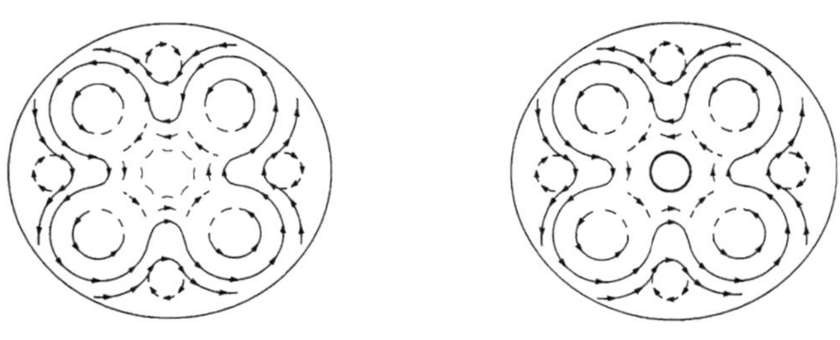

(a) The eddy field with decentralization (b) The eddy field with centralization

Fig. 11.7 The yoyo field of a well-established organization. (**a**) The eddy field with decentralization. (**b**) The eddy field with centralization

compete for approximately the same limited resources, the attention of the leadership, and the support of the administration so that the efforts and commitments of each division cannot be totally focused on what the division thinks is critical. Also, the relatively long chain of command enables the firm to react slowly to market changes. That is how formalism and centralized decision-making weakens the innovativeness of the firm.

The same systemic modeling and analysis explain why such variables as "flexible structure," "empowerment of employees," and "interaction between firm's units," have significant positive impact on innovation. Specifically, a young firm without established bureaucratic hierarchy can be innovative through formalizing its rules and procedures; a well-established company with centralized decision-making has to assure, if it wishes to compete in the same play field with all young"firm', that it has a flexible structure, that decision-making is decentralized, and that interdivisional functional communication and coordination are stimulated.

11.7 The Leadership of a Firm

This section introduces the definition of leadership, explains why leadership commitment is a vital and the essential key for the innovativeness of a firm, and discusses the effects of the following variables on the innovativeness of a firm: "presence of a project leader," "CEO's characteristics," "CEO change," and "CEO's qualification and experience."

11.7.1 Leadership: The Concept

Leadership depicts one of the most notable contents in the organizational context that is hard to define. For example, Chemers (2001) defines leadership as the process of social influence in which one person can enlist the aid and support of others in the accomplishment of a common task; Kouzes and Posner (2007) describe leadership as an ultimate way of creating an environment for people to work together in creating something extraordinary.

The topic of leadership has been well researched by many authors, who have developed correspondingly different theories of leadership. The trait theory, for example, attempts to identify talents, skills, and physical characteristics of men that are associated with effective leadership (House, 1996). In lieu of criticism of such theories, more recent studies have identified leadership skills, not simply a set of traits, but as a pattern of motives. That suggests that successful leaders tend to have an increasing need for power, a low need for affiliation, and a high level of self-control (McClelland, 1975). Spencer (1841) argues that great leaders emerge with time, suggesting that different situations demand for different leadership qualities. Hence, a single optimal psychographic profile for all leaders does not exist; and, an individual's actions as a leader primarily depend upon characteristics of the situation in which he operates (Hemphill, 1949). Van Wormer et al. (2007) demonstrate three leadership styles: the authoritarian style, the democratic style, and the laissez faire style, each of which has its own pros and cons and is applicable only under specific circumstances.

According to the functional theory (Wageman et al., 2008), a leader is responsible for ensuring the needs of his group. So, he is responsible for the group's effectiveness and how cohesive the group is. When the leader promotes his unit's effectiveness, there are five broad functions he provides: environmental monitoring, organizing subordinate activities, teaching and coaching subordinates, motivating others, and intervening actively in his group's work. A formal organization is defined (Cecil, 1970, pp. 884–889) as a hierarchy of people, established for accomplishing defined objectives. The hierarchy consists of divisions, departments, sections, positions, jobs, and tasks so that all members would behave impersonally toward clients and other members. Employees are ranked based on either merit or seniority so that the higher a member's position in the hierarchy, the greater his presumed expertise and social status. Within such managerial structure heads are chosen and endowed with authority for administrative purposes. Beyond these chosen heads, informal leaders generally surface, according to Theorem 11.1, within the underlying informal organizational structure that consists of the personal objectives and goals of individual employees.

All of the implicit requirements, such as personal security, maintenance, protection, and survival, of the employees are met within the informal organization through the official leaders (Knowles & Saxberg, 1971, pp. 884–889). And, each informal leader without any endowed authority provides supports for a group of employees and is acknowledged by his concern for others, open communication, and persistent commitment (Hoyle, 1995). Although appointed managers have the authority to command and administer orderliness, they still need to possess adequate personal attributes to match their authority. When personal competence is inadequate, a manager will have to confront emergent unofficial or informal leader(s). They challenge the manager and diminish his role to that of a nonentity. Hence, leadership can be defined as one's ability to get others to willingly follow. Each organization needs leaders at every level to achieve functionality and efficiency.

The concept of leadership, be it official or informal, can be systemically modeled and analyzed as follows. Based on the definitions of Chemers (2001) and Kouzes and Posner (2007), leadership is one's capability to adjust his underlying yoyo field structure in such a way that many other neighboring yoyo fields will spin in similar fashions without much difficult readjustment. In particular, if a person can use social influence to acquire aids and supports of others in accomplishing a common task (Chemers, 2001), it implies that there has appeared a big whirlpool spinning around a defined axis—the common task. Although this pool may initially be conceptual and physically weak, it covers a large territory, within which many smaller yoyo fields—individual people, relevant resources—are located. Now, a so-called leader, official or not, is such a person who is able to realign sufficient number of individual eddy fields in such a way that the conceptual large yoyo field becomes a visible and

Fig. 11.8 The yoyo field of a leader

functional reality, Fig. 11.8. In this figure, the central pool is capable of aligning the neighboring fields so that jointly a much greater pool of eddy fields is formed.

This systemic model of leadership unifies all relevant studies into one organic, holistic theory. Specifically, to function as a leader, a person needs to possess some key elements, such as talents, skills, and physical characteristics, as claimed in the trait theory (House, 1996), and drive, leadership motivation, honesty, integrity, self-confidence, cognitive ability, and knowledge of the business, as argued by Kirkpatrick and Locke (1991). It is the movement pattern of the yoyo field of a person that is the fundamental reason why the person can become a leader: his overreaching field influence on others makes him seen as having a high need for power, a low need for affiliation, and a strong self-control. This systemic modeling at the same time explains why, as argued by Spencer (1841), it is the times that produce leaders and not the other way around and that different situations call for different leadership characteristics. For relevant discussions in more details, see Lin and Forrest (2011).

11.7.2 Leadership Commitment and Innovativeness

The leadership of a company has the potential to draw out and emphasize the harmonic aspects of individual employees' systems of philosophical values and beliefs by clearly stating and rigidly following the mission of the firm. Apart from that, the leadership commitment is the essential key to success. Indeed, leadership represents the core of the organizational system, a slight change or vibration of which creates shock waves throughout the entire system. That is, a firm with a true leadership is a centralized system (Hall & Fagen, 1956). Particularly, when the leadership embraces, endorses, and actively seeks after the goal of realizing the mission, a focused effort throughout the organization will appear (Theorem 11.1).

As mentioned in the prior subsection, leadership commitment represents a process of social influence where the leader(s) can consolidate assistance from others to carry out a common task. And, when the organization wants to realize its ambition, its chosen leaders will conceivably possess the key traits and demonstrate patterns of motives, as discussed earlier, such as a burning desire, energy, tenacity, and initiative to achieve, an ability to rally supporters, strong self-confidence backed by emotional stability, a necessary vision for the future, and sufficient knowledge of the business. Leadership commitment is systemically and critically important because it represents the organization's willingness and ability to adjust its underlying field structure so that all or most of the individual employees' fields will spin in necessary fashions, Fig. 11.8. The coordinated movements of the individual yoyo fields naturally give rise to the appearance of a much greater field that spins around the common task—the big ambition (Lin & Forrest, 2011).

In a nutshell, irrespective of what venture a firm is engaged in and which particular strategy the firm adopts, everything needs to be clearly associated with the mission and the effort of realizing the established ambition with clear leadership commitment. Through conducting business with such tenacious consistency, the firm clearly institutes a goal for all employees to work toward and a comforting point for customers of the firm to look up to.

One definite indication of the needed leadership commitment is the presence of a "project leader" in the company, as empirically established by Souitaris (2002). Such a leader enthusiastically supports and is committed to innovative projects. At the same time, when the firm is committed to its long-term, unwavering ambition, its selected leadership will presumably possess the corresponding key characteristics and abilities to achieve and to motivate with an adequate vision for the future and knowledge of the business, as indicated by the levels of education, qualifications, and cumulative experience. That provides a theoretical explanation as to why the Chief Executive Officers' (CEO) characteristics have a significant positive impact on the innovativeness of the firm (Jung et al., 2003). That is, when the CEO is entrepreneurial, a transformational leader, and has a strong desire to achieve, he will most likely set high goals, strive to work harder, and be willing to commence upon innovation projects since only such projects can provide the company opportunities to achieve the established challenging goals.

Regarding the significance of the CEO's term on a firm's innovativeness, CEO's stable tenure indicates the firm's commitment to its established mission and ambition. It is because only an internal stability, including those of mission, long-term ambition, and personnel, can ensure that the firm withstands the chaotic impact of the external world. Alternately, only when the firm is sufficiently stable endogenously, it will be able to internalize chaos from its environment and alter its pre-determined path of development (Forrest & Nightingale, 2017). That is, CEO's term in the firm has a positive impact on innovation.

In summary, all such variables that are related to the stability and presence of the leadership as "presence of a project leader," "CEO's characteristics," "CEO change," and "CEO's qualification and experience" are secondary when compared to having a long-term, unwavering ambition.

11.8 Managerial Recommendations

Individual company attributes can differ from the discussion in the earlier sections. However, the theoretical framework of this chapter provides a general set of recommendations for managers to adopt in order to enhance the innovativeness of their companies. It further encourages research scholars to analyze how different strategies can positively affect and encourages innovation in the manufacturing sector.

Specifically, to foster innovation, the leaders in a company's management need to establish clearly stated mission and commit to a long-term resolute ambition. The mission and ambition are the central driving forces for obtaining the desired level of innovativeness that a firm aims for. They consolidate seemingly incoherent credence of individual employees and amplify the harmonic aspects of the individuals' values and beliefs. Along with developing the mission and building upon the ambition, the leadership at the firm needs to demonstrate its dedication to the chosen mission and ambition. The firm also needs to perpetrate in cultivating an organizational culture that is suitable for changes, assists efforts of innovation, and strives for recognizing resolute ambition.

In order to stimulate innovation, it is important to begin with an explicit definition of how to realize the mission and the ambition of the firm. For a compelling implementation of a diversification strategy, managers need to direct their attention to continuous improvement of the process development of existing products. This is to lure successfully customers away from rival firms. Whenever possible, the firm need to engage in international trade, preferably involving both import and export, and in the event that is too ambitious, the firm need to still aim at either import or export. In strengthening association with outside partners, the firm needs to concentrate on knowledge, and embrace new technologies, without causing much disruption to the already established product li"es.

Because managers, regardless of their levels, are the ones within a firm who push for the realization of the mission and achievement of long-term ambition, they are required to possess specific characteristics such as emotional stability and cognitive abilities. That is, managers need to have futuristic visions, knowledge of the business, and strong ambition, stamina, and initiatives to achieve, to lead, and to rally supports. Firms need to preserve such quality managers as long as they remain competent.

The emphasis of developed growth strategies needs to be on establishing specialization on the firm's unique advantages, with the idea of contrasting business strategies. Among the most recommended ideas will be the creation of a special task force to determine the current market competition, what that specifically means for the firm, and what strategies the firm need to adopt to maximize the impact of such potential strategies. Since any protectionist ideas primarily target to preserve differentiation, managers need to have the main target of creating new ways of differentiating their products, as improving upon such differentiation, rather than spending too much on resources to fortify protections. With regard to specific strategies aimed at cost minimization, managers need to emphasize on the efficiency of production and that of the routines of business operation.

To realize the long-term ambition, managers need to sustain, at the operational level, secondary variables, such as "firm size" and good "performance," and implement strategies, such as in-house R&D activities, hiring and retaining experienced employees who are experts in advanced technologies, at the operational level. A competent rule regarding personnel decisions needs to be developed such that whenever required, the firm has flexibility in hiring additional labor or firing workers, in accordance with market demand. The mechanism also needs to outline specific ways for managers to change the sizes of their divisions through internal movements of people or through mergers and acquisitions, through disinvestment, downsizing, reengineering, and/or outsourcing. Because better performance is good news for investors, and a fair indicator of the quality of the firm, maintaining performance is of utmost importance. And, the process of continuous improvement as well as retraining programs need to be implemented at a regular basis for each employee. There is a need for persuasive marketing of products and constant check on rivals' strategies in order to cater to the growing and forever changing needs of consumers. Managers also need to secure financial competence of their company by ensuring they do not indulge in disproportionate debts.

Further from developing particular strategies to implement operational routines, the next step in boosting innovation is to ensure that the administrative structure is adaptable; the decision-making process is either centralized or decentralized in such a manner that it can efficiently assist in focusing efforts and scarce resources on things that are vital for endurance and growth of each division, by explaining roles of individuals and by lessening uncertainty. If the firm is a strong-rooted and large corporation, it is recommended to have a decentralized decision-making process in order to enhance the innovativeness of each division. Communication between employees of different divisions need to be highly encouraged.

Since the recommendations in this chapter are based on rigorous reasoning, rather than reliance on the methods of data analysis, data mining, and anecdotes, these are more reliable in practical applications to manufacturing firms. These sets of recommendations are the substantial contributions of this work to the existing literature. They are also improvements from the results of the empirical literature, which indicate mere suggestions and not assertions. Generally, conjectures based on empirical evidence suffer from the limitations of generalizability. Further detailed discussion of this can be found in Chap. 10 of Volume 1 and in Forrest et al. (2019).

11.9 A Few Final Words

As evidenced by the literature, the innovativeness of a manufacturing firm is a convoluted occurrence, affected by a number of different factors and has been studied by a plethora of scholars from varieties of angles (Marzi et al., 2017). In order to have a better understanding of this process, this chapter undertakes a theoretical analysis of (a) the strategy-related factors and their impact on innovation and (b) the impacts of manufacturing firms' culture, structure and leadership on their innovativeness. Owing to the power of the holistic thinking of systems science, we are able to bring all the empirical investigations on the strategic determinants of innovation in the manufacturing sector to the height of sound scientific abstraction and navigate through the 16 variables, representing different aspects of manufacturing firms' culture, structure, and leadership, and recognize the ones which are essential for encouraging and promoting innovation in a manufacturing firm, ones which are primary factors behind the innovativeness of the firm, and distinguish the secondary factors that simply appear due to the creation of the primary forces.

For practical purposes of managerial decision-making, apart from developing many useful insights, the thinking logic and method of systems science employed herein enable us to theoretically explain why previous conclusions have been mixed with some showing positive impact on innovation, some negative, while others insignificant (Becheikh et al., 2006). Beyond such explanation, this chapter effectively validates many of the empirically established conjectures as generally true, leading to solid managerial recommendations rather than merely suggestions. In a nutshell, due to the particular holistic method of reasoning applied in this chapter, the established theoretical results are expected to help a firm's attempt of enhancing its innovativeness become a practical possibility.

In particular, previous literature empirically isolated a good number of strategy-based variables and organizational factors that can certainly increase a manufacturing firm's innovativeness. Yet, the empirically established results are inconclusive with some variables and factors having positive, while others negative impacts on innovativeness (Becheikh et al., 2006). Hence, the majority of these empirical results do not have valid real-life applications due to the uncertainties involved in how the results were derived. Opposite to such ambiguity and uncertainty, this chapter clarifies the strategic and organizational complexity of innovation by determining and distinguishing between primary and secondary strategy variables and organizational factors. That means, managers can devote their time and energy on establishing the primary variables and factors in their efforts to elevate the level of their company's innovativeness.

In conclusion, two primary limitations of this study need to be acknowledged:

- All results are based on the definition of innovativeness in the manufacturing sector developed in this chapter; and
- An implicit assumption is that each firm in the manufacturing sector aims to conquer a particular market niche by creating a positive cash flow, either from the profits of the marketplace, or investments, or both.

Particularly, the concept of innovation considered in this chapter does not incorporate incremental improvements, which stands for a major omission of studies on disruptive break-throughs as consequences of incremental progresses (Kuhn, 1962; Rostow, 1960). The second limitation also excludes firms that exist for purposes other than satisfying any market niche. In other words, it is still unclear as to how a firm's culture, structure, and leadership will affect the innovativeness of the firm, if the firm exists for a purpose other than that of attempting to satisfy a market niche.

Appendix: Firm Size and Market Demand

To analytically understand these two variables, assume that a manufacturer sells a specific product for $\$p_{\mathrm{s}}$ per unit. The total cost for the product from production to eventual sale is $\$p_{\mathrm{p}}$ per unit. If the number of units produced and sold at the price $\$p_{\mathrm{s}}$ is $n = n(p_{\mathrm{s}})$, then the profit of this manufacturer from this product is

$$P = \text{profit} = n(p_{\mathrm{s}})\left(p_{\mathrm{s}} - p_{\mathrm{p}}\right).$$

Maximizing this profit subject to the budget constraint $n(p_{\mathrm{s}})p_{\mathrm{p}} = I$, where $I > 0$ is the total available funds for the manufacturer to invest in this line of product, leads to the following solution:

$$n(p_{\mathrm{s}}) = \frac{n(p_{\mathrm{s}0})p_{\mathrm{s}0}}{p_{\mathrm{s}}},$$

where $n(p_{\mathrm{s}0})$ is the initial market demand when the product is sold at $\$p_{\mathrm{s}0}$ per unit. So, the profit of the manufacturer is

$$P = \frac{n(p_{\mathrm{s}0})p_{\mathrm{s}0}}{p_{\mathrm{s}}}\left(p_{\mathrm{s}} - p_{\mathrm{p}}\right) = n(p_{\mathrm{s}0})p_{\mathrm{s}0}\left(1 - \frac{p_{\mathrm{p}}}{p_{\mathrm{s}}}\right).$$

Similar to what is seen above, each employee the manufacturer hires generates as much profit as $\left(p_{\mathrm{s}}^{W} - p_{\mathrm{p}}^{W}\right)$, where the average revenue the employee is expected to make is $\$p_{\mathrm{s}}^{W}$ while her total expected cost of employment is $\$p_{\mathrm{p}}^{W}$. So, the total profit of the manufacturer is

$$P_{\mathrm{total}} = P^{p} + P^{W} = n_{\mathrm{p}}\left(p_{\mathrm{s}}^{p}\right)\left(p_{\mathrm{s}}^{p} - p_{\mathrm{p}}^{p}\right) + n_{W}\left(p_{\mathrm{s}}^{W}\right)\left(p_{\mathrm{s}}^{W} - p_{\mathrm{p}}^{W}\right), \tag{11.1}$$

where P^{p} stands for the profit from the product directly, P^{W} the profit from employees, $n_{\mathrm{p}}\left(p_{\mathrm{s}}^{p}\right)$ the number of units of the product produced and sold at the unit price p_{s}^{p} with p_{p}^{p} being the unit cost, and $n_{W}\left(p_{\mathrm{s}}^{W}\right)$ the number of employees hired at the expected average revenue $\$p_{\mathrm{s}}^{W}$ per employee.

This profit is subject to the following budget constraint, where $I > 0$ is a constant representing the total amount of funds available to the company,

$$n_{\mathrm{p}}\left(p_{\mathrm{s}}^{P}\right)p_{\mathrm{p}}^{P}+n_{W}\left(p_{\mathrm{s}}^{W}\right)p_{\mathrm{p}}^{W}=I. \tag{11.2}$$

Solving the maximization problem of Eq. (11.1) subject to Eq. (11.2) leads to the following:

$$n_{\mathrm{p}}\left(p_{\mathrm{s}}^{P}\right)=\frac{n_{\mathrm{p}}\left(p_{\mathrm{s0}}^{P}\right)p_{\mathrm{s0}}^{P}}{p_{\mathrm{s}}^{P}},$$

$$n_{W}\left(p_{\mathrm{s}}^{W}\right)=\frac{n_{W}\left(p_{\mathrm{s0}}^{W}\right)p_{\mathrm{s0}}^{W}}{p_{\mathrm{s}}^{W}},$$

and

$$P_{\mathrm{total}}=n_{\mathrm{p}}\left(p_{\mathrm{s0}}^{P}\right)p_{\mathrm{s0}}^{P}\left(1-\frac{p_{\mathrm{p}}^{P}}{p_{\mathrm{s}}^{P}}\right)+n_{W}\left(p_{\mathrm{s0}}^{W}\right)p_{\mathrm{s0}}^{W}\left(1-\frac{p_{\mathrm{p}}^{W}}{p_{\mathrm{s}}^{W}}\right), \tag{11.3}$$

where all the symbols with a subscript 0 stand for the corresponding initial values.

References

Aas, T. H., Breunig, K. J., Hydle, K. M., & Pedersen, P. E. (2015). Innovation management practices in production-intensive service firms. *International Journal of Innovation Management, 19*(5), 1–28.

Adner, R., & Levinthal, D. (2001). Demand heterogeneity and technology evolution: Implications for product and process innovation. *Management Science, 47*(5), 611–628.

Ahuja, G., & Katila, R. (2001). Technological acquisitions and the innovation performance of acquiring firms: A longitudinal study. *Strategic Management Journal, 2*(3), 197–220.

Alegre, J., & Chiva, R. (2008). Assessing the impact of organizational learning capability on product innovation performance: An empirical test. *Technovation, 28*(6), 315–326.

Amara, N., & Landry, R. (2005). Sources of information as determinants of novelty of innovation in manufacturing firms: Evidence from the 1999 statistics Canada innovation survey. *Technovation, 25*(3), 245–259.

Becheikh, N., Landry, R., & Amara, N. (2006). Lessons from innovation empirical studies in the manufacturing sector: A systematic review of the literature from 1993 to 2003. *Technovation, 26*(5), 644–664.

Belderbos, R. (2001). Overseas innovations by Japanese firms: An analysis of patent and subsidiary data. *Research Policy, 30*, 313–332.

Bjerknes, V. (1898). Uber einen hydrodynamischen Fundamentalsatz und seine Anwendung besonders auf die Mechanik der Atmosphare und des Weltmeeres. *Kongl Sven. Vetensk. Akad. Handlingar, 31*, 1–35.

Cecil, A. G. (1970). *Leadership (handbook of social psychology)*. Addison-Wesley.

Chemers, M. M. (2001). Cognitive, social, and emotional intelligence of transformational leadership: Efficacy and effectiveness. In R. E. Riggio, S. E. Murphy, & F. J. Pirozzolo (Eds.), *Multiple intelligences and leadership* (pp. 139–160). Lawrence Erlbaum.

Christensen, C. M., Anthony, S. D., & Roth, E. A. (2004). *Seeing what's next: Using the theories of innovation to predict industry change*. Harvard Business School Press.

Czichos, H., Saito, T., & Smith, L. (Eds.). (2011). *Springer handbook of metrology and testing* (2nd ed.). Springer.

Damanpour, F. (1987). The adoption of technological, administrative, and ancillary innovations: Impact of organizational factors. *Journal of Management, 13*(4), 675–688.

Damanpour, F. (1992). Organizational size and innovation. *Organization Studies, 13*, 375–402.

Darroch, J., & McNaughton, R. (2002). Examining the link between knowledge management practices and types of innovation. *Journal of Intellectual Capital, 3*(3), 210–222.

De Massis, A., Frattini, F., Pizzurno, E., & Cassia, L. (2015). Product innovation in family versus nonfamily firms: An exploratory analysis. *Journal of Small Business Management, 53*(1), 1–36.

Debackere, K., Clarysse, B., & Rappa, M. A. (1996). Dismantling the ivory tower: The influence of networks on innovative output in emerging technologies. *Technological Forecasting and Social Change, 53*, 139–154.

Duez, P. (2012). From competitive advantage to differential advantage: A new model of strategic management. In *Proceedings of the 6th International Management Conference*, November 15–16, 2012, Bucharest, Romania (pp. 9–24).

Ettlie, J. E., Bridges, W. P., & O'Keefe, R. D. (1984). Organization strategy and structural differences for radical versus incremental innovation. *Management Science, 30*(6), 682–695.

Forrest, J. Y.-L., & Nightingale, J. (2017). Successfully transition into the era of transient competitive advantages. In *Proceedings of 2017 NABET Annual Conference*, October 26–27, 2017, State College, PA (pp. 57–79).

Forrest, J. Y.-L., & Orvis, B. (2016). Principles of management efficiency and organizational inefficiency. *Kybernetes: The International Journal of Cybernetics, Systems and Management Sciences, 45*(8), 1308–1322.

Forrest, J. Y.-L., Mondal, S., Tucker, R., & Lin, C. C. (2018a). Effects of manufacturing firms' strategies on innovation: A holistic view. In *Proceedings of the 2018 Annual Conference of NABET*, November 1–2, 2018, State College, PA (pp. 74–94).

Forrest, J. Y.-L., Tucker, R., Lin, C. C., & Mondal, S. (2018b) Impacts of manufacturing firms' culture, structure and leadership on innovation: A systemic approach. In *Proceedings of the 2018 Annual Conference of NABET*, November 1–2, 2018, State College, PA.

Forrest, J. Y.-L., Lin, C. C., Mondal, S., & Tucker, R. (2019). Environmental forces underneath the innovativeness of manufacturing firms. *Theoretical Economics Letters, 9*, 1353–1382.

Francois, J. P., Favre, F., & Negassi, S. (2002). Competence and organization: Two drivers of innovation: A micro-econometric study. *Economics of Innovation and New Technology, 11*(3), 249–270.

Freel, M. S. (2003). Sectoral patterns of small firm innovation, networking and proximity. *Research Policy, 32*, 751–770.

Galende, J., & De la Fuente, J. M. (2003). Internal factors determining a firm's innovative behaviour. *Research Policy, 32*, 715–736.

Hall, L. A., & Bagchi-Sen, S. (2002). A study of R&D, innovation, and business performance in the Canadian biotechnology industry. *Technovation, 22*, 231–244.

Hall, A. D., & Fagen, R. E. (1956). Definitions of systems. *General Systems, 1*, 18–28.

Hemphill, J. K. (1949). *Situational factors in leadership*. Ohio State University Bureau of Educational Research.

Herrera, M. E. B. (2015). Creating competitive advantage by institutionalizing corporate social innovation. *Journal of Business Research, 68*(7), 1468–1474.

Hitt, M. A., Hoskisson, R. E., & Johnson, R. A. (1996). The market for corporate control and firm innovation. *Academy of Management Journal, 39*, 1084–1119.

Holmstrom, J., Holweg, M., Khajavi, S. H., & Partanen, J. (2016). The direct digital manufacturing (r) evolution: Definition of a research agenda. *Operations Management Research, 9*, 1–10.

House, R. J. (1996). Path-goal theory of leadership: Lessons, legacy, and a reformulated theory. *The Leadership Quarterly, 7*(3), 323–352.

Hoyle, J. R. (1995). *Leadership and futuring: Making visions happen*. Corwin Press.

Jung, D. I., Chow, C., & Wu, A. (2003). The role of transformational leadership in enhancing organizational innovation: Hypotheses and some preliminary findings. *The Leadership Quarterly, 14*, 525–544.

Kanter, R. M. (2001). *Evolve! Succeeding in the digital culture of tomorrow*. Harvard Business School Press.

Keizer, J. A., Dijkstra, L., & Halman, J. I. M. (2002). Explaining innovative efforts of SMEs. An exploratory survey among SMEs in the mechanical and electrical engineering sector in The Netherlands. *Technovation, 22*, 1–13.

Kirkpatrick, S., & Locke, E. (1991). Leadership: Do traits matter? *Academy of Management Executive, 5*(2), 48–60.

Knowles, H. P., & Saxberg, B. O. (1971). *Personality and leadership behavior*. Addison-Wesley.

Koberg, C. S., Uhlenbruck, N., & Sarason, Y. (1996). Facilitators of organizational innovation: The role of life-cycle stage. *Journal of Business Venturing, 11*, 133–149.

Kouzes, J., & Posner, B. (2007). *The leadership challenge*. Jossey Bass.

Kuhn, T. (1962). *The structure of scientific revolutions*. University of Chicago Press.

Landry, R., Amara, N., & Lamari, M. (2002). Does social capital determine innovation? To what extent? *Technological Forecasting and Social Change, 69*, 681–701.

Leonidou, L. C., Fotiadis, T. A., Christodoulides, P., Spyropoulou, S., & Katsikeas, C. S. (2015). Environmentally friendly export business strategy: Its determinants and effects on competitive advantage and performance. *International Business Review, 24*(5), 798–811.

Li, L. (2018). China's manufacturing locus in 2025: With a comparison of "Made-in-China 2025" and "Industry 4.0". *Technological Forecasting and Social Change, 135*, 66–74. https://doi.org/10.1016/j.techfore.2017.05.028

Li, D. Y., & Liu, J. (2014). Dynamic capabilities, environmental dynamism, and competitive advantage: Evidence from China. *Journal of Business Research, 67*(1), 2793–2799.

Lieberman, M. B., & Montgomery, D. B. (1988). First-mover advantages. *Strategic Management Journal, 9*, 41–58.

Lin, Y. (1988). An application of systems analysis in sociology. *Cybernetics and Systems: An International Journal, 19*, 267–278.

Lin, Y., & Forrest, B. (2011). *Systemic structure behind human organizations: From civilizations to individuals*. Springer.

Lin, Y., & OuYang, S. C. (2010). *Irregularities and prediction of major disasters*. CRC Press.

Lin, R. J., Tan, K. H., & Geng, Y. (2013). Market demand, green product innovation, and firm performance: Evidence from Vietnam motorcycle industry. *Journal of Cleaner Production, 40*, 101–107.

Liu, S. F., & Lin, Y. (2006). *Grey information: Theory and practical applications*. Springer.

MacPherson, A. D. (1994). Industrial innovation among small and medium-sized firms in a declining region. *Growth and Change, 25*, 145–163.

Makadok, R. (2010). The interaction effect of rivalry restraint and competitive advantage on profit: Why the whole is less than the sum of the parts. *Management Science, 56*(2), 356–372.

Malerba, F., Orsenigo, L., & Peretto, P. (1997). Persistence of innovative activities, sectoral patterns of innovation and international technological specialization. *International Journal of Industrial Organization, 15*, 801–826.

Martinez-Ros, E. (1999). Explaining the decisions to carry out product and process innovations: The Spanish case. *The Journal of High Technology Management Research, 10*(2), 223–242.

Marzi, G., Dabic, M., Daim, T., & Garces, E. (2017). Product and process innovation in manufacturing firms: A 30-year bibliometric analysis. *Scientometrics, 113*, 673. https://doi.org/10.1007/s11192-017-2500-1

McClelland, D. (1975). *Power: The inner experience*. John Wiley & Sons.

McGrath, R. G. (2013). *The end of competitive advantage: How to keep your strategy moving as fast as your business*. Harvard Business Review Press.

Michie, J., & Sheehan, M. (2003). Labour market deregulation, 'flexibility' and innovation. *Cambridge Journal of Economics, 27*(1), 123–143.

OECD. (1997). *The measurement of scientific and technological activities, proposed guidelines for collecting and interpreting technological innovation data*. Organization for Economic Cooperation and Development.

Peng, M. W., Lee, S. H., & Tan, J. J. (2001). The *keiretsu* in Asia: Implications for multilevel theories of competitive advantage. *Journal of International Management, 7*(4), 253–276.

Porter, M. E. (1980). *Competitive strategy: Techniques for analyzing industries and competitors*. Free Press.

Porter, M. E. (1985). *Competitive advantage: Creating and sustaining superior performance*. Free Press.

Robertson, P. L., & Langlois, R. N. (1995). Innovation, networks, and vertical integration. *Research Policy, 24*, 543–562.

Rostow, W. W. (1960). *The stages of economic growth: A non-communist manifesto*. Cambridge University Press.

Rothwell, R. (1992). Successful industrial innovation: Critical factors for the 1990s. *R&D Management, 22*(3), 221–239.

Schumpeter, J. A. (1934). *The theory of economic development*. Transaction Publishing.

Schumpeter, J. A. (1942). *Capitalism, socialism and democracy*. Harper.

Senn-Delaney Leadership Consulting Group. (n.d.) *Interview with Atmos Energy CEO Bob Best*. Retrieved February 7, 2020, from www.senndelaney.com/bobbestarticle.html

Smith, A. (1776). *The wealth of nations*. Bantam Classics; annotated edition edition (March 4, 2003).

Smith, W. K., & Tushman, M. L. (2005). Managing strategic contradictions: A top management model for man-aging innovation streams. *Organization Science, 16*(5), 522–536.

Sobel, R. (1999). *When giants stumble: Classic business blunders and how to avoid them*. Prentice Hall.

Sørensen, J. B., & Stuart, T. E. (2000). Aging, obsolescence, and organizational innovation. *Administrative Science Quarterly, 45*(1), 81–112.

Souitaris, V. (2002). Technological trajectories as moderators of firm-level determinants of innovation. *Research Policy, 31*, 877–898.

Spencer, H. (1841). *The study of sociology*. D. A. Appleton.

Stock, G. N., Greis, N. P., & Fischer, W. A. (2002). Firm size and dynamic technological innovation. *Technovation, 22*, 537–549.

Utterback, J. M., & Abernathy, W. J. (1975). A dynamic model of process and product innovation. *Omega, 3*(6), 639–656.

Van Wormer, K. S., Besthorn, F. H., & Keefe, T. (2007). *Human behavior and the social environment: Macro level: Groups communities and organizations*. Oxford University Press.

Veugelers, R., & Cassiman, B. (1999). Make and buy in innovation strategies: Evidence from Belgian manufacturing firms. *Research Policy, 28*(1), 63–80.

Visnjic, I., Wiengarten, F., & Neely, A. (2016). Only the brave: Product innovation, service business model innovation, and their impact on performance. *Journal of Product Innovation Management, 33*(1), 36–52.

Wageman, R., Nunes, D. A., Burruss, J. A., & Hackman, J. R. (2008). *Senior leadership teams: What it takes to make them great*. Harvard Business School Press.

Wagner, J. (2013). Exports, imports and firm survival: First evidence for manufacturing enterprises in Germany. *Review of World Economics, 149*, 113–130.

Wu, D., Rosen, D. W., Wang, L., & Schaefer, D. (2015). Cloud-based design and manufacturing: A new paradigm in digital manufacturing and design innovation. *Computer-Aided Design, 59*, 1–14.

Zahra, S. A. (1993). *New product innovation in established companies: Associations with industry and strategy variables* (pp. 47–69). Entrepreneurship Theory and Practice.

Zollo, L., Marzi, G., Boccardi, A., & Ciappei, C. (2016). Gli effetti della Stampa 3D sulla competitivita aziendale. Il caso delle imprese orafe del distretto di Arezzo. *Piccola Impresa/Small Business, 2*(2), 80–100.

Chapter 12
The Decision of Either Going International or Staying Domestic

Jeffrey Yi-Lin Forrest, Michael E. Trebing, Anindya Chatterjee, and Joachim Wagner

Abstract In recent years, the number of studies on international trade and firm performance has been increasing exponentially. Aiming at unifying the conclusions of these studies, this chapter, which is mainly based on Forrest et al. (Theor Econ Lett 9:649–674, 2019), presents a general theory regarding how trades internationally can either negatively or positively affect the performance of the firm of concern. It accomplishes this goal by employing the logic of systemic thinking and game theory.

By revisiting two theorems on the dynamics of competition of the domestic market, as established in the previous chapters, the present chapter focuses on discussions and results on exports to either lesser developed or more advanced foreign markets. Although the formulated general theory is about international trades, it emphasizes on both exports and imports, while considering firm performance in terms of productivity, profitability, employee wages, and survival.

Other than re-confirming some of the previously established empirical findings, this chapter also outlines suggestions for future research. Due to the introduction of the logic of systemic thinking into the study of international trades, this chapter provides a much-needed framework for public debates and policy decision-making.

Keywords Export market · Foreign direct investments · Foreign market · Product life cycle · Productivity advantage · Sunk costs

Jeffrey Yi-Lin Forrest (Department of Accounting Economics Finance, Slippery Rock University, Slippery Rock, PA, USA; Email: Jeffrey.forrest@sru.edu), Michael E. Trebing (Federal Reserve Bank of Philadelphia, Philadelphia, PA, USA; Email: mike.trebing@phil.frb.org), Anindya Chatterjee (Department of Accounting Economics Finance, Slippery Rock University, Slippery Rock, PA, USA; Email: anindya.chatterjee@sru.edu), and Joachim Wagner (Institute of Economics, Leuphana University, Lueneburg, Germany; Email: wagner@leuphana.de) are equally contributed to this chapter.

J. Y.-L. Forrest, *Systemic Principles of Applied Economic Philosophies II*,
Translational Systems Sciences 39, https://doi.org/10.1007/978-981-99-7939-4_12

12.1 Introduction

International business activities and performance of firms have been a hot topic of research in recent years; and the relevant literature, both empirical and theoretical, has been growing exponentially (Melitz & Redding, 2014; Wagner, 2016). The empirical branch of the literature was initiated by Bernard and Jensen (1995), and the theoretical branch by Melitz (2003). Due to the ongoing globalization of regional and natural economies from around the world, investigations on this research topic have been helping not only relevant academic discussions but also public debates and policy decision-making. Evidently, such studies are vitally important for local, regional, national, and international economic developments. Therefore, it is both theoretically and practically important for us to establish a general theory that integrates the findings reported in the literature while providing guidelines for practical applications and future research.

To limited by the length of this chapter, which is mainly based on Forrest et al. (2019), however, any such attempt needs to be carefully choosy and attentive to only a few related topics. By employing systems science and game theory, this chapter unambiguously concentrates on the following topics:

- The dynamics of competition of the domestic market;
- Exports to either less developed markets or more advanced markets or both; and
- Development of a general theory regarding the relationship between international trades and the performance of firms, where such firms' outcomes as productivity, profitability, employees' wages, and survival are specifically considered.

One of the most important contributions this chapter makes to the existing international business literature is the introduction and application of systems science (especially, the systemic yoyo model) to the study of international activities and how such activities affect the involved firms in terms of their economic performance. In addition to creating a brand-new perspective of looking at the international business activities, the employment of the systemic logic of reasoning and the methodology of systems science makes it more intuitive, specifiable, predictable, and repeatable for decision makers to determine what kinds of international activities—export, import, or both, their firms should be engaged in. By utilizing the systemic yoyo model, frontline managers and entrepreneurs will be able to make their important decisions in a timelier and more reliable fashion. These advantages of course have tremendous practical implications considering the fact that competitive advantages in the present business world are no longer sustainable, and have been becoming transient (McGrath, 2013).

Completely different from the approaches employed by various scholars in the past, the specific systemic perspective taken in this chapter stands for how a decision maker can look at the issues in hands from a holistic, system-based view. Because the essence of how firms survive and grow is really about how the firms interact externally with each other and mature internally so that the best can be brought out of each division and every employee, our adopted holistic, system-based perspective focuses on how organizations, as entities with internal structures, exert forces and constraints on each other. And due to the novelty of this approach, this chapter is able to develop theoretically interesting and practically significant conclusions.

The rest of this chapter is organized as follows. Section 12.2 provides a literature review and outlines specific contributions this paper makes. Section 12.3 revisits two characteristics of domestic competition. Section 12.4 looks at the situation of exporting to (a) a less developed market and (b) a more advanced market. Section 12.5 develops the suggested general systemic theory of productivity, employees' wages, and survival for domestic firms, exporters, importers, and two-way traders. Section 12.6 draws some conclusions based on the discussions in this chapter and suggests a few directions for future research.

12.2 Literature Review

The literature relevant to this chapter can be roughly divided into two areas. One area consists mostly of empirical studies using transaction level data on exports and imports; and the other area deals generally with theoretical investigations.

For the first area—empirical studies, it finds (Bernard & Jensen, 1995, 1999) that firms participating in international trades perform better in a number of dimensions, while exporters are larger, more productive, more capital intensive, more skill intensive, and pay higher wages than non-exporters within the same industry. As for importers, many of these characteristics identified for exporters also hold true, while those firms that simultaneously export and import typically exhibit the highest levels of performance (cf., Bernard et al., 2007a, b, 2009). More specifically, the top 1% of exporters dominate the export market, covering the lion's share of all exports (Freund & Pierola, 2012; Wagner, 2012c). Similarly, a high degree of concentration is also found with importers (Bernard et al., 2009, 2013; Muuls & Pisu, 2009; Manova & Zhang, 2009; Wagner, 2012c). On the other hand, most firms export to and import from a small number of countries, involving a small number of goods only (cf., Arkolakis & Muendler, 2013; Eaton et al., 2004; Eriksson et al., 2009). Prior experience in exporting a certain product or exporting to a specific market increases the chance for the firms to export these products to new markets or new products to the same markets (cf., Blum et al., 2013; Buono & Fadinger, 2012; Békés & Muraközy, 2012; Rahu, 2015).

It is found that firm characteristics, such as productivity, credit constraints, firm age, innovation, and profitability, are closely linked to the extensive margins of international trade. For example, productivity is positively related to export (respectively, import) participation and also to the number of goods exported, and the number of export destination countries (Andersson et al., 2008; Bernard et al., 2014; Casas et al., 2015; Muuls & Pisu, 2009; Wagner, 2012d). In terms of credit constraints, it is discovered that exporting and/or importing firms are less financially constrained than non-exporting firms (Wagner, 2014a, b). As for the age of firms, it is documented that older firms export and import more different goods to and from more different countries (Bastos & Dias, 2013; Wagner, 2015). And, innovative firms are more likely to participate in foreign trades (Halpern & Muraközy, 2012). Most importantly, firms that have less diversified export sales over goods or more diversified export sales over destination countries seem to enjoy higher levels of profits; in terms of imports, firms that import more goods and from more countries do not necessarily produce higher levels of profits (Wagner, 2014c).

The second area of the literature—theoretical studies on international trade—emphasizes on the causes and consequences of aggregate trade by looking at firm-level decisions. Relevant studies examine the heterogeneity in productivity, size, and other characteristics of the economy through investigating related features of firms, as motivated by empirical findings. As shown both empirically and theoretically, this heterogeneity is closely correlated to trade participation such that exporters are larger and more productive than non-exporters even before they entered a foreign market. Entry into export market induces expansions in firm scales, which consequently enhances the return of investments in technologies and innovations that improve productivity. See Melitz and Redding (2014) for related references.

In these theoretical studies, various models are developed to provide explanations for as many empirically revealed patterns as possible; and these models produce predictions of those patterns of trade and production that are not revealed by micro-level data on plants and firms. For example, Melitz (2003) and Melitz and Redding (2014) develop models of monopolistic competition to reflect product differentiation and increasing returns to scale at the level of individual firms. By neglecting strategic interactions between firms, these models provide a way to analyze a host of firm decisions in general equilibrium. Bernard et al. (2003) develop a heterogeneous firm framework to describe the head-to-head competition between firms. For a good survey on studies of oligopoly and trade in general equilibrium, see Neary (2010). In short, these theoretical studies are especially important from a policy perspective in terms of how trades should be liberated, who might be the potential winners and losers of the liberation, and in which way new trade policies should be designed and introduced.

Enriching the literature, this chapter establishes a series of generally-true conclusions that confirm many of the empirically observed patterns. Although some of these results developed herein had also been derived by certain theoretical investigations (Melitz & Redding, 2014; Neary, 2010), our results do not suffer from the same methodological deficiencies as the previous theoretical works do. In particular, for a constructed model to function properly, the modeler has to make a few basic assumptions, although they are not true in real life. For example, to investigate the impact of trade on intra-industry reallocations and aggregate industry productivity, Melitz (2003) assumes, among others, that (1) the collection of all goods (indexed by ω) considered by a representative consumer is a continuum; and (2) there is a continuum of firms, each of which produces a different variety ω of product. Evidently, the total number of goods considered by any consumer has to be a natural number, while the same is true for the number of firms that produce the products a consumer is interested in consuming. The reason for Melitz and others to introduce these and or similar assumptions is to fit the situation of concern into the framework of the calculus-based methodology. In comparison, the conclusions developed in this chapter does not suffer from these methodological deficiencies.

12.3 Stability in Domestic Market

This section establishes the fact that to expand into foreign market(s), it is necessary for an exporting firm to first stabilize its domestic market position. To do this and to make our discussion here self-contained, let us quote Theorem 4.1 in Chap. 4 as follows:

Theorem 12.1 In Nash equilibrium of the domestic market that is described below, a sufficient and necessary condition for at least one firm to enter the market profitably, as a competitor of the incumbent firms, is that the consumer surplus satisfies $\beta = 1 - \alpha > 0$, where the market is assumed to satisfy the following conditions:

- It is oligopolistic, occupied by m incumbent firms, $m = 1, 2, \ldots$;
- These incumbent firms provide consumers with mutually substitutable products;
- Each of the incumbent firms has its respective base of loyal consumers who make their purchases only from their respective firms, as long as the price is no more than the reservation value;
- There are such consumers, known as (price) switchers in the market, who make their purchases depending on whose price is the lowest;
- To protect their turfs while potentially increase their consumer bases, these incumbent firms compete over the switchers with adjustable prices charged to their customers in order to deter the potential entrance of new competitions (Theorem 12.1);
- The incumbent firms produce their products at constant marginal costs, which is set to zero without loss of generality;
- The managements of these incumbent firms know the pricing strategies of each other and establish their best responses by playing the Nash equilibrium through pure self-analyses.

The assumed market conditions in this theorem generally mean that the technology involved and the relevant business operations have been standardized. Hence, for a new small firm to enter such a market with profit potential, it is reasonable to assume that this firm has come up with a more efficient technology and/or operation that can greatly reduce the overall business expenditure.

As for the systemic intuition for why such a theoretical result holds true in general, please consult with Chap. 6. All the relevant details are omitted here.

The practical significance of Theorem 12.1 is that although the market is entirely occupied by the incumbents that compete over the switchers, who at the same time are not content with the existing product, there is still a chance for a new company to enter the market profitably. And the size of the entrant will be proportional to that of the market segment of switchers.

The following result necessary for the discussions of this chapter is Theorem 10.1 in Chap. 10.

Theorem 12.2 In Nash equilibrium, when the competition of the afore-described market grows with an increasing number of firms entering the market, the base of loyal customers for each incumbent firm will gradually and eventually diminish.

Jointly Theorems 12.1 and 12.2 paint a very dynamic picture of competition in the domestic market. In particular, if incumbent firms do not compete within the domestic market over the consumer surplus, then new competitions will enter the market. Additionally, when the number of firms that compete within the market increases, the market share of each firm will diminish. In other words, no matter whether a firm plans to export into any foreign market or not, it has to first stabilize its domestic market share for the primitive purpose of survival, which is its home base on which bigger plans can be dreamed of and can next be implemented. In terms of the systemic yoyo model, what these two theorems say is that when the market competition intensifies, the number of eddy leaves in Fig. 12.1, where the dish models the domestic market (for details, see Fig. 8.2b in Chap. 8), will increase while the size of each of the leaves gets smaller until they become not clearly visible. This result is exactly what is shown in the laboratory in the name of dishpan experiment. That is, when the difference between the periphery and the center of the spinning dish increases, the number of eddy leaves will increase until the leaves become so small that they are no longer visible (Lin & OuYang, 2010).

By summarizing the discussions above, we have the following conclusion:

Proposition 12.1 No matter whether a firm plans to enter a foreign market or not, it needs to stabilize its market territory domestically.

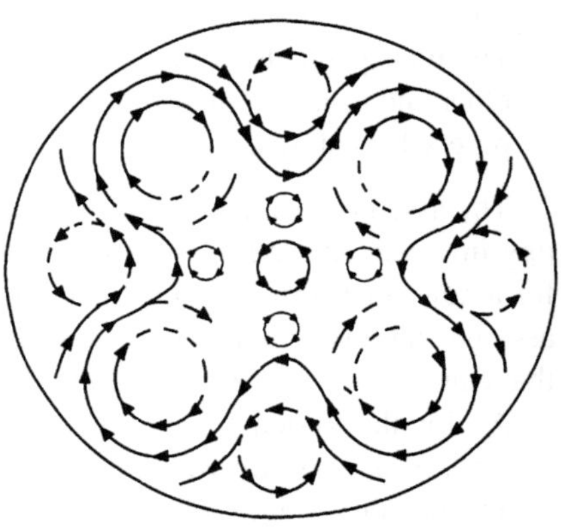

Fig. 12.1 The systemic yoyo model of the domestic market

12.4 Foreign Markets That Are Either Less Developed or More Advanced

This section looks at the market characteristics of a foreign market into which a firm plans to enter profitably. Due to differences in the relevant circumstances, this section considers the potential foreign market in two cases: it is either less developed than or at least as advanced as the domestic market.

12.4.1 Entry into a Less Developed Market

In this chapter, by a less developed foreign market it represents a foreign market that it is not as well developed economically and is not as well serviced with quality products as is the domestic market. That is, the functionality of the products, exported into such a foreign market, can be adjusted according to the existing market situation so that sufficient savings can be generated to cover all the sunk costs of entering the foreign market. The range of extra sunk costs includes those of transportation, distribution, marketing, and personnel with skill to manage foreign networks. These costs provide an entry barrier into foreign markets for less resourceful firms to overcome. That indirectly implies that for a firm to successfully export its products into a foreign market, the firm has to be more productive than non-exporting firms of the same size from the same industry before it starts to export successfully with the additional sunk costs comfortably absorbed. See Bernard and Jensen (1995) and Wagner (2012a) for relevant empirical confirmations of this conclusion. Here, productivity stands for the efficiency with which the firm turns inputs (labor, physical capital, energy, materials, managerial know-how) into outputs (goods, services).

In other words, when competing with local firms i $(= 1, 2, \ldots, m)$ of the receiving economy, we can also assume that our exporting firm and local firms produce their products that are horizontally differentiated at constant marginal costs, which is set to zero without the loss of generality. Assume that each local firm enjoys a base of loyal customers of size α, $\beta = 1 - m\alpha$ is the size of the market segment of price switchers, and that the managements of these $m + 1$ firms are well aware of the pricing strategies of the other firms and have established their best responses by playing the Nash equilibrium through pure self-analyses. Because our exporting firm comes from a more advanced market, its products naturally carry a brand name in the less developed market. That is, assume that a percentage r of the customers of the receiving market are brand chasers; and from being well aware of its advantageous position, the exporting firm sells its product at k (≥ 1) times more than the market price P, $0 \leq P \leq 1$, of the local firms.

Theorem 12.3 In the Nash equilibrium, if the consumer surplus of the local market satisfies $\beta = 1 - m\alpha > \alpha$, then the exporting firm will make the same level α of profits as any of the local firms in this less developed foreign market by randomizing the local firms' price P within the interval [0,1].

Corollary 12.1 In the Nash equilibrium, if the consumer surplus of the local market satisfies $\beta = 1 - m\alpha > 0$, then the exporting firm will make profits that is proportional to β in this less developed foreign market by randomizing the local firms' price P within the interval [0,1] even if the foreign market does not have any brand chasers.

For the technical proofs of these results, see the appendix of this chapter.

What Theorem 12.3 says is that only when the consumer surplus of the less developed foreign market is sufficiently large, exporting into such market will be profitable with profits equaling at least k times of how much any of the local firms had made before any foreign competitor appeared. Otherwise, the profits will be so, so very small that it is not worth the effort of exporting into such a foreign market as indicated in Corollary 12.1 considering the potential risk associated with the sunk costs.

The reason why the exporting firm randomizes the market price P of the local firms over the interval [0,1] is that without any first-hand knowledge of the new market, the firm just aims at making profits and develop its customer base. Hence, as the initial pricing strategy it is a reasonable market approach.

The conclusion of Theorem 12.3 can be seen readily from the systemic yoyo model. For instance, let us model the said foreign market of our concern as the entire spinning dish in Fig. 12.1, and each of the m firms a local eddy pool. Then, the symmetry that is assumed to exist in the market place, just like that that exists in the dishpan experiment, suggests that it is impossible that.

1. A large blank space, which is at least as big as the area occupied by one of the local eddy leaves, will appear within the circular chain of the local eddy pools. That is, the local eddy leaves have to be evenly distributed within the spinning dish along the periphery and around the center of the dish. And,
2. The total area that borders between adjacent local eddy leaves and between the periphery of the dish and circular chain of the local eddy leaves is too big, because the appearance of the local eddy leaves is caused by uneven distributions of forces that act on the fluid particles located at different distances from the center of the dish.

By summarizing the discussions above, the conclusion below follows:

Proposition 12.2 For a less developed foreign market, if the magnitude of the consumer surplus of that market is greater than that of the loyal customer base of one of the local firms, then exporting into this market will be profitable with the amount of profits equaling at least k times of how much any of the local firms had made before any foreign competitor appeared. The multiple k is at least 1.

12.4.2 *Entry into a More Advanced Market*

In this chapter, by an advanced foreign market it implies a foreign market in which the quality and functionality of products imported into the market have to be the best possible of all options that are available to consumers. In other word, to export into an advanced foreign market, the sunk costs of the exporting firm have to be greater than zero. In this case, other than the costs of transportation, distribution, marketing, and personnel with the skill to manage foreign networks, the sunk costs also include those of production in improving current domestic products for the consumption of the advanced foreign market. At the same time, within the advanced foreign market, the imported products represent just another alternative and do not naturally enjoy any advantage of being foreign.

Theorem 12.4 Assume that the consumer surplus β of the foreign market satisfies $\beta = 1 - m\alpha \geq \alpha$. If this foreign market is in Nash equilibrium, then there is an expected opportunity for the exporting firm to make at least as much profits as (α – sunk costs) in the said foreign market by uniformly randomizing its price *P* over the interval [0,1].

For the technical proof of this result, see the appendix of this chapter.

What Theorem 12.4 says is that when entering an advanced foreign market, to develop the necessary consumer base and to generate the baseline revenue, the exporting firm can use such a sales' strategy that it materially randomizes the selling price uniformly over the interval [0,1], the interval from the cost of producing and selling one unit of the product to the reservation price of the customers of the foreign market. At the same time, this theorem and its proof imply that although it is advanced, if the market in the foreign land is expanding, one can expect capable foreign firms to enter and to compete with the incumbent local firms. On the other hand, the sunk costs for the exporting firm cannot be too big in terms of how much each local firm has been making.

After the initial foray into the advanced foreign market by randomizing its selling price over the interval [0,1], the exporting firm can treat itself as one of the local firms as soon as it establishes a base of loyal customers. By doing so, the firm will be able to double its revenue in the foreign market by employing different pricing strategies (Forrest & Anderson, 2017).

12.5 International Trades: A Systemic Theory

This section presents a general theory on international trades and firms' productivity, survival, and employees' wages based on the theorems established in the previous sections and the systemic yoyo model. What is significant here is that we theoretically derive conclusions that are observed earlier by various scholars from data mining, while provide conclusions that can potentially be confirmed by data analysis in the years to come.

12.5.1 Relationship Between Productivity and Trades in Foreign Market

The dynamic nature of the domestic market competition, developed by Theorems 12.1 and 12.2, clearly shows that it is not easy for any firm to stay afloat domestically without actively trying to attract additional customers while improving its products. Otherwise, increasing competition will wear away the established consumer base of the firm and push the firm over the edge of the market. Hence, such important issues as exporting goods to international markets have to be in the making years ahead of the actual implementation of the idea. (It is well known that most consumer products in the advanced countries are in the maturity stage of the product life cycle facing intense competition and eroding market shares. As such, firms look to exporting as an option to extend their product life cycles.) The leadership of the firm has to be a major part of such ambition and export market entry decision. Please refer to Sobel (1999) for a historical account and McGrath (2013) for recent reviews on the importance of leadership in export management. In other words, we expect the quality and vision of the management team of an export starter to be different from that of a domestic firm, i.e., a firm that buys and sells only domestically.

All firms with an ambition of international reach can be categorized into two groups: those that are successful and those that are not successful. To be successful, there are definitely many hurdles to overcome. One of the first hurdles will be to muster the necessary financial resources to cover the sunk costs of potentially going abroad. Before anything else, some of the first initial sunk costs will be those used to acquire the knowledge of the particular foreign markets, the technology needed for modifying current domestic products for foreign consumption, the development of distribution centers and retail outlets, and all other strategic ground works. If all goes well, a second round of heavy investments will be needed to actually arrange transportation, purchase equipment for product modifications, establish distribution or marketing networks, and hire and train personnel that will be skillful enough to manage foreign networks.

No matter how an exporter's investments are financed, either by cash or bank loans or a combination of both, a potentially successful export starter has to be efficient in turning its inputs (labor, physical capital, energy, materials, managerial know-how) into outputs (goods) years before taking the leap into a foreign market (Bernard & Jensen, 1999; Bernard & Wagner, 1997). Otherwise, the needed finance for international reach cannot be secured. In order to facilitate a much greater output requirement, the export starter firm will be better equipped than non-exporters in terms of its technology and skills of its workers to accelerate its productivity growth when called for (Melitz & Redding, 2014; Wagner, 2007a; Baldwin & Robert-

Nicoud, 2004). That explains why exporters that have low productivity will fail when compared to successful exporters (Wagner, 2007b, 2008). In short, our theory confirms the following hypothesis with some modification on why exporters can be generally expected to be more productive than non-exporting firms (Bernard & Jensen, 1999; Bernard & Wagner, 1997): Among all the firms that self-select themselves into export markets, only more productive ones tend to be successful within these markets (or only more productive firms go abroad successfully).

Likewise, in terms of the management quality of export starters, export starters will be superior to non-exporters in terms of their ability to produce with sufficiently high productivity, analyze foreign markets accurately and timely, keep abreast of technological advancements seamlessly, establish transportation and distribution centers, and recruit and train the necessary personnel to manage foreign networks. It is important to note that any of these areas of planning can either go wrong or operate inefficiently.

The knowledge acquired from foreign markets and interacting with international customers and foreign competitors motivates exporting firms to advance its post-entry performance by improving its products via additional functionalities, adopting more efficient systems, becoming more user-friendly, among others. With successful entry into export market(s), exporting firms have to increase their outputs in order to satisfy the expanding needs of their global customer base. At the same time, the intense competition in foreign markets, which is additional to that of the domestic market, forces exporting firms to make changes faster than firms that sell their products domestically only. That is, competitive advantages become truly transient for exporting firms; they need to be disengaged with obsolete technology in timely fashion and new advantages have to be uncovered and adopted quickly. This rapid cycle of innovation is at times difficult to accomplish for many firms (McGrath, 2013). As discussed in the preceding two sections, a difficult aspect of exporting is figuring out how to overcome the sunk costs of exporting, which can be affected by many extraneous factors, including international politics, policy changes, etc. In short, our theory supports the following hypothesis: Successful exporters are expected to be more productive than non-exporting firms (Bernard & Jensen, 1999; Bernard & Wagner, 1997) due to the enhanced learning experience acquired through exporting and drastically increased market demands in terms of management strategy and productivity. That actually also explains why exporting does not necessarily improve the firms in general (Singh, 2010, p. 1537), because increasing frequency of disengaging and adopting strategic advantages can practically lead to uncertainties and business disruptions (McGrath, 2013).

Our theoretical framework offers an explanation for why there exists a difference in terms of exporter premiums, the ceteris paribus percentage difference of labor productivity. It is expected that on average, the premiums will be larger for countries with lower export participation rates, with more restrictive trade policies, lower per capita GDP, less effective government and poor regulatory quality, and for countries exporting to relatively distant markets (ISGEP, 2008). That is because these characteristics, either individually or jointly, make it more difficult to finance the sunk costs of exporting compared to those countries without these characteristics. In sum, to successfully finance export activities, the exporter premiums for countries with these characteristics must be high.

Similarly, the reason why firms that export to a larger number of foreign markets have to be more productive than firms that serve a smaller number of foreign markets is because of the recurrent nature of some of the sunk costs for each market. For example, transportation costs will be incurred for each destination market, local language related materials, such as user's manual and direct marketing publications, need to be prepared for each destination. Likewise, recurrent costs will be incurred to comply with local regulations in each target market and so on.

Theorems 12.3 and 12.4 jointly explain why exporters to developed economies have superior ex ante productivity levels than non-exporters and firms exporting to less developed countries. It is because when exporting to relatively developed economies, none of the sunk costs can be easily recovered simply by modifying the products for foreign consumption; at the same time, additional expenses are incurred for upgrading the products designed and produced for domestic consumption to the need of consumers of the developed economies. That is, superior ex ante productivity levels are needed for firms to finance their exporting initiatives. In terms of different learning-by-exporting effects by varying export destinations, these theorems imply that exporting to advanced economies foster higher levels of productivity than exporting to less developed countries, because the former destinations force exporters to satisfy more advanced consumer demands along with greater challenges of the local competitors than the latter.

In terms of the relationship between import and productivity, a similar theory as the one just developed above also holds true, because for a firm to start importing, it also has to first cover the relevant sunk costs, including, but not limited to, finding potential foreign suppliers, inspection of goods, negotiations, contract formulation, learning and acquisition of customers, etc., (Kasahara & Lapham, 2013; Andersson et al., 2008; Castellani et al., 2010). In other words, in order to import goods successfully, higher productivity has to be a prerequisite for the importing firm. That is, more productive firms have the potential to foray into import markets *successfully*.

At the same time, through importing, the firm can exploit global specialization and use inputs from the forefront of knowledge and technology. That will surely impact the productivity of the firm positively. That is, other than desired goods that are either not available or better than those available in the domestic market, the importing firm also acquires new knowledge and technology that are useful and advantageous for the firm to compete domestically.

Because importing successfully requires high levels of productivity and helps further increase productivity, it will very well lead the importing firm into export markets. That is why successful two-way traders tend to be the most productive firms on average (Andersson et al., 2008; Castellani et al., 2010; Muuls & Pisu, 2009; Altomonte & Békés, 2010). Hence, the conclusion below follows:

Proposition 12.3 In terms of productivity, all firms in any one regional economy can be placed in the following descending order: Two-way (import and export) traders, one-way players (either import or export), and domestic firms.

12.5.2 Relationship Between Employee Wages and Trades in Foreign Market

Based on what has been discussed in Sect. 12.5.1 we can generally conclude that exporters tend to be more productive than domestic firms even before the former enter export markets for the reason that they need to muster sufficient financial resources to cover the sunk costs that domestic firms do not ever have to worry about. So, we can assume collectively (not individually) that exporters have more financial resources than do domestic firms at least during those several years prior to their entry into export markets.

Theorem 12.5 If a firm is well funded, assuming all other aspects of the business operation stay the same, then

1. The market demand for the firm's product increases as the unit selling price drops close to the unit cost basis, while the total profits increase drastically; and
2. The firm will hire additional employees at higher than competitive wage rates and better benefits with the total profits soaring.

For the technical proof of this result, see the appendix of this chapter. Here the systemic intuition behind the profit function and the staffing need function of Firm A, a "would-be" or successful exporter (or Eqs. (12.2) and (12.5) in the appendix of this chapter) is that beside the fact that products of Firm A generate profits, other main stakeholders of the firm also more or less and directly or indirectly contribute to the profits making.

Let Firm B be a non-exporter that produces only one product that is horizontally differentiated with that produced by Firm A. Then the analysis in the appendix of this chapter under the title of "Analysis of a Non-Exporter" indicates that to expand the market demand, Firm B has to decrease its unit selling price, Eq. (12.8). Because its financial resources are limited, Firm B has a limited ability to invest in its product. That is, Firm B cannot afford to compete with Firm A that has way more resources. Similar to the situation of Firm A, Firm B can also increase its profits by reducing its selling price (p_s^{Bp}), if it can keep the unit profit $\left(p_s^{Bp} - p_p^{Bp}\right)$ constant. However, unlike the case with Firm A, the level of profits for Firm B is capped (at $n^{Bp}\left(p_{s_0}^{Bp}\right)p_{s_0}^{Bp}$, Eq. (12.10)). A comparison between Firms A and B, we can see the following:

1. While Firm A is promoting its product to expand its market share and appearance, Firm B cannot afford to devote much of its scarce resources to do so. One reason

is that it does not have much money to allocate for the purpose of promotion. And another reason is that, as Eq. (12.10) indicates, an excessive amount of spending will keep its unit selling price (p_s^{Bp}) high. So, to increase its profits, Firm B has to control its spending so that its profits can be maximized by lowering its unit selling price (p_s^{Bp}).

2. While Firm A is placing large orders at much reduced wholesale price, Firm B just cannot take such opportunities. Similarly, other volume-related savings are not available to Firm B.

And, to hire more employees, Firm B has to lower the average expected per-worker revenue, as indicated by Eq. (12.9). Because of its limited financial resources, this result implies that Firm B has to limit how many workers it can afford to hire. To maximize its profits in the dimension of human resources, Eq. (12.10) implies that $p_s^{Bw} \gg p_p^{Bw}$ must hold true. So, for Firm B, it can either hire a relatively large number of employees at low wage rates or hire a relatively small number of high-quality employees at a relatively high wage rates. For the latter to occur, the employees' productivity has to be very high, which in general means that Firm B needs to invest a great deal in technology that needs to be constantly updated. And this end may not be possible due to Firm B's limited financial resources. That is, the high-quality employee option may never be practically possible for Firm B to take.

By comparing Eqs. (12.6) and (12.10), the following results can be seen:

1. Firm A can spend extra money on employees' retraining programs to lower the average per-employee cost basis p_p^{Aw}, while Firm B cannot. This is because in the latter case, extra spending on employees' training programs increase both p_s^{Bw}- and p_p^{Bw}-values. So, the ratio p_p^{Bw}/p_s^{Bw} may not change in the favorable direction to Firm B. (Parallel to this conclusion is that Firm A can drastically reduce the average per-employee costs basis by simply engaging in outward foreign direct investments, which can very possibly involve investments in capital goods).
2. Similar reasoning indicates that Firm A can afford to invest in programs that make its employees feel good and to raise employee morale, while Firm B cannot afford such luxuries. Consequently, employees of Firm A produce more than those of Firm B.
3. While Firm A hires a larger number of employees so that it can easily reduce its per-employee benefits costs, Firm B with fewer employees has to pay the inflated market prices for the same benefit packages. That is, volume savings are not available to Firm B.

This analysis explains why in a firm, if one occupation is highly paid, so are all other occupations. In particular, if one occupation is paid at a level above the competitive wage rate, then all other occupations within the firm, including those playing supporting roles, will most likely be also paid at levels above their corresponding competitive wage rates. The increased productivity from the central occupation will be more than enough to finance the supporting occupations so that their respective wages are higher than those occupations' competitive market rates. For a relevant study and the literature on inter-industry wage differentials, see Lin (2009).

Now, let us look at the relationship between international trade and employee wages. From Theorem 12.5, it follows that if we look at successful exporters of all sizes from economies at different developmental stages, they will tend to pay higher wages and better benefits than those of non-exporters (Bernard & Jensen, 1995; 1999; Schank et al., 2007; 2010; Serti et al., 2010). It needs to be emphasized that for this conclusion to hold true, the key words are "successful exporters." Since not all exporters are successful and not all successful exporters are financially resourceful at all times (Theorems 12.3 and 12.4), what is developed above only holds true for "successful exporters."

12.5.3 Relationship Between a Firm's Survival and Trades in Foreign Market

In this subsection, we consider the following two questions:

Question 12.1 Does the productivity advantage of firms involved in international trade lead to a profitability advantage for these firms when compared to otherwise identical domestic firms even though international firms incur extra costs and pay higher wages?

Question 12.2 Would firms involved in international trades be more likely to survive as a business compared to those that are domestic-only firms?

It is clear that profitability has to be supported by productivity. However, productivity is only one of several possible idiosyncratic factors that determine profits (Foster et al., 2008). In other words, the success of firms in general depends directly on profitability instead of productivity. This explains the importance of Question 12.1.

Based on Theorems 12.3 and 12.4 and the discussion in Sect. 12.5.1, it can be concluded that as long as the conditions of export markets and relevant exchange rates stay constant, then yes, the productivity advantage of firms involved in international trade naturally leads to profitability advantage over identical domestic firms. However, conditions of the export markets can change for the worse, exchange rates can and do fluctuate in unfavorable directions, and damaging events can break out unexpectedly at the height of international politics. Therefore, originally profitable operations can easily and quickly turn into losing propositions. This explains why empirical studies on Question 12.1 have been mixed without any definite conclusion (Wagner, 2012b).

On the other hand, by comparing Theorems 12.3 and 12.4, one can see clearly that exporting into less developed foreign markets can more likely turn productivity advantage into profitability advantage. It is because the sunk costs of exporting into

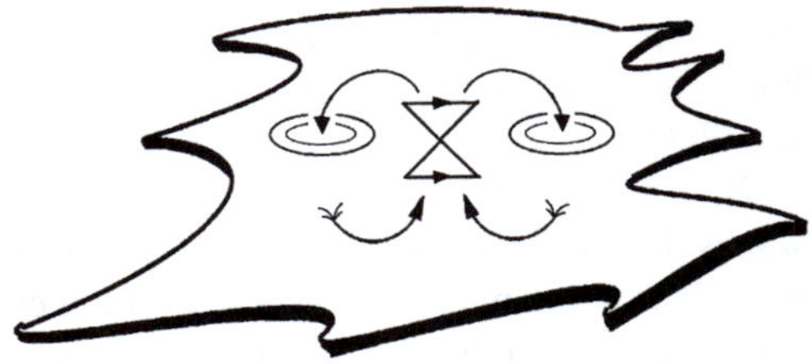

Fig. 12.2 A domestic firm

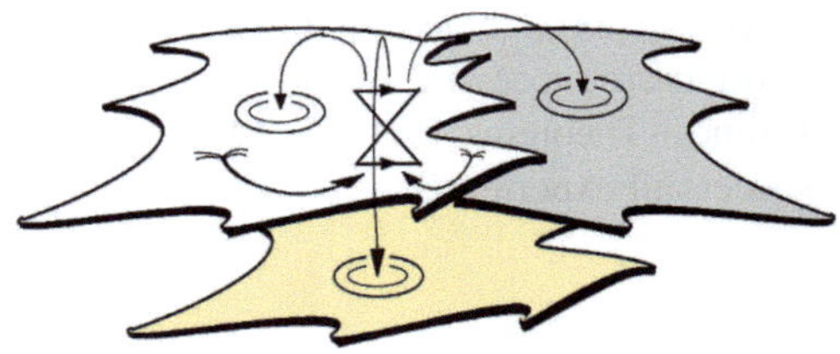

Fig. 12.3 An exporting only firm

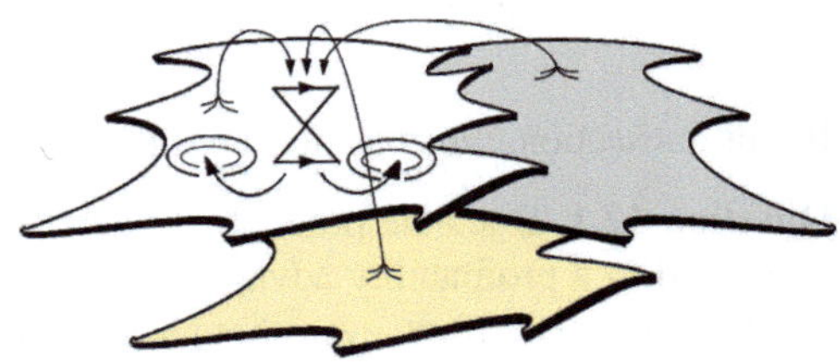

Fig. 12.4 An importing only firm

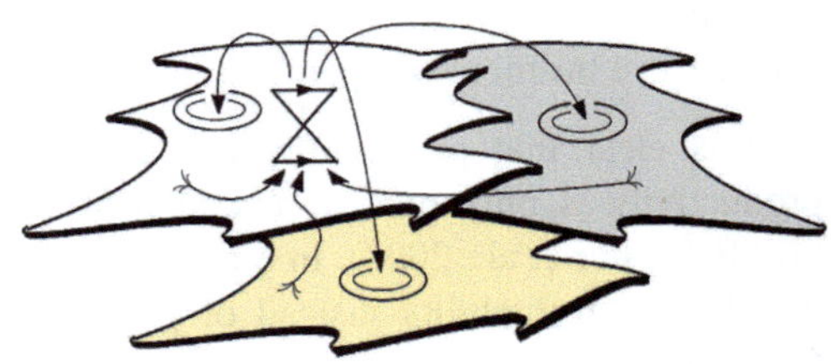

Fig. 12.5 An importing and exporting firm

such markets can be more easily covered, while the effect of the naturally built-in brand name can be employed to amplify the magnitude of profits. On the other hand, exporting into advanced markets does not naturally carry any built-in advantages other than facing intensified competition and rising costs. This end in fact is well confirmed by Wagner's empirical study (Wagner, 2012a, b, 2016), where data from manufacturing enterprises of Germany show that any productivity advantages of international trading firms are eaten up by extra costs related to selling and buying in foreign markets.

To address Question 12.2, let us model a firm as an abstract yoyo, because each firm is an input–output system. Then we have one of the four scenarios shown in Figs. 12.2, 12.3, 12.4, and 12.5. Specifically, in Fig. 12.2 the abstract firm is seen as the spinning yoyo with its inputs from the domestic market and its outputs provided to the same market, where the curved arrows represent how the outputs of the firm are offered to the domestic market, while various inputs are drawn from the same market.

Figure 12.3 depicts how the firm acquires its supplies from the domestic market. At the same time, other than selling its offers to the domestic market, the firm also sells its products to two overseas markets, where the foreign markets are the shaded areas. As shown in Fig. 12.2, the curved arrows stand for the directions about how inputs and outputs of the firm move.

Continuing the conventions in Figs. 12.2 and 12.3, and 12.4 the firm sells its products in the domestic market only, while it imports at least some of its inputs from foreign markets.

Similarly, Fig. 12.5 depicts how the firm acquires inputs and sells outputs internationally and domestically. By comparing this figurative description of a more globalized market to what is ongoing in the business world, it can be seen that when any of the curved input trajectories is broken, the established routine of operation of the firm will be disrupted. The worst situation will be that the firm is run out of business, because its production can no longer continue, while its markets are blocked. The best scenario will be that all foreign supplies can be substituted by domestic ones, while the domestic market is large enough to absorb the lost foreign markets. In other words, Fig. 12.5 provides an intuition for politicians to either strengthen the international trades or interrupt an existing international business order.

For an input–output system to be stable there must be enough market forces to maintain the system so that both inputs and outputs of the system will be in equilibrium (Lin, 1999). And for a spinning yoyo field to sustain itself there must be sufficient unevenness in the "material" distribution in the field of the yoyo body and the surrounding areas so that appropriate supplies are absorbed into the field and that abundant products are produced out of the field (Lin, 2009). Hence, the domestic firm in Fig. 12.2 and the multinational firm in Fig. 12.5 are most stable, while the firm in export markets in Fig. 12.3 is least stable depending on how long the domestic resources and supply of the firm can afford to sustain the international consumption, assuming all other conditions stay constant.

As for the difference between the domestic firm in Fig. 12.2 and the firm with multinational exchange in Fig. 12.5, because the latter is expected to experience more challenges than the former, that is, there is more unevenness in the "material" distribution in the yoyo field of the firm in Fig. 12.5 than that of the domestic firm in Fig. 12.2, if all other conditions stay constant, the latter firm is expected to enjoy a longer life span than the domestic firm. In the terminology of business, firms involved in both imports and exports diversify their sales over different markets that have different business cycle conditions and/or in different phases of the product life cycle (Wagner, 2013), and enjoys the benefit of combining the relative price and technology embodied in the imported products (Gibson & Graciano, 2011). Consequently, firms involved in both imports and exports spread their risk while increasing their price and non-price competitiveness when compared to domestic firms. Additionally, based on the discussion in Sect. 12.5.1, as domestic firms are generally less efficient in terms of productivity and management than firms with international reach, one can expect that the former are more likely to fail than the latter (Baldwin & Yan, 2011, p.135).

As for the firm in Fig. 12.3, which exports only, although it is the least stable among the four kinds of firms, the instability can potentially occur any moment when the national resources are drained over an exhaustively long-time span. So, in the foreseeable future within which the supply of the needed resources is abundant, this firm is expected to do better than the domestic firm in Fig. 12.2, because the export markets expand the magnitude of the domestic market (Theorems 12.3 and 12.4) and help to diversify the risk of the domestic market.

As for the firm in Fig. 12.4, which imports only, although it is not as stable as those firms in Figs. 12.2 and 12.5, it is more stable than the firm in Fig. 12.3. It is because the input–output yoyo field in Fig. 12.4 always has abundant supplies (inputs), which can include capital, talents, better priced inputs, advanced technology, etc.

Based on what has been discussed above, the proposition below follows:

Proposition 12.4 Assume that all other conditions remain constant. Then the probability for firms involved in two-way trades to survive is expected to be the highest, followed by firms that only import, then firms that only export, and finally domestic firms.

This result is also empirically shown in parts by Wagner (2013), Gibson and Graciano (2011), Vogel and Wagner (2010), López (2006), and Namini et al. (2011).

12.6 A Few Final Words

Recent theoretical or empirical studies on international trade and firm performance have enriched the knowledge on these related issues. Empirical works help uncover potential facts that hold true over space and time, while theoretical investigations confirm among the potential facts which are truly facts and which are not, and provide capabilities for policy decision makers to reason beyond what available data are telling. Considering what has been established in the literature both theoretically and empirically, this chapter introduces systemic thinking and the systemic yoyo model into the literature. Consequently, we are able to confirm in theory the following big picture:

- Exporters and importers are more productive than non-exporters and non-importers, and that is true even in years prior to their start of exporting or importing;
- The number of export markets served increases with the firm's productivity, and exporters to more developed economies have superior ex ante productivity levels than non-exporters and firms exporting to less developed countries;

- Domestic firms are the least productive group, followed by firms that export and by firms that engage in outward foreign direct investment;
- Firms involved in exports and/or imports tend to be more profitable and pay higher wages and benefits than domestic firms; and
- The probability for firms involved in two-way trades to survive is expected to be the highest, followed by firms that only import, then firms that only export, and then domestic firms, assuming all other conditions stay constant.

Although the first three conditions stated above were supported by a large number of empirical studies using data from different countries, previous works suffered from the absence of a reasonably high degree of comparability due to differences in the unit of analysis (establishment vs. enterprise), the sampling frame (all firms versus only firms with a number of employees above a certain threshold only), the specification of the empirical models estimated, and the econometric methods applied, as pointed out by Wagner (2012a, b).

The present work is able to fill in voids in the literature where empirical studies are lacking due to unavailability of suitable data or in some cases inconsistent empirical conclusions were discovered (Silva et al., 2012). For example, this chapter confirms the presence of the effect of learning by exporting (and learning by importing), while pointing out the fact that exporting/importing does not necessarily improve the involved firms in general.

What is established in Sect. 12.5 helps clarify some of the empirical research topics regarding firms' survival. For example, one important topic for future research will be: Under what conditions will the given order of firms' survival in Proposition 10.1 be reversed?

The bottom line here is that by employing systemic thinking and the systemic yoyo model, we were able to develop a general theory on international trade and firm performance. Additionally, the theory also points to subareas where further empirical and theoretical studies are needed to uncover finer details.

Before we conclude this chapter, let us make a last remark. In the two sets of different symbolic modellings of the product markets, either domestic or foreign, developed in this chapter, the demand side does not have to be made of households, although it seems to be throughout the previous sections, because the not-specified consumers (or buyers) can also be profit-maximizing firms as long as they make purchases. In other words, our models developed here also naturally cover the large and increasing share of exports and imports of intermediate goods that are part of international value chains.

As for limitations of this presentation, they are related to the implicit assumption employed throughout this chapter: firms strive to succeed in the product marketplace. As a matter of fact, in the business world, not all firms are established in such ways. So, this fact opens up a large territory and space for future explorations.

Appendix: Proofs of Results

The Proof of Theorem 12.3 For local Firm *i*, its objective function is

$$\max_{F_i(P)} E(\Pi_i) = (1-r)\int_0^1 \left\{\alpha P + \prod\nolimits_{j\neq i}^{m}[1-F_j(P)]\beta P\right\} dF_i(P)$$

with the equilibrium indifference condition being

$$\alpha \times P + \beta \times P \prod\nolimits_{j\neq i}^{m} (1-P)\left[1-F_j(P)\right] = \alpha \times 1.$$

So, the symmetric equilibrium pricing strategy is

$$F(P) = 1 - \left(\frac{\alpha}{\beta P}\right)^{\frac{1}{m-1}},$$

which is defined only for $1 \geq P \geq \alpha/\beta$. Now, the expected profits of the exporting firm are

$$E[\Pi] = \int\limits_{\alpha/\beta}^{1} rkPdP = \frac{rk}{2}\left(1 - \frac{\alpha^2}{\beta^2}\right),$$

which is positive only when $\beta = 1 - m\alpha > \alpha$.

The Proof of Corollary 12.1 The expected profits $E[\Pi]$ of the exporting firm will be equal to $k\beta Q$, for $0 < Q < P$, where P is the price at which local firms sell their products and Q the price the exporting firm charges.

The Proof of Theorem 12.4 From $\beta = 1 - m\alpha \geq \alpha$, it follows that $\alpha/\beta \leq 1$. So, for any price P, satisfying $\alpha/\beta \leq P \leq 1$, the following function $F(P)$:

$$F(P) = 1 - \left(\frac{\alpha}{\beta P}\right)^{\frac{1}{m-1}}, \tag{12.1}$$

represents a well-defined strategy for each of the m local firms existing in the foreign market of concern. It satisfies the following equilibrium indifference condition of Firm i, $i = 1, 2, \ldots, m$,

$$\alpha \times P + \beta \times P \prod\nolimits_{j\neq i}^{m} (1-P)\left[1-F_j(P)\right] = \alpha \times 1,$$

which implies that for the m incumbent firms in the foreign market, their lowest allowed price is α/β.

Next, we show that there is such an opportunity that the exporting firm can expect to make at least as much revenues as α in the said foreign market. To this end, Eq. (12.1) implies that

$$\lim_{P \to 1^-} F(P) = 1 - (\alpha/\beta)^{\frac{1}{m-1}} \neq F(1) = 1.$$

So, the cumulative price distribution function $F(P)$ has a jump discontinuity at the reservation value $P = 1$, where the amount of jump is $(\alpha/\beta)^{\frac{1}{m-1}}$. So, the expected revenue of the exporting firm in the said foreign market is the following:

$$\begin{aligned} E(\Pi) &= \int_0^{\alpha/\beta} \beta P dP + \int_{\alpha/\beta}^{+\infty} \beta P[1 - F(P)]^m dP \\ &= \int_0^{\alpha/\beta} \beta P dP + \int_{\alpha/\beta}^{1} \beta P[1 - F(P)]^m dP + \beta\left(\frac{\alpha}{\beta}\right)^{\frac{m}{m-1}} \\ &= \begin{cases} \dfrac{-m}{2(m-2)} \dfrac{\alpha^2}{\beta} + \dfrac{m-1}{m-2} \dfrac{\alpha^{\frac{m}{m-1}}}{\beta^{\frac{1}{m-1}}} + \beta\left(\dfrac{\alpha}{\beta}\right)^{\frac{m}{m-1}}, & \text{if } m \geq 3 \\ \dfrac{\alpha^2}{2\beta} - \dfrac{\alpha^2}{\beta} \ln \dfrac{\alpha}{\beta} + \beta\left(\dfrac{\alpha}{\beta}\right)^{\frac{m}{m-1}}, & \text{if } m = 2 \end{cases} \end{aligned}$$

And because $\frac{\partial}{\partial \alpha}[E(\Pi) - \alpha] > 0$ and when $\alpha = 1/(m+1) = \beta$, $E(\Pi) - \alpha > 0$, it follows that there is $\alpha_\Pi^* \in (0, 1/(m+1))$ such that when $\alpha \geq \alpha_\Pi^*$, $E(\Pi) > \alpha$. Therefore, there is an opportunity when the expected profits of the exporting firm in the said foreign market are at least as much as (α – sunk costs) by uniformly randomizing its price P over the interval [0,1].

The Proof of Theorem 12.5 Let Firm A be a "would-be" or successful exporter and Firm B a non-exporter. Assume that each of them produces only one product. Then the profits of each firm i (= A, B) from the product are given by

$$P^{\text{ip}} = n^{\text{ip}}\left(p_{\text{s}}^{\text{ip}}\right)\left(p_{\text{s}}^{\text{ip}} - p_{\text{p}}^{\text{ip}}\right), \tag{12.2}$$

where p_{s}^{ip} is the unit selling price, p_{p}^{ip} the total unit cost, and $n^{\text{ip}}\left(p_{\text{s}}^{\text{ip}}\right)$ the number of units sold at price p_{s}^{ip}.

For Firm A, its market demand for its product is given as follows by maximizing Eq. (12.2):

$$n^{\text{Ap}}\left(p_{\text{s}}^{\text{Ap}}\right) = n^{\text{Ap}}\left(p_{\text{s}_0}^{\text{Ap}}\right) \frac{p_{\text{s}_0}^{\text{Ap}} - p_{\text{p}}^{\text{Ap}}}{p_{\text{s}}^{\text{Ap}} - p_{\text{p}}^{\text{Ap}}} \text{ (units)}, \tag{12.3}$$

where $n^{\mathrm{Ap}}\left(p_{\mathrm{s_0}}^{\mathrm{Ap}}\right)$ is the initial market demand at the initial selling price $p_{\mathrm{s_0}}^{\mathrm{Ap}}$. And the profits are

$$P^{\mathrm{Ap}} = n^{\mathrm{Ap}}\left(p_{\mathrm{s_0}}^{\mathrm{Ap}}\right)\left(p_{\mathrm{s_0}}^{\mathrm{Ap}} - p_{\mathrm{p}}^{\mathrm{Ap}}\right). \tag{12.4}$$

So, as the sales price $p_{\mathrm{s}}^{\mathrm{Ap}}$ lowers to the cost $p_{\mathrm{p}}^{\mathrm{Ap}}$, the demand approaches infinity. If $\left(p_{\mathrm{s_0}}^{\mathrm{Ap}} - p_{\mathrm{p}}^{\mathrm{Ap}}\right)$ stays constant, then the lower the sales price $p_{\mathrm{s}}^{\mathrm{Ap}}$ $\left(> p_{\mathrm{p}}^{\mathrm{Ap}}\right)$, the greater the demand $n^{\mathrm{Ap}}\left(p_{\mathrm{s}}^{\mathrm{Ap}}\right)$, and the greater the total profits P^{Ap}.

Similarly, Firm A's staffing need is given by

$$n^{\mathrm{Aw}}\left(p_{\mathrm{s}}^{\mathrm{Aw}}\right) = n^{\mathrm{Aw}}\left(p_{\mathrm{s_0}}^{\mathrm{Aw}}\right)\frac{p_{\mathrm{s_0}}^{\mathrm{Aw}} - p_{\mathrm{p}}^{\mathrm{Aw}}}{p_{\mathrm{s}}^{\mathrm{Aw}} - p_{\mathrm{p}}^{\mathrm{Aw}}} \text{ (persons)} \tag{12.5}$$

and the total profits from hiring $n^{\mathrm{Aw}}\left(p_{\mathrm{s}}^{\mathrm{Aw}}\right)$ are

$$P^{\mathrm{Aw}} = n^{\mathrm{Aw}}\left(p_{\mathrm{s_0}}^{\mathrm{Aw}}\right)\left(p_{\mathrm{s_0}}^{\mathrm{Aw}} - p_{\mathrm{p}}^{\mathrm{Aw}}\right), \tag{12.6}$$

where $n^{\mathrm{Aw}}\left(p_{\mathrm{s_0}}^{\mathrm{Aw}}\right)$ stands for the firm's initial need for additional staffing to be hired at the initial expected revenue $p_{\mathrm{s_0}}^{\mathrm{Aw}}$ per employee, $p_{\mathrm{p}}^{\mathrm{Aw}}$ the per-employee cost, and $p_{\mathrm{s}}^{\mathrm{Aw}}$ the ongoing expected revenue generated by an employee.

Equations (12.5) and (12.6) imply that when the difference $\left(p_{\mathrm{s}}^{\mathrm{Aw}} - p_{\mathrm{p}}^{\mathrm{Aw}}\right)$ decreases, the need for more employees increase and the profits generated by the employees grow. Now, $\left(p_{\mathrm{s}}^{\mathrm{Aw}} - p_{\mathrm{p}}^{\mathrm{Aw}}\right) \to 0$ implies that when the $p_{\mathrm{s}}^{\mathrm{Aw}}$-value is relatively stable, $p_{\mathrm{p}}^{\mathrm{Aw}}$ will be increased as much as possible. That is, employees' wages and benefits can go up so that the total per-employee cost can approach the expected per-employee revenue $p_{\mathrm{s}}^{\mathrm{Aw}}$ as much as possible.

When the $p_{\mathrm{p}}^{\mathrm{Aw}}$-value increases, the per-unit product cost $p_{\mathrm{p}}^{\mathrm{Ap}}$ will also rise accordingly. But Eqs. (12.3) and (12.4) indicate that as long as the difference $\left(p_{\mathrm{s_0}}^{\mathrm{Ap}} - p_{\mathrm{p}}^{\mathrm{Ap}}\right)$ does not change much while $\left(p_{\mathrm{s}}^{\mathrm{A}} - p_{\mathrm{p}}^{\mathrm{A}}\right)$ drops, the total profits from the product will continue to go higher. That is, this analysis shows that Theorem 12.5 holds true.

Analysis of a Non-exporter For Firm B, assume that it is of limited financial resources. In this case, its profits are given by the following:

$$P_{\mathrm{total}}^{\mathrm{B}} = P^{\mathrm{Bp}} + P^{\mathrm{Bw}} = n^{\mathrm{Bp}}\left(p_{\mathrm{s}}^{\mathrm{Bp}}\right)\left(p_{\mathrm{s}}^{\mathrm{Bp}} - p_{\mathrm{p}}^{\mathrm{Bp}}\right) + n^{\mathrm{Bw}}\left(p_{\mathrm{s}}^{\mathrm{Bw}}\right)\left(p_{\mathrm{s}}^{\mathrm{Bw}} - p_{\mathrm{p}}^{\mathrm{Bw}}\right)$$

subject to the budget constraint

$$n^{\mathrm{Bp}}\left(p_{\mathrm{s}}^{\mathrm{Bp}}\right)p_{\mathrm{p}}^{\mathrm{Bp}}+n^{\mathrm{Bw}}\left(p_{\mathrm{s}}^{\mathrm{Bw}}\right)p_{\mathrm{p}}^{\mathrm{Bw}}=I \tag{12.7}$$

where I stands for the total financial resources available to Firm B. By maximizing this problem, we establish the following results:

$$n^{\mathrm{Bp}}\left(p_{\mathrm{s}}^{\mathrm{B}}\right)=\frac{n_{\mathrm{p}}^{\mathrm{Bp}}\left(p_{\mathrm{s_0}}^{\mathrm{Bp}}\right)p_{\mathrm{s_0}}^{\mathrm{Bp}}}{p_{\mathrm{s}}^{\mathrm{Bp}}} \tag{12.8}$$

$$n^{\mathrm{Bw}}\left(p_{\mathrm{s}}^{\mathrm{Bw}}\right)=\frac{n^{\mathrm{Bw}}\left(p_{\mathrm{s_0}}^{\mathrm{Bw}}\right)p_{\mathrm{s_0}}^{\mathrm{Bw}}}{p_{\mathrm{s}}^{\mathrm{Bw}}} \tag{12.9}$$

and

$$P_{\mathrm{total}}^{\mathrm{B}}=n^{\mathrm{Bp}}\left(p_{\mathrm{s_0}}^{\mathrm{Bp}}\right)p_{\mathrm{s_0}}^{\mathrm{Bp}}\left(1-\frac{p_{\mathrm{p}}^{\mathrm{Bp}}}{p_{\mathrm{s}}^{\mathrm{Bp}}}\right)+n^{\mathrm{Bw}}\left(p_{\mathrm{s_0}}^{\mathrm{Bw}}\right)p_{\mathrm{s_0}}^{\mathrm{Bw}}\left(1-\frac{p_{\mathrm{p}}^{\mathrm{Bw}}}{p_{\mathrm{s}}^{\mathrm{Bw}}}\right), \tag{12.10}$$

where $p_{\mathrm{s_0}}^{\mathrm{Bp}}$, $n^{\mathrm{Bp}}\left(p_{\mathrm{s_0}}^{\mathrm{Bp}}\right)$, $p_{\mathrm{s_0}}^{\mathrm{Bw}}$, and $n^{\mathrm{Bw}}\left(p_{\mathrm{s_0}}^{\mathrm{Bw}}\right)$ are defined similarly as in the analysis of Firm A above.

References

Altomonte, C., & Békés, G. (2010, September). *Trade complexity and productivity* (CeFiG Working Papers 12).

Andersson, M., Lööf, H., & Johansson, S. (2008). Productivity and international trade: Firm level evidence from a small open economy. *Review of World Economics, 144*, 774–801.

Arkolakis, C., & Muendler, M. A. (2013). Exporters and their products: A collection of empirical regularities. *CESifo Economic Studies, 59*(2), 223–248.

Baldwin, R. E., & Robert-Nicoud, F. (2004). *The impact of trade on intraindustry reallocations and aggregate industry productivity: A comment* (NBER Working Paper Series, 10718).

Baldwin, J., & Yan, B. L. (2011). The death of Canadian manufacturing plants: Heterogeneous responses to changes in tariffs and real exchange rates. *Review of World Economics, 147*, 131–167.

Bastos, P., & Dias, D. A. (2013). *The life cycle of exporting firms*. Mimeo.

Békés, G., & Muraközy, B. (2012). Temporary trade and heterogeneous firms. *Journal of International Economics, 87*, 232–246.

Bernard, A. B., & Jensen, J. B. (1995). Exporters, jobs, and wages in U.S. manufacturing: 1976–1987. *Brookings Papers on Economic Activity, Microeconomics* (pp. 67–119).

Bernard, A. B., & Jensen, J. B. (1999). Exceptional exporter performance: Cause, effect, or both? *Journal of International Economics, 47*, 1–25.

Bernard, A. B., & Wagner, J. (1997). Exports and success in German manufacturing. *Weltwirtschaftliches Archiv, 133*, 134–157.

Bernard, A. B., Eaton, J., Jensen, J. B., & Kortum, S. S. (2003). Plants and productivity in international trade. *American Economic Review, 93*(4), 1268–1290.

Bernard, A. B., Jensen, J. B., Redding, S. J., & Schott, P. K. (2007a). Firms in international trade. *Journal of Economic Perspectives, 21*(3), 105–130.

Bernard, A. B., Redding, S. J., & Schott, P. K. (2007b). Comparative advantage and heterogeneous firms. *Review of Economic Studies, 74*, 31–66.

Bernard, A. B., Jensen, J. B., & Schott, P. K. (2009). Importers, exporters, and multinationals: A portrait of firms in the U.S. that trade goods. In T. Dunne, J. B. Jensen, & M. J. Roberts (Eds.), *Producer dynamics: New evidence from micro data*. University of Chicago Press.

Bernard, A. B., Moxnes, A., & Ulltveit-Moe, K. H. (2013). *Two-sided heterogeneity and trade*. Mimeo.

Bernard, A. B., Beveren, I. V., & Vandenbussche, H. (2014). Multi-product exporters and the margins of trade. *Japanese Economic Review, 65*(2), 142–157.

Blum, B. S., Claro, S., & Horstmann, I. J. (2013). Occasional and perennial exporters. *Journal of International Economics, 90*(1), 65–74.

Buono, I., & Fadinger, H. (2012). The micro dynamics of exporting: Evidence from French firms. *Banca D'Italia Temi di Discussione*, Number 880.

Casas, C., Díez, F. J., & González, A. (2015). Productivity and export market participation: Evidence from Colombia. *Banco de la Republica Colombia, Borradores de Economía*, Núm. 876.

Castellani, D., Serti, F., & Tomasi, C. (2010). Firms in international trade: Importers' and exporters' heterogeneity in the Italian manufacturing industry. *The World Economy, 33*, 424–457.

Eaton, J., Kortum, S., & Kramarz, F. (2004). Dissecting trade: Firms, industries, and export destinations. *American Economic Review Papers & Proceedings, 94*(2), 150–154.

Eriksson, T., Smeets, V., & Warzynski, F. (2009). *Small open economy firms in international trade: Evidence from Danish transactions-level data* (Aarhus University Department of Economics Working Paper 09-7).

Forrest, J. Y. L., & Anderson, M. (2017). Customers' indecisiveness: A pricing strategy approach. *Pennsylvania Economic Review, 24*(2), 46–64.

Forrest, J. Y. L., Trebing, M. E., Chatterjee, A., & Wagner, J. (2019). Domestic firms, exporters and importers: A systemic perspective. *Theoretical Economics Letters, 9*, 649–674.

Foster, L., Haltiwanger, J., & Syverson, C. (2008). Reallocation, firm turnover, and efficiency: Selection on productivity or profitability? *American Economic Review, 98*, 394–425.

Freund, C., & Pierola, M. D. (2012). *Export superstars* (The World Bank Policy Research Working Paper 6222).

Gibson, M. J., & Graciano, T. A. (2011). *Costs of starting to trade and costs of continuing to trade*. Washington State University.

Halpern, L., & Muraközy, B. (2012). Innovation, productivity and exports: The case of Hungary. *Economics of Innovation and New Technology, 21*(2), 151–173.

ISGEP (International Study Group on Exports and Productivity). (2008). Understanding cross-country differences in exporter premia: Comparable evidence for 14 countries. *Review of World Economics, 144*, 596–635.

Kasahara, H., & Lapham, B. (2013). Productivity and the decision to import and export: Theory and evidence. *Journal of International Economics, 89*, 297–316.

Lin, Y. (1999). *General systems theory: A mathematical approach*. Plenum and Kluwer Academic Publishers.

Lin, Y. (2009). *Systemic yoyos: Some impacts of the second dimension*. Auerbach Publication.

Lin, Y., & OuYang, S. C. (2010). *Irregularities and prediction of major disasters*. CRC Press.

López, R. A. (2006). Imports of intermediate inputs and plant survival. *Economics Letters, 92*, 58–62.

Manova, K., & Zhang, Z. W. (2009). *China's exporters and importers: Firms, products and trade partners* (National Bureau of Economic Research NBER Working Paper Series 15249).

McGrath, R. G. (2013). *The end of competitive advantage: How to keep your strategy moving as fast as your business*. Harvard Business Review Press.

Melitz, M. J. (2003). The impact of trade on intra-industry reallocations and aggregate industry productivity. *Econometrica, 71*, 1695–1725.

Melitz, M. J., & Redding, S. J. (2014). Heterogeneous firms and trade. *Handbook of International Economics, 4*, 1–54.

Muuls, M., & Pisu, M. (2009). Imports and exports at the level of the firm: Evidence from Belgium. *The World Economy, 32*, 692–734.

Namini, J. E., Facchini, G., & López, R. (2011). *Export growth and factor market competition: Theory and evidence*. Erasmus University.

Neary, J. P. (2010). Two and a half theories of trade. *The World Economy, 33*(1), 1–19.

Rahu, S. (2015). *The role of uncertainty for export survival: Evidence from Estonia* (The University of Tartu FEBA Working Paper).

Schank, T., Schnabel, C., & Wagner, J. (2007). Do exporters really pay higher wages? First evidence from German linked employer-employee data. *Journal of International Economics, 72*, 52–74.

Schank, T., Schnabel, C., & Wagner, J. (2010). Higher wages in exporting firms: Self-selection, export effect, or both? First evidence from linked employer-employee data. *Review of World Economics, 146*, 303–322.

Serti, F., Tomasi, C., & Zanfei, A. (2010). Who trades with whom? Exploring the links between firms' international activities, skills, and wages. *Review of International Economics, 18*, 951–971.

Silva, A., Africano, A. P., & Afonso, Ó. (2012). Learning-by-exporting: What we know and what we would like to know. *The International Trade Journal, 26*, 255–288.

Singh, T. (2010). Does international trade cause economic growth? A survey. *The World Economy, 33*, 1517–1564.

Sobel, R. (1999). *When giants stumble: Classic business blunders and how to avoid them*. Prentice Hall.

Vogel, A., & Wagner, J. (2010). Higher productivity in importing German manufacturing firms: Self-selection, learning from importing, or both. *Review of World Economics, 145*, 641–665.

Wagner, J. (2007a). Exports and productivity: A survey of the evidence from firm-level data. *The World Economy, 30*, 60–82.

Wagner, J. (2007b). Exports and productivity in Germany. *Applied Economics Quarterly, 53*, 353–373.

Wagner, J. (2008). Export entry, export exit and productivity in German manufacturing industries. *International Journal of the Economics of Business, 15*, 169–180.

Wagner, J. (2012a). International trade and firm performance: A survey of empirical studies since 2006. *Review of World Economics, 148*, 235–267.

Wagner, J. (2012b). Exports, imports and profitability: First evidence for manufacturing enterprises. *Open Economies Review, 23*, 747–765.

Wagner, J. (2012c). German multiple-product, multiple destination exporters: Bernard-Redding-Schott under test. *Economics Bulletin, 32*(2), 1708–1714.

Wagner, J. (2012d). Productivity and the extensive margins of trade in German manufacturing firms: Evidence from a non-parametric test. *Economics Bulletin, 32*(4), 3061–3070.

Wagner, J. (2013). Exports, imports and firm survival: First evidence for manufacturing enterprises in Germany. *Review of World Economics, 149*, 113–130.

Wagner, J. (2014a). Low-productive exporters are high-quality exporters: Evidence from Germany. *Economics Bulletin, 34*(2), 745–756.

Wagner, J. (2014b). Extensive margins of imports, productivity and profitability: First evidence for manufacturing enterprises in Germany. *Economics Bulletin, 34*(3), 1669–1678.

Wagner, J. (2014c). Is export diversification good for profitability? First evidence for manufacturing enterprises in Germany. *Applied Economics, 46*(33), 4083–4090.

Wagner, J. (2015). A note on firm age and the margins of exports: First evidence from Germany. *The International Trade Journal, 29*(2), 93–102.

Wagner, J. (2016). A survey of empirical studies using transaction level data on exports and imports. *Review of World Economics, 152*, 215–225.

Part IV
Management of Large-Scale Business Forces

Chapter 13
A Few Important Issues Regarding Child Labor

Jeffrey Yi-Lin Forrest and Dillon Forrest

Abstract This chapter investigates several issues related to a child's accumulation of human capital by focusing on three variables—child labor, formal schooling, and level of maturity. Due to the novelty of employing these variables, this chapter is able to establish some important results that are significantly different from all those works that do not consider possible interactions of these variables. Among others, this chapter shows that (a) as long as the child's disutility or utility of labor or formal schooling is concerned with, the laissez faire triple of child labor, formal schooling, and level of maturity, which maximizes the parents' utility function, can never be efficient; (b) if the parents are altruistic and save in period 1 and bequeath their wealth in period 2, or if the adult children are altruistic and transfer to their parents, then efficiencies of child labor, formal schooling, and level of maturity can be possibly achieved; and (c) if the child's feelings toward labor or formal schooling in period 1 matter, the inefficiencies of child labor, formal schooling, and level of maturity become unavoidable. To potentially reduce the severity of the inefficiency, it is suggested the government imposes a marginal ban on child labor and mandates a marginal increase in child's formal schooling.

Keywords Disutility · Formal schooling · Human capital · Level of maturity · Lifetime earnings · Poverty · Rotten parents · Transfer of wealth

---

Jeffrey Yi-Lin Forrest (Department of Accounting Economics Finance, Slippery Rock University, Slippery Rock, PA, USA; Email: Jeffrey.forrest@sru.edu) and Dillon Forrest (Steady Capital, LLC., Verona, NJ, USA; Email: dillon@steady.capital) are equally contributed to this chapter.

J. Y.-L. Forrest, *Systemic Principles of Applied Economic Philosophies II*, Translational Systems Sciences 39, https://doi.org/10.1007/978-981-99-7939-4_13

13.1 Introduction

This chapter shows how the systemic yoyo model (Chap. 2, or see Wu & Lin, 2002) and its methodology (see volume 1 or Lin, 2007) can be meaningfully employed to study problems on child labor in economics. What is new in this chapter from the mainstream literature in economics is that we look at various problems related to child labor as problems of (general) systems and spinning yoyos in the light of whole evolution of these systems (Lin, 1999).

Particular to this chapter, we now consider the situation that the rotten members of the family are the parents instead of the kids (Bommier & Dubois, 2004; Lin, 2009), so that the problem of child labor and its efficiency arises. Using the systemic yoyo model as a justification, this chapter, which is mainly based on Lin and Forrest (2008b), introduces three independent variables—child labor, formal schooling, and level of maturity—into the study of child labor. Then, it is shown that as long as children's disutility of labor or utility of labor or formal schooling is concerned, the laissez faire triple of child labor, formal schooling, and level of maturity, which maximizes the parents' utility function, can never be efficient. In particular, such a laissez faire triple is always inefficiently too high. Conversely, if the efficiency of parent's chosen (for their children) levels of child labor, formal schooling, and level of maturity is determined by the impact on the children's lifetime earnings potential, we can show:

1. The laissez faire triple of child labor, formal schooling, and level of maturity is efficient either if the parents' savings and bequests are interior when the capital markets are imperfect, or if the parents' bequests are interior and the capital markets are perfect. That is, all externalities of the parents' decision made for the children would be internalized by their interior transfers in terms of savings (if the capital markets are imperfect) and bequests in order for the children to obtain their optimal lifetime earnings.
2. When the capital markets are perfect, the laissez faire triple of child labor, formal schooling, and level of maturity is efficient if the adult child's transfers to his parents are interior and he lives on a fixed budget. This result implies that when the parents could borrow money in the capital markets, if the child lives below his means when he is an adult, then the parents' decision made for the child, when he was a kid, about the child's labor, formal schooling, and level of maturity, would be efficient in terms of the child's lifetime earnings potential. However, see number 3.
3. When the parents' bequests are at a corner or their savings are at a corner (if the capital markets are imperfect), the laissez faire triple of child labor, formal schooling, and level of maturity is inefficiently high.

To help resolve some of the inefficiencies, which cannot be resolved by individual families, we place family yoyos in a much mightier yoyo, representing the government. In this way, the spin field of the government yoyo forces families and individuals to modify their behaviors accordingly. In particular, if a government regulation is introduced to impose a marginal ban on child labor, then such a ban could be either welfare reducing for both the child and the parents or a Pareto improvement for both the child and the parents, under different sets of specific conditions.

This chapter is organized as follows: Sect. 13.2 provides the necessary preparation for the reader to go through the rest of this presentation smoothly. It consists of two subsections: one focusing on the literature review and the other the needed systemic intuitions and an example that points to the question this chapter addresses. Section 13.3 investigates child labor and work's disutility by considering one-sided altruism and the efficiency of child labor, formal education, and level of maturity. Section 13.4 examines how different definitions of efficiency can lead to different conclusions regarding the efficiency of child labor, formal education, and level of maturity. Section 13.5 studies various equilibrium effects of marginal ban on child labor, and how such a ban affects parents, child, and firms. And, the chapter is concluded in Sect. 13.6.

13.2 Preparations

This section prepares the reader to enjoy a smooth navigation through the rest of this presentation by providing (1) a literature review, and (2) a few motivations on why this work is important both theoretically and practically.

13.2.1 Literature Review

Studies on child labor represent the opposite of those on rotten kids (cf., Becker, 1991; Lin & Forrest, 2008b). The latter considers how selfish kids take advantage of the benevolence of parents, while the former looks at issues on how parents take advantages of their children by forcing them to bring income into the family (Bommier & Dubois, 2004; Lin, 2009).

The literature relevant to this chapter employs two kinds of models in terms of the concept of time. One kind of model involves only one period of time. During this single time period, the parents decide how they would mobilize their children for immediate financial gains without considering the lifelong consequences for the children and the parents themselves beyond the considered time period. For related details, see, for example, Basu and Van (1998) and Ravallion and Wodon (2000). Comparing these studies with what generally happens in real life, it can be readily seen that conclusions of these studies cannot be adequately applied to address most challenges facing those children who are forced to be laborers. It is because people, either in business or academia, know that the decision maker can only control what actions he takes without much or any control on what will follow next as reactions to what he does (Lin & Forrest, 2011).

Because of such weakness with the models involving only one time period, many scholars develop models with two time periods, during the first of which the children are little and cannot live on their own without support from certain adults, such as parents or caretakers. And during the second time period, the children who were little in the first time period are now adults who live independently from their parents and caretakers. Some of such improved studies include, for example, Baland and Robinson (2000), Bommier and Dubois (2004), Dessy (2000), Lin (2009), and Ranjan (2001). In comparison, this chapter adopts the approach with two time periods, as just described.

Other than theoretical investigations, it needs to be pointed out that child labor is an age-old phenomenon and represents some facet of poverty, as well established empirically, see, for example, Rosenzweig (1981), Labenne (1997), Chakraborty and Das (2005), Baland and Robinson (2000), while Bommier and Dubois (2004) establish a straightforward welfare argument to suggest that child labor can be inefficient. Corresponding to the estimate by the International Labor Organization (ILO, 1996) that worldwide 120 million children between the ages of 5–14 work fulltime, Krueger and Donohue (2005) examined the effects of child labor legislation on human capital accumulation and distribution of wealth and welfare. These authors find that (1) those households that hold significant amounts of financial assets unmistakably lose from any government intervention, (2) high-wage earners benefit most from a ban on child labor, while low-wage workers benefit the most from free education, and (3) a ban on child labor induces welfare losses because it reduces income opportunities for poor families without being effective in stimulating education attainment.

Related to these conclusions, Canagarajah and Coulombe (1997) state in their study of Ghana that "poverty is significantly correlated with the decision to send children to school, and there is a significant negative relationship between going to school and working." To the contrary, Weiner (1991, p. 195) reports, "In India the proprietors of large businesses have not opposed child-labor laws ... one of the complaints of managers of large firms is that their labor force is not sufficiently educated, that too many workers are unable to read manuals or follow the simple instructions written on machines." In terms of social and cognitive skills, Ennew (1982, p. 560) notes that "when relatively young children are forced to care for even younger siblings ... the old child loses the educational opportunity at school, but in addition the younger child may be prevented from developing sufficient verbal and conceptual skills to benefit from formal education." Facing such more or less controversial empirical literature about the effects of child labor, this chapter attempts to clear up such inconsistencies revealed by anecdotes and data analyses.

Regarding the transfer of wealth from the first time period to the second, Becker and Murphy (1988) and Nerlove et al. (1988) observe that nonnegativity constraints on bequests could lead to inefficiencies in the family's resource allocation. As for how the first period can be indirectly affecting the second period, it is noted (Bommier & Dubois, 2004) that childhood is often related to as the time when one had the largest amount of long-lasting memory of both positive and negative experiences. It is the childhood quality of life that has the greatest impact on the valuation of lifetime utility, even though childhood is only a small fraction of life. Also, during childhood, individuals acquire a large part of their human capital, which is a major determinant of the ability to raise lifetime earnings potential.

Comparing to the literature, this chapter uses models of two time periods to theoretically confirm some of the known conclusions established empirically, strengthen a few weakly stated results derived earlier by different scholars without considering child's disutility of work from period 1 and levels of maturity. For example, among others, although it is trade unions that have been influentially pushing for a ban on child labor in order to avoid the potential of depressing wages (Davin, 1982; Zelizer, 1994; Doepke & Zilibotti, 2005), this chapter shows that (1) a ban on child labor is not Pareto improving, and (2) if the laissez faire levels of child labor l_c^* or formal schooling e_c^* are not zero, then it leads to the rotten parents effect, as so named by Bommier and Dubois (2004). In other words, when the condition in (2) holds true, the parents will rationally sacrifice the childhood utility of their children by making them work and study beyond their limits. They anticipate that doing so will result in higher future earnings of the children and consequently larger transfers from the children.

In short, other than clearing up inconsistencies that exist in the relevant literature, this chapter provides a unified theory of child labor.

13.2.2 Interactions Between a Benevolent Parent and a Selfish Kid

To help make the rest of this chapter convenient to follow, assume that the family of concern has only two members, a benevolent head H and a selfish kid K. In this case, the interactions between the yoyo fields of these two people can be depicted in Fig. 13.1, where the benevolence of the head H is represented as a divergent whirlpool and the selfishness of the kid K as a convergent whirlpool. If both m_1 and m_2 stand for the voluntary money transfers from the head, the spin field of K in Fig. 13.1 will accept gift m_1 happily and transfer m_2 unwillingly or even reject such a monetary gift. Here, m_1 is given to the selfish kid K without violating his own

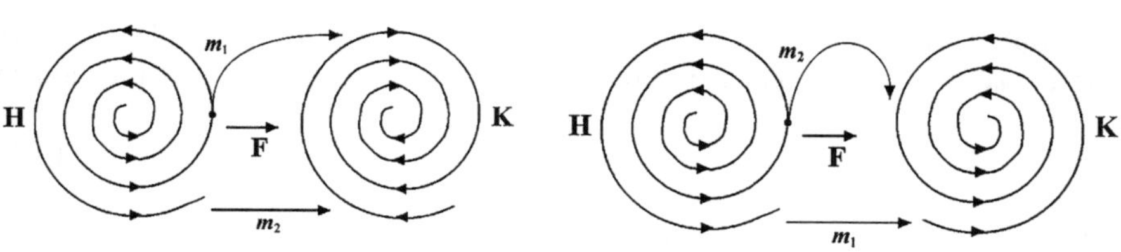

Fig. 13.1 Interactions between benevolent head H and a selfish kid K. Parts (**a**) and (**b**) respectively depict the situations of similar and dissimilar personalities of H and K

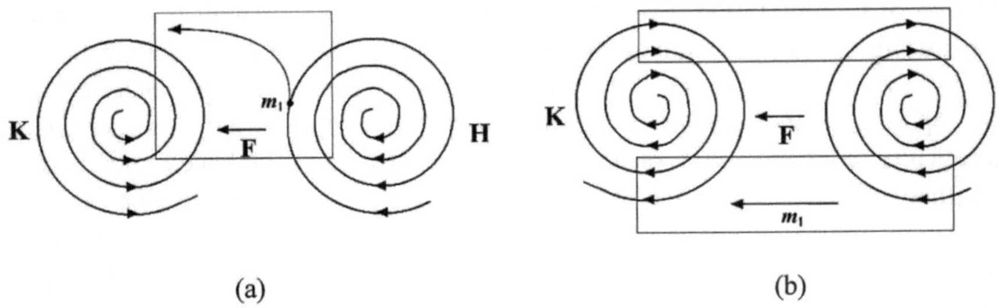

Fig. 13.2 Interactions of the other side of the head's and the kid's yoyo fields. Parts (**a**) and (**b**) respectively depict the situations of similar and dissimilar personalities of H and K

preference of consumption, while m_2 is forced on K against his will or personal preferences. That is the reason why in general Becker's rotten kid theorem does not hold true (Lin & Forrest, 2008a), where Becker's (1974) theorem states that if a family has a head who cares about all other members so much that he transfers his resources to them automatically, then any redistribution of the head's income among members of the household would not affect the consumption of any member, as long as the head continues to contribute to all. Additionally, other members are also motivated to maximize the family income and consumption, even if their welfare depends on their own consumption alone. For additional related discussions, see Theorem 13.1 below in this chapter.

The other side of the spinning yoyos in Fig. 13.1 without standing to the other side of the structures is shown in Fig. 13.2. Here, the head's yoyo field spins convergently, meaning that he needs to make money to support his family. And kid K's yoyo field rotates divergently, representing the fact that other than taking in his share of the family's income, he is also willing to do something to help out the family. In particular, Becker's rotten kid theorem holds true in the enclosed areas in the interactions between kid K's yoyo and head H's yoyo fields (Lin & Forrest, 2008a). In these areas, H's transfers (m_1) are happily accepted by kid K, and kid K actively helps out head H to suck in more resources. At the same time, the interactions outside the enclosed areas might not be very cooperating. In fact, in some areas, kid K's yoyo might be spinning against the spinning direction of head H's yoyo. This observation is well illustrated by the following example.

Example 13.1 Assume that a family is made up of a parent p and a child c. Similar to what is studied in Baland and Robinson (2000), let the parent's utility function be

$$W_{\mathrm{p}} = c_{\mathrm{p}} + \delta W_{\mathrm{c}}(c_{\mathrm{c}}), \tag{13.1}$$

where c_{p} stands for the parent's total consumption on various commodities, $W_{\mathrm{c}}(c_{\mathrm{c}}) = c_{\mathrm{c}}^2 + 8$ the child's utility function of consuming as much as c_{c} on the numeraire of goods, and $\delta \in (0,1)$ a parameter measuring the degree of the parent's altruism toward the child.

The constraints are given as follows:

$$c_p = 8 + l_c - (l_c + 1) \quad \text{and} \quad c_c = l_c + 1, \tag{13.2}$$

where 8 is the parent's income from his work, $l_c \in [0,1]$ the child's income as a child laborer working as much time as l_c out of his endowed unity of available time, and (l_c + 1) the transfer from the parent to the child. Then, from Eqs. (13.1) and (13.2), the parent's utility function is

$$W_p = 7 + \delta\left[(l_c + 1)^2 + 8\right],$$

which reaches its maximum at $l_c = 1$, where the child's utility is also optimized. That is, as shown in the enclosed areas in Fig. 13.2, the parent's transfers and the kid's willingness to help maximize the family income work out perfectly. However, there is a problem left open here: the child spends his entire endowed unity of time to work as a child laborer. He has no time for school or any other activities, as a kid would enjoy doing. Because of this, the parent is known as a rotten parent (Lin, 2009, p. 184).

13.3 Child Labor and Work's Disutility

In this section, we look at the situation in two cases: one contains only one-sided altruism and the other two-sided altruism.

13.3.1 Modeling the Scenario of One-Sided Altruism

Similar to the fact that the enclosed areas in Fig. 13.2 do not cover the entire spin fields of parent H's and kid K's yoyos, the situation constructed in Example 13.1 does not consider the possibility that to some degree, kid K may not like to spend all his available time to work as a child laborer for income. He may very much like to go out to play with his friends instead of working. To capture this scenario, going along with Baland and Robinson (2000), Bommier and Dubois (2004), Dessy (2000), and Ranjan (2001), let us assume that there are two time periods, labeled $t = 1, 2$, without any discount of the future.

Models with only one time period ignore the fact that parental decisions made for children when they are little have lifelong consequences for the children and the parents themselves. See, for example, Basu and Van (1998) and Ravallion and Wodon (2000). The family of our study consists of parents and children who live through both time periods. In the first period, parents decide how to allocate the children's unit time endowment among work as child labor, formal schooling, and other activities, such as play, sports, and socializing with others. Parents have A efficiency units of labor in each period. In period 1, the children provide $l_c \in [0, 1]$ amount of time at work (child's work includes not just salaried occupations outside the home, but also domestic tasks imposed on children), $e_c \in [0, 1]$ for formal schooling, and $p_c \in [0, 1]$ for other activities, satisfying that $l_c + e_c + p_c = 1$. In this period, parents control all income, including that earned by children. Let

$$a_c = a_c(l_c, e_c, p_c, m_c) = a_c(l_c, e_c, m_c)$$

stand for a child's human capital accumulation acquired through schooling e_c, work l_c, and other activities p_c, where m_c represents the child's level of maturity. Assume a_c is strictly increasing and strictly concave upward with respect to each independent variable. Because the sum of l_c, e_c, and p_c is the unity, we can think of a_c as a function of l_c, e_c, and m_c only without having p_c explicitly included.

A word about the variable "maturity" m_c: Different children have different levels of maturity no matter what age they are. The level of maturity can be determined partially by a person's ability to interact with others in a socially appropriate manner, and how well he or she takes on his or her responsibilities. The reason for us to introduce the function a_c for children's accumulation of human capital is that from all activities, children acquire knowledge and experience, both positive and negative, that in general will benefit them for the rest of their lives.

In period 2, children are now called adults and working for a living. Their total labor supply in this period is $h(a_c)$, where $h(a_c)$ represents the number of human capital units possessed by an adult who worked for a fraction l_c and attended formal school for a fraction e_c of his time endowment when a child with a level of maturity m_c. The functions h and a_c are differentiable as needed and strictly increasing and strictly concave upward. In period 2, adults control their own income. We assume that labor markets are all competitive and pay $1 for each unit of human capital.

We assume that both parents and adult children consume one (aggregate) commodity with unit price 1. For simplicity, we assume that the family has only one child and the parents' and child's utility functions W_p and W_c are related as follows:

$$W_p = U\left(c_p^1\right) + U\left(c_p^2\right) + \delta W_c(c_c), \tag{13.3}$$

where $\delta \in (0, 1)$ is a parameter measuring the extent to which parents are altruistic toward the child, U and W_c are differentiable as needed, strictly increasing and strictly concave upward, c_p^i is the total consumption of the parents in period $i = 1, 2$, and c_c is the consumption of the adult child in period 2.

Other than choosing the time allocation l_c, e_c, and p_c for the child during period 1, parents in period 2 only decide on monetary transfers to the child, called bequests and denoted $b \geq 0$. Between the periods, they use savings, denoted s, to transfer their income. So, the parents and child face the following budget constraints:

$$c_{\mathrm{p}}^{1}=c_{\mathrm{p}}^{1}(l_{\mathrm{c}},e_{\mathrm{c}},m_{\mathrm{c}})=A+C(a_{\mathrm{c}})-s(a_{\mathrm{c}}) \tag{13.4}$$

$$c_{\mathrm{p}}^{2}=c_{\mathrm{p}}^{2}(l_{\mathrm{c}},e_{\mathrm{c}},m_{\mathrm{c}})=A-b(s)+s(a_{\mathrm{c}})=A-b(a_{\mathrm{c}})+s(a_{\mathrm{c}})$$

and

$$c_{\mathrm{c}}=c_{\mathrm{c}}(l_{\mathrm{c}},e_{\mathrm{c}},m_{\mathrm{c}})=h(a_{\mathrm{c}})+b(s)=h(a_{\mathrm{c}})+b(a_{\mathrm{c}}), \tag{13.5}$$

where we assume that the functions c_{p}^{1}, c_{p}^{2}, c_{c}, C, s, and b are all differentiable increasing functions in each of their independent variables; $C=C(a_{\mathrm{c}})$ is the units of the child's human capital from working as much time as l_{c}, having formal schooling e_{c}, and having a level of maturity m_{c}; $s=s(a_{\mathrm{c}})$ is the parents' savings in period 1; and $b=b(s)=b(a_{\mathrm{c}})$ is the parents' bequests in period 2. If we assume that the capital markets are imperfect, then s will have to be nonnegative.

The first-order conditions of maximizing the parents' utility W_{p}, Eq. (13.3), subject to the budgetary constraints in Eqs. (13.4) and (13.5) with respect to b, l_{c}, s, e_{c}, and m_{c}, are given, respectively, below:

$$U'\left(c_{\mathrm{p}}^{2}\right)\begin{cases}=\delta W_{\mathrm{c}}'(c_{\mathrm{c}}), & \text{if } b>0\\ >\delta W_{\mathrm{c}}'(c_{\mathrm{c}}) & \text{if } b=0\end{cases} \tag{13.6}$$

$$U'\left(c_{\mathrm{p}}^{1}\right)\left[\frac{\partial C}{\partial l_{\mathrm{c}}}-\frac{\partial s}{\partial l_{\mathrm{c}}}\right]+U'\left(c_{\mathrm{p}}^{2}\right)\left[\frac{\partial s}{\partial l_{\mathrm{c}}}-\frac{\partial b}{\partial l_{\mathrm{c}}}\right]+\delta W_{\mathrm{c}}'(c_{\mathrm{c}})\left[\frac{\partial h}{\partial l_{\mathrm{c}}}+\frac{\partial b}{\partial l_{\mathrm{c}}}\right]=0 \tag{13.7}$$

$$U'\left(c_{\mathrm{p}}^{1}\right)\begin{cases}=U'\left(c_{\mathrm{p}}^{2}\right), & \text{if } s>0\\ >U'\left(c_{\mathrm{p}}^{2}\right), & \text{if } s=0\end{cases} \tag{13.8}$$

$$U'\left(c_{\mathrm{p}}^{1}\right)\left[\frac{\partial C}{\partial e_{\mathrm{c}}}-\frac{\partial s}{\partial e_{\mathrm{c}}}\right]+U'\left(c_{\mathrm{p}}^{2}\right)\left[\frac{\partial s}{\partial e_{\mathrm{c}}}-\frac{\partial b}{\partial e_{\mathrm{c}}}\right]+\delta W_{\mathrm{c}}'(c_{\mathrm{c}})\left[\frac{\partial h}{\partial e_{\mathrm{c}}}+\frac{\partial b}{\partial e_{\mathrm{c}}}\right]=0 \tag{13.9}$$

$$U'\left(c_{\mathrm{p}}^{1}\right)\left[\frac{\partial C}{\partial m_{\mathrm{c}}}-\frac{\partial s}{\partial m_{\mathrm{c}}}\right]+U'\left(c_{\mathrm{p}}^{2}\right)\left[\frac{\partial s}{\partial m_{\mathrm{c}}}-\frac{\partial b}{\partial m_{\mathrm{c}}}\right]+\delta W_{\mathrm{c}}'(c_{\mathrm{c}})\times\left[\frac{\partial h}{\partial m_{\mathrm{c}}}+\frac{\partial b}{\partial m_{\mathrm{c}}}\right]=0. \tag{13.10}$$

13.3.2 Efficiency of Child Labor, Formal Education, and Maturity

The triple $\left(l_c^*, e_c^*, m_c^*\right)$ of child labor, formal schooling, and level of the child's maturity is said to be efficient if the triple maximizes the child's lifetime earnings. That is, $\left(l_c^*, e_c^*, m_c^*\right)$ maximizes the following function:

$$E_c(l_c, e_c, m_c) = C(a_c) + h(a_c). \tag{13.11}$$

Because work experience and formal schooling are always positive to those involved in terms of human capital accumulation, it is reasonable to assume that $l_c^*, e_c^* > 0$. And because m_c measures a person's level of maturity, we can also assume $m_c^* > 0$.

Proposition 13.1 If the parents' bequests and savings are interior, then the laissez faire triple $\left(l_c^*, e_c^*, m_c^*\right)$ of child labor, formal schooling, and level of maturity is efficient.

Proof Solving Eq. (13.7) for $\partial h(a_c)/\partial l_c$ produces

$$\begin{aligned}
\frac{\partial h(a_c)}{\partial l_c} &= \frac{-1}{\delta W_c'(c_c)}\left\{U'\left(c_p^1\right)\left[\frac{\partial C}{\partial l_c} - \frac{\partial s}{\partial l_c}\right] + U'\left(c_p^2\right)\left[\frac{\partial s}{\partial l_c} - \frac{\partial b}{\partial l_c}\right] + \delta W_c'(c_c)\frac{\partial b}{\partial l_c}\right\} \\
&= \frac{-1}{\delta W_c'(c_c)}\left\{U'\left(c_p^2\right)\left[\frac{\partial C}{\partial l_c} - \frac{\partial b}{\partial l_c}\right] + \delta W_c'(c_c)\frac{\partial b}{\partial l_c}\right\} (\text{from Eq.}(13.8)) \\
&= \frac{-1}{\delta W_c'(c_c)}\delta W_c'(c_c)\frac{\partial C}{\partial l_c} (\text{from Eq.}(13.6)) \\
&= -\frac{\partial C(a_c)}{\partial l_c}.
\end{aligned} \tag{13.12}$$

Similarly, solving Eq. (13.9) for $\partial h(a_c)/\partial e_c$ and Eq. (13.10) for $\partial h(a_c)/\partial m_c$ leads to

$$\frac{\partial h(a_c)}{\partial e_c} = -\frac{\partial C(a_c)}{\partial e_c} \tag{13.13}$$

and

$$\frac{\partial h(a_c)}{\partial m_c} = -\frac{\partial C(a_c)}{\partial m_c}. \tag{13.14}$$

Combining Eqs. (13.12)–(13.14), we have shown that the laissez faire triple (l_c^*, e_c^*, m_c^*), which maximizes the parents' utility, also maximizes the child's lifetime earnings. That is, the triple is efficient.

Proposition 13.2 If the parents' bequests are at a corner, then the laissez faire triple (l_c^*, e_c^*, m_c^*) of child labor, formal schooling, and level of maturity is inefficiently high, meaning that the potential child's lifetime earnings are decreasing at the level of the triple.

Note It is initially observed by Becker and Murphy (1988) and Nerlove et al. (1988) that nonnegativity constraints on bequests could lead to inefficiencies in the family's resource allocation.

Proof Because the parents' bequests are at a corner, Eqs. (13.7) and (13.8) lead to

$$\begin{aligned}\frac{\partial h(a_c)}{\partial l_c} &\le \frac{-1}{\delta W_c'(c_c)}\left\{U'\left(c_p^2\right)\left[\frac{\partial C}{\partial l_c} - \frac{\partial b}{\partial l_c}\right] + \delta W_c'(c_c)\frac{\partial b}{\partial l_c}\right\} \\ &< \frac{-1}{\delta W_c'(c_c)}\left[\delta W_c'(c_c)\frac{\partial C}{\partial l_c}\right] \text{(from Eq.(13.6))} \\ &= -\frac{\partial C(a_c)}{\partial l_c}.\end{aligned}$$

Similarly, based on Eqs. (13.9) and (13.10), we have

$$\frac{\partial h(a_c)}{\partial e_c} < -\frac{\partial C(a_c)}{\partial e_c} \quad \text{and} \quad \frac{\partial h(a_c)}{\partial m_c} < -\frac{\partial C(a_c)}{\partial m_c}.$$

That is, the laissez faire triple (l_c^*, e_c^*, m_c^*) is inefficiently high.

What is implied in Proposition 13.2 is that when the family is poor, even though the parents are altruistic toward the child, the desired contribution from the child will surely decrease the child's lifetime earnings potential. (This result is similar to what is obtained in Basu and Van (1998) and Eswarran (1996).) The fact that child labor is a facet of poverty has been well established in the empirical literature (see, for example, Rosenzweig, 1981; Labenne, 1997; Chakraborty & Das, 2005; Baland & Robinson, 2000; Bommier & Dubois, 2004 establish a clear-up welfare argument that suggests that child labor can be inefficient). A natural question at this junction is: Would the child be willing to make the wanted contribution to the family? According to the recent work (Lin & Forrest, 2008a) on Becker's rotten kid theorem (1974), the answer is both yes and no, depending on how the parents treat the child and what the child's consumption preferences are.

Going back to our case of the poor family, if the child's consumption preference coincides with the desire of the parents, then Becker's rotten kid theorem applies, for the self-containment of this chapter, the referenced theorem is cited below. That is, the child will be willing to meet the parents' demand. Consequently, Proposition

13.2 implies that the child might repeat his parents' lifestyle, being financially poor. Conversely, if the child's consumption preference is in conflict with how he is treated or demands made on him at home (because in this case, the parents do not have many financial resources to transfer to the child), the child might likely work for the demanded amount of time l_c^* to survive at home. At the same time, he might very well explore other opportunities through formal schooling e_c^* or other activities $p_c^* = 1 - l_c^* - e_c^*$. In this case, the child's level of maturity might rise drastically to have his own consumption preference satisfied.

Theorem 13.1 (Lin & Forrest, 2008a). Becker's rotten kid theorem holds true if and only if the distribution of the benevolent head's resources is not in conflict with the consumption preferences of any selfish member.

Proposition 13.3 If the parents' savings are at a corner, then the laissez faire triple (l_c^*, e_c^*, m_c^*) of child labor, formal schooling, and level of maturity is inefficiently high.

Proof Because the parents' savings are at a corner, Eqs. (13.7) and (13.8) lead to

$$\begin{aligned}\frac{\partial h(a_c)}{\partial l_c} &< \frac{-1}{\delta W_c'(c_c)}\left\{U'\left(c_p^2\right)\left[\frac{\partial C}{\partial l_c} - \frac{\partial b}{\partial l_c}\right] + \delta W_c'(c_c)\frac{\partial b}{\partial l_c}\right\} \\ &\leq \frac{-1}{\delta W_c'(c_c)}\left[\delta W_c'(c_c)\frac{\partial C}{\partial l_c}\right] (\text{from Eq.}(13.6)) \\ &= -\frac{\partial C(a_c)}{\partial l_c}.\end{aligned}$$

Similarly, from Eqs. (13.9) and (13.10), we can produce

$$\frac{\partial h(a_c)}{\partial e_c} < -\frac{\partial C(a_c)}{\partial e_c}$$

and

$$\frac{\partial h(a_c)}{\partial m_c} < -\frac{\partial C(a_c)}{\partial m_c}.$$

That is, the laissez faire triple (l_c^*, e_c^*, m_c^*) is inefficiently high.

The inefficiency pointed to in Proposition 13.3 is more likely to arise if the family is poor or lives an extravagant lifestyle in period 1. In the former case, imperfect capital markets prevent the parents from borrowing in the marketplace. So, they borrow from their child's future earnings in period 1. Then, in period 2, they try to internalize the negative effects of child labor on period 2 income through their bequests. In the latter case, where the family lives in extravagant lifestyle in period 1, the capital markets surely will not be perfect enough for the parents to borrow indefinitely. So, they borrow from their child's future earnings. They value period 1 income higher than that of period 2. In such a case, it will be difficult to imagine that the parents will even try to internalize the negative effects of child labor in the second period by bequeathing their child.

Similar to the inefficiency described in Proposition 13.2, if the child's consumption preference in the situation of Proposition 13.3 does not agree with how he is treated at home, but as a child he has to comply with his parents' demand, his level of maturity would potentially rise drastically to have his own consumption preference met while keeping the demanded values of child labor l_c^*, formal schooling e_c^*, and other activities $p_c^* = 1 - l_c^* - e_c^*$.

Both Propositions 13.2 and 13.3 say that when parents leave their children no bequests or transfer no assets from period 1 to period 2 when capital markets are imperfect, the parents fail to internalize the socially efficient trade-off between the levels of child labor, formal schooling, and maturity and the children's lifetime earning potential.

13.3.3 Modeling an Adult Child's Altruism Toward Parents

All assumptions in the previous section are kept the same in this subsection, except that the child is simultaneously altruistic toward his parents. (Because the inefficiencies of child labor, formal schooling, and level of maturity, as studied in the previous section, are caused partly by the nonnegativity constraint of bequests, we wanted to see if, by introducing filial altruism, the inefficiencies could be eased. Proposition 13.7 shows that they can be if capital markets are perfect. However, when capital markets are imperfect, the same inefficiencies persist.) That is, we assume that the utility function of the child is given as follows:

$$W_c = V(c_c) + \lambda W_p, \tag{13.15}$$

where $\lambda \in (0, 1)$ measures the degree of the child's filial altruism and V is differentiable as needed, strictly increasing and strictly concave upward. In this case, we can solve Eqs. (13.3) and (13.15) for W_c and W_p and obtain:

$$W_p = \frac{1}{1-\delta\lambda}\left[U\left(c_p^1\right) + U\left(c_p^2\right) + \delta V(c_c)\right] \tag{13.16}$$

and

$$W_c = \frac{1}{1-\delta\lambda}\left[V(c_c) + \lambda U\left(c_p^1\right) + \lambda U\left(c_p^2\right)\right] \tag{13.17}$$

subject to the budgetary constraints:

$$c_{\mathrm{p}}^{1}=c_{\mathrm{p}}^{1}(l_{\mathrm{c}},e_{\mathrm{c}},m_{\mathrm{c}})=A+C(a_{\mathrm{c}})-s(a_{\mathrm{c}}) \tag{13.18}$$

$$c_{\mathrm{p}}^{2}=c_{\mathrm{p}}^{2}(l_{\mathrm{c}},e_{\mathrm{c}},m_{\mathrm{c}})=A-b(a_{\mathrm{c}})+s(a_{\mathrm{c}})+\tau(a_{\mathrm{c}}) \tag{13.19}$$

and

$$c_{\mathrm{c}}=c_{\mathrm{c}}(l_{\mathrm{c}},e_{\mathrm{c}},m_{\mathrm{c}})=h(a_{\mathrm{c}})+b(a_{\mathrm{c}})-\tau(a_{\mathrm{c}}), \tag{13.20}$$

where $\tau(a_{\mathrm{c}}) \geq 0$ is a monetary transfer from the child to the parents in period 2. As before, we assume that the functions c_{p}^{1}, c_{p}^{2}, c_{c}, C, s, and b are all differentiable and increasing in each of their independent variables. Different from Baland and Robinson (2000), we do not assume that the value $\tau(a_{\mathrm{c}})$ is dependent on the parents' savings s and bequests b.

In this new model, the parents make their choices on l_{c}, e_{c}, m_{c}, s, and b, in both periods to maximize W_{p} in Eq. (13.16). And the child determines his monetary transfers τ to maximize his utility function W_{c} in Eq. (13.17) conditional on l_{c}, e_{c}, m_{c}, and s subject to constraint (13.20). So, the child's first-order condition is given by

$$V'(c_{\mathrm{c}})\begin{cases} =\lambda U'\left(c_{\mathrm{p}}^{2}\right), & \text{if } \tau>0 \\ >\lambda U'\left(c_{\mathrm{p}}^{2}\right), & \text{if } \tau=0. \end{cases} \tag{13.21}$$

The first-order conditions of maximizing the parents' utility function W_{p} (Eq. (13.16)) subject to the budgetary constraints in Eqs. (13.18)–(13.20) with respect to b, l_{c}, s, e_{c}, and m_{c} are given, respectively, below:

$$U'\left(c_{\mathrm{p}}^{2}\right)\begin{cases} =\delta V'(c_{\mathrm{c}}), & \text{if } b>0 \\ >\delta V'(c_{\mathrm{c}}), & \text{if } b=0 \end{cases} \tag{13.22}$$

$$\begin{aligned} &U'\left(c_{\mathrm{p}}^{1}\right)\left[\frac{\partial C}{\partial l_{\mathrm{c}}}-\frac{\partial s}{\partial l_{\mathrm{c}}}\right]+U'\left(c_{\mathrm{p}}^{2}\right)\left[\frac{\partial s}{\partial l_{\mathrm{c}}}-\frac{\partial b}{\partial l_{\mathrm{c}}}+\frac{\partial \tau}{\partial l_{\mathrm{c}}}\right]+\delta V'(c_{\mathrm{c}}) \\ &\times\left[\frac{\partial h}{\partial l_{\mathrm{c}}}+\frac{\partial b}{\partial l_{\mathrm{c}}}-\frac{\partial \tau}{\partial l_{\mathrm{c}}}\right]=0 \end{aligned} \tag{13.23}$$

$$U'\left(c_{\mathrm{p}}^{1}\right)\begin{cases} =U'\left(c_{\mathrm{p}}^{2}\right), & \text{if } s>0 \\ >U'\left(c_{\mathrm{p}}^{2}\right), & \text{if } s=0 \end{cases} \tag{13.24}$$

$$U'\left(c_{\mathrm{p}}^{1}\right)\left[\frac{\partial C}{\partial e_{\mathrm{c}}}-\frac{\partial s}{\partial e_{\mathrm{c}}}\right]+U'\left(c_{\mathrm{p}}^{2}\right)\left[\frac{\partial s}{\partial e_{\mathrm{c}}}-\frac{\partial b}{\partial e_{\mathrm{c}}}+\frac{\partial \tau}{\partial e_{\mathrm{c}}}\right]+\delta V'(c_{\mathrm{c}})$$
$$\times\left[\frac{\partial h}{\partial e_{\mathrm{c}}}+\frac{\partial b}{\partial e_{\mathrm{c}}}-\frac{\partial \tau}{\partial e_{\mathrm{c}}}\right]=0 \tag{13.25}$$

$$U'\left(c_{\mathrm{p}}^{1}\right)\left[\frac{\partial C}{\partial m_{\mathrm{c}}}-\frac{\partial s}{\partial m_{\mathrm{c}}}\right]+U'\left(c_{\mathrm{p}}^{2}\right)\left[\frac{\partial s}{\partial m_{\mathrm{c}}}-\frac{\partial b}{\partial m_{\mathrm{c}}}+\frac{\partial \tau}{\partial m_{\mathrm{c}}}\right]+\delta V'(c_{\mathrm{c}})$$
$$\times\left[\frac{\partial h}{\partial m_{\mathrm{c}}}+\frac{\partial b}{\partial m_{\mathrm{c}}}-\frac{\partial \tau}{\partial m_{\mathrm{c}}}\right]=0. \tag{13.26}$$

Proposition 13.4 If the parents' bequests and savings are interior, then the laissez faire triple $\left(l_{\mathrm{c}}^{*}, e_{\mathrm{c}}^{*}, m_{\mathrm{c}}^{*}\right)$ of child labor, formal schooling, and level of maturity is efficient.

Proof From Eq. (13.23), it follows that

$$\frac{\partial h}{\partial l_{\mathrm{c}}}=\frac{-1}{\delta V'(c_{\mathrm{c}})}\left\{U'\left(c_{\mathrm{p}}^{1}\right)\left[\frac{\partial C}{\partial l_{\mathrm{c}}}-\frac{\partial s}{\partial l_{\mathrm{c}}}\right]+U'\left(c_{\mathrm{p}}^{2}\right)\left[\frac{\partial s}{\partial l_{\mathrm{c}}}-\frac{\partial b}{\partial l_{\mathrm{c}}}+\frac{\partial \tau}{\partial l_{\mathrm{c}}}\right]\right.$$
$$\left.+\delta V'(c_{\mathrm{c}})\left[\frac{\partial b}{\partial l_{\mathrm{c}}}-\frac{\partial \tau}{\partial l_{\mathrm{c}}}\right]\right\}$$
$$=\frac{-1}{\delta V'(c_{\mathrm{c}})}\delta V'(c_{\mathrm{c}})\frac{\partial C}{\partial l_{\mathrm{c}}}(\text{from Eqs.}(13.22)\text{ and}(13.24))=-\frac{\partial C}{\partial l_{\mathrm{c}}}.$$

Similarly, from Eqs. (13.25) and (13.26), we get

$$\frac{\partial h}{\partial e_{\mathrm{c}}}=-\frac{\partial C}{\partial e_{\mathrm{c}}}\quad\text{and}\quad\frac{\partial h}{\partial m_{\mathrm{c}}}=-\frac{\partial C}{\partial m_{\mathrm{c}}}.$$

That is, from Eq. (13.11), we have shown that the laissez faire triple $\left(l_{\mathrm{c}}^{*}, e_{\mathrm{c}}^{*}, m_{\mathrm{c}}^{*}\right)$ is efficient.

13.3.4 Inefficiency of Child Labor, Formal Schooling, and Maturity

This subsection looks at when inefficiencies might appear with a child's labor, formal education, and level of maturity.

Proposition 13.5 If the parents' bequests are at a corner, then the laissez faire triple (l_c^*, e_c^*, m_c^*) of child labor, formal schooling, and level of maturity is inefficiently high.

Proof Let us assume that the parents' bequests are at a corner. Then, Eq. (13.23) implies that

$$\begin{aligned}\frac{\partial h}{\partial l_c} &= \frac{-1}{\delta V'(c_c)}\left\{U'\left(c_p^1\right)\left[\frac{\partial C}{\partial l_c}-\frac{\partial s}{\partial l_c}\right]+U'\left(c_p^2\right)\left[\frac{\partial s}{\partial l_c}-\frac{\partial b}{\partial l_c}+\frac{\partial \tau}{\partial l_c}\right]\right.\\ &\quad\left.+\delta V'(c_c)\left[\frac{\partial b}{\partial l_c}-\frac{\partial \tau}{\partial l_c}\right]\right\}\\ &\leq \frac{-1}{\delta V'(c_c)}\left\{U'\left(c_p^2\right)\left[\frac{\partial C}{\partial l_c}-\frac{\partial b}{\partial l_c}+\frac{\partial \tau}{\partial l_c}\right]+\delta V'(c_c)\left[\frac{\partial b}{\partial l_c}-\frac{\partial \tau}{\partial l_c}\right]\right\}(\because \text{Eq.}(13.24))\\ &< \frac{-1}{\delta V'(c_c)}\delta V'(c_c)\frac{\partial C}{\partial l_c}(\text{from Eq.}(13.22)) = -\frac{\partial C}{\partial l_c}.\end{aligned}$$

Similarly, based on Eqs. (13.25) and (13.26), we can show that

$$\frac{\partial h}{\partial e_c} < -\frac{\partial C}{\partial e_c} \quad \text{and} \quad \frac{\partial h}{\partial m_c} < -\frac{\partial C}{\partial m_c}.$$

From Eq. (13.11), it follows that the laissez faire triple (l_c^*, e_c^*, m_c^*) is inefficiently high.

What is implied in Propositions 13.4 and 13.5 is that as long as the filial altruism exists, the child's decision to make monetary transfers to his parents in period 2 has nothing to do with whether the parents' demanded laissez faire triple (l_c^*, e_c^*, m_c^*) in period 1 helps to maximize his lifetime earnings or not. His decision will be purely based on Eq. (13.21) to maximize his utility W_c and is determined by his degree of filial altruism. For example, when the condition

$$V'\left(h\left(a_c^*\right)+b\left(a_c^*\right)\right) > \lambda U'\left(A-b\left(a_c^*\right)+s\left(a_c^*\right)\right),$$

where $a_c^* = (l_c^*, e_c^*, m_c^*)$, is satisfied, the adult child would not make monetary transfers to his parents even though the parents' bequests $b\left(a_c^*\right)$ could be interior.

Proposition 13.6 The adult child's transfers and the parents' bequests cannot both be interior at the laissez faire triple (l_c^*, e_c^*, m_c^*) of child labor, formal schooling, and level of maturity.

Proof By contradiction, assume that at the laissez faire triple (l_c^*, e_c^*, m_c^*), both the child's transfers and the parents' bequests are interior and the child's utility is maximized. Then, Eqs. (13.21) and (13.22) imply that

$$V'(c_c) = \lambda U'\left(c_p^2\right) = \lambda\delta V'(c_c), \quad 0 < \lambda\delta < 1.$$

That is, we must have $V'(c_c)=0$, which contradicts the hypothesis that V is strictly increasing.

Proposition 13.7 If capital markets are perfect and the adult child's transfers are interior such that the child lives on a fixed budget, then the laissez faire triple $\left(l_c^*, e_c^*, m_c^*\right)$ of child labor, formal schooling, and level of maturity is efficient.

Proof The assumption that capital markets are perfect implies that the equalities in Eqs. (13.22) and (13.24) hold, even though b might be negative. So, Eq. (13.23) leads to

$$\begin{aligned}
\frac{\partial h}{\partial l_c} &= \frac{-1}{\delta V'(c_c)}\left\{U'\left(c_p^1\right)\left[\frac{\partial C}{\partial l_c} - \frac{\partial s}{\partial l_c}\right] + U'\left(c_p^2\right)\left[\frac{\partial s}{\partial l_c} + \frac{\partial \tau}{\partial l_c}\right] - \delta V'(c_c)\frac{\partial \tau}{\partial l_c}\right\} \\
&= \frac{-1}{\delta V'(c_c)}\left\{U'\left(c_p^2\right)\left[\frac{\partial C}{\partial l_c} + \frac{\partial \tau}{\partial l_c}\right] - \delta V'(c_c)\left[\frac{\partial C}{\partial l_c} + \frac{\partial \tau}{\partial l_c}\right] + \delta V'(c_c)\frac{\partial C}{\partial l_c}\right\} \\
&= \frac{-1}{\delta V'(c_c)}\left\{\left[U'\left(c_p^2\right) - \delta V'(c_c)\right] \times \left[\frac{\partial C}{\partial l_c} + \frac{\partial \tau}{\partial l_c}\right] + \delta V'(c_c)\frac{\partial C}{\partial l_c}\right\},
\end{aligned}$$

where $b(a_c) = 0$ is a consequence of Proposition 13.6. Therefore,

$$\frac{\partial h}{\partial l_c} + \frac{\partial C}{\partial l_c} = \frac{-1}{\delta V'(c_c)}\left[U'\left(c_p^2\right) - \delta V'(c_c)\right] \times \left[\frac{\partial C}{\partial l_c} + \frac{\partial \tau}{\partial l_c}\right]. \tag{13.27}$$

By differentiating Eq. (13.21) with respect to l_c, we obtain

$$V''\left[\frac{\partial h}{\partial l_c} - \frac{\partial \tau}{\partial l_c}\right] = \lambda U''\left[\frac{\partial s}{\partial l_c} + \frac{\partial \tau}{\partial l_c}\right]$$

and

$$\frac{\partial s}{\partial l_c} + \frac{\partial \tau}{\partial l_c} = \frac{V''}{\lambda U''\left(c_p^2\right)}\left[\frac{\partial h}{\partial l_c} - \frac{\partial \tau}{\partial l_c}\right]. \tag{13.28}$$

Based on Eq. (13.24), we can rewrite Eq. (13.21) as follows:

$$V'(c_c) = \lambda U'\left(c_p^1\right).$$

Differentiating this equation with respect to l_c provides

$$V''\left[\frac{\partial h}{\partial l_{\mathrm{c}}}-\frac{\partial \tau}{\partial l_{\mathrm{c}}}\right]=\lambda U''\left[\frac{\partial C}{\partial l_{\mathrm{c}}}-\frac{\partial s}{\partial l_{\mathrm{c}}}\right]$$

and

$$\frac{\partial C}{\partial l_{\mathrm{c}}}-\frac{\partial s}{\partial l_{\mathrm{c}}}=\frac{V''}{\lambda U''\left(c_{\mathrm{p}}^{1}\right)}\left[\frac{\partial h}{\partial l_{\mathrm{c}}}-\frac{\partial \tau}{\partial l_{\mathrm{c}}}\right]. \tag{13.29}$$

Adding Eqs. (13.28) and (13.29) leads to

$$\frac{\partial C}{\partial l_{\mathrm{c}}}+\frac{\partial \tau}{\partial l_{\mathrm{c}}}=\frac{V''}{\lambda}\left[\frac{1}{U''\left(c_{\mathrm{p}}^{1}\right)}+\frac{1}{U''\left(c_{\mathrm{p}}^{2}\right)}\right]\left[\frac{\partial h}{\partial l_{\mathrm{c}}}-\frac{\partial \tau}{\partial l_{\mathrm{c}}}\right]. \tag{13.30}$$

The assumption that the adult child lives on a fixed budget implies that $h(a_{\mathrm{c}}) - \tau(a_{\mathrm{c}})$ is a constant, his fixed budget. So, we have

$$\frac{\partial h(a_{\mathrm{c}})}{\partial l_{\mathrm{c}}}-\frac{\partial \tau(a_{\mathrm{c}})}{\partial l_{\mathrm{c}}}=0.$$

This end means, as indicated by Eqs. (13.27) and (13.30),

$$\frac{\partial C}{\partial l_{\mathrm{c}}}+\frac{\partial \tau}{\partial l_{\mathrm{c}}}=0 \quad \text{and} \quad \text{hence } \frac{\partial h}{\partial l_{\mathrm{c}}}+\frac{\partial C}{\partial l_{\mathrm{c}}}=0.$$

Similarly, based on Eqs. (13.25) and (13.26), we can prove

$$\frac{\partial h}{\partial e_{\mathrm{c}}}+\frac{\partial C}{\partial e_{\mathrm{c}}}=0 \quad \text{and} \quad \frac{\partial h}{\partial m_{\mathrm{c}}}+\frac{\partial C}{\partial m_{\mathrm{c}}}=0.$$

This end implies that the laissez faire triple $\left(l_{\mathrm{c}}^{*}, e_{\mathrm{c}}^{*}, m_{\mathrm{c}}^{*}\right)$ is efficient.

In fact, the proof of Proposition 13.7 also shows the following implication:

$$\frac{d(h-\tau)}{da_{\mathrm{c}}}>0 \rightarrow \frac{\partial E_{\mathrm{c}}}{\partial l_{\mathrm{c}}}<0, \quad \frac{\partial E_{\mathrm{c}}}{\partial e_{\mathrm{c}}}<0 \text{ and } \frac{\partial E_{\mathrm{c}}}{\partial m_{\mathrm{c}}}<0.$$

That is, the laissez faire triple $\left(l_{\mathrm{c}}^{*}, e_{\mathrm{c}}^{*}, m_{\mathrm{c}}^{*}\right)$ is inefficiently high. And, the following also holds:

$$\frac{d(h-\tau)}{da_{\mathrm{c}}}<0 \rightarrow \frac{\partial E_{\mathrm{c}}}{\partial l_{\mathrm{c}}}>0, \quad \frac{\partial E_{\mathrm{c}}}{\partial e_{\mathrm{c}}}>0 \text{ and } \frac{\partial E_{\mathrm{c}}}{\partial m_{\mathrm{c}}}>0.$$

That is, the laissez faire triple $\left(l_{\mathrm{c}}^{*}, e_{\mathrm{c}}^{*}, m_{\mathrm{c}}^{*}\right)$ is inefficiently low, meaning that even though the triple $\left(l_{\mathrm{c}}^{*}, e_{\mathrm{c}}^{*}, m_{\mathrm{c}}^{*}\right)$ maximizes the parents' and the adult child's utilities, it does not optimize the child's lifetime earnings potential.

Proposition 13.8 When capital markets are imperfect and the parents' savings are at a corner, the laissez faire triple $\left(l_{\mathrm{c}}^{*}, e_{\mathrm{c}}^{*}, m_{\mathrm{c}}^{*}\right)$ of child labor, formal schooling, and level of maturity is inefficiently high.

Proof Both Eqs. (13.23) and (13.24) imply that

$$\begin{aligned}\frac{\partial h}{\partial l_{\mathrm{c}}} &< \frac{-1}{\delta V'(c_{\mathrm{c}})}\left\{U'\left(c_{\mathrm{p}}^{2}\right)\left[\frac{\partial C}{\partial l_{\mathrm{c}}}+\frac{\partial \tau}{\partial l_{\mathrm{c}}}\right]-\delta V'(c_{\mathrm{c}})\frac{\partial \tau}{\partial l_{\mathrm{c}}}\right\} \\ &\leq \frac{-1}{\delta V'(c_{\mathrm{c}})}\delta V'(c_{\mathrm{c}})\frac{\partial C}{\partial l_{\mathrm{c}}}\,(\text{from Eq.}(13.22)) \\ &= -\frac{\partial C}{\partial l_{\mathrm{c}}}.\end{aligned}$$

That is, $\partial E_{\mathrm{c}}/\partial l_{\mathrm{c}} < 0$. Similarly, based on Eqs. (13.25) and (13.26), we can prove that $\partial E_{\mathrm{c}}/\partial e_{\mathrm{c}} < 0$ and $\partial E_{\mathrm{c}}/\partial m_{\mathrm{c}} < 0$. That is, the laissez faire triple $\left(l_{\mathrm{c}}^{*}, e_{\mathrm{c}}^{*}, m_{\mathrm{c}}^{*}\right)$ is inefficiently high.

The proof of Proposition 13.8 implies that the laissez faire triple $\left(l_{\mathrm{c}}^{*}, e_{\mathrm{c}}^{*}, m_{\mathrm{c}}^{*}\right)$ is inefficiently high even if the adult child's transfers or the parents' bequests are interior.

13.4 Different Definition of Efficiency Leads to Different Conclusion

Walking along the same path as what we have done so far in this chapter, let us look at Fig. 13.1 and consider such a question: When the spin field and the yoyo structure of kid K are weak, meaning that K is a minor child, the family head H, say a parent, might purposely feed the kid with various gifts or opportunities, such as monetary, educational, or other kinds, in the hope that the kid's yoyo could soon be strong enough to become self-sufficient and independent. As shown in Fig. 13.1, not all kinds of gifts the kid wants to accept (the difference between m_1 and m_2), and for a specific kind of gift, the kid's willingness to accept does depend on how it is represented to the kid. So, how can we model the situation that when the parent makes decision regarding the kid, we know if the decision and its inevitable consequences are good for the kid or not?

As Bommier and Dubois (2004) state, childhood is often related to as the time when one had the largest amount of long-lasting memory of both positive and negative experiences. It is the childhood quality of life that has the greatest impact on the valuation of lifetime utility, even though childhood is only a small fraction of life. Also, during childhood, individuals acquire a large part of their human capital, which is a major determinant of the ability to raise lifetime earnings potential. So, following Bommier and Dubois (2004), let us in this section add a child's disutility from period 1 into our model. In particular, all assumptions in previous sections will be kept the same in this section, except that the child's utility function W_c is given by

$$W_c = V_1(1 - l_c - e_c) + V_2(c_c) + W_p, \tag{13.31}$$

where $\lambda \in (0,1)$ is defined as before, the child's degree of his filial altruism; V_2 is the child's selfish utility function, dependent on his adult consumption in period 2; and $V_1(1 - l_c - e_c)$ is the child's disutility of working l_c and formal schooling e_c.

Assume that V_1 and V_2 are strictly increasing, strictly concave upward, and differentiable as needed. In this section, if the child's utility W_c reaches its maximum at $\left(l_c^*, e_c^*, m_c^*\right)$, then we say that the laissez faire triple $\left(l_c^*, e_c^*, m_c^*\right)$ of child labor, formal schooling, and level of maturity is efficient.

Combining Eqs. (13.3) and (13.31), we are able to see that the parents are willing to maximize their utility,

$$W_p = \frac{1}{1 - \lambda\delta}\left[U\left(c_p^1\right) + U\left(c_p^2\right) + \delta V_1(1 - l_c - e_c) + \delta V_2(c_c)\right], \tag{13.32}$$

under their first and second period budgetary constraints in Eqs. (13.18) and (13.19). And, the child's objective is to maximize his utility,

$$W_c = \frac{1}{1 - \lambda\delta}\left[V_1(1 - l_c - e_c) + V_2(c_c) + \lambda U\left(c_p^1\right) + \lambda U\left(c_p^2\right)\right], \tag{13.33}$$

under the budgetary constraints in Eq. (13.20).

The respective first-order conditions for the parents to maximize their utility W_p with respect to l_c, e_c, and m_c are given as follows:

$$\delta V_1'(1 - l_c - e_c) - \delta V_2'(c_c)\frac{\partial c_c}{\partial l_c} = U'\left(c_p^1\right)\frac{\partial c_p^1}{\partial l_c} + U'\left(c_p^2\right)\frac{\partial c_p^2}{\partial l_c} \tag{13.34}$$

$$\delta V_1'(1 - l_c - e_c) - \delta V_2'(c_c)\frac{\partial c_c}{\partial e_c} = U'\left(c_p^1\right)\frac{\partial c_p^1}{\partial e_c} + U'\left(c_p^2\right)\frac{\partial c_p^2}{\partial e_c} \tag{13.35}$$

$$-\delta V_2'(c_c)\frac{\partial c_c}{\partial m_c} = U'\left(c_p^1\right)\frac{\partial c_p^1}{\partial m_c} + U'\left(c_p^2\right)\frac{\partial c_p^2}{\partial m_c}. \tag{13.36}$$

Proposition 13.9 The laissez faire triple $\left(l_c^*, e_c^*, m_c^*\right)$ of child labor, formal schooling, and level of maturity is inefficiently high.

Proof From Eq. (13.33), it follows that

$$\begin{aligned}\frac{\partial W_c}{\partial l_c} &= \frac{1}{1-\lambda\delta}\left[V_1'(1-l_c-e_c)(-1)+V_2'(c_c)\frac{\partial c_c}{\partial l_c}+\lambda U'\left(c_p^1\right)\frac{\partial c_p^1}{\partial l_c}+\lambda U'\left(c_p^2\right)\frac{\partial c_p^2}{\partial l_c}\right]\\ &=\lambda-\frac{1/\delta}{1-\lambda\delta}\left[U'\left(c_p^1\right)\frac{\partial c_p^1}{\partial l_c}+U'\left(c_p^2\right)\frac{\partial c_p^2}{\partial l_c}\right]\text{(from Eq. (13.34))}<0.\end{aligned}$$

Similarly, from Eqs. (13.35) and (13.36), it follows that

$$\frac{\partial W_c}{\partial e_c}<0 \quad \text{and} \quad \frac{\partial W_c}{\partial m_c}<0.$$

So, we have proven that the laissez faire triple $\left(l_c^*, e_c^*, m_c^*\right)$ is inefficiently high.

The inefficiency described in Proposition 13.9 holds true no matter whether capital markets are perfect or not, no matter whether the parents' bequests or savings are interior or at a corner, and no matter whether the child's transfers are interior or not. This result shows that one obtains an inefficiency as soon as children's utility and disutility become the criterion. The inefficiency of a child's time allocation and his level of maturity results only from communications internal to the family between the child and the parents. Driven by two-way altruism, adequate communication between the parents and the child would help to achieve Pareto improving allocation of child labor l_c^* and formal schooling e_c^* while helping the child to become more mature. In particular, the inefficiency described in Proposition 13.9 is caused by a conflict between the parents' altruism toward the child and the child's consumption preference (Theorem 13.1, Lin & Forrest, 2008a, b). Here, the parents first decide how the child is treated in period 1, and then the child determines if he is willing to help out the family or meet the demand of the parents by deciding whether he should join the workforce as a child laborer, and how he would deal with his formal schooling, and consequently, his maturity would land at an appropriate level.

Also, our analysis above holds true if the child's disutility $V_1(1 - l_c - e_c)$ of working and formal schooling is replaced by either the disutility $V_1(1 - l_c)$ of working only or the disutility $V_1(1 - l_c)$ of formal schooling only, respectively. These individual cases would cover the following situations:

1. The child does not like to work for the purpose of making money but prefers going to school and any other activities.
2. The child does not like to experience the required formal schooling but prefers working for money and any other activities.

13.5 When Child Labor Is Marginally Banned

This section examines the equilibrium effects of marginal bans on child labor. It also studies how such bans may bring forward Pareto improvements to parents, child, and firms of the economy. The section consists of three subsections. The first subsection looks at the partial equilibrium effect of marginal bans on child labor. The second subsection investigates the general-equilibrium effects of such bans on child labor. And, the third subsection addresses the Pareto improvement of such bans to parents, child, and firms of the economy.

13.5.1 Partial Equilibrium Effect of Marginal Bans on Child Labor

As analyzed above, especially in Proposition 13.9, it is highly unlikely that individual families are capable of resolving the inefficiencies found in this chapter. So, a natural thinking is to introduce government regulations to mandate some behavioral changes of all citizens, such as imposing a reduction of child labor. (Historically, trade unions were influential in pressing for banning child labor. One reason is that it is thought to depress wages (Davin, 1982; Zelizer, 1994; Doepke & Zilibotti, 2005).)

In terms of the yoyo model, this thinking implies that we place individual family yoyo collections in the influence of the spin field of a much mightier yoyo, which is the government. The reason this government yoyo is much mightier than the individual family yoyo or an individual person's yoyo is because the government yoyo has the court system, legal system, police force, etc., at its disposal. Figure 13.3 shows how such a mightier spin field could affect individuals differently. Briefly, it flattens all small yoyos in the same direction. No matter whether the spin field influence of the government yoyo goes upward or downward, the effect of a partial ban on child labor will be mixed, depending on the specific circumstances that

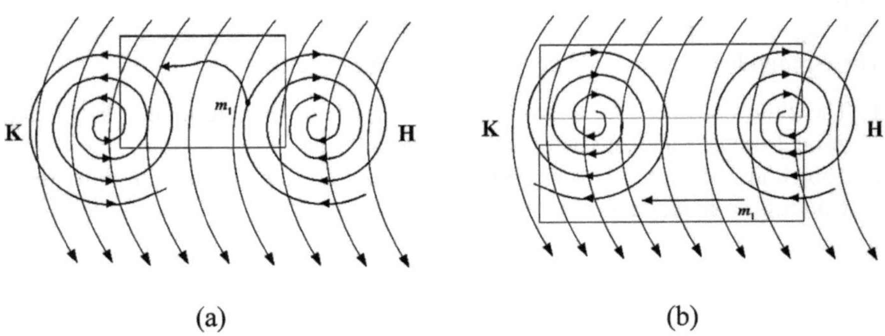

Fig. 13.3 Government yoyo's influence on individual's behavior and preferences. Parts (**a**) and (**b**) respectively depict the situations of similar and dissimilar personalities of H and K

individuals are in. For example, in the enclosed area in Fig. 13.3a, if the government's spin field goes downward, a partial ban on child labor will be welfare reducing for both the child K and the parent H. And, in the enclosed area in Fig. 13.3b, a partial ban on child labor will raise the welfare for both child K and parent H. This is a case where we assume that a linear technology is in place, meaning that the field of H spins at a constant speed.

Let us first analyze the partial equilibrium (or linear technology) effect of a marginal ban on child labor. Here, the partial equilibrium (or linear technology) is defined to mean that any variation of child labor supply has no effect on child and adult wages and firms' profits. Then, we have the following results.

Proposition 13.10 For all three models studied above, the model of one-sided altruism, that of two-sided altruism, and that with a child's disutility or utility, at partial equilibrium (or with linear technology), a marginal ban on child labor is welfare enhancing for the child but not for the parents if, for the first two models, the parents' bequests or savings are at a corner.

Proof For both the one-sided and two-sided altruism models, Propositions 13.2, 13.3, 13.5, and 13.8 imply that if the parents' bequests or savings are at a corner, the laissez faire triple $\left(l_{\mathrm{c}}^{*}, e_{\mathrm{c}}^{*}, m_{\mathrm{c}}^{*}\right)$ of child labor, formal schooling, and level of maturity is inefficiently high. So, when the child labor l_{c}^{*} is marginally reduced, the parents' utility W_{p} will be short from its maximum, while the efficiency of child labor will be accordingly improved.

For the model with child's disutility or utility from period 1, Proposition 13.9 and the discussions earlier imply that the laissez faire triple $\left(l_{\mathrm{c}}^{*}, e_{\mathrm{c}}^{*}, m_{\mathrm{c}}^{*}\right)$ is inefficiently high. So, the same reasoning as given in the previous paragraph applies here, which ends the proof.

Proposition 13.11 If either of the following conditions holds, then a marginal ban on child labor is welfare enhancing for the child but not for the parents.

1. Capital markets are perfect and $d(h - \tau)/da_{\mathrm{c}} > 0$;
2. Capital markets are imperfect and parents' savings are at a corner.

Proof The result follows from the remarks beneath Propositions 13.7 and 13.8.

Proposition 13.12 If capital markets are perfect and $d(h - \tau)/da_{\mathrm{c}} < 0$, then a marginal ban on child labor is welfare reducing for both the child and the parents.

Proof The proof of Proposition 13.7 implies that when capital markets are perfect and $d(h - \tau)/da_{\mathrm{c}} < 0$, the laissez faire triple $\left(l_{\mathrm{c}}^{*}, e_{\mathrm{c}}^{*}, m_{\mathrm{c}}^{*}\right)$ maximizes the parents' utility, but not enough to optimize the child's lifetime earnings potential. So, in this case, a marginal ban on child labor will not only make the parents' utility W_{p} short from its maximum, but also pull the child farther away from reaching his maximum lifetime earnings potential.

Proposition 13.13 If one of the following conditions holds true, then a marginal ban on child labor is welfare reducing for both the child and the parents.

1. for both one-sided and two-sided altruism models, the parents' bequests and savings are interior;
2. for the two-sided altruism model, capital markets are perfect, the child's transfers are interior, and the child lives on a fixed budget.

Proof The conclusion follows from Propositions 13.1, 13.4, and 13.7.

13.5.2 More General-Equilibrium Effects on Child Labor

Suppose next that a marginal ban on child labor is accompanied by a government legislation requiring an additional amount of formal schooling for each child. Then the child's human capital accumulation $a_c = a_c(l_c, e, m_c)$ might not necessarily drop with the marginal ban on child labor. For example, let

$$a_c = a_c(l_c, e_c, m_c) = l_c + (1 + e_c)^2 + m_c^2,$$

where we assume that the level of child's maturity m_c is of an order ≥ 2. If the marginal ban on child labor reduces the total available child labor supply by Δl_c ($>$ 0) and the government legislation requires an increasing amount of formal schooling by this available time slot Δl_c, then we have

$$\begin{aligned} a_c(l_c - \Delta l_c, e_c + \Delta l_c, m_c) &= (l_c - \Delta l_c) + (1 + e_c + \Delta l_c)^2 + m_c^2 \\ &= a_c(l_c, e, m_c) + 2e_c \Delta l_c + \Delta l_c + \Delta l_c^2 \\ &> a_c(l_c, e, m_c). \end{aligned}$$

In this case, both the total child income $C(a_c)$ and the adult child income $h(a_c)$ will in fact be increased.

At the same time, when the child labor drops by Δl_c (> 0) and formal schooling increases by Δl_c, if the child's level of maturity drops as much as $2\Delta l_c$ as a consequence of the marginal ban on child labor, then we have

$$\begin{aligned} a_c(l_c - \Delta l_c, e_c + \Delta l_c, m_c - 2\Delta l_c) &= a_c(l_c, e, m_c) + \Delta l_c(2e_c + 1 + 5\Delta l_c - 4m_c) \\ &< a_c(l_c, e, m_c). \end{aligned}$$

That is, in this case, both child income $C(a_c)$ and adult income $h(a_c)$ will drop. And both the parents and child are worse off.

Therefore, to guarantee success of any marginal ban on child labor, the corresponding levels of formal schooling and maturity should be kept up. Additionally, this analysis also suggests that a complete ban on child labor might not be a good idea. Here, by *complete ban* we mean that children are not allowed to work for income in any possible manner. It is because working experience, both positive and negative, surely helps to increase the value of m_c, the level of maturity.

Third, let us look at the general-equilibrium (or nonlinear technology) effects of a marginal ban on child labor, where a ban on child labor reduces the supply of child labor in period 1 and increases the supply of adult labor in period 2. As a result, period 1 wages might rise and period 2 wages might fall. (If we position this situation on an infinite timeline, it can be seen that all individuals are first children and then adults. So, the transition from a situation where there is no ban on child labor to a situation where there is a ban on child labor will be costly for the generation that spend their childhood before the transition and their adulthood after the transition. So, in a partial equilibrium approach or with linear technology, the introduction of a ban on child labor does not induce Pareto improvement, even though such a ban will benefit all the subsequent generations, because it is costly only to one generation. This remark also implies that when such government legislation as a ban on child labor is introduced, it should be implemented gradually to reduce the cost of the generation that lives across the transition.)

To develop our analysis, assume that there are agents in the economy who run firms and use labor to produce the numeraire good. For simplicity, we assume that only one such agent (a representative firm) exists, who lives through both time periods, has no children, and is endowed with nonlinear technologies for converting efficiency units of labor into commercial good. The firm's profit is given by

$$\pi = \sum_{t=1}^{2} \sum_{\mathrm{i}=\mathrm{p},\,\mathrm{c}} [f_{\mathrm{i}}(L_{\mathrm{i}t}) - w_{\mathrm{i}t}L_{\mathrm{i}t}], \tag{13.37}$$

where $L_{\mathrm{i}t}$ represents the firm's demand of i (= p, c) kind of labor, p = parents and c = children, in period t (= 1, 2); $w_{\mathrm{i}t}$ is the wage rate of i kind of labor in period t; and f_{i}, i = p, c, is the firm's economic output of the parental or child labor so that $f_{\mathrm{p}}(AL_{\mathrm{p}})$ is the output produced by parents in each time period, and $f_{\mathrm{c}}(C(a_{\mathrm{c}})L_{\mathrm{p}})$ and $f_{\mathrm{c}}(h(a_{\mathrm{c}})L_{\mathrm{p}})$ are the outputs produced by children in periods 1 and 2, respectively. Assume that the production functions f_{i}, i = p, c, are differentiable as needed, strictly increasing and strictly concave upward. The firm's objective is to choose $L_{\mathrm{i}t}$ to maximize its profit π given in Eq. (13.37). So, the optimal labor demand $L_{\mathrm{i}t}$ satisfies

$$f_{\mathrm{i}}'(L_{\mathrm{i}t}) - w_{\mathrm{i}t} = 0.$$

Considering available labor supplies in periods 1 and 2 (in efficiency units), equilibrium wages $w_{\mathrm{i}t}^*$ should satisfy the following market-clearing conditions:

$$\left.\begin{array}{ll} L_{\mathrm{p}1}\left(w_{\mathrm{p}1}\right) = AL_{\mathrm{p}}, & L_{\mathrm{c}1}\left(w_{\mathrm{c}1}\right) = L_{\mathrm{p}}C\left(a_{\mathrm{c}}^*\right) \\ L_{\mathrm{p}2}\left(w_{\mathrm{p}2}\right) = AL_{\mathrm{p}}, & L_{\mathrm{c}2}\left(w_{\mathrm{c}2}\right) = L_{\mathrm{p}}h\left(a_{\mathrm{c}}^*\right) \end{array}\right\}, \tag{13.38}$$

where $a_c^* = a_c(l_c^*, e_c^*, m_c^*)$ for the laissez faire triple (l_c^*, e_c^*, m_c^*) of child labor, formal schooling, and level of maturity.

We now study when a marginal ban of child labor will be Pareto improving to the parents, the child, and the representative firm in the economy under the general-equilibrium effects.

First, for the model of one-sided altruism, the parents maximize their utility W_p in Eq. (13.3) subject to the following budgetary constraints:

$$\left.\begin{array}{c} c_p^1 = c_p^1(l_c, e_c, m_c) = w_{p1}A + w_{c1}C(a_c) - s(a_c) \\ c_p^2 = c_p^2(l_c, e_c, m_c) = w_{p2}A - b(a_c) + s(a_c) \\ c_c = c_c(l_c, e_c, m_c) = w_{c2}h(a_c) + b(a_c) \end{array}\right\}.$$

where as before, c_p^1, c_p^2, c_c, C, s, and b are all differentiable increasing functions in each of their independent variables. So, the first-order conditions in Eqs. (13.6) and (13.8) still hold true.

For the firm, from Eq. (13.37) it follows that the effects of a small ban of child labor on its profits are given by

$$\frac{\partial \pi}{\partial l_c} = -\frac{\partial w_{c1}}{\partial l_c} L_{c1} - \frac{\partial w_{c2}}{\partial l_c} L_{c2}. \tag{13.39}$$

Differentiating the market-clearing conditions in Eq. (13.38) provides

$$L'_{c1}(w_{c1}) \frac{\partial w_{c1}}{\partial l_c} = L_p \frac{\partial C}{\partial l_c} \quad \text{and} \quad L'_{c2}(w_{c2}) \frac{\partial w_{c2}}{\partial l_c} = L_P \frac{\partial h}{\partial l_c}.$$

So, Eq. (13.39) can be rewritten as

$$\frac{\partial \pi}{\partial l_c} = -L_p \left(\frac{\partial C}{\partial l_c} w_{c1} \varepsilon_{c1} + \frac{\partial h}{\partial l_c} w_{c2} \varepsilon_{c2} \right), \tag{13.40}$$

where

$$\varepsilon_{it} = \frac{\partial w_{it}}{\partial L_{it}} \frac{L_{it}}{w_{it}}, \quad \text{for i} = \text{p, c}, t = 1, 2,$$

is the elasticity of the wage rate to the amount of labor demanded. So, $\partial \pi / \partial l_c$ is nonpositive if

$$\frac{\partial C}{\partial l_c} w_{c1} \varepsilon_{c1} + \frac{\partial h}{\partial l_c} w_{c2} \varepsilon_{c2} \geq 0. \tag{13.41}$$

For parents, the effects of the ban are given by

$$\frac{\partial W_{\mathrm{p}}}{\partial l_{\mathrm{c}}} = U'\left(c_{\mathrm{p}}^{1}\right)\left[w_{\mathrm{c}1}\frac{\partial C}{\partial l_{\mathrm{c}}}(\varepsilon_{\mathrm{c}1}+1)+w_{\mathrm{c}2}\frac{\partial h}{\partial l_{\mathrm{c}}}(\varepsilon_{\mathrm{c}2}+1)\right],$$

assuming that the parents' bequests and savings are interior. That is, if we have the following, then the effects on the parental welfare are nonpositive:

$$w_{\mathrm{c}1}\frac{\partial C}{\partial l_{\mathrm{c}}}(\varepsilon_{\mathrm{c}1}+1)+w_{\mathrm{c}2}\frac{\partial h}{\partial l_{\mathrm{c}}}(\varepsilon_{\mathrm{c}2}+1)\leq 0. \tag{13.42}$$

For the child, the effects of the ban are

$$\frac{\partial W_{\mathrm{c}}}{\partial l_{\mathrm{c}}} = W_{\mathrm{c}}'(c_{\mathrm{c}})\left[w_{\mathrm{c}2}\frac{\partial h}{\partial l_{\mathrm{c}}}(\varepsilon_{\mathrm{c}2}+1)+\frac{\partial b}{\partial l_{\mathrm{c}}}\right],$$

which are nonpositive if

$$w_{\mathrm{c}2}\frac{\partial h}{\partial l_{\mathrm{c}}}(\varepsilon_{\mathrm{c}2}+1)+\frac{\partial b}{\partial l_{\mathrm{c}}}\leq 0. \tag{13.43}$$

13.5.3 Pareto Improvement to Parents, Child, and the Firm

This subsection develops conclusions on when a marginal ban of child labor will be Pareto improving to the parents, the child, and the representative firm in the economy under the general-equilibrium effects.

Proposition 13.14 For the one-sided altruism model, no ban on child labor can be a Pareto improvement.

Proof If the parents' bequests and savings are interior, then a ban on child labor is a Pareto improvement if Eqs. (13.41)–(13.43) hold true simultaneously. But Eqs. (13.41) and (13.42) cannot hold true at the same time.

If the parents' bequests or savings are not interior, then the first-order conditions (13.6) and (13.8) imply that

$$\begin{aligned}\frac{\partial W_{\mathrm{p}}}{\partial l_{\mathrm{c}}} &\geq \delta W_{\mathrm{c}}'(c_{\mathrm{c}})\left[w_{\mathrm{c}1}\frac{\partial C}{\partial l_{\mathrm{c}}}(\varepsilon_{\mathrm{c}1}+1)+w_{\mathrm{c}2}\frac{\partial h}{\partial l_{\mathrm{c}}}(\varepsilon_{\mathrm{c}2}+1)\right]\\ &= \delta W_{\mathrm{c}}'(c_{\mathrm{c}})\left[\left(w_{\mathrm{c}1}\varepsilon_{\mathrm{c}1}\frac{\partial C}{\partial l_{\mathrm{c}}}+w_{\mathrm{c}2}\varepsilon_{\mathrm{c}2}\frac{\partial h}{\partial l_{\mathrm{c}}}\right)+\left(w_{\mathrm{c}1}\frac{\partial C}{\partial l_{\mathrm{c}}}+w_{\mathrm{c}2}\frac{\partial h}{\partial l_{\mathrm{c}}}\right)\right].\end{aligned}$$

So, if Eq. (13.40) holds true, we must have $\partial W_{\mathrm{p}}/\partial l_{\mathrm{c}} > 0$.

Proposition 13.15 For the one-sided altruism model, a marginal increase on formal schooling is a Pareto improvement, if

$$E = \frac{\partial C}{\partial e_c} w_{c1}\varepsilon_{c1} + \frac{\partial h}{\partial e_c} w_{c2}\varepsilon_{c2} \leq 0 \tag{13.44}$$

$$E + \left(w_{c1}\frac{\partial C}{\partial e_c} + w_{c2}\frac{\partial h}{\partial e_c} \right) \geq 0 \tag{13.45}$$

and

$$w_{c2}\frac{\partial h}{\partial e_c}(\varepsilon_{c2} + 1) + \frac{\partial b}{\partial e_c} \geq 0.$$

Proof The details are similar to those used in the proof of the previous proposition and are omitted.

Second, for the model of two-sided altruism, the parents' and child's utilities are given in Eqs. (13.16) and (13.17) subject to the following constraints:

$$\left. \begin{array}{r} c_p^1 = c_p^1(l_c, e_c, m_c) = w_{p1}A + w_{c1}C(a_c) - s(a_c) \\ c_p^2 = c_p^2(l_c, e_c, m_c) = w_{p2}A - b(a_c) + s(a_c) + \tau(a_c) \\ c_c = c_c(l_c, e_c, m_c) = w_{c2}h(a_c) + b(a_c) - \tau(a_c) \end{array} \right\}, \tag{13.46}$$

where c_p^1, c_p^2, c_c, C, s, b, and τ are the same as before with the first-order conditions in Eqs. (13.22) and (13.24) holding true for the parents to maximize their utility W_p.

Proposition 13.16 For the two-sided altruism model, no ban on child labor can be a Pareto improvement.

Proof If a ban on child labor is a Pareto improvement, then its effects on the firm's profit π, the parents' utility W_p, and the child's utility W_c must satisfy

$$\frac{\partial \pi}{\partial l_c} \leq 0, \quad \frac{\partial W_p}{\partial l_c} \leq 0, \quad \frac{\partial W_c}{\partial l_c} \leq 0.$$

However, based on Eqs. (13.16), (13.22), and (13.24), it can be shown that

$$\frac{\partial W_c}{\partial l_c} \geq \frac{\delta V'(c_c)}{1 - \delta\lambda}\left[w_{c1}\frac{\partial C}{\partial l_c}(\varepsilon_{c1} + 1) + w_{c2}\frac{\partial h}{\partial l_c}(\varepsilon_{c2} + 1) \right].$$

Therefore, if $\partial\pi/\partial l_c \leq 0$ or Eq. (13.41) holds true, we have $\partial W_p/\partial l_c > 0$.

Proposition 13.17 For the two-sided altruism model, a marginal increase on formal schooling is a Pareto improvement, if Eqs. (13.44) and (13.45) and the following hold true:

$$w_{c2}\frac{\partial h}{\partial e_c}(\varepsilon_{c2}+1)+\delta\lambda w_{c1}\frac{\partial C}{\partial e_c}(\varepsilon_{c1}+1)\geq(1-\delta\lambda)\left(\frac{\partial\tau}{\partial e_c}-\frac{\partial b}{\partial e_c}\right). \tag{13.47}$$

Proof Both Eqs. (13.44) and (13.45) imply that

$$\frac{\partial\pi}{\partial e_c}\geq 0 \quad \text{and} \quad \frac{\partial W_p}{\partial e_c}\geq 0.$$

The effects of a marginal increase of formal schooling on the child are given by

$$\begin{aligned}
\frac{\partial W_c}{\partial e_c} &= \frac{1}{1-\delta\lambda}\left[V'(c_c)\frac{\partial c_c}{\partial e_c}+\lambda U'\left(c_p^1\right)\frac{\partial c_p^1}{\partial e_c}+\lambda U'\left(c_p^2\right)\frac{\partial c_p^2}{\partial e_c}\right]\\
&\geq \frac{V'(c_c)}{1-\delta\lambda}\left[\frac{\partial c_c}{\partial e_c}+\delta\lambda\frac{\partial c_p^1}{\partial e_c}+\delta\lambda\frac{\partial c_p^2}{\partial e_c}\right]\\
&= \frac{V'(c_c)}{1-\delta\lambda}\left[\varepsilon_{c2}\frac{\partial h}{\partial e_c}(\varepsilon_{c2}+1)+\delta\lambda w_{c1}\frac{\partial C}{\partial e_c}(\varepsilon_{c1}+1)+(1-\delta\lambda)\left(\frac{\partial b}{\partial e_c}-\frac{\partial\tau}{\partial e_c}\right)\right].
\end{aligned}$$

So, Eq. (13.47) implies $\partial W_c/\partial e_c \geq 0$. That is, when the required conditions are satisfied, any marginal increase on formal schooling is a Pareto improvement.

Third, for the model with a child's disutility from period 1, the parents' and child's utilities are given in Eqs. (13.32) and (13.33) subject to the budgetary constraints in Eq. (13.46). So, Eqs. (13.24), (13.34), and (13.35) hold true as the first-order conditions of the parents' utility maximization with respect to s, l_c, and e_c.

The effects of a small ban of child labor on parental welfare are given by

$$\begin{aligned}
\frac{\partial W_p}{\partial l_c} &= \frac{1}{1-\delta\lambda}\left\{U'\left(c_p^1\right)\frac{\partial c_p^1}{\partial l_c}+U'\left(c_p^2\right)\frac{\partial c_p^2}{\partial l_c}-\left[\delta V_1'(1-l_c-e_c)-\delta V_2'(c_c)\frac{\partial c_c}{\partial l_c}\right]\right\}\\
&\leq \frac{1}{1-\delta\lambda}\left\{U'\left(c_p^1\right)\left[\frac{\partial c_p^1}{\partial l_c}+\frac{\partial c_p^2}{\partial l_c}\right]-\left[U'\left(c_p^1\right)\frac{\partial c_p^1}{\partial l_c}+U'\left(c_p^2\right)\frac{\partial c_p^2}{\partial l_c}\right]\right\}\\
&\quad (\because \text{Eqs.}(13.24) \text{ and } (13.34))\\
&\leq \frac{1}{1-\delta\lambda}\left[U'\left(c_p^1\right)-U'\left(c_p^2\right)\right]\cdot\left[\frac{\partial c_p^1}{\partial l_c}+\frac{\partial c_p^2}{\partial l_c}\right],
\end{aligned}$$

where the equality holds true when parents' savings are interior or capital markets are perfect.

The effects of the ban on the child labor are

$$\begin{aligned}\frac{\partial W_c}{\partial l_c} &= \frac{\delta\lambda - 1}{(1-\delta\lambda)\delta}\left[U'\left(c_p^1\right)\frac{\partial c_p^1}{\partial l_c} + U'\left(c_p^2\right)\frac{\partial c_p^2}{\partial l_c}\right] \text{(from Eq.(13.34))} \\ &< 0 \text{ (because } \delta\lambda - 1 < 0).\end{aligned}$$

Therefore, we have partially shown the following result.

Proposition 13.18 For the model with a child's disutility or utility from period 1, if the parents' savings are interior or capital markets are perfect and Eq. (13.41) holds true, then a ban on child labor is a Pareto improvement.

Note: Results in Propositions 13.10–13.14 and 13.16 agree with Basu and Van (1998), who also find that a ban on child labor is not Pareto improving. The result in Proposition 13.18 roughly agrees with what is obtained by Bommier and Dubois (2004).

Proof For the case where the child's utility in period 1 is considered, discussions in Sect. 13.4 beneath Proposition 13.9 apply here.

Similar to this analysis, Eq. (13.35) implies the following.

Proposition 13.19 For the model with a child's disutility or utility from period 1, no marginal increase on formal schooling is a Pareto improvement.

Proof The result follows from the fact that based on Eq. (13.35), we have

$$\frac{\partial W_c}{\partial e_c} = \frac{\delta\lambda - 1}{(1-\delta\lambda)\delta}\left[U'\left(c_p^1\right)\frac{\partial c_p^1}{\partial e_c} + \mathrm{U}'\left(c_p^2\right)\frac{\partial c_p^2}{\partial e_c}\right] < 0.$$

13.6 A Few Final Words

In this chapter, we emphasize on the importance of all three variables—child labor, formal schooling, and level of maturity—in the context of a child's accumulation of human capital. Because these variables may well interact with each other, we establish some both theoretically and practically important results, differing significantly from all those works that do not consider such possible interactions.

The results in this chapter show that when the parents are altruistic and well-disciplined in their lives, for example, they save in period 1 and bequeath in period 2, or if the adult children are altruistic and transfer to their parents, then efficiencies of child labor, formal schooling, and level of maturity can be achieved, assuming that the children have no feelings about their childhood experiences. However, if the children's period 1 feelings toward labor or formal schooling matter, the inefficiencies of child labor, formal schooling, and level of maturity become unavoidable. This is where the situation becomes challenging. In particular, if the laissez faire levels of child labor l_c^* or formal schooling e_c^* are not zero, then it leads to the rotten parents effect, as so named by Bommier and Dubois (2004), where the parents rationally sacrifice some of the children's childhood utility by making them work and study too much with the anticipation that this will result in higher future earnings of the children and consequently larger transfers from the children.

One possible method to reduce the size of inefficiencies is to introduce government legislations for a marginal ban on child labor and a marginal mandate on child's formal schooling. By doing so, there is a possible chance to achieve a Pareto improvement for all parties involved: the parents, children, and firms. This is because with more formal education, the children's level of maturity can be expected to rise and the human capital accumulation to accelerate. So, the earnings power as a child laborer or as an adult will accordingly increase.

The analysis in this chapter, in fact, also indirectly shows the reason why it is difficult or impossible to abolish child labor in reality. (The phenomenon of child labor is age old. In the contemporary world, the International Labor Organization estimates that worldwide 120 million children between the ages of 5 and 14 work fulltime. See, for example, ILO (1996). And in 2005, Krueger and Donohue (2005) quantified the effects of child labor legislation on human capital accumulation and distribution of wealth and welfare. They found that households with significant financial asset holdings unambiguously lose from any government intervention, high-wage workers benefit most from a ban on child labor, while low-wage workers benefit the most from free education, and that a child labor ban induces welfare losses because it reduces income opportunities for poor families without being effective in stimulating education attainment.) This is because under different circumstances, the laissez faire triple $\left(l_c^*, e_c^*, m_c^*\right)$ of child labor, formal schooling, and level of maturity can be efficient, inefficiently high, or inefficiently low. And in reality, these circumstances can easily evolve from a state where the laissez faire triple is efficient to one where the triple becomes inefficient. And not even government legislations on a ban of child labor can be guaranteed to be Pareto improving.

References

Baland, J. M., & Robinson, J. (2000). Is child labor inefficient? *Journal of Political Economics, 108*(4), 663–679.

Basu, K., & Van, P. H. (1998). The economics of child labor. *The American Economic Review, 88*(3), 412–427.

Becker, G. (1974). A theory of social interactions. *Journal of Political Economics, 82*(6), 1063–1093.

Becker, G. S. (1991). *A treatise of the family*. Harvard University Press.

Becker, G., & Murphy, K. (1988). The family and the state. *The Journal of Law & Economics, 31*(1), 1–18.

Bommier, A., & Dubois, P. (2004). Rotten parents and child labor. *Journal of Political Economics, 112*(1), 240–248.

Canagarajah, R., & Coulombe, H. (1997). *Child labor and schooling in Ghana. Human development technical report (Africa Region)*. World Bank.

Chakraborty, S., & Das, M. (2005). Mortality, fertility, and child labor. *Economics Letters, 86*(2), 273–278.

Davin, A. (1982). Child labour, the working class family, and domestic ideology in 19th century Britain. *Development and Change, 13*(4), 633–652.

Dessy, S. (2000). A defense of compulsive measures against child labor. *Journal of Development Economics, 62*(1), 261–275.

Doepke, M., & Zilibotti, F. (2005). The macroeconomics of child labor regulation. *The American Economic Review, 95*(5), 1492–1524.

Ennew, J. (1982). Family structure, unemployment and child labour in Jamaica. *Development and Change, 13*(4), 551–563.

Eswarran, M. (1996). *Fertility, literacy and the institution of child labor.* Manuscript, Department of Economics, University of British Columbia.

ILO. (1996). *Child labor: Targeting the intolerable.* ILO.

Krueger, D., & Donohue, J. (2005). On the distributional consequences of child labor legislation. *International Economic Review, 46*(3), 785–815.

Labenne, S. (1997). *The determinants of child labor in India. Manuscript, C.R. E.D.* University of Namur.

Lin, Y. (1999). *General systems theory: A mathematical approach.* Plenum and Kluwer Academic Publishers.

Lin, Y. (2007). Systemic yoyo model and applications in Newton's, Kepler's laws, etc. *Kybernetes: The International Journal of Systems, Cybernetics and Management, 36*(3/4), 484–516.

Lin, Y. (2009). *Systemic yoyos: Some impacts of the second dimension.* CRC Press.

Lin, Y., & Forrest, D. (2008a). Economic yoyos and Becker's rotten kid theorem. *Kybernetes: The International Journal of Systems, Cybernetics and Management, 37*(2), 297–314.

Lin, Y., & Forrest, D. (2008b). Economic yoyos, parasites and child labor. *Kybernetes: The International Journal of Systems, Cybernetics and Management, 37*(6), 757–767.

Lin, Y., & Forrest, B. (2011). *Systemic structure behind human organizations: From civilizations to individuals*. Springer.

Nerlove, M., Razin, A., & Sadka, E. (1988). A bequest constrained economy: Welfare analysis. *Journal of Public Economics, 37*(2), 203–220.

Ranjan, P. (2001). Credit constraints and the phenomenon of child labor. *Journal of Development Economics, 64*(1), 81–102.

Ravallion, M., & Wodon, Q. (2000). Does child labour displace schooling? Evidence on behavioural responses to an enrollment subsidy. *The Economic Journal, 110*(462), C158–C175.

Rosenzweig, M. (1981). Household and non-household activities of youths: Issues of modeling, data and estimation strategies. In G. Rodgers & G. Standing (Eds.), *Child work, poverty and unemployment.* International Labour Organization.

Weiner, M. (1991). *The child and the state in India.* Princeton University Press.

Wu, Y., & Lin, Y. (2002). *Beyond nonstructural quantitative analysis: Blown-ups, spinning currents and modern science*. World Scientific.

Zelizer, V. A. (1994). *Pricing the priceless child: The changing social value of children*. Princeton University Press.

Chapter 14
Industry Sizes and Wage Differentials

Jeffrey Yi-Lin Forrest

Abstract This chapter, which is mainly based on Lin (Systemic yoyos: impacts of the second dimension, Auerbach Publications, 2008), studies the structure of inter-industrial wages and provides a fresh look at inter-industrial wage differentials. To accomplish this end, the chapter models each commercial firm as a specific spinning yoyo and reveals how these economic yoyos interact with each other through combinations and breakups on the basis of the evolution of a flow of such yoyos. Similar analysis shows why at any chosen moment of time in history, there are economic sectors and industries of various scales. With such a dynamic systemic analysis, which points to certain key structures for each existing commercial entity, such as a firm, economic sector, or industry, in place, this chapter establishes a simple profit maximization model to study large and small firms and their differences in areas of production, determination of product selling prices, and the cost basis of their products. Among other conclusions, it is found that when a firm has limited resources, its potential level of profits experiences a glass ceiling.

Keywords Capital markets · High-wage industries · Law of one price · Need for additional personnel · Rotten kid theorem · Supporting occupations · Unionization · Wage differentials

14.1 Introduction

For over half a century in the most recent past, many first-class economists, including Nobel laureates George Stigler of 1982 (Stigler, 1958), Robert Solow of 1987 (Solow, 1979), George Akerlof of 2001, and Daniel Kahneman of 2002 (Kahneman et al., 1986), have contributed to the understanding of inter-industrial wage pattern. However, as Thaler (1989) shows, none of the established attempts seems to explain the existing pattern in a satisfactory manner without assuming something difficult to accept. To answer this call, the current chapter provides an intuitive and plausible explanation without assuming anything difficult to swallow, thanks to the systemic yoyo model and the methodology of systems science.

More specifically, over a half century ago, economists started to notice stable wage differentials existing inter-industrially over time and across national borders.

J. Y.-L. Forrest, *Systemic Principles of Applied Economic Philosophies II*,
Translational Systems Sciences 39, https://doi.org/10.1007/978-981-99-7939-4_14

Some industries pay their workers more than other industries (Slichter, 1950). And the differentials apply across all occupations. That is, if one occupation in an industry is highly paid, then all other occupations of the same industry tend to be so too, and such wage differentials appear stably over time and exist internationally.

To successfully answer Thaler's (1989) call, this chapter models each commercial firm as a specific spinning yoyo and reveals how these economic yoyos interact with each other through combinations and breakups on the basis of the evolution of a flow of such yoyos. Then, it develops a simple profit maximization model to study large and small firms and their differences in areas of production, determination of the selling prices, and cost bases of their products. By employing this simple profit maximization model to the study of inter-industry wage differentials, it is found that financially resourceful companies have a large array of advantages over those companies that are limited by their resources. One example of such advantage is that the former companies bring in handsome profits in two dimensions—the product dimension and the personnel dimension, while the latter companies could only produce their profits from a single dimension—the products—with an invisible glass ceiling. Note: According to discussions in the first volume of this monograph series, not all firms attempt to maximize its profit. Instead, they all maximize the realization of their respective missions. However, considering the fact that the present world of business is still mostly composed of such firms that aim at maximizing profits. Therefore, the simple profit maximization model developed for the described purpose above is appropriate for our need.

To maximize their profit in the human resource dimension, financially resourceful companies need to spend extra money on their employees. This end provides the long-sought-after explanation for the stable wage differentials existing inter-industrially over time and across national borders (Thaler, 1989). Beyond this wonderful outcome, the model derived herein also provides plausible economic reasons for other relevant questions, including, but not limited to,

- Why high-wage industries tend to have low quit rates,
- Why profits and market power are reliable predictors of industry wages,
- Why the association between wages and labor's share of costs in an industry is negative,
- Why industries with high capital-labor ratios tend to pay higher wages,
- Why unionization rate increases wages for both union and nonunion members in a firm, etc.

What is worth mentioning here is that in the labor market, the law of one price does not hold true for job opportunities that look identical in their job descriptions.

The rest of the chapter is organized as follows: Sect. 14.2 provides the reader with all the necessary background information, including a literature review and the systemic modeling of business firms and their interactions. Section 14.3 examines why there are different industrial sizes by using the concept of economic eddies. Section 14.4 investigates the phenomenon of stably and internationally existing wage differences from one industry to another. Based on what are developed in these sections, Sect. 14.5 pays a revisit to some of the main theories regarding this phenomenon and provides a self-contained and plausible theory while shedding new light on the law of one price. The chapter concludes in Sect. 14.6.

14.2 Preparations

The purpose of this section is to make the chapter as self-contained as possible by providing the reader with a literature review, showing how this chapter makes it contribution and then deriving a systemic yoyo model for business firms and their interactions.

14.2.1 Literature Review

To comprehend the inter-industrial wage structure and to discover the mechanism behind it, many scholars over the past decades have looked at the topic from various angles and made a lot of important progress. Even so, the wage differentials still cannot be fathomed in its entirety without introducing some hypotheses that are difficult to accept by the community of economists. These hypotheses include, but are not limited to:

1. Firms are choosing not to maximize their profits (Krueger & Summers, 1987).
2. Firms pay attention to perceived equity in setting wages (Akerlof & Yellen, 1990).
3. High-wage firms find that lowering wages would decrease their profits (Krueger & Summers, 1987).
4. A high-paying industry involves unpleasant and unsafe working environment.
5. Higher wages are employed for the purpose of hiring better workers for their both measurable and immeasurable labor quality.
6. Compensation differences naturally exist between industries.
7. Each employee's effort $e(w)$ is an increasing function of his wage rate w.
8. Firms engage in monitoring their workers' performance—those who are caught shirking will be fired.
9. Higher wages are used to reduce the rate of employees quitting, because hiring and training workers can be expensive (Hamermesh, 1993).
10. Making employees feel that they are paid fairly.
11. Firms that pay higher wages are able to expend its resources in such a way.
12. Higher wages are positively related to labor union density, etc.

The idea that firm managers would choose not to maximize profits and instead have highly paid employees, including the blue-color workers far removed from the managers' milieu, is a real enigma. Due to this reason, there has not been any attempt to explain inter-industrial wage differentials using any agency model. Conversely, several attempts (for example, Stiglitz, 1976; Akerlof & Yellen, 1990; Berlinski,

2000) have been made to apply the concept of norms of internal equity in setting wages as constraints. They lead to the appearance of persistent inter-industrial wage differentials and uniformity across occupations of the inter-industrial wage structure. However, such an assumption seems to be controversial to economists (Thaler, 1989).

For hypothesis 3 to hold, one has to assume either that higher wages can increase production output, which is the foundation of the efficiency wage models (Yellen, 1984), or that higher wages are offered as a natural response to the threat of possible collective actions (Dickens, 1986).

The uniformity of wage differentials across occupations works against both explanations 4 and 5 (Thaler, 1989). And although explanation 6 is undoubtedly true to a degree (Rosen, 1986), it still cannot explain why such compensation differences exist from one industry to another. Murphy and Topal (1987) support explanation 5, believing that the unexplained variance is due to employees' unobserved abilities. By identifying "the unobserved abilities" as intelligence, in particular as IQ test scores, Blackburn and Neumark (1988) find that there is a negative relationship between an industry's wage and the average IQ scores of its employees.

Explanations 7–10 are the fundamental premises of the so-called efficiency wage models using the rigor of mathematics (Yellen, 1984). These models have attracted a great deal of attention and tend to prove that higher than competitive wages can be profitable.

By specifying the positive effort-wage relationship, as described in explanation 7, four main classes of efficiency wage models have been established. More specifically, shirking models (Shapiro & Stiglitz, 1984) are developed to describe how hard employees work at their jobs where piece rates are impractical due to either the difficulty of counting "pieces" or high costs of monitoring, or both. By paying above market wages, firms engage in monitoring their workers and fire those who are caught shirking. As expected, these models indicate that high-wage industries are those with high monitoring costs or those bearing high costs of employee shirking. About shirking models, Thaler (1989) casts the following natural questions: Do employees work harder when they think they are in danger of losing a high-paying-job? Do employees work enough harder to justify the higher wages? Are the firms that pay high wages those that would gain the most from an increase in workers' effort? The analysis in this chapter will address these important questions from a new angle completely and definitely.

The so-called turnover models are established on the assumption that explanation 9 holds true (Salop, 1979; Stiglitz, 1974). Consequently, these models predict that high-wage industries are those with the highest costs associated with quitting. Because data on quit rates are published, it has been confirmed that paying high wages does decrease quit rates. Adverse selection models (Stiglitz, 1976; Weiss, 1980) are established based on explanations 5 and 7 by assuming that the average quality of the applicant pool increases with the wage rate. These models imply that industries that are sensitive to labor quality or spend a lot on measuring quality offer high wages. Evidently, these models do not provide a convincing explanation for the inter-industrial wage patterns.

On explanation 10, fair-wage models are created (Akerlof & Yellen, 1990; Solow, 1979) by assuming that employees will exert more effort if they think they are being paid fairly. Under this premise, firms pay wages above competitive levels whenever their workers' perceived fair wage exceeds the competitive wage. As a result, these models lead to such conclusions as industries with high profits or where teamwork and employee cooperation are particularly important will pay high wages (Kahneman et al., 1986). Even though both common sense and social psychological research on equity theory suggest that workers are more productive if the morale is high, the following practical problem remains open: Is the true efficiency wage that sets the marginal gains from increased morale equal to marginal costs (Thaler, 1989)? To this end, Raff and Summers (1987) evaluated Ford's decision in 1913 to double wages.

Evidently, explanation 11 does not make sense, because each dollar wage increase means a dollar dividend less for the stockholders. As for explanation 12, the analysis in this chapter below will show that labor unions are attracted to high-wage industries instead of the other way around, even though studies find that industry wage rates are corrected to union density (the percentage of workers in an industry who belong to a union), and that the unionization rate increases wages for both union and nonunion members in an industry.

Evidently, these listed hypotheses, provided to explain the inter-industrial wage differentials, seem difficult for an economist to accept (Thaler, 1989). Facing this challenge, this chapter turns to the systemic yoyo model and the logic of thinking of systems science to see what one can develop beyond what is known now in this area of research. This methodological choice is made based on the fact that these unconventional tools can be effectively employed to analyze nonlinear interactions (Lin, 2008).

14.2.2 Abstract Economic Yoyos and Their Interactions

Let us model a commercial company as a spinning yoyo, as shown in Fig. 14.1, where the input side sucks in all the basic supplies to sustain the vitality of the company, such as all needed raw materials, utilities, human resources, various services, and, most importantly, the profit. The output side emits the company's products. Through marketing effort, the company establishes its reputation for quality and occupies a certain percentage of the consumer market. With the help of its R&D efforts, the company continuously eyes on expansions in new areas of business. Various internal decision-making units, including the board of directors, the CEO, and other executives, connect the two sides of the spinning yoyo (Gillan, 2006).

The force necessary for such a yoyo to exist is the continued inflow of profits (or investment) at and above the minimum sustainable level. Without the profits or

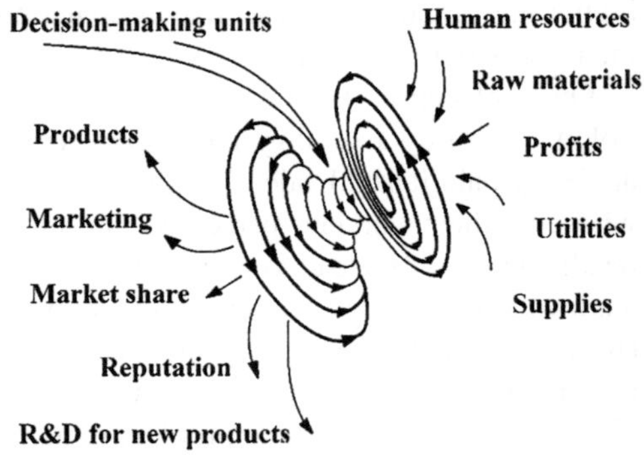

Fig. 14.1 The yoyo model for a viable commercial company

the ability to generate the adequate profits, the company will fail and its economic yoyo will disappear. When the opportunity to generate adequate profits exists in the marketplace, many entrepreneurs will enter the same sector of the economic actions to fight for their share of the potential pool of profits. Therefore, an industry or economic sector starts to emerge. If we imagine all the possible spinning yoyos of an industry, each of which stands for a company, floating against each other, we then can see the fact that some yoyos will have the tendency to combine into greater yoyos, and other yoyos may break up into smaller yoyos or simply disappear, depending on the yoyos' spinning directions, speeds, and angles of tilt. For details on how spinning yoyos could interact with each other, please consult with Lin (2008). As long as the flow of demands is unstable, the economic yoyos will continue to fight for their own:

1. Existence,
2. Survival, and
3. Possible expansion.

When the picture of demands begins to crystallize, that is, when the acting and reacting forces start to stabilize, the intensive struggles for market shares between the economic yoyos will decline to a minimum and the entire economic sector begins to stabilize. This description is based on studies of fluid motions (OuYang, 1994) without using any of the terminology.

Now, if each economic yoyo, representing an individual company, in the previous imagined picture is replaced by such a bigger economic yoyo that represents an economic sector or industry, then a similar evolution of struggles for market share or available resources and profit opportunities between industries or economic sectors would exist. This evolution of struggle would be dynamic if we place it in the flow of time. In particular, some yoyos, representing economic sectors or industries, will have the tendency to combine into greater yoyos, and others may break apart into smaller yoyos or simply disappear. This evolutionary process is similar to that of a current of water rushing down a high land. If the boundary conditions are complicated, the state of the flow patterns of the current will be difficult to model using the traditional mathematics. It is because the overall state of motion is moving downward mixed with local variations, such as jet streams, whirlpools of different sizes, strengths, and directions, etc. So, if we take a snapshot for the evolution of economic power struggle between the economic yoyos of various industries, in the still momentary picture, we can expect to see spinning yoyos of different sizes, meaning some industries (yoyos) suck in more profits and human resources than others. It is reasonable to expect that industries whose yoyo structures suck in more profits and other available resources behave differently than other industries.

The qualitative analysis of economic yoyos, as given above, can continue along a line parallel to the evolution process of a fluid motion, and a corresponding mathematical analysis can be introduced to support such a qualitative analysis. In the following, we will establish a simple analytic model based on the premise of the yoyo model to see that the analysis above actually works out mathematically. Also, this analytic model provides a platform for us to study the inter-industrial wage differentials without introducing any hard-to-accept hypothesis.

14.3 Economic Eddies and Industrial Sizes

This section investigates the profit picture of a firm that sells a particular product directly to the marketplace. To this end, it consists of two subsections with the first one assuming that the firm has unlimited financial resources, while the second one greatly constrained by its financial capability.

14.3.1 A Differential Model Description of Perfect Capital Markets

Assume that a retailer sells a specific product for $\$p_s$ each unit. The total cost for the entire process of acquiring the product, shipping and handling, insurance, storage, salesperson's salary, etc., is $\$p_p$ each unit. Let $n = n(p_s)$ be the total number of units sold at the price $\$p_s$ per unit. Then, for this particular retailer, his profit from this single line of product is given by

$$P = \text{profit} = n(p_s)\left(p_s - p_p\right). \tag{14.1}$$

If the capital markets are perfect, meaning that the retailer can borrow as much funds to purchase or produce as many units of the product as he needs to at any desirable time, then he would determine such a selling price $\$p_s$ so that his profit P in Eq. (14.1) will be maximized. The first-order condition for this maximization problem is given as follows:

$$\frac{\partial P}{\partial p_s} = n'(p_s)(p_s - p_p) + n(p_s) = 0.$$

For each fixed p_s- and p_p-value, we have

$$n'(p_s) = -\frac{n(p_s)}{p_s - p_p}.$$

This is a separable differential equation; its solution is

$$n(p_s) = \frac{C}{p_s - p_p}, \tag{14.2}$$

where C is the constant of integration. If at the price level p_{s0} the initial market demand for the product is $n(p_{s0})$ units, then Eq. (14.2) implies that $C = n(p_{s0})(p_{s0} - p_p)$. Substituting this C-value and Eq. (14.2) into Eq. (14.1) leads to

$$P = \text{profit} = n(p_{s0})(p_{s0} - p_p). \tag{14.3}$$

Equation (14.2) implies that if the retailer plans to make a profit on each unit of his product, meaning $p_s > p_p$, then the constant C will be positive and $n(p_s)$ increases indefinitely as the selling price $p_s \to p_p^+$. For reasons like competition or clearing out the specific product line, the retailer could choose to get rid of the product by selling it at a price p_s below the cost p_p. In this case, the constant C will be less than 0. If the retailer is involved in a competition to occupy a greater market share for his product, then Eq. (14.2) also implies that he has to keep the unit price p_s as close to the cost basis p_p as possible to maximize the market demand $n(p_s)$.

To maximize his profit P, Eq. (14.3) indicates that if the difference $(p_{s0} - p_p)$ stays constant, the lower the p_{s0}-value, the greater the demand $n(p_{s0})$ and the greater the total profit P. So, to generate as much profit as possible, the retailer has to keep his per-unit cost p_p as low as possible. Because costs like shipping and handling, insurance, storage, salesperson's salaries, etc., are exogenous to the retailer and are quite robust, the retailer's efficient strategy to drastically reduce the cost basis p_p is to locate a manufacturer who can massively produce the needed product at a price below all other competitors. There are many ways to achieve this goal. For example, the manufacturer can hire a labor force at a below-the-market price, purchase his raw materials at extremely low prices, or introduce a revolutionary technology to drastically increase the labor's productivity.

Because raw materials and energies are international commodities mostly traded on global markets, and due to the advances of information technology, all competing manufacturers can quite easily catch up with technological innovations, to purchase products at below-the-market prices, the retailer would naturally go to places where the labor quality is adequate and the labor costs are as low as possible. When many retailers look for such ideal labor markets, manufacturing businesses naturally start to relocate in different geographic locations with as close to ideal labor bases as possible. That is, the sea of economic yoyos starts to flow, caused by the uneven force of competition. This end explains why the current trend of moving manufacturing operations from industrialized nations to third world countries does not seem reversible in the foreseeable future, as long as international transportation costs stay low and the global economic system stays open and competitive. In fact, this end is simulated well by the fluid patterns found in the dishpan experiment.

Assume in Eq. (14.1) that the selling price p_s drops an increment $\Delta p_s > 0$ per unit. If the retailer does not pick up any additional market demand for his product at this reduced price ($p_s - \Delta p_s$), then he would have a loss in the amount of $n(p_s)\Delta p_s$. So, if at the lower unit price level, the retailer expands the market demand $n(p_s)$ to that of $n(p_s - \Delta p_s)$, and if the profit increment $P(p_s - \Delta p_s) - P(p_s)$ is greater than the theoretical loss $n(p_s)\Delta p_s$, that is,

$$n(p_s - \Delta p_s)(p_s - \Delta p_s - p_p) - n(p_s)(p_s - p_p) > n(p_s)\Delta p_s, \tag{14.4}$$

then the retailer would rather reduce his unit selling price p_s to maximize his profit. Equation (14.4) is equivalent to the following:

$$\frac{dP(p_s)}{dp_s} = \lim_{\Delta p_s \to 0^+} \frac{P(p_s - \Delta p_s) - P(p_s)}{-\Delta p_s} < -n(p_s). \tag{14.5}$$

Now, instead of reducing the per-unit selling price p_s by an increment $\Delta p_s > 0$, the unit cost basis p_p is increased by an increment $\Delta p_p > 0$. If the retailer does not pick up any additional demand for his product with his increased cost basis, then he would experience a loss in the amount of $n(p_p)\Delta p_s$. However, if such an increase in his cost basis produces a new market demand $n(p_p + \Delta p_p)$ and the change in profit P satisfies

$$P(p_p + \Delta p_p) - P(p_p) > n(p_p)\Delta p_p, \tag{14.6}$$

then the retailer would rather increase his unit cost basis by as much as necessary to maximize his profit. Now, Eq. (14.6) is equivalent to the following:

$$\frac{dP(p_p)}{dp_p} = \lim_{\Delta p_p \to 0^+} \frac{P(p_p + \Delta p_p) - P(p_p)}{\Delta p_p} > n(p_p). \tag{14.7}$$

Combining Eqs. (14.5) and (14.7) provides the following conclusions.

Proposition 14.1 Assume that the capital markets are perfect. If at a unit selling price $p_s = p_{s0}$ and a unit cost basis $p_p = p_{p0}$, the total profit $P(p_s, p_p)$ from selling the product satisfies:

1. The retailer can reduce his unit selling price p_{s0} to increase his total profit, when

$$\left.\frac{dP}{dp_s}\right|_{p_s=p_{s0}} < -n(p_{s0});$$

2. The retailer can increase his unit cost basis p_{p0} to reap in additional profits, when

$$\left.\frac{dP}{dp_p}\right|_{p_p=p_{p0}} > n(p_{p0});$$

3. The retailer can both reduce his unit selling price p_{s0} and increase his unit cost basis p_{p0} to boast his total profit from his specific line of product, when

$$\left.\frac{dP}{dp_s}\right|_{p_s=p_{s0}} < -n(p_{s0}) \quad \text{and} \quad \left.\frac{dP}{dp_p}\right|_{p_p=p_{p0}} > n(p_{p0}).$$

What is implied in the previous analysis includes the fact that if by reducing his unit profit ($p_s - p_p$) the retailer can greatly increase his total profit by gaining additional market demand, he will try all he can to accomplish that goal. More specifically, he might:

1. launch an aggressive commercial campaign where p_s is increased to expand the market demand,
2. acquire a larger number of units of the product at a much lower price, where p_p is decreased so that p_s can be accordingly lowered to attract more customers,
3. lower per-unit shipping and handling costs with increased volume of business,
4. lower per-unit insurance costs with increased volume of business so that the savings can be passed on to the customers to create a healthier market demand, and
5. increase the salesperson's wages. With such a potential of drastically increasing take-home pays, the salesperson would work harder and smarter so that the market demand is consequently pushed to new extremes.

Example 14.1 Assume that for a special product, the unit cost basis $p_p = \$5.00$ and its market demand is determined by $n(p_s) = 1000\exp(5 - p_s)$, where p_s is the unit selling price. So, the total profit from selling $n(p_s)$ units at $\$p_s$ each is

$$P = n(p_s)(p_s - 5) = 1000e^{5-p_s}(p_s - 5).$$

If $p_s > 7$, then we have $\partial P/\partial p_s < -n(p_s)$. Proposition 14.1(1) implies that if the retail company is well funded, it can increase its profit by reducing the unit selling price as close to \$7+ as possible.

Similar examples can be constructed for the scenarios in Proposition 14.1 (2) and (3).

14.3.2 A Differential Model Description of Imperfect Capital Markets

In this section, we analyze the simple model established in the previous section for the case of imperfect capital markets. That is, the profit P in Eq. (14.1) is subject to the following constraint:

$$n(p_s)p_p = I, \tag{14.8}$$

where I is the total available funds for the retailer to invest in his line of product and $n(p_s)$ is seen as the size of the inventory. The first-order conditions for maximizing the profit P subject to the constraint in Eq. (14.8) are given by

$$\frac{\partial P}{\partial p_s} = n'(p_s)(p_s - p_p) + n(p_s) = \lambda n'(p_s)p_p \tag{14.9}$$

and

$$\begin{aligned}\frac{\partial P}{\partial p_p} &= n'(p_s)\frac{dp_s}{dp_p}(p_s - p_p) + n(p_s)\left(\frac{dp_s}{dp_p} - 1\right)\\ &= \lambda\left[n'(p_s)\frac{dp_s}{dp_p}p_p + n(p_s)\right],\end{aligned} \tag{14.10}$$

where λ is the Lagrange multiplier. Substituting Eq. (14.9) into Eq. (14.10) leads to

$$(1+\lambda)n(p_s) = 0.$$

Equation (14.8) implies that $n(p_s) \neq 0$ so that the previous equation indicates $\lambda = -1$. So, Eq. (14.9) becomes

$$n'(p_s)p_s = -n(p_s).$$

Solving this equation for $n(p_s)$ gives us

$$n(p_s) = \frac{n(p_{s0})p_{s0}}{p_s}, \tag{14.11}$$

where $n(p_{s0})$ is the initial market demand when the product is sold for $\$p_{s0}$ per unit. So, the retailer's profit P is given by

$$P = \text{profit} = \frac{n(p_{s0})p_{s0}}{p_s}(p_s - p_p) \tag{14.12a}$$

$$= n(p_{s0})p_{s0}\left(1 - \frac{p_p}{p_s}\right). \tag{14.12b}$$

Equation (14.11) indicates that to expand the market demand, the retailer has to decrease his unit selling price. Because the capital markets are imperfect, this means that the retailer has a limited resource to invest in his product. That is, he cannot afford to compete with a retailer who has unlimited resources. Similar to the situation of a financially powerful retailer, our small retailer can also increase his profit by reducing his selling price p_s, if he can keep the unit profit ($p_s - p_p$) constant. However, unlike the powerful retailer in Sect. 14.3.1, our small retailer has a cap, $n(p_{s0})p_{s0}$ (Eq. 14.12b), on how much he can expand his potential of total profit. This comparison tells us the following two facts:

Proposition 14.2 When financial resources are limited, any venture will have a glass ceiling for its maximum level of profits.

Proposition 14.3 Small retailers or poorly funded ventures do not have many opportunities to locate extremely low-priced manufacturers.

This conclusion follows from the implied limitations of resources and Proposition 14.2. Speaking differently, because of their limited resources, small retailers or poorly funded ventures do not have the ability to place large orders, and also, they do not have the financial strength to create their own low-priced manufacturing operations to strengthen their ability to compete.

By comparing Eqs. (14.12a) and (14.12b) to conclusions (1)–(5) in the previous section, we can see the following facts:

Proposition 14.4 Companies with limited resources cannot afford to devote much of their scarce resources to promote their products to expand their market shares and appearances.

One reason, among others, is that these companies do not have much money and resources to allocate for the purpose of promotion. Another reason is that, as Eq. (14.12b) indicates, an excessive amount of spending will keep their unit selling price p_s high. To increase their profit potential, companies with limited resources have to control their spending so that their profit can be maximized by lowering their unit selling price p_s. Speaking slightly differently, companies with limited resources just cannot place large orders at much reduced wholesale prices while also missing out other volume-related savings.

14.4 Inter-industrial Wage Differentials

As the title suggests, this section develops a theory for why the phenomenon of inter-industrial wage differentials exists widely and internationally. It consists of two subsections, considering, respectively, the situation of unlimited financial resources and that of limited resources.

14.4.1 Opportunities of a Financially Resourceful Company

Assume that a company produces and sells a line of special product. Then, the company has two sources of income: (1) producing and selling the product and (2) hiring each worker. In particular, from each unit of the product produced and sold, the company makes as much profit as $p_s^p - p_p^p$, where p_s^p is the selling price per unit and p_p^p the unit cost. And for each worker it hires, the company generates as much profit as $p_s^W - p_p^W$, where p_s^W is the average revenue the worker is expected to make and p_p^W the average cost associated with the worker.

To help us uncover the underlying mechanism of the inter-industrial wage differentials, we will analyze the company in two situations:

1. The company has strong financial backings. That is, the model in Sect. 14.3.1 applies to this company.
2. The company's financial network and resources are limited. That is, the company does not have a perfect capital market available to it. So, the model in Sect. 14.3.2 applies here.

For situation 1, according to Eq. (14.2), for the company's product, the market demand is given by

$$n_p\left(p_s^p\right) = n_p\left(p_{s0}^p\right)\frac{p_{s0}^p - p_p^p}{p_s^p - p_p^p} \text{ (units)} \tag{14.13}$$

and the total profit from selling its product, based on Eq. (14.3), is

$$P^p = \text{profit of its product} = n_p\left(p_{s0}^p\right)\left(p_{s0}^p - p_p^p\right), \tag{14.14}$$

where $n_p\left(p_{s0}^p\right)$ is the initial market demand for the product selling at $\$p_{s0}^p$ each unit. Equation (14.13) implies that when $p_s^p \to \left(p_p^p\right)^+$, the demand will approach infinity. Equation (14.14) indicates that if the unit profit $\left(p_{s0}^p - p_p^p\right)$ stays constant, the lower the p_{s0}^p-value, the greater the demand $n_p\left(p_{s0}^p\right)$ and the greater the total profit P^p. For details, see the analysis of Eqs. (14.2) and (14.3).

Similarly, the company's staffing need is given by

$$n_W\left(p_s^W\right) = n_W\left(p_{s0}^W\right)\frac{p_{s0}^W - p_p^W}{p_s^W - p_p^W} \text{ (persons)} \tag{14.15}$$

and the total profit from hiring $n_W\left(p_s^W\right)$ employees is given by

$$P^W = \text{profit of personnel} = n_W\left(p_{s0}^W\right)\left(p_{s0}^W - p_p^W\right), \tag{14.16}$$

where $n_W\left(p_{s0}^W\right)$ stands for the company's initial need for additional personnel, hired at the initial expected revenue $\$p_{s0}^W$ per worker.

Different from Eq. (14.13), in Eq. (14.15) the higher the initial p_{s0}^W -value, the more workers the company would like to hire initially. After then, the smaller the difference $\left(p_s^W - p_p^W\right)$ is and the less p_p^W is controlled, the greater number $n_W\left(p_s^W\right)$ of workers will be needed. When Eqs. (14.15) and (14.16) are combined, it can be seen that if the difference $\left(p_{s0}^W - p_p^W\right)$ can stay constant, the closer $p_s^W \to \left(p_p^W\right)^+$, the greater the $n_W\left(p_s^W\right)$-value will be and the greater the total profit P^W will become. Now, $p_s^W \to \left(p_p^W\right)^+$ means that when the p_s^W-value is relatively stable, p_p^W should be increased as much as possible. That is, workers' wages can go up so that the total per-employee cost can approach the expected per-employee revenue p_s^W as much as possible.

When the p_p^W-value is increasing, the per-unit product cost p_p^p will also increase accordingly. But Eqs. (14.13) and (14.14) indicate that as long as the difference $\left(p_{s0}^W - p_p^W\right)$ does not decrease and $\left(p_s^W - p_p^W\right)$ drops, the total profit from the line of product will still go higher. That is, our analysis leads to the following result.

Proposition 14.5 If a business venture is well funded, assuming all other aspects of the operation stay the same, then:

1. The market demand for the product increases as the unit selling price drops close to the unit cost basis, while the total profit increases drastically.
2. The company taking on the venture will hire additional employees at higher than competitive wage rates with the total profit soaring.

Corresponding to Proposition 14.1 in terms of hiring employees, we have the following:

Proposition 14.6 Assume that the company has all necessary funds for its operation. If at the expected revenue level $p_s^p = p_{s0}^p$ a new hire would generate for the company and at a total cost $p_p^W = p_{s0}^W$, the total profit $P^W\left(p_s^W, p_p^W\right)$ all employees together are expected to generate satisfies

1. $\left.\frac{\partial P^{\mathrm{W}}}{\partial p_{\mathrm{s}}^{\mathrm{W}}}\right|_{p_{\mathrm{s0}}^{\mathrm{W}}} < -n_{\mathrm{W}}\left(p_{\mathrm{s0}}^{\mathrm{W}}\right)$

   then the company can reduce its expected per-employee revenue $p_{\mathrm{s0}}^{\mathrm{P}}$ to increase its total profit; or
2. $\left.\frac{\partial P^{\mathrm{W}}}{\partial p_{\mathrm{p}}^{\mathrm{W}}}\right|_{p_{\mathrm{p0}}^{\mathrm{W}}} > n_{\mathrm{W}}\left(p_{\mathrm{p0}}^{\mathrm{W}}\right)$

   then the company can raise its expected per-employee cost basis $p_{\mathrm{p0}}^{\mathrm{P}}$ to reap in additional profit; or
3. $\left.\frac{\partial P^{\mathrm{W}}}{\partial p_{\mathrm{s}}^{\mathrm{W}}}\right|_{p_{\mathrm{s0}}^{\mathrm{W}}} < -n_{\mathrm{W}}\left(p_{\mathrm{s0}}^{\mathrm{W}}\right)$ and $\left.\frac{\partial P^{\mathrm{W}}}{\partial p_{\mathrm{p}}^{\mathrm{W}}}\right|_{p_{\mathrm{p0}}^{\mathrm{W}}} > n_{\mathrm{W}}\left(p_{\mathrm{p0}}^{\mathrm{W}}\right)$

   then the company can both reduce its expected per-employee revenue $p_{\mathrm{s0}}^{\mathrm{P}}$ and raise its per-employee cost basis p_{p0}^{P} to maximize its overall profit.

14.4.2 Limitations of a Company with Resource Constraints

For situation 2, where the company's resources are limited, our model in Sect. 14.3.2 applies. The total profit is given by

$$\begin{aligned} P_{\text{total}} &= P^{\mathrm{P}} + P^{\mathrm{W}} \\ &= n_{\mathrm{P}}\left(p_{\mathrm{s}}^{\mathrm{P}}\right)\left(p_{\mathrm{s}}^{\mathrm{P}} - p_{\mathrm{p}}^{\mathrm{P}}\right) + n_{\mathrm{W}}\left(p_{\mathrm{s}}^{\mathrm{W}}\right)\left(p_{\mathrm{s}}^{\mathrm{W}} - p_{\mathrm{p}}^{\mathrm{W}}\right) \end{aligned} \tag{14.17}$$

subject to the budget constraint

$$n_{\mathrm{P}}\left(p_{\mathrm{s}}^{\mathrm{P}}\right)p_{\mathrm{p}}^{\mathrm{P}} + n_{\mathrm{W}}\left(p_{\mathrm{s}}^{\mathrm{W}}\right)p_{\mathrm{p}}^{\mathrm{W}} = I, \tag{14.18}$$

where I stands for the total funds available to the company. By solving the maximization problem of Eq. (14.17) subject to Eq. (14.18), we establish the following results:

$$n_{\mathrm{P}}\left(p_{\mathrm{s}}^{\mathrm{P}}\right) = \frac{n_{\mathrm{P}}\left(p_{\mathrm{s0}}^{\mathrm{P}}\right)p_{\mathrm{s0}}^{\mathrm{P}}}{p_{\mathrm{s}}^{\mathrm{P}}} \tag{14.19}$$

$$n_{\mathrm{W}}\left(p_{\mathrm{s}}^{\mathrm{W}}\right) = \frac{n_{\mathrm{W}}\left(p_{\mathrm{s0}}^{\mathrm{W}}\right)p_{\mathrm{s0}}^{\mathrm{W}}}{p_{\mathrm{s}}^{\mathrm{W}}} \tag{14.20}$$

and

$$
\begin{aligned}
P_{\text{total}} &= P^{\mathrm{p}} + P^{\mathrm{W}} \\
&= \frac{n_{\mathrm{p}}\left(p_{\mathrm{s0}}^{\mathrm{p}}\right)p_{\mathrm{s0}}^{\mathrm{p}}}{p_{\mathrm{s}}^{\mathrm{p}}}\left(p_{\mathrm{s}}^{\mathrm{p}} - p_{\mathrm{p}}^{\mathrm{p}}\right) + \frac{n_{\mathrm{W}}\left(p_{\mathrm{s0}}^{\mathrm{W}}\right)p_{\mathrm{s0}}^{\mathrm{W}}}{p_{\mathrm{s}}^{\mathrm{W}}}\left(p_{\mathrm{s}}^{\mathrm{W}} - p_{\mathrm{p}}^{\mathrm{W}}\right), \\
&= n_{\mathrm{p}}\left(p_{\mathrm{s0}}^{\mathrm{p}}\right)p_{\mathrm{s0}}^{\mathrm{p}}\left(1 - \frac{p_{\mathrm{p}}^{\mathrm{p}}}{p_{\mathrm{s}}^{\mathrm{p}}}\right) + n_{\mathrm{W}}\left(p_{\mathrm{s0}}^{\mathrm{W}}\right)p_{\mathrm{s0}}^{\mathrm{W}}\left(1 - \frac{p_{\mathrm{p}}^{\mathrm{W}}}{p_{\mathrm{s}}^{\mathrm{W}}}\right)
\end{aligned}
\tag{14.21}
$$

where $p_{\mathrm{s0}}^{\mathrm{p}} n_{\mathrm{p}}\left(p_{\mathrm{s0}}^{\mathrm{p}}\right)$ and $p_{\mathrm{s0}}^{\mathrm{W}} n_{\mathrm{W}}\left(p_{\mathrm{s0}}^{\mathrm{W}}\right)$ are defined the same as in the analysis of situation 1.

Equation (14.19) is the same as Eq. (14.11). So, for its analysis, refer to that of Eq. (14.11). Equation (14.20) indicates that to hire more employees, the company has to lower the average expected per-worker revenue. Because the capital markets are not perfect for the company, this result implies that the company has to limit how many workers it can afford to hire. To maximize its profit in the dimension of human resources, Eq. (14.21) implies that $p_{\mathrm{s}}^{\mathrm{W}} \gg p_{\mathrm{p}}^{\mathrm{W}}$. So, in such a company with limited resources, it can either hire a relatively large number of employees at low wage rates or hire a relatively small number of high-quality workers at relatively higher wage rates. For the latter case to occur, the workers' productivity must be very high, which in general means that the company needs to invest a great deal in technology. And this end might not be possible. Together with the company's weak financial standing, the high-quality worker option may never be practically possible for the company to take.

When Eq. (14.21) is compared to Eq. (14.16), the following proposition can be seen.

Proposition 14.7 Financially resourceful companies can spend extra money on workers' retraining programs to lower the average per-worker cost basis $p_{\mathrm{p}}^{\mathrm{W}}$, while firms with limited resources cannot.

The reason behind this conclusion is that for firms with limited resources, extra spending on workers' training programs increases both $p_{\mathrm{s}}^{\mathrm{W}}$- and $p_{\mathrm{p}}^{\mathrm{W}}$-values. So, the ratio $p_{\mathrm{p}}^{\mathrm{W}}/p_{\mathrm{s}}^{\mathrm{W}}$ may not change in the favorable direction to the firms.

Proposition 14.8 Financially resourceful companies can afford to invest in programs to make their workers feel good and to raise their morale, while firms with limited resources just cannot afford such luxuries.

The argument for this conclusion is similar to that for the previous conclusion. Consequently, workers in financially strong firms produce more and are less likely to quit when compared to those hired by financially strained companies.

Proposition 14.9 While financially resourceful companies hire large numbers of workers so that these companies can easily reduce per-employee benefit costs, companies with few workers have to pay the inflated market prices for the same benefit packages.

Speaking differently, volume savings are not available to firms with limited resources.

The analysis above explains why in a firm, if an occupation is highly paid, then so are all other occupations when compared to those of other firms. In particular, if one occupation is paid at a level above the competitive wage rates, then all other occupations within the firm must play supporting roles. The increased productivity from the central occupation will be more than enough to finance the supporting occupations so that their respective wages are higher than those occupations' competitive market rates. For more detailed discussion about this end, please refer to the section below.

14.5 Looking Back at Some of the Past Milestones

The purpose of this section is to employ the theory developed in the previous sections to pay a revisit to the known theories, established by different authors in varied angles to explain the phenomenon of inter-industrial wage differentials, so that as many of them as possible can be unified into a grander theory. The section consists of two subsections. The first subsection sorts through a list of known theories, while the second subsection looks back on why the law of one price does not work in general.

14.5.1 A Revisit to Some of the Previous Works

Our analysis, together with our yoyo model, in fact provides a plausible economic explanation for:

1. Why high-wage industries tend to have low quit rates (Katz & Summers, 1989; Akerlof et al., 1988).

   It is because of a sense of job security (financially strong firms), being treated with respect (because each of them brings profit to the company), and the feeling of being paid in excess of their opportunity costs. In terms of our yoyo model, high-wage industries are those yoyos that spin powerfully so that fewer objects can escape their spin fields.
2. Why firm sizes are an indicator of the levels of compensation (Brown & Medoff, 1989; Groshen, 1988).

   It is because large firm sizes reflect the market share the firms occupy and how much they make from the head count of their workers. In terms of our yoyo model, the large size of an industry shows its large volume of materials, including profits, being sucked in from the input side.
3. Why accounting profits and market power are reliable predictors of industry wages (Thaler, 1989).

It is because they indicate how fast the firms' products and their workers generate revenue. From the angle of spinning yoyos, they are indicators of the speed of materials being sucked into the yoyo of the industry.

4. Why the association between wages and labor's share of costs in an industry is negative (Slichter, 1950).

   It is because in Eq. (14.15), to reduce the difference $\left(p_s^W - p_p^W\right)$, the firm may well spend a good amount of money to improve productivity while raising its workers' wages disproportionably slowly. In the economic yoyo of an industry, the overall spinning strength has to be distributed among all aspects of the output side. And workers' wages are only one aspect of the many.

5. Why industries with high capital-labor ratios tend to pay higher wages (Lawrence & Lawrence, 1985; Dickens & Katz, 1987).

   Our model indicates that if a firm requires a high level of capital investment for its operation, the unit product cost of the firm must be high compared to that of firms operating on relatively much lower budgets. Equation (14.14) implies that for such a capital-intensive firm, the initial unit profit $\left(p_{s0}^p - p_p^p\right)$ must be enough high for the investors to put up the necessary venture capital. After achieving the firm's initial business success, continued high level of capital investment will be needed to reduce the unit cost basis p_p^p by heavily investing in advanced and innovative technology to increase the workers' productivity. For a long period of time, the delicate technology may require large amounts of capital to maintain its working conditions.

6. Why the unionization rate increases wages for both union and nonunion members in a firm.

   Based on our model in Eqs. (14.13)–(14.16), the firm will have a lot of weight in both its product market and the labor market. The large number of employees is good for the firm in the sense that the firm actually generates profits in the dimension of human resources. But this same crowd of workers is also, or could also be, a problem and a source of troubles. The first reason is that when the firm is small, its workers are few in numbers and low in quality (relatively speaking). So, they can be replaced relatively easily. Using our yoyo model, the small group of workers could not form a strong enough whirlpool to overthrow or severely interrupt the operation of the economic yoyo of the firm. When the number of workers reaches a critical mass, and when these employees discover the lucrative cash flows in and out of the firm's bank accounts because of their work, they will see the need to take collective actions to share a greater proportion of the firm's profits. This end is simulated well by the dishpan experiment, where only with enough water, asymmetric and nonuniform flow patterns will appear. Our analysis here explains why Dickens (1986) predicts that industries with high wages suffer from the highest threat of union actions.

To make the following discussion go forward smoothly, let us quote two important theorems from Lin (2008, pp. 156, 162).

Theorem 14.1 (Becker's (1974) Rotten Kid Theorem). If a family has a head who cares about all other members so much that he transfers his resources to them automatically, then any redistribution of the head's income among members of the household would not affect the consumption of any member, as long as the head continues to contribute to all. Additionally, other members are also motivated to maximize the family income and consumption, even if their welfare depends on their own consumption alone.

Theorem 14.2 Becker's rotten kid theorem holds true if and only if the distribution of the benevolent head's resources is not in conflict with the consumption preferences of any selfish member.

Similar to the situation of making a snowball on a cold, snowy winter day (a kind of yoyo action), firms or industries that pay wages above the competitive rates can reap in profits with added advantage and convenience: high workers' morale, desirable work ethics, low quit rates, better-quality people, etc. To see this end, let us identify our firm, which pays its workers wages above the competitive rates, with the benevolent head in Theorems 14.1 and 14.2, and all employees with those selfish members of the family. Then, Theorem 14.2 says that as long as the distribution of the firm's resources to all employees is not in conflict with the consumption preferences of any (selfish) employees, then all the employees will be motivated to maximize the firm's income. Because the employees can tell by comparison that their wages are above the competitive market rates, their consumption preferences—getting paid more than others in the same occupation—are not in conflict with the need for the firm to pay its employees as much as possible (Eqs. 14.15 and 14.16). So, Theorem 14.1 implies that of course none of the workers would quit, except for those who have different consumption needs and preferences beyond wages, and of course, the workers would have high morale toward their work and company, because they are motivated to maximize the firm's income.

Beyond what is said above, what Theorem 14.1 says also provides an answer to Thaler's (1989) question:

> Consider the case of two large firms with plants located in the same community. The firms have clerical staffs that perform virtually identical services. Firm H is in a high-wage industry and pays its clerical staff W_H, while Firm L is in a low-wage industry and pays its clerical staff only W_L ($<W_H$). Suppose that Firm H decides to save money by cutting the wage of its clerical workers to W_L. Is this action profitable?

Proposition 14.10 If H's cut of the wages of its clerical workers is temporary and is for savings that will be used to finance some crisis H faces, then the wage cut will still be profitable to firm H.

This conclusion follows directly from Theorems 14.1 and 14.2. And, our analysis based on the yoyo model and that developed in Sects. 14.2 and 14.3 indicates that if Firm H plans to hang on to its competitive edge, meaning that it will continue to occupy similar market share for its products and reap similar profits from its human resources, it will naturally not make the cut permanent, because the firm also expects to generate profit from each and every employee it hires.

What we have obtained in this section shows that what Krueger and Summers (1987) said is correct: for some reason, high-wage firms find that lowering wages would decrease profits. What is different, though, is that our analysis shows that wages above opportunity costs for the workers are consistent with profit maximization without any prerequisite like:

- Higher wages can increase output as assumed in efficiency wage models.
- Higher wages are a rational response to the threat of collective actions.

At the same time, our analysis provides a theoretical explanation for the following conclusion:

Proposition 14.11 When a high-wage firm outsources an activity, it generally does not pay the same high wages to the outside contractor.

This result reconfirms what is observed by Berlinski (2000). As for why this conclusion holds true generally, it is because the contractor is not in the human resource equation of the firm's profit maximization.

14.5.2 Remarks on the Law of One Price

Even though we provided a plausible explanation for the existence of inter-industrial wage differentials, this phenomenon still seems to violate the law of one price, a fundamental component of the theory of competitive markets. In terms of the literature, Pratt et al. (1979) show that the law of one price may not hold true in product market. And, Lamond and Thaler (2003) cited sources that indicate that this law might be violated in financial markets, too.

To see what has gone wrong with this law in our situation at hand, let us first recite the law from a standard textbook and look at its background reasoning.

> **Law of one price** (Bodies & Merton, 2000): In a competitive (and efficient) market, if two assets are equivalent, they will have the same market price.

The intuition for this law is that all sellers will flock to the highest prevailing price and all buyers to the lowest current market price. So, if the market is efficient and competitive, the convergence to one price is instant.

The long-lasting and stable existence of inter-industrial wage differentials indicates that this law does not apply to the situation of wage structures. In particular, when, say, janitor positions with identical job descriptions are for sale by various companies, each selling price of these positions is the unseen (to the buyers, the job applicants) expected revenue each prospective janitor will bring to the specific hiring company. For example, a janitor working for a small dentist's office is expected to save the owner dentist time from cleaning the clinic complex and related works. So, the expected revenue the janitor creates is the additional revenue the dentist actually produces from his relieved cleaning responsibilities. If this value were \$100/day on the average, then the selling price for this janitor position would be \$3000/month.

So, if the dentist hires a janitor for $1500/month, he still pockets $1500/month more than before hiring the janitor. Conversely, if the same janitor works for a large and extremely profitable law firm, his work might help the firm produce an additional $3000/day, even though he would carry exactly the same responsibilities as if he worked for the dentist. In this case, this janitor position's selling price would be tagged at $90,000/month. If the law firm paid a janitor $10,000/month, a purposely exaggerated number for such an occupation to make a point here, the firm would still make $80,000/month extra compared to before the firm hired any janitor.

Because the selling prices in our job market situation are hidden either purposely or unconsciously, there is no way for all sellers, the hiring firms, to flock to the highest prevailing price. Conversely, even when these selling prices are known to everyone, the sellers still will not flock to the highest prevailing price due to varied productivities and price tags being involved. Because of this reason, those companies that are most profitable can easily offer the highest market wages to occupations like janitor. At the same time, all job applicants flock to the advertised positions with the highest wages and best benefits, assuming that such information of advertisement can reach all potential job applicants in exactly the same fashion. Also, our analysis indicates that the highest advertised wages could well be the lowest expenses the hiring companies would pay to the advertised positions compared to other positions with identical job descriptions available in the marketplace, considering how much revenue the workers generate for their companies.

14.6 A Few Final Words

Thaler (1989) calls for a better explanation for the stable wage differentials existing inter-industrially over time and across national borders. Although many attempts have been tried before, they all assumed something difficult to accept. Therefore, this chapter focuses on providing another explanation for the said phenomenon without assuming anything that is difficult for anyone, be it an economist or a random person waking on the street, to accept.

Comparing to studies of the past in this area, the main contribution of this chapter is its success with the development of models and analysis that evolve naturally without based on any empirically confirmed hypotheses. And, the maximization of the established models is achieved through using the simple Lagrange method and some elementary knowledge of differential equations. A second contribution is how the understanding of the purpose of hiring workers is expanded as a new dimension of profit making. By analyzing the major differences between perfect and imperfect capital markets, this chapter uncovers some of the invisible differences between firms and consequently between industries. These subtle differences lead firms and industries to varied opportunities, causing relevant business entities to behave differently in terms of wage setting and other practical aspects of daily operations.

References

Akerlof, G., & Yellen, J. (1990). The fair wage-effort hypothesis and unemployment. *The Quarterly Journal of Economics, 105*(2), 255–283.

Akerlof, G., Rose, A., & Yellen, J. (1988). Job switching and job satisfaction in the US labor market. *Brookings Papers on Economic Activity, 1988*(2), 495–594.

Becker, G. S. (1974). A theory of social interactions. *Journal of Political Economy, 82*(6), 1063–1093.

Berlinski, S. (2000). *Contracting-out and the interindustry wage structure: Do norms of internal equity matter in wage determination?* Paper presented at Economic Society World Congress 2000, Contributed Papers 1053.

Blackburn, M., & Neumark, D. (1988). *Efficiency wages, inter-industry wage differentials, and the returns to ability. Finance and economics discussion series*. Federal Reserve Board.

Bodies, Z., & Merton, R. (2000). *Finance*. Prentice Hall.

Brown, C., & Medoff, J. (1989). The employer size-wage effect. *Journal of Political Economy, 97*(5), 1027–1059.

Dickens, W. (1986). *Wages, employment and the threat of collective action by workers* [Unpublished]. University of California, Berkeley.

Dickens, W., & Katz, L. (1987). Inter-industry wage differences and industry characteristics. In K. Lang & J. S. Leonard (Eds.), *Unemployment and the structure of labor markets* (pp. 48–89). Basil Blackwell.

Gillan, S. (2006). Recent developments in corporate governance: An overview. *Journal of Corporate Finance, 12*(3), 381–402.

Groshen, E. L. (1988). *Sources of wages dispersion: The contribution of interemployer differentials within industry* (Working Paper No. 88-02). Federal Reserve Bank of Cleveland.

Hamermesh, D. (1993). *Labor demand*. MIT Press.

Kahneman, D., Knetsh, J., & Thaler, R. (1986). Fairness as a constraint on profit seeking: Entitlements in the market. *The American Economic Review, 76*(4), 728–741.

Katz, L., & Summers, L. (1989). Industry rents and industry policy. *Brookings Papers on Economic Activity, 1989*, 209.

Krueger, A. B., & Summers, L. (1987). Reflections on the inter-industry wage structure. In K. Lang & J. S. Leonard (Eds.), *Unemployment and the structure of labor markets* (pp. 17–47). Basil Blackwell.

Lamond, O., & Thaler, R. (2003). Anomaly: The law of one price in financial markets. *Journal of Economic Perspectives, 17*(2), 191–202.

Lawrence, C., & Lawrence, R. (1985). Manufacturing wage dispersion: An end game interpretation. *Brookings Papers on Economic Activity, 1985*(1), 45–106.

Lin, Y. (2008). *Systemic yoyos: Impacts of the second dimension*. Auerbach Publications.

Murphy, K., & Topal, R. (1987). Unemployment, risk, and earnings: Testing for equalizing wage differences in labor market. In L. Lang & J. S. Leonard (Eds.), *Unemployment and the structure of labor markets* (pp. 103–139). Basil Blackwell.

OuYang, S. C. (1994). *Break-offs of moving fluids and several problems of weather forecasting*. Press of Chengdu University of Science and Technology.

Pratt, J., Wise, D., & Zechhauser, R. (1979). Price differences in almost competitive markets. *The Quarterly Journal of Economics, 93*(2), 189–211.

Raff, M., & Summers, L. (1987). Did Henry Ford pay efficiency wages? *Journal of Labor Economics, 5*(4), S57–S86.

Rosen, S. (1986). The theory of equalizing differences. In O. Ashefelter & R. Layard (Eds.), *Handbook of labor economics* (Vol. 1, pp. 641–692). Elsevier Science Publishers BV.

Salop, S. (1979). A model of the natural rate of unemployment. *The American Economic Review, 69*(1), 117–125.

Shapiro, C., & Stiglitz, J. (1984). Equilibrium unemployment as a worker discipline device. *The American Economic Review, 27*(3), 433–444.

Slichter, S. (1950). Notes on the structure of wages. *The Review of Economics and Statistics, 32*(1), 80–91.

Solow, R. M. (1979). Another possible source of wage stickiness. *Journal of Macroeconomics, 1*(1), 79–82.

Stigler, G. (1958). The economics of scale. *The Journal of Law and Economics, 1*(1), 54–71.

Stiglitz, J. E. (1974). Alternate theories of wages determination and unemployment in L.C.D.'s: The labor turnover model. *The Quarterly Journal of Economics, 88*, 194–227.

Stiglitz, J. E. (1976). *Prices and queues as screening devices in competitive markets* (IMSSS Technical Report 212). Stanford University.

Thaler, R. (1989). Interindustry wage differentials. *Journal of Economic Perspectives, 3*, 181–193.

Weiss, A. (1980). Job queues and layoffs in labor markets with flexible wages. *Journal of Political Economy, 88*(3), 526–538.

Yellen, J. (1984). Efficiency wage models of unemployment. *The American Economic Review, 74*(2), 200–205.

Chapter 15
Clashes of Currencies

Jeffrey Yi-Lin Forrest, Zackary Hopkins, and Sifeng Liu

Abstract This chapter, which is mainly based on Forrest et al. (Adv Syst Sci Appl 13:198–217, 2013a; Adv Syst Sci Appl 13:299–316, 2013b), highlights the power and usefulness of the systemic yoyo model, concepts of the conventional control theory, and Bernanke–Gertler model of fundamental value of capital by looking at the movements of money. By going along with the common knowledge that money can easily destroy a person, a family, and a healthy business enterprise, it demonstrates the reason why currency conflicts (or wars) are inevitable and the fact that each economic system is defenseless against financial attacks so that money can be purposefully and strategically employed as a weapon of mass destruction. This fact was materially confirmed by the case of Drexel Burnham Lambert, where the relevant bankers were able to attack any business entity if they deemed the attacks were profitable (Sobel, When giants stumble: classic business blunders and how to avoid them, Prentice Hall, 1999).

Keywords Controllability · Financial crises · International reserve · International speculative capital · Observability · Speculative attacks · Weapon of mass destruction

---

Jeffrey Yi-Lin Forrest (Department of Accounting Economics Finance, Slippery Rock University, Slippery Rock, PA, USA; Email: Jeffrey.forrest@sru.edu), Zackary Hopkins (Institutional Research, Assessment and Analytics, Gannon University, Erie, PA, USA; Email: hopkins013@gannon.edu), and Sifeng Liu (School of Economics and Management, Nanjing University of Aeronautics and Astronautics, Nanjing, China; Email: sfliu@nuaa.edu.cn) are equally contributed to this chapter.

J. Y.-L. Forrest, *Systemic Principles of Applied Economic Philosophies II*,
Translational Systems Sciences 39, https://doi.org/10.1007/978-981-99-7939-4_15

15.1 Introduction

The focus of this chapter, which is mainly based on Forrest et al. (2013a, b), is on financial crises caused or created purposefully by certain group(s) of people in order to acquire economic and political gains. Here, financial crises include all those with respect to, either individually or jointly, currency, credit, bank, debt, and the markets of stocks, bond, and financial derivatives. They generally mean severe fluctuations that appear in the financial area of an economy. The chaos interferes negatively with the operation of the real economy. Each of such crises is accompanied by sudden deterioration of all or most financial indexes, stock market crash, capital flight, credit destruction, extremely tight money supply, rising interest rate, bank runs, bankruptcy of a large number of financial institutions, major decrease in the official reserves, inability to repay the interest and principal of maturing debt, currency devaluation both internally and externally, etc.

Because the present-day regional economies are closely intertwined with each other due to a high degree of globalization, when a nation or geographic region suffers from economic and financial shocks, in terms of their damaging effects and adverse impacts, the shocks tend to possess international and global characteristics. Since the 1920s, there had appeared many large-scale financial crises (Hein et al., 2016; Wang & Hu, 2005).

This chapter makes use of the systemic yoyo model, concepts of control theory, and Bernanke–Gertler model of fundamental value of capital to show that when a large amount of foreign investments gathers in one place over either a long period or a short period of time and then leaves suddenly and massively, that local economy will suffer through a positive bubble, caused by the increased money supply as a consequence of the foreign investments, and then a following negative, disastrous bust, caused by the sudden dry-out of the money supply. Because a large number of economic activities are either unexpectedly delayed or totally impossible to complete, the local investors are actually unable to continue to collect their originally expected dividends for many time periods to come. In other words, foreign investments can be employed as a weapon of mass destruction, if they leave strategically and suddenly, no matter whether they come quickly in a short period of time or slowly over a relatively longer period of time.

The rest of this chapter is organized as follows: Sect. 15.2 provides a literature review that examines how currencies interact with each other in the presently globalizing economy. Section 15.3 considers the concepts of controllability and observability of economic systems and how these concepts are in fact duals of each other. Section 15.4 explores the structural forms of economic systems' controllability and observability. Section 15.5 shows how each economy, when modeled as a constant coefficient linear system, can be decomposed into subsystems, where only one of them can be controlled and observed. Section 15.6 shows how currency wars can be launched purposefully. Section 15.7 concludes the discussion of this chapter by providing an explanation for how each general economic system is vulnerable to external influences.

15.2 Literature Review

The financial crises can be grouped into four classes: currency, bank, foreign debt, and systems. Here, by currency crisis it represents such a situation that due to purposeful and targeted speculative activities against a nation, the nation's currency suffers from drastic devaluation, or the nation's government is forced to drastically increase its interest rate or spend a large amount of the foreign reserves to defend its currency. By bank crisis, it means actual and/or potential bank runs or such a scenario that a number of banks stop repaying their debts because of their falling into bankruptcy or the government is forced to interfere by providing large amounts of support. By foreign debt crisis it implies such a case that a nation can no longer repay its foreign debts on time, no matter whether the debtors are governments or private individuals. By systemic financial crisis, it stands for the destructive effects on the real economy due to severe damages of the financial infrastructure so that the efficiency of the financial markets is greatly affected. The connotation of systemic financial crises might overlap with those of other kinds of crises, while currency and bank crises might not lead to severe damage to a nation's payment system. So, neither currency crises nor bank crises can be identified with systemic financial crises.

In many circumstances, the specific definition of financial crises simply means currency crises. The early investigation of currency crises can be traced back to at least Krugman (1979). Paul Krugman treats a currency crisis as an international balance-of-payments crisis. He believes that in order to prevent their currencies to devaluate, countries with either a fixed exchange rate system or pegged exchange rate system would pay the price of either spending their international reserves or increasing inflation due to their raising domestic interest rates; when the governments give up on the fixed exchange rate system or the pegged exchange rate system, their currencies experience drastic drops in value. That leads to currency crises. Each currency crisis is generally indicated by the collapse of the fixed exchange rate system or forced adjustment to the system, such as official devaluation of the local currency, expanded floating range of the exchange rate, drastic decrease in international reserves, noticeable rise in the interest rate of local currency, etc.

According to the literature, there are four main criteria for judging currency crises:

1. Sudden and large-scale changes in exchange rate;
2. The weighted average of exchange rate and foreign reserves fluctuates widely;
3. The weighted average of exchange rate, foreign reserves, and interest rate vibrates wildly;
4. Import drops drastically.

The second criterion was established by Kaminsky et al. (1998) who believe that a currency crisis represents such a scenario that is caused by either devaluation of the nation's currency or drastic drop in the nation's international reserve or both as a consequence of an attack on a nation's currency. Because of this reason, currency crises can be verified afterward by using the index named exchange market pressure (EMP). This index stands for a weighted average between the monthly percentage change in the exchange rate of the local currency and that of the international reserves. Because this index increases with the devaluation of the local currency and the loss of international reserve, major increases in this index indicate a strong pressure to sell off the local currency. Because of its practical operationality, this second criterion has been employed most widely among these four criteria.

Most of the financial crises that occurred since the 1990s have shown clear characteristics of currency crises, and an outstanding feature of currency crises is that they are accompanied by bank crises. Since the 1980s, with the globalization of the capital markets, international capital flows have been developed unprecedentedly with ever increasing magnitude, velocity, and accompanying dangers and risks. Large amounts of short-term capitals that are not under the watch of any national government and international financial organization have been moving freely in the international financial markets to pursue after profit opportunities by using various financial tools, trading platforms, and advanced trading technologies. These characteristics of the capital have led to frequent occurrence of turmoil in the international financial markets; speculative attacks happen often with ever increasing strength and duration of impact. The Asian currency crises that started in 1997 further indicate that the currency crises caused by speculative attacks can also develop into full scale financial and social disasters of large magnitude.

The so-called international speculative capital or hot money represents such capital that is frequently moved within and between various markets in pursuit of short-term, high levels of profits without any particular fields of investment focus. Such capital tends to be short term even though there are exceptions to this rule of thumb. One characteristic of international speculative capitals is their camouflage. At the same time, these capitals can also travel along the market cycles by pursuing mid- and long-term investments. Of course, not all short-term capitals are speculative, some of which, for example, could be involved in the financial intermediation and settlement of international trades, short-term interbank funds, banks' short-term positions for allocation, etc.

With the expansion in the size, circulation speed, and the coverage of international capital markets, international speculative capitals have grown quietly. Based on their predictions on the changes in exchange rate, interest rate, security prices, gold price, or the prices of certain commodities, speculative capitals could be suddenly involved in large scale in both long and short trades in a short period of time. By substantially altering the composites of their portfolios and by affecting the confidence of the holders of other assets, these speculative capitals cause severe instability in the market prices so that short-term high profit opportunities could be created. Such market behaviors that appear suddenly while disturbing the market prices are known as speculative attacks. Due to the need of pursuing after quick gains, international speculative capitals generally choose to attack such economic sectors and geographic areas that can hold large amount of capitals and allow fast movements of funds with expected high returns and few financial regulations. These economic fields include (foreign) currencies, futures, options, precious metals, real estates, etc.

From what happened in the past, it seems that international speculative capitals have been fond of attacking the currency of one nation or the currencies of several nations at the same time. Most often seen speculative attacks are those that assault either fixed exchange rate systems or regulated exchange rate systems. Under the conditions of either fixed or pegged exchange rate system, as long as there appears either a domestic inflation or recession accompanied with sustained current account deficits, the governmental promise on the fixed exchange rate would lose its reliability. It is because in these situations there is heavy pressure to devaluate the local currency; in order to maintain the promised exchange rate, the government will be forced to mobilize and spend its international reserve. Even with the support of the international financial markets, the fundamental imbalances existing in the economic states still cannot be corrected, which can most likely delay the occurrence of the devaluation of the local currency, although the devaluation will sooner or later happen inevitably. If speculators predicted this forthcoming event, they would mobilize their capitals ahead of time and launch their speculative attack in order to position themselves for quick profits. By using the spot and forward transactions, futures contracts, options trades, and swaps of various financial tools, speculators carry out their multi-dimensional speculative strategy. They position their capitals at the same time on the markets of foreign exchanges, securities, and all different forms of financial derivatives. Because of the fixed exchange rate or the promise that the government would maintain the rate fixed, the risk to the speculators is actually quite low, because the direction along which the exchange rate would move is clear. To say the least, even if the prediction is incorrect, the worst is that the exchange rate parity did not change so that the most the speculators could lose is their minimal amounts of trade costs. Hence, once a speculative wave is started, the magnitude in general is large, leading to the expected consequences, as a self-fulfilling prophecy of a humongous scale.

Due to the fact that the relevant literature is huge, this section only summarizes what is known without citing any particular reference.

15.3 An Economy's Controllability and Observability

According to Forrest et al. (2013a), any economy, when seen as a system, can be *approximately* written as an n-dimensional constant coefficient linear system:

$$\begin{cases} \frac{dx}{dt} = Ax + Bu \\ y = Cx + Du \end{cases}, \tag{15.1}$$

where x describes the state of the system, y stands for the output, and u the policy input. Let X represent the state space of this system so that $x \in X$. If the matrices A, B,

C, and D are constant, Eq. (15.1) is an approximate representation of the control system of the economy within a neighborhood of the initial time moment. In this case, the pair (C, A) of matrices describe the relationship of the economic system between the output y and the state x when there is no policy input, while the pair of matrices (A, B) describe the relationship between the policy input u and the state x.

The concepts of controllability and observability of the economic system are very important. They, respectively, describe the relationship between the policy input and the state of the economy and the relationship between the output and the state of the economy. When A, B, C, and D are constant matrices, the controllability of the system in Eq. (15.1) roughly means whether or not for any given state x there is always a policy control u such that within a limited time interval the state x can be transformed to the desired state. As for the observability of the economic system, it is about whether or not the initial state of the system can be determined by the knowledge of some known output of the system. Formerly, we have

Definition 15.1 If the state $x(t_0)$ of the economy at a given time t_0 can reach the expected state $x(t_f)$ within a finite time interval $[t_0, t_f]$ by adopting an appropriate policy input, then the economic system is said to be controllable at time moment t_0. If any of the state of the economy, as represented by the constant matrix system given by the first equation in Eq. (15.1), is controllable, then the economy is known as completely controllable, written as (A, B) controllable.

The following result (Perko, 2013) provides several equivalent conditions for the controllability of the economy if it can be represented by a constant matrix system. This result also reveals some characteristics of economic controllability.

Theorem 15.1 Each of the following is a sufficient and necessary condition for the economy, which is modeled by the n-dimensional constant matrix system in Eq. (15.1), to be completely controllable:

1. The following controllability matrix is of rank n:

$$U = \left[B|AB|A^2B|\ldots|A^{n-1}B\right];$$

2. All rows of $e^{-At}B$ are linearly independent on the interval $[0, \infty)$;
3. For any $t_1 > t_0$, the following controllability Cramer's matrix is non-singular:

$$W(t_0, t_1) = \int_{t_0}^{t_1} e^{-A\tau}BB^{T}e^{-A^{T}\tau}d\tau;$$

4. For every eigenvalue λ of A (hence for any complex number), the rank of the matrix $[\lambda I - A|B]$ is n.

The concept of controllability of the economic system in Eq. (15.1) can also be defined as follows: Assume that x_0 is the state of the economic system at time t_0 and x_1 an arbitrary state of the system. If there are a finite time moment $t_1 > t_0$ and $u(t)$, for $t_0 \leq t \leq t_1$, such that under the effect of $u(t)$ the state x_0 of the system can be transformed into x_1, then the state x_0 is known as controllable.

It can be shown that this definition and the earlier definition are equivalent. In fact, it can be shown that for a controllable economic system under Definition 15.1, for any given $t_1 > t_0$ and two arbitrary states x_0 and x_1, there is a control vector $u(t)$, for $t_0 \leq t \leq t_1$, such that under the effect of $u(t)$ the system's state $x(t_0) = x_0$ is transformed to the state $x(t_1) = x_1$. The control vector that materializes this state transformation is

$$u(t) = B^{\mathrm{T}} \mathrm{e}^{-A^{\mathrm{T}} t} \{ W^{-1}(t_0, t_1) \left[\mathrm{e}^{-At_1} x_1 - \mathrm{e}^{At_0} x_0 \right] \}.$$

Definition 15.2 For the economic system

$$\begin{cases} \frac{dx}{dt} = Ax + Bu, \\ y = Cx \end{cases} \tag{15.2}$$

assume the input is zero. If for any given initial state x_0 there is finite time $t_1 > t_0$ such that the initial state x_0 can be uniquely determined by the output $y(t)$ on the time interval $[t_0, t_1]$, then the economic system is known as completely observable, or (C, A) observable in short.

For the constant coefficient linear economic system in Eq. (15.2), the following theorem holds true (Perko, 2013).

Theorem 15.2 The following are sufficient and necessary conditions for the n-dimensional constant coefficient linear system in Eq. (15.2) to be completely observable:

1. The rank of the following observability matrix is n:

$$V = \left[C^{\mathrm{T}} | A^{\mathrm{T}} C^{\mathrm{T}} | (A^{\mathrm{T}})^2 C^{\mathrm{T}} | \ldots | (A^{\mathrm{T}})^{n-1} C^{\mathrm{T}} \right]^{\mathrm{T}};$$

2. All rows of the matrix Ce^{At} are linearly independent on the internal $[0, \infty)$;
3. For any $t_1 > t_0$, the following observability Cramer's matrix is non-singular:

$$W(t_0, t_1) = \int_{t_0}^{t_1} e^{A\tau} C^{\mathrm{T}} C e^{A^{\mathrm{T}} \tau} d\tau;$$

4. For each eigenvalue λ of A, the rank of the matrix $\begin{bmatrix} \lambda I - A \\ C \end{bmatrix}$ is n.

As for any economic system, there is a duality relationship between controllability and observability. In particular, for the following continuous time constant coefficient linear economic system

$$S:\begin{cases}\dfrac{dx}{dt}=Ax+Bu\\ y=Cx\end{cases}$$

define its dual system as follows:

$$S^{\mathrm{T}}:\begin{cases}\dfrac{dx}{dt}=A^{\mathrm{T}}x+C^{\mathrm{T}}u\\ y=B^{\mathrm{T}}x\end{cases}.$$

Then for the dual systems, the following result (Perko, 2013) holds true:

Theorem 15.3 If system S is completely controllable, then its dual system S^{T} is observable; if system S is observable, then its dual system S^{T} is completely controllable. The opposite of these statements also holds true.

Let U and U_T, respectively, stand for the controllability matrices of S and S^{T}, and V and V_T, respectively, the observability matrices of S and S^{T}. Then the following relationships hold true:

$$U_T = V^{\mathrm{T}} \quad \text{and} \quad V_T = U^{\mathrm{T}}.$$

From Theorems 15.1 and 15.2 it follows that

controllability of $S \Leftrightarrow$ rank $U = n \Leftrightarrow$ rank $U^{\mathrm{T}} = n \Leftrightarrow$ rank $V_T = n \Leftrightarrow S^{\mathrm{T}}$ is observable.

Similarly, we have that

observability of $S \Leftrightarrow$ rank $V = n \Leftrightarrow$ rank $V^{\mathrm{T}} = n \Leftrightarrow$ rank $U_T = n \Leftrightarrow S^{\mathrm{T}}$ is controllable.

15.4 Structures of Economic Systems' Controllability and Observability

When investigating a real-life economic system, its control-theory model might not be controllable or observable. In such a situation, it will be difficult to obtain the system's controllability through the method of altering the input vector and difficult to know the state of the system through observing the output. So, a natural question is: Can we somehow decompose the control-theory model of the economic system into two or more subsystems such that one of the subsystems is observable or controllable, and so, the original system can be investigated through the analysis of regional observability and regional controllability? In this section, we will address this question fully.

15.4.1 Controllable Subspaces

Based on the analysis above, it follows that the state x_0 is controllable, if and only if there are t_1 and $u(t)$, $0 \leq t \leq t_1$, such that

$$x_0 = -\int_0^{t_1} e^{-A\tau} Bu(\tau) d\tau.$$

Therefore, the following results follow (Perko, 2013):

Theorem 15.4 The controllable subspace X_c is generated by B, AB, ..., $A^{n-1}B$, that is,

$$X_c = \text{span}\{B, AB, \ldots, A^{n-1}B\}.$$

Theorem 15.5 The controllable subspace is an invariant subspace.

For the constant coefficient linear economic system, given in Eq. (15.2), if $x' = Tx$ is a non-singular transformation, then this given system can be rewritten as follows:

$$\begin{cases} \dfrac{dx'}{dt_{y=C'x'}} = A'x' + B'u \end{cases},$$

where $A' = TAT^{-1}$, $B' = TB$, and $C' = CxT^{-1}$.

The controllability matrix of this second system is

$$U' = \left[B', A'B', \ldots, A'^{n-1}B'\right] = TU.$$

Similarly, the observability matrix is $V' = T^{-1}V$. Hence, non-singular linear transformations do not change the controllability and observability of the economic system.

15.4.2 Decomposition of the State Space

Assume that X_C is the subspace of X that consists of all controllable states and X_{Nc} the subspace that consists of all non-observable states. Let

$$e_1', e_2', \ldots, e_{nc}' \quad \text{and} \quad e_{nc+1}', \ldots, e_n',$$

respectively, be a base of X_C and X_{Nc}. Then

$$\Sigma_c = \left\{e'_1, e'_2, \ldots, e'_{n_c}, e'_{n_c+1}, \ldots, e'_n\right\}$$

constitutes a new base of the state space X. Let the base transformation from the original coordinate system to the new system be $x = Tx'$, where

$$T = \begin{bmatrix} t_{11} & t_{12} & \cdots & t_{1n} \\ t_{21} & t_{22} & \cdots & t_{2n} \\ \vdots & \vdots & \ddots & \vdots \\ t_{n1} & t_{n2} & \cdots & t_{nn} \end{bmatrix},$$

so that the ith column is the coordinate of e'_i in the original coordinate system of X, and for any $x \in X$, its coordinate in the new base system Σ_c is

$$x' = \left[x'_c, x'_{Nc}\right]^T, \quad \text{for } x'_c \in X_C \quad \text{and} \quad x'_{Nc} \in X_{Nc}.$$

Assume that the original economic system is written in the base system Σ_c as follows:

$$\begin{bmatrix} \frac{dx'_c}{dt} \\ \frac{dx'_{Nc}}{dt} \end{bmatrix} = \begin{bmatrix} A_1 & \vdots & A_{12} \\ \cdots & \cdots & \cdots \\ A_{21} & \vdots & A_2 \end{bmatrix} \begin{bmatrix} x'_c \\ \cdots \\ x'_{Nc} \end{bmatrix} + \begin{bmatrix} B_1 \\ \cdots \\ B_2 \end{bmatrix} u, y = [C_1 \ \vdots \ C_2] \begin{bmatrix} x'_c \\ \cdots \\ x'_{Nc} \end{bmatrix}.$$

Then the following result holds true:

Theorem 15.6 The constant coefficient linear system in Eq. (15.2) takes the following form in the new base system Σ_c:

$$\begin{bmatrix} \frac{dx'_c}{dt} \\ \frac{dx'_{Nc}}{dt} \end{bmatrix} = \begin{bmatrix} A_1 & \vdots & A_{12} \\ \cdots & \cdots & \cdots \\ 0 & \vdots & A_2 \end{bmatrix} \begin{bmatrix} x'_c \\ \cdots \\ x'_{Nc} \end{bmatrix} + \begin{bmatrix} B_1 \\ \cdots \\ B_2 \end{bmatrix} u \tag{15.3}$$

$$y = [C_1 \ \vdots \ C_2] \begin{bmatrix} x'_c \\ \cdots \\ x'_{Nc} \end{bmatrix}$$

and is (A_1, B_1) controllable.

Proof Denote $T_1 = \left[e'_1, e'_2, \ldots, e'_{n_c}\right]$ and $T_2 = \left[e'_{n_c+1}, \ldots, e'_n\right]$. Then $T = [T_1, T_2]$. If $T^{-1} = [Q_1, Q_2]^T$, then we have

$$A' = T^{-1}AT = \begin{bmatrix} Q_1 \\ Q_2 \end{bmatrix} A[T_1, T_2] = \begin{bmatrix} Q_1AT_1 & Q_1AT_2 \\ Q_2AT_1 & Q_2AT_2 \end{bmatrix}$$

and

$$B' = T^{-1}B = \begin{bmatrix} Q_1B \\ Q_2B \end{bmatrix}.$$

Because

$$T^{-1}T = \begin{bmatrix} Q_1 \\ Q_2 \end{bmatrix}[T_1, T_2] = \begin{bmatrix} Q_1T_1 & Q_1T_2 \\ Q_2T_1 & Q_2T_2 \end{bmatrix} = \begin{bmatrix} I_{n_c} & 0 \\ 0 & I_{n-n_c} \end{bmatrix},$$

we have $Q_2T_1 = 0$. Because T_1 consists of the base vectors of X_c as columns, $Q_2T_1 = 0$ implies that for any $x \in X_c$, $Q_2x = 0$. Because the columns of B belong to X_c, we have $Q_2B = 0$. That is, $B_2 = 0$. Because X_c is an invariant subspace of A, AT_1 belongs to X_c so that $Q_2T_1 = 0$ implies that $Q_2AT_1 = 0$, that is $A_2 = 0$.

In the following, we show the (A_1, B_1) controllability. The controllability matrix of the system in Eq. (15.3) is

$$U' = \begin{bmatrix} B_1 & A_1B_1 & \cdots & A_1^{n-1}B_1 \\ 0 & 0 & \cdots & 0 \end{bmatrix}.$$

From Theorem 15.4, it follows that rank $U' =$ the dimension of $X_c = n_c$. So, rank $[B_1|A_1B_1|\ldots|A_1^{n-1}B_1] = n_c$. That is, rank $[B_1|A_1B_1|\ldots|A_1^{n_c-1}B_1] = n_c$. So, the (A_1, B_1) controllability follows.

The expression

$$X = X_c \bigoplus X_{Nc}$$

means that the state space X can be decomposed into controllable subspace X_c and non-controllable subspace X_{Nc}. Therefore, the economic system in Eq. (15.2) can be decomposed into controllable subsystem

$$S_c : \frac{dx'_c}{dt} = A_1x'_c + B_1u + A_{12}x'_{Nc}$$

and non-controllable subsystem

$$S_{Nc} : \frac{dx'_{Nc}}{dt} = A_2x'_{Nc},$$

where these two subsystems are coupled together through the matrix A_{12}, as shown in Fig. 15.1.

Theorem 15.6 guarantees that the system

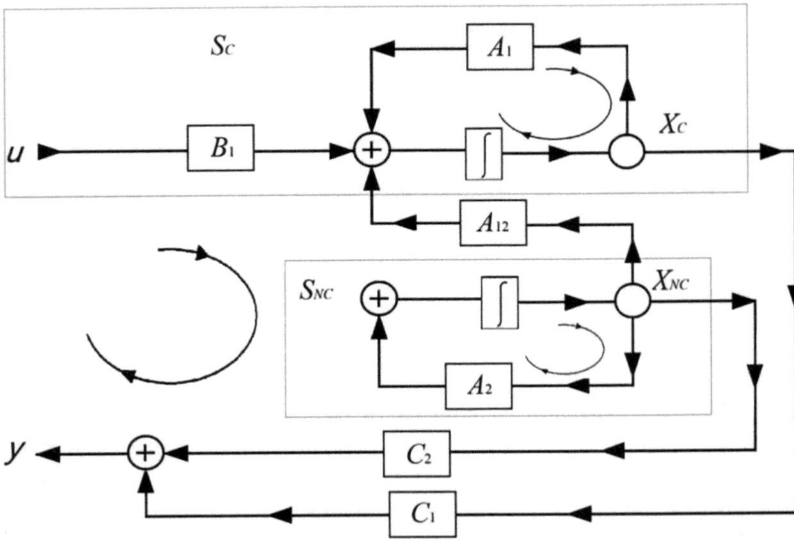

Fig. 15.1 The structural form of the economic system's controllability

$$\frac{dx_c'}{dt} = A_1 x_c' + B_1 u$$

is controllable, and by letting $f(t) = A_{12} x_{Nc}'$, we see the controllability of the subsystem S_c.

15.4.3 The Subspace of Unobservable States

When $u(t) = 0$ and the initial state is x_0, assume that the state trajectory that corresponds to the initial state x_0 is $x(t)$. If the corresponding output of the system is $y(t) = Cx(t) = 0$, then the output $y(t)$ cannot uniquely determine the initial state x (except for the zero state). In this case, x_0 is known as a not-observable state. The set of all not-observable states within the state space forms a subspace, which is known as not-observable subspace, denoted as X_{No}. For the structure of the not-observable subspace, we have the following results, for related proofs, see Perko (2013):

Theorem 15.7 The not-observable subspace X_{No} is equal to the intersection of all the kernels of the matrices C, CA, …, CA^{n-1}. That is, the following holds true:

$$X_{\text{No}} = \bigcap_{i=0}^{n-1} \ker\left(CA^i\right).$$

Theorem 15.8 The economic system in Eq. (15.2) is observable, if and only if $X_{\text{No}} = \{0\}$.

Theorem 15.9 The not-observable subspace X_{No} of the economic system in Eq. (15.2) is an invariant subspace of A.

Assume that the dimension of the not-observable subspace X_{No} is n_1 and X_{O} a subspace of the state space X such that $X = X_{\text{O}} \oplus X_{\text{No}}$. Select a base of X_{No} and one of X_{O}, respectively, as follows:

$$e'_1, e'_2, \ldots, e'_{n_1} \quad \text{and} \quad e'_{n_1+1}, \ldots, e'_n.$$

Let the coordinate system of X, based on the base $e'_1, e'_2, \ldots, e'_{n_1}, e'_{n_1+1}, \ldots, e'_n$, be Σ_{O}. Then within this coordinate system, for any state $x \in X$, it can be written as

$$x' = \begin{bmatrix} x_{\text{No}} \\ x_{\text{O}} \end{bmatrix}^{\text{T}},$$

where

$$x_{\text{No}} = \left[x'_1, x'_2, \ldots, x'_{n_1}\right]^{\text{T}} \quad \text{and} \quad x_{\text{O}} = \left[x'_{n_1+1}, x'_{n_1+2}, \ldots, x'_n\right]^{\text{T}}.$$

The transformation from the original coordinate system to the new system Σ_{O} is $x = Tx'$, where the ith column of T is the coordinate of the base vector e'_i in the original coordinate system, $i = 1, 2, \ldots, n$.

After applying this coordinate transformation, the economic system can be rewritten as follows:

$$\begin{cases} \dfrac{dx'}{dt} = \begin{bmatrix} \dfrac{dx_{\text{No}}}{dt} \\ \dfrac{dx_{\text{O}}}{dt} \end{bmatrix} = \begin{bmatrix} A_1 & A_{12} \\ A_{21} & A_2 \end{bmatrix} \begin{bmatrix} x_{\text{No}} \\ x_{\text{O}} \end{bmatrix} + \begin{bmatrix} B_1 \\ B_2 \end{bmatrix} u \\ y = \begin{bmatrix} C_1 & C_2 \end{bmatrix} \begin{bmatrix} x_{\text{No}} \\ x_{\text{O}} \end{bmatrix} \end{cases}.$$

Then, the following result holds true (Perko, 2013):

Theorem 15.10 The constant coefficient linear economic system in Eq. (15.2) under the new base system Σ_{O} takes the following form:

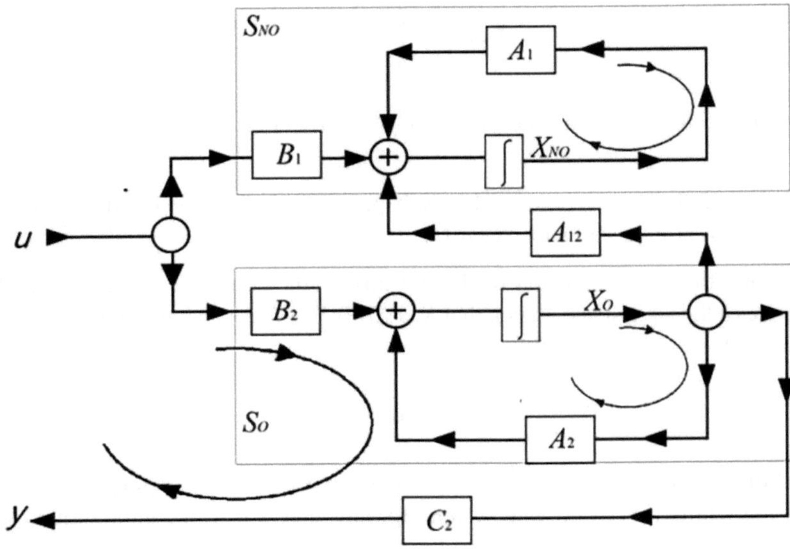

Fig. 15.2 The observability structure of a linear economic system

$$\begin{cases} \begin{bmatrix} \frac{dx_{No}}{dt} \\ \frac{dx_{O}}{dt} \end{bmatrix} = \begin{bmatrix} A_1 & A_{12} \\ 0 & A_2 \end{bmatrix} \begin{bmatrix} x_{No} \\ x_{O} \end{bmatrix} + \begin{bmatrix} B_1 \\ B_2 \end{bmatrix} u \\ y = \begin{bmatrix} 0 & C_2 \end{bmatrix} \begin{bmatrix} x_{No} \\ x_{O} \end{bmatrix} \end{cases},$$

which is (C_2, A_2) observable.

Figure 15.2 depicts the observability structure of an economic system written in the form of Eq. (15.2).

Similar to the controllability decomposition, the constant coefficient linear economic system in Eq. (15.2) can be decomposed by using a non-singular transformation into an observable subsystem:

$$S_O : \begin{cases} \frac{dx_{No}}{dt} = A_2 x_O + B_2 u \\ y = C_2 x_O \end{cases}$$

and a not-observable subsystem:

$$S_{No} : \frac{dx_{No}}{dt} = A_1 x_{No} + A_{12} x_O + B_1 u.$$

These two subsystems are coupled together by A_{12}.

15.5 Decomposition of an Economic System

If the state of an economic system is holistically and completely described by employing a control-theory model, the state vector most likely would contain a very good number of variables. In such a situation, the established model will be extremely complex and will be difficult to use for analyzing the characteristics of the economic system. Additionally, as a complex system, even after the state equation of the economic system is established, it will still be difficult to judge whether or not the system is observable and controllable. As a matter of fact, as a state equation that perfectly describes the complexity of an economic system, most likely the equation is neither observable nor controllable. Therefore, in this section we see how we can decompose the established state equation of the economic system into the following four parts: observable and controllable subsystem, controllable but not-observable subsystem, not controllable but observable subsystem, and not-observable and not controllable subsystem.

For the n-dimensional constant coefficient linear economic system in Eq. (15.2), let us decompose its state space X as follows:

$$X_1 = X_{\text{No}} \cap X_{\text{C}},$$

X_2 such that $X_{\text{C}} = X_1 \bigoplus X_2$,
X_3 such that $X_{\text{No}} = X_1 \bigoplus X_3$, and
X_4 such that $X = X_1 \bigoplus X_2 \bigoplus X_3 \bigoplus X_4$.

If we assume the dimensionality of X_i is n_i, then we have $n_1 + n_2 + n_3 + n_4 = n$. By choosing a basis $\left\{e'_1, \ldots, e'_{n_1}\right\}$ in X_1, $\left\{e'_{n_1+1}, \ldots, e'_{n_1+n_2}\right\}$ in X_2, $\left\{e'_{n_1+n_2+1}, \ldots, e'_{n_1+n_2+n_3}\right\}$ in X_3, and $\left\{e'_{n_1+n_2+n_3+1}, \ldots, e'_n\right\}$ in X_4, we can introduce the following coordinate system:

$$\Sigma_{\text{CO}} = \left\{e'_1, \ldots, e'_{n_1}, e'_{n_1+1}, \ldots, e'_{n_1+n_2}, e'_{n_1+n_2+1}, \ldots, e'_{n_1+n_2+n_3}, e'_{n_1+n_2+n_3+1}, \ldots, e'_n\right\}.$$

For any $x \in X$, denote its coordinates in the new coordinate system Σ_{CO} as

$$x' = \left[x_1^{\text{T}}, x_2^{\text{T}}, x_3^{\text{T}}, , x_4^{\text{T}}\right],$$

where

$$x_1 = \left[x'_1, \ldots, x'_{n_1}\right],$$

$$x_2 = \left[x'_{n_1+1}, \ldots, x'_{n_1+n_2}\right],$$

$$x_3 = \left[x'_{n_1+n_2+1}, \ldots, x'_{n_1+n_2+n_3}\right],$$

and

$$x_4 = \left[x'_{n_1+n_2+n_3+1}, \ldots, x'_{n}\right].$$

Let T be the transformation from the original coordinate system to the new system Σ_{CO} so that $x = Tx'$, where the ith column is the coordinates of e'_i in the original system. So, T is obviously non-singular. Now, with this transformation, the original system is rewritten as follows:

$$\begin{cases} \dfrac{dx'}{dt} = \begin{bmatrix} \dfrac{dx_1}{dt} \\ \dfrac{dx_2}{dt} \\ \dfrac{dx_3}{dt} \\ \dfrac{dx_4}{dt} \end{bmatrix} = \begin{bmatrix} A_{11} & A_{12} & A_{13} & A_{14} \\ A_{21} & A_{22} & A_{23} & A_{24} \\ A_{31} & A_{32} & A_{33} & A_{34} \\ A_{41} & A_{42} & A_{43} & A_{44} \end{bmatrix} \begin{bmatrix} x_1 \\ x_2 \\ x_3 \\ x_4 \end{bmatrix} + \begin{bmatrix} B_1 \\ B_2 \\ B_3 \\ B_4 \end{bmatrix} u. \\ y = [\, C_1 \quad C_2 \quad C_3 \quad C_4 \,] x' \end{cases}$$

Theorem 15.11 (Kalman Canonical Decomposition). The constant coefficient linear economic system in Eq. (15.2) can be simplified into the following canonical form in the new coordinate system Σ_{CO}:

$$\begin{cases} \dfrac{dx'}{dt} = \begin{bmatrix} A_{11} & A_{12} & A_{13} & A_{14} \\ 0 & A_{22} & 0 & A_{24} \\ 0 & 0 & A_{33} & A_{34} \\ 0 & 0 & 0 & A_{44} \end{bmatrix} x' + \begin{bmatrix} B_1 \\ B_2 \\ 0 \\ 0 \end{bmatrix} u \\ y = [\, 0 \quad C_2 \quad 0 \quad C_4 \,] x' \end{cases}$$

and the original economic system is decomposed into the following four subsystems:

$$S_1 : \begin{cases} \dfrac{dx_1}{dt} = A_{11}x_1 + B_1u + f_1 \\ y_1 = 0x_1 = 0 \end{cases}, \quad \text{where } f_1 = A_{12}x_2 + A_{13}x_3 + A_{14}x_4$$

$$S_2 : \begin{cases} \dfrac{dx_2}{dt} = A_{22}x_2 + B_2u + f_2, & \text{where } f_2 = A_{24}x_4 \\ y_2 = C_2x_2 \end{cases}$$

$$S_3 : \begin{cases} \dfrac{dx_3}{dt} = A_{33}x_3 + f_3, & \text{where } f_3 = A_{34}x_4 \\ y_3 = 0x_3 = 0 \end{cases}$$

$$S_4 : \begin{cases} \dfrac{dx_4}{dt} = A_{44}x_4 \\ y_4 = C_4x_4 \end{cases}$$

where the subsystem S_1 does not have any observable output, the subsystem S_2 can be completely observed and controlled, the subsystem S_3 does not have any output and cannot be affected by any control variable, and the subsystem S_4 is not influenced by any control variable.

Notice that although the subsystem S_1 has control input, it does not guarantee that this subsystem is (A_{11}, B_1) controllable. And, the subsystem S_4 has observable output. However, it is not guaranteed that this subsystem is (C_4, A_{44}) observable. In terms of the possibility of economic interactions, the portion(s) of the economic system that are not fully controllable represent the vulnerability of the economy for hostile attacks from outsiders, for relevant discussions on hostile attacks at the micro-firm level, see Sobel (1999). In the following section, we will present one possible way for a currency war to be launched.

15.6 One Possible Form of Currency Wars

According to Bernanke and Gertler (1999), the fundamental value of a particular capital is equal to the present value of the dividends the capital is expected to generate throughout the indefinite future. Symbolically, the fundamental value Q_t of a depreciable capital in period t is given by

$$\begin{aligned} Q_t &= E_t\left(\sum_{i=0}^{\infty}\left[\frac{(1-\delta)^i D_{t+1+i}}{\prod_{j=0}^{i} R^q_{t+1+j}}\right]\right) \\ &= E_t\left(\frac{D_{t+1}}{R^q_{t+1}} + \frac{(1-\delta)^1 D_{t+2}}{R^q_{t+1}R^q_{t+2}} + \frac{(1-\delta)^2 D_{t+3}}{R^q_{t+1}R^q_{t+2}R^q_{t+3}} + \ldots\right) \end{aligned}, \tag{15.4}$$

where E_t stands for the mathematical expectation as of period t, δ the rate of physical depreciation of the capital, D_{t+i} the dividends, and R^q_{t+1} the relevant stochastic gross discount rate at t for dividends received in period $(t + 1)$. Then, we can rewrite Eq. (15.4) as follows:

$$Q_t = E_t\left(\frac{D_{t+1} + (1-\delta)Q_{t+1}}{R^q_{t+1}}\right). \tag{15.5}$$

Because of various reasons, such as fads, the market price S_t of the capital differs persistently from the capital's fundamental value Q_t. When $S_t \neq Q_t$, we say, as in Bernanke and Gertler (1999), there is a bubble. However, to be more specific, when $S_t > Q_t$, we say that there is a positive bubble in the marketplace, and a negative bubble, when $S_t < Q_t$. In the realistic market place, asset prices mostly like deviate from the fundamental values due to various reasons, such as liquidity trading or to waves of alternating optimism and pessimism.

If a bubble exists at period t with probability p to persist into the next period, then by using the mathematical expectations the difference between the market price and the fundamental value of the capital in period $(t + 1)$ satisfies the following:

$$p(S_{t+1} - Q_{t+1}) + (1-p)\cdot 0 = a\left[(S_t - Q_t)R^q_{t+1}\right] + (1-a)\cdot 0. \tag{15.6}$$

It means that the mathematically expected $(S_{t+1} - Q_{t+1})$ value with probability p for $S_{t+1} \neq Q_{t+1}$ to happen is equal to the expected growth of the t-period difference $(S_t - Q_t)R^q_{t+1}$ with probability a $(>p)$ for $S_t - Q_t \neq 0$. That is, what is expected is a more severe "bubble," since $a/p > 1$. So, if we assume $a/p < 1$, it means that the bubble in period $(t + 1)$ is expected to be less severe than in period t.

From Eq. (15.6), it follows that we know the following expression is true:

$$p\cdot\frac{S_{t+1} - Q_{t+1}}{R^q_{t+1}} = a(S_t - Q_t).$$

Now by taking the mathematical expected value for $(S_{t+1} - Q_{t+1})/R^q_{t+1}$ in period t, we have the following:

$$E_t\left(\frac{S_{t+1} - Q_{t+1}}{R^q_{t+1}}\right) = p\cdot\left(\frac{S_{t+1} - Q_{t+1}}{R^q_{t+1}}\right) + (1-p)\cdot 0 = a(S_t - Q_t). \tag{15.7}$$

Equation (15.5) implies that

$$
\begin{aligned}
Q_t &= E_t\left\{\frac{D_{t+1} + (1-\delta)S_{t+1} - (1-\delta)S_{t+1} + (1-\delta)Q_t}{R^q_{t+1}}\right\} \\
&= E_t\left\{\frac{D_{t+1} + (1-\delta)S_{t+1}}{R^q_{t+1}} - (1-\delta)\frac{S_{t+1} - Q_{t+1}}{R^q_{t+1}}\right\} \\
&= E_t\left\{\frac{D_{t+1} + (1-\delta)S_{t+1}}{R^q_{t+1}}\right\} - (1-\delta)E_t\left\{\frac{S_{t+1} - Q_{t+1}}{R^q_{t+1}}\right\} \\
&= E_t\left\{\frac{D_{t+1} + (1-\delta)S_{t+1}}{R^q_{t+1}}\right\} - (1-\delta)a(S_t - Q_t), \text{(from Eq.(15.7))}.
\end{aligned}
$$

Therefore, we have

$$
Q_t + (1-\delta)a(S_t - Q_t) = E_t\left\{\frac{D_{t+1} + (1-\delta)S_{t+1}}{R^q_{t+1}}\right\},
$$

which is the equivalent to:

$$
\frac{S_t[Q_t + (1-\delta)a(S_t - Q_t)]}{S_t} = E_t\left\{\frac{D_{t+1} + (1-\delta)S_{t+1}}{R^q_{t+1}}\right\}.
$$

By isolating the factor S_t in the numerator and cross multiplying the rest from the left-hand side onto the right-hand side produce the following:

$$
\begin{aligned}
S_t &= E_t\left\{\frac{[D_{t+1} + (1-\delta)S_{t+1}]S_t}{R^q_{t+1}[Q_t + (1-\delta)a(S_t - Q_t)]}\right\} \\
&= E_t\left\{\frac{[D_{t+1} + (1-\delta)S_{t+1}]S_t}{R^q_{t+1}\{[a(1-\delta)S_t - a(1-\delta)Q_t] + Q_t\}}\right\} \\
&= E_t\left\{\frac{[D_{t+1} + (1-\delta)S_{t+1}]S_t}{R^q_{t+1}[bS_t + (1-b)Q_t]}\right\}, \quad \text{where } b = a(1-\delta) \\
&= E_t\left\{\frac{D_{t+1} + (1-\delta)S_{t+1}}{R^q_{t+1}\left[b + (1-b)\dfrac{Q_t}{S_t}\right]}\right\} \\
&= E_t\left\{\frac{D_{t+1} + (1-\delta)S_{t+1}}{R^{s.}_{t+1}}\right\}.
\end{aligned}
$$

Therefore, we have derived at

$$
S_t = E_t\left\{\frac{D_{t+1} + (1-\delta)S_{t+1}}{R^s_{t+1}}\right\},
$$

where the return on stocks R^s_{t+1} is related to the fundamental return of the capital R^q_{t+1} as follows:

$$R^s_{t+1} = R^q_{t+1}\left[b + (1-b)\frac{Q_t}{S_t}\right].$$

If $S_t > Q_t$, then $R^s_{t+1} < R^q_{t+1}$, meaning that the expected stock return is less than the fundamental return. That is,

$$E_t\left\{\frac{D_{t+1} + (1-\delta)S_{t+1}}{R^s_{t+1}}\right\} < E_t\left\{\frac{D_{t+1} + (1-\delta)S_{t+1}}{R^q_{t+1}}\right\}.$$

From Eq. (15.6), it follows that

$$(S_t - Q_t) = \frac{p}{a} \times \frac{(S_{t+1} - Q_{t+1})}{R^q_{t+1}}, \tag{15.8}$$

which implies that at period $(t + 1)$, there is a positive bubble if and only if there is a positive bubble at period t. Because $0 < p < a < 1$, if $S_{t+1} > Q_{t+1}$ (assuming a positive bubble), then from $0 < \frac{p}{a} < 1$, Eq. (15.8) implies that the current bubble $(S_t - Q_t)$ is smaller than the fundamental return of the bubble in period $(t + 1)$. In other words, the bubble in period $(t + 1)$ gets more severe than when in period t.

Now, if $S_{t+1} < Q_{t+1}$ with $0 < p < a < 1$, then Eq. (15.8) implies that the underpricing S_{t+1} of the asset Q_{t+1} in period $(t + 1)$ is more severe than that in period t. Moreover, this equation also indicates that at period $(t + 1)$ there is a negative bubble if and only if there is a negative bubble at period t.

These two conclusions evidently contradict the efficient market hypothesis, because these analogies indicate that if in period t the market overprices the asset, then the overpricing will continue forever, and if in period t the market underprices the asset, then the underpricing will also continue forever. That is, neither positive nor negative bubble will ever crash. So, there are two possibilities: (1) The model in Eq. (15.8) does not hold true in general or (2) the efficient market hypothesis is not *ever* true.

Evidence appears to show that the efficient market hypothesis holds true at least occasionally and also bubbles, both positive and negative, do burst (Beechey et al., 2000; Smith et al., 1988). So, the model in Eq. (15.8) needs to be modified in order to describe the more realistic market situation better.

If in Eq. (15.8) we assume $0 < a < p < 1$, then a similar analysis as above indicates that the phenomenon of overpricing or underpricing disappears over time. And, if $0 < a = p < 1$ is assumed, then the model in Eq. (15.8) implies that the existing underpricing or overpricing stays fundamentally stable.

If $0 < a < p < 1$ and $a \approx 0$ are assumed, then Eq. (15.8) implies that $p/a \approx +\infty$ so that the fundamental return $(S_{t+1} - Q_{t+1})/R^q_{t+1}$ of the asset approaches 0, meaning that the existing bubble gradually disappears with time.

Next, let us focus on the analysis of Eqs. (15.4) and (15.5). In particular, assume that in the $(t + i)$th period foreign investments are suddenly increased drastically due to expected appearance of activities from the current weak economic state and weak local currency. So, for this period, δ (= the physical depreciation rate of capital) would increase due to the increased amount of money supply, which in turn pushes up the inflation. So, $(1 - \delta)^i$ would decrease drastically if the influx of foreign investments is large. At the same time, R^q_{t+i} (= the stochastic gross discount rate of the $(t + i)$th period) would also increase, because of the increased inflation, while the dividends D_{t+i} would generally decrease due to the reason that everybody would like to reinvest much of the available capital back into the market in order to capture the rising book values, including stocks, real estate, and others with impressive increasing prices. That is, the present value of the return of the $(t + i)$th period

$$\frac{(1-\delta)^i D_{t+i}}{R^q_{t+1} \cdots R^q_{t+i}}$$

would drop from the level of expectation. In reality, the investor would hold onto the increased book value by receiving less tangible return, hoping that the book value would continue to rise drastically.

Due to the wide and convenient availability of capital, as caused by the increased money supply, the local economic activities pick up, too, in large quantities, while the interest rate also goes up because the central bank, to control the inflation, revises the interest rate and attempts to limit the money supply.

At this very moment of financially prosperity, assume that a huge amount of foreign investments suddenly leaves in the $(t + j)$th period, where $j > i$, because of the much higher prices in assets, in capital investments, etc., for them to take profit in order to move their capitals to other regions to capture new economic opportunities. So, in the $(t + j)$th period, when a huge amount of foreign investment leaves, most of the economic activities that got started because of the foreign investments become stalled and/or negatively impacted. Therefore, a good portion of the local investments is forced to be retained with the interrupted economic activities. That is, the investors of the local investments can no longer receive their expected dividends, and at the same time a large amount of the investments evaporates totally if many of the stalled activities can no longer be continued until their expected completion or are indefinitely delayed. That of course costs additional local capital to do the cleanup of what is left behind unfinished and unusable ruins. In particular, in Eqs. (15.4) and (15.5), the dividends D_{t+j} of the $(t + i)$th period decrease drastically and the remaining future dividends, if they still come fortunately as expected, would have to be used to bail out (to finish up) some of the other potentially possibly profitable projects.

That is, right before the large amount of foreign investments leaves suddenly and strategically, the local economy is more active than ever before. Hence, the stochastic gross discount rate R^q_{t+i} of the $(t + i)$th period would be much lower than R^q_{t+j} of the $(t + j)$th period, because much higher returns on earlier investments are optimistically expected. So, the present ratio:

$$\frac{(1-\delta)^i D_{t+i}}{R^q_{t+1} \cdots R^q_{t+i} \cdots R^q_{t+j}}$$

would in reality be very close to zero.

Summarizing what is just analyzed above, one can see that when a large amount of foreign investments gathers in one place over either a long period or a short period of time and then leaves suddenly and massively, that local economy has to suffer through a positive bubble, caused by the increased money supply as a consequence of the foreign investments, and then a following negative, disastrous bubble, caused by the sudden dry-out of the money supply. And due to the reason that a large number of economic activities are either unexpectedly delayed or totally impossible to complete, the local investors are actually unable to continue to collect their originally expected dividends for many periods to come. That is, foreign investments can be employed as a weapon of mass destruction, if they leave strategically and suddenly, no matter whether they come quickly in a short period of time or slowly over a relatively longer period of time.

15.7 A Few Final Words

Through the concepts of economic systems' observability and controllability, the theoretical results in the first part of this chapter imply that in the most general circumstance, each economic system is vulnerable to external influences through first the subsystem S_1 and then the subsystems S_3 and S_4. And, domestic monetary policies and fiscal policies can only effectively affect the subsystem S_2 and the consequent results on S_2 can also be readily observed. What is worse is that the base vectors in Σ_{CO} are chosen by the attacker; that makes self-defense more challenging.

By using the systemic intuition of the yoyo model and the Bernanke–Gertler model of the fundamental value of capital, the second portion of this chapter demonstrates theoretically how financial crises could be caused and/or created purposefully by certain group(s) of people in order to acquire economic and political gains through the use of movements of money across national borders. Because of the present-day globalization of the world economy, national and regional economies have been closely intertwined with each other. Hence, when one nation or geographic region suffers from economic and financial crises, the consequent damaging effects and adverse impacts tend to spread internationally. In particular, the discussion here indicates that when a large amount of foreign investments gathers in one place over either a long period or a short period of time and then leaves suddenly and massively, that local economy will suffer through a positive bubble, caused by the increased money supply as a consequence of the foreign investments, and then a following negative, disastrous burst, caused by the sudden dry-out of the money supply. And because a large number of economic activities are either unexpectedly delayed or totally impossible to complete, the local investors can no longer continuously collect their originally expected dividends for many time periods to come. If we look at such situations differently, this result indicates that foreign investments can be potentially employed as a weapon of mass destruction, if they leave strategically and suddenly, no matter whether they come quickly in a short period of time or slowly over a relatively longer period of time.

References

Beechey, M., Gruen, D., & Vickrey, J. (2000). The efficient markets hypothesis: A survey. *Reserve Bank of Australia in its series RBA Research Discussion Papers* numbered rdp2000-01.

Bernanke, B. S., & Gertler, M. (1999). Monetary policy and asset price volatility. *Economic Review, Federal Reserve Bank of Kansas City*, fourth quarter (pp. 17–51).

Forrest, J. Y. L., Hopkins, Z., & Liu, S. F. (2013a). Currency wars and a possible self-defense (I): How currency wars take place. *Advances in Systems Science and Application, 13*, 198–217.

Forrest, J. Y. L., Hopkins, Z., & Liu, S. F. (2013b). Currency wars and a possible self-defense (II): A plan for self-protection. *Advances in Systems Science and Application, 13*, 299–316.

Hein, E., Detzer, D., & Dodig, N. (Eds.). (2016). *Financialisation and the financial and economic crises: Country studies*. Edward Elgar Publishing.

Kaminsky, G. L., Lizondo, S., & Reinhart, C. M. (1998). Leading indicators of currency crises. *IMF Staff Papers, 45*(1), 1–48.

Krugman, P. (1979). A model of balance-of-payments crises. *Journal of Money, Credit, and Banking, 11*, 311–325.

Perko, L. (2013). *Differential equations and dynamical systems* (Vol. 7). Springer.

Smith, V. L., Suchanek, G. L., & Williams, A. W. (1988). Bubbles, crashes, and endogenous expectations in experimental spot asset markets. *Econometrica, 56*(5), 1119–1151.

Sobel, R. (1999). *When giants stumble: Classic business blunders and how to avoid them.* Prentice Hall.

Wang, R. X., & Hu, G. H. (2005). *International finance*. Press of Wuhan University of Science and Technology.

Chapter 16
Several Strategies of Self-Defense

Jeffrey Yi-Lin Forrest, Zackary Hopkins, Sifeng Liu, Bohua Yang, Sailau Baizakov, and Oinarov Azamat Ryskulovich

Abstract Continuing the previous chapter on how a currency war can be raged against a nation or a region, this chapter, which is mainly based on Forrest et al. (Adv Syst Sci Appl 13:299–316, 2013), makes use of the results of feedback systems (Lin, J Syst Eng 1(1):32–38, 1994) to develop a self-defense mechanism that can conceivably protect the nation or region under siege. In particular, this chapter studies the problem that when the control-theory model of an economic system is established with the parameters determined, how can one design the corresponding economic policy based on the feedback of the system so that the performance indicator would approach the pre-determined objective. By identifying the "invisible hand" that adjusts the economic market automatically as the feedback controller that regulates the economy's supply and demand, this chapter focuses on the design of feedback controls that could withstand disturbances of the environment. It establishes a feedback control model for the economic system, provides confirmations for how well this proposed control method could perform in practice, and expands this method to design the linear multivariable feedback control and the feedback control of discrete variables.

To show the practical significance of the conclusions presented in this chapter, an empirical analysis is constructed for the purpose of showing that the established control design can make the regulated economic indicator(s) approach the ideal targets well even when an environmental disturbance exists. This chapter establishes results that are expected to provide practical guidance for developing and adopting appropriate economic policies that could withstand external shocks.

Jeffrey Yi-Lin Forrest (Department of Accounting Economics Finance, Slippery Rock University, Slippery Rock, PA, USA; Email: Jeffrey.forrest@sru.edu), Zackary Hopkins (Institutional Research, Assessment and Analytics, Gannon University, Erie, PA, USA; Email: hopkins013@gannon.edu), Sifeng Liu (School of Economics and Management, Nanjing University of Aeronautics and Astronautics, Nanjing, China; Email: sfliu@nuaa.edu.cn), Bohua Yang (Business School, Jiangsu Normal University, Xuzhou, Jiangsu, China; Email: mathyang@126.com), Sailau Baizakov (Institute of Mathematics and Mathematical Modeling, Almaty, Kazakhstan; Email: Baizakov37@mail.ru), and Oinarov Azamat Ryskulovich (Economic Research Institute, Astana, Kazakhstan; Email: Azamat.oinarov@gmail.com) are equally contributed to this chapter.

J. Y.-L. Forrest, *Systemic Principles of Applied Economic Philosophies II*,
Translational Systems Sciences 39, https://doi.org/10.1007/978-981-99-7939-4_16

Keywords Allocation of money demand · Categorized monetary policies · Currency warfare · Economic policies · Feedback controller · Optimal economic adjustment · Purchasing power of money

16.1 Introduction

By combining the theoretical analysis in the previous chapter with the recent cases of speculative attacks in the arena of international finance, one can surely see the following predicament. When a nation tries to develop economically, due to its loosening economic and monetary policies, large amounts of foreign investments would be welcomed, and at the same time, a lot of such foreign investments would strategically rush into the nation in order to ride along with the forthcoming economic boom. Now what we have shown earlier is that if a large amount of foreign investments leaves suddenly, then the nation would most likely suffer from a burst of the economic bubble with a large percentage of economic activities interrupted either temporarily or indefinitely. So, a natural question at this junction is: How could policy makers possibly design a measure to counter such sudden leaves of foreign investments in order to avoid the undesirable disastrous consequences? This chapter, which is mainly based on Forrest et al. (2013), will address this problem.

This chapter is organized as follows: Sect. 16.2 provides a quick literature review and demonstrates how this chapter contributes to the literature. Section 16.3 symbolically formulates the problem of concern and introduces the basic models. Section 16.4 examines how to categorize the overall economy into different sectors for the purpose of directing consumption behaviors and how to design feedback controls with pure gain. Section 16.5 outlines the procedures on how to design feedback controllers and linear multivariable regulators. Two examples of applications are given in Sect. 16.6 to demonstrate how one can employ the theory developed in this chapter to resolve real-life problems. Section 16.7 concludes the chapter.

16.2 Literature Review

Historically, it is Adam Smith, the initiator of modern quantitative economics, who treated economy as a self-regulating (or self-adjusting) system, where "an invisible hand" automatically adjusts the markets' supply and demand so that the system reaches and maintains its equilibrium. For the purpose of this chapter, the so-called invisible hand will be identified with the feedback controller. It bridges the production of products and the exchanges that take place in the marketplace by regulating the relationship between the system's supply and demand and by making this relationship as balanced as possible through adjusting prices, profits, competition, and other factors. Because of this identification, methods of control theory can be readily applied to resolve problems of economics and business (Chow, 1975; Shefrin & Thaler, 1981). They provide economists with practically operational procedures for the theoretical research and real-life applications (Kendrick, 1981; Seierstad & Sydsaeter, 1986). That explains why control theory has been increasingly employed in the research of economic policies (McKinnon, 1993).

For example, Pindyck (1977), a control theorist, resolved the control problem of deterministic secondary tracking of a mathematical model developed for the American economy, where the model contains 28 state variables, by using such control variables as excess tax, government spending, and money supply. This work illustrates the importance of the methods of feedback control in the design of financial policies and fiscal policies. Moe (1985) presented an empirical analysis of the National Labor Relations Board by use of feedback control by focusing on the balance the agency strikes to achieve between the interests of businesses and those of labors. Kydland and Prescott (1980) presented recursive methods for designing optimal taxation plan. Because most economic systems are nonlinear, the so-called economic model predictive control (MPC) system, which is capable of optimizing closed loop performance with respect to general economic considerations in the construction of the cost function, was used to design an estimator for nonlinear economic systems (Diehl et al., 2011; Ellis et al., 2014; Heidarinejad et al., 2012; Rawlings et al., 2012).

Corresponding to the characteristics of the target entities of a regional economic policy, such as large inertia, long time delay, etc., we can use the state feedback to offset the time delay and inertia of the entities so that these entities would have good quality dynamic response characteristics and excellent regulation performance (Hu & Hu, 2005). Considering the theoretical continuity and practical discreteness of time in terms of the operation and regulation of economic systems, Wu and Liu (2004) employed the methods of systems theory and control theory to simulate the operational mechanism of macroeconomic systems and developed their replaceable cyclic control model and discrete successive input control decision model for macroeconomic systems. For dynamic input–output economic systems, Chow (1976) investigated a general production strategy based on monitors of consumption while developing particular strategies for structurally adjusting productions for several specific circumstances of consumption. Based on the methods of control theory, Yang et al. (2004) derived an optimal economic adjustment scheme for the optimization control problem of linear quadratic forms of the dynamic input–output model with integral inequality of the state by using the maximization principle. This scheme can be employed to materialize the optimal tracking of the actual output compared to the ideal output.

Because economic systems entail a large amount of nonlinearity and seemingly chaotic interactions, how to transform the seemingly chaotic dynamics of the systems into orderly matters has become the goal of research on the control and regulation of chaotic economic systems. The control method of prediction feedback, developed by Yao and Sheng (2002), can effectively control discrete chaotic systems and provide a sufficient and necessary condition for the stability of the systems. In fact, as a dynamic system, each model of the macroscopic economy is incomplete and suffers from errors of parameters' estimation and from signal interference from the environment. In other words, each general physical system inevitably involves uncertainty, and when the uncertainty varies within a pre-determined range, Xiao and Lu (2002) successfully analyzed and optimally controlled a general macroeconomic system while guaranteeing that the controlled variables could accurately trace the pre-determined objectives. These scholars accomplished the goal by simplifying the linear Gauss problem of quadratic form into a general optimization control problem of quadratic form and by obtaining the gain matrix of the Kalman filter. As for the control systems of macroscopic economies (Pindyck, 1977), they are sometimes not only required to track the expected paths but also desired to have the controlled variables to be as close to the ideal measures as possible. That is the so-called ideal control strategy. By making the quadratic performance index equivalent to observation information of control, Wang and Wang (2006) transformed the original problem of regulating the macroscopic economy into one of solving for the optimal estimation of the controlled variable.

To enrich this literature and to address the question posed earlier, the present chapter proposes two different defense strategies against currency attacks. One is based on manipulating exchange rate, and the other using the feedback mechanism of the economy under siege.

16.3 Formulation of the Problem and Model Development

This section consists of two subsections. The first one shows how to categorize the purchasing overall power of the economy into different categories in the language of differential equations. The second subsection symbolically formulates the problem of how to appropriately regulate the activities that take place within the economy.

16.3.1 Categorization of Purchasing Power

Let us consider the following model that relates the purchasing power of money with the demand and supply of the money of a national economy:

$$\frac{dP}{dt} = k(D - S), \tag{16.1}$$

where D stands for the demand for money, S the money supply, P the purchasing power of money, $k > 0$ is a constant, and t represents time.

What this model says is that with all other variables staying constant, if the money supply S increases by a large amount and satisfies $S > D$, then the purchasing power of the money P decreases so that more money is needed to buy essentials of living and inflation will rise due to the increase in the money supply S. Now, let us divide the overall national economy into three sectors E_1, E_2, and E_3 as follows: E_1 stands for the goods, services, and relevant production of these goods and services that are needed for maintaining the basic living standard, E_2 the goods, services, and relevant productions that are used to acquire desired living conditions, and E_3 the goods, services, and relevant productions that are used for the enjoyment of luxurious living conditions.

The reason why we divide the economy in such a way is that according to Allen and Goldsmith (1972), the following are four base requirements for a society to maintain its stability.

1. Minimum disruption of ecological processes;
2. Maximum conservation of materials and energy, or an economy of stock rather than flow;
3. A population in which recruitment equals loss; and
4. A social system in which individuals can enjoy rather than feel restricted by the first three conditions.

So, in terms of economics, for a society to maintain its stability, economic sector E_1 has to be stable.

Next, let us accordingly divide the overall demand D of money into three corresponding categories as follows:

D_1 = the demand of money for meeting the minimum requirement to maintain the basic living standard;
D_2 = the demand of money for acquiring desired living conditions; and
D_3 = the demand of money for enjoying luxurious living conditions.

Assume that in a stable economy, we have the following allocation of money demand:

$$D = D_1 + D_2 + D_3 = \alpha_1 D + \alpha_2 D + \alpha_3 D,$$

where the weights α_i, $i = 1, 2, 3$, stand for the average allocation of the citizens of the economy over the three categories as described above, satisfying $\alpha_1 + \alpha_2 + \alpha_3 = 1$ and $D_i = \alpha_i D$, $i = 1, 2, 3$. For instance, in the stable economy, an average family allocates half of its monthly income on necessities of living, such as food, utilities, etc., four tenth of the income on acquiring the desired quality of life, and one-tenth of the income on luxurious items, then $\alpha_1 = 0.5$, $\alpha_2 = 0.4$, and $\alpha_3 = 0.1$.

If the money supply S increases drastically, along with the decreasing purchasing power of money, all goods will cost more. If somehow the goods in the category of living necessities rise more rapidly, then a reallocation of household income will appear. For instance, due to rumors about potential interruptions in the supply of food and clean water accompanying a substantial increase in the money supply, the average family has to reallocate its income as follows: $\alpha_1 = 0.625$, $\alpha_2 = 0.3$, and $\alpha_3 = 0.075$.

When such a reallocation of income of the average family is forced to take place, the stability of the economy would very likely be in trouble. So, to stabilize the economy, the purchasing power of money in category D_1 should stay relatively constant, while in D_2 increases somehow slightly, and in D_3 it should be allowed to increase in order to attract and trap the additional money supply away from category D_1. So, let P_i = the purchasing power of money in category D_i, $i = 1, 2, 3$.

Similarly, let us define S_i = the money supply that goes into category D_i, $i = 1, 2, 3$. Hence, Eq. (16.1) would look as follows:

$$\begin{cases} \dfrac{dP_1}{dt} = k_{11}(D_1 - S_1) + k_{12}(D_2 - S_2) + k_{13}(D_3 - S_3) + \sum_{j=1}^{n} q_{1j}x_j \\ \dfrac{dP_2}{dt} = k_{21}(D_1 - S_1) + k_{22}(D_2 - S_2) + k_{23}(D_3 - S_3) + \sum_{j=1}^{n} q_{2j}x_j , \\ \dfrac{dP_1}{dt} = k_{31}(D_1 - S_1) + k_{32}(D_2 - S_2) + k_{33}(D_3 - S_3) + \sum_{j=1}^{n} q_{3j}x_j \end{cases} \tag{16.2}$$

where k_{ij} and q_{ij} are constants and x_j stands for monetary policies, $i = 1, 2, 3$, and $j = 1, 2, \ldots, n$. By using matrix notations, Eq. (16.2) can be rewritten as follows:

$$\dot{P} = Kz + Qx, \tag{16.3}$$

where $P = [P_1\ P_2\ P_3]^{\mathrm{T}}$, $\dot{P}$ is Newton's notation for derivatives such that

$$\dot{P} = \left[\frac{dP_1}{dt}\ \frac{dP_2}{dt}\ \frac{dP_3}{dt}\right]^{\mathrm{T}},$$

and

$$K = \left[k_{ij}\right]_{3\times 3} \quad \text{and} \quad Q = \left[q_{ij}\right]_{3\times n}$$

are, respectively, the coefficient matrices of the variables $(D_i - S_i)$, $i = 1, 2, 3$, and x_j, $j = 1, 2, \ldots, n$.

In terms of systems research, the model in Eq. (16.3) can be seen as a feedback system as depicted in Fig. 16.1, where S represents the initial state of the economy. After the monetary policies $x_1, x_2, \ldots, x_n$ are introduced, the participants of the economy introduce either consciously or unconsciously a feedback component system S_f so that the overall system with the added feedback produces the desired output P_1, P_2, and P_3.

What is shown in Fig. 16.1 is the fact that each and every market economy, where the participants are allowed to design their own methods (without violating the established laws) to achieve their individually defined financial successes, then the economy constitutes a "rotational" field. Here, the word of rotation means that as

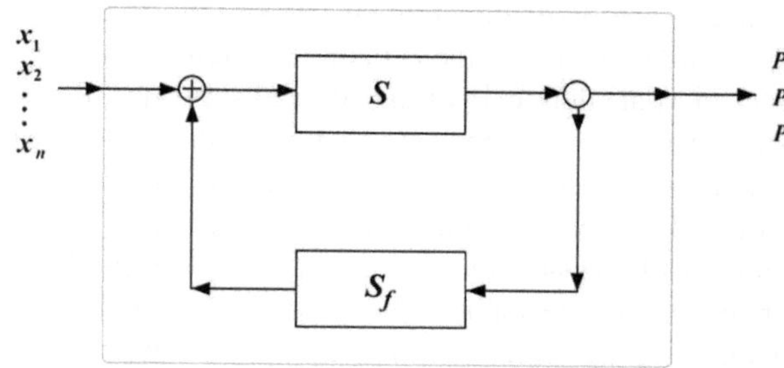

Fig. 16.1 The feedback loop between monetary policies and categorized purchasing powers

soon as a monetary policy is introduced, the market participants will find ways to take advantage of the policy so that the policy and the individually designed methods jointly produce the individually desired outputs.

16.3.2 The Problem of Economic Regulation

Assume that x_1 is the state variable of the economy that is to be regulated, x_2 the variable that reflects how the environment interferes with the economic system, u and y represent the control (or regulation) vector and the output vector, respectively. Then the state equation of the economic system that is to be regulated is

$$\frac{dx_1}{dt} = A_1x_1 + A_3x_2 + B_1u, \tag{16.4}$$

where the interference variable satisfies the following state equation:

$$\frac{dx_2}{dt} = A_2x_2. \tag{16.5}$$

the output equation is

$$y = C_1x_1 + C_2x_2. \tag{16.6}$$

When the natural evolution of the state variables of the economic system is affected by the external environment, the people who are charged with the responsibility to overlook the health of the system will often adopt certain policies to reduce the deviation of the state variables from their targeted values. For example, during a currency attack when the currency and the exchange rate of the economy that is under attack are greatly affected, the policy makers tend to adopt the strategy of selling its target currency to lower the rate of change in its currency so that the exchange rate of the system's currency would gradually recover to a certain desired level. As a matter of fact, when the regulator of the economy adopts countermeasures to reduce the influence of external factors, the strength of the effect of the adopted strategies is roughly directionally proportional to the control deviation of the observable state variables of the economic system. That proportionality constant we will refer to as the pure gain of the adopted strategies. Because the state variables of the original economic system and changes in these variables when the economic system is under influence of some external factors can be readily observed, we can use these observed state variables and the relevant changes as inputs in controlling the action strength of the adopted strategies. Here, the product of the gain of the control strategies and the input value is referred to as the feedback gain, and when the changes in the state variables are used as input, the product is known as pure feedback gain. So, the simplest situation is to use both x_1 and x_2 as feedback to design a feedback controller of pure gains as follows:

$$u = K_1 x_1 + K_2 x_2, \tag{16.7}$$

so that the resultant closed loop system is stable while reaching the following goal of regulation of the output:

$$\lim_{t \to \infty} y(t) = 0.$$

Figure 16.2 figuratively shows this closed loop system. Because we only consider regulating the output, and because the solutions that correspond to the eigenvalues with negative real parts do not have any effect on the regulation of the output, without loss of generality, we assume $\sigma(A_2) \subset C^{+}$, meaning that the real parts of all the extreme points are positive, where $\sigma(A_2)$ stands for the set of the extreme points of the interfering system. As a matter of fact, if none of the extreme points has positive real part, then the interfering system is asymptotically stable. In this case, the interfering system does not affect the stability of the original system. Hence, we

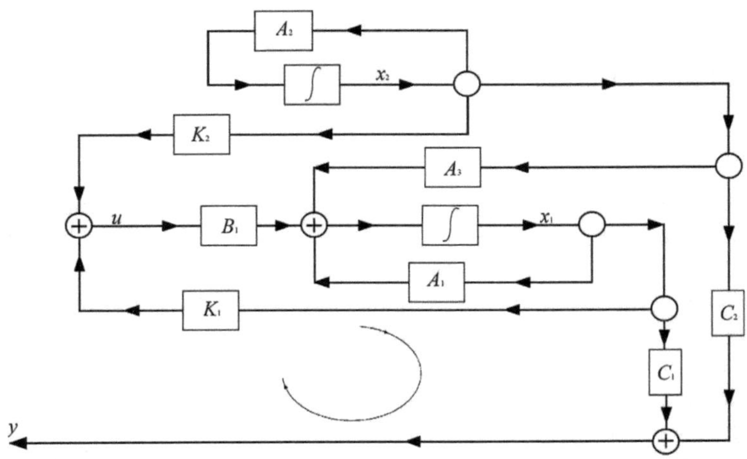

Fig. 16.2 The feedback controller with pure gains

only consider the case when the extreme points of the interfering system have positive real parts.

16.4 Categories of Economy and Feedback Control

This section applies the models developed in the previous section to (1) roughly divide the whole of the economy into different sectors so that consumers would most likely exhibit very different consumption behaviors in these individual sectors, (2) design feedback controls with pure gains.

16.4.1 Dividing an Economy into Categories

Let the categorized purchasing power $P = [P_1\ P_2\ P_3]^T$ of money and categorized difference $D - S = [D_1 - S_1\ D_2 - S_2\ D_3 - S_3]^T$ of the demand and supply of money be related as follows: $P = R_{3\times3}(D - S) + \varepsilon$, where $R_{3\times3}$ is a constant square matrix with real entries and $\varepsilon = [\varepsilon_1\ \varepsilon_2\ \varepsilon_3]^T$ a random vector with a none zero mean. Then, we have

$$\begin{bmatrix} P_1 \\ P_2 \\ P_3 \end{bmatrix} = A_{3\times3} \begin{bmatrix} D_1(t) - S_1(t) \\ D_2(t) - S_2(t) \\ D_3(t) - S_3(t) \end{bmatrix} + \begin{bmatrix} c_1 \\ c_2 \\ c_3 \end{bmatrix}, \tag{16.8}$$

where $E(\varepsilon_i) = c_i \neq 0$, $i = 1, 2, 3$. Substituting Eq. (16.8) into Eq. (16.3) leads to

$$R_{3\times3}\dot{z} = Kz + Qx. \tag{16.9}$$

Without loss of generality, assume that $R_{3\times3}$ is invertible. That is, we assume in general the categorized purchasing power of money is completely determined by the categorized differences of demand and supply of money. Then, Eq. (16.9) can be rewritten as follows:

$$\dot{z} = Az + Bx, \tag{16.10}$$

where $A = R^{-1}K$ and $B = R^{-1}Q$. To make the model in Eq. (16.10) technically manageable, we assume without loss of generality that B is a 3×3 matrix, meaning that the monetary policies $x_1, x_2, \ldots, x_n$ are accordingly categorized into three groups:

X_1 = the set of all those monetary policies that deal with the population meeting the minimum need to maintain the basic living standard;

X_2 = the set of all those monetary policies that deal with the population's need for acquiring desired living conditions; and

X_3 = the set of all those monetary policies that deal with the population's need for enjoying luxurious living conditions.

Without causing confusion, we will still use the same symbol x to represent the vector $[X_1\ X_2\ X_3]^T$ of categorized monetary policies.

Similar to the concept of consumer price index (CPI), let us introduce an economic index vector $y = [y_1\quad y_2\quad y_3]^T$ such that y_i measures the state of the economic sector i, $i = 1, 2, 3$. Then from Eq. (16.10) we can establish the following model for the national economy of concern:

$$\begin{cases} \dot{z} = Az + Bx \\ y = Cz + Dx \\ z(0) = 0 \end{cases}, \tag{16.11}$$

where z is the 3 × 1 matrix $[D_1 - S_1\ D_2 - S_2\ D_3 - S_3]^T$ of the categorized difference of demand and supply of money, referred to as the state of the economic system, symbols A, B, C, and D are, respectively, constant 3 × 3 matrices, such that D is non-singular (meaning that each introduction of monetary policies does have direct, either positive or negative, effect on the performance of the economy), and the input space X and output space Y are following:

$$X = Y = \{r : [0, +\infty) \to \boldsymbol{R}^3 : r \text{ is a piecewise continuous function}\},$$

where $\boldsymbol{R}$ stands for the set of all real numbers and $\boldsymbol{R}^3$ the nth dimensional Euclidean space.

What is described by Eq. (16.11) is that the state of the national economy is representable through the use of the state variable z that helps the economy to absorb the positive and negative effects of the monetary policies X_1, X_2, and X_3. Then, both the internal mechanism z of the economy and the monetary policies x jointly have a direct effect on the overall performance y of the economy. The condition, as imposed on the input space X and the output space Y means that monetary policies, which form the input space X, are introduced based on the effects of the previously implemented policies, while the overall performance, indexes of which constitutes the output space Y, of the economy evolves from previous states mostly continuous. Such assumptions, historically speaking, are not always true, while failures occur rarely in terms of frequencies. For instance, in modern China, the so-called Cultural Revolution occurred abruptly (MacFarquhar & Schoenhals, 2008), and several times in the history of Russia, the Tsars had introduced rushed social reforms creating a torn country (Huntington, 1996).

Geometrically, the systemic model in Eq. (16.11) of the national economy is depicted in Fig. 16.3. The monetary policy input X splits into two portions $F_1F_2F_3F_4$ and $F_5F_6F_7F_8$. The former portion directly affects the performance Y of the economy. The other portion is fed into the initial state of the economy S, leading to the

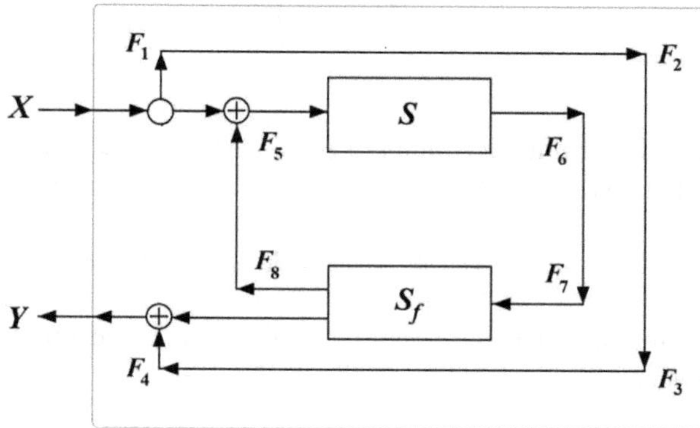

Fig. 16.3 The geometry of the systemic model of the national economy

introduction of the feedback component system S_f, which stands for the market reactions to the introduced monetary policies and the formation of a feedback loop within the economy. This feedback loop in fact constitutes the main body of the economy, while the overall performance vector Y of indexes is merely an artificially designed measure. What needs to be noted is that within each of our three economic sectors E_1, E_2, and E_3, the market reactions, which constitute parts of the feedback component system S_f, to monetary policies in general are unique and economic sector specific. That is, the market reactions in one economic sector are different from those of another sector. The outer most loop $F_1F_2F_3F_4$ is the second stage of the economy after the introduction of new monetary policies. They by the joint effect of the market reactions (S_f) and the non-reactionary aspects ($F_5F_6F_7F_8$) of the monetary policies, the final numerical readings Y of the economy are produced.

To see how monetary policy input X could have two aspects, one is reactionary and the other non-reactionary, let us assume that X stands for such a monetary policy that it allows the inflation to inch higher. Therefore, the price of crude oil is expected to rise accordingly. Now, the reactionary aspects of the policy X make the gradual and calculated increase in the price of crude oil more or less random. Conversely, the expected outcome of the policy is the theoretical, non-reactionary aspect of the policy. When the actual outcome deviates from the expectation, the difference is caused by the market reactions to the policy.

According to Lin (1994), the three-dimensional system in Eq. (16.11), meaning that both the input x and the output y are elements from $\boldsymbol{R}^3$, can be decoupled into three independent systems of the same kind with one-dimensional input and output. Specifically, if we let

$$\begin{aligned} S &= \{(x, y) \in X \times Y : \exists z \in Z \text{ such that } x, y, z \text{ satisfy Eq.}(16.11)\} \\ &= \text{the system of all the ordered pairs}(x, y) \text{ satisfy Eq.}(16.11) \end{aligned},$$

where the state space $Z = \{r : [0, +\infty) \to \boldsymbol{R}^3 : r \text{ is a piecewise continuous function}\}$, and for each $i = 1, 2, 3$, define a system S_i as follows:

$$\begin{cases} \dot{z} = Az + B_i x_i \\ y_i = C_i z + D_i x_i \\ z(0) = 0 \end{cases},$$

where B_i is the ith column of B, C_i the ith row of C, D_i a non-zero constant, and the input space X_i and the output space Y_i are given as follows:

$$X_i = Y_i = \{r : [0, +\infty) \to \boldsymbol{R} : r \text{ is a piecewise continuous function}\}.$$

In particular, the system S can be decoupled through feedback into the factor systems S_i, $i = 1, 2, 3$, as follows. Let

$$\alpha = \begin{bmatrix} A & 0 & 0 \\ 0 & A & 0 \\ 0 & 0 & A \end{bmatrix}, \quad \beta = \begin{bmatrix} B_1 & 0 & 0 \\ 0 & B_2 & 0 \\ 0 & 0 & B_3 \end{bmatrix}, \quad \gamma = \begin{bmatrix} C_1 & 0 & 0 \\ 0 & C_2 & 0 \\ 0 & 0 & C_3 \end{bmatrix}, \quad \delta = \begin{bmatrix} D_1 & 0 & 0 \\ 0 & D_2 & 0 \\ 0 & 0 & D_3 \end{bmatrix}.$$

Then, the Cartesian product system $S_d = S_1 \times S_2 \times S_3$ is represented by the set of all ordered pairs (x, y) satisfying

$$\begin{cases} \dot{z} = \alpha z + \beta x \\ y = \gamma z + \delta x \\ z(0) = 0 \end{cases}.$$

Because δ is non-singular, the inverse system S_d^{-1} is obtained as follows:

$$S_d^{-1} = \{(y, x) : (y, x) \text{satisfies Eq.}(16.12)\},$$

where Eq. (16.12) is given as follows:

$$\begin{cases} \dot{z} = (\alpha - \beta\delta^{-1}\gamma)z + \beta\delta^{-1}y \\ x = -\delta^{-1}\gamma z + \delta^{-1}y \\ z(0) = 0 \end{cases}. \quad (16.12)$$

The particular feedback component system $S_f : Y \to X$ used in this decoupling is given as follows:

$$\begin{cases} \begin{bmatrix} \dot{z} \\ z' \end{bmatrix} = \begin{bmatrix} A - BD^{-1}C & 0 \\ 0 & \alpha - \beta\delta^{-1}\gamma \end{bmatrix} \begin{bmatrix} z \\ z' \end{bmatrix} + \begin{bmatrix} BD^{-1} \\ \beta\delta^{-1} \end{bmatrix} y \\ x = \begin{bmatrix} -D^{-1}C & \delta^{-1}\gamma \end{bmatrix} \begin{bmatrix} z \\ z' \end{bmatrix} + (D^{-1} - \delta^{-1})y \\ \begin{bmatrix} z \\ z' \end{bmatrix}(0) = 0 \end{cases}.$$

In terms of economics, what the concept of decoupling the three-dimensional system S into component systems S_i, $i = 1, 2, 3$, as discussed above, implies is that when monetary policies are established individually and, respectively, for each of the three economic sectors E_1, E_2, and E_3, although these economic sector specific policies will most definitely have joint effects on the economy, there is at least one way to design a feedback component system S_f so that the overall feedback system $F(S, S_f)$, which represents the whole system as depicted in Fig. 16.1, can be controlled through adjusting individually each of the economic sectors E_1, E_2, and E_3.

16.4.2 Design of Feedback Control with Pure Gain

To accomplish such a design in order to address the problem of economic regulation, substituting Eq. (16.7) into Eq. (16.4) provides the following closed loop system:

$$\frac{dx_1}{dt} = (A_1 + B_1K_1)x_1 + (A_3 + B_1K_2)x_2. \tag{16.13}$$

For the system in Eq. (16.13) that is to be controlled, as long as we can appropriately choose such a matrix that makes the eigenvalues of the state matrix in Eq. (16.13) all have negative real parts, we then can apply the control strategy as given in Eq. (16.7) to make the controlled variable eventually approach the target value accurately. If some or all of the elements of A, B, and C of the system change, or the interference input x_2 also experiences changes, as long as the real parts of the eigenvalues of the state matrix in Eq. (16.13) stay negative, then the control strategy in Eq. (16.7) can guarantee that the controlled variable will accurately approach the target value. That implies that the control strategy in Eq. (16.7) possesses good quality, is considered "very strong," and is of the robustness.

As a matter of fact, if (A_1, B_1) is controllable, we can then find K_1 such that $A_1 + B_1K_1$ can have any chosen value as its extreme. As long as we place the extreme values at appropriate places on the left-half open plane, we can make the closed loop system in Eq. (16.13) asymptotically stable. As for how to find K_2 in order to gradually approach the problem of regulation, we will come back to this problem after we first establish the lemma in the next section.

When both x_1 and x_2 can be used as feedback, our problem will be resolved as long as we can find K_1 and K_2. When x_1 and x_2 cannot be all used as feedback, then for the following augmented system:

$$\frac{dx}{dt} = \begin{bmatrix} A_1 & A_3 \\ 0 & A_2 \end{bmatrix} x + \begin{bmatrix} B_1 \\ 0 \end{bmatrix} u \equiv Ax + Bu \tag{16.14}$$

$$y = \begin{bmatrix} C_1 & C_2 \end{bmatrix} u \equiv Cx, \tag{16.15}$$

we need to design the following observer:

$$\frac{dz}{dt} = (A + GC)z + Bu - Gy \tag{16.16}$$

and estimate the state $x = \begin{bmatrix} x_1^{\mathrm{T}} \; x_2^{\mathrm{T}} \end{bmatrix}$ of the augmented system in Eq. (16.14). If (C, A) is observable, then we can find G such that $A + GC$ has the pre-determined extreme points located on the left-half open place. In this case, we use

$$u = [K_1 \; K_2]z$$

as the feedback instead of Eq. (16.7). Such a feedback controller with an observer attached is referred to as a linear multivariable regulator. Additionally, we can use the following general dynamic compensator:

$$\begin{cases} \dfrac{dz}{dt} = Ez + Fy \\ u = Kz + Ly \end{cases}$$

to substitute for the observer. In this case, we obtain the following closed loop system:

$$\begin{cases} \dfrac{dx_1}{dt} = \begin{bmatrix} A_1 + B_1FC_1 & B_1K \\ FC_1 & E \end{bmatrix} x_1 + \begin{bmatrix} A_3 + B_1FC_2 \\ FC_2 \end{bmatrix} x_2 \equiv A_1x_1 + B_1x_2 \\ \dfrac{dx_2}{dt} = A_2x_2 \\ y = \begin{bmatrix} C_1 & 0 \end{bmatrix} x_1 + C_2x_2 \equiv C_1x_1 + C_2x_2 \end{cases}.$$

16.5 Feedback Controllers and Multivariable Regulator

As suggested by the title, this section presents a few specific ways to design feedback controllers and multivariable regulators. It consists of three subsections with the first one devoted to the development of a necessary lemma.

16.5.1 A Preliminary Result

As for the question of whether or not the output of the previous closed loop system can still be successfully regulated under the influence of the interference variable, let us first establish the important lemma.

Lemma 16.1 For the following system with $x_l = \begin{bmatrix} x_1^{\mathrm{T}} & z^{\mathrm{T}} \end{bmatrix}^{\mathrm{T}}$:

$$\frac{dx_l}{dt} = A_l x_l + B_l x_2 \tag{16.17}$$

$$\frac{dx_2}{dt} = A_2 x_2 \tag{16.18}$$

$$y = C_l x_l + C_2 x_2. \tag{16.19}$$

If $\sigma(A_l) \subset C^-$ and $\sigma(A_2) \subset C^+$, then the following hold true:

1. The following matrix equation has a unique solution X:

$$A_l X - X A_2 = B_l. \tag{16.20}$$

For any given initial values $x_l(0)$ and $x_2(0)$, a sufficient and necessary condition for $\lim_{t \to \infty} y(t) = 0$ is

$$C_l X = C_2. \tag{16.21}$$

Proof

1. Because $\sigma(A_l) \subset C^-$ and $\sigma(A_2) \subset C^+$, we have $\sigma(A_l) \cap \sigma(A_2) = \varnothing$. So, from results of algebra, it follows that the matrix equation in Eq. (16.20) has a unique solution.
2. Let us first prove the sufficiency. If the matrix equation in Eq. (16.20) has solution X such that $C_l X = C_2$, then by direct checking it follows that for any solution x_2 of the interference equation in Eq. (16.18), $-Xx_2$ is a solution of Eq. (16.17). So, we have

$$y = C_l x_l + C_2 x_2 = C_l x_l + C_l X x_2 = C_l [x_l - (-Xx_2)].$$

And because both x_l and $-Xx_2$ are solutions of Eq. (16.17), $x_l - (-Xx_2)$ is a solution of the corresponding homogeneous equation

$$\frac{dx_l}{dt} = A_l x_l. \tag{16.22}$$

From the assumption that A_l is a stable matrix, it follows that when $t \to \infty$, $[x_l - (-Xx_2)] \to 0$. That is, we have $\lim_{t \to \infty} y(t) = 0$.

Next, we show the necessity. If for any initial conditions $x_l(0)$ and $x_2(0)$, $\lim_{t \to \infty} y(t) = 0$, then assume the solutions that satisfy the initial conditions are $x_l(t)$ and $x_2(t)$. Let $\tilde{x}_l = x_l - (-Xx_2)$, then $\tilde{x}_l$ satisfies the homogeneous equation in Eq. (16.22) and so we have $\lim_{t \to \infty} \tilde{x}_l = 0$. Conversely, from Eq. (16.19) and $\lim_{t \to \infty} y(t) = 0$, it follows that

$$\begin{aligned}\lim_{t\to\infty} y(t) &= \lim_{t\to\infty} (C_l x_l + C_2 x_2)\\ &= \lim_{t\to\infty} [C_l \widetilde{x}_l + (C_2 - C_l X)x_2]\\ &= \lim_{t\to\infty} [(C_2 - C_l X)x_2] = 0.\end{aligned}$$

Because of the arbitrariness of $x_2(0)$, $x_2(t)$ stands for an arbitrary solution of the interference equation. And, because of $\sigma(A_2) \subset C^+$, the previous equation implies $C_2 - C_l X = 0$, that is, $C_l X = C_2$.

Under certain specific conditions, such as when large amounts of money suddenly enter into or withdraw from an economic system, the domestic currency system of the economy would have to experience disturbances of the outside world. Some of the state variables of the economic system, which describe the movement of the domestic currency within the economy, would have to undergo drastic changes, causing major impacts on the originally normal operation of the currency system of the economy. More often than not, the impacts bring forward huge economic losses to the domestic currency system. For example, the 1997 financial crisis of Thailand represents a real-life scenario where the control on the economic stability was eventually lost when the domestic currency system of the economy was first disturbed by external factors. To this end, the previous result indicates that even under the influence of an interfering system, if the coefficient matrices of the state variables of the original economic system and of the interfering system satisfy Eqs. (16.20) and (16.21), then the output of the original economic system can still reach a stable state. As a matter of fact, this result also indirectly provides a method on how to stabilize the economic system when the system is interfered by an external environment. That is, if the regulator of the economic system could learn the laws of evolution of the interfering system and the effects of the interfering system on the state variables and the output variables of the original economic system, then he could design an appropriate countermeasure of control to keep the original economic system stable. In particular, the countermeasure of control only needs to guarantee that under the effect of the adopted strategies (policies) the coefficient matrices of the state variables of the economic system and the interfering system satisfy satisfy Eqs. (16.20) and (16.21).

Therefore, in order to introduce appropriate measures in a timely fashion to counter the adverse effects of external interferences on the development of the economic system, the economic decision maker has to promptly acquire the knowledge on how the external interferences affect the state variables and output variables of the economic system. Then he could design his corresponding strategies (policies) according to the previous result in order to keep the economic system within effective control. In the following, we will provide specific method and steps on how to design such countermeasures (policies).

16.5.2 Pure Gain Feedback Controllers

Assume that the state equation, interference equation, and the output equation of the economic system of concern are given, respectively, by Eqs. (16.4), (16.5), and (16.6), and that (A_1, B_1) is controllable so that $\sigma(A_2) \subset C^{+}$. Let us design the following pure gain feedback controller so that the closed loop system is stable and accomplishes the desired regulation of the output.

$$u = K_1 x_1 + K_2 x_2.$$

This end can be accomplished in two steps.

Step 1: Use the method of how to replace the extreme points to compute K_1 so that the closed loop system

$$\frac{dx_1}{dt} = (A_1 + B_1 K_1)x_1 + (A_3 + B_1 K_2)x_2$$

is stable. In order to accomplish this objective, all we need to do is to replace all the extreme points of $A_1 + B_1K_1$ on the appropriate locations in the left-half open plane.

Step 2: Apply Lemma 16.1 on the system in Eq. (16.21). In order to guarantee that the output is adjustable, solve the matrix equation

$$\begin{cases} A_1 X - X A_2 = B_l \\ C_l X = C_2 \end{cases}$$

For its solution X by considering the facts that $A_l = A_1 + B_1K_1$, $B_l = A_3 + B_1K_2$, and $C_l = C_1$. The previous two matrix equations can then be simplified into

$$A_1 X - X A_2 + B_2 U = A_3 \tag{16.23}$$

$$C_1 X = C_2, \tag{16.24}$$

where

$$U = K_1 X - K_2,$$

which leads to

$$K_2 = K_1 X - U. \tag{16.25}$$

Because K_2, which is computed out of Eq. (16.25), satisfies satisfy Eqs. (16.20) and (16.21), it is guaranteed that the system's output reaches the desired adjustment. Based on this analysis, we obtain the particular steps for designing a pure gain feedback controller as follows.

Step 1: Solve for K_1 so that the extreme points of $A_1 + B_1K_1$ are located at the n pre-determined locations in the left-half open plane.

Step 2: Solve the following matrix equation for X and U:

$$\begin{cases} A_1X - XA_2 + B_1U = A_3 \\ C_1X = C_2 \end{cases}.$$

Step 3: Calculate $K_2 = K_1X - U$ and let $u = K_1x_1 + K_2x_2$, which is the desired pure gain feedback controller.

The pure gain feedback controller, as designed above, consists of two parts: K_1x_1 and K_2x_2. The former is the state feedback, while the latter the feedback of interference variable. In particular, the state feedback K_1x_1 plays the role of making the closed loop system stable with good dynamic responses, while the feedback of interference variable K_2x_2 plays the role of eliminating the effect of the environmental disturbance in order to reach the purpose of adjusting the output.

16.5.3 Linear Multivariable Regulator

The pure gain feedback controller designed by using the previous scheme needs the feedbacks of the state variables and the interference variables. If some of these variables cannot be employed as feedback for various reasons, such as they are not observable, then we have to use the augmented system in Eqs. (16.14) and (16.15) to design the observer in Eq. (16.16). In this case, the resultant closed loop system is

$$\frac{dx_1}{dt} = A_1x_1 + A_3x_2 + B_1u$$

$$\frac{dx_2}{dt} = A_2x_2$$

$$\frac{dz}{dt} = (A + GC)z + Bz - Gy$$

$$u = \begin{bmatrix} K_1 & K_2 \end{bmatrix} z \equiv Kz$$

$$y = C_1x_1 + C_2x_2.$$

By letting $x_l = \begin{bmatrix} x_1^{\mathrm{T}} & z^{\mathrm{T}} \end{bmatrix}^{\mathrm{T}}$, the previous five equations can be rewritten as follows:

$$\frac{dx_l}{dt} = \begin{bmatrix} \frac{dx_1}{dt} \\ \frac{dz}{dt} \end{bmatrix} = \begin{bmatrix} A_1 & B \\ -GC_1 & A + GC + BK \end{bmatrix} \begin{bmatrix} x_1 \\ z \end{bmatrix} = A_lx_l + B_lx_2 \qquad (16.26)$$

$$\frac{dx_2}{dt} = A_2 x_2 \tag{16.27}$$

$$y = \begin{bmatrix} C_1 & 0 \end{bmatrix} x_l + C_2 x_2 = C_1 x_l + C_2 x_2. \tag{16.28}$$

By letting

$$A = \begin{bmatrix} A_1 & A_3 \\ 0 & A_2 \end{bmatrix}, \quad B = \begin{bmatrix} B_1 \\ 0 \end{bmatrix}, \quad C = \begin{bmatrix} C_1 & C_2 \end{bmatrix}, \quad K = \begin{bmatrix} K_1 & K_2 \end{bmatrix}, \quad G = \begin{bmatrix} G_1 \\ G_2 \end{bmatrix},$$

we obtain

$$A_l = \begin{bmatrix} A_1 & B_1 K_1 & B_1 K_2 \\ -G_1 C_1 & A_1 + G_1 C_1 + B_1 K_1 & A_3 + G_1 C_2 + B_1 K_2 \\ -G_2 C_1 & G_2 C_1 & A_2 + G_2 C_2 \end{bmatrix}$$

$$B_l = \begin{bmatrix} A_3 \\ -G_1 C_2 \\ -G_2 C_2 \end{bmatrix}.$$

So, the characteristic polynomial of the closed loop system is

$$\begin{aligned}
|sI - A_l| &= \begin{vmatrix} sI - A_1 & -B_1 K_1 & -B_1 K_2 \\ G_1 C_1 & sI - (A_1 + G_1 C_1 + B_1 K_1) & -(A_3 + G_1 C_2 + B_1 K_2) \\ G_2 C_1 & -G_2 C_1 & sI - (A_2 + G_2 C_2) \end{vmatrix} \\
&= \begin{vmatrix} sI - A_1 & -B_1 K_1 & -B_1 K_2 \\ G_1 C_1 & sI - (A_1 + G_1 C_1 + B_1 K_1) & -(A_3 + G_1 C_2 + B_1 K_2) \\ G_2 C_1 & -G_2 C_1 & sI - (A_2 + G_2 C_2) \end{vmatrix} \\
&= \begin{vmatrix} sI - (A_1 + B_1 K_1) & -B_1 K_1 & -B_1 K_2 \\ sI - (A_1 + B_1 K_1) & sI - (A_1 + G_1 C_1 + B_1 K_1) & -(A_3 + G_1 C_2 + B_1 K_2) \\ 0 & -G_2 C_1 & sI - (A_2 + G_2 C_2) \end{vmatrix} \\
&= \begin{vmatrix} sI - (A_1 + B_1 K_1) & -B_1 K_1 & -B_1 K_2 \\ 0 & sI - (A_1 + G_1 C_1) & -(A_3 + G_1 C_2) \\ 0 & -G_2 C_1 & sI - (A_2 + G_2 C_2) \end{vmatrix} \\
&= \begin{vmatrix} sI - (A_1 + B_1 K_1) & B_1 K \\ 0 & sI - (A + GC) \end{vmatrix}
\end{aligned}$$

That indicates that the set of all extreme points of the closed loop system is

$$\sigma(A_1 + B_1K_1) \cup \sigma((A + GC)).$$

This end shows that the closed loop system with an observer in Eq. (16.26) is stable. Now, by using Lemma 16.1 on Eqs. (16.29) and (16.26)–(16.28), it follows that the matrix equation

$$A_l\overline{X} + \overline{X}A_2 = B_l \tag{16.29}$$

has a unique solution $\overline{X}$. If we can also prove $C_l\overline{X} = C_2$, then Lemma 16.1 guarantees that $\lim_{t \to \infty} y(t) = 0$.

Before we establish the fact that $C_l\overline{X} = C_2$, let us first check that for any X that satisfies the matrix equations in Eqs. (16.23) and (16.24), the following matrix

$$\overline{X} = \begin{bmatrix} X \\ X \\ -I \end{bmatrix}$$

satisfies matrix equation in Eq. (16.29). By direct substitution, we have

$$A_l\begin{bmatrix} X \\ X \\ -I \end{bmatrix} - \begin{bmatrix} X \\ X \\ -I \end{bmatrix}A_2$$

$$= \begin{bmatrix} A_1X + B_1(K_1X - K_2) - XA_2 \\ -G_1C_1X + (A_1 + G_1C_1 + B_1K_1)X - (A_3 + G_1C_2 + B_1K_2) - XA_2 \\ -G_2C_1X + G_2C_1X - (A_2 + G_2C_2) + A_2 \end{bmatrix}$$

$$= \begin{bmatrix} A_3 \\ -G_1C_2 \\ -G_2C_2 \end{bmatrix} = B_l.$$

Next, let us check $C_l\overline{X} = C_2$:

$$C_l\overline{X} = \begin{bmatrix} C_1 & 0 \end{bmatrix}\begin{bmatrix} X \\ X \\ -I \end{bmatrix} = C_1X = C_2.$$

So, Lemma 16.1 implies that $\lim_{t \to \infty} y(t) = 0$.

16.6 Examples of Applications

The purpose of this section is to demonstrate how the theory and relevant discussions developed in the previous sections can be practically applied to address real-life problems. In particular, Sect. 16.6.1 presents a strategy on how to develop a national defense system to fence off hostile currency attacks. And, Sect. 16.6.2 examples how one can employ what is established in this chapter to address the control problem of production inventory systems.

16.6.1 A Method of National Defense

The significance of the previous discussion is that we can now propose based on the sound analytical reasoning presented above a strategy for national defense against currency warfare in case that initial "friendly" foreign investments turn out to be an aggressive act of war by suddenly withdrawing all or significant amount of the investments.

In particular, let us assume that at time period t, the total money supply of the specific nation of our concern is \$1000, \$100 of which is from foreign investments. That is, the foreign investments amount to 10% of the total domestic money supply. With the additional money supply (due to the foreign investments) the speed of money circulation increases, signaled by increased spending and elevated levels of economic activities. If these foreign investments leave the nation suddenly, then it is reasonable to expect that more than 10% of the economic activities from around the nation will be more or less affected adversely due to the sudden exhaustion of the money flow, because accompanying the foreign investments there tends to be domestic investments attached too, making the total investments on the related economic activities more than 10% of the national economy.

Now, if before the foreign investments depart while leaving behind disastrous aftermath, the national government has been keeping the exchange rate (to this end not all nations from around the world are currently able to do this successfully) the same while gradually and strategically increased its money supply, say, to the level of \$10,000, then in the entire monetary circulation around the nation the proportion of the foreign investments shrinks to about 1% from the original 10%. And if the money supply had been increased to the level of \$1000,000, then the proportion of the foreign investments would have shrunk from the original 10% to about 0.01%, which is nearly zero. So, if at this moment of time the foreign investments are suddenly withdrawn as an aggressive act of war, only around 1% or 0.01% of the consumption and economic activities of the nation will be affected adversely and the overall economic health of the nation will be relatively stable.

Conversely, along with the drastically increased money supply, all prices in the nation will most certainly go through the roof, placing a large portion of the national population in financial crises due to the run-away inflation. For instance, a certain commodity A, which is piece of living necessity, used to cost \$1.00 a unit; now it requires \$10.00 or even \$1000 to purchase. Such a dramatic increase in prices will surely cause hardships for a good number of citizens of the nation. To this end, the national government needs to work on how to redistribute the additional money supply. In fact, as long as the distribution of the increased money supply does not cause social upheaval, then to this nation, nothing disastrous will really happen and the potentially damaging impacts of sudden departure of the foreign investments will be under control, too.

However, in reality, the distribution of the extra money supply could easily lead to major societal instabilities to the nation due to the increased unevenness in the economic scene: The rich become richer, while the poor become poorer. The situation here is similar to that of the normal inflation, which has been employed to make the economic structure more uneven than before so that the yoyo structure of the economy spins with more strength. In other words, with additional money supply injected into the economy, the redistribution of wealth that is represented by the increased money supply is surely uneven, where some people receive more than their share, some simply keep pace with the decrease in the purchasing power of their income, while others fall behind or further behind with their financial status. So, if our suggested measure is adopted to counter the damaging effects of sudden departure of foreign investments, the nation needs to develop a practical plan to redistribute the extra money supply in order to:

1. Keep societal peace and national stability so that a normal and operational economy can be maintained.
2. Increase the nation's economic prosperity by taking advantage of the foreign investments even though they leave sooner or later either slowly or suddenly.

Specifically, as suggested by the systemic model in the previous section, to help protect the innocent citizens of the nation from suffering from the potential economic turmoil, the national government could purposely divide the economy into three sectors E_1, E_2, and E_3 as described earlier to meet the following goals. In Sector E_1, which consists of living necessities, the sector performance, such as the sector specific CPI, evolves as normally as possible; in Sector E_2, which consists of such goods, services, and relevant productions that are used by citizens to acquire desired living conditions, the sector performance index, say the particular CPI of E_2, could outpace that of Sector E_1 by a large amount; and critically, the national government needs to manage to trap most of the additional money supply in the economic sector E_3, which consists of such goods, services, and relevant productions that are used by the citizens for their enjoyment of luxurious living. The previous discussion on the systemic model of the national economy indicates that by managing the market reactions correctly, that is the design of the feedback component system S_f, these three economic sectors can be well separated from each other.

When the economic sector E_1 evolves normally as expected based on the history of the nation, the citizens would not need to worry about their basic living and survival. That naturally leads to the desired societal stability and peace. Although the prices in the economic sector E_2 increase drastically when compared to those in E_1, that in general should not affect the mood or the happiness of the population much, because desired living conditions change from time to time and vary from one family to another. In other words, isolated, temporary personally desires, which are not yet satisfied and which are generally inconsistent with each other and even contradictory to each other, could not amalgamate into a political force to cause turmoil. Now, the key is how to keep most of the additional money supply in the economic sector E_3. To address this problem, let us pay attention to our earlier assumption that a large amount of foreign investments entered the nation. That means commercial products and services that are new to the people in the specific nation are expected to and will become available soon. Because these products and services are brand new to the region, high prices can of course be charged for these commercial goods and services. The situation is similar to the scenarios with developed nations, where the focus has been placed on innovations, design, and production of unprecedented products and services. It is these never-before-seen products and services that generate the most profits.

At this junction, let us address the problem of how to classify a product or a service into one of the three economic sectors E_1, E_2, and E_3. First of all, goods and services that should be classified into E_1 are clear. They represent such commodities that directly relate to the survival of any human being, such as foods, utilities, and shelters of the basic quality. Now, if a family lives in a rented two-bedroom apartment and wants to own a house, then houses to that particular family will be in the economic sector E_2. If the people in a community go to work, shopping, and entertainment mostly on foot, then individually owned transportation tools, such as bicycles, motorcycles, cars, private jets, etc., will belong to the economic sector E_3. That is, as time evolves forward, what belongs to the economic sector E_3 gradually lowers itself into the economic sector E_2, and what used to be in E_2 also gradually moves to E_1. That is, the classification of one particular product or service is a function of time and space. Just by looking at shopping centers, one can see vividly that such classification of commercial goods and services has been successfully done by merchants throughout the world without much trouble.

Now, let us consider the scenario that when the nation purposefully and strategically increases its money supply in order to prevent disastrous aftermaths that could be potentially left behind by sudden withdrawals of foreign investments, additional foreign investments could continue to pour in. In this case, if the nation could not pick up its corresponding speed of economic development, then it will be taken over by the run-way high rate of inflation. In this case, if the foreign investments depart strategically, then the nation will be in real major political, societal, and economic crises. To prevent such disastrous consequences, the continued inflow of foreign money has to be managed so that they cannot depart quickly.

Another practical scenario that is different of what has been discussed above is that at a high speed the nation develops itself into a super economic power such that there is no longer such a single number of foreign investments that can amount to an influencing percentage in the nation's domestic consumption and/or economic activities. In this case the nation will be safe in the face of any potentially sudden withdrawal of foreign investments.

16.6.2 Control of Production Inventory System

The basic equation for the production inventory system is

$$\frac{dI}{dt} = P(t) - S(t),$$

where $I(t)$ stands for the inventory in the storage of the production at time t, $P(t)$ the productivity of the particular product, and $S(t)$ the speed at which the product is sold. The meaning of this equation is that any change in the inventory is equal to the production minus the sale.

Assume that we desired productivity is $u(t)$. Then the equation that reflects the process for the actual productivity $P(t)$ to reach the necessary level is

$$\frac{dP}{dt} = \theta[u(t) - P(t)],$$

where θ is a positive constant. So, the state equation of the production inventory system is

$$\begin{cases} \dfrac{dP}{dt} = \theta[u(t) - P(t)] \\ \dfrac{dI}{dt} = P(t) - S(t) \end{cases}. \tag{16.30}$$

By introducing the state vector $x_1(t) = \begin{bmatrix} P(t) & I(t) - Z \end{bmatrix}$ and the interference vector $x_2(t) = S(t)$, Eq. (16.30) can be rewritten as the following state equation:

$$\frac{dx_1}{dt} = \begin{bmatrix} -\theta & 0 \\ 1 & 0 \end{bmatrix} x_1(t) + \begin{bmatrix} \theta \\ 1 \end{bmatrix} x_2(t) + \begin{bmatrix} 0 \\ -1 \end{bmatrix} u(t), \tag{16.31}$$

where Z stands for the required level of inventory, which is assumed to be a constant. As a matter of fact, in practical applications, the actual values of both $P(t)$ and $S(t)$ are determined once per unit time period, such as once per day or once per month. So, we can discretize Eq. (16.31) into the following state equation:

$$x_1(k+1) = \begin{bmatrix} q & 0 \\ r & 1 \end{bmatrix} x_1(k) + \begin{bmatrix} 0 \\ -1 \end{bmatrix} x_2(k) + \begin{bmatrix} 1-q \\ 1-r \end{bmatrix} u(k), \tag{16.32}$$

where $q = \exp(-\theta)$, $r = (1 - \exp(-\theta))/\theta$. When the speed of sale $S(t)$ is assumed to be a constant, then $x_2(t)$ satisfies the following interference equation:

$$x_2(k+1) = x_2(k). \tag{16.33}$$

And the objective of control $P(k) \to u(k)$, $I(k) \to Z$, can be expressed as follows:

$$y(k) = \begin{bmatrix} P(k) - u(k) \\ I(k) - Z \end{bmatrix} = x_1(k) + \begin{bmatrix} -1 \\ 0 \end{bmatrix} u(k) \to 0,$$

so that the output equation can be obtained as follows:

$$y(k) = x_1(k) + \begin{bmatrix} -1 \\ 0 \end{bmatrix} u(k). \tag{16.34}$$

Therefore, the problem of control of the production inventory system becomes: Design a feedback control strategy

$$u(k) = K_1 x_1(k) + K_2 x_2(k), \tag{16.35}$$

so that the closed loop system is stable and its output is controllable. This is a problem of designing a linear multivariable regulator for a discrete control system.

To obtain the solution of the problem, assume that the state equation of the system that is to be controlled is

$$x_1(k+1) = A_1 x_1(k) + A_3 x_2(k) + B_1 u(k) \tag{16.36}$$

with an interference equation and output equation, respectively, being

$$x_2(k+1) = A_2 x_2(k) \tag{16.37}$$

and

$$y(k) = C_1 x_1(k) + C_2 x_2(k) + Du(k). \tag{16.38}$$

Now, the problem of designing a linear multivariable regulator of discrete time is: Find a pure gain feedback controller as given in Eq. (16.35) such that the closed loop system is stable and satisfies the following goal of output adjustment: $\lim_{k \to \infty} y(k) = 0$. When either $x_1(k)$ or $x_2(k)$ cannot be employed as feedback variables, we need to design an observer to estimate the variable(s) that cannot be employed as feedbacks.

For this problem of designing linear multivariable regulator of discrete time, we have the following result: If in the system, as expressed in Eqs. (16.34), (16.36)–(16.38), (A_1, B_1) is completely reachable and the eigenvalues of A_2 are not located within the unit circle, then a sufficient and necessary condition for there being a pure gain feedback controller in Eq. (16.35) that makes the closed loop system stable and the output is controllable is that there are matrices X and U satisfying the following equation:

$$A_1X - XA_2 + B_1U = A_3 \tag{16.39}$$

$$C_1X + DU = C_2. \tag{16.40}$$

Therefore, we obtain the following specific steps for designing a pure gain feedback controller:

Step 1: Select a matrix K_1 such that the eigenvalues of $A_1 + B_1K_1$ are located at some appropriate points within the unit circle of the complex plane.

Step 2: Solve the matrix equations in Eqs. (16.39) and (16.40) to obtain matrices X and U.

Step 3: Compute

$$K_2 = K_1X - U$$

and so, $u(k) = K_1x_1 + K_2x_2$ is the desired pure gain feedback controller.

If necessary, we further design an observer to form a linear multivariable regulator.

To solve the control problem of production inventory system, let us try the previous result. To this end, let us look at the system given in Eqs. (16.32)–(16.34), where

$$A_1 = \begin{bmatrix} q & 0 \\ r & 1 \end{bmatrix}, \quad B_1 = \begin{bmatrix} 1-q \\ 1-r \end{bmatrix}, \quad A_3 = \begin{bmatrix} 0 \\ -1 \end{bmatrix}, \quad A_2 = 1, \quad C_1 = I, \quad C_2 = 0, \quad D = \begin{bmatrix} -1 \\ 0 \end{bmatrix}.$$

Step 1: Select a matrix K_1 so that the eigenvalues of $A_1 + B_1K_1$ are equal to $\lambda_1 = \lambda_2 = 0$. So, we have

$$K_1 = \frac{1}{(1-q)^2}\begin{bmatrix} q^2 - r & q-1 \end{bmatrix}.$$

Step 2: Solve the following matrix equation:

$$\begin{bmatrix} q & 0 \\ r & 1 \end{bmatrix}X - X + \begin{bmatrix} 1-q \\ 1-r \end{bmatrix}U = \begin{bmatrix} 0 \\ -1 \end{bmatrix},$$

$$X + \begin{bmatrix} -1 \\ 0 \end{bmatrix}U = 0$$

and obtain

$$X = \begin{bmatrix} -1 \\ 0 \end{bmatrix} \quad \text{and} \quad U = -1.$$

Step 3: Compute

$$K_2 = K_1 X - U = \frac{r - q^2}{(1-q)^2} + 1.$$

So, the desired pure gain feedback controller is

$$u(k) = \frac{1}{(1-q)^2} \begin{bmatrix} q^2 - r & q - 1 \end{bmatrix} x_1(k) + \left[\frac{r - q^2}{(1-q)^2} + 1 \right] x_2(k).$$

By letting

$$x_1(k) = \begin{bmatrix} P(k) \\ I(k) - Z \end{bmatrix} \quad \text{and} \quad x_2(k) = S(k),$$

we obtain

$$u(k) = \frac{q^2 - r}{(1-q)^2} P(k) + \frac{1}{q-1} [I(k) - Z] + \left[\frac{r - q^2}{(1-q)^2} + 1 \right] S(k). \tag{16.41}$$

When the input is an unknown disturbance, we design a reduced order observer to estimate $S(k)$, say, the estimation is $\widehat{S}(k)$. Now, we substitute this estimated value $\widehat{S}(k)$ into the previous equation for $S(k)$.

In order to design a reduced order observer, let us consider the following augmented system:

$$\begin{bmatrix} x_2(k+1) \\ c \\ x_1(k+1) \end{bmatrix} = \begin{bmatrix} 1 & \vdots & 0 & 0 \\ 0 & \vdots & q & 0 \\ \cdots & \vdots & \cdots & \cdots \\ -1 & \vdots & r & 1 \end{bmatrix} \begin{bmatrix} x_2(k) \\ \cdots \\ x_1(k) \end{bmatrix} + \begin{bmatrix} 0 \\ \cdots \\ 1-q \\ 1-r \end{bmatrix} u(k)$$

$$\bar{y}(k) = \begin{bmatrix} 0 & 1 \end{bmatrix} \begin{bmatrix} x_2(k) \\ x_1(k) \end{bmatrix} = x_1(k),$$

which takes the identical form of Eq. (16.29). That is, we have

$$A_{11}=1,\quad A_{12}=\begin{bmatrix}0 & 0\end{bmatrix},\quad A_{21}=\begin{bmatrix}0\\-1\end{bmatrix},\quad A_{22}=\begin{bmatrix}q & 0\\ r & 1\end{bmatrix},\quad B_1=0,\quad B_2=\begin{bmatrix}1-q\\1-r\end{bmatrix}.$$

We next place the extreme points of the observer at the origin. That is, solve for G such that the extreme values of A_{11} + GA_{21} are equal to 0. That is equivalent to solving $G=\begin{bmatrix}g_1 & g_2\end{bmatrix}$ such that

$$1+\begin{bmatrix}g_1 & g_2\end{bmatrix}\begin{bmatrix}0\\-1\end{bmatrix}=1-g_2=0.$$

So, we can simply take $G=\begin{bmatrix}0 & 1\end{bmatrix}$. Because Eqs. (16.33) and (16.34) are also applicable to discrete time systems, the state equation of the reduced order observer should be

$$\begin{aligned}w(k+1)&=(A_{11}+GA_{21})w(k)+(B_1+GB_2)u(k)\\&\quad+[A_{12}+GA_{22}-(A_{11}+GA_{21})G]\bar{y}(k)\end{aligned}$$

$$\widehat{x}_2(k)=w(k)-G\bar{y}(k).$$

So, we obtain the following reduced order observer of the augmented system:

$$w(k+1)=(1-r)u(k)+\begin{bmatrix}r & 1\end{bmatrix}\bar{y}(k)=rP(k)+[I(k)-Z]+(1-r)u(k)$$

$$\widehat{x}_2(k)=w(k)-\begin{bmatrix}0 & 1\end{bmatrix}\bar{y}(k)=w(k)-[I(k)-Z].$$

By substituting $\widehat{x}_2(k)$ for $x_2(k)$ as the feedback, the pure gain feedback controller in Eq. (16.41) becomes

$$\begin{aligned}u(k)&=\frac{q^2-r}{(1-q)^2}P(k)+\frac{1}{q-1}[I(k)-Z]+\left[\frac{r-q^2}{(1-q)^2}+1\right]\widehat{x}_2(k)\\&=\frac{q^2-r}{(1-q)^2}P(k)+\left[\frac{1}{q-1}-\frac{r-q^2}{(1-q)^2}\right][I(k)-Z]+\left[1+\frac{r-q^2}{(1-q)^2}\right]w(k).\end{aligned}$$

When $q = 0.5$, $r = 0.72$, $P(0) = 10$, $I(0) - Z = 0$, $S(k) = 11$, the result of the control is depicted in Fig. 16.4.

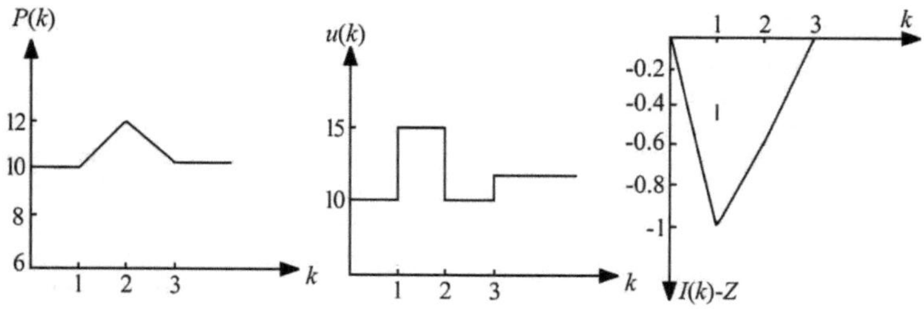

Fig. 16.4 The control and the state trajectory of the production inventory system

16.7 A Few Final Words

This chapter investigates how policy makers could possibly design measures to counter currency attacks, such as sudden withdrawals of foreign investments, in order to avoid undesirable disastrous consequences. The purpose of doing so is to potentially protect innocent people who simply work hard to make a living. At the same time, one should always be prepared for the worst that might be imposed upon him by those who always look for ways to take advantage of others.

In particular, after a control-theory model for an economic system is established with its parameters determined, one can readily design measures to regulate the economic system by employing relevant methods of the control theory. The complexity and dynamics of any real economy tend to make the estimates of the model's parameters inaccurate or change without any advanced notice. So, it is necessary under such circumstances to introduce effective strategies into the theoretical model so that the controlled variables could approach the target values accurately in order to guarantee the stability of the economic system. Based on this kind of thinking, on the basis of the feedback control method, this chapter symbolically formulates the problem of designing regulatory policies and establishes a feedback control model for the economic system. It provides proofs and symbolic reasonings for how well this developed theory could perform in practice. Then, by using examples, this chapter constructs two examples to confirm the feasibility and applicability of the developed theory.

References

Allen, R., & Goldsmith, E. (1972). Towards the stable society: Strategy for change. *The Ecologist Archive, The Ecologist*. Retrieved May 22, 2012, from http://www.theecologist.info/page32.html

Chow, G. C. (1975). *Analysis and control of dynamic economic systems*. Wiley.

Chow, G. C. (1976). Control methods for macroeconomic policy analysis. *Journal of American Economic Association, 66*, 340–345.

Diehl, M., Amrit, R., & Rawlings, J. B. (2011). A Lyapunov function for economic optimizing model predictive control. *IEEE Transactions on Automatic Control, 56*(3), 703–707.

Ellis, M., Zhang, J., Liu, J., et al. (2014). Robust moving horizon estimation based output feedback economic model predictive control. *Systems & Control Letters, 68*, 101–109.

Forrest, J. Y. L., Hopkins, Z., & Liu, S. F. (2013). Currency wars and a possible self-defense (II): A plan for self-protection. *Advances in Systems Science and Application, 13*, 299–316.

Heidarinejad, M., Liu, J., & Christofides, P. D. (2012). State-estimation based economic model predictive control of nonlinear systems. *Systems & Control Letters, 61*(9), 926–935.

Hu, G. Y., & Hu, A. G. (2005). Application of the state variable control theory to regional economic policy adjustment and control. *Journal of Tsinghua University (Science and Technology Edition), 45*(9), 1273–1276.

Huntington, S. P. (1996). *The clash of civilizations and the remaking of world order*. Simon & Schuster.

Kendrick, D. A. (1981). *Stochastic control for economic models*. McGraw-Hill.

Kydland, F. E., & Prescott, E. C. (1980). Dynamic optimal taxation, rational expectations and optimal control. *Journal of Economic Dynamics and Control, 1980*(2), 79–91.

Lin, Y. (1994). Feedback transformation and its application. *Journal of Systems Engineering, 1*(1), 32–38.

MacFarquhar, R., & Schoenhals, M. (2008). *Mao's last revolution*. Harvard University Press.

McKinnon, R. I. (1993). *The order of economic liberalization: Financial control in the transition to a market economy*. Johns Hopkins University Press.

Moe, T. M. (1985). Control and feedback in economic regulation: The case of the NLRB. *American Political Science Review, 79*(4), 1094–1116.

Pindyck, R. S. (1977). Optimal economic stabilization policies under decentralized control and conflicting objectives. *IEEE Transactions on Automatic Control, 2*, 517–530.

Rawlings, J. B., Angeli, D., & Bates, C. N. (2012). Fundamentals of economic model predictive control. In *Proceedings of 2012 IEEE 51st Annual Conference on Decision and Control* (pp. 3851–3861).

Seierstad, A., & Sydsaeter, K. (1986). *Optimal control theory with economic applications*. Elsevier.

Shefrin, H. M., & Thaler, R. H. (1981). An economic theory of self-control. *The Journal of Political Economy, 89*(2), 392–406.

Wang, Z. S., & Wang, D. B. (2006). Optimal control with ideal control strategy and expected trajectory. *Control and Decision, 21*(1), 100–103.

Wu, J. L., & Liu, F. (2004). Control and decision model of macro-economy movement. *Control and Decision, 19*(5), 550–553.

Xiao, D. R., & Lu, Z. Y. (2002). Analysis of macroeconomic system using robust control theory. *Control and Decision, 17*(5), 629–630.

Yang, F., Zhang, Q. L., & Zhai, D. (2004). Optimal control of dynamic economic systems with state constraint. *Journal of Northeastern University, 25*(5), 475–477.

Yao, H. X., & Sheng, Z. H. (2002). Improved method for feedback control in economic chaotic model. *Journal of Systems Engineering, 17*(6), 507–511.

Index

J. Y.-L. Forrest, *Systemic Principles of Applied Economic Philosophies II*,
Translational Systems Sciences 39, https://doi.org/10.1007/978-981-99-7939-4

MIX
Papier aus verantwortungsvollen Quellen
Paper from responsible sources
FSC® C105338
www.fsc.org

If you have any concerns about our products,
you can contact us on
ProductSafety@springernature.com

In case Publisher is established outside the EU,
the EU authorized representative is:
Springer Nature Customer Service Center GmbH
Europaplatz 3, 69115 Heidelberg, Germany

Printed by Libri Plureos GmbH
in Hamburg, Germany